RIM OF CHRISTENDOM

RIM OF CHRISTENDOM

A Biography of Eusebio Francisco Kino
Pacific Coast Pioneer

Herbert Eugene Bolton

FOREWORD BY JOHN L. KESSELL

THE UNIVERSITY OF ARIZONA PRESS
Tucson, Arizona

About the Author

Herbert Eugene Bolton (1870–1953) established the Spanish Borderlands as a significant area of research in North American history. In 1917 he published his seminal essay "The Mission as a Frontier Institution in the Spanish-American Colonies." He was named head of the history department at the University of California, Berkeley, in 1919 and director of the Bancroft Library in 1920; he held both positions until 1940. Bolton was a pioneer in the use of Spanish and Mexican archives, where he studied the lives of his favorite subjects, Spanish missionaries and explorers of the Borderlands. Among his numerous publications are *Fray Juan Crespi, Explorer on the Pacific Coast, 1769–1774* (1927), *Outpost of Empire: The Story of the Founding of San Francisco* (1931), and *Coronado, Knight of Pueblo and Plains* (1949).

THE UNIVERSITY OF ARIZONA PRESS
First Printing 1984

Copyright © 1984
The Arizona Board of Regents
Manufactured in the U.S.A.

Library of Congress Catalog in Publication Data

Bolton, Herbert Eugene, 1870 –1953.
Rim of Christendom.

Reprint. Originally published: New York : Macmillan, 1936.
Bibliography: p.   Includes index.
1. Kino, Eusebio Francisco, 1644 –1711. 2. Explorers —
Southwest, New — Biography. 3. Explorers — Spain — Biography.
4. Jesuits — Southwest, New — Biography. 5. Southwest, New
— History — To 1848. 6. Pima Indians — Missions.
7. Indians of North America — Southwest, New — Missions.
I. Title.
F799.K57B65   1984   266'.2'0924 [B]   84-8814
ISBN 0-8165-0863-1

To

HERBERT BOLTON, Jr.

My good companion on the trail

Contents

ON THE TRAIL

PIONEER OF CIVILIZATION

Illustrations

Facsimiles of Documents

Maps

Foreword

The writing of *Rim of Christendom* was an adventure on the trail as well as in the archives. I wanted to see Kino's world as Kino saw it, understand the words of his diaries and letters, know the scene of his labors, visualize the conditions under which he worked, relive the experiences which he recorded. So I literally followed his footsteps from the cradle to the grave.

—Herbert Eugene Bolton, 1936[1]

HISTORIAN HERBERT EUGENE BOLTON (1870–1953) liked a winner. Praise came easier to him than deprecation. One good hero, stretching for lofty goals, was worth a pack of misfits. And biography, founded on solid scholarship, was the highest form of the historian's craft. Pioneer archival researcher, promoter of the Spanish Borderlands, enthusiastic teacher, eager trail-finder, Bolton did history as adventure. In restless, rugged Eusebio Francisco Kino, S. J. (1645–1711), native of the Italian Tyrol and missionary in the Sonora Desert, he found a kindred spirit and an absorbing subject.

Bolton first met Kino in Mexico City in 1907. Already at work surveying Mexican archives, he chanced upon Kino's "Favores Celestiales," a manuscript of more than four hundred closely written folios describing the works and visions of this extraordinary frontiersman. He was caught. He told in print of his discovery in 1911, produced a scholarly translation as *Kino's Historical Memoir of Pimería Alta* in 1919, publicized his subject in *The Padre on Horseback* (1932), and in 1936 related the full story. Placing *Rim of Christendom* in the context of

Bolton's long and prodigious career, John Francis Bannon, his student and biographer, calls the "carefully reconstructed life of his favorite Black Robe" Bolton's "most original piece of scholarship."[2]

Over the years, Bolton developed a plan that featured Kino as a central figure, a plan "to do for New Spain something like Parkman did for New France."[3] But he did not write as well as Francis Parkman. His style was more folksy than epic. Some wag is supposed to have said of Bolton that "he couldn't write worth a damn, but he wrote, and he wrote, and he wrote." That is patently unfair: *Rim of Christendom* is good reading. If the average schoolchild in Boston knows of Father Marquette and not of Father Kino, other factors—the anti-Spanish Black Legend and remoteness, for two—are more to blame than literary style.

Bolton did not live to observe the two-hundred-and-fiftieth anniversary in 1961 of Kino's death. He should have. There was much ado. *Arizona Highways* dedicated a special issue to Padre Kino, the state's historical society put out a commemorative publication, and the legislature in Phoenix, quoting Bolton at length, urged Congress to accept the "pioneer missionary, explorer, and cartographer" as the state's second representative in the Statuary Hall collection at the Capitol. (Arizona's other representative, installed in 1930, was Gen. John C. Greenway.) Acceptance followed. Since no portrait of Kino was known, Tucson artist Frances O'Brien, by analysis of recurrent characteristics evident in photographs of four generations of the Chini (Kino) family, created a no-nonsense, robustly handsome face. Of the twenty-six entries in the statue competition, that of Suzanne Silvercruys was judged most faithful. Her seven-foot tall, Arizona-copper likeness, unveiled in the Rotunda in 1965, put Kino in "this shrine of American achievement" in the company of another Jesuit explorer, a detail that would not have escaped Bolton. The other Black Robe, representing the historian's home state of Wisconsin, was Jacques Marquette.[4]

Later in 1965, prompted by all this attention to Kino north of the border, the Mexican government resolved to locate the famous missionary's grave and erect a fitting monument. Kino's bones, buried at Magdalena, Sonora, in 1711 in a chapel that had since fallen down over them, were long the object of vain probes and conflicting conjecture, some on the part of Bolton himself. The new polytechnic team of researchers from both sides of the international line, headed by Wigberto Jiménez Moreno, was no mere token. By the spring of 1966 its members had assembled clues from a variety of archives. They had narrowed trenching in search of the lost chapel to part of Magdalena's central plaza, which looked like a war zone. Guided by documentary evidence, the archaeologists identified a wall foundation, a corner, then a known burial at the entrance to the chapel. And, on May 19, they found Kino, unearthing first his skull and then the rest of his skeleton. A small eroded bronze crucifix lay on the right clavicle. Asked what the renowned missionary had looked like in life based on his skeletal remains, physical anthropologists agreed. The O'Brien sketch—and hence the statue in Washington—could not be a better likeness.[5]

Today the town is officially Magdalena de Kino. In its thoroughly remodeled fifteen-acre plaza, the bones of Father Kino, treated with preservatives and protected in a sealed glass vault, lie in situ beneath a domed monument. Mexico's President Luis Echeverría made the trip north in 1971 to inaugurate the Kino memorial complex. Today there are twin bronze equestrian statues of Kino by Julián Martínez in the capitals of Sonora and Arizona. Hermosillo has its Boulevard Padre Eusebio Kino and its Hotel Kino; Phoenix its Kino Junior High School and Kino Institute and Library. In Tucson, where the Kino Community Hospital, the Kino Station Post Office, and the Kino Learning Center share the name with a dozen other businesses, a Kino Boulevard has been planned to connect the International Airport with downtown. Elsewhere in the Pimería the list goes on—Kino Ranch, Kino Springs, Kino Peak, Kino Bay, radio station KINO (Winslow, Arizona). Pedro Domecq of Mexico markets a table wine labeled "Padre Kino." Geologists have even named a hydrous copper calcium silicate mineral ($Cu_2Ca_2Si_3O_{10} \cdot 2H_2O$) for him. First observed in the northern Santa Rita Mountains (Pima County), whose silhouette he knew so well, it is called kinoite.[6]

More than the commissions and ceremonials and contests and statues and things named Kino, what would have excited Bolton is the resurgence of Kino studies and a number of notable Kino finds. The prime scholarly mover has been, not surprisingly, an indefatigable Jesuit, research historian Ernest J. Burrus. His books bearing on Kino, documentary and narrative, fill a shelf: for example, *Kino Reports to Headquarters* (1954); *Correspondencia del P. Kino con los Generales de la Compañía de Jesús* (1961); Kino's *Vida del P. Francisco Saeta, S. J.* (1961); *Kino's Plan* (1961); *Kino escribe a la Duquesa* (1964); *Kino Writes to the Duchess* (1965); *Kino and the Cartography of Northwestern New Spain* (1965); *La obra cartográfica de la Provincia Mexicana* (1967); *Kino and Manje* (1971).

In 1967 the Archbishop of Sonora appointed Father Burrus chairman of a historical commission charged with gathering and submitting to the Congregation of Rites in Rome material for the cause of Kino's beatification. Bolton had served on a similar commission for the cause of California's Fray Junípero Serra. He would have applauded both causes and enjoyed the competition. A couple of Borderlands saints, why not?

Research into the life and times of Kino continues. So does the promotion. At the Arizona State Museum in Tucson ethnohistorian Charles W. Polzer, S. J., translator of *Kino's Biography of Francisco Javier Saeta, S. J.* (1971) and author of the popular *Kino Guide* (1968) and *Kino Guide II* (1982), regularly interrupts his studies and his administration of the Documentary Relations of the Southwest to lead mission tours. The allied Southwestern Mission Research Center, through the *SMRC Newsletter,* monitors activities in and publications about the entire Spanish Borderlands.[7]

As writer and lecturer, Bolton made the most of "human interest" stories. There is one he missed. At the Archivo General de Indias in Spain he had searched for the passenger list of Kino and his fellow Jesuits with its precious brief physical descriptions, the forerunners of passport photos. But he failed to find it. Because Kino's contingent included more foreign-born missionaries than the government quota allowed, some of them had been given false Spanish names and birthplaces. Kino, Father Burrus discovered, sailed aboard the dispatch boat *San Fernando* in 1681 as "Eusebio de Chaves, native of Córdoba, 21 years old [he was 35], well-built, dark-complexioned, curly black hair."[8]

Bolton loved maps. Yet it remained for the persistent Burrus in 1962 to find in Paris at the Bibliothèque Nationale a 1724 copy of Kino's 1710 map, the graphic culmination of the missionary's entire career as explorer and cartographer.[9] Father Polzer uncovered in the Archivo Histórico de Hacienda in Mexico City a 1707 order from the Jesuit Provincial forbidding Kino, because of a change in policy, to carry out further explorations. Bolton did not know that. Things keep turning up.[10]

One question the devil's advocate is bound to ask. How objective are all these Jesuits writing about a fellow Jesuit? How objective was Bolton when it came to "his favorite Black Robe"? How objective was Juan Mateo Manje, Spanish officer and trail companion of Kino, who eulogized the missionary after his death? Manje noted that Kino "was by nature of a fiery temperament," but that he kept it under saintly self-control.[11] Whatever further evidence or scrutiny may have to say about his personality and his motives, Kino by his acts assured himself a lasting fame.

A half-century after its publication, *Rim of Christendom* is still the standard biography. It is a monument to Bolton's scholarship and vision. If no new standard appears in the next half-century, it will not be for lack of new material but for lack of a new Bolton, and it will be a disservice to Kino. Whether one sees the missionary expansionist's life as a welcome gift to "the abandoned souls" of Baja California and Pimería Alta, or whether one considers him an aggressor violating the most sacred inner precincts of other beings, Eusebio Francisco Kino did with unusual energy, earnestness, and success what he set out to do. And it was with these same qualities that Bolton told his story.

John L. Kessell

Notes

1. "Archives and Trails," *California Monthly,* vol. 37 (Oct. 1936), quoted by John Francis Bannon, *Herbert Eugene Bolton, The Historian and the Man, 1870–1953* (Tucson, The University of Arizona Press, 1978), pp. 196–97.

2. Bannon, *Bolton,* p. 195. Bannon provides a listing of all Bolton's published scholarship from 1900 to 1950 (pp. 275–82).

3. Bolton writing in 1931, quoted ibid., p. 192.

4. U.S. Congress, *Acceptance of the Statue of Eusebio Francisco Kino Presented by the State of Arizona,* Proceedings in the Rotunda, United States Capitol, February 14, 1965, 89th Cong., 1st Sess., House Doc. No. 158 (Washington, U.S. Government Printing Office, 1965). Patricia Paylore, *Kino...A Commemoration* (Tucson, Arizona Pioneers' Historical Society, 1961). *Arizona Highways,* vol. 37, no. 3 (Mar. 1961).

5. In his *Kino Guide II: A Life of Eusebio Francisco Kino, S. J., Arizona's First Pioneer and A Guide to His Missions and Monuments* (Tucson, Southwestern Mission Research Center, 1982), pp. 58–72, Charles W. Polzer, S. J., conveys some of the excitement of the quest for Kino's bones.

6. John W. Anthony and Robert B. Laughon, "Kinoite, A New Hydrous Copper Calcium Silicate Mineral from Arizona," *The American Mineralogist,* vol. 55, nos. 5–6 (May–June 1970), pp. 709–15.

7. Since the appearance of *Rim of Christendom* in 1936, with its extensive bibliography, the outpouring of material about Kino has been phenomenal. Peter Masten Dunne, S. J., *Black Robes in Lower California* (Berkeley, University of California Press, 1952), adds to the story of Kino's time in and his continuing influence on Baja California. Other works, including those of Burrus and Polzer mentioned above, are listed by Francis J. Fox, S. J., "Bibliography," in Fay Jackson Smith, John L. Kessell, and Fox, *Father Kino in Arizona* (Phoenix, Arizona Historical Foundation, 1966), pp. 99–122; by Burrus in *Kino and Manje, Explorers of Sonora and Arizona* (Rome, Jesuit Historical Institute, 1971), pp. 737–45; by Polzer in *Kino Guide II,* p. 73; and in the serial bibliography of the *SMRC Newsletter.* An offering by a fellow Trentino is Bonifacio Bolognani, O.F.M., *Padre e Pioniere: Eusebio Francesco Chini, S. J., Missionario-Scrittore-Geografo, 1645–1711* (Trento, Edizioni Biblioteca PP. Francescani, 1983).

8. Burrus, *Kino and the Cartography of Northwestern New Spain* (Tucson, Arizona Pioneers' Historical Society, 1965), p. 10, n. 15. The age must have been a slip of the pen. A twenty-one-year-old could not have received full Jesuit training or been ordained a priest.

9. The map is reproduced in Burrus, *Kino and the Cartography,* between pp. 50 and 51. An inventory of other Burrus finds and his assessment of their importance is found in "An Essay on Sources," *Kino and Manje,* pp. 5–15.

10. In 1981 the University of Arizona purchased from a dealer a signed, sixteen-page Kino diary of the Oct. 24–Nov. 18, 1699, expedition (see below, pp. 424–28, 557).

11. Burrus, *Kino and Manje,* p. 14.

An Adventure in Archives and on the Trail

EUSEBIO FRANCISCO KINO was the most picturesque missionary pioneer of all North America—explorer, astronomer, cartographer, mission builder, ranchman, cattle king, and defender of the frontier. His biography is not merely the life story of a remarkable individual; it illuminates the culture history of a large part of the Western Hemisphere in its pioneer stages. Born in Italy, educated in Germany, sojourner in Spain and Mexico City, missionary and royal cosmographer in California, Kino was with the first expedition which ever reached the Pacific Ocean by crossing the Peninsula. This was in 1684, just when LaSalle landed his colony in Texas; when England annulled the charter of Massachusetts and thereby raised a storm; when Philadelphia was three years old and Charleston was celebrating its fourteenth birthday. This California episode in Kino's romantic career closed with a pirate-chasing voyage on the Pacific to protect the treasure-laden Philippine Galleon on its return from Manila to Mexico.

For a quarter of a century Kino was the outstanding figure on the Sonora-Arizona-California frontier. A score of present-day towns and cities began their history as mission pueblos founded by him or directly under his influence. Over a vast area in the Southwest and adjacent Mexico, cattle ranching and the introduction of European cereals and fruits owe to him their beginnings. Wheat raising in Alta California, to give a single example, was begun with a handful of seed sent by Kino from Mexico across the Arizona desert to a giant Yuma chieftain whom he had formerly visited on the Colorado River. Kino's maps of Western North America made him famous in Europe even in his own day, and with or without acknowledgment they were copied there by cartographers for nearly a century after his death. His manuscripts now brought to light constitute by far the best contemporary historical record of the regions where he labored.

A born individualist, Kino was happiest on the border. A dreamer of dreams, his more conventional associates sometimes thought him queer. When he persisted in the building of a boat in the desert he was called crazy. The notion may have been quixotic, but such a man as he was entitled to at least one impractical hobby. Perhaps it helped him to maintain his sanity when troubles threatened to drive him to distraction. In spite of his boundless visions, he was a thrifty man of affairs, and his mission farms and ranches were the most prosperous in all Sonora. Because of his personal influence over the natives, in the defence of the Spanish settlements he was declared to be more potent than a whole garrison of soldiers. By the Pimas he was so loved that among them his word was law.

The writing of *Rim of Christendom* has been an adventure both in foreign archives and on the trail. In my search for unpublished Kino letters, diaries, maps, and other manuscripts of whatsoever nature, I have personally and by correspondence ransacked the repositories of America and Europe. Spain, Mexico, Perú, Italy, Germany, England, France, and other countries have contributed unsuspected quotas. My first success of capital importance in Kino *heuristic* was the discovery in 1907 of the long lost manuscript of his autobiography called by him *Favores Celestiales*. Its publication in 1919 started a veritable renaissance of interest in the prodigious missionary, and created a soaring market for original Kino writings. Continued nosing into musty bundles has proved equally successful. The facsimiles of unpublished Kino holographs and related manuscripts thus accumulated now reach a total of several thousand pages. They give the completest revelation of the daily career of a missionary pioneer in America ever made available. They have afforded a vast fund of fresh material now utilized for the first time, making possible a comprehensive biography of Kino, placed in the setting of a dramatic period in the history of Mexico and the Pacific Coast.

Equally as intriguing as my adventures in archives has been my odyssey on Kino's trail—from his birthplace in the Italian Alps, through Germany, to Spain, to Mexico, to Lower California, up the West Coast of Mexico to the Gila and Colorado Rivers, and thence by a network of routes over the Sonora mountains to the Sierra Madre of

Chihuahua. By water on ocean liner and Gulf steamer, by land on horseback, on muleback, by team, by automobile, and *á pie,* by air in a monoplane, I have retraced nearly all his endless trails and identified most of his campsites and water holes—all this in an endeavor to see Kino's world as Kino saw it.

In the course of so long and so exacting a task I have inevitably contracted heavy debts of gratitude. The University of California has generously given me leaves of absence for field work and travel. A summer in European archives was partly financed by the Native Sons of the Golden West and the Del Amo Foundation. The Huntington Library on my request and at a cost of more than $18,000 purchased the eighty-page Maggs Collection of original Kino letters to the Duchess of Aveiro y Arcos, and put them at my service. Part of the cost of photostating manuscripts in foreign archives and of assistance in editing them for future publication has been generously borne by Mr. Sidney M. Ehrman, and by grants from the Board of Research and the Institute of Social Sciences of the University of California.

For their remarkable generosity, courtesy, and co-operation I am deeply grateful to the custodians of all the archives, libraries, and collections, public and private, on which I have drawn. Not one to whom I have applied has denied me access. By their help several persons especially have imposed on me a debt of gratitude which I can never adequately repay—Helen Salisbury Carr, for secretarial aid and for successful scouting in European archives while Native Sons Traveling Fellow in Pacific Coast History; Dr. Marion Reynolds for editorial assistance; Dr. Beatrice Cornish Quijada for expert aid with difficult Spanish documents; and Josephine Fessenden for assistance in preparing the manuscript for the press. After all the rest of us had done our best with the proof reading, the sharp eye of Mary Ross reaped a profitable harvest of typographical errors. Not by any means the least helpful has been the stimulating interest of my closest associates in the University—my students—on whom I must rely to carry on much work which I shall have time only to start. *Messis quidem multa.*

PROLOGUE

The Jesuits in Spain

I

THE COMING OF THE BLACK ROBES

NO PHASE OF WESTERN HEMISPHERE HISTORY reveals greater heroism, and few have greater significance, than that of the Jesuit missions. The story of the Black Robes in Paraguay and other parts of South America has been told by many writers. The deeds of the Jesuits in New France have been made widely known to English readers by the scintillating pages of Parkman.

It would be presumptuous for one to attempt greatly to modify what the brilliant New England historian wrote. Indeed, aside from its narrow geographical horizon and the Puritan assumptions on which it is based, the chief fault to be found with the masterpiece is its title. Parkman called his classic *The Jesuits in North America,* meaning only those of New France. In the book there is scarcely a hint that there were any Jesuits in colonial America except those who labored in Canada and the Mississippi Valley. He wrote so brilliantly that he conveyed to lay readers a grossly erroneous impression; for, because of Parkman's facile pen, nine out of ten persons in English speaking circles, when they hear the phrase "the Jesuits in North America," think instinctively and exclusively of the Black Robes of New France; and many of them would be surprised, perhaps skeptical, if told that there were any Jesuits in colonial days other than those of whom Parkman wrote.

But the Black Robes of New France were by no means the only sons of Loyola in the North American colonies. Indeed, they were not the earliest nor the most numerous group, for they were long preceded and greatly outnumbered by those of New Spain. The French Jesuits suffered martyrdoms which made them justly famous among the mar-

3

tyrs of all the missionary world. But they were far exceeded in numbers by the Black Robe martyrs of Nueva España.

Judged by their own criteria, the Canadian Jesuits were not by any means the most successful sons of Loyola in colonial America. The primary aim of the missionary was to save souls. To baptize a dying babe nearly any of them would go through fire or water. Their first measure of success was the number of baptisms solemnized, the number of pagan mortals brought into the Christian fold. Thus computed, the success of the Canadian Jesuits was relatively small. This was no fault of theirs. They labored in a most difficult land, where Satan and all his imps were particularly rampant. The Black Robes of New France counted their conversions by hundreds, or at best by thousands; those of New Spain, working in a more propitious vineyard, numbered their baptisms by hundreds of thousands, or even by millions. And their achievements in other directions were similarly disparate.

These comparisons are by no means made to exalt one group of noble men over another group equally worthy. They are intended merely to bring to the attention a momentous episode in American history which has remained obscure. The height of one great mountain can best be realized by comparing it with another towering peak of known elevation. The imposing stature of the Jesuits of New France is widely known because they had Parkman as their historian. The Spanish Jesuits in North America await their Parkman.

To indicate the magnitude of their achievements, it is necessary only to sketch in broadest outline the two-hundred-year sweep of Jesuit missionary work in New Spain. It will be the more impressive if it is borne in mind that each page of mine calls for at least a full-length volume, each of which in turn must rest on many volumes of documentary materials, known to exist, but most of which have not been utilized.[1]

The pioneer Jesuits in North America labored on the Atlantic sea-

---

[1] In preparing a sketch so broad and so general as the one contained in these introductory chapters, it has not been deemed advisable to give specific citations to all the vast materials drawn upon. Besides the general authorities such as Florencia, Pérez de Ribas, Alegre, Ortega, Venegas, Baegart, Pfefferkorn, Decorme, Astrain, Cuevas, and Bancroft, extensive use has been made of documentary materials, most of which are still unpublished. See also Bolton, Herbert E., "The Mission as a Frontier Institution in the Spanish-American Colonies," *American Historical Review*, XXIII, 42–61 (October, 1917). A part of this Prologue was printed in an article in the *Catholic Historical Review*, XXI, 257–282 (October, 1935).

board, all of which was then comprised in the vast region called La Florida. Father Martínez, the first Black Robe to arrive, was martyred by a Florida chief in September, 1566, just sixty years before Lallemand and his band reached Canada. Father Segura and his followers were slain near Chesapeake Bay not far from the site where the English first settled thirty-six years later. Virginia history thus opened not with the founding of Jamestown, but with giving to the world eight Jesuit martyrs.[1]

The Black Robes who escaped a Carolina revolt and the Virginia massacre were soon transferred to a happier field. Mexico, or New Spain, was early a Jesuit province. Pedro Sánchez came from Europe as Provincial with fifteen companions, who were soon joined by the Florida survivors. In the fall of 1572 Sánchez and his band reached Mexico City, and began an unbroken work of almost two centuries. Sánchez was a "sturdy beggar" and a gifted man of affairs. Generously endowed by private citizens, the viceroy, and the city, the Jesuits soon had a substantial residence and a church. More Black Robes came from Spain, an American novitiate was opened, and recruits were drawn from the "flower of Mexico."

For nearly a score of years effort was directed mainly toward establishing educational institutions, for which the young Order was already famous. Four colleges and a seminary were followed by the Colegio Máximo of San Pedro y San Pablo, which received its papal charter sixty years before Harvard opened its doors, and soon took its place as one of the three or four leading universities in all America. Father Kino, fresh from Europe in 1680, just before Philadelphia was founded, remarked that it had fifteen hundred students and a respectable debt of $40,000. Schools and colleges outside Mexico City were established in quick succession, at Pátzcuaro, Valladolid, Oaxaca, Puebla, Vera Cruz and other places. Some of them were maintained especially for the natives. Conversion evidently bred humility, for one of the young chieftains became a professor, and taught for more than forty years in the college of San Gregorio.[2]

[1] Their story has just been told in an excellent volume by the Reverend Dr. Michael Kenny, entitled *The Romance of the Floridas* (New York, 1934).

[2] The Reverend Dr. Jerome V. Jacobsen has set forth this important chapter in the history of America in a book, now awaiting publication, entitled *Educational Foundations of the Jesuits in New Spain*.

II

PIONEERS OF CIVILIZATION

Such were some of the foundations and ministries of the Black Robes in and near the capital of New Spain, among Spaniards and sedentary Indians, in the early years of their apostolate. Two decades had not passed when they began to push beyond the border to found missions among the less civilized tribes—the work in New Spain for which they ultimately became most famous.

Their maiden effort in missions *entre infieles* was at San Luís de la Paz, where they were sent to help tame the wild Chichimecos, those people who terrorized the highway leading from the capital to the mines of Zacatecas. Under the gentle influence of the Black Robes roving Indians now settled down to village life, warriors became farmers, and the roads were made safe. Spaniards came to live in the vicinity, and the present city of San Luís de la Paz is the result. Thus the first Jesuit mission among the wild Indians of Mexico was typical of all: it became the nucleus of a Christian colony and a center of civilization.

The Chichimec mission was but a step toward the great heathendom of Nueva Vizcaya, that immense jurisdiction embracing all the country beyond Zacatecas, and extending a thousand miles or more, to New Mexico and California. Before the Jesuits arrived, Spain had made considerable beginnings toward the occupation of this vast Northwest. Coronado had opened a road to Cíbola, Guzmán and Ibarra had conquered Sinaloa, thousands of cattle roamed the plains, haciendas flourished here and there in the fertile valleys, and silver mines were thinly scattered through the mountains of Durango.

Jesuit Land, for such the Northwest might well be called, comprised the modern districts of Nayarit, the four great states of Durango, Chihuahua, Sinaloa and Sonora, Baja California, and part of Arizona, a domain larger than all of France. And the Black Robes did not merely explore this vast area, they occupied it in detail.[1]

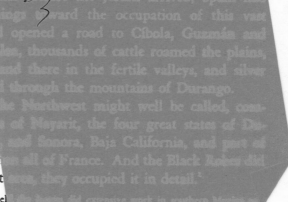

[1] Outside of this northwestern field the Jesuits did extensive work in southern Mexico, in Central America, not to mention their vast enterprises in Spanish and Portuguese South America.

This extensive region was chiefly a mountain country. It embraced four rather distinct geographic areas: the Central Plateau, the Sierra Madre, the Coastal Plain, and the California Peninsula, each with features which greatly influenced Jesuit activities. The Central Plateau, seven thousand feet high in southern Durango, gradually slopes northward and extends to and beyond the Río Grande. On the west this table-land is walled in by one of the roughest portions of the entire Hemisphere—so rough indeed that south of the United States border there is a stretch of nearly a thousand miles which, after three centuries of occupation, has never yet been crossed by a wheel track. On its precipitous western slope this Sierra Madre is cut by numerous rivers which tumble through immense barrancas—veritable Grand Canyons —some of them several thousand feet deep and many miles long.

The Indians of this vast expanse were of various linguistic stocks and of many tribes. They occupied fairly definite areas, but with a few exceptions they did not lead a highly sedentary life. For food most of the mainland peoples within the area raised maize, beans, and calabashes by primitive methods; the Peninsula Indians practiced no agriculture at all. The natives of the mainland coast and the foothills were the most numerous, and offered the best missionary field.[1]

The pioneer missionaries in Nueva Vizcaya were the Franciscans. But the sons of Loyola now entered the field (1591), and became almost its sole evangelists during the next century and three quarters. Then the Franciscans came back. In two wide-fronted columns the Jesuits marched northward up the mainland, one up the eastern and one up the western slope of the imponderable Sierra Madre, meeting generally west of the Continental Divide. At the end of the seventeenth century they crossed the Gulf and advanced in a third phalanx into the Peninsula of California.

River by river, valley by valley, canyon by canyon, tribe by tribe, these harbingers of Christian civilization advanced into the realm of

[1] Beals, Ralph, *The Acaxee. A Mountain Tribe of Durango and Sinaloa* (Berkeley, 1933); Hervas, Lorenzo, *Catálogo de las Lenguas* (Mexico, 1860); Kroeber, A. L., *Uto-Aztecan Languages of Mexico* (Berkeley, 1934); McGee, W. J., *The Seri Indians* (Washington, 1898); Orozco y Berra, M., *Geografía de las Lenguas* (Mexico, 1864); Pimentel, Francisco, *Cuadro Descriptivo de las Lenguas* (Mexico, 1862–1865); Sauer, C., *The Road to Cíbola* (Berkeley, 1932); Sauer, C., *The Distribution of Aboriginal Tribes and Languages in Northwestern Mexico* (Berkeley, 1934); Sauer, C., and Brand, D., *Aztatlán* (Berkeley, 1932); Thomas, C., and Swanton, J. R., *The Indian Languages of Mexico* (Washington, 1911).

heathendom. They gathered the natives into villages, indoctrinated them in the Faith, trained them in agriculture, in the care of stock, and in the simpler crafts. Under the tutelage of the patient Jesuits, barbarians who formerly had constructed only the meanest huts now built fine Christian temples, some of which still stand as architectural monuments. The natives were generally well-disposed toward the missionaries. But secular Spaniards exploited their labor in mines and on haciendas; and native priests were jealous of their white competitors. The result was a series of periodic Indian revolts in which a score or more of Black Robes in New Spain won the crown of martyrdom. But in spite of this the march went on.

It was a colorful pageant. Black Robes moved into the wilderness beside or ahead of prospector, miner, soldier, cattleman, and frontier trader. Land travel chiefly was on horseback, muleback, or on foot, and land transportation by pack train or by Indian carriers. As the frontier expanded, here and there a town, a mining camp, an hacienda, a garrison, was pitched on the border of settlement. Still beyond, in the midst of heathendom, Christian missions were planted. As the Spaniards advanced northward, the Indians were reduced to sedentary life or driven back. The spread of European culture in North America was not by any means wholly a westward movement.

The central feature of the mission was the pueblo. The Black Robe went into the wilds seeking out heathen, making them his friends, telling them the Gospel story, baptizing the children of such parents as were willing, and adults who were dangerously ill. But this did not suffice. In order properly to indoctrinate the whole body of natives, drill them in the rudiments of Christian civilization, and give them economic status on a civilized plane, they were assembled in pueblos, or towns, organized to achieve these aims. Customarily each missionary had charge of three pueblos, a *cabecera* and two *visitas*. With the wilder tribes pueblo forming was often a difficult task, for they preferred to live in freedom in caves or huts. The mountain Tarahumares especially opposed reduction to pueblo life.[1]

---

[1] The difficulties of gathering these mountain people into pueblos are set forth by Father Joseph Neumann in an unpublished letter written during his first months among them: "Our labors consist in converting and baptizing the natives, founding settlements, persuading the Indians to leave their caves and scattered hovels, and to adopt a civilized life, thus

As a nucleus of a new pueblo, it was customary to bring a few families of Christianized Indians from an older mission, to help tame and domesticate the raw recruits. The heart of the mission and the pride of the padre was the church. Near by was the residence of the pastor. Close at hand, in another quadrangle, perhaps, were the houses of the Indians, which constituted the pueblo. In a fully developed mission there were carpenter shops, blacksmith shops, spinning and weaving rooms, corrals for the stock, fields, irrigation ditches, and everything going to make a well-ordered and self-supporting agricultural unit. All this was supervised by the missionary himself, assisted sometimes by a lay brother expert in the mysteries of farm and shop. At first all buildings were of the most flimsy character. These in time were replaced by substantial adobe structures, larger and more beautiful churches, generally of adobe but sometimes built of stone. In hostile country it was customary to erect a strong protecting wall around the pueblo, or at least around the missionary's residence, and to provide it with military towers. Such a mission was a veritable frontier fortification.

To help supervise the labor of the Indians, keep them in order, punish minor offenses, and drill the neophytes in the rudiments of civilized life, native officers were appointed—governor, captain, alcaldes, madores, topiles, chief herdsman, head muleteer, head plowman,[1] etc. According to their respective spheres, some of these functionaries were named by the missionary, others by the provincial governor or some other secular representative of the king.

Instruction of the neophytes provided a daily round of drill in the Catechism, prayers, and sacred music. Many a missionary was as proud

forming them, so to speak, into a corporate body. We compel them to live in villages near the churches, which we build in convenient locations where the country is more open. This is a very difficult task. For,—to explain their character a little—while these people were still heathen . . . they were accustomed to live, not in groups, but separately, one from another. With their wives and children they dwelt in mountain caves or in huts built of straw, which seemed more suitable for catching birds than for human habitation." (Neumann, Joseph, Letter to an unknown father, Sisoguichic, Feb. 2, 1682. Manuscript in the Strahov Monastery, of the Praemonstratensian Order, Prague. Another copy is in the private library of Dr. E. Lange, Branau, Bohemia.)

[1] In a book which he wrote after the Jesuit Expulsion, Father Pfefferkorn describes the functions of the native mission officials. Pfefferkorn, Ignaz, *Beschreibung der Landschaft Sonora samt andern merkwürdigen Nachrichten von den innern Theilen Neu-Spaniens, und Reise aus Amerika bis in Deutschland, nebst einer Landcharte von Sonora.* Köln am Rhein (1794–95). 2 vols.

of his native choir and orchestra as of his church.[1] Promising youths were trained as altar boys, and as temastianes or catechists, to help in the routine of drilling neophytes. Many of them were taught to read and write. Several of the central missions—those at San Felipe, Mátape, Parral, Chihuahua, and other places—had seminaries designed to give such training.

The religious life of a mission included attendance at Mass, the regular prayers, the Sunday sermon, the celebration of holidays with processions, pageantry, and other suitable exercises, in imitation of the Spanish settlements. These Church fiestas, often attended by the Spaniards of the vicinity, were combined with the jollities of secular sports —foot races, horse races, bull fights, and other healthful releases for the nervous system. On his own testimony, one Black Robe, at least, is known to have engaged in a race with his Indians—he on horseback, they on foot—and to have been beaten.

The Black Robe story is one of Homeric quality. The missionaries were the adventurers of the seventeenth and eighteenth centuries, successors to the conquistadores of an earlier day. They traveled vast distances, coped with rugged nature and the fickle savage, performed astounding physical feats, won amazing victories over mountains, rivers, hunger, cold and thirst. The story is filled with picturesque men, like Santarén, who vied with the Pied Piper of Hamelin; Ruíz, who was arrow proof; Azpilcueto, who bluffed an Indian horde with blunderbuss and machete; Contreras, who led the defense of Cocóspora against an Apache attack; Kino, the hard riding cowman; Glandorff, the Black Robe with the magic shoes. The tale is full of diverting humor and of exalting edification. The actors were human beings, who either had a sense of humor or were humorous because they lacked it.

The missionary calling demanded the highest qualities of manhood —character, intelligence, courage, resourcefulness, health, and endurance. Missionaries were required to face physical dangers and hardships almost beyond belief. They went among heathen without es-

---

[1] Pfefferkorn writes: "In all the missions of the Opatas and Eudebes, also in some among the Pimas, Solemn High Mass was celebrated on Sundays and feast days. Some of the choirs consisted of Indians who were so skillful in singing that many European churches might well wish such choristers. I had eight of them in my mission of Cucurpe, four men and four women. Among the latter, one especially was noted for her incomparable voice." (*Op. cit.*)

corts, into places where soldiers dared not tread. They were liable at any time to hear the blood-curdling war whoop or to see the destroying fire by night. They were ever at the mercy of the whims of sensitive Indians, or of jealous and vengeful medicine men. Even to baptize a child was often perilous, for if it died the death might be charged to the "bad medicine" of the padre. Martyrdom was always a very distinct possibility. Most Black Robes came to America hoping to win this glorious crown; many still coveted it after seeing real Indians; and when martyrdom stared them in the face they met it with transcendent heroism. Their hardest trial, more to be feared than death, was loneliness, for they lived leagues apart and saw their own kind only at long intervals. Hence they treasured visits from distant neighbors, and looked forward with the eagerness of a homesick boy to the church dedications and celebrations which brought them for a brief time together; or to the annual journey to a neighbor mission to fulfill their religious obligations.

Not every Black Robe was fit for service in the missions. Some lacked the temperament or the physical stamina, some could not learn the Indian languages. Such were given employment of a different sort. More than one Jesuit who found himself unsuited for the frontier was sent to be professor or president in some college, amid softer surroundings. Many of these Jesuits were of the best blood of Europe. Such were Hernando Tobar, grandnephew of Viceroy Mendoza; Pedro Velasco, relative of another viceroy; Ratkay, the Hungarian noble who had been a page at the Court of Vienna; and Salvatierra, son of a noble house of Spain and Italy.

The Black Robes belonged to their age. They had an unfaltering faith in God and His omnipotence. Miracles were not only possible, but often passed before their eyes. They believed in and talked much of predestination. Indeed, they recognized it every time they came upon and baptized a dying ancient. The man and his wife, each two hundred and fifty years old, whose baptism is narrated by Ribas, were clear examples of this exercise of divine mercy.

Being theologians and spiritual practitioners, they were naturally interested in all religious and spiritual phenomena. True to their time, they believed not only in a personal God, but also in a personal Devil, the same Devil so well known to Cotton Mather. The missionaries saw all around them patent evidence of the malice and of the mischief done by His Satanic Majesty. They believed in signs and portents. Eclipses, earthquakes, epidemics, and all unusual phenomena were interpreted as divine or diabolic manifestations, with supernatural cause and significance. Witchcraft was taken for granted by seventeenth century Jesuits, and its evils were often encountered, just as was the case in Puritan New England and in all contemporary Europe. Spaniards brought with them all the European phraseology of witchcraft, and the usual machinery for rooting it out.

A catalogue of the manifold services of the missionaries would be long and varied. In their daily routine, like the monks of old, they performed the most menial tasks. They cooked, washed, plowed, planted, harvested, handled stock, made adobes, built houses and erected churches. They served as nurses and doctors in the huts of the natives. During epidemics they were called from pillar to post, lacking time even to eat or sleep. The Black Robes converted the natives to Christianity, baptizing in New Spain alone before the Expulsion probably not less than two millions. They also brought to the Indian the rudiments of Christian civilization, teaching them decent habits, agriculture, stock raising, the handicrafts, building, and myriad other things. The less civilized natives were the ones most remolded by mission life.

Another comparison will help us. The Jesuits of New France played a highly important part in the religious, educational, and social life of the French part of the colony. But by reason of circumstances beyond their control, they did relatively little toward changing the society of the Indian population of the vast areas over which they traveled. The Jesuits of New Spain, on the other hand, were primary agents during a century and three quarters in the transformation of a large native population from a roving to a sedentary life, with attendant cultural changes. Indeed, a considerable part of the inhabitants of western Mexico today are descended from ancestors, on one side or the other, who got their first contact with European civilization as neophytes in a Jesuit mission. That this was possible in one case and not in the other, was due largely to the contrasting views of the respective nations under whom the Jesuits worked. Spain considered the Indian worth civilizing as well as converting, and proceeded with zeal and firmness to bring it about. In the process the missionaries were her best agents.

For the border Spaniards as well as for the neophytes the Black Robes performed many services. The mission was the agricultural unit for a large part of frontier Spanish America. There the missionary organized and directed most of the agricultural labor. The mission not only raised produce for its own subsistence, but from the surplus it supplied neighboring soldiers, miners, and cattlemen with agricultural products. The missionaries, by gentle means, subdued and managed the Indians, went as diplomats to hostile tribes, and helped to pacify the frontier in time of trouble. The mission itself, with its fortified plant and its usually loyal native defenders, often served as a bulwark against hostile neighbors. Regarding frontier matters, religious or secular, including international relations, the missionaries helped to mold the opinions of central officials, and were often called to Mexico, or even to Spain and Rome, to give advice. Instructions issued from Europe on such matters were both shaped and interpreted by the men on the frontier, for they were the ones who knew conditions.

The importance of the Black Robes as teachers and founders of colleges has been touched upon in earlier paragraphs. But their scholarly services were not confined to teaching. They wrote learned books on a great variety of subjects. Incidentally to their frontier work they were explorers, cartographers and ethnologists. Ribas declared them linguists by divine gift, and certain it is that they did much to reduce to grammar and to preserve the languages of many tribes, some of which have long since disappeared.

Finally, the Jesuits were the principal historians of early western North America. Ribas, Kino, Venegas, Alegre, Ortega, Baegert, Neumann, Pfefferkorn and the author of the *Rudo Ensayo,* all wrote chronicles which will never be displaced. The Black Robes of New France left us as a legacy the famous *Jesuit Relations* which were assembled by Cramoisy and put into English by Thwaites. These precious records of life in the wilderness are justly celebrated among the treasures of pioneer days in heathen America. They constitute a noble body of historical literature. Equally noble in quality, and vastly greater in bulk, are the similar writings left behind by the Black Robes of New Spain. Most of these have yet to be assembled and edited, a gigantic task toward which a few scholars are now directing their attention.

The number of the men who accomplished these things was not large. At the time of the Expulsion in 1767 there were six hundred and seventy-eight Jesuits in all New Spain, not half of whom were in the missions. The rest were engaged in teaching and other services. During the two centuries of their stay there were perhaps three thousand Black Robes in Mexico all told, whose average term of service in America may have been twenty or twenty-five years.

III

NORTHWARD THE COURSE OF EMPIRE

The pioneer Jesuit in Nueva Vizcaya was Gonzalo de Tapia, of eternal fame.[1] With one companion in 1591 he crossed the perilous Sierra Madre. His precise destination was San Felipe, on Sinaloa River, then the very last outpost of European civilization in northwestern New Spain. San Felipe became and long continued to be the Jesuit capital on the Pacific Coast. Taking their lives in their hands, the two apostles undertook a gigantic task. Their touch was magic. Within six months several pueblos had been formed and more than a thousand natives baptized. Undaunted by poisoned arrows and yawning chasms, Tapia recrossed the Sierra to Mexico for additional help.

Four years passed, and the Faith was taking firm root on Sinaloa River. But in the same degree, the chronicler tells us, the wrath of Satan grew. Tapia was marked for destruction. Nacabeba, a native medicine man, who saw his power waning, brained Father Gonzalo with a war club and celebrated his triumph with pagan orgies. Tapia thus became the proto-martyr of Jesuit New Spain. But the work went

---

[1] His inspiring career has recently been made known to English readers through the excellent biography by Rev. Dr. William Eugene Shiels, entitled *Gonzalo de Tapia, 1561–1594* (New York, 1934).

on. The confidence of the natives regained, conversions struck a new pace. By the end of the first decade there had been 10,000 baptisms, and the Jesuits had eight missions with substantial churches, serving thirteen pueblos along Sinaloa and Mocorito rivers.

People sometimes raise their eyebrows at such stories of wholesale baptisms. But the explanation is simple. Infant heathen were baptized without catechism, the same as children of Christians. When the padres first arrived there was a large crop of infants awaiting them. There-after baptisms proceeded at a slower rate, for the annual increment of babes was smaller than the first accumulation; and older children and adults must first be instructed.

Almost simultaneously the Black Robes began their work on both slopes and in the heart of the Sierra Madre. With a gift of $22,000 from Governor del Río and others, a college was established in Durango in 1593–4. By the end of the century six Jesuits of this house were founding missions among the Acaxees in Topia, among the Tepehuanes in central Durango, and among the Laguna tribes of Coahuila. Here was a field as large as that of Sinaloa. Father Santarén became the saint of Topia; but Ruíz did not fall far behind him in prowess and fame. Together they assembled crowds, destroyed heathen idols, built churches, and baptized thousands. At first the natives were friendly. But Topia was a mining district, Indian labor was exploited, and a typical revolt followed. In the crisis Father Ruíz performed a prodigy. Eight hundred Acaxees besieged forty Spaniards at San Andrés. The beleaguered settlers struck back. In one of the sorties Ruíz marched ahead of the soldiers protected only by his Crucifix. "Clouds of arrows were discharged at the holy man, but not one struck him," we are told. The chronicler regarded this as evidence of divine protection —a scoffer might suspect bad native marksmanship.

Governor Urdiñola rushed from Durango with soldiers to relieve the siege. But Santarén became the hero of the episode. Going almost alone among the hostiles, by diplomacy he won them over and marched back to Topia at the head of a thousand natives, bearing a cross and the white flag of peace. There was a love feast and the Indians rebuilt their churches. The conversion now spread to the Xiximes and other tribes, where there were baptisms by added thousands. The name of

Santarén is still a household word in all that western Sierra, where he has become a legendary figure.

Fonte and Ramírez had similar fortunes in central and northern Durango, among the virile Tepehuanes. Other evangelists turned northeast to the Laguna region of Coahuila called Parras. The Lake People were friendly and the success of the Black Robes was flattering. But like other missions, those of Parras had their full measure of pioneer troubles. Smallpox carried off four hundred neophytes in 1608, shortly before Jamestown's "starving time." The Nazas River went on a rampage, destroyed the church of one mission, forced the people to flee from another, and nearly cost the life of a Black Robe. First it was too wet, then too dry. Drought was followed by famine. But in spite of these calamities baptisms multiplied to thousands, and Parras became a precious jewel in Loyola's crown.

The scene shifts back to Sinaloa.[1] On nearly every frontier the Black Robes found and relied on some secular champion. Such were Del Río and Urdiñola in Durango. More famous in this rôle was Hurdaide, defender of the Faith in Sinaloa, contemporary of Canada's Champlain, of Virginia's John Smith, and of Plymouth's John Alden. His appointment as Captain at San Felipe was a decisive event in Jesuit history. For nearly three decades this bandy-legged soldier ruled the Pacific Coast like a medieval Count of the March. El Capitán, as he was known, was famous far and wide for the wax seals with which he authenticated his orders. Any naked Indian messenger bearing a bit of paper stamped with these symbols had safe passage among friends or foes.

Hurdaide's part was to make safe the northward advance of the Black Robes. The Sinaloa River vineyard had been firmly planted by Tapia and his successors. But the way to the Fuerte, the next main stream north, was blocked by hostile Suaquis, Sinaloas, and Tehuecos. One by one El Capitán subdued these tribes, by methods which were sometimes harsh and always spectacular. Ribas the historian, Méndez, and Villalta followed where Hurdaide led. Villalta baptized four hundred Sinaloas the very first day, Méndez gleaned a similar harvest, Ribas

[1] In a forthcoming book on the Jesuit missions of Sinaloa Rev. Dr. Peter M. Dunne has taken up the story where Father Shiels left off.

made his name enduring at Ahome, and within a year the whole river valley west of the mountains had been added to Christendom. By placating the sturdy Yaquis and subduing the defiant mountain Tepahues, El Capitán opened the way to Mayo River. Venerable Father Méndez headed a procession of Black Robes, three thousand children were baptized within two weeks, and seven pueblos were founded within a stretch of eighteen leagues. The 30,000 Mayos had come into the Christian fold.

All the North Country now received a terrific shock, and the mountain streams of Durango ran red with the blood of missionaries and settlers. In the Tepehuán missions the Black Robes had labored with gratifying success for more than two decades. Pueblos had been formed, churches built, thousands of Indians baptized. Then suddenly the Tepehuanes, led by a self-styled Messiah, rose in savage rebellion. In the fall of 1616 the natives of Santa Catalina sprung the trap and murdered Father Tobar. Two hundred Spaniards fell at Atotonilco. At Santiago Papasquiaro Fathers Orozco and Cisneros, with some Spanish families, were brutally slain in the cemetery. At Zape nearly a hundred victims fell, including Fathers Alavez, Del Valle, Fonte, and Moranta. Santarén, the saint of Topia, who chanced to be in the vicinity, also went down in this bloody rebellion. Soldiers hurried north, punished the rebels, gathered up the remains of the martyred missionaries, and took them to Durango, where they were buried with solemn honors. The Tepehuán uprising was at an end. Undaunted, new Black Robes entered the field and the missions were restored.

On the West Coast the missions now began the period of their greatest prosperity. The Tepehuán revolt caused uneasiness in Sinaloa, lest the Yaquis should join the rebels. Instead, they welcomed the Black Robes to their own territory and became one of the most faithful Christian communities. Ribas moved up the map once more and became the apostle to this manful tribe, among whom he set up the Cross in May, 1617. Four thousand children and five hundred adults were baptized within a few weeks. More workers came, eight missions were founded, and soon most of the populous tribe were converted. As a granary for sterile California, these Yaqui missions later played a distinctive rôle.

From the Yaquis it was but a step to the Lower Pimas and Opatas, higher up on the Yaqui River, where flourishing missions were begun in 1620, year of the *Mayflower*. Venerable Méndez, like Daniel Boone, ever on the frontier, went into the mountains to the Sahuaripas. Miners were not far behind. Azpilcueto, at Batuco, was a fighting padre long remembered in this region. Hostile neighbors threatened to kill him and drive away his fellow Jesuits. "Hurry up" was the message he sent them; then he coolly awaited their approach. When he fired a musket and brandished a machete they bolted and fled, to return soon afterward as loyal neophytes.

By now the Sinaloa-Sonora missions had reached impressive proportions. Baptisms there in 1621 alone were over 17,000. As a consequence of this great expansion, a new rectorate was formed in the north, with its capital at the Yaqui town of Tórin, where the thick-walled old Jesuit church, today in ruins, looks down from its height like a Roman fortress. The rectorate at this time employed eleven Jesuits and embraced 60,000 Mayos, Yaquis, and Lower Pimas. On the whole West Coast there were now 86,340 converts in fifty-five pueblos. Three years later the number was more than 100,000. The Christian harvest was exceeding great.

Several veterans now left the scene. In 1620 Ribas retired after sixteen years on the coast, to become provincial in Mexico and to write his great history. Six years later died Martín Pérez, veteran of all the West, for he had come with Tapia, the Founder. At the same time Sinaloa lost by death its matchless soldier, El Capitán Hurdaide, who was mourned and missed by seculars and religious alike. Few regions in America have had more colorful pioneers than these.

Notwithstanding the loss of the Old Guard—or perhaps because of it, for Old Guards have a way of becoming impedimenta—the boom in the West continued. At Chínipas, high up in the barranca-gouged mountains, Julio Pascual won several thousand converts. In 1632 he was joined by Father Martínez. As he climbed the mountain trail to his new destination, Martínez rode to his death. A week after his arrival both Black Robes were martyred by hostile Chief Cambeia. It will help us to keep our chronology straight if we remember that this was just a century before George Washington was born on the other coast of

From drawing by Montenegro

Yaqui face mask

Photo by Bennett and Zingg

Tarahumares today

America. The Chínipas mission was now closed, to be reopened four decades later.

Martyrdom but fanned the apostolic flame. The Black Robes now pushed into Valle de Sonora, and to the upper waters of the many-forkéd Yaqui, thus carrying the Gospel to the border of the lands of the Apaches and the Upper Pimas. Valle de Sonora, site of Coronado's ill-fated San Gerónimo, was the most historic spot in all that region. It is from this charming little valley, peopled by gentle and industrious Opatas, that the vast state of Sonora gets its name. Castaño came here to live among the Opatas in 1635, shortly after Roger Williams fled from religious persecution to his Rhode Island wilderness. Within a year Castaño had baptized three thousand natives, who lived in pueblos which still bear the names by which they then were known. Soon the northernmost missions, mainly of Opatas, were formed into a new rectorate,[1] where seven Jesuits were ministering to fourteen pueblos, and where already there had been a total of more than 20,000 baptisms.[2]

When Ribas published his famous *Triunfos de Nuestra Santa Fé* in 1645, the showing for a half century of labors was most impressive. West of the Sierra, in a continuous stretch of some six hundred miles, there were now thirty-five head missions, each with from one to four towns—a hundred or more in all. Each of the head missions, and many of the visitas, or sub-stations, had fine churches, generally of adobe, and prosperous farms and well-stocked ranches. The mission books showed a total of more than 300,000 baptisms in the West to date. These are astounding figures, but of their accuracy there can be no doubt.

Again the scene shifts. The Jesuit frontier west of the Sierra Madre had far outrun that on the eastern slope, a fact which may be explained in part by three circumstances. The Tepehuán revolt had caused a setback on the Central Plateau; hostile Tobosos and Conchos made mission life precarious there; and the field was partly covered by the zealous Franciscans, who were active on the right flank of the Jesuits. But the Black Robes now made a new thrust forward, to work among the Tarahumares, those fleet-footed mountain people who lived

[1] In 1646.

[2] To the outermost Opata missions a few Upper Pimas (at the time called Imuris) now began to be attracted.

on both slopes of the Sierra Madre in western Chihuahua. Before his martyrdom Fonte had made a small beginning there in 1611, and another nibble at the same bait was taken in 1630. Nine years later the Tarahumar missions were begun in earnest. Meanwhile the prosperous mining town of Parral was founded (1632) and became for a century the residence of the governors of Nueva Vizcaya and the seat of a Jesuit College. For these reasons it played a vital part in subsequent frontier history.

Men of parts continued to come forth. Gerónimo Figueroa and José Pascual launched the new drive in 1639 (year of the Fundamental Orders of Connecticut, if you please), when they founded missions on Conchos River north and west of Parral. A corps of Black Robes followed in their train, reaped a large harvest, and by 1650 carried the Cross to the upper Yaqui River in Tarahumara Alta. But they had come to a most difficult frontier, quite in contrast with that of Sonora. The incursions of wild Tobosos made life unsafe for priest, secular, or neophyte. Then the savage yells of the murderers of Brebeuf and Lallemand in the forests of Canada were echoed back from the craggy mountains of Chihuahua. The Tarahumares, led by haughty Chief Tepóraca, rose in revolt, destroyed several missions, murdered Father Godínez (Beudin) at Papigochic, and massacred all the Spanish settlers at the near-by town of Aguilar (1650). The city of Guerrero marks the approximate site today. In a second onslaught Father Basile was decapitated and hanged to a cross (1652). Indian legend has it that as he expired, his spirit, in the form of a beautiful child, was seen to issue from his mouth and ascend to Heaven attended by two Angels. Thus was lengthened the list of Jesuit martyrs. With a courage which commands more than admiration, the Black Robes reoccupied the southern missions. But with Papigochic destroyed, Tarahumara Alta, the region of the high Sierra, was still solidly heathen.

For two decades the Tarahumara field remained stationary. Then, in 1673, another forward movement was begun. This, by the way, was the very year when Marquette reached the Mississippi River. French and Spanish Black Robes were approaching each other from opposite sides of the continent. The Tarahumara Alta missions were now reopened. Apostles Tardá and Guadalajara entered the Sierra as far as

Yepómera and Tutuaca. The region was inconceivably difficult; mountains and barrancas were inexpressibly rough; only the hardiest men could endure the winter cold. Yet the missions flourished. Eight Jesuits in Tarahumara Alta were serving 4,000 natives in thirty-two pueblos in 1678, and within the next four years more than thirty new churches were built.

New names now appear on the honor roll. Foronda and Picolo,[1] Neumann and Ratkay, led a procession of Black Robes from Italy and North Europe who greatly vitalized the work. For ten years they toiled in the midst of privation and danger. Then another revolt burst forth. There was a gold rush to Santa Rosa,[2] Spaniards summoned the Indians to forced labor, and the story of Papigochic was repeated. In 1690 the natives murdered Fathers Foronda and Sánchez, expelled the rest of the Black Robes from the Sierra, and destroyed six mountain missions.[3] But peace was restored, the fearless Black Robes returned to their craggy exile, and rebuilt their churches "larger and better than before."

Seven years later peace was disturbed by an outburst of wizardry. This was precisely the time when witch baiting was epidemic in New England. If we can believe the evidence, there were more broom voyages then than airplane flights today. Feminism seems to have been at the zero hour in Tarahumara, for nothing is said of witches. But many wizards were captured and executed by the soldiery, for Spaniards were as silly as Englishmen or Germans of their day. The result was still another uprising. Rebels destroyed four mountain missions and again the Jesuits fled. War was followed by the submission of the natives, and the return of the Black Robes to their posts. Their courage was sublime.[4]

It had been a bitter conflict. However, says Father Neumann, who was a witness of it all, not half of the Tarahumar nation had taken

[1] This Italian usually or always signed his name Piccolo, but the Spaniards generally wrote and printed his name as Picolo, and I have adopted their usage.

[2] Santa Rosa de Cusihuiriachic.

[3] Yepómera, Tutuaca, Cahurichic, Tomochic, Matachic, and Cocomorachic.

[4] Neumann, Joseph, *Historia Seditionum quas Adversùs Societatis Jesu Missionarios, Eorúmqu; Auxiliares Moverunt Nationes Indicae, ac Potissimùm Tarahumara in America Septemtrionali, Regnóque Novae Cantabriae, Jam toto ad fidem Catholicam propemodùm redacto, Authore P. Josephe Neymanno Ejusdem Societatis Jesu in Partibus Tarahumarorum Missionario.* Pragae, Typis Univers. Carolo-Ferd. Soc. Jesu ad S. Clem. N.d. Preface dated April 15, 1724.

up arms or deserted Christianity. In the midst of disorder they had been steadfast in the Faith. The whole situation was now changed by a new Indian policy. Henceforth no effort was made to move Tarahumares from their mountain homes to the plains. Henceforth they remained peaceful, and the Jesuits went forward with their apostolic labors among them. The circumstance carries a moral. The transplantation policy as applied to these people had been a mistake from the outset.

On the eastern edge of the Tarahumara, Chihuahua now became a flourishing city and the seat of a Jesuit college, where a lay brother wrote a widely used treatise on medicine.[1] Among the colorful Black Robes in the Tarahumara at a later date was Glandorff, who served some forty years at Tomochic. Famous for his gentle sanctity, he was even better known as the great hiker. Like Serra of California, he was a poor horseman, but he could climb a mountain like a goat, and in a cross country run would put a mule to blush. He was a marvel even to the fleet-footed Tarahumares, who still have world-wide renown for their own speed and endurance. According to legend Glandorff had magic shoes. An Indian servant worn with travel fell exhausted. Glandorff loaned him his moccasins, and behold, he sprang up revived as if from a refreshing sleep and without further halt continued his journey. This happened not once but many times. So runs the diverting legend.[2]

Other frontiers were pushing simultaneously forward. The Chínipas missions, after a blank of four decades, were restored by the Italians Prado and Pecoro in 1676. At the end of four years they had gathered into pueblos and converted 4,000 Indians. Square-jawed Salvatierra now joined his countrymen in the district and became its most distinguished missionary. One of his exploits was his descent into the mammoth canyon of Urique, in size and awesomeness a close competitor of the Grand Canyon of the Colorado. His naïve account of the adventure is refreshing. With a Cerocahui Indian he set forth to visit the stupendous gorge. The guide told him he could ride three leagues,

---

[1] Brother Joseph Steinheffer, from the Province of Bohemia. His book, written in Spanish, was called *A Medical Anthology* (Neumann, *Historia Seditionum*).
[2] A sketch of Glandorff's life is given in *Carta del P. Bartholomé Braun, Visitador de la Provincia Tarahumara, a los PP. Superiores de esta Provincia de Nueva España, sobre la Apostólica Vida, Virtudes, y Santa Muerte del P. Francisco Hermano Glandorff* (Mexico, 1764).

then he would have to walk. The admonition was unnecessary. "On seeing the precipice," says Salvatierra, "such was my terror that I immediately asked . . . if it was time to dismount. Without waiting for an answer I did not dismount but let myself fall off on the side opposite the precipice, sweating and trembling all over from fright. For there opened on the left a chasm whose bottom could not be seen, and on the right rose perpendicular walls of solid rock." He was on a mantel shelf suspended in mid-air. This account by Father Juan in 1684 should interest all twentieth century "discoverers" of Urique canyon.[1]

The northward tide was now deflected. By this time the Black Robes had established Christianity in the Sierra Madre and on both its slopes, all the way from southern Durango to northern Chihuahua, and from Culiacán to the Arizona border. Now, on the northeast, they were blocked by the Apaches, as by a Chinese wall. But the way was open to the west and northwest, in California and Pimería Alta, where large populations lay still beyond the rim of Christendom. To cultivate these extensive vineyards now came Kino, Campos, Salvatierra, Ugarte, and a valiant host of only less notable figures. Conspicuous among them all was Kino, pioneer in California and Apostle to the Upper Pimas. His story, which we now relate, is typical of the careers of many who had gone before and of many who came after him. He comes on the stage in the middle of the Jesuit drama, and nearly a century ahead of Serra, his great Franciscan successor.

[1] Alegre, Francisco Javier, *Historia de la Compañia de Jesús en Nueva-España.* Edited by Carlos Bustamante (Mexico, 1842). Tomo III, p. 51.

KINO IN EUROPE AND MEXICO

A Dream of the Orient

IV

VAL DI NON

A FEW MILES NORTHWEST OF THE FAMED ITALIAN CITY OF TRENT, in the Tyrolese Alps, lies the miniature basin known as Val di Non. It was the Anaunia of Roman days. This picturesque inter-mountain vale, hemmed in on the west by a sierra that seems to touch the sky and on the east by a less ambitious range, is a veritable amphitheater, as a classic writer once called it. At its southern end the valley is entered by a road which winds through a narrow gap by which the river Noce finds its tortuous exit from Val di Non to join the fuller flooded Adige. The floor of the valley and the enclosing slopes are dotted with little villages, some of which pride themselves on an antiquity that carries them back to pre-Roman days. Cles, the principal town, is distinguished among its almost jealous neighbors for the discovery there in 1869 of the now celebrated Tavola Clesiana, the beautiful bronze tablet on which is inscribed the edict of Emperor Claudius granting Roman citizenship to the inhabitants of Val di Non in the year 46 of the Christian era.[1]

Proudest of all these old towns is Segno, a snug little hamlet which nestles in a fold of the hillside on the eastern border of the valley midway of its length. And Segno's boast is not of her antiquity nor of her archaeological treasures, but of the simple fact that within her precincts was born Eusebio Kino, the renowned Jesuit missionary explorer of the Pacific Coast of North America.

Kino's biography starts off with a tantalizing question mark. We do not know the exact day of his birth—a matter, 'tis true, rather of curiosity than of importance. His baptism took place on August 10,

---

[1] Claudius ruled 41–54 A.D.

1645. This much is certain. Moreover, official records of the Jesuit Order, of which Kino was long a member, give this baptismal date as his birthday, and we may accept it as probably correct. In that case, in keeping with good old custom, Eusebio was christened on the very day that he was born.

The original record of Kino's baptism may still be seen, for it is carefully preserved in the church archives of Torra, a little village on the hillside close to Segno and now head of the parish to which Segno belongs. To view the venerable document was well worth my journey thither, for, apart from the surrounding halo of age and association, it contains interesting information. It is not a long document:

"On the 10th of August, 1645, Eusebius, the son of Franciscus Chinus and his wife Donna Margherita, was baptized in the presence of the god-parents, the worthy rector, the very reverend Father Don Arnoldus Thay, and Donna Rosa, wife of Don Eusebius Chinus of Segno." [1] The priest who performed the ceremony little realized what a prodigious man child he had christened that day.

Kino's name is still represented at Segno by a numerous family. They are of a collateral branch, for with the missionary his direct line ended. He had sisters but no brother. The family have long lived in the valley—continuously since the early sixteenth century at least. In the course of the decades thereafter the name was variously spelled— Chini, Chino, Chinus. Today the family write it Chini—pronounced Kini—which has been the generally established form since the later eighteenth century. In his early manhood Eusebio usually wrote his name Chino or Chinus. But when in middle life he went to Spain and to Spanish-America he faced a problem. In Spain Chino meant Chinaman. In Mexico it was often applied contemptuously to persons of mixed and low caste. In order, therefore, to avoid ambiguous suggestions, and to preserve the Italian sound of his proud old family name, in Spain and Spanish-America the missionary generally wrote his name Kino. But this did not end the trouble. Kino is now the German word for cinematograph, or "movie"; and Keno, pronounced the same, is the feminine gambling game familiar to all who have traveled by sea. One of the missionary's relatives recently wrote me

[1] Original Latin manuscript in the baptismal register of the parish archive at Torra.

from Segno begging me to restore the Italian form of the name because "over here Kino smacks of Hollywood." But there might be something worse, so I shall adopt the spelling used in America by the missionary himself. In this form it has been fixed in Western Hemisphere history. To change it in English books to Chini, or Chino, or Chinus, would be quite as pointless as to change Columbus to Colón.

Kino's people were villagers of good stock. The family now point with pride to a title of nobility which was once bestowed on one of their ancestors. That the missionary's parents were well-to-do is evidenced by the considerable property which by his will and testament, made at the age of twenty-two, he conveyed to the Jesuit Order.

Since the publication of Kino's autobiography[1] in 1919 there has been a veritable renaissance of interest in the great Jesuit. On both sides of the Atlantic Kino's work as missionary explorer and pioneer of civilization is coming to be appreciated as it richly deserves. In America a society has been formed for the purpose of erecting a monument to Father Kino in Arizona, where he left so resounding a name. Italy is now eagerly doing honor to Kino as an illustrious if a long forgotten son. In Segno, his birthplace, a plaque recording his prodigious deeds has been affixed in a conspicuous place on the front of the village church. At Trent, where he went to school, his fame has been celebrated by the erection of a monument in the public park. The Chini family of Segno, stimulated by the missionary's renown, have brought forth and trimmed up their family tree. More important still are the numerous sketches that have been written and the serious studies accomplished in recent years in Italy to make Father Kino known as an Italian hero. Weber, Tacchi-Venturi, Rossaro, Chini, Ricci, Trozzi, Rizzatti, and others, by their writings have helped in a significant way to make known the facts of Kino's early life or to spread his fame in his homeland.

One phase of the Kino renaissance has been especially diverting. On both sides of the Atlantic a discussion has raged, ever since the

---

[1] Kino, Eusebio Francisco, *Favores Celestiales.* Original manuscript in the Archivo General y Público, Mexico, Sección de Misiones, Tomo 27. This long-lost autobiography is the most important single documentary account of Kino's life work. It was discovered, edited and published in English by the present writer as *Kino's Historical Memoir of Pimería Alta, 1683–1711* (Cleveland, 1919). 2 vols. Cited hereafter as Kino, *Hist. Mem.* Printed in Spanish under the title, *Las Misiones de Sonora y Arizona* (Mexico, 1922).

publication of Kino's autobiography, as to whether the missionary was Italian or German. In the course of the debate much heat and some light have been generated. In the outcome the Italian claim has been fully established. That is to say, it is now clear that the missionary's name was Chino (or Chini) and not Kühn, and that his ancestral stock and his native tongue were Italian.

The German contention was not altogether baseless, however. Kino's connection with Germany was close and long continued. In his day the ecclesiastical principality of Trent was within the Holy Roman Empire. The bishop of Trent was a vassal of the Emperor. Trent, with the Val di Non, was included in the Jesuit Province of Upper Germany, to which Kino belonged. Before he came to America he had spent more than half of his life in Bavaria, where the German language prevailed.

Moreover, Kino often spoke of himself and his Jesuit companions as "we Germans," in the same sense, no doubt, that collegians call themselves Harvard men, Oxford men, Yale men, or Californians, wherever they may hail from. Just as there are German-Americans, he regarded himself as an Italo-German. In fact, there has recently been discovered a letter written by Kino on his way to America in which he says he hardly knows whether he is German or Italian.[1] "As for what your Excellency wishes to know about me," says Kino, "I am very glad to write about my nation and my country. I am from Trent in the Tyrol, but I am in doubt whether I should call myself an Italian or a German. The city of Trent uses almost entirely the language, customs, and laws of the Italians. However, it is in the very edge of the Tyrol, and the Tyrol belongs to Germany. Besides, the college at Trent is a college of the province of Upper Germany, although we were instructed in our classes and talked together in Italian. Still, for the last eighteen years of my life I have lived almost in the center of Germany."[2] Under these circumstances there is little wonder that Germany is ambitious to share in the glory shed on Europe by the great missionary.

[1] In the same way Carl Schurz might have said he hardly knew whether he was American or German.

[2] Kino to the Duchess of Aveiro y Arcos, Cádiz, November 16, 1680. Original Latin manuscript in the Huntington Library, San Marino, California.

V

A YOUTH SEEKS HIS FORTUNE

In Kino's day, as now, Segno was a village of farm laborers, and in all likelihood young Eusebio, even though relatively well-to-do, shared in the rural toil of a hard-working peasantry. His hands were probably rough and red.[1] But the boy was destined for a wider sphere. The friendly mountain walls of Val di Non could not contain a youth so richly endowed. He had qualities of head and heart and will not to be confined to so narrow a scene. The urge of adventure was in him. A larger world called.

Down the valley a few miles to the south lay mountain-girt Trent. Here was a city with a resounding history. Here was a castle which had heard the clangor of arms. Here were churches already venerable with age. Here, indeed, had been held the celebrated Council of Trent, where great matters of Church doctrine and reform had been debated and settled. More immediately to the point, here was a college which offered an ambitious young man an education.

So to Trent Kino made his way. No one has told us whether he trudged thither on foot with a bundle on his back, or rode on a horse, in a diligence, or in a two-wheeled cart; whether he went alone, or accompanied by a fond and over-anxious parent. But we do know and we have followed the trail which he probably took— the road which winds beside the deep-gorged river Noce.

A short journey down the Val di Non took the young adventurer to the narrow exit. Behind him now lay boyhood and all the boy-hood scenes—Segno in the fold of the hillside, the Chino hearth, play-mates, the familiar fields, the smokes of the valley towns, the high mountain wall in the west—all friendly and belovéd. Ahead of him lay a boy's dream world, uncertain, and therefore boundless and allur-ing. Homesick he doubtless was, but he would not face about. If home called him back, the big world in louder tones urged him for-ward. So now, threading the rugged canyon, he emerged into the

---

[1] The Chini family are still a sturdy breed, as is plain from the twenty-one members whom I photographed at the old family home in Segno in 1931.

valley of the noisy Adige. Following its course, a few miles further down he entered the city whose heavy gates opened to the village lad a way to enduring fame.

At Trent Kino entered the Jesuit College. Ricci brands as "simply conjectural" Rossaro's statement to this effect. If so, it was a fortunate guess, for Kino himself confirms it in the letter quoted above. Rossaro writes of Kino's student life at Trent: "In the walls of the austere institute, where in the long thoughtful silence the most arduous study alternated with the practice of exquisite piety, and where penetrated the echo of the astonishing progress of the Jesuit missions, by this time scattered over all the world, the sensitive soul of Chini developed amid the keen enthusiasm and the ardent dreams which were the food of the very bright faith of those times." [1] These words, true in spirit, are mainly impressionistic, for we have the scantiest of data for this period of Kino's life, and Rossaro adduces none.

When we next hear of Eusebio he was a student in the Jesuit college of Hala, or Hall, near Innsbruck, on the German frontier. [2]

VI

A MORTAL ILLNESS AND A SOLEMN VOW

Kino now entered the Jesuit Order. The circumstances under which he did so were dramatic. For some time he had experienced a desire to become a soldier in Loyola's army and to go as missionary to

[1] Rossaro, D. A., *Brevi Cenni sul Gesuita P. Eusebio Francesco Chini di Segno in Val di Non* (Rovereto, 1929).

[2] See Holweck, F. J., Letter of May 9, 1920, concerning Kino's nationality, in *The Catholic Historical Review*, Vol. VI (October, 1929), 378–379; Weber, letter of June 21, 1920, *ibid.*, 379–380. Data relative to Kino's early life are contained in Ricci, Eugenia, *Il Padre Eusebio Chini, Esploratore Missionario della California e dell' Arizona* (Milano, 1930); Ricci, Eugenia, *P. F. E. Chini* (Trento, 1930); Rizzatti, Ferraccio, "L'Italiano Padre Eusebio Chini, Pionere, Esploratore, Civilizzatore," in *L'Illustrazione Italiana*, VIII, 911–913 (Milano, May 25, 1930); Rossaro, D. Antonio, *Brevi Cenni sul Gesuita P. Eusebio Francesco Chini di Segno in Val di Non* (Rovereto, 1929); Tacchi-Venturi, Pietro, "Sei Lettere Inédite del P. Eusebio Chino al P. Gian Paolo Oliva, Gen. d.C.d.G.," in *Studi Trentini di Scienze Storiche,* Annata XI, 3–17 (Trento, 1930); Trozzi, Ugo, "P. Eusebio Francesco Chini, Grande Esploratore Trentino," in *Trentino: Rivista della Legione Trentina* (Trento, 1930), Anno VI, N.S., 73–77; Weber, Simone, "P. Eusebio F. Chini, Apostolo ed Esploratore del Nord America," in *Bolletino del Clero dell' Arcidiocesi di Trento* (Trento, Luglio-Agosto, 1930). Weber, Simone, *Nazionilità e Cognomen di P. Eusebio Chini* (Trento, 1930). Most of these writings were elicited by the publication of Kino's autobiography and the consequent Kino celebration held in Trento in 1930.

Entrance to Val di Non, Kino's birthplace

The Kino family at the old Kino residence

Jesuit monastery at Ingolstadt

foreign lands. The latter was not wholly a secondary objective, for the urge to roam was strong within the breast of this young Italian. Presumably the idea of becoming a Jesuit came to him while he was a student in the college at Trent. It may have even antedated that event, for his relative, Father Martini, had won fame as a missionary in China, and his name was a household word at Segno.

While Eusebio was a student at Hala—in 1663, to be exact—his inclination was crystallized into a resolve. He was then a youth of eighteen. In some way that is not disclosed he was stricken with a "mortal illness." Whatever the circumstance, the case was alarming, and the physicians despaired of the young collegian's life. It was an anxious moment. By the bedside stood a Jesuit father who knew of Kino's ambition. He offered a suggestion to the imperiled youth. Acting upon it, Eusebio made a vow that determined his career. He solemnly promised his patron saint, San Francisco Xavier, Apostle of the Indies, that if his life were spared he would seek admission to the Society of Jesus and employment in a mission to foreign lands.

Kino recounts this incident in a letter written in 1670 to Father Oliva, the Father General at Rome. "Seven years ago, when a student of rhetoric, and confined to my bed by a mortal illness, at the persuasion of one of our Fathers, to whom was already known my ardent desire to enter the Society of Jesus and go to the Indian Mission, I made a vow that if I recovered my health I would seek both the Society and the Indian Mission." [1] Years later, when a veteran missionary in the wilds of America, Kino told this story in more graphic language. He was still passionately loyal to his patron saint. "To the most glorious and most pious thaumaturgus and apostle of the Indies, San Francisco Xavier, we all owe very much. I owe him first my life, of which I was caused to despair by the physicians of the city of Hala, of Tirol, in the year 1663; second, my entrance into the Society of Jesus; third, my coming to these missions. . . . And because I know that I owe, and do not know whether or not I pay,

---

[1] Kino to Oliva, Ingolstadt, June 1, 1670. Original Latin manuscript in Fondo Gesuitico al Gesù di Roma, Codex Germaniae Superiori Indipetae, 1661–1730, folio 69. Printed in Tacchi-Venturi, Pietro, "Sei Lettere Inédite del P. Eusebio Chino al P. Gian Paolo Oliva Gen. d.C.d.G.," in *Studi Trentini di Scienze Storiche,* Annata XI, 9–10 (Trento, 1930).

I beg and entreat all the celestial court and all the earthly universe to aid me in giving him due thanks for so many celestial favors bestowed upon the most unworthy of all the earth." [1]

This solemn vow Kino held sacred. At the end of two years he carried out the first part of his promise by entering the Jesuit Order.[2] He began his novitiate in the autumn of the year 1665.[3] Now followed twelve long years of arduous study and hard discipline, such as all Jesuits were and still are required to undergo in preparation for their life work. To equip young Kino the best colleges of south Germany were laid under tribute. Freiburg, Ingolstadt, Innsbruck, München, and Oettingen contributed their respective quotas. And St. Ignatius himself could not have wished for a more zealous disciple.[4] Meanwhile, out of gratitude to his patron saint, Kino added "Francisco" to his own name.

The novitiate and scholastic studies passed, in October, 1667, Kino began his three years' course in Philosophy at the celebrated university of Ingolstadt, the most important in the Jesuit province of Upper Germany. That his mind was now fully made up regarding a career is evidenced by the fact that two months later, there at Ingolstadt, he willed all his property to the Jesuit Order. The gift was "for the better maintenance of poor persons dedicated to God." Eusebio had burned all his worldly bridges behind him and joined Loyola's army.[5] Strangely enough, this will is the earliest of his writings known to us.

[1] Kino, *Favores Celestiales*, Prologo; Kino, *Hist. Mem.*, I, 97–98. The date in the original manuscript heretofore has been read 1669, a mistake for 1663.

[2] Beristáin y Souza, José Mariano, *Biblioteca Hispano-Americano Septentrional, Adiciones y Correcciones* (Mexico, 1898), 392, says he entered on November 20; Tacchi-Venturi ("Sei Lettere") says it was November 10. In 17th century manuscripts the numerals 1 and 2 often are very much alike and are mistaken for each other.

[3] In one place Kino says that he began his novitiate at Lansperga (Landsberg), and in another that it was at Freiburg.

[4] The primary facts of Kino's student career after he became a Jesuit are set forth in the manuscript *Libro de Profesiones* of the Province of Mexico, quoted by Beristáin. These are supplemented by Father Tacchi-Venturi who, by utilizing "the old manuscript catalogues of the Province of Upper Germany," was able to establish the outline of a *curriculum studiorum* for Kino. In his *Favores Celestiales* and other writings Kino himself contributes supplementary data (Beristáin, *op. cit.*, 393; Tacchi-Venturi, *op. cit.*).

[5] Kino's manuscript will, dated at Ingolstadt, December 10, 1667 (Latin manuscript in the possession of Father Simone Weber, Trento, Italy). The document recites that Kino made his will "by deliberate and mature decision . . . for the greater glory of the Divine Majesty and for the salvation not only of my own soul but also of the souls of my dear parents," both of whom had passed beyond. See also the record of the division of the Chini family property, Enneberg, August 27, 1668. Original manuscript (Latin, Italian, and German) in the possession of Maestro Benedetto Chini, Rovereto, Italy.

The young scholar now became a teacher, as was required of all Jesuits. In the autumn of 1670, when he had finished his course in Philosophy, he was sent to give instruction in what Tacchi-Venturi calls belles lettres—the official Jesuit record calls it grammar—in the college of Hala, at Innsbruck. His return thither aroused vivid memories, for this was the very place where as a student he had experienced his "mortal illness" and made his solemn vow. This period as pedagogue, called the Regency, lasted till 1673, when he returned to the University of Ingolstadt, to spend four years in Theology.

In the course of all these studies Kino took special interest in mathematics. One of his teachers at Ingolstadt was Father Adam Aigenler, the cartographer, who in Kino's time at the University published there "a very beautifully executed general map of all the terrestrial world." "My father master of mathematics" Kino affectionately called him many years later. Another of his famous mentors was Father Scherer, also geographer and map maker. Endowed with natural gifts, and stimulated by such teachers, Kino excelled in mathematics. Indeed, while still a student he attained such proficiency in the branch that he attracted the attention of the Duke of Bavaria, and was invited to become a professor under ducal patronage. He tells the story:

"I discussed various mathematical sciences with his Lordship the Duke of Bavaria, who rules today, and with his Lordship his father, when their highnesses together, in the year 1676, came from the Electoral Court of Munich to see that great fortification, city, and university of Ingolstadt, and our greatest college of that city and province of Bavaria in Upper Germany, and was invited to give courses in these sciences, arts, and occupations there in Europe." [1] This was doubtless a great temptation to the village-bred boy, but he had his eyes set on mysterious lands beyond the seas, so he declined.

Eusebio's days in college cubicles were now nearly over. The long course in Theology was finished. To complete the arduous Jesuit discipline he went in 1677 to Oettingen, to the *schola affectus,* as Saint Ignatius called the third probation, prescribed for his aspiring disciples

[1] Kino, *Favores Celestiales,* Parte I, Lib. ii, Cap. 4; Kino, *Hist. Mem.,* I, 330–333.

before they make their final solemn profession. This test over, the
humble son of Segno was ready to find his place in the world.[1]

VII

PIOUS GAMBLING

Student life gave wings to Kino's dream of a mission to foreign
lands. The Jesuits during these years were filling the air with tales
of their apostolic adventures in Asia, the Americas, and the islands
of the seas. They were the greatest travelers and best geographers of
their day. Their letters and their annual relations set young Kino on
fire. He would go and do likewise. So, when his course in Philosophy
was hardly finished, he addressed the Father General. He would
gladly go abroad as missionary, even in the humblest capacity. "I feel
so endowed with the spirit," he wrote, "that in any place or office
whatsoever, even though it be most lowly, where I may be sent at the
command of my superior, there I shall be most content." He preferred a mission to the Indies, "or to China, or some other very
difficult one of like nature, if indeed, to the Divine Grace anything is
difficult."

This was in 1670, when Kino was nearly twenty-five. His petition
not being granted, it was oft repeated. His letters to Father Oliva became almost a refrain. Spurred by the sending of two of his associates
to Asia, a second time he addressed the Father General. Ever obedient,
he said, if his superiors so willed he was content to continue his
studies and perfect his preparation. But his eyes were turned toward
the Orient. "I can say that from the moment I heard that Fathers
Beatus Amrhyn and Adamus Aigenler were appointed to China . . .
desires arose in me of obtaining a similar mission such that I could
scarcely be satisfied until the matter had been commended to God
and . . . to my most reverend Father." Amrhyn and Aigenler both
lost their lives during the voyage, but this merely fanned the flame.

---

[1] Tacchi-Venturi, *op. cit.* The *Libro de Profesiones* as quoted by Beristáin (*op. cit.*, 392)
gives the following sketch of Kino's Jesuit career: "Entered the society in the novitiate of
Lansperga, of the Province of Upper Germany, November 20, 1665; he made his vows; he
finished his studies, made his third probation, and has taught grammar three years."

Once more Eusebio's appeal was in vain. Another year passed and again he petitioned. Another year and another letter. Father Oliva gave encouragement but no appointment. A fifth and a sixth time Kino importuned. What a persistent youth the Father General must have thought him. Still a seventh time Kino wrote. Success at last, after eight years of waiting! We can readily imagine his delight when word now came that his oft-repeated request had been granted. He would after all become a missionary in foreign lands! [1]

Kino's fondest wish had always been that he might go to the Far East. This field of missionary adventure had intrigued him ever since in his early boyhood he had read of the martyrdom of Carolus Spinola. China was the scene of the renowned labors and death of his patron, San Xavier. To China had gone his relative, Father Martin Martini. Both had made their names immortal there. So Kino dreamed of China. He tells us that while a student at Ingolstadt his window faced the east, and that, like a love-sick swain, he spent much of his leisure time gazing in that direction in order that he might thus become oriented. "It was always a most agreeable pleasure to me"— these are his own words—"to live in the rooms of our college whose windows looked toward the East, so that I might be comforted, at times oft-repeated during the day, by the mere sight of the East." [2] Between gazings he devoted himself assiduously to mathematics, for in China the Jesuits had found favor with the rulers because of their mathematical learning. They had helped to revise the Chinese calendar and they had made maps. So Kino prepared himself for a similar service. [3]

[1] Kino to Oliva, Ingolstadt, June 1, 1670; same to same, Ala, Innsbruck, January 31, 1672; same to same, Ala, June 18, 1673; same to same, Ingolstadt, February 25, 1675; same to same, Ingolstadt, April 7, 1676; same to same, Old Oettingen, March 17, 1678. Original Latin manuscripts in Codex Germaniae Superiori Indipetae, 1661–1730, folios 69, 99, 121, 139, 141, 190. Printed by Tacchi-Venturi, *op. cit.*, and Tacchi-Venturi, Pietro, "Nuove Lettere Inédite del P. Eusebio Francesco Chino," in *Archivum Historicum Societatis Jesu, III*, pp. 248–264 (Roma, 1934).

[2] Kino to the Duchess of Aveiro y Arcos, Cádiz, December 14, 1680. Original Latin manuscript in the Huntington Library. One day at Ingolstadt, in the summer of 1931, during the noon hour, in order to get an unobstructed snap-shot of the east window of the old Jesuit College building out of which Kino had gazed, I raised a neighborhood crew and by hand we moved a loaded coal truck around the corner and out of the line of vision. It cost me only the Trinkgeld for the men. Fortunately no policeman appeared on the scene.

[3] "I have always had an especially strong leaning toward the conversions of Great China, and at the suggestion of the superiors I applied myself to the mathematical sciences, which are very general there, and in the beginning I asked to go to the missions there, because in that great vineyard of the Lord had lived and worked my kinsman, Father Martin Martini, who wrote the celebrated volumes and made geographical maps of the great empire and monarchy of Great

Now, at last, his dream had come true. He was to become a missionary in foreign lands. But his joy was not unmixed, for he found himself in a predicament. The mission to which he was assigned by Father Oliva was partly for America and partly for Asia. With Kino another Tyrolese, Father Antonio Kerschpamer, was sent from Ingolstadt. The provincial, who attended to the details, was ordered that one of the two should go to Mexico, the other to the Philippines. The provincial in turn left the choice to be settled by the two men between themselves.

What was Kino to do? He was burning with a desire to go with the party bound for the Orient. But God's will must be done. Not to be selfish, he asked Father Antonio to choose. But Father Antonio was quite as caballero as himself. It was a case of Alphonse and Gaston. Neither one would make the choice. But it could be left to Chance. Perhaps God would manifest His wish through this means. So, "while we were engaged in this pious argument," Kino writes to a friend, "it occurred to us to settle our devout quarrel by lots." Therefore, two slips of paper were prepared. On one was written, "Mexico," on the second, "Philippines." Alas, Father Antonio drew "Philippines"; to Father Eusebio fell "Mexico." Chance had failed him and his hopes were dashed. All his mathematics would go to waste. But he prayed for grace, and peace came to his mind. He humbly accepted his fate,— but he still hoped. Perhaps something would turn up.[1]

China." (Kino, *Favores Celestiales*, Parte III, Lib. ii, Cap. 13; *Hist. Mem.*, II, 77–78. List of Martini's works in footnote, 78.)

Kino's ground for thinking that mathematicians were at a premium in China was well founded. The Jesuits had made a great impression at the Chinese court, and not the least reason was their mathematical skill. Fathers Ricci, Langobardi, Schaal, and Verbiest were all men of mathematical and scientific training and they made themselves useful to the Ming dynasty. "They prepared correct maps of the provinces. They reformed the calendar. They taught the Chinese how to manufacture brass cannon. They . . . translated numerous mathematical and scientific treatises." Later they transferred their allegiance to the Manchu dynasty, and continued in favor by continued usefulness. Under Emperor K'anghsi, they made a careful survey of the empire and prepared maps of the provinces which remain today the source of most of the maps of China" (E. T. Williams, *A Short History of China*, New York and London, 1928, 207–208, 215).

[1] Kino to the Duchess of Aveiro y Arcos, Cádiz, November 16, 1680.

The Way to the Indies

VIII

BAGS AND BOXES

BOTH THE PHILIPPINE AND THE AMERICAN MISSION were to sail from Cádiz, for both were to work in Spanish lands. The rendezvous assigned for the voyage to Spain was Genoa, and thither Kino and Kerschpamer made their way without loss of time. Father Eusebio has left us a record of the journey. They set out from Oettingen on March 30, going first to Munich. Here they remained six days while the "necessary things" were prepared for the journey. There was hammering of boxes and stuffing of bags. The last goodbyes were said, and the adventurers were off. Their coach rolled across the wide, level plains of Bavaria and soon reached Hala at Innsbruck. It was now fifteen years since there he had suffered his "mortal illness" and made the solemn vow that fixed the course of his life.

But Kino's eager spirit was facing the future, not the past. We have a letter which he wrote from Innsbruck to Father Schnurnberg. It was all about the mission to the Philippines. It contained new information regarding that exotic land which started anew his dreams of the Orient. "In that place Beelzebub is worshipped." And "for those who go thither there is an adamantine law that they must never return; secondly, that they must abstain from wines." Yet for all that he would give his head to go.[1]

Germany was now left behind. Threading Brenner Pass, the travelers descended the slopes of the Alps to sunny Italy. Kerschpamer bade his old friends good bye at Salorno, and Kino shed his farewell tears amid the scenes of his boyhood in Val di Non. Then they pushed forward once more. En route they passed through Trent, Brescia, and

---

[1] A recent biographer of Kino applies to the pious town of Ala instead of to the Orient, Kino's account of Beelzebub, wine, drunkenness, marauding, and murder. I feel it my solemn duty to restore Ala's good name.

Milan, and on May 2 reached Genoa. The old city then looked much as the intra-mural portion appears today. From the heights as they approached they beheld the tall masts of the ships gracefully anchored in the harbor of the famous port that claimed Columbus as its son. Passing the gate that admitted them through the massive walls, they threaded the narrow, canyon-like streets to the Casa Profesa, where they found hospitality with their Jesuit brethren. On the way from Germany they had been "always safe, and everywhere . . . courteously received and entertained."

Kino and his companion were the first of the missionary band to reach the rendezvous. Two days behind them seven arrived from Bohemia. Next came two from Naples. They were still awaiting six from Austria, then they could start. But no chance for sailing was in sight. So, eager to be on their way, they talked of going overland to Spain.

Father Eusebio gives us one more glimpse of himself before leaving Genoa. On May 10 he wrote to his friend and patron, D. Pietro Lucca, of Caldaro. He did not have time to visit him on his way, so he wrote a hasty but fond goodbye. "If we do not see each other again in this life, we shall hope to meet in another and better one, in Heaven." This was Kino's farewell to Italy, land of his birth.[1] Thereafter, in all his long correspondence, I have found no expression on Kino's part of a hope or even a desire to return. He was fully committed to the will of God and the whims of Destiny.

IX

PIRATES AND SEA MONSTERS

For the journey of Kino and his companions from Genoa to Spain we have the excellent diary kept by Kino himself.[2] It is written in

[1] Kino to Schnurnburg, Ala, Innsbruck, April 12, 1678. Original Latin manuscript in Bayerische Staatsbibliothek, München, Codex Latinus Monacensis, No. 26472, fol. 259; Kino to Oliva, Genoa, May 6, 1678. Original Latin manuscript in Cod. Germ. Sup. Indipetae, 1661–1730, fol. 179; Kino to Lucca, Genoa, May 10, 1678. Original Italian manuscript in the possession of Maestro Benedetto Chini, Rovereto, Italy.

[2] Kino, diary of his voyage from Genoa to Sevilla, Genoa, June 12, 1678–Sevilla, July 27, 1678. Original Latin manuscript in Bayerische Hauptstaatsarchiv, München, Jesuitica.

Latin and addressed to the father provincial. We also have a good account of the sea voyage by Adam Gerstl, one of Kino's traveling companions. Their experiences were typical of Jesuit travel to America. Nineteen Black Robes left Genoa on June 12. Gerstl gives us the names of eighteen.[1] It was the plan that all should go to Spain and thence to Mexico. There seven would remain; the other twelve would go on mule-back to Acapulco and sail thence across the broad Pacific to the Philippines. It was no soft journey which these voluntary exiles were facing.

Before noon of the fateful sailing day the nineteen travelers, accompanied by many Genoese priests, went from the Casa Profesa down to the harbor. From the shore they were rowed four German miles[2] out to the flagship, a goodly craft commanded by Captain Francesco Columbus, said by Kino to be a relative of the great discoverer. On this vessel, counting crew, soldiers, and passengers, there were two hundred persons besides the Jesuit band. A smaller vessel, the San Nicolás, was there ready to sail in company.

Travel by sea in that day was not so bad as one might imagine. The price of each passage to Cádiz, including meals, was sixty imperials, "which sum had to be paid at once to the Master Captain." That was rather stiff. But Columbus certainly spread a good table. "In my opinion we were fed well, and even sumptuously," Kino remarks, "with at least four courses at each meal, often five, and frequently six, not counting the customary fruit served at both dinner and supper." There was little to complain of here. Father Gerstl gives additional details. "As for beds, each of us had his own mattress, which we spread out at night in our very comfortable room, covering ourselves with our cloaks."

The landlubbers soon got a typical initiation into sea travel. On the day after starting there was a violent wind, followed by thunder, lightning, rain, and a heavy sea. Kino proved to be a good sailor. He was not altogether exempt from *mal de mar,* but he quickly re-

---

[1] They were Fathers Calvanese, Borgia, De Angelis, Mancker, Borango, Gerstl, Tilpe, Strobach, Neumann, Cuculinus, Klein, Christman, Ratkay, Revel (Reidl), Fischer, Kerschpamer (Kerschbaumer), Kino and Brother Poruhradiski. See also Huonder, Anton, S. J., *Deutsche Jesuitenmissionäre des 17. und 18. Jahrhunderts* (Freiburg, 1899).

[2] A German mile was a little longer than a Spanish league, but the two terms were sometimes used interchangeably.

covered. Like most good sailors he was rather proud of it. "Three of us said Mass in the morning; I commenced but was unable to finish. However, in a short time I was quite well again, and so remained during the rest of the voyage, praise God." Some others, poor Kerschpamer among them, were not so fortunate, as entries in the diary show. "June 13.—Many persons became weak from seasickness and disorders of the stomach, and were unable to attend the regular meals." June 15, because of a calm, "we were all present at dinner." Evidently this was considered an event worth noting.

There was more than one storm, and housekeeping on board ship was sometimes seriously upset. "The manner in which we ate both dinner and supper today was very peculiar," Kino wrote on June 17. "We had to eat our food on the floor, because the dishes could not be kept securely enough in their places at the table. Therefore a large carpet was spread on the floor in the dining hall. Over this a tablecloth was laid and set with goblets, spoons, plates, knives, forks, and napkins for each,—a very low table at which we were able to sit only by getting down on the floor. Our most distinguished Master Captain came in during the meal to . . . console us."

There were other diversions than storms and seasickness. Fear of pirates kept everybody free from excessive ennui. It need not surprise one that there should be soldiers on this merchant vessel on which Kino was sailing, for the Mediterranean was still infested by Algerine pirates, then commonly called Turks. The worst days were over, but the memory of them was yet vivid. Every Italian schoolboy could tell how Barbarossa had ravaged the coast, sacked Reggio, burned ships in a score of harbors, captured eleven thousand Christians and made them slaves; and how he had barely failed to capture Julia Gonzaga, "the loveliest woman in Europe" because she managed to escape in her night-dress on the back of a galloping horse.

That raid of the "Sea Wolf" was now long past, but the mention of his name still hushed Italian children when nights were dark and the bleak wind howled. After Spain's Don Juan had won his decisive victory at Lepanto there was no Barbarossa, and no Dragut the Rover. But there had been an Ochiali. Lesser Algerine pirates even yet overhauled merchant fleets on the Mediterranean, and levied blackmail on

European powers. Christian captives still served Turks as slaves or rotted in Moorish dungeons. Not long since, three thousand Englishmen had languished in Algerine prisons, and English wives and daughters had besieged Parliament with prayers and tears for their release. Captain Columbus was too good a sailor to go unprepared. And every seaman, soldier, and passenger regarded a voyage on the Mediterranean as a chance for adventure. It is not strange that every sail was feared as a pirate ship.[1]

They were nearly a week out of harbor when the first scare occurred. On the morning of June 18, when in view of the Island of Minorca, from the lookout they caught sight of two large ships approaching from the south. Taking them to be Turkish freebooters, the captain ordered everything in the flagship made ready for a fight. The missionaries contributed their share. "In accordance with a custom observed at sea, we handed over the coverings and mattresses of our beds, in order that the soldiers and sailors might so suspend and dispose them as to form a breastwork." Thus sheltered, the soldiers were ready to fight. The Jesuits now withdrew to a place of safety. "We gathered up our other personal belongings as well as we were able, and most of us betook ourselves to the Captain's quarters, in order that the officers and men might have a freer field for discharging the guns and performing the other maneuvers of war."

For a long time everybody was in suspense. It was not plain whether the pirate ships were approaching or receding. But nothing happened. Dinner was served. Suddenly, at the end of the meal, the men were all ordered again to their posts, for the strange vessels were close at hand. But soon there was a sigh of relief, for it was now seen that the ships bore the flag of England. They were friendly craft; Captain Francesco saluted them with seven guns, and the Jack Tars returned the compliment with five.

Kino's comment reveals the insecurity of the Mediterranean at that date, and England's part in policing it. "They were royal ships, furnished with full armament, and with other equipment as well, and they zealously defended these seas from the insolence of Turks and

---

[1] See Stanley Lane-Poole, *The Barbary Corsairs* (New York and London, 1902); E. Hamilton Currey, R.N., *Sea-Wolves of the Mediterranean* (New York, 1910).

pirates." There were other scares of this kind before Cádiz was reached.

On the voyage the Jesuits did not slacken their accustomed religious routine. Mass was said every morning by several fathers, sometimes as many as seven, unless the sea was rough and stomachs were squeamish. There were sermons, confessions, and communion. Kino tells us of the Vesper services. "In the evening twilight, in accordance with a custom which thereafter we observed daily, litanies were chanted by all on board, preceded by the Antiphon Salve Regina, and followed by the Responsory of San Antonio de Padua, as they call it; followed also by the psalm De Profundis, by another hymn to the Blessed Virgin, and finally by prayers for the success of the voyage, for the prevention of storms, for souls in Purgatory, and for all who are in mortal sin. When these had been concluded the ship's bell sounded, very much as our own bells sound in Ingolstadt, and the signal was given for the Angelus."

Sailor's oaths on this voyage were milder than usual. The fathers were bound for missions to the heathen. But on board they did not miss their splendid opportunity to hold a mission *entre fieles*. Among a hundred or more sailors and soldiers there were hardened fellows who had not gone to confession for months or even years. The zealous young evangelists rose to the occasion, and through their influence some of the crew were smitten with contrition. Kino writes on June 15, "Among the sailors there was one who after darkness had fallen sought me out to atone for his sins by the sacrament of confession." One night after supper Father Calvanese preached a powerful sermon from the prow of the ship. He must have been eloquent, for next day the harvest was bounteous. Seventy took communion that day.[1]

Kino was born with the instincts of a traveler, and he took an interest in all he saw. His diary was kept like a veteran's. He described seasickness, ship routine, meals, storms, strange vessels. One day he amused himself watching dolphins, and there was a whale "which

---

[1] June 23 was Eve of the Feast of San Juan Bautista, and a special ceremony was in order. After Father de Angelis had preached a sermon the priests lit the festal lamps and hung them about the ship, where they were kept burning till nearly midnight. A rocket was thrown into the waves, "and it went out in smoke."

exceeded in size even the larger ships which came to Ingolstadt on the Danube and to Hala on the Oenus for wine."

Speed varied according to wind and weather. The first morning after starting, the Capitana was scarcely more than a mile from its anchorage at Genoa. On June 14 they saw at their left the island of Corsica. Next day and the next they were becalmed for hours. On the 18th they caught a glimpse of Minorca, which they kept at their right. Two days later they reached Formentor, asylum of a Spanish penal colony. "This island, covered with very tall trees, is like a great forest, and abounds in wild beasts of all kinds. To it are banished many persons found guilty of certain crimes; and there, in the felling of trees or in other hard labor, they suffer punishment throughout a large part of their lives, indeed, often until death."

X

THE VEIL OF SANTA VERONICA

On the morning of June 25 the vessels arrived at the harbor of Alicante, or Alona, as it was often called. There, in plain sight when Kino awoke, were the light house, the high perched castle, and the flat roofed city itself. The landing was made with due ceremony. Captain Francesco sent an officer ashore in a boat with health certificates and other papers necessary for entry. Salutes were fired and anchors cast. When the launch returned from the town it brought two fathers from the Jesuit College of Alicante, who had come to welcome the visitors. Before night all the missionaries went ashore, taking most of their baggage, for there was talk of continuing the journey to Cádiz overland. They reached tierra firme about seven o'clock, and were conducted to the College.

Kino was quite overcome by the reception extended to the visitors. It gave him a new sense of his place in the world. Others besides the Jesuits wished to do them honor. One of the canons of the Cathedral begged the privilege of lodging half a dozen of the voyagers in his quarters. Other priests in the city likewise offered their hospitality, "in an indulgence similar to that of our hosts." In fact, the arrival was an event for the little coast town. For, said Kino, "we fathers of the Society were here in numbers never before seen in this place, and in many persons our presence aroused admiration and piety." But in spite of the universal hospitality, the travelers preferred to remain with their own brethren in the College, even though it was so crowded that some of the visitors had to sleep in the gymnasium.

The halt of a week in Alicante gave Kino his first touch with Spanish life. The place was well worth stopping to see, for it held a shrine of wide-spread fame. Just outside the town was the monastery of Santa Veronica, where was kept under three keys the sacred Sudarium, or handkerchief, or veil, with which, on the way to Calvary, the compassionate woman had wiped the brow of Christ, whose suffering features were left imprinted on the fabric. Who would not turn aside to behold such a rare treasure? At the moment the relic was in the principal church of the city, brought there to avert a threatened plague.

Besides several regular feast days which fell during the visit, there were special occasions which offered novelty. On the very night of their arrival, without awaiting supper, the visitors all went out on the street to see a procession organized to counteract the plague, which was prevalent in neighboring towns, and to avert threatened war. With the brilliantly lighted torches, and the procession of monks carrying the sacred Veil of Santa Veronica, the spectacle was impressive. One day Kino said Mass in the church where the Sudarium was preserved. In the afternoon all the visiting Jesuits, accompanied by the Rector of the College, went to the same church to kiss the sacred relic. These were memorable experiences for the devout traveler.

There were diversions a little more secular in character. One afternoon some of the visitors went down to the beach, and walked around the town to see the sights. On this occasion Kino and a companion were "asked to seat ourselves on benches and invited to view public spectacles which gave us much pleasure. These were being enacted not far away in the streets, while a bull of great size, which was to be sacrificed in honor of San Juan Bautista, was being driven up and down." During one of his walks in the town, seeing some little crosses which were sold very cheap, Kino purchased a large supply of them for use in his future missionary work.

The stop in Alicante was not long. The day after arrival a council was held to decide whether the journey to Cádiz should be continued by sea or by land. It was hoped to sail from Spain in the annual Flota, or merchant fleet, that went to Vera Cruz. Through letters received by the rector it was learned that the Flota expected to leave for America that summer on July 2, although it might be delayed till the 10th or the 12th. There was need for haste, and as the land journey was uncertain it was decided to continue by sea. So the Jesuits kept in readiness for a summons by Captain Francesco. To insure admission to the port of Cádiz, one day they went down to the curia to get health certificates.[1]

On July 2 the Captain notified the Jesuits to be ready to go aboard next morning. Eight of them did not wait that long, but went out to the ship the same night. Next morning the rest, Kino among them, arose before sunrise, said Mass, drank some chocolate, and were rowed to the Capitana, which was already outside the harbor. "Some of the fathers of Alona accompanied us to the port," says Kino, "and we left them forty-three imperials, because they had entertained and fed us so liberally and with such great kindness for eight days."

Alicante lay behind.

XI

STRANGE SHAPES IN THE CLOUDS

Progress was slow. All day on July 3, for lack of favorable wind, the ships remained in sight of Alicante. On the 5th they had in view on the right the sierras of Granada, covered with snow, "even as the mountains of Tyrol are covered in the months of March and April." As they passed Málaga the blue bay smiled, but the massive old Moorish fortification frowned down at them from its mountain

---

[1] Here Kino saw things that interested him. "In the main entrance of this building, near a large and majestic altar, some very beautiful pictures were hung, portraying separately and in a most splendid and elegant manner, each and every king of Aragón."

height, just as it glowers on travelers today. On the 8th, when near the towering rock of Gibraltar, the voyagers began to see the shores of Africa, topped by the twin peaks of Ceuta. Now came a serious setback. A west wind blew up so strong that the sails of the *San Nicolás* were torn away. Next morning the gale was so furious that no one could say Mass, and both vessels were driven back to the vicinity of Málaga. In the space of three hours they had lost all the distance made in four days.

Kino, with his scientific turn of mind, was interested in all natural phenomena. The bright sea fish especially engaged him. One evening some dolphins played very near the ship, "their great size exceeding that of an ox." Another sea-monster chasing the dolphins, and easily surpassing them in weight, swam entirely round the ship. "Its color was such as we had never seen before. It was dazzlingly white, yet partly green and alternately yellow, deep red and blue, and of such extraordinary brilliance that even when two or three feet, or more, below the surface of the water it seemed to rival the beauty of the rainbow."

One day fishermen caught a monster that would outweigh a large horse. It had a tail on its back, and by the Italians was called mola. Another fish caught "was a beauty to be admired by all," says Kino. "The color of its head and back was coral, strewn, so to speak, with silver stars, and the hue was exceedingly brilliant. Its belly was white, or rather ivory. Its sides were golden, variegated with green and blue. Its eyes were marvellously bright. You might have described them as splendid sapphires set in topaz and gold. In a word, the plumage of no bird, however gorgeous, could rival the beauty of this fish, so resplendent it was and so diversified with colors of every hue. Wonderful, we said, is God in His works."

Kino the mathematician now had opportunities to try out his astronomy. One evening, before the moon rose, he observed several constellations, "especially those of the south . . . Ara, Lupus, Centaurus, and similar ones which cannot so easily be seen in Germany." On board Kino played with his mathematical instruments. One day he and some companions measured the Capitana. It was 168 feet long, 38 feet wide, 52 feet high, and had a mast 150 feet tall. Several times

Part of the first page of Kino's diary of his voyage from Genoa to Sevilla, in June and July, 1679.

(From the original Latin manuscript in the archives of Munich)

An old fort at Cadiz, where Kino was shipwrecked

he assisted in taking latitudes. On one occasion his fellow astronomer was Captain Columbus.

Sometimes Kino and his companions amused themselves watching fanciful shapes in the clouds. Who that has sailed has not? Their imaginations were especially stirred when they faced the mysterious borders of Mohammedan Africa. One evening while "four of us were gazing at the near-by shores," he says, "one of our party exclaimed that he saw a dragon on the summit of one of the mountains. I looked for it with the rest. Both with the naked eye and with the telescope I saw above the top of the mountain a kind of monster, the form of which, though shifting, was very like that of a dragon. Presently the whole thing disappeared. Then, while we were still watching the mountain, which itself had suffered no change, we began to see something like a forest of very tall trees, of which not a trace had hitherto been apparent. A little later this forest was transformed into the likeness of a great ship, which had two beaks, or prows, as it were, one facing the south, the other north, which by turns increased and diminished by forty or fifty feet. It was all very vague, but its shape was roughly as described. At length it changed into the form of a huge anvil; upon this last we who were standing in the stern were all agreed. Finally it vanished completely from sight." Things began to look awesome. "There was no one who could explain to us this mystery," says Kino, "but there was one who ascribed it to the magic art of the Turks, in which the African Turks are said to be very clever."

The 13th was unlucky. A mist that night caused a deviation from the true course. Just at the mouth of the Straits the pilot mistook an African mountain for one in Spain, and consequently steered south, straight to the African shore near Ceuta. Next morning the error was corrected, and the Straits were passed. But disappointment lay ahead. That evening, when near the harbor of Cádiz, they saw a Spanish fleet of forty-four ships only a short distance away. It was the Flota, sailing for the Indies.

The hearts of the Jesuits sank. This was the fleet in which they hoped to take passage for New Spain. But they were too late. As it passed before them the fleet eclipsed the setting sun, a sinister omen.

"When we saw this melancholy spectacle, we at once guessed its import, and most of us abandoned the hope of departing from Europe during the coming year."

There were still other delays. At dark that night they were almost at the entrance to the harbor of Cádiz. But it took four days to get inside, on account of bad weather and the strictness of immigration laws, particularly during the epidemic that was in progress. In attempting to enter, the sails were twice broken and the ship left in danger of going on the rocks. At last the storm abated. On the morning of the 19th port officials boarded the Capitana and examined ship and goods. "After an entertainment at the expense of our most illustrious Captain they granted to everybody the privilege of entering the city." Columbus knew the ropes.

Meanwhile Father Pedro Espinar, a procurator of missions for the Indies, came out in a boat to conduct the missionaries to the Jesuit college. He had eagerly awaited their arrival, for he had already paid 22,500 florins for their passage to Mexico. The fleet had sailed away without them and Father Espinar had to get his money back. He had also to write to the Father General in Rome to ask what to do with the missionaries until he could send them to their destination—which might be at least a year hence. And who would feed them during all this time? The procurator indeed had his troubles.

A week later Kino was at Sevilla. Whether he went by land or up the Guadalquivir River by boat we are not informed. Closing his diary on July 27 he told his provincial in Germany, "We shall wait for this decision [about sailing] in Sevilla, where we shall stay, just as if in a separate college, in the buildings and garden of the College of San Hermenegildo, whither our reverend father Pedro de Espinar conducted us from Cádiz four days ago." With his diary Kino sent a "crude geographical map" of their route. If they were not "too inelegant," he requested that both diary and map be sent to his dear old college at Ingolstadt.[1]

---

[1] Kino, diary of his voyage from Genoa to Sevilla, Genoa, June 12, 1678—Sevilla, July 27, 1678: Bayerische Hauptstaatsarchiv, München, Jesuitica, Nos. 293–294.

XII

"SI NO HA VISTO SEVILLA"

From the pen of Father Ratkay we have a succinct statement of what the Jesuits did to occupy their time while they were waiting in Sevilla for passage to America. The sojourn there, Father Neumann tells us, was "like a second novitiate," during which they prepared for their missions. "We not only busied ourselves with mathematics, astronomy, and other sciences, but also made many different things for future use. Some made compasses or sundials, or cases for these things; still others acquired a knowledge of distilling brandy, or of carving or turning. We did all this in order to impress the minds of the heathen with our commodities and with our arts, and thus make them more willing to accept the Christian faith."[1] One of the sundials was made by Kino for Father Thirso González, who later become Father General of the Order and a strong supporter of the man from Segno at a time when he needed help.

Father Gerstl's letters give a graphic account of some phases of Sevillan life. He heard and quoted with approval the old adage, still in use today, "Si no ha visto Sevilla no ha visto maravilla." The beauty of the churches impressed Father Adamo. "The Cathedral is so large that St. Stephen's church at Vienna could easily be placed inside it." He commented on customs unfamiliar to German eyes. "In Spain they do not ring the bells with a taut and a slack cord as in Germany. . . . On ordinary days they fasten the cord on the clapper and thus slowly beat with it just one side of the bell."

Gerstl was especially interested in the monopoly of industry and commerce by the Dutch and the French, of the latter of whom forty thousand lived in Sevilla; in the amazing number of clergy and monastic houses there; in the terrible pestilence which was raging in the country; in the prevalence of poverty and the multitude of beggars, of whom the archbishop regularly fed twenty-two thousand out of

[1] Ratkay to Father Nicolaus Avancinus, Mexico, November 16, 1680. In Stöcklein, Joseph, *Der Neue Welt-Bott, mit allerhand Nachrichten dern Missionariorum Soc. Jesu* (Augsburg and Gratz, 1726), Part I. No. 28. Cited hereafter as *Neue Welt-Bott*. Neumaun, Joseph, *Historia Seditionum*, chapter II.

his income; in the havoc wrought by the bloodletters, at whose hands one of the nineteen Jesuits, Father Fischer, succumbed; in the crude methods of public execution, and the premature burials; in the bull-fights, in which the nobles participated but on which the Church frowned; and in the depreciation of silver on the arrival of a treasure fleet from America. He comments, "The Spaniards themselves admit that so much silver has already been brought that with it they could build a bridge from Cádiz to the West Indies." [1] In fact, this had become a saying.

The delay in Spain was unexpectedly long. Some royal ships sailed for America, but as they went by way of the African coast to get slaves, the Jesuits did not embark. Private vessels also sailed, but their charge for the passage was higher than the procurator was willing to pay, consequently he awaited the departure of the next royal fleet for the West Indies.

We have a letter written by Kino from Sevilla to his old friend Father Leinberer at Landsberg. [2] Naturally he reported news about missions. A band of Jesuits had recently been sent to Paraguay. Procurators were planning to raise a mission, especially of Germans, for New Granada. And there was a little personal news. Two months previously, when Kerschpamer, his companion, had made his final profession of faith, Kino had tried to express his Pythagorean joy by presenting him with some mathematical instruments, "symbols, as it were, of virtue and religious excellence."

XIII

SHIPWRECK

Late in March, Gerstl, Kino, and their companions returned by water to Cádiz, preparatory to sailing. Ratkay was one of the party, and a letter which he wrote supplements the accounts given by Kino

---

[1] Extracts of Gerstl's letters to his father, June 30, 1678–July 14, 1681. In Stöcklein, *Neue Welt-Bott,* I, No. 31.
[2] Kino to Father Leinberer, Sevilla, October 17, 1679. Original Latin manuscript in Bayerische Hauptstaatsarchiv, München. Jesuitica, Nos. 293–294.

and Gerstl. There was another three months' wait. Then, on July 7, with all their belongings, the Jesuits boarded the *Nazareno,* one vessel of the large West Indian fleet that was preparing to sail for Mexico. Of the twenty-three Jesuits now sailing, eighteen were bound for the Philippines and five for Mexico. Ratkay was one of the latter.

The missionaries felt unusually honored, and well they might. The Viceroy of New Spain and his wife, the lordly Conde and the gracious Condesa de Paredes,[1] were sailing for Mexico in the same fleet. With numerous attendants the viceregal pair boarded the Capitana or flagship. They were given a pompous send-off by the old seaport city. Cannons boomed, and for a time Kino and his companions were shrouded in a cloud of smoke.

The viceroy's presence gave the fleet prestige, but for three days the poor Jesuits were uncomfortable, nevertheless. They were required to find their own food till the *Nazareno* should leave the harbor, and they had been hurried on board so fast that the procurator had lacked time to supply them properly. So, says Ratkay, "like traveling journeymen in the cold inns," they had no food except bread and water. Belts were tightened. The three days seemed interminable, but at last they came to an end. On July 10 the new superior took charge, and he soon remedied the food situation. Life was more cheerful now.

Next day all the ships were towed out of the harbor. In order to avoid the large obstruction called "the Big Diamond," the pilot ran the ship on a sand bar and the wind finished the work by driving it on another rock. Water poured in and the passengers had to climb out on the upper deck. Confusion reigned and the crew was helpless. The Captain fired signals of distress. "We had recourse to God," says Ratkay, "and honored the Holy Virgin by the Lauretanian Litany and other prayers." Not alone the Jesuits looked above for help. The captain held before him the picture of the Virgin and prayed amid tears, "Oh, Most gracious Mother! Why wilt thou desert me in this time of tribulation!"

---

[1] Don Antonio de la Cerda, Conde de Paredes, Marqués de la Laguna, was viceroy of Mexico for six years, 1680–1686. His rule was marked especially by raids of English and French pirates, who sacked Vera Cruz in 1683, Tampico and Campeche in 1684, and West Coast ports in succeeding years.

To all appearances the *Nazareno* was lost. So the admiral ordered the cargo thrown overboard and commanded that all attention be given to saving the passengers. Boats came to the rescue, and fortunately all were saved. The missionaries were now a disheveled looking band. Deprived of their baggage, some without cloak or hat, they were loaded on a launch, and returned to Cádiz and to the Jesuit college. Kino, characteristically, attributed the rescue to his patron, San Francisco Xavier.

When the news reached the procurator he was shocked. But he was not a quitter. On the contrary, he bent every energy to get passage for his missionaries. He had lodged them long enough, and they were needed among the heathen. If they did not sail now there would be another long wait. So he hurried back and forth between the port authorities and the admiral of the fleet, trying to arrange for passage. Finding some encouragement, he aroused the sleeping Jesuits after midnight. As they rubbed their eyes they were surprised enough, for they had assumed that their chances for the voyage had vanished. Moreover, they had lost most of their baggage. "We were all without cloaks, caps or breviaries," says Kino. But not on this account did the energetic procurator stop. In a launch he hurried his charges to the fleet, which was already outside the harbor. There, with the admiral's permission, he went from vessel to vessel begging space for his men. The captains demurred, for the ships were already overcrowded. But the viceroy interceded, and eleven missionaries obtained passage.

Twelve disappointed Jesuits were left behind. Among them were Father Kino and his companion, Father Kerschpamer. Kino, who for eight years had waited for permission to go to the Indies, now had another lesson in patience. Gerstl writes of his own disappointment, "Eleven of us thus being luckily taken in, I, unhappy fellow, and eleven others, were rejected, and had to remain in spite of all my begging and praying." Commenting later on the loss of their baggage in the wreck of the *Nazareno*, Ratkay remarks: "Under such circumstances we have often regretted our unnecessary preparations during the two years in Sevilla." He was alluding to all the things they had so laboriously made for their missionary work during the delay. "For

God had preferred to sink into the sea all our tools, our labor, and our goods."

Gerstl and seven companions now returned to Sevilla to wait, and to minister during an epidemic. Kino and Revel remained as workers in the Jesuit college at Cádiz. They too were in the midst of an epidemic. Meanwhile the procurator conducted a lawsuit to recover six thousand dollars which he had paid in advance for passage for the wrecked missionaries. Let us hope that he was successful.[1]

XIV

THE DUCHESS

Several letters by Kino give us intimate knowledge of his doings in Cádiz. Shortly after the shipwreck he began a correspondence with the Duchess of Aveiro y Arcos, of Madrid.[2] The Duquesa was a bountiful patroness, keenly interested in promoting Jesuit missions in the Orient. Kino turned to her as to one destined to help him escape from the decision made against him by Fate, who had spoken through a slip of paper bearing the word "Mexico." He desired most of all to abide by God's will, but in his inmost heart he hoped that the

[1] Extract of letters from Adam Gerstl to his father, Sevilla, June 30, 1678–Mexico, July 14, 1681. Printed in German in Stöcklein, *Neue Welt-Bott,* I, No. 31; Ratkay to Avancinus, Frontiers of New Mexico, February 25, 1681. Printed in German in Stöcklein, *ibid.,* I, No. 29; Kino to the Duchess of Aveiro y Arcos, Cádiz, August 18, 1680. Original Italian manuscript in the Huntington Library.

[2] María Guadalupe de Lancaster, Duchess of Aveiro, Arcos, y Maqueda, was by birth a Portuguese of very noble blood. She was a descendant of the princely English adventurer John of Gaunt, hence the name Lancaster. From a Portuguese ancestor she inherited the Duchy of Aveiro, and in 1665, at the death of her brother, she succeeded to the Duchy of Maqueda. The third title came through her marriage with the Spanish Duke of Arcos. To the advantages of birth were added those of great wealth. She and her husband held vast estates, and shared with the dukes of Medina Sidonia and Feria the distinction of being the chief landowners of Granada, Estremadura, and Jaén. At the court of Madrid the Duchess was a person of influence. Her interests were manifold. She was an accomplished linguist, patroness of letters, and a painter of repute. It is even intimated that she was once a pupil of the great Velásquez. Her charities were proverbial, and she was a patroness of missions in all parts of the world. Famed for her piety, she was especially devoted to the Virgin of Guadalupe, whose name she bore. The celebrated shrine of Guadalupe, in the mountains of Estremadura, repeatedly enjoyed her generosity. Among other benefactions, she financed the building there of a beautiful *camarín,* or wardrobe, for the sacred statue; and after she died (in 1715), her body was buried at the shrine, where it still rests, beneath the throne of Our Lady. The vast, imposing, and historic old monastery of Guadalupe now offers delightful hospitality to travelers, to whom the priests in charge relate the story of the celebrated Duquesa.

little paper might not contain the last word which God had to say about the matter. Perhaps he might yet go to China. Something might turn up after all. To the Duchess Kino told his story. She in turn pinned her hopes on him as an instrument ready at hand for her plans. The common bond between them was their burning interest in saving souls of heathen in the Far East.

Their acquaintance was almost fortuitous. The go-between, who made Kino and the Duchess known to each other, was Father Theophilus de Angelis. This Jesuit, who had come from Genoa to Spain on the same ship with Kino, was on his way to the Orient. He visited the Duchess in Madrid, planned to go to the South Sea with her aid, and named Kino as his choice for a companion. On his return to Sevilla he wrote to the Father General at Rome about the matter and urged Kino to write to both the Duchess and the Father General. Kino modestly delayed writing to the lady, but he did write to Rome, though "with the indifference which seemed necessary as coming from a father missionary already assigned to his mission." That slip of paper bearing the word "Mexico" was still in his way.

Hitherto Kino had relied on Father Theophilus to effect arrangements. But now Father Theophilus was removed from the scene. He was one of the lucky ones who had sailed with the Flota, after the wreck of the *Nazareno*. Not only was Kino left behind, but the question of the South Sea mission was still unsettled. But Kino did not give up hope. Instead, he now took the matter into his own hands, and wrote to the Duchess. He recounted the story of the shipwreck, his failure to sail with Father de Angelis, and his boyhood dreams of the Orient.[1]

Thus was begun an interchange of ideas, hopes, and confidences between the Duchess and himself which constituted an epoch in Kino's life. In the course of the six months which yet remained before Kino left Spain we have ten letters by him to the Duquesa. Her replies have not come to light, but from Kino's letters we can infer what she wrote. Father Eusebio's enthusiasm gave the Duchess a new impulse. She wrote to him frequently and without reticence—three

---

[1] Kino to the Duchess of Aveiro y Arcos, Cádiz, August 18, 1680. Original Italian manuscript in the Huntington Library.

letters in one mail—setting forth her zeal for missions in Austral lands. In return Kino opened his heart. He wrote of many things, but his major theme was the Oriental mission. The Duchess was to him a new ray of hope.[1]

Father Eusebio at once revealed his personal disappointment at not being sent to the East. "All of us missionary fathers who for the last two years have lived in Spain would have considered it a special happiness if the superiors had sent us to the Marianas." Only the virtue of obedience could mitigate his own sorrow. "Some of us had from Rome our orders to go to New Spain, and this disposition for me [that slip of paper again] was and will be a reason why I do not dare request to go to other parts, unless the superiors so order and dispose it, although I have never lacked the desire or the spirit." The Duchess promised to try to find a way for Kino to embark at Lisbon for China, to go by the Portuguese route to join Father Theophilus. For this Kino devoutly thanked her. The great question now was permission to go. But obedience must be put first. "I do not request it unless the superiors so order it."

The Duquesa complained of the want of enthusiasm for missions. For the lack of zeal, Kino replied, "your anger hath a just complaint." But he at least was not lacking in zeal. "As for myself," he said, "I confess that from my earliest youth and especially after reading the life and martyrdom of our Father in Christ, Carolus Spinola, I have been consumed with a great eagerness to go to the East Indies, and with this in view I have devoted myself constantly to the study of mathematics." But obedience must come first. "May His most holy will be done; may His most holy will be done, now and for Eternity."[2]

It is in this letter that Kino tells of his ill luck in drawing lots with Father Kerschpamer. But he had not yet given up hope of getting to the Orient. His good stomach might yet land him there. On the voyage to Spain he had found himself a better sailor than his companion. Now, if in crossing the Atlantic this experience should be repeated, Father Antonio might be glad to forego the long voyage to

[1] Kino to the Duchess, Cádiz, September 15, 1680. Original Spanish manuscript in the Huntington Library.
[2] Kino to the Duchess, Cádiz, November 16, 1680. Original Latin manuscript in the Huntington Library.

the Orient and let him go instead. "Nevertheless, may the will of the Most High be done."

Kino was delighted with the Duquesa's prophecy of glorious martyrdoms in the East. To illustrate the point he told a story. A bishop of Milan once said to a canon that if he were Pope he would make the canon a saint. The canon replied, "that would be fine for me, for then your Most Reverend Lordship would be Pope and I should be a saint." Similarly, said Kino, "since your most Excellent Ladyship has foretold to me toil and martyrdom in Japan and China . . . I reply that this would be well for me, for then your Excellency would be a prophetess, and in due time I should be a martyr." [1] Kino was not without a sense of humor.

Father Eusebio had ideas about a route to the Orient. His study of astronomy was not mere theory. He thought he saw a practical use to make of the *Primum Mobile.* Go with it and not against it. "I believe that the journey into China would be more easily and comfortably made by way of the West Indies and the Philippines than by going around the Cape of Good Hope and crossing the Equator through the East Indies, Goa, etc. On the other hand, I believe that the return journey from China to Europe would very probably be easier if it were made through the East Indies instead of the West Indies. The reason in both cases appears to be that the movement of the ship and the trend of navigation are thus in conformity with the movement of the *Primum Mobile,* which revolves continually from east to west." [2] This reasoning seems simple enough. And if applied in practice it gave more chance for a missionary in Mexico to get to the Orient.

The Duchess feared a shortage of missionaries. But Kino had a suggestion. His own beloved province of Upper Germany could furnish them. Now, perhaps, in imagination Kino saw himself in China working, not with strangers, but beside his dear brothers, Hans, Jacob, Friedrich, Gottlieb, *und so weiter.* "In Germany our Company," said Kino, "esteem very greatly the missions of the Marianas Islands, with no less desire to be sent to convert those people. The province of

[1] Kino to the Duchess, Cádiz, December 6, 1680. Original Latin manuscript in the Huntington Library.

[2] In the Ptolemaic system the *Primum Mobile* was the tenth or outermost of the crystalline spheres. It was supposed to revolve from east to west every twenty-four hours, carrying the other spheres with it.

Upper Germany has more than two hundred applicants. Our Lord will not fail to hear the fervent desires of so many who truly would rather suffer and labor hard for their Redeemer and for the salvation of those Indies than to enjoy at once happiness in heaven with the Angels." [1] The provinces of Bohemia and Austria, said Kino, had more members than his own. But mere numbers did not count. German hardihood must not be overlooked. His brethren were the most rigorously trained for the privations of missionary life. "The majority . . . are men who truly love the cross of Christ and toil for His glory and the bringing of souls to salvation. They do not seek many bodily or temporal comforts, either in matters of food and clothing, or of dwelling place. They know they are voluntarily undertaking to endure cold and heat, hunger and thirst, and they are prepared to suffer such other hardships as are apt to occur at any time during pilgrimages to the Indies. [2]

The correspondence of Kino and the Duchess was not all quite so impersonal as what they wrote about China, the Marianas, the Philippines, and Terra Australis. Kino was lonely in a strange land and the Duchess extended to him a friendly welcome. The Duquesa, on the other hand, found in Kino some one who stirred her religious nature. It is not strange that a warm friendship sprang up between the two, although apparently they never met.

In his first letter Kino had told of his shipwreck in the *Nazareno*. This tale at the very start was a good tweak at the lady's heart strings. In the lively exchange of letters that ensued, numerous chatty bits were interspersed between martyrdoms, the saints, and the salvation of souls. Kino writes that all his companions in Spain are in good health, except that Father Pablo Klein "had to be bled a few days ago." He puts in a pious lesson for the Duquesa's edification: "The greater one's faith, the greater one's reward." He discusses his changing prospects for sailing to Mexico, and passes on the news as it comes to him.

Then there was a little contest in mutual remembrances. Pledges at first were restricted and special. In closing one of his letters Kino

---

[1] Kino to the Duchess, Cádiz, September 15, 1680.
[2] Kino to the Duchess, Cádiz, November 16, 1680.

asked to be remembered in the prayers of the Duchess, and as a recipro-
cal favor promised to remember her during Mass of the Feast of San
Xavier. As time went on these pledges became more sweeping. The
Duchess said a prayer for Kino on the Feast of his patron, and promised to do so on each anniversary of that day. Kino now promised to
offer a prayer for the Duquesa on the Feast of the Immaculate Conception "every year as long as I live." In a later epistle his pledge
became more extravagant. He would not be satisfied to set aside
merely one day in the year in which to pray for her, "but daily"—
Kino was still young—"God willing, wherever the Divine Will and
my obedience shall send me, I shall diligently make it my concern
to commend your Grace, and your beloved children, and your
apostolic zeal for converting infidels to the heavenly Father of
Light."

Gifts as well as pledges passed both ways. The Duchess took compassion on the band of Jesuit strangers, Kino included, and provided
some of the comforts of life—socks, handkerchiefs, and jellies, perhaps—during their two years' stay in Spain. Kino's gifts could only
be simple and pious expressions of his gratitude and esteem. The
Duquesa sent Kino a picture, which he treasured and pasted in his
Breviary. In return he, too, sent some pictures. "And pardon me for
the boldness with which I send to your Excellency the little vellum
bearing the name of one who has so greatly influenced the natives."
This was a picture of the Virgin of Guadalupe, patron saint of the
Mexicans. Again, "That I may be mindful of my vows . . . I wrote
them down on the well-loved picture which I have in my Breviary.
And that they may sometimes be pleased to remember me in their
devout prayers, I am sending three other pictures for your three noble
children, whose names and ages I should like much to know."

The Duquesa replied that her children were Joachin, Gabriel, and
Elizabeth, and sent Kino another present. It was an image of Mary,
her patron saint, "the Great Mother, the thrice admirable Mother
of God, crowned with stars, and cherishing her own Creator, God,
made man for our sake, etc." As a final memento, just before leaving
Spain for America, Kino sent, or at least promised to send, to the
Duchess "some little images of San Xavier for your Excellency and

your dear, dear children." The good Duquesa, I have no doubt, sent as her goodbye substantial comforts for the missionary's hard voyage.

XV

A CELESTIAL TRAMP

While Kino was in Cádiz a prime opportunity was afforded him for the exercise of his knowledge of mathematics and astronomy. It came through the appearance of a brilliant comet. This heavenly wanderer was observed by several scholars in Europe and America. Its orbit time has been computed by astronomers as approximately 575 years. If this is correct it will be seen again about the year 2256. At Cádiz the visitor began to be visible in the evening hours late in December. Kino thought it was the same one which had been seen in the morning hours several weeks earlier. He tells us that he saw, observed, and took the course of the comet every day for two or more weeks. He does not inform us what instruments he used, but his language shows that he knew what he was talking about. His views are gleaned from four letters which he wrote while at Cádiz, three to the Duchess and one to Father Espinosa.[1]

Kino first mentions the apparition in his letter of December 28, 1680. "Here for the last five days now we have seen a huge comet very plainly during the evening hours of six, seven, and eight. I have no doubt it can be seen at Madrid, and will be visible there perhaps an hour before it sets for us. Those of us who live here in the College began to see and observe it on the 23rd of this month, although some others had already seen it three or four days earlier. In my mind there is no question but that this comet is the same one that many

---

[1] The comet of 1680, called the *Great Comet* and also *Heaven's Chariot*, made a profound impression upon the minds of those who saw it. Its unusual brilliancy quickened superstitious terrors, but at the same time stimulated scientific enquiry. In particular, it enabled Newton to make observations which proved that comets revolve around the sun in conic sections; hence, that the same force which regulates the movements of the planets also retains the comets in their orbits.

This comet is believed to be identical with the one which appeared at about the time of Caesar's death; with another that became visible in 531 A.D.; and with a third that was seen in the year 1106.

claim they saw four or five weeks ago at four or five o'clock in the morning. That one was seen in the east before sunrise, with its tail turned toward the west. Those who deny that the two can be the same comet give as reasons the difference in time at which they were seen and the difference in the positions of their tails."

Father Luís Espinosa heard of Kino's attainments as a mathematician and wrote to him about the topic of the times. Father Eusebio replied: "We have seen and observed the comet here every day, and the course which it has taken in the sky. Having traversed the constellations of Sagittarius, Antinous, and Delphinus, it is now passing by Pegasus, where it was yesterday afternoon, at night being at 6°, in the breast of the constellation of Pegasus with 60° of length for its tail and with 328° of right ascension, and with 17° 18' of boreal declination or distance from the equator. The self-movement which the comet has made every day since December 24 has been four or five degrees. This self-movement was from southwest to northeast, with some declination to the east. The comet apparently will last for many days more. I judge that its distance from the earth must be about three thousand leagues and more, which is more than three times the radius of the terraqueous globe." This would now be regarded as uncomfortably close.

Of more interest to the layman than Kino's rather technical description of the comet and its movements are his ideas regarding its significance. The good Jesuit was clearly quite medieval in his notions of the dire portent of the celestial body. "God over all," he wrote to Father Espinosa—how German that sounds— "But connaturally it appears that this comet, which is so large that I do not know whether or not the world has ever seen one like it or so vast, promises, signifies, and threatens many fatalities, and as your Reverence very well says, its influence will not be favorable. And therefore it indicates many calamities for all Europe, especially for three or four kingdoms, and signifies many droughts, hunger, tempests, some earthquakes, great disorders for the human body, discords, wars, many epidemics, fevers, pests, and deaths of a great many people, especially of some very prominent persons. May God our Lord look upon us with eyes filled with pity.

"And because this comet is so large it signifies that its fatalities will be more universal and involve more peoples, persons, and countries. And since it is lasting so long a time as it has already lasted (this being the same one which has been seen at four or five o'clock in the morning for more than six or seven weeks), and since it appears that it will still endure, it indicates that its evil influence will afflict mortals for many years."[1]

By the end of January the disturbing visitor was becoming dim, and people's fears were accordingly subsiding. On the 26th Kino wrote to the Duchess in a tone of reassurance: "With regard to the comet nothing unusual has happened which I should mention, except that it continues to get smaller as the days go by, and I believe it should disappear during the first part of February, as I conjectured eight days ago. Now it is moving from the constellation of Andromeda to the constellation of the Triangle in the north, called Deltoton. The fear of a plague is also lessened, but it is not yet entirely allayed."[2] The Duquesa felt relieved.

This is not the last we shall hear from Father Kino about the comet.

XVI

THE WIDE ATLANTIC

During all this time Kino was anxiously awaiting his chance to sail for Mexico, either to take up his work there if he must, or, if Fortune favored him, to go thence to the Orient. His delay illustrates the uncertainty of communication between Europe and America in the later seventeenth century. We get most of our information from Kino's letters to the Duchess. Nearly every one of them discusses his chances for sailing: all show him to be champing at the bit.

After the wreck of the *Nazareno* there was hope for a time that

[1] Kino to the Duchess, Cádiz, December 28, 1680. Original Latin manuscript in the Huntington Library; Kino to Espinosa, Cádiz, January 8, 1681. Original Spanish manuscript in the Huntington Library.

[2] Kino to the Duchess, Cádiz, January 11, 1681; same to same, Cádiz, January 26, 1681. Original Latin manuscripts in the Huntington Library.

some vessel of the Flota might have to return to Cádiz, and that the stranded Jesuits might thereby get passage. "But these hopes were vain"; none of the vessels returned. So, while Kino and Revel remained as workers in the Jesuit college at Cádiz, the rest waited in Sevilla.[1] In August there was a prospect that some of the missionaries might sail on the Windward Fleet,[2] others on vessels bound for Honduras. But news that buccaneers had sacked Puerto Bello and besieged Panamá kept sailing craft in port. Various makeshifts were thought of. Kino was granted permission from Rome to go as missionary either to Paraguay or to New Granada. But the Paraguay mission had already sailed, and he preferred Mexico to South America. Thus Kino was saved for North America.

November prospects were better. The Galleons—the fleet bound for Panamá—were being prepared at Cádiz. With them a dispatch boat would sail for Vera Cruz, and on this vessel the procurator decided to send the stranded Jesuits. On January 11, 1681, Kino was packing his belongings ready to sail, and he asked the Duchess if she could help him obtain some little crosses for his prospective neophytes —"thirty or forty dozen little Spanish or Caravacensian crosses, that is, from Caravaca, which I hear they are selling in great numbers in Madrid." He would gladly pay for them. He knew very well he would not be permitted to do so. At the same time he sent "some little rings of San Xavier for your Excellency and your dear, dear children, before my departure from Europe."[3]

Gerstl and his companions now came down from Sevilla, arriving on January 18. Cádiz was still quarantined, and they had to leave their baggage outside the city. There were now eighteen missionaries awaiting embarkation. Gerstl gives a broad hint at the reason for the long delay of the galleons. "There was a rumor in Cádiz that the Capitana . . . must be fastened to a gold or a silver anchor put into the pockets of the General [of the fleet] with the intention of keeping him there as long as their business required it." On January 26 Kino wrote to the Duquesa his "last, or almost last, farewell." And yet

---

[1] Kino to the Duchess, Cádiz, August 18, 1680. Original Italian manuscript in the Huntington Library.

[2] The Armada de Barlovento, the armed fleet which patrolled the West Indies.

[3] Kino to the Duchess, Cádiz, November 16, 1680; same to same, Cádiz, January 11, 1681. Original Latin manuscripts in the Huntington Library.

in a "P.S." he wrote, "There are some who say that the galleons will not leave so soon." But they did raise anchor—next day.[1]

Before Kino sailed from Cádiz the eleven Jesuits who had clung to the viceroy's fleet after the wreck of the *Nazareno* on the 11th of July had already safely reached Mexico. Of their voyage we have an excellent account by Father Ratkay, the Hungarian baron. The first vessel of the fleet overhauled by the procurator after the wreck that strenuous night consented to take fathers Calvanese and Borgia; the second refused to take any; on the third embarked Tilpe and Mancker; on the fourth went Borango and Sarzosa; on another Strobach and Neumann. The procurator was especially anxious to get aboard the men bound for the Philippines lest they should miss their ship on the Pacific. Father Ratkay, who was assigned to New Spain, here reminded him that Christ had shed his blood for the Indians of Mexico as well as for the Filipinos. The procurator was moved by this appeal, and by extraordinary effort he obtained passage for Ratkay and De Angelis on another vessel. Poor Father Ratkay was most grateful for being taken aboard, but this did not prevent him from fainting early that morning from hunger and fatigue.

The strict vows of obedience did not reduce Jesuit resourcefulness in a pinch. Witness Brother Simon Poruhradiski. This Bohemian had been left by the procurator on the wrecked *Nazareno* to look after the baggage and get it safely back to Cádiz. Next morning at seven o'clock he learned that some of his brethren had found passage. "Then remembering that the procurator wanted to keep him as an assistant, against his will, he hired a boat and hurried to the fleet, where by his entreaties he got a place on the third vessel," with Mancker and Tilpe.[2] Brother Simon was determined to see the world.

The vessel on which Fathers de Angelis and Ratkay found passage was the *San Diego*. Theirs was a fortunate catch, and they were well cared for. Before leaving the harbor the procurator besought and obtained for them the special protection of the knightly captain, and

[1] Gerstl to his father, Puebla, July 14, 1681. Printed in German in Stöcklein, *Neue Welt-Bott*, I, No. 31. Kino to the Duchess of Aveiro y Arcos, Cádiz, January 26, 1681; same to same, near the Canary Islands, February 24, 1681. Original Latin manuscripts in the Huntington Library.

[2] Ratkay to Avancinus, Mexico, November 16, 1680. Printed in German in Stöcklein, *Neue Welt-Bott*, I, No. 28; Gerstl to his father, Puebla, July 14, 1681. *Ibid.*, I, No. 31.

of a distinguished fellow passenger, none other than the new bishop of Manila, "a very dignified prelate of the Dominican Order." When Father Ratkay fainted that morning in the bishop's cabin the prelate not only nursed him, but also provided both him and Father Theophilo with all things necessary, "so that we soon forgot the wreck and the loss of our belongings. . . . After we had rested we were invited to the table of the bishop, where we were more comforted by his pious conversation than by the excellent meal." Ratkay adds, "The Captain was a real gentleman. He gave us quarters in his own room, and allowed us to promenade on the bridge as often as we wished." Not everybody was so privileged.

Ratkay gives us a good picture of ship routine in the royal fleet. There are many things of interest to a modern voyager across that same sea. "Now I must say a few words about order and discipline on the ship," he remarks. "Very early a soldier aroused the captain and asked permission to relieve the night watch, whereupon a drum was beaten and two guns discharged. The sailors and soldiers were aroused from their sleep, and the mate set the sails. Then followed Mass, or at least a morning prayer. At nine o'clock a bell announced breakfast." It was on a caste basis. "The bishop, with another priest of his order, and we two Jesuits, took ours in the captain's room. At another table ate the captain with twenty prominent passengers, while the first mate with the other officers took the same meal at a side table. At a third table ate those whose means allowed only scant fare. The rest of the men on the ship ate when and where they wished. After breakfast chocolate was served to those who desired it, and then the passengers did whatever they pleased. . . . At four in the afternoon dinner was eaten in the same manner as breakfast. After sunset the signal was given for evening prayer, which included the singing of the Lauretanian Litany and the Salve Regina.[1]

"We were much surprised to get so many good things for our meals," says Ratkay. "For breakfast we had the wing or a leg of a chicken, a piece of beef or pork, and candy or preserves. For dinner the meal consisted of lapary cabbage, mutton, olla (or meat stew),

---

[1] Ratkay to Avancinus, Mexico, November 16, 1680. Printed in German in Stöcklein, *Neue Welt-Bott*, I, No. 28, pp. 77–81.

rice, a piece of tart, and finally, cheese and olives. On fast days they served the same number of dishes of smoked or salted sea fish. There was also no lack of lemonades and wines."

This good living was not unwelcome, and it deserved a mark of gratitude. "In order to show our appreciation and to occupy our time," says Father Ratkay, "we missionaries devoted our free hours to spiritual duties. Our endeavors were so far successful that all our companions at least once received the Holy Sacrament, and thus reformed their lives." We trust he was not too optimistic. He adds, in a tone of apparent surprise—he came from turbulent Hungary—"I observed that the Spaniards were careful in talking to each other, so that there was never any disagreement or fighting."

The monotony of the long voyage was broken by a variety of occurrences. One day a council of the whole fleet was called. The admiral's ship hoisted flags, turned about, and struck sail, whereupon all the other vessels gathered around, like a flock of great white swans. It was an imposing sight in the wilderness of waves. There was ample time for religious observances. On July 25 they celebrated the feast of Santiago, Spain's patron saint. In the morning the bishop said High Mass and preached a sermon. In the evening the passengers were entertained by a "merry spectacle." All the flags were hoisted to the breeze and several cannon shots boomed forth. On this same day the fleet divided. Seventeen ships left the main body, some going to Cape Verde, some to other colonies.

In mid-ocean a terrific storm occurred, for it was the hurricane season. Four long days it lasted. It was so violent that the captain of the *San Diego* ordered thrown overboard "not only old rubbish, but also many valuable things." The ship was so filled with water that the portholes had to be opened to get rid of it. The vessel listed till the masts almost touched the sea. Even hardened seamen feared a wreck. "Not until the waves had washed a young man overboard did the storm abate, as if the sea had waited for this sacrifice."

The terrors of the hurricane gave way to joy. On the day after the storm ceased[1] there were loud cheers at the first sight of land in the West Indies. Cannons roared. "Many birds came flying to our ship,"

[1] August 15.

says Ratkay, "as if they wished to invite us to their country." The rejoicing was mingled with a solemn religious ceremony, for it was the
Feast of the Assumption. The devotional exercises over, in the evening the sailors performed a drama by Beaumont and Fletcher called
"Duke Frederick of Naples."

The first stop was made at Puerto Rico, where the fleet arrived on
August 18th. It was ten days behind time. Santo Domingo was
reached on the 24th. Six days later they saw Jamaica "which the English took away from Spain"—this was sixteen years before—"and
which is now so well settled and organized that it can be compared
with European countries," says Ratkay. Cuba was left behind, and
on September 6 the fleet entered the Sound. Here they were in a fish-
erman's paradise. "The water is full of fish, and of turtles whose
shells are sometimes as wide as a medium-sized table. The stupid fish
could easily be caught. Within half an hour we hauled about forty
on board, each of twenty to thirty pounds in weight, not to mention
four much larger ones which are called burones and weigh about four
hundred pounds each." Ratkay's next comment does not speak well
for the sportsmanship of the day. "These they either gutted or cut out
their eyes, an empty barrel was attached to their fins, and then they
were set free to rage in the sea."

A week later from the crow's-nest sails were descried in the west.
There was a flurry of excitement, and the crew began preparations for
any event. Were they pirate ships or friendly craft? Everybody was
relieved when they proved to be the Armada de Barlovento, "the
Spanish fleet of nine men-of-war which cruises the Mexican Gulf
watching for enemies and sea-robbers," says Ratkay. "Both fleets were
very cautious until they recognized each other, whereupon the commander of the other fleet showed his respect for the new viceroy by
discharging the heavy pieces."

Then came Vera Cruz, reached on September 25, after a voyage of
sixty-five days. As they stretched their legs on American soil, the
Jesuits marveled at the tropical verdure of the *Tierra Caliente*. That
night they went to the college of their order, arriving at a distressing
moment, for next day the rector died. This bereavement had one
mitigating feature. "There was no question as to who should be the

new rector, because there were left, besides the lay brothers, only one priest and one magistrate." There was nobody to quarrel over the office. "Vera Cruz is about as large as Wiener Neustadt," says Ratkay, "and has about as many cloisters. But they are peopled by other orders, namely the Dominicans, Augustinians, Franciscans, and Hippolitans." They braved the climatic terrors of even the "graveyard of Europeans."

Old Mexico

XVII

IN THE AZTEC CAPITAL

A T THE COLLEGE THE BLACK ROBES WERE MET by two procurators from Mexico City with a letter from the Jesuit provincial there. After a week's rest they set out for the capital. On the first day, crossing the river in small boats, they reached old Vera Cruz. From there they traveled close to Cortés's trail across *Tierra Caliente,* up the steep slopes of *Tierra Templada,* and over the mountains to *Tierra Fría.* It is a thrilling ride even today in a Pullman. How much more so then in the saddle! "We made the journey on mules, which the two procurators had brought for us, while our baggage was carried by burros. We were well treated on the road, especially at the two haciendas which belong to our college in Puebla de los Angeles. In one of these they have 80,000 hogs, 20,000 sheep, and many thousands of cattle, as well as other animals and fowls." Who said the Spaniards in America were merely explorers and gold seekers? There were hundreds of plantations like these in New Spain, and they were not all owned by Churchmen by any means.

Puebla was reached early in October. The coming of the Jesuits was an event. The father provincial, who had come from Mexico City for the occasion, met them near the town with coaches and drove them to the college. "When we arrived all the fathers, about forty in number, assembled at the gate and welcomed us in the most kindly manner. We were then led into the church, which surpassed in beauty and amount of gold anything I have ever seen in Germany." This was not Ratkay's only surprise.

From Puebla the Jesuits proceeded to Mexico, over a road and through country at whose beauty travelers hold their breath today.

"The city is not nearly so large as Vienna," says Ratkay. "The houses are very low on account of the many earthquakes, and the streets are very straight. In the city there is so much gold and silver that the interiors of the churches are magnificently adorned with it. . . . The so-called Casa Profesa is more beautiful than the college but not so large. The church of the former shines with gold, and contains so many fine pictures that there is hardly any empty space on the walls." "They have here a college where priests and members of the order lecture to each other"—perhaps a means of penance for the listeners. "Philosophy is represented thrice, the other schools twice; yet there are not more than fifteen hundred students." Not a bad start for 1680, before Philadelphia was founded. He adds, "The college is highly endowed but has nevertheless a debt of almost 40,000 guldens." This note has a modern sound.

"The Spaniards form the ruling class. Mexicans are considered their serfs. They are usually men of moderate intelligence, yet they are so clever that they easily imitate everything they see. There are good painters and carvers among them."

Ratkay noticed some of the more ordinary things of life. Cabbages and onions were not too lowly for the nobleman's comment. "A pound of beef costs only one kreutzer and a fat ox four reichsthalers. . . . Chocolate is very common here even among the lower classes; we receive monthly three pounds each from our superior." No wonder Mexican priests were so often fat. "There are all kinds of birds in this country. Sparrows can be taught to talk much easier than parrots, though they look exactly like the European sparrows."

Anything but soft, this Hungarian baron was soon on his way again. "Tomorrow," he wrote on November 16, "I shall start for the mission which has been assigned to me." It was away to the north in the Tarahumar country. Neumann accompanied him to the same field. "It is, like all the others in this province, well provided with everything; a fact, however, which I value very little because all my thoughts are directed to the conversion of the heathen. The king of Spain gives every new missionary three hundred thalers, from which he has to equip himself. The same amount is paid every year. There are at present about seventy missionaries who receive this sum." He meant seventy Jesuits.[1]

Kino reached Mexico more than eight months behind Ratkay. Few of the details of his voyage have come to us. The galleons sailed from Cádiz on the 27th of January, 1681. On the 24th of February Kino wrote on board ship a short note to the Duchess from a place in the blue Atlantic "not far from the Canary Islands." The galleons directed their voyage to Panamá; the despatch boat, on which Kino crossed the Atlantic, came by way of Puerto Rico. Gerstl, who was on the same vessel, says, "At all places in the West Indies they received me with the greatest love and civility," and, "by the wonderful grace of God" they landed safely at Vera Cruz early in May, after a difficult voyage lasting ninety-six days. Ocean liners now make it in a week.

Riding over the same mule trail that Ratkay had followed, Kino reached Mexico City about the first of June. Almost immediately he wrote to the Duchess letters "telling of our entire journey and voyage to the Indies." These precious documents have not come to our hands. A month later, July 4, he wrote her another letter from Mexico City. This one by good fortune we have.

The band of devoted Jesuits who had set out from Genoa together three years before were destined now to scatter to the ends of the earth. The romantic story of their personal experiences in America and the islands of the western seas occupies large space in the pages of Stöcklein's *Neue Welt-Bott,* one of the great adventure books of all time. Eight of the companions were sent to South America. Ten came to Mexico, whence some went to the Philippines; others to the Marianas Islands and to China. Fathers Borango, Tilpe, Strobach, De Angelis, and Cuculinus went to work among the heathen of the Marianas. Mancker and Klein sailed to the Philippines and Gerstl to China. Neumann and Ratkay labored in Chihuahua among the Tarahumares, where the former became a great figure and lived to be a veteran. Ratkay, the good story teller, soon died at his mission. Of the four who went to the Marianas Islands, three—Borango, Strobach, and De Angelis—won the martyr's crown.[2]

---

[1] Ratkay to Avancinus, Mexico, November 16, 1680. In Stöcklein, *Neue Welt-Bott,* I, No. 28.
[2] Kino to the Duchess, near the Canary Islands, February 24, 1681. Original Latin manuscript in the Huntington Library; Gerstl to his father, Puebla, July 14, 1681. Gerstl says the

XVIII

THE SLIP OF PAPER WINS

Kino was in the metropolis of America. But America was not his heart's desire. He was still hopeful of going to the Orient, and his optimism had some foundation. In the first place, he had a noble patroness. In the second place, he found a new friend, Father Baltasar de Mansilla. Father Baltasar was procurator of the missions of the Philippines and the Marianas Islands. To him Kino told the same story he had told the Duchess. Could he help? Yes, he thought he could. He was gathering up a mission, including many of Kino's companions, to be sent in March across the Pacific from Acapulco. He would be glad to enlist such an enthusiast and such a mathematician as Kino, if he were free to go. Father Eusebio wrote to the Duchess, "the Reverend Father Baltasar is urging that I be sent to China. In fact, many days ago he even spoke about the matter to the reverend father provincial of this province of Mexico. He is trying to obtain me for work in his Orient."

But this was no certainty. Bernardo Pardo, the provincial, had projects of his own that might defeat this one. In the same letter Kino added, "the reverend father provincial is planning to send me with some veteran missionaries into California in a few months, when ships and men and an extraordinary expedition are to be dispatched to that place to determine as far as possible whether it is an island or perhaps a very huge and vast peninsula. Thus far he has not given his final decision to the Most Reverend Father Baltasar. He will probably decide within two or three weeks, when Father Antonio Cereso" —this was Kerschpamer's Spanish name [1]—"will arrive here from Angelopolis, or the city of the Angels," now Puebla.

Kerschpamer's bad record as a sailor offered Kino a third chance. Father Antonio's insides had behaved badly on the long Atlantic voy-

voyage lasted ninety-six days. This would take them to May 1. The *Libro de Profesiones* in Mexico stated that Kino and Revel reached Vera Cruz on May 3. The discrepancy might be accounted for by delays in landing. The above account of the voyage confirms Ortega's statement that Kino arrived in America in 1681, Sommervogel and others to the contrary notwithstanding. See Kino, *Hist. Mem.*, I, 34.

[1] An approximation to a translation.

age, as Father Eusebio had more than half hoped they would, we fear. "Although he was destined for work in the Philippines," Kino wrote, "nevertheless, because of the very great difficulties which he experienced on the sea voyage he will perhaps remain here in this very province of Mexico, and so perhaps I shall manage to be sent in his place to the Orient. Meanwhile I dare not anticipate, seek, or desire one place rather than another lest someone should rebuke me with the words, 'You know not what you ask.' "

So Kino put the matter of his destiny in the hands of the Virgin of Guadalupe, patron saint of the Duchess. To this end he went every week to say Mass at the famous shrine north of the city, scene of the miraculous appearance of the Virgin to the Indian Juan,—and likewise scene of the treaty which three centuries later assigned to a new and alien nation a large portion of the region where Kino was destined to make himself famous.

Distance did not lessen his loyalty to the Duchess. "Whether they keep me for work in California or not," he continued, "your Excellency will always know that I am most faithfully and obediently doing my work. And both in my prayers and during the celebration of Mass I shall always think of you. Moreover, that sacred picture of the Blessed Virgin Mary—the picture which you autographed and deigned to send me from Madrid to Cádiz and which I placed in my Breviary —will daily remind me of you." In closing Kino commended to the prayers of the Duchess himself "together with the missions of the East as well as of the West, particularly those of the vast land of China."

China was still Kino's refrain. But his destiny had been written on that slip of paper when he piously gambled with Father Antonio. An expedition to California was being prepared, as Kino said, and he was marked for the California frontier. Father Mansilla's friendly efforts and Father Antonio's unstable stomach were of no avail to reverse the dictum of Chance.

For a century and a half the Spaniards had made attempts to Christianize and colonize the Peninsula of California. In spite of repeated set-backs, another essay at settlement was decided upon. By an agreement of December, 1678, confirmed by a royal cédula of December, 1679, the enterprise was entrusted to Don Isidro Atondo y Antillón, a former governor of Sinaloa and Sonora, mainland provinces opposite the Peninsula. The spiritual ministry, a primary consideration since this was to be chiefly a missionary venture, was assigned to the Jesuits, by agreement with Bernardo Pardo, the father provincial.

In the midst of Atondo's preparations Kino arrived in Mexico, and before many weeks were passed he was named missionary to California. As his companion, Pardo appointed Father Matías Goñi, a friend of Atondo, and missionary at Yécora,[1] in the mountains of Sonora. Kino's mathematical learning would not be lost after all, for the viceroy made him royal cosmographer, that is astronomer, surveyor, and map maker of the expedition. Before leaving for his new destination he prepared himself for this scientific task by studying California geography, borrowing maps for the purpose from a friend and from the viceroy's palace and taking them to the Jesuit Colegio Máximo of San Pedro y San Pablo to copy.[2] Indeed, a manuscript map of western New Spain which he made at this time has just come to light.[3]

Meanwhile Father Eusebio was getting in touch with the currents of life and gossip in Mexico—the things which now would constitute headlines in the daily papers, but which then were announced by the ringing of the multitude of church bells of the city. Just before he arrived, imposing funeral services had been held in the cathedral in honor of the twenty-one Franciscan missionaries who fell in New Mexico the previous September in the terrible Pueblo Revolt. It was still a live topic of conversation. Martyrdom, with this nearer view, now had for Father Eusebio a less theoretical aspect than when he was living in a Bavarian cloister. But it in no wise checked his missionary zeal. On April 2 the church bells called the people of the city to public prayers for the China Ship, or Manila Galleon, which had recently sailed from the port of Acapulco, carrying some of Kino's beloved student mates to the Orient. The prayers were justified when on June 2 the city was stirred by reports of eight pirate ships near Acapulco. June 23—"Earthquake! Today the earth trembled severely at

---

[1] Now within the State of Chihuahua.

[2] Kino, *Hist. Mem.,* I, 38.

[3] The viceroy of Mexico to the King of Spain, August 3, 1678; Atondo to the viceroy, Mexico, November 8, 1678; same to same, November 23, 1678 (all in A.G.I. 58–4–18, Mexico 51); Escritura de asiento de la California, 1678–1679 (A.G.I. 1–1–2/31, Patronato 31); the king to the viceroy, Madrid, October 8, 1679 (A.G.I. 58–4–18, Mexico 51).

six in the afternoon, it having previously rained. It lasted about three *Credos.*" Next day "the earth trembled at the same hour, it having just stopped raining." On June 27 Viceroy Rivera resigned his authority to the city Cabildo, to be transferred in turn to the Conde de Paredes.

Three days later Rivera started for Spain, "a sad day for Mexico," for he was beloved by his people. He was accompanied as far as the Shrine of Guadalupe by the new viceroy, the Audiencia, and the judges of the high tribunals. Many tears were shed and the church bells rang for public prayers. July 21 at four in the afternoon all the bells rang to announce the arrival of a public news-letter from Spain. It reported the Spanish sovereigns in good health, but there were fears of a breach with Portugal, France, and England. Thus did Mexico keep in touch with European politics. Four days later the new viceroy honored the Jesuits by attending services at the Casa Profesa, where Kino was staying. On the occasion his friend, Florencia, the famous Jesuit historian—a native of Florida, by the way—said the Mass of the Feast of San Ignacio. On August 6, 7, and 8 the viceroy was bled in the leg, and a few days later, when the Royal Audiencia met, was still too ill to attend. Strangely enough, the three days' weakening process had not made him strong. A nun of the Convent of La Encarnación and one of its founders died on August 17 at the age of one hundred and two years. Three days later a frigate arrived from Havana at Vera Cruz with a cargo of 200,000 bushels of cacao. The Jesuits in their distant missions would not lack chocolate for breakfast next winter. On September 21 there was another earthquake —and a silver lamp was stolen from the Hospital de Jesús, the place where the bones of the Conqueror Cortés long lay buried. Next day the Inquisition held an Auto de Fé at the Church of Santo Domingo, in which a half-breed was given two hundred lashes for having two wives. Some people thought this a rather heavy penalty for so slight an offence.[1]

[1] Rivera, Juan Antonio, "Diario Curioso de México," *Documentos para la Historia de México.* Primera série, Tomo VII, pp. 319 *et seq.*

XIX

A TEMPEST IN A TEAPOT

Kino had scarcely arrived in the Aztec capital when he made the acquaintance of the noted Mexican scholar, Sigüenza y Góngora. This was but natural. Sigüenza had been educated by the Jesuits, though he was not a member of the order. He was now a professor of astrology and mathematics in the Royal University of Mexico.[1] An astronomer of repute, he enjoyed the patronage of the viceroy's wife, the Condesa de Paredes, to whom Kino had a letter of introduction from the Duquesa. Father Eusebio's renown as a scholar ran ahead of him. So it was not long before he was a welcome guest at Sigüenza's modest residence. Sigüenza introduced him to his friends and helped to spread his fame. He loaned the missionary some maps needed in preparation for his work in California. This friendship ran along smoothly for a few weeks, when it was disrupted by the recent comet. Here was one baleful consequence such as Kino had predicted from its ominous presence.

That celestial tramp was visible in Mexico at the same time that Kino had observed it in Cádiz. In America superstitious notions regarding it spread among the populace the same as in Europe. Like the people of New England, those in Mexico shuddered at its portent. Sigüenza, who was a man of science with a remarkably modern spirit, took little stock in what he regarded as ignorant superstitions. He had read Kepler with approval. In order to allay these fears in Mexico, and perhaps to air his astronomical knowledge—for he had no slight touch of vanity—he wrote a pamphlet called *Philosophical Manifest against Comets stripped of their dominion over the Timid.*[2] In this long-titled work he gave a hard whack at some brands of astrology, although he was a professor of that subject himself.

The *Philosophical Manifest* was published while Kino was still in

---

[1] This venerable institution was already more than a century old, having been founded in 1551, the first university in North America. It is now the National University of Mexico.
[2] For an excellent account of the relations of Kino and Sigüenza, see Leonard, Irving A., *Don Carlos de Sigüenza y Góngora, a Mexican Savant of the Seventeenth Century* (Berkeley, 1929), 55–73, on which I have drawn freely in this chapter.

Cádiz.[1] Since it rapped astrologers it brought forth a reply from a dabbler in astrology. As a comeback Martín de la Torre published a pamphlet called *Christian Manifest in favor of the Comets maintained in their Natural Significance.* Pugnacious Sigüenza accepted the challenge and swept De la Torre into oblivion—or rather into remembrance—by publishing a reply with the resounding title of *Mathematical Bellérophon against the Astrological Chimera of Don Martín de la Torre.* All that was left of De la Torre was fit only for the waste basket—and for the historian. Dr. Escobar, Sigüenza's colleague in the University faculty, now entered the Joust of the Comets. His weapon was called *Cometological Discourse,* in which he set forth the rather nauseating proposition that the comet was composed of the exhalations of dead bodies and human perspiration. Don Carlos evidently considered this unsavory emanation too disgusting even to merit a reply.[2]

Kino now arrived in Mexico. His repute was heralded, and at the instance of friends he proceeded to write a little book on the great comet of 1680. He called it *Exposición Astronómica de el Cometa,*[3] and dedicated it in fulsome terms to the viceroy, the Conde de Paredes. While in Spain Kino had expressed his opinions about the import of comets in his correspondence with the Duchess and Father Espinosa. Comets were things of ominous portent. But in the introduction to his book the hope was expressed that the present comet augured nothing sinister for the great Conde or for his rule. Kino apologized for the "lack of rhetorical figures to purify the style" of his work, yet he was able to say, "And as for the comet, though it is of such baleful reputation, yet despite its ill-omened splendor may it be the happy messenger of your good fortune; may it find your royal lilies ever more brightly in bloom; your lions more and more a terror to the rage and vagaries of heretics; while ever better defended be the truth, the faith, the justice and the integrity of the noble bastions and towers which crown the device upon your arms!" Not so very bad at that!

But in the body of the little book Kino reasserted, with qualifica-

[1] January 13, 1681.
[2] Leonard, *op. cit.,* 59–62.
[3] For the full title of the book see the Bibliography at the end of this work.

EXPOSICION
ASTRONOMICA
DE EL COMETA,

Que el Año de 1680. por los meses de
Noviembre, y Diziembre, y este Año de 1681. por los meses
de Enero y Febrero, se ha visto en todo el mundo,
y le ha observado en la Ciudad de Cadiz,

EL P. EUSEBIO FRANCISCO KINO
De la Compañia de Jesvs.

Con LICENCIA, en Mexico por Francisco Rodriguez Lupercio, 1681.

Title Page of Kino's book on the comet 1680–1681, written and printed in
Mexico City, in 1681

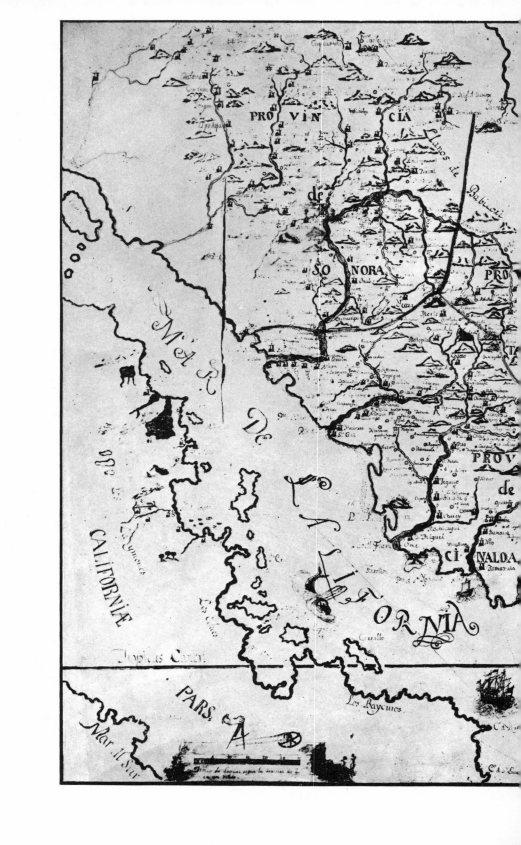

Map of the Jesuit Missions in New Spain, made in 1760
(From the original manuscript, which is in colors)

Jesuit Novitiate at Tepotzotlán near Mexico City

tions, the ideas which he had expressed in his letters written in Europe. The dire portent of comets, he said, was patent to everybody, "unless there be some dull wits who cannot perceive it." Was he referring to dull wits in general, or to some dull wit in particular? Be that as it may, these words had a resounding echo.

The *Exposición* before publication readily won the approval of the Church authorities in Mexico. Father Ximénez wrote, "It is a work which implies in its author a perfect knowledge of Geometry, Arithmetic, Optics, and the fundamental sciences of Astrology, and is worthy of being made the ideal and model for those who write on the subject in the future." This might seem a little lavish. "It does not contain anything contrary to our Holy Faith or to good morals. On the other hand, it implants a holy fear of God in our souls, His comet being something like a lash, or a sword of justice which God suspends from Heaven, terrifying all mortals, so that each one may endeavor to improve his habits." With this and other testimonials, the book was approved for printing, went through the press at once, and was published in the autumn of 1681.[1] Here was efficiency.

During all this time, Sigüenza tells us, Kino had said nothing to him about his forthcoming book, although they had often discussed the comet. Don Carlos's friends heard rumors of the proposed treatise, warned him that it was to be an attack on his own writings, and urged him to be prepared for a reply. But the first certain knowledge that Sigüenza had of it was obtained on the day when Kino left Mexico for California. That day Father Eusebio went to Sigüenza's house to say goodbye to his friend. Before he departed he asked Don Carlos what he was writing those days. "Nothing," was the reply. Then handing over a copy of his new book, just off the press, Kino said in effect, "Read this and you'll have something to write about."

When the professor read the missionary's work he went up in the air. He considered it a direct attack on his *Manifest*. Moreover, though he was not named in the book, he regarded it as a very personal attack on himself. Sigüenza these days was courting the patronage of the Condesa. What would she think now of his standing as

---

[1] It was approved for publication on September 24, and was published apparently in October.

an astronomer? By this visit of Kino, he tells us, "I confirmed the truth of those who had told me about it, and I considered myself challenged to a literary duel." This is Sigüenza's version of the case.[1]

Kino went on his way, innocent, it would seem, of any intention to assail any particular individual in his *Exposición,* and most of all, blissfully ignorant that he had given any offense to his friend Sigüenza. Meanwhile Sigüenza sharpened his quill, dipped it in a mixture of acid and vitriol, and went out to demolish the mathematical reputation of the unsuspecting missionary. The result was another book, aimed frankly at Kino, as was made patent in the very title. He called it *Libra Astronómica,*[2] or "Astronomical and Philosophical Balance in which Don Carlos de Sigüenza . . . examines not only the objections to his *Philosophical Manifest* against Comets raised by the Reverend Father Eusebio Francisco Kino . . . but also what the same Reverend Father pretended to have demonstrated in his *Exposición Astronómica de el Cometa."* This was no "veiled" attack on Father Eusebio. It was open as day.

We are not concerned here with the technical aspects of Sigüenza's treatise. This would require the gifts of a trained astronomer. The result would doubtless give a competent twentieth century audience more merriment than Sigüenza hoped to furnish his contemporary readers. And not all the fun would be at Kino's expense. Both writers were exponents of seventeenth century science. The views expressed, the arguments used, and the books cited illuminate with diverting effect the history of notions regarding comets. Sigüenza cited some eighty "authorities" on comets, including twenty classic writers and many of the Church Fathers.

Don Carlos may or may not have been a better astronomer than Father Eusebio. He confessed that he was. He did take a more modern view than Kino of the portent of comets. But it was not his main interest to determine the scientific soundness or unsoundness of what Kino had written. He thought he had been attacked. His reputation with scholars and his noble patroness would suffer. He wanted to discredit Kino and save himself. And then, a reply would give him

---

[1] Leonard, *op. cit.*
[2] Sigüenza y Góngora, *Libra Astronómica y Philosóphica* (Mexico, c. 1690).

a grand opportunity to display his literary gifts, of which he was vain. A nephew of the prototype of Góngorism, he was a Góngorist himself. In short, his book was quite as much a rhetorical performance as a scientific treatise.

The *Libra Astronómica* was sarcastic in the extreme, and Sigüenza bore throughout an injured air. Kino the European was patronizing him, as just an American, for Europeans "think those of us who were born here by chance . . . walk on two legs only by divine dispensation." Sigüenza said he had freely shown Kino his own observations on the comet, but no attention was given them because they were not "made in Germany." Kino had spoken of dull wits and of crazy people. Whom did he mean? "Nobody but myself," said Sigüenza. Don Carlos had befriended the newcomer, and this was a base return. Father Eusebio had borrowed his maps and then forgotten to bring them back. That might be expected of a professor, but Kino was no longer a pedagogue. When, through a third party, the maps were recovered, they were badly tattered and torn. "Does he think me crazy because of the hospitality which I showed him? It may well be that! It may well be that!"

Kino had dedicated his book to the viceroy. Why did he do this when he knew that Sigüenza "was paying some compliments" to that nobleman's wife? Was he trying to discredit him in the eyes of the lady? How would Kino like to be called crazy in the presence of the Duchess? What if Sigüenza, having written a book opposing Kino's views, should dedicate it to the Duke, the husband of the Duchess of Aveiro? Was it good manners for Kino to come to America to set right a professor in the Royal University? Was it right to injure his reputation? Was it in Germany that such manners were taught? In this vein Sigüenza proceeds to combat Kino's offensive propositions, one by one. He ridicules Kino's knowledge of Latin, his history, and his logic. He charges him with duplicity for a flattering introduction which contradicts the text of his book.[1] He even questions Kino's claim to have made observations in Cádiz. This charge of course was absurd.

Says Leonard, "Judgment may be suspended as to the relative merits

[1] Leonard, *op. cit.*

of the books written by these two learned men, one from the Old and one from the New World. We are not concerned here with the technical and scientific aspects of the debate."

Just here is the point. Was it a debate? Sigüenza so regarded it. But it takes two to make an argument. And if we may believe Kino he was entirely unconscious of this aspect of his book. Sigüenza wrote his sarcastic treatise in the latter part of 1681, after Kino left Mexico for California. It was not published till nine years later. During all this time Kino was as busy as a bee on a distant missionary frontier. There is no evidence that he ever heard of Sigüenza's work till after it was published, though this is not certain. In all his writings there has been found only one single reference to it, and that was made still later. In a book written by Kino in 1695 he wrote these significant words:

"I beg the sovereign Lord that this my little treatise [1] may have a happier fate than that experienced by my *Exposición Astronómica.* . . . For Don Carlos de Sigüenza is very much offended, charging me in his *Libra Astronómica* that I wrote my *Exposición Astronómica* as an attack on his *Manifiesto Philosóphico,* the fact being that it never entered my mind to pretend to write or to print a single letter in opposition to that *Manifiesto Philosóphico,* nor do I know that I ever read it. And I should not fail to have scruples against wasting time so precious and so necessary for better and more urgent occupations, such as those which brought me to the Indies and which I have now in hand, in order to devote myself to contentions and quarrels of such futility and of such little edification.

"And so Don Carlos de Sigüenza performed a labor and task which he might well have spared himself when he attacked my *Exposición Astronómica.* For I wrote it at the request and urging of some fathers and friendly gentlemen of Mexico during the few weeks of my stop in that city. They thanked me for it from Rome, and it was approved by the very learned fathers Francisco Ximénez and Francisco Florencia, and especially by the very erudite, able, and most religious mother, Juana Inez de la Cruz, in her most ingenuous and

[1] Kino, Inocente, Apostólica y Gloriosa Muerte del V. Pe. Francisco Xavier Saeta, 1695. Original manuscript in the Biblioteca Nacional, Mexico.

most learned printed volume, with special verses, all of whom praise, support, and defend it with apparent sufficiency."

If Kino is to be believed, then, Sigüenza's extravagant invective and his biting sarcasm were beside the point, because based on an imaginary grievance. Be that as it may, the episode is both diverting and instructive. From it we learn something about the comet and a good deal about astronomers.

IN CALIFORNIA

Preliminaries

XX

ATONDO

MEANWHILE ATONDO WAS PREPARING HIS EXPEDITION. Don Isidro was a Navarrese who had seen active service both as seaman and soldier. He knew a jib from a topsail and a mortar from a pedrero. For three years he had been a successful governor of Sinaloa and Sonora, and had proved his ability to cut red tape. While governor he had come in touch with California affairs, for the Peninsula lay just across the Gulf. When he learned that the viceroy was looking for some one to head a new expedition to California, he offered to undertake the task and outlined a plan. On the face of things, certainly, he was suited to the undertaking. With very little change, but not without verbose reports such as lawyers are prone to write, his proposal was accepted by Viceroy Rivera and approved by the king. Rivera sent to Madrid a copy of the agreement. In his dispatch he misspelled Atondo's name, writing it "Otondo," and this blunder has been perpetuated to this day.[1]

By the terms of his contract Atondo was made governor of Sinaloa and admiral of California and its armada for a term of five years. In order that he might command all available resources, he insisted upon and was granted full military and civil power in Sinaloa, which would be his base of operations. This concession was a bid for a row

---

[1] Atondo signed his proposal on November 8, 1678 (A.G.I. 58–4–18, Mexico 51.) It was approved by the viceroy in December, 1678, and by the king on December 29, 1679. On February 12, 1679, Rivera sent to Madrid a copy of the contract he had made with Atondo. Don Isidro, he said, was considered "most suitable" for the undertaking, as was proved by his success as governor of Sinaloa, he "never having given cause for complaint." (Viceroy to king, Feb. 12, 1679, A.G.I. 1–1–2/31, Patronato 31.) By royal cédula of October 8, 1679, the king approved all that the viceroy had done (A.G.I. 58–4–18, Mexico 51). For the Atondo-Kino expedition, see Venegas, Empressas Apostólicas, paragraphs 104–143; Venegas (Burriel), *Noticia de la California*, I, 218–240; Bayle, Constantino, S.J., *Historia de los Descubrimentos y Colonización de los Padres de la Compañia de Jesús en la Baja California* (Madrid, 1934), 89–108.

with the governor of Nueva Vizcaya at Parral, but Atondo was willing to take the consequences.

Don Isidro agreed to lead a colony to the Peninsula, fortify himself, explore the interior, pacify the Indians, promote their conversion, and make Spanish settlements if water and suitable lands could be found. Two of the five years would be spent in preparations, and Atondo pledged himself to remain in California at least a year in order to give the project a fair trial. Private ventures into the Peninsula had often been tried and they had failed. So Atondo's expedition was equipped at royal expense.

Thus financed, Don Isidro agreed to build in Sinaloa two frigates of sixty and seventy tons, a launch for each, and a barco luengo or longboat. This need not surprise us, for shipbuilding on the west coast had been a common enterprise ever since the days of Balboa. Within three decades after he discovered the Pacific Ocean, the entire coast of both North and South America, from the Strait of Magellan to the Oregon border, was explored by mariners in vessels built on the Pacific Coast. Then why did a famous historian, not ten years ago, write of a vessel built on the coast of Maine in 1607 as "the first boat built in America"? Atondo's ships were designed to carry the colony to California and to ply back and forth across the Gulf to get supplies and dispatches. To man and equip the craft the viceroy authorized funds for twenty-four seamen, four pilots, three carpenters, two caulkers, a gunsmith, ship tackle, rigging, and cordage. For defence there were to be thirty soldiers, eight cannons, fifty flintlock arquebuses, a hundred pikes, twenty-four "strong pieces," and six hundred pounds of gunpowder. Atondo would furnish the shot at his own expense. Other equipment included four hundred pounds of iron and twenty-five of steel. The list of tools and utensils provided for shovels, augers, hoes, six copper cauldrons, six copper pots, eighty water barrels, and two church bells. This was a real pioneer outfit. Other needs Atondo was to report as they arose, for the government—especially Rivera, who was both viceroy and archbishop of Mexico—was anxious to leave no stone unturned to convert the California Indians.

The Admiral was granted an extra 6000 pesos to be spent for presents for the natives: "food, coarse woolen cloth, women's chemises, short coats, petticoats, hats, knives, and other trifles with which to win the good will of the heathen in order to attract them to conversion to our holy Faith." For this amount Atondo would give a bond, and he was to distribute the gifts under the supervision of the missionaries. The Admiral's personal salary was fixed at two thousand pesos a year. But in spite of a protest on his part, half of it must be paid back to the government as income tax, under the head of the *media anata*. This has a modern sound.

Atondo agreed to take christianized Indians from Sinaloa to California at his own expense,—men to do the manual labor of pioneering and women to grind corn, make tortillas, cook, wash, and perform other domestic service. Until the colony should be securely established no Spanish women were to be taken, since they might "be the cause of disturbances,"—of just what kind it is not stated. We wish the viceroy had been a little more explicit.

With this outfit Don Isidro would sail to California, find a spot with water and irrigable land, erect a fort, win the good will of the heathen, and learn their language. He would then explore the interior for fifteen leagues, and if suitable water and land should be found, from a new fort he would penetrate ten leagues further. If no satisfactory site were discovered he would strike inland from another base, "always looking for a place that has a stream and is fertile, in order to be able to plant crops and make a settlement." This would seem to be a sensible plan.

It was clearly stipulated that the reduction of California was to be made "not by force of arms, but rather by the gentle means of persuasion and evangelical preaching." Hence missionaries would be in the center of the picture. Special care was taken that the Indians should not be abused through the greed of Spaniards, as sometimes had occurred. So it was urged that the soldiers chosen be experienced men, accustomed to work, and of good character, "for on other occasions, when wicked men of evil behavior have been taken, they have terrorized the Indians, taking from them by violence the pearls which they had hanging from their ears and noses." Pearl snatching must be no part of this venture. Trade was to be only a secondary consideration. Such was the will of both the king and Rivera. Nevertheless, if legitimate commerce resulted, the royal interest must not be overlooked. It was therefore stipulated that if by means of goods provided by the $6000, "pearls, amber, gold, or silver" were obtained, all the proceeds would belong to the king. If private individuals acquired such treasures they must render to his Majesty his royal fifth.

Atondo urged haste so that the timber for the ships might be cut during the third quarter of the moon, for, he said, "by cutting it at any other time there may be unforeseen risk in these navigations." Was this some sailor's superstition, like that which requires the catching of fish in the dark, or the planting of potatoes when Fair Luna is full? Let a seaman answer.

The terms of his contract settled, Atondo started for Sinaloa with his crew to begin his two years of preparation. His instructions from the viceroy bore the date of March 23, 1679. Before leaving the city he repaired with his men to the famous shrine of Los Remedios to asks the favor of its patron saint. On March 25th they set forth. As they traveled the long stretch of nearly a thousand miles, they encountered "bad roads, precipices, rain, cold, and hail. And from that time they were made to realize that in this enterprise there would be no lack of trials and crosses, and that it is by the Camino Real of the Holy Cross that one wins the laurels of rest." [1]

Don Isidro built his ships at Pueblo de Nío, a village on Sinaloa River, midway between the coast and his capital at San Felipe, now the city of Sinaloa. Nío was already an old town, for it was nearly ninety years since Father Pérez had begun his mission there. It is now a *triste* little pueblo just below Bamoa, through which the Southern Pacific Railroad runs. It was here at Bamoa that Cabeza de Vaca in 1536, after his hike across the continent from Texas, parted from his band of Pima followers from the far north, whose descendants still live where he left them. A league or less below Nío are the ruins of Pueblo Viejo, or old town. There, on the river bank, Atondo's ships were fashioned. Unless the region was better forested then than now, timber must have been cut in the mountains and floated downstream during

---

[1] Kino, San Bruno Diary, March 25, 1684, recounting the celebration of the fifth anniversary of Atondo's departure from Mexico (Archivo General y Público, Mexico, Historia, Tomo 17); Consulta of Governor Bartolomé Estrada, Parral, Nov. 27, 1680, and related documents. Autos sobre la Entrada Primera, A.G.I. 58–4–23, Mexico 56.

the freshets. For many months the settlement, now so dead, was alive with the hum of labor, the noise of hammer and saw, the songs and oaths of seafaring men, the shouts of ox and mule drivers, and the mellow peal of the bells of the old church whose ruins still recall the days of yore when Nío was for a time a boom town.

While the Admiral was laying his keels in the northwest, officials in Mexico City were gathering equipment, enlisting seamen and soldiers, and sending them across the continent. Couriers galloped back and forth between Sinaloa and Mexico City carrying letters and dispatches. The viceroy and the royal fiscal in Mexico, the naval establishment at Vera Cruz, and the president of the royal audiencia at Guadalajara were especially busy purchasing, manufacturing, packing, and shipping. Most manufactured articles had to be obtained in Vera Cruz, and the royal officials there were called upon to prepare and forward tools, ship stores, and nautical equipment. Transportation was effected by contract with private pack train owners, or on mules rented by the officials. Government mules were evidently not in vogue. In the seasoned seaport of Palos, in Old Spain, Columbus's task of equipping his vessels for his historic voyage to America was comparatively easy beside Atondo's. Here every pound of paraphernalia had to be carried a thousand miles over tropical lowlands and rugged mountains on the backs of patient animals. For the heaviest items the freight charges were almost prohibitive.

Part of the equipment was shipped directly to Nío for Atondo's immediate use. The rest was sent to a less distant depot on the west coast to await the arrival of the Admiral with his fleet when it should be ready to sail to California. The port selected for assembling supplies was Chacala, a little harbor near Compostela, first capital of the kingdom of Nueva Galicia, and the city whence Coronado a hundred and forty years before had set forth to conquer the Seven Cities.[1]

As the time approached for starting to California more men were

[1] Behind Atondo from time to time went more workmen and supplies. For example, in January, 1680, we learn, the Vera Cruz officials sent to Mexico City for Sinaloa four additional ship carpenters, two caulkers and six sailors for Atondo's service. Their advance pay and the rent of saddle and pack mules to Mexico amounted to $3216. Two months later lateen, tackle, and other supplies for Nío were sent from Vera Cruz to Mexico at a cost of $7977 and twenty tomines. From the capital all these were forwarded to Atondo. (Officials of Vera Cruz to Viceroy, April 23, 1681. Two letters. Originals in the Clark Library, University of California at Los Angeles.)

raised and sent to Chacala. From documents available we get interesting details of the enlistment and transportation of some of the seamen who crossed Mexico to join the expedition. Manuel Luque, "one of the best of mariners," volunteered and was put at the head of a band of eight sailors bound for the rendezvous. From the capital they rode to Guadalajara on mules hired by the viceroy for the purpose. Luque appealed to Zevallos, president of the audiencia at Guadalajara, for twelve new mounts to carry his men and their baggage to Chacala, some three hundred miles further west. Zevallos complied, hired from Francisco Rodríguez the necessary twelve mules—eight for the men and four for the baggage—at $6.00 per mule for the round trip, paid in gold cash. The seamen ate at government expense, so Zevallos advanced funds for rations—for the armorer and caulker at the rate of four reales (half a dollar) a day, and for the common sailors at three reales. The royal chest at Guadalajara being empty, Zevallos had to borrow the cash from Miguel de Pordia, a citizen. Seven of Luque's men thus provided were hastened to Chacala to join the expedition. One remained ill in the hospital at Guadalajara, but soon recovered, was put on a mule, and sent forward. The anticipated duration of the tedious journey over barrancas and mountains from Guadalajara to Chacala is indicated by the fact that the men were given rations for twenty-four days.[1]

XXI

A FULL-FLEDGED MISSIONARY

Kino left Mexico City to join Atondo and Goñi about the middle of October, 1681.[2] When he first arrived in America he had approxi-

---

[1] Testimonio de Auttos sobre los Socorros, A.G.I. 58-4-21, Mexico 54; Paredes to the king, July 12, 1681 (A.G.I. 1-1-2/31, Patronato 31). As late as March, 1683, enlistments were being made at Vera Cruz. Men applied, were accepted, and hurried to Mexico. There they were formally given an examination in seamanship. Since they were "very expert" and passed high, they were accepted, each given $100 advance salary, supplied with rations and mules and sent over the trail behind Luque (Auttos sobre los Socorros, A.G.I. 58-4-21, Mexico 54). Original Spanish manuscripts.

[2] Joseph Gregorio to the Duchess of Aveiro y Arcos, Mexico, October 9, 1681; Paulus Klein to the superior at Ingolstadt, Mexico, February 16, 1682. Original Latin manuscripts in the Huntington Library.

mated the historic route of Cortés from Vera Cruz to the City of the Aztecs. He now resumed the Conqueror's trail and followed it westward across the continent. The old camino led over the towering sierras that form the western wall of the Valley of Anáhuac, in which lies Mexico City; across the wide plateau that is watered by the west-flowing Santiago River and its affluents; past Lake Chapala, a noble sheet of water five thousand feet above the level of the sea, and on whose shores Cortés found a Tarascan civilization scarcely inferior to that of the Aztecs. Today in places the roads he traveled are narrow lanes or stock drives hemmed in for miles at a stretch by stone walls that look centuries old. On November 5 Kino was in Guadalajara, the beautiful capital of Nueva Galicia, whose history had already covered fourteen decades.

Here, in the metropolis of the West, Kino had important business. California lay within the jurisdiction of the bishop of Guadalajara, at least the bishop so maintained, and Kino came from Mexico instructed to obtain from him a license for his prospective missionary work. Spiritual jurisdiction over the Peninsula, as a matter of fact, was at this very time in dispute between Juan Garabito, bishop of Guadalajara, and Fray Bartolomé de Escañuela, bishop of Durango. Escañuela was a Franciscan, and between him and the Jesuits there was bad blood. A few months previously Bishop Juan had heard that Bishop Bartolomé had licensed a priest to go with Atondo to California as chaplain of the vessels and as Escañuela's vicar on the Peninsula. He was surprised! He protested in emphatic terms. Bishop Bartolomé replied in equally vigorous language. California, he said, was in the diocese of Nueva Vizcaya. This being the case there was but one question. "Am I or am I not the bishop of Nueva Vizcaya?" "You are not bishop of California," thundered Bishop Juan, and referred the matter to the king's representative.[1] Pardo, the Jesuit provincial, also protested, and Viceroy Paredes sustained him. The chaplain should be a Jesuit. So he ordered Escañuela to rescind the obnoxious commission and not meddle in California affairs.

When Kino arrived in Guadalajara the dispute was still going on,

[1] Bishop Garabito to Bishop Escañuela, Zacatecas, Guadalajara, July 14, 1681; reply, July 26, 1681. Original Spanish manuscripts, A.G.I. 67–1–30, Guadalajara 63.

and gossip about it was buzzing round the halls of the great cathedral where the bishop held sway. But that was not Kino's affair. His mission was the salvation of souls. And he doubtless knew of the viceroy's decision. So he showed his credentials and applied for a license. Bishop Juan was absent that day, but Peña, his vicar, issued the desired document. It declared that "since Fathers Eusebio Francisco Quino and Mathias Goñi, . . . will soon depart for these islands [of California], and in view of the good parts, virtue, and letters which are combined in the person of Father Eusebio Quino," he was appointed curate and *juez eclesiástico vicario* of California, as representative of the bishop. By the same document license was granted to Father Goñi, as Kino's assistant, to perform the same offices. This paper, duly signed by Peña, was delivered on the same day to Father Kino, "who received it and took it into his possession."[1] As he read it he must have felt a conflict of emotions. He was one step nearer to California, where there were multitudes of heathen to save and where adventure was awaiting him, but his chances for going to China were getting slimmer each day.

Three Jesuits instead of two were now needed, two as missionaries and one to serve as chaplain of the vessels. Without reference to previous arrangements the viceroy asked the provincial to nominate the missionaries. Pardo replied that in anticipation of such an order he had already selected Kino and Goñi, one because of his mathematics and the other at Atondo's instance. Both, he said, were now on the northern frontier awaiting orders. For the third Jesuit, Pardo nominated Father Antonio Suárez, an experienced missionary then residing at San Luís Potosí, ordering him to go at once to Guadalajara and prepare for the journey.[2] The three were duly approved by the viceroy. It was agreed that one should be paid by the Order out of a famous legacy left the Jesuits by Fernández de la Torre; the others by the government, one as missionary, the other as chaplain. Suárez repaired to Guadalajara.[8]

---

[1] Testimonio de Título de Cura y Vicario, Guadalajara, November 15, 1681. Sobre Pertenencia, A.G.I. 67–4–2.

[2] Atondo to the Viceroy, Shipyard of Nío, Jurisdiction of Sinaloa, Feb. 12, 1682.

[8] There on August 13 he was given a license by Bishop Garabito as missionary to California. The above account is a brief summary of the expediente regarding the appointment of the California missionaries.

XXII

WHERE SHIPS WERE BUILDING

From Guadalajara Kino jogged on his way, and in March, 1682, we find him at Nío, where Atondo's ships were being built. His experiences there must have stirred him. He had spent half his life dreaming of missionary work among heathen, and now the goal was close at hand. At this moment he was in the very cradle of Jesuit history on the Pacific Slope. The Sinaloa River was the scene of the labors and death of Father Tapia, protomartyr of the sons of Loyola in New Spain. Nío itself, and many of the settlements round about, had begun their existence as Jesuit missions. The church at Guasave, just down stream, was a famous shrine, whose statue of the Virgin was "one of the most beautiful that human eye had seen." Just across the Gulf lay California, toward which Kino's eyes were now turning.

But Father Eusebio lost little time in mere contemplation. He seldom did. He was on the move these days, and as he darted in and out of the tangled *monte* that hides the Sinaloa trails, it was difficult to keep track of him. On March 25 he was at Pueblo de Nío; thence he returned to Guadalajara. On June 3 he was at the famous old mining town of Rosario near Mazatlán, now so eloquent of past splendors, and so in danger of falling into its own cellar. To avoid this fate for its most precious monument to colonial culture, the superb church is being carefully taken down, the stones numbered, to be rebuilt outside the city on a spot not honeycombed with mines. Kino passed through Rosario just too soon to be an eye-witness of the miracle which made the Holy Cross of Rosario a famous shrine. It occurred the following April.

While in Rosario Kino indited a letter to the Duchess. He wrote in Spanish now. He was in good health and "hoped she was the same." Well, he had not succeeded in going to China after all. The slip of paper had spoken with oracular effect. Father Antonio's weak stomach had not availed him. But Kino was an optimist, and he had already become a booster for California. "My superiors, the viceroy himself, and the bishop of Guadalajara, are sending me to the new conquest and new missions of the Great Kingdom of the Californias, which, in my opinion, is the largest island which the Orb contains." A Native Son of the Golden West could hardly do better.

Visions of the Orient were becoming dimmer. "To Father Baltasar de Mansilla I owe sincere thanks for the efforts which he made to send me to Gran China, a mission which I have so much desired for so many years. But I am sure that it is a divine disposition that I should go to the Californias, and so may the holy will be done of Him who always knows what is best. And I confess that I go with very great pleasure." In fact, California stocks had risen. "Recently the bishop of Guadalajara told me that as soon as it is known that in the Californias we have begun to conquer and to convert souls and to settle, he must go in person and aid us in *captura piscium,* for he signs himself and is bishop of the Californias, and he has done me the honor of making me his vicar." [1]

His letter writing finished, Father Eusebio saddled up, hit the north-bound trail, and jogged his way once more to Nío. There preparations were coming to a head. In the autumn the little fleet was finished—two fragatas and a balandra, this last instead of the barco luengo at first planned. Unfortunately we do not know what señorita, if any, broke the wine bottles at the christening. But we may be sure that Kino and Goñi gave appropriate blessings. The Almiranta, or Admiral's ship, was called the *San José y San Francisco Xavier;* the Capitana bore the much favored name of *La Concepción.* In the ancient documents from which our tale is gleaned, these little vessels generally figure as Almiranta, Capitana, and Balandra, and so we shall designate them as we follow their intriguing fortunes. What would one give if we might discover a contemporary picture of them!

Amid the cheers of the natives the ships were pushed into the stream. From the bridge Atondo bowed in acknowledgment of the compliment and waved a smiling goodbye. Then the armadilla floated down the river to the Gulf and sailed over its blue waters to Chacala to get provisions and the rest of the crew. Kino was on board the

---

[1] Klein to the superior at Ingolstadt, Mexico, February 16, 1682; Kino to the Duchess, El Rosario, June 3, 1682. Original Spanish manuscripts in the Huntington Library. That Kino had returned to Guadalajara is an inference. When he was there in November, 1681, the Bishop was absent. Now, on June 3, he says he "recently" talked with Bishop Juan.

A pack train descending into the Barranca, west of Guadalajara

Ruins of a Jesuit Mission at Pueblo Viejo, Nio, Sinaloa

The Plaza at Ahome, Sinaloa

La Paz, where Atondo and Kino built their settlement, 1683

Island in La Paz Bay, showing the salt bed described by Kino

Almiranta. The moment he arrived he reported to the Duchess. "On October 28 of this year of 1682 we sailed with the Capitana, the Almiranta, and the Balandra for this Sea of the South, and on November 3, after a safe although somewhat long voyage of seven days, we arrived at this port of Chacala. . . . Here we are taking on supplies for a six months' voyage, . . . to the Californias, which I very, very sincerely commend, and myself as well, to the holy prayers of your Excellency and to your holy Marian and angelic family, Gabriel, Joachín, and Isabel."[1]

XXIII

TOO MANY LICENSES

While in Sinaloa Kino had taken a step that involved him innocently in the controversy between the two bishops. From Pueblo de Nío he wrote to the bishop of Durango[2] requesting a license to administer the sacraments in his diocese, saying that because of his many tasks and other circumstances he had not presented himself personally before the bishop. To do so he would have had to ride a mule over the rugged Sierra Madre, which even now terrifies all but the most hardy.

Letters traveled slowly over that difficult trail. But the wonder is that the mail service was so efficient. Two months passed, and then Bishop Bartolomé granted the request.[3] "Because of the qualities of this reverend father, and from the account which they have given of his efficiency, and since he tells us that he has a license to confess both men and women in the dioceses of Germany and in the archdiocese of Mexico; and because he also tells us that he is about to go on a voyage to the Californias, we grant our authority and license to said reverend Father Eusebio Francisco Quino" to confess, absolve, and preach the Word of God, "in this diocese."[4] Likewise, Bishop

[1] Kino to the Duchess, Chacala, November 3, 1682. Original Spanish manuscript in the Huntington Library.
[2] On March 25.
[3] On May 24.
[4] Sobre Pertenencia, A.G.I. 67-4-2.

Bartolomé continues, because Kino says he is going to California, and that he has a license from the bishop of Guadalajara "where right to said California is in *litiz pendencia*"—that is to say, in litigation— therefore, "for the security of our conscience and that of Father Eusebio Francisco Quino and for the legalization of sacraments," Kino is granted the desired permission to administer them in California.

This was in May. Then something else happened. In August Kino was superseded as superior of the California missions by Father Antonio Suárez. The reason is not clear. Was there any connection between the two events? The change, of course, was made by Father Pardo, the provincial. Bishop Juan was "informed" of the change, but he may have had something to do with making it. At any rate Kino was displaced.

We learn the fact from Father Suárez's license. On August 13, 1682, Father Antonio was in Guadalajara. On that day Bishop Juan wrote that whereas in his absence, his vicar, Peña, had given Kino and Goñi a commission, "and since Father Antonio Suárez, religious of the same Society, is about to go to that mission as superior of these fathers, Eusebio Francisco Quino and Mathías Goñi, as we have been informed both by that father and by the others who are in his college of this city"; therefore, without revoking the license given to Kino and Goñi, Bishop Juan appointed Suárez his vicar and *juez eclesiástico* in California, it being understood that when Suárez and Kino were together the latter was not to exercise his powers as vicar or as *juez*, "but only Father Antonio Suárez, his regular superior, because it is our wish." But whenever they were separated, each one might exercise those functions independently. This commission was delivered to Suárez in Guadalajara the same day. Father Antonio now proceeded over the mule trail to Chacala to join Atondo.

Bishop Juan was still concerned over his authority. It must be maintained. The viceroy had decreed it. So the bishop issued to Suárez, Kino, and Goñi an order forbidding them to permit any one to administer the sacraments in California without a license from himself.[1] Of course he had Bishop Bartolomé in mind. This command was rushed to the coast to catch the three fathers before they sailed.

[1] November 26, 1682.

The energetic bishop did not stop here. He would make assurance doubly sure. He would check trouble at the source. If no interloper reached California there would be no trouble. To this end, on December 5 he issued a supplementary order to Suárez, Kino, and Goñi, not to permit any other priest to embark with them for California without a license from himself.[1] That was that.

Soon after starting for the coast the bishop's messenger must have met Kino, for three days later Father Eusebio was in Guadalajara. What special errand took him there is not clear. One wonders if he had been sent for. Or did he go voluntarily to show Escañuela's license, in which he claimed jurisdiction over California, and which Kino knew to be contrary to the viceroy's decision? Be that as it may, the bishop added to the already thick pile of documents regarding the controversy over jurisdiction a copy of the offensive permit issued by Bishop Bartolomé, and after it he wrote, "This license was presented by Father Francisco Eusebio Quino." Beneath it he wrote that Kino might use it within the diocese of Guadalajara, but that "with respect to . . . the Islas Californias . . . to which this license pretends to extend" it was invalid, "because the territory of California pertains to this diocese of Guadalajara." Moreover, he charged Kino to deliver this Durango license into the hands of Bernardo Pardo, at the same time begging the provincial to revoke the obnoxious paper, in order to avoid disputes over jurisdiction.[2] Bishop Garabito might well be called thorough, to say the least. From this interesting file of old papers with their rubrics and seals we learn much about administration and something about bishops.

[1] License to Suárez, Guadalajara, August 13, 1682; Auto, November 26, 1682; Auto, Dec. 5, 1682; letter to Suárez, Dec. 7, 1682. Original Spanish manuscripts, Sobre Pertenencia, A.G.I. 67–4–2.

[2] Auto, December 10, 1682. Sobre Pertenencia, A.G.I. 67–4–2.

La Paz

XXIV

FULL SAIL FOR CALIFORNIA

HAVING FINISHED HIS BUSINESS WITH BISHOP JUAN, Father Kino faced westward once more. As he wound his way through the yawning barranca, and threaded the dizzy mule path over the rough sierras that lay between Guadalajara and the Pacific Ocean, he must have felt like a veteran on that historic trail, for within the past year he had been over it several times. He was soon back in Chacala.

Atondo completed his preparations there in the middle of January and was about to sail, when he learned that Luque and his six seamen were hastening to join the expedition. Short of men, the Admiral was disposed to wait for them. But he was already behind schedule, so he decided to sail at once, leaving the Balandra under Captain Parra to await Luque and then follow in his wake. Father Suárez was not at Chacala at this time. Kino thought him to be on his way to Sinaloa by land.

The long-awaited moment had at last arrived. It was now more than four years since Atondo had signed his contract. At midnight on January 17, 1683, the two fragatas opened sail to the breeze and started for California.[1] Another adventure in colonization was under way. The Capitana was commanded by Blas de Guzmán, the Almiranta by Francisco de Pereda y Arze. On the former vessel went the Admiral, and with him Father Goñi, his personal friend. Kino sailed on the Almiranta, the ship which bore the name of his patron saint. The surgeon of the expedition was Fray Joseph de Guijosa, a brother of the Order of San Juan de Dios. Joseph de Castro went as master blood-letter. Besides these persons of prominence there were more

---

[1] Because they sailed at midnight some participants reported that they started on the 17th, others said it was the 18th.

than a hundred men on board. In the company there were Christianized Indians, men and women, to serve as laborers, cooks, and at
other household tasks. Moraza, the Veedor, or royal watchdog, because of illness was left behind to follow with the Balandra.

Before crossing to California Atondo headed north to the mouth
of the Sinaloa River, the stream on whose banks the two vessels had
been built. We have Kino's account of the voyage in two graphic
letters written to Father Pardo.[1] Winds were contrary. The Capitana fell behind and was lost to view. To await the lagging consort,
after eleven days of sailing the Almiranta put in at Mazatlán, "town
of the Mulattos," making her way gingerly up the passage between
the steep, rocky islands and anchoring near the shore. There she lay
to for four or five days, but no Capitana appeared. She must have
passed by unobserved. But just as the Almiranta was about to leave
the harbor to pursue her way alone[2] the Capitana hove in sight.
There were cheers, the Almiranta went out to meet her companion,
and on the 4th of February both vessels put in at Mazatlán, whence
Kino recounted to Pardo the voyage thus far.

Equipped with a new supply of wood and water, and leaving
orders for the Balandra to follow—they could wait no longer because of an epidemic of *baruadillo*[3]—the vessels continued up the
coast. Unintentionally they ran a zigzag race. For ten days they kept
company, then separated. Now it was the Capitana which got ahead.
The lagging Almiranta sailed in her wake—as was supposed—for
more than two weeks. When she reached the harbor at Sinaloa River
no Capitana was in sight. She must already have crossed to California, it was thought. But this was an error; the Capitana had again
fallen behind. Two days later, however,[4] she sailed into the harbor.
Again hats were in the air and vivas resounded. "And it gave very

---

[1] We have also a contemporary manuscript sketch called Relación Puntual de la Entrada
. . . en la Grande Isla de la California. Biblioteca Nacional, Mexico, Californias, Legajo 53.
This account was printed in Mexico in 1686. A fragment of the rare print is in the private collection of Henry R. Wagner (see Bibliography). The Relación Puntual is clearly the document
of which the *Descent Made by the Spaniards,* published by Lockman, is a rough translation. A
French version by Father Verbiest was printed under the title *Nouvelle Descente des Espagnols,*
etc. (Paris, 1685). See also Kino to Zingnis, August 30, 1683.

[2] On February 3.

[3] Testimonio de Auttos sobre los Socorros hechos a la Armadilla. Original Spanish manuscript, A.G.I. 58–4–21, Mexico 54.

[4] March 10.

great consolation to both vessels to find ourselves reunited," says Kino. He adds "the voyage to this place has been much longer and more tedious than we had expected, for we had very contrary northwest winds on the way."[1] Father Suárez was not at Sinaloa, where Kino expected to find him.

XXV

WITH BEAT OF DRUM

Ten busy days were spent here on the mainland coast in getting new supplies. Messengers hurried inland, and pack trains plodded heavy-laden to the landing. The Jesuit missions in the vicinity gave generous aid, and Atondo replenished his larder with sheep, fowls, and other welcome provisions. Then, on March 18, at sunset, the vessels weighed anchor and sailed. As California came closer, China receded from Kino's ambitions.

Because of unfavorable winds they stood for five days near the mainland shore, visible no doubt from the noble heights at Topolobampo. On March 25, Feast of the Annunciation, they got a glimpse of California. Kino's pulse quickened at the sight. He would soon be a missionary *entre infieles,* not in China, 'tis true, but in the "largest island in the world." Six days later, last day of a novena rendered to San José, they entered the great bay named La Paz, the spacious haven where since the day of Cortés so many expeditions had gone to pieces—for its history, belying its name, had been anything but peaceful.

Swinging south, on April 1 they entered the inner harbor and anchored. Looking eastward they gazed on a beautiful fringe of tall palms stretching gracefully for half a league along the beach. Just behind the grove ran a narrow mesa, terminated on the east by hills that soon rose into bare-topped mountains.[2]

---

[1] Kino to Pardo, Sinaloa, March 16, 1683. Original Spanish manuscript in the central archives of the Jesuit Order.

[2] Kino tells the story of the voyage in a letter to Father Juan Martínez, dated April 20, 1683, put in the form of a brief diary. Original Spanish manuscript in the Huntington Library. In a letter to Father Paul Zingnis, August 30, 1683, he gives a fuller account of some particulars. Original Latin manuscript in Bayerische Hauptstaatsarchiv, München, Jesuitica Nos. 293–294.

Before anybody went ashore Atondo issued an impressive proclamation. The great trouble in all previous expeditions to the Peninsula had been the abuse of the Indians by the pearl fishers. But this was not a pearl fishing enterprise; the principal object of Atondo's efforts was to establish the Christian Faith. This must be made clear to everybody. So, on the Capitana, to assemble all the men a drum was beat by Juan de Zavala, a mulatto who was official *pregonero,* or public crier. When crew and passengers had come together Diego de Salas, royal scribe, "in a loud and clear voice" read Atondo's *bando.*

The document recited that the king had spent much money for the expedition, for the building of the fleet, equipping it with provisions, and the purchase of clothing for the Indians, for the sole purpose of reducing them to the Holy Faith and obedience to his Majesty. All this had been done by the king without hope of other return— unless of their own accord and out of gratitude the Indians might freely give gold, silver, pearls, amber, and other valuable things. Such a contingency was provided for. In that case these free gifts must be put in the royal chest brought for the purpose, locked with three keys, and kept securely for his Majesty, to reimburse him for his outlay.

To the same purpose the scribe, continuing to read the bando, proclaimed that nobody should presume to vex the Indians under pain of death. Nor might they trade with them. Experience had shown, he recited, that disputes over small matters of property had often led to rebellions. The Tepehuanes, for example, had revolted because of being defrauded of a chicken. The California Indians had rebelled against Vizcaíno, and had killed eighteen of his Spaniards, for the sole reason that one of them snatched a single paltry pearl from a native damsel. To prevent such misunderstandings, nobody must even dare to enter an Indian's house or hut without the owner's permission,—this, too, under pain of death.

To Father Eusebio these Spanish laws must have appeared rather harsh. But there was a softer side to the bando. Nobody might take a pearl from any Indian. But each man might have all the wealth gathered by his own industry—pearls, gold, silver, amber,—paying the fifth due to the king; and each man in the expedition was assured of honors according to his merit. It was in order that none might

sin through ignorance that Atondo was now having the bando published "a son de cajas y a voz de pregonero," in all parts of the Capitana.[1] This done, the same formality was repeated on board the
Almiranta. Things looked—or sounded—promising for the Indians.

Atondo now went ashore and selected a site for a settlement. The
one chosen was at the very place where La Paz stands today. It was
in a palm grove—still there—beside a fine well of water, also still
there. Next day all landed, made a cross from a large palm tree,
and set it up on the mesa which overlooks the beach. On the 4th
the little estuary south of the main bay was explored in the launches,
and fish were caught in a net.

On the 5th Atondo took formal possession of the country in the
name of King Carlos II, with pageantry as pompous as the primitive
circumstances permitted. The soldiers, ranged in military order, were
fully armed with all their cumbrous weapons and trappings. Next
to the Admiral, who wore his best, Ensign Verástegui was the most
conspicuous personage, for he carried a scarlet banner, painted and
embroidered on one side with the image of Our Lady of Remedios,
and on the other with the royal arms. Fuses were lighted, and when
the Admiral gave the order to fire, the ensign three times hoisted the
banner and shouted "Long live Carlos Segundo, Monarch of the Spains,
our king and lord." The soldiers joined in the vivas and the hills
echoed them back. Atondo in the name of the sovereign declared that
he took possession of the Province of the Most Holy Trinity of the
Californias. "This ceremony," the record reads, "was repeated three
times, with the banner and the arquebuses, the joyous vivas repeating
again and again, 'Long live Carlos Segundo.' " Atondo now had the
royal banner set up in the shade of a palm tree and there established
a guard.

This scene finished, another, less noisy but equally solemn, was
enacted. Fathers Kino and Goñi, dressed in their most formal robes,
took spiritual possession of California in the name of Bishop Garabito,
"whom all recognize as their legitimate pastor and us . . . as his lieutenants." Another chapter in the history of California had begun.[2]

---

[1] "By the beat of the drum and the voice of the public crier."
[2] Act of Possession, and Declaration at La Paz. Original manuscripts, A.G.I. 67–4–2.

XXVI

FIRST DAYS

Pioneer beginnings are always interesting, and those at La Paz yield to none. In the course of the next three weeks the bay and its environs were explored, a church and a fort begun, planting started, and the Capitana careened preparatory to a voyage up the Gulf to Yaqui for supplies and horses and to carry mail. Meanwhile the provisions brought in the vessels were supplemented by hunting and fishing.

For five days the timid Indians kept out of sight. But at last they appeared, and through the gentle efforts of the missionaries they were gradually coaxed by sweet morsels and relieved of their fear. The soldiers, on the other hand, felt quite as much concerned that the natives should be impressed with the Spaniard's power and prowess, and not become too bold. In their efforts to learn the Indian language, Kino and Goñi went about eagerly "with inkwell in their hands," noting down "their vocables and their pronunciation." [1]

No account of these first days in California, when the Spaniards were alone with nature and the aborigines, can be quite so interesting as the one which Kino himself wrote to Father Martínez on April 20. He put it in the form of a brief diary, from which we have already drawn. At the risk of a little repetition it is reproduced here from the day of leaving the mainland.

"After we had sailed from the bar of Río de Sinaloa on March 18, for lack of favorable winds we remained five days in the vicinity of the Peaks and Islands of San Ignacio." The peaks and islands still have the same name.[2] "But on the 25th of that month of March, Feast of the Annunciation of Our Lady, His Divine Majesty willed that we should come to get a glimpse of California, without losing sight of the Sinaloa mainland and the Serros de San Ignacio, since the distance across is not more than thirty-five leagues. On the 31st of March, the

[1] Relación Puntual de la Entrada. Manuscript in the Biblioteca Nacional, Mexico. Californias, Legajo 53.
[2] On the modern map two long islands lying between Sinaloa River and Topolobampo are called Macapule and San Ignacio.

day on which we finished a novena to the glorious San Joseph, we entered the great bay of Nuestra Señora de la Paz, whose entrance[1] is in 24 degrees and 55 minutes north latitude." Kino's estimate was a little too high. "Next day, the 1st of April, we entered, sailing south as far as the mouth of the Puerto de la Paz. Some of the men went ashore and found a beautiful well of water, a plentiful supply of fire wood, a marsh, a pretty grove of palms, and tracks of Indians.

"On the 2d of April nearly all of us went ashore, made a very large cross, set it up on a little elevation, and returned to the ships to sleep. On Saturday, April 3, we again went ashore, but did not encounter or see a single Indian, which for us was a matter of great disappointment. On Sunday, in the two launches, we went farther into the gulf of this Puerto de la Paz, which is in 24 degrees and 10 minutes north latitude. But still we neither met nor saw any Indian. In the afternoon we caught with the net a very large quantity of fine fish. And we saw some smokes, although far away. On Monday we began to build a small church and a little fort or Real de Nuestra Señora de Guadalupe, and from this day we began to sleep and live on the land." This was the day when formal possession was taken.[2]

It was next day that Kino got his first sight of real wild Indians, the kind of people he had come so far to teach.[3] They lived up to his expectations. "On Tuesday morning, at the time when nearly all the men were clearing the brush from a little elevation and cutting timber for our buildings, they heard some whoops of Indians who were coming toward this harbor. Immediately all the soldiers stood by their arms. The Indians arrived shouting loudly, armed with bows and arrows, painted as a sign of war, at least defensive, and making signs that we should leave their lands— ['*Auric, auric,* Begone, begone,' they shouted][4]—We tried to make them understand that we came in peace and begged them to lay their weapons down on the ground, promising that we would do likewise, but they refused. Father Gony and I then

---

[1] This was San Lorenzo Channel. It is about twelve miles north of the inner harbor.
[2] They entered the Ensenada, westward of the harbor.
[3] At the time Kino was raising a portable altar. Kino to Zingnis, San Lucas, August 30, 1683. Original Latin manuscript in Bayerische Haupstaatsarchiv, München, Jesuitica Nos. 293–294.
[4] The words in brackets are in Kino's letter to Zingnis, San Lucas, August 30, 1683, in which the same story is told.

went up to them, gave them maize, biscuits, and glass beads, which they refused to take from our hands, asking us to lay them down on the ground; but afterward they began to take them directly from our hands." At last Kino was a real missionary.

"We now began to be very friendly and familiar and they gave us roasted mescal heads, which were very good, little nets very well made, and feathers of birds which they wore on their heads, etc. We showed them a crucifix, and next day a statue of Our Lady of Guadalupe, but they gave no sign of ever having had either of these things or anything else relating to the Catholic faith. In the afternoon they went away very well content, although some of our men suspected that they could not be trusted."[1] When a man carries a gun he is prone to use it.

"On Wednesday the men continued cutting trees and very large palms, laying out and building a little fort in the shape of a crescent and building our little church. On Thursday they caught a great quantity of very fine fish, there being enough for a very liberal supply for all the men for three days and more.

"On Friday the Indians returned, accompanied by many others, in all more than eighty, all being peaceful and very friendly. They asked for maize, which for them is a great luxury, and they ate it as if it were some sweetmeat. After we gave them the maize we taught them to make the sign of the Holy Cross. The sun having set, they went away very well satisfied, to sleep in the woods, saying they would return next day. They did return [on Saturday] and we succeeded in making them much more familiar, friendly, and docile."

Pioneer tasks occupied the time of soldiers and missionaries. The centers of interest were the tiny chapel, the slender fortress, exploration, planting, the voyage to Yaqui, and dealings with the natives. Religious rites were observed and Church holidays celebrated. The diary continues: "On Palm Sunday we blessed and arranged many very pretty palms. On Monday and the succeeding days they continued with the building of the little church and of the fort or real, and careened the Capitana preparatory to going to Hyaqui for provisions and horses. On Tuesday the admiral sent nine soldiers inland to see if

---

[1] Kino learned that Aini meant water (Kino to Zingnis, San Lucas, August 30, 1683). The edge of the original manuscript is lacking, but the Martínez copy supplies the omission.

there was any river, lake, or village. Since they were on foot they did not go more than three leagues, and they found neither river nor ranchería,[1] but from a small hill they saw some smokes, a lake, and pretty plains. Very soon, God willing, we shall go farther inland, as far as the opposite coast, which cannot be more than twenty leagues from here.

"On Wednesday many of the Spaniards confessed. On Thursday others confessed, and Communion was received by the Admiral, the captains, and many soldiers and sailors. In the afternoon more than forty Indians came to see us, over half of them being people who had not come to visit us before. They learned how to make the sign of the Holy Cross and were very docile and friendly. We gave them maize, pinole, and pozole, and they went to the woods to sleep under the trees. And there was a sermon for the Spaniards.

"On Friday the Indians returned with a little load of firewood, for they had noticed that the day before we had rewarded those who had brought wood. At midday they returned to their villages. In the afternoon there was a sermon on the Passion of Our Lord. On Holy Saturday we chanted the litanies and said Mass, according to custom, and at the Gloria in Excelsis and five other times during the Mass all the muskets were fired, with peal of bells and much ceremony.

"The land is good and it has a fine climate. There are plentiful fish, firewood, birds, deer, rabbits, etc. We planted maize, muskmelons, watermelons, etc. We hope that all will bear fruit, and we trust that within a few months we may begin to baptize, for these Indians appear to be the most docile, laughing, and jovial of all those in all America."[2] Of course he had not seen it all.

Clearly, Kino was pleased with the prospect. And his account of these pioneer days at La Paz will be cherished for all time.

There were many other things of interest to the soldiers as well as to the missionaries. Right near the camp they found the skeleton of a whale "so large that one jawbone was five yards long." In the intervening two and a half centuries the skeleton has disappeared and

---

[1] A *ranchería* is a small village.
[2] Kino to Martínez, La Paz, April 20, 1683. Original Spanish manuscript in the Huntington Library. For other details see Kino to Zingnis, San Lucas, August 30, 1683.

in 1932 at La Paz I found no memory of it. Some of the men, when walking for diversion along the beach, discovered caves containing human bones, and concluded that the caverns must be Indian burial places. From these caves and their hoard of skulls the high hill just north of La Paz is still called La Calavera. "They also found a piece of grappling iron, which must be from the vessels which in the years of '33 and '34 were lost near that port in the third expedition which was made to California by Captain Ortega."[1] Kino had read his history. They found likewise rocks showing signs of precious metals,— this made their eyes shine, for the Spaniards dearly loved "una mina" —and "many shells of nacre, which are the mother of pearls in which it is certain that this great gulf abounds. But up to now they have not seen any pearls, nor any Indians possessing any such as are praised by the old narratives."[2] Was it possible that the old chronicles had exaggerated? This has happened.

Kino did his best to keep his friends in Mexico and Europe informed of his doings, for he was exuberant over his work. Three days after closing the foregoing diary he wrote again to Father Martínez, promising to send him some large mother of pearl shells, "some of which I already have in my little house [ranchito]." He was not forgetful of his commission as cosmographer for the viceroy. In honor of the king he rechristened the Peninsula. "I am continuing to write a little book about this our enterprise and of these Carolinas, with a map," he says, "and as the superiors wish it I shall send it from here in a few months, when at the same time it may be possible to give some news of some baptisms." Perhaps Kino did not know that England had recently christened another American colony with the name Carolina; possibly that would make no difference.

Near the end of April—it was the 25th—the Capitana sailed for Yaqui, two hundred miles north up the Gulf, to obtain supplies, and horses with which to continue explorations. In it went Kino's letters, and others by the Admiral.[3]

---

[1] For the entrada of Ortega, see Venegas, *Empressas Apostólicas*, paragraph 76; Venegas (Burriel), *Noticia de la California*, I, 205–208. See also Hubert Howe Bancroft, *History of the North Mexican States*, Vol. I.

[2] *Relación Puntual de la Entrada*.

[3] Kino to Martínez, La Paz, April 23, 1683. Original Spanish manuscript in the Huntington Library; Kino to Zingnis, San Lucas, August 30, 1683.

XXVII

THE CALIFORNIANS AT CLOSE RANGE

Having dispatched the Capitana on its errand, Atondo and Kino undertook new explorations. A principal purpose of these jaunts was to make friends with the natives, in the hope that they would bring their children to camp, so that the Fathers might learn the native tongue and begin to teach the Catechism. And of course they were looking for sites for missions and settlements.

The first expedition was made toward the southwest, because it was from that direction that the Guaicuros generally had come to the camp. With Atondo went Father Kino, Captain Pereda, other principal men, twenty-five soldiers, some domestics, and a few peones or laborers, to clear the trails.[1]

For Kino this was the humble beginning of a remarkable career of exploration, for hitherto he had been traveling old trails. The first day they went seven leagues in a winding direction, and came before night to a fair-sized plain, on one side of which were some villages. The Indians, seeing the soldiers, hastened to hide their women and children. To gain time, some of the gandules or braves went out to meet and delay the visitors. By signs they said that the water hole, for which every man in the desert may be assumed to be looking, was in another direction. Time enough having been gained, a messenger came forth saying that the strangers might now come and drink. Going forward now, they found at the village two hundred men, armed with bows and arrows. But there were no women or children in sight, an ominous sign, indicative of preparations for a fight.

Atondo tried to make friends with the naked warriors, but they were suspicious, and refused to lay down their weapons. On his side, too, Atondo felt it wise to maintain military discipline. The hosts were again sparring for time, as it was afterward learned. While the conference was going on the chief secretly sent a band of twelve men to the Spanish settlement to see if it were left unguarded. Finding a gar-

[1] Venegas, in his unpublished Empressas Apostólicas, paragraph 112, gives a more detailed account of these explorations round about La Paz than is contained in any of the contemporary documents that have come to me. He says that Atondo was accompanied on this occasion also by Fray Joseph de Guijosa, the friar of San Juan de Dios.

rison there they returned as stealthily as they had gone.[1] Near the Indian village Atondo camped for the night, with sentinels carefully placed. Next day, after distributing a few presents, he returned to the fort, fearing to go any farther for lack of water. It must be remembered that he and his men were on foot.

Early in June [2] Atondo made another excursion, taking with him Father Goñi, besides a goodly squad of soldiers. This time he went east, into the country of the Coras, bitter enemies of the Guaicuros. Evidently Kino was learning the Guaicuro language, while Goñi specialized in the Cora tongue. This road was much rougher than the one to the southwest, but scouts reported that from the top of a high range ahead they had seen a beautiful valley. With quickened pulses Atondo and Goñi followed. To their disappointment they found no paradise, but only a rough canyon, indeed the worst country they had seen in California. With tired limbs and dampened ardor they returned to camp. But their journey had not been fruitless. In fact, from it they eventually reaped a harvest of trouble, for they had made friends with the gentle Coras, foes of the Guaicuros, and thus the wires got crossed. Accepting Atondo's invitation, the Coras now began to frequent the Spanish settlement in peaceable intercourse, "and without any fear whatever, they were accustomed to remain and sleep in the fortification among the soldiers."

Near the end of June Kino wrote again to Father Martínez, and from his letter we can carry his story forward. It deals largely with the Indians, his main concern. The soldiers were distrustful of the Guaicuros, but Kino saw them through a missionary's eye. What to them was black to him was white. Devils to the soldiers, to Kino they were potential angels. In spite of some friction, the Guaicuros remained outwardly bland. They came frequently to camp, bringing "presents of pitahayas, mescales, and sometimes of little pearls." The Spaniards in return gave them "maize, glass beads, belts, ribbons, and little knives."

Father Eusebio gives us an excellent description of the Guaicuros. "These Indians are of a very lively and friendly disposition, of good

---

[1] Atondo learned about this trick after he returned to camp. Venegas, *Empressas Apostólicas*, paragraphs 112–114.

[2] After the disturbance of June 6.

stature, strength, and health, and are very happy, laughing and jovial. The men wear no clothing whatever, unless it be a cupi of feathers on the head. The women wear skins which reach from the breasts to the ground. They are whiter than the Indians of New Spain.[1] A few days ago, indeed, there came to see us a little boy who was very pink-skinned. They live on sea foods and other products of the country, such as deer, rabbits, and birds, of which there is an abundance. Recently a soldier, with the permission of the Admiral, went with his arquebus to the woods, and in a short time brought back three pigeons.

"The weapons of these Indians are bows and arrows, flint-pointed but without poison, for they do not know this art. . . . The chiefs carry reed flutes hanging from their necks, but they do not use them except when they are actually fighting, and for this reason they do not like our guitar, or our little harps and flutes. They are very fond of knives, anything made of iron, coscates or glass beads, and all kinds of little beads or of red ribbons. Their wives and children are very timid."

Then a word for the linguist: "Their language, which is not very difficult to learn, has all the sounds of the alphabet except *s* and *f*, but they learn and pronounce prettily the salubrious word *Jesús* and other such words of the Castilian language, even though they may have the *s* sound. When they inquire of us about anything, they are very careful to ask what it is called in our language. We have greatly lacked and still lack an interpreter, for if we had possessed one doubtless we could have done many things and by now we should have many baptisms. But we leave this to His Divine Majesty and trust that everything will be arranged, only I wish things might move a little faster." Kino was getting restless.[2]

XXVIII

PANTOMIMES AND A SHOOTING MATCH

This lack of an interpreter was less noticeable than it otherwise would have been if it had not been for the cleverness of the natives in

---

[1] He means the mainland.
[2] Kino to Martínez, San Lucas, July 27, 1683. Original Spanish manuscript in the Huntington Library. Part of this letter was written at La Paz in June.

sign language. Kino and Atondo give diverting accounts of the way they made themselves understood.

"A good old man among them set himself to tell them in his own language, accompanied by signs which made clear what he was saying, that he had five sons, and that one little one had died a few days before. In order to explain that he had buried him he made a hole in the ground, took a little stick, which represented his boy, and buried it.

"The Spaniards asked them by signs if there was any river in that country. One of them, understanding the question, explained as follows: He took a dart, and, pointing steadily to the west, began to go on the trot peculiar to the Indians, and after going once and a half around the camp he again pointed toward the sun. By this he signified that in a turn and a half of the sun through its course there was a river, from which they understood that a day and a half's journey from there we would find it.

"The Spaniards took a little salt in their hands, tasted it, and then giving some of it to the Indians to taste, they asked them by signs if they had any of this article and where it was. The Indians tasted it but gave to understand that they did not know of it." In view of what Kino said about a fine salt bed on an island in the bay, this sign language does not seem to have been a perfect success. He continues: "Then, twisting their faces and putting their hands to their cheeks and shutting their eyes, they said good night, indicating in this way that they were going to sleep."

When the Indians became too familiar they began to pilfer things from the Spaniards, at which they showed great dexterity. This had to be stopped. "The Admiral, seeing their bold actions, decided to put a little fear into them through an experiment which he tried." He invited them to a shooting match. "Setting up a shield called a *chimale* and made of rawhide, against a very large skeleton of a whale which they found there, by signs he told the Indians to shoot at it with their arrows. The most mettlesome and courageous among them took their bows and shot their arrows at the shield, but they hardly broke the skin of it, and some of the arrows were shattered with the impact. At this they were surprised, because the arrows are so pene-

trating and sharp that they usually pierce any animal through and
through."

But the real surprise was yet to come. "The Admiral now by signs
asked them whether they wished to see what our weapons would do.
They apparently thought that the arquebus was our bow, the ramrod
the arrow, and that the worm was what served as a flint. In order that
they might see what a powerful weapon the arquebus was, the Admiral ordered the alférez, Martín de Verástegui, to fire an arquebus
ball at the chimale. In order to make them understand that it would
carry farther than their bows, he stood six paces back of the place from
which they had shot. Then, firing, he not only pierced the chimale
through and through, but also the bone of the whale against which
it was leaning."

The success was complete. The barbarians were astonished to see
the shot. But they were progressives and eager to learn. "They asked
for a ball, in order to put it on the point of a dart. Thinking that the
noise of the arquebus was what did the work, and that they might make
one like it, they put the ball there, gave a puff—and immediately it
fell at their feet. With this demonstration they were somewhat frightened, and their freedom was repressed." [1]

XXIX

A CALIFORNIA BOOSTER

Nobody who ever went to La Paz escaped the lure of pearls. This
is as true today as when Cortés risked life and reputation to found a
colony there; or as when the Dutch pirate Spillberg overhauled and
robbed the pearl fishing vessel of Iturbi. Even Kino was not immune.
Atondo's expedition was designed to be free of the abuses incident to
pearl fishing. To prevent them he had issued that high-sounding and
wordy proclamation. But his men, when they were not playing the
guitar, spent their spare time in gathering *las perlas*.

---

[1] Relación Puntual de la Entrada; Lockman, *Descent Made by the Spaniards;* Verbiest,
Nouvelle Descente des Espagnols.

Kino wrote about pearls to Father Martínez. The Indians, he said, "do not greatly esteem or pay much attention to them, nor do they devote themselves to fishing for them, although pearls really are plentiful and of good luster in all this bay. In fact, many of them have been gathered. More than two hundred have been given as alms to the most Holy Virgin"—himself the custodian—"and some persons have more than this. It is true that after selecting a few which have proved to be of very good quality and larger than chick peas, nearly all the rest are very small. Yet if his Majesty or the Señor Viceroy, or their officials, would send divers who know how to dive in five, six, eight, or ten fathoms of water,"—this was asking a good deal—"no doubt they would produce a large royal income, for the pearls which they have gathered here during these two months have come from the shells which are on the shores of the sea and in shallow water. May Our Lord will that they may all serve for the more celestial conquest of the best pearls, namely souls saved by the precious blood of Our Redeemer." In his optimism no doubt Kino was one hundred per cent sincere. But he was also shrewd in appealing to royal interest in profit making. In this way the pearls would promote royal interest in the missions, and in the "conquest of the best pearls"—*ad majorem Dei gloriam.*

The country promised other treasure. "In one of the little islands of this great bay we found a very fine bed or lake of salt. The island must be about two leagues in circumference, and the salt lagoon a quarter of a league in periphery. It has been named Ysla de Santo Tomás de la Laguna," in honor of the viceroy. "From this lake could be taken a great quantity of very fine salt, with which to load many ships." Today steamers bound for La Paz run close by this island, with Kino's salt bed in plain sight.

And there was the California climate. Kino informed Martínez that La Paz had good water and was a pleasant land to live in, even in mid-summer! "The two wells which we have close to this fort or camp have very fine, abundant, and healthful water." One of the wells is used to this day. "And although last week we buried Don Lorenzo de Córdova, may he be with God in Heaven, his death was from a disease which he brought from Chacala. The rest, although they had ague [achaques] and other ills when they arrived, now enjoy good health, and all of us are well thank God, although we are rather short of biscuits and meat, and shall be until the Capitana returns." This vessel, it will be remembered, had left for Yaqui near the end of April to get supplies and horses. "Nevertheless, the men play on their harps and guitars, and sing, and most of them have a good time and enjoy themselves. We have very good weather, for although from ten in the morning to three or four in the afternoon it is usually pretty hot, it is no worse than in Sinaloa." This, in summer, is not the highest praise. "And all the other eighteen or twenty hours of the day and night are temperate, and the water which we drink gets so cool"—hung in ollas, no doubt,—"that all declare that they have never drunk better water in all New Spain, and in few places so good." As an early California promoter Kino takes high rank, notwithstanding his dream of China.[1]

XXX

THE SLAUGHTER OF THE INNOCENTS

Though the Guaicuros kept coming to the Spanish settlement and received presents, at times they were sullen and threatening. The friendship of Spaniards with the Coras did not improve the temper of the men from the southwest. As is so often true of weaklings, this timid tribe were trouble makers.

On the feast of Espíritu Santo (June 6) over a hundred naked warriors came to camp. They advanced in two divisions and in warlike mood "to drive us from their land and get possession of our provisions. In the interval while we were hesitating and debating whether or not we should shoot, we saw a very patent sign and demonstration of hostility," says Kino. "One of the troops of Indians came clear into the enclosure, and although our valorous soldiers placed the muzzles of the arquebuses at the breasts of the Indians, the latter, perhaps through not having experienced and not knowing fully the force of these weapons, neither retreated nor fired. Therefore it was to all of

[1] Kino to Martínez, San Lucas, July 27, 1683.

us a special gift of the Holy Spirit that the peace was not broken by such circumstances." [1]

A crisis had been averted, and affairs went on much as usual till near the end of June. At that time the Capitana had not yet returned and the supply of biscuits was running low. It was now proposed to send the Almiranta to Sinaloa to carry mail, get news of the Capitana, and bring provisions. But some of the men so distrusted the Indians that they objected to remaining marooned on the Peninsula without a vessel in sight. To decide the matter a council of war was held. There was hard-headed reasoning and heated debate. Most of the men of the council favored waiting ten or twelve days. Castellanos and Briviesca favored going at once. Kino and Goñi were for remaining till orders to the contrary should send them elsewhere. Atondo therefore decided to hold on. [2]

All of a sudden, an incident occurred which gave the timid more ground for their fears. The day after the council an Indian shot a soldier with a dart. The weapon did not even draw blood, but the act was rebellion, and Atondo ordered the offender taken first to the stocks, then to the bilboes on the ship. At this the Guaicuros became excited and loudly protested. To complicate matters it was reported that the Guaicuros had killed in the interior a ship boy who had run away. The fugitive was no other than Zavala, the mulatto drummer boy. The report at first was that he had absconded with a band of Guaicuros. Now came some Coras to tell the Spaniards that he had been killed by his desert hosts. [3]

Frightened men are prone to rashness, and they seldom lack an occasion to exhibit it. So it was in this case. One day early in July [4] sixteen Guaicuro warriors came to camp. They made signs of peace, but it was feared that they had come to rescue their tribesman, or perhaps to attack the settlement. Atondo decided to act. He ordered the

---

[1] Kino to Martínez, July 27, 1683. Venegas (Empressas Apostólicas, paragraph 116), says that Atondo ordered the soldiers to fire on the advance guard of the Guaicuros with a pedrero, but when they were about to do so they discovered that Atondo was outside the trinchera, having gone to meet the second band of Indians, whom he frightened off by shouting at them.

[2] Declarations at La Paz. Autos sobre la Entrada Primera, A.G.I. 58–4–23, Mexico 56.

[3] Venegas says that Atondo now arrested a Guaicuro chief (Empressas Apostólicas). Kino tells only of the arrest of the Indian who shot the dart.

[4] About July 3. See Atondo's account from San Lucas, September 25, 1683. A.G.I. 58–4–23, Mexico 56.

visitors given pozole, or corn meal mush, of which they were very fond. In a friendly mood, feeling secure in the white man's hospitality, the naked guests sat down on the ground to eat. While they were thus occupied, and suspecting no evil, Atondo ordered the soldiers to fire into their midst with the little cannon. The match was applied. A moment later three of the Indians lay dead on the ground and the rest had fled, some of them wounded. This was a sad beginning for a missionary enterprise.

The story of the killing of the mulatto by the Guaicuros, fully believed by Atondo and his men, years afterward proved to be false. When the pedrero was fired Zavala was still alive. What happened was this. The mulatto, fearing punishment for some misdemeanor, sought to escape, and he found the means. There was a bark on the California coast. Going to the captain of the vessel—evidently some pearl hunter—Zavala offered him a fine pearl for a canoe. The captain took the bribe. In this frail craft Zavala crossed the full width of the Gulf in spite of its perils. Many years afterward Father Juan de Ugarte, then rector of the college of San Gregorio in the City of Mexico, happening to be at the hacienda of Oculma, met Zavala, who told him the story. Father Salvatierra learned of it, and told it in a letter dated October 10, 1716—a third of a century after the event.[1]

XXXI

LA PAZ ABANDONED

This needless slaughter was the beginning of the end. "From that time forward," Kino wrote,[2] "we were greatly worried, fearful by day and especially by night, the more so because we did not hear anything from the Capitana or the Balandra"—for it must be remembered that the Balandra had not been seen since Atondo had sailed from Chacala nearly six months before, and the Capitana had been absent more than

---

[1] Kino to Martínez, San Lucas, July 27, 1683. Venegas supplements Kino here with a good deal of detail. After giving another version of the story he accepts Kino's, which he learned through the letter by Father Salvatierra (Empressas Apostólicas, paragraphs 118–123).
[2] Only July 7. Kino to Martínez, San Lucas. July 27.

two months. Two or three days after the massacre Atondo called another council,[1] reported that provisions would last little more than a week, and that he had decided to send Captain Andrés with five men in the launch of the Almiranta to Sinaloa to get provisions and inquire for the missing craft. All the members of the junta, including plucky Andrés, voted favorably.

But the rank and file emphatically said "No." Learning of the plan they presented Atondo with a petition. Reviewing the events since April 1, they reminded the Admiral that the Indians were hostile, had killed the drummer boy (as they supposed), kept the soldiers under arms, invited the recent slaughter, and could easily set fire to the palm huts of the settlement. They begged Atondo to embark at once, sail to Cape San Lucas at the end of the Peninsula, and from there send the Almiranta to Sinaloa for help. Atondo denied the request and declared he would hold out a week longer. But he ordered the sick men put on board the Almiranta ready for an emergency. He was a little nervous himself.

On July 13 the week was up. The day was indeed unlucky. Provisions were exhausted, no ship was in sight, the men were frightened. So Atondo decided to pull up stakes. Before sailing he took the depositions of ten men regarding La Paz events since the sailing of the Capitana on April 25. They would serve as his justification.[2] On the 14th the eighty-three colonists went aboard, and next day Atondo set sail. For several days he hovered near the entrance to the bay, still hoping that he might meet the Capitana or the Balandra. Finally he sailed across the Gulf and anchored on July 21 in what he called the new harbor of San Lucas. It was Agiabampo Bay, north of Fuerte River.

This drab chapter in the California story is crisply epitomized by Venegas: "God permitted or disposed that this ill-considered decision of the Admiral, or of the men in his squadron,"—the firing on the natives—"should prove a boomerang and fall upon his own head. For, far from quieting the consternation of the men of the camp by the slaughter of the innocent Indians, it increased until it became a sort

[1] On July 6.
[2] Petition, July 6, 1683; Declarations at La Paz, July 13.

of panic, in which most of the men persuaded themselves that all the tribes of California would fall upon them, to cut them in pieces and avenge the deaths."

In a spirit of fairness Venegas continues: "To this it must be added that they had been three months in that port in excessive discomfort, and without any profit. The provisions were now extremely scanty, and most of them damaged and spoiled. The Capitana, which had gone for provisions to Río Hiaqui, distant only a little over eighty leagues, failed to appear after an absence of two months, and all regarded it as having sunk. The bitterness and discontent of many grew to such a point that in the guise of despair they went to the Admiral weeping and clamoring for him to take them away from there, even if only to leave them on the islands near by. The Admiral may have feared some conspiracy against his person—unless he was confident from sad experience that the men did not possess enough valor even for this. He tried to quiet them by a useless appeal to their honor, and by faint hopes of succor from the Capitana. All these efforts proving in vain, he was forced to prepare to depart, and he abandoned the Puerto de la Paz on July 14."

Kino tells the story of the withdrawal from La Paz in more laconic terms. After the slaughter, he says, "plans were changed, and because the soldiers did not wish to remain without having a ship in sight, we all came in the Almiranta to this coast of Cinaloa." His letter was written on July 27 from San Lucas, on the Sinaloa coast, where they had arrived six days previously.[1]

XXXII

PARRA VIEWS THE REMAINS

Atondo and Parra now played a game of hide and seek. By a strange trick of Fate, as the Admiral sailed from La Paz harbor he barely missed the Balandra, for whose arrival he had been praying.

---

[1] Kino to Martínez, July 27, 1683; Atondo to the viceroy, San Lucas, Sept. 25, 1683; Kino to Pardo, San Lucas, August 10, 1683. Autos sobre la Entrada Primera, A.G.I. 58–4–23, Mexico 56. Venegas, Empressas Apostólicas, paragraphs 111, 127, 128. Venegas confuses San Lucas with Cape San Lucas.

Parra's story was a bizarre one. Twelve days behind Atondo he had sailed from Chacala in the Admiral's wake.[1] At Chametla his launch was wrecked, and he returned to Chacala for a new one, which he was enabled to purchase by borrowing money from the curate of Compostela.

With Father Suárez now on board—for the Jesuit had returned to Chacala—Parra again raised anchor. Thirty terrible days were spent in reaching Mazatlán, and there the Balandra was nearly wrecked. Before a new start could be made it was necessary to obtain help from Chametla and Rosario. Suárez and Parra now quarreled, and when the Balandra was ready to continue its voyage Suárez refused to go aboard. He regarded the voyage as unsafe. Someone said "that the previous night he had talked with a Christian saint which he held in his hand, and the saint told him that the ship and he and all the rest would drown."

Leaving Suárez behind, Parra again weighed anchor on July 1, and on the 7th he reached the California coast. This was just when Atondo, facing starvation, was holding on at La Paz with grim courage. For ten days Parra explored near and in the bay, looking for the Admiral, and on the 19th he reached the site of the abandoned settlement. It was during these very days that Atondo had sailed out of the harbor. They had missed each other by a hair.

Parra's visit gave us a picture of the remains of Atondo's frail settlement, which the Indians had ransacked. Landing, he found "the fort and seven or eight palm-roofed huts, a fence made of pieces of palm leaves tied together with hide, a cross on top of a small elevation, and three wells inside the very fosse." He adds, "I went to the well which was below the four palms, covered on the sides with pieces of palm and uncovered in the middle, and containing wonderful water. About five varas further in there was another well that was not so good. I saw inside the fort two small gardens encircled by a bamboo fence, and the maize was more than a palm high. I also saw calabashes and string beans." Agriculture had made a small beginning.

[1] Moraza to the viceroy, Compostela, Feb. 24, 1683. In his report to Atondo in September Parra says he left Chacala nine days behind Atondo, which would be the 26th. But in letters to the viceroy written in February soon after the event, Moraza and Parra give the date as the 28th or 29th.

Leaving the bay, Parra now sailed up and down the coast, still looking for the Admiral. Some of his experiences were amusing, others tragic. One day some Indians went aboard the Balandra and remained as overnight guests—without invitation. Parra was a troubled host, for he even had to share his bed with his lodgers. "As I spread the mat on which to lie down," he says, "one of the chiefs by signs asked if I were going to sleep on it? I answered in the affirmative and he said that he, too, wanted to sleep on it. Thereupon he raised the blanket, crawled under the covers in the middle of the mat, and then called a son of his and made him sleep there also. I tried to get up, but he told me not to move, so you can well imagine what a night I spent." One wonders if the captain was afraid or just hospitable.

After coasting to Cape San Lucas and north again to latitude 26° 23', Parra was compelled by mutiny to abandon the search. One night they saw a huge fire on shore. Four days more they coasted the Peninsula, without losing sight of the conflagration. By now the seamen were in open rebellion, and when Parra ordered his men to go ashore for water they refused. So he steered for the mainland, and anchored near the mouth of Sinaloa River. At this moment Atondo was at San Lucas only a few leagues up the coast, but Parra did not know it. So he turned south to Mazatlán. His chase had cost him more that half a year.

By now the Balandra was nearly dismantled. It lacked sails, ropes, and anchors, and was almost too ruinous to be worth careening; few men were left, and those few disheartened. Parra had not a cent. Ill and discouraged, he asked for sick-leave or for discharge from his captaincy. "I have spent many years in the service of the king," he wrote, "but it is axiomatic that he who serves best obtains the least reward." He did, however, receive a kind word, and that counted. When the fiscal in Mexico read Parra's report, he remarked that his discoveries were really more promising than those of the Admiral.[1]

[1] Atondo to the viceroy, San Lucas, September 25, 1683. Testimonio de Auttos sobre los Socorros hechos a la Armadilla, A.G.I. 58–4–21, Mexico 54. In this expediente there is extensive correspondence concerning the Parra voyage. The documents reveal with vivid detail the hostility between Parra and Suárez. Parra is outspoken but we lack Suárez's side of the story. Learning at Mazatlán of Atondo's whereabouts, Parra wrote an extended account of his voyage and sent it with a letter to the admiral at San Lucas.

XXXIII

STILL HOPEFUL AND CHATTY

Kino was not disheartened. From San Lucas, on board the Almiranta, he wrote to Father Martínez, who had requested California curios. "I am leaving with Father Rentero, vice-rector of Cinaloa, twelve very large mother of pearl shells, since your Reverence said I should send none unless they were gigantesque. I am sending them immediately to your Reverence at Mexico, for in the Californias there are mountains of them and many with pearls."

From San Lucas he wrote also to the Duchess.[1] He was still enthusiastic for California, and he had kept his promise. "The first and up to now the only post which we have founded in the very great island of California we called Our Lady of Guadalupe." The Duchess with her thick-walled castles could hardly have imagined what a pathetic little thing this fortress was. "The reason for giving it that best of names . . . I wrote to you last year. May this sovereign Lady be pleased to accompany us with all her celestial gifts and favors." He still needed the Duquesa's aid. She had offered to help him convert China. She surely would not be deaf to a cry from California. "I beg also that . . . in Madrid you may arrange according to your pious and most prudent judgment for the promotion of the conversion of the largest island of the world, filled with so many souls . . . and the natives of such good qualities that in no other part of the world can the many royal funds and the holy zeal of Europe be better employed than now in this vast California, . . . for I perceived that they had good souls—*videns enim sortiti animas bonas.*"

Father Eusebio had already begun that series of maps of the Pacific Coast of North America for which he will ever be famous. He now writes to the Duquesa. "I am sending herewith a little map of a part of California, the Puerto de Guadalupe and its vicinity. Your Excellency must pardon its small size. Perhaps through the help and intercession of the Holy Virgin María de Guadalupe His Divine Majesty will

---

[1] Kino to the Duchess of Aveiro y Arcos, San Lucas, Sinaloa, August 12, 1683. Original Spanish manuscript in the Huntington Library.

show me such grace that in time I may be able to send other and better and larger maps."

The trouble in California, Kino thought, was partly due to the celestial wanderer about which he had written so much. "I hope you have received the little books about the comet, or the comets [he had seen Halley's brilliant comet,[1] which appeared that year], for over here we have not failed to see and experience many of their effects."

[1] See Charles P. Olivier, *Comets* (Baltimore, 1930), pp. 94–126.

San Bruno

XXXIV

A NEW DEAL

ATONDO AND HIS COMPANY SPENT TWO MONTHS AT SAN LUCAS—hot midsummer months they were.[1] He had failed of his main purpose at La Paz, perhaps through his own fault, though it must not be forgotten that his colony was forced to leave there by impending starvation as well as by fear. At any rate, the Indians were now hostile, and nothing would be gained by going back. But he had not given up. Far from it. His contract, indeed, provided that he was to try, and then to try again if need be. So he planned to continue his enterprise, perhaps at San Bernabé, near the point of the Peninsula, of which he had heard favorable reports.

For this he needed fresh supplies and more equipment. There was no time for awaiting the results of slow correspondence with Mexico, so he must take the bull by the horns, and make his own arrangements in Sinaloa. Immediately on arrival he sent out couriers and soon learned that the Capitana was safe in Yaqui. This was cheering news. While Atondo visited his capital at San Felipe to assemble an outfit, Kino and Goñi sallied forth to gather supplies among the Jesuit missions.

A new wind now blew both hot and cold. Atondo heard in one breath bad news and good. A month after the Almiranta reached San Lucas the Capitana sailed into the same harbor and Guzmán told his story.[2] It was April 25—exactly three months before—when he left La Paz for Yaqui—then spelled Hyaqui—to get horses and supplies, and to carry mail. He had a hard voyage. For fourteen days his little vessel was tossed about like a cork on the waters of the Gulf. Head

[1] One day when I was there in the summer of 1932 the thermometer stood at 112° in the shade.
[2] On August 25.

winds forced him to take shelter at the islands of San Joseph and El Carmen; and he was unable to reach his destination till the 8th of May. By the Yaqui missions Guzmán was promptly supplied with provisions and with one hundred and forty head of stock, including cattle, sheep, and nineteen horses. But when he veered around for La Paz he had new trouble with contrary winds and boisterous seas. Three times he was driven back to Yaqui after having sighted the California coast. On a fourth attempt, when near Coronados Island, he was forced by heart-breaking tempests to throw overboard cattle, horses, sheep, and other animals in order to save the ship and the lives of his men. This was no less than a calamity to the colony at La Paz. Guzmán now learned from a fishing bark on the coast that Atondo had gone to San Lucas, so he turned his prow southward and went there to join him. Like Atondo, he barely missed meeting Parra in the Balandra.

This tale of disaster was offset by one of encouragement. Guzmán told of a Río Grande near the place where the horses and cattle had been thrown overboard. In fact it was shown on the old maps. In its vicinity he had seen and dealt with numerous affable Indians. The Admiral's troubled countenance now relaxed. Forthwith he gave up his plan to go to San Bernabé, and prepared instead to make his next venture at the Río Grande.

Renewed hope released a fresh flood of energy. But the Admiral was hard up. His credit was already stretched to the limit, and he was forced to imitate good Queen Isabel. In short, he pledged his jewels, his silverware, and even his own clothing to pay for provisions needed.[1] With Kino's approval he sold at auction at San Felipe ten bales of the clothing destined as presents for the Indians before it should become moth-eaten and worthless. Captain Anguís, Atondo's lieutenant at San Felipe, gave all the aid possible. From the presidio there Atondo took fifteen soldiers. In the vicinity he obtained fourteen horses and thirty-eight civilian recruits, including peones, tortilleras, servant boys, and female slaves.[2] Meanwhile Kino and Goñi were busy soliciting aid among the Jesuit missions. Kino worked in Sinaloa. Goñi

---

[1] Atondo to the viceroy, San Lucas, Sept. 25, 1683; same to same, San Bruno, Dec. 13, 1684. In Autos sobre Parajes, A.G.I. 1–1–2/31, Patronato 31. Venegas erroneously says that Atondo went to Yaqui to sell his goods (Empressas Apostólicas, paragraph 129).

[2] Atondo to the viceroy, Sept. 27; Anguís to the viceroy, Sept. 28. Autos sobre la Entrada Primera. A.G.I. 58–4–23, Mexico 56.

rode across the vast cactus and mesquite flat to Mayo River and up that stream to the flourishing mission of Conicari, whence he returned in due time with generous supplies and a band of Mayo Indian laborers.

Besides refitting for the immediate voyage, Atondo planned for the future. As soon as possible he would send the vessels from the Río Grande back to Matanchel to be careened. With this in view he made a contract with Rafael El Inglés,—"Ralph the Englishman"—an excellent craftsman whom he had picked up on the coast and employed in building the fleet. Where this Nordic hailed from, *quién sabe?* He was perhaps a member of some band of freebooters who had anchored on the Sinaloa shore. Rafael agreed to go to Matanchel, get out the timber needed for careening, and make thirteen canoes for the fleet. Heretics had their uses.

Atondo's pen now flew over the pages. The dispatches which he wrote made "the new Port of San Lucas" a notable place on the map, and the archives of Spain still jealously guard bulky correspondence with the name San Lucas on the date line. It is now called Agiabampo Bay. Atondo asked the viceroy for a fresh supply of ship stores, to be ready when the vessels should return to the main—ropes, sailcloth, cables, needles, thread, steel axes, augers, and such other things as a ship and its crew might need. One of the items was "an anchor weighing ten of twelve arrobas [250–300 pounds] for the Almiranta." Don Isidro's sad experience at La Paz with timid soldiers and hostile natives moved him to ask for more men, to bring the total up to 177. Even docile Indians could not be trusted. He requested also fifty young horses, estimated at fifteen pesos each, for foot soldiers make poor explorers. And what Spaniard was happy without his caballo? Both steeds and men would need protection from Indian arrows, so he asked for helmets, coats of mail, and horse armor. Give him these and the Indians might shoot arrows to their hearts' content. His list of needs included arquebuses, flints, horseshoes, blacksmith's tools, saddles, horse hair xaquimas (hackamores), shot moulds, chains and collars—these last for prospective prisoners.[1]

Before September ended Atondo was ready for his new voyage.

[1] Atondo to the viceroy, Sept. 19, 1683. Autos sobre la Entrada Primera. A.G.I. 58–4–23, Mexico 56.

Kino and Goñi had said goodbye to the Jesuits in the vicinity. On the 24th the Admiral was waiting for the swollen rivers to subside so that he could send mail to Mexico. He enclosed a memorandum of provisions needed for a year, asking that they be purchased in Sonora in order that they might be fresh, for on the long voyage to La Paz the supplies had spoiled. Three days later he had everybody on board and was ready to set sail.[1] Father Suárez did not appear, and Kino was once more left as superior of the California missions.

XXXV

THE RÍO GRANDE THAT SOMETIMES HAD WATER

While his couriers galloped toward the capital with dispatches, Atondo was sailing to the California coast on his new venture. Defeat was now a memory, hope gave life new savor. Kino tells the story of the voyage to the Río Grande and the beginnings of the new enterprise in a short diary sent to the provincial and in a much longer one which he kept for himself—precious documents these!

"On September 29 of this rapidly passing year of 1683 we set sail from the port of San Lucas in Sinaloa, bound for the largest island in the world." Pious booster, all Californians will forgive and love him! As before, Kino went with Captain Pereda on the Almiranta, Goñi with Atondo on the Capitana. Friar Joseph, the *médico,* was still in the party. The voyage was not an easy one. Like all sail ships on that long tricky Gulf in the autumn, the vessels were at the mercy of fickle winds. The second night out they caught sight of California. Sunday morning they awoke off the island of Santa Cruz, well south of their goal. "And," says Kino, "notwithstanding that we did not yet have certain information of any good port in that place, we turned the prows toward the Río Grande." Head winds came up, the Almiranta sprang a leak, and Atondo ran before the gale toward La Paz.

---

[1] Atondo to the viceroy, Sept. 24, 1683; Atondo to the viceroy, Sept. 27; Atondo to the viceroy, Sept. 18, 1683; Respuesta fiscal, Nov. 3, with accompanying lists of supplies needed. Autos sobre la Entrada Primera. A.G.I. 58–4–23, Mexico 56. Venegas erroneously says that Atondo went to Yaqui. (Empressas Apostólicas, par. 129.)

Photo by Bolton

The Río Grande, now Arroyo de San Bruno

Photo by Bolton

San Bruno, looking north. The settlement was on the hill at the right.

Photo by Bolton, Jr.

Ruins of San Bruno

HYAQVI

Rio de Huyqui

Rhaum
Las Missiones
de Hyaqui

la Gaviota

259

258

257

NORTE.

253

252

261

27

MAR DE LAS CAL

S. Ildefonso.

Punta del Mazon

Rio Gande semagua enmurien.

P.r de los S.s Coronados.

Is. de

LOS DIDIOS

Pta. de S.
Juan

PROVINCIA DE S. ANDRES.

Llanos de
S.Pablo

Laguna de S.
Salvador.

Valle de
S.Joseph.

Llanos de
S.Xauier

La Sierra
Giganta.

LOS EDVES.

LOS

NOES

Serro de S.
Eulalia

Serro de
S.Mig.l

Valle de S.
Ratista

Laguna de S.
Ignacio.

Valle del
agua Angua

R.o de

PON

Delineacion de la Nueva Provincia de Andres,
del Puerto de la Paz, y de las Islas circum-vecinas
de las Californias, o Carolinas, que
Al Excell.mo Señor D. Thomas Antonio Lorenzo
Manuel Manrique de la Zerda, Enriquez Afan de Ribera,
Corto-Carrero, y Cardenas, Conde del Paredes, Marques de la Laguna...
Consuegra de la Morraja en la Vega, y Señor de Maulalan...
del Con. sejo de la Magestad, Camara, y Junta de Guerra de Indias...
su Pres... Lugar-teniente Guernador, y Capitan General de la Nueba España...
y Presidente de la R.l Audiencia, y Chancellaria, della...
Didos, y arreglan la Magen de la Cosa, de Borgo de Andre, Califormia...
Carolinas, onocerli... dia del Senon Sapte lla de Indias P. Thomas, de 1685 ani.

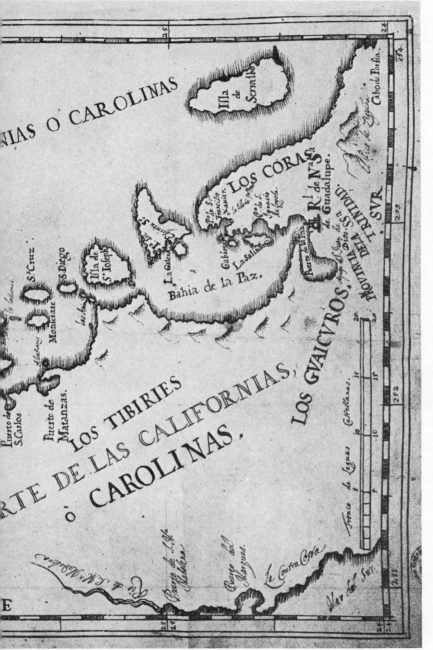

Kino's Plan of the Settlement at San Bruno, December 21, 1683

(From the original manuscript)

Ruins of Jesuit Mission at Tórin, Sonora

Sierra La Giganta, west of San Bruno

Next day the wind shifted, dampened spirits revived, and they again turned north. On October 5th, after a Mass said in honor of San Joseph, a good breeze wafted the adventurers before night to the mouth of the Río Grande. The place was just north of Coronados Island.[1]

Next day was the feast of San Bruno, and that saint's name was accordingly given to the settlement which they now founded. The name has persisted, though the Río Grande today goes by the humble name of Arroyo de San Bruno. The scene enacted when Atondo and Kino went ashore that morning reminds one of the first landing of Columbus on American soil. "A little before noon," says Kino, "the Admiral with Father Goñi in the launch of the Capitana, and Captain Don Francisco Pereda and I with other persons in the launch of the Almiranta, went ashore. There we set up a cross, and all kneeling down we venerated it, begging of his Divine Majesty a successful outcome of this conversion and conquest of California."

The hard work now began. It was next in order to find fresh water and examine the site. So Kino and the officers ascended the stream a league to the place where the natives of the vicinity had a village. The water was good, but there was no Indian to be seen. Where were those affable people whose docility had been so heralded? For two hours Kino and his friends rested "in a pretty shade," and still no Indians. What had Guzmán to say for himself? Then the scene changed, Guzmán was vindicated, and Kino's heart rejoiced. For now about twenty Indians hove in sight, "among them two boys of ten or twelve years, and all so gentle and so extremely friendly, affable, and familiar that at once they sat down in our midst just as if they had always lived among Spaniards."

Father Eusebio did not delay his Christian message. "I showed them a crucifix and the Admiral exhibited some pictures which I had in my *reso* or breviary. And although we noticed that they had never heard of or seen any signs of our holy Catholic faith, they gave us great hopes of their conversion. And when we talked of going back to the sea they came with us, all loaded with very good green grass for our

[1] Relación de la Segunda Navegazión a las Californias del Año de 1683 y de las entradas de 20 leguas la tierra adentro. Manuscript in the central archives of the Jesuit Order.

horses." The little procession, as it descended the stream, was watched with interest by the men on the ships.

During this journey a location for the settlement was chosen. "On the way to the sea," says Kino, "the Admiral pointed out on an elevation a good site for the camp which we had to make, and from which one gets a very fine view of all the plain of the valley through which descends this Río Grande." Atondo was pleased with the view, which indeed is still charming, even though seen as I saw it, in the heat of midsummer. "This valley must be more than five leagues wide and even more than that in length, and it is all very green with many trees and grass and with very good pasturage for the horses and cattle." He did not mention the imposing sierra which walled in the valley on the west.

While ashore that day Kino saw other signs of friendship on the part of the natives. "A little after we had reached the sea, when the Admiral and all of us were resting in the shade and in the good company of the Indians, awaiting the launch, there came another Indian, who must be about ninety years old." They usually are a hundred. "When we embarked in the launches they followed after us, and he and all of them asked if we would return, saying that they would return also, and that they were sorry that we did not stay with them. And there they remained, looking at and showing each other the little presents which we had given them."

The Indians and the country were promising. But the Río Grande soon took on a different aspect. Less than a week after the landing Kino remarked, "although the river which runs through the valley may be called the Río Grande, it flows only in the rainy season, and the water which we are now drinking we get from the vatequites or little wells which are dug in the sands, into which during past weeks the river has sunk." Such are California rivers—they sometimes have water.[1]

News of the coming of the white men spread, and the natives flocked in to see them. They were treated generously, and the number of visitors grew. The Indians north of San Bruno were called Didius, and their language the Nebe. Their principal chief was one dubbed by

---

[1] Relación de la Segunda Navegazión, entry for October 11 (*ibid.*).

the Spaniards Leopoldo. To the west, over the mountains, lived the Noys. South of San Bruno were the Edues, whose speech was called the Noe. Their head cacique was Ibo, "The Sun." He lived at Conchó, on a bay down the coast some twenty miles to the south. Guzmán visited him there in the launch on October 9, and in honor of the day named him Dionisio and his estuary San Dionisio. It was here that Loreto was founded a few years later. The people of the vicinity were called Los Danzantes or the Dancers, and the larger bay of which San Dionisio is an affluent was called the Bay of Los Danzantes.

Kino thus describes Ibo. "The capitanejo of those who speak the Lengua Noe, who are the Edues, is called Dionisio. He is a man of very tall stature and is very peaceful." He was a real man, famed for his hearty appetite. He became a staunch friend of the Spaniards, soon moved a part of his people to San Bruno, established a village in the vicinity, and with his followers aided greatly in the building of fort and mission. He was a personage, and so stories were told about him. One day when an Indian at San Bruno stole a silver snuffbox from the Admiral's table, The Sun, being informed of the theft, made after the culprit, brought back the box and received as a reward a clasp-knife, "a thing which they greatly esteem" and a fit present for a cacique.

XXXVI

DRIVING DOWN STAKES

The little valley had been suddenly awakened from its sleepy habits. Europeans had come with their blessings and their curses. During the next few weeks San Bruno presented the busy scene of founding a presidio and a mission, designed as outposts of Christianity and of Spanish civilization. Naked Californians and armored Spaniards now mingled together in a curious blend.

The day after landing, the fifteen horses and mules brought by Atondo were lowered from the ships and taken ashore. They caused astonishment but no terror to the natives on the beach, who soon were bringing them water and herding them in the near-by pastures. But not all the Californians were so friendly. Before night it was reported that other Indians had stoned the horses and ordered the Spaniards out of the country. They had acquired a taste for horseflesh in preceding months, when Guzmán dumped his live stock overboard a few miles down the coast. So Atondo sent the soldiery ashore with a cannon, "and with hides for a barricade, on a slight elevation, something like a little fort was arranged." This was but a temporary site, near the beach.

The permanent location which Atondo had chosen for the settlement was a mesa about a league up the arroyo, close to, and just below, the Indian village.[1] Kino was greatly edified when, on October 10, a large cross to mark the spot was carried up the hill "on the shoulders of the Admiral, Captain Don Francisco, and other principal personages." To celebrate the event they all said the Rosary.

For a time everybody continued to live on the flat just below the chosen site, in hastily constructed ramadas or bowers, or slept in the open, or on the ships. One such ramada was used as a temporary chapel. During these early days the men worked hard at clearing the ground of brush, and at building the fort, the church, and the more permanent dwellings. Through it all the Indians aided generously, carrying timbers, stone, and other materials, "some on foot, and others on mules and horses, mounting them almost in the same manner as the Mayo Indians whom we brought in our company, and who have been of very great assistance in our many and continuous tasks." These were the Mayos whom Goñi had obtained in Conicari. Having been Christianized in their own country, they were now serving as pioneers of civilization in a new outpost. This was a typical process on every Spanish frontier in America.

By October 28 the new site on the mesa was ready for occupation, and the transfer to it was signalized by a ceremony. In the afternoon everybody left the temporary camp, and, carrying the royal standard, "went up to live on the hill of the fortification and new Real de San Bruno."[2] Two days later the first Mass was said in the little church,

---

[1] The site is clearly marked today. In the summer of 1932, with my son Herbert Bolton, Jr., I identified the exact location beyond question. The mission ruins are still plainly to be seen.
[2] Atondo to the viceroy, Oct. 10, 1683. Autos sobre la Entrada Primera, A.G.I. 58–4–23, Mexico 56; Kino, Relación de la Segunda Navegazión, *passim*.

not yet finished. Crude and small, to Kino it was a matter of pride, especially when he placed on its altar "a very pretty statue of Our Lady of Guadalupe," a present from the Duchess.

Conspicuous among the dwellings was "the house of the Society, in building which the Indians, big and little, cheerfully aided." This structure, too, was a source of pride to Kino. It had "a small hall, an azotea [or flat roof], and three good-sized sleeping rooms. And in one of these, two little boys, Californians or Carolinians, have begun to sleep nights, with all friendliness, confidence, and familiarity, leaving and almost forgetting their fathers and mothers, and remaining very content with the Spanish mode of living." Like more sophisticated people, the parents grieved but held their peace, in order to give the boys a chance. Kino knew full well that his most profitable work would be among the children. Of the older Indians he could say with the Great Teacher, "A little child shall lead them."

XXXVII

SUPPLIES FROM YAQUI

Until it should get on its feet, the little California colony was dependent on the mainland for subsistence. So while soldiers and Indians were building the town, sailors and other Indians were unloading the ships and preparing them for new voyages, the Capitana to hasten to Yaqui for horses and provisions, the Almiranta to Matanchel to be careened, carry dispatches for the viceroy, and bring more men and supplies. On the way it was to stop at Mazatlán to pick up the crippled Balandra, taking it tar, tallow, pitch, and tow to enable it to make the voyage. Among the things now requested of the viceroy Atondo listed "eighteen pack mules equipped with lasso and reata." These, he said, would cost forty pesos each. He also asked for "two dozen wrought-iron mule shoes, with their nails and a thousand nails extra." Mules without shoes in this stony country would be of little use.

By October 15 the Almiranta was ready. In preparation for the voyage some of the seamen confessed and received Communion. Next day goodbyes were said and Captain Pereda, Pilot Andrés, and Fray Joseph, the *médico,* embarked. About ten o'clock at night anchors were raised and the Almiranta set sail for Matanchel. With a fine land breeze she made good headway, and next morning was completely lost to view. This was Fray Joseph's farewell to California.

Four days after the Almiranta left the anchorage Captain Guzmán was ready to sail for Yaqui. That morning Kino went on board to say Mass for the success of the voyage. Some of the sailors confessed and received Communion, and many letters were written to the fathers of Sonora and Sinaloa. In the afternoon Guzmán embarked and about midnight anchor was raised. The little Spanish colony was now alone on the Peninsula without means of retreat or communication. Atondo felt slightly heroic. One feels sorry that he had to express himself in writing, without histrionic effects. "I am sending the Capitana to the Yaqui coast for more provisions," he wrote to the viceroy, "and to try, before necessity demands that it be careened, to purchase, even if I go without a shirt, more horses and mules, equipped with harness, for they are very important for the continuation of the conversion, to penetrate the country, and to carry provisions, munitions, and tools."[1]

The Capitana was gone just a month. On November 20 an Indian reported that a ship was in sight. At first not much credit was given to the story, but when some soldiers climbed the eastern ridge to get a good view, there indeed the Capitana was gliding swanlike toward the anchorage. To spread the news the soldiers fired their muskets. "Very great was the joy of everybody in camp," says Kino, "and especially of the natives." The arrival of the ship made a good show, and they knew that food and presents were coming. To celebrate the event a large cross, carried thither on the shoulders of the natives, was set up along the new road which had been opened over the ridge to the anchorage. Conspicuous among those who helped was Ibo, The Sun, the tall and lusty chief from the south.

What news, what needed things did the ship bring from the mainland? For the settlers were there letters from home? For the Fathers, tidings from Mexico, or Spain, or Germany? Had some prince or prel-

---

[1] Atondo to the viceroy, San Bruno, Oct. 10, 1683, and Oct. 15, 1683. Autos sobre la Entrada Primera, A.G.I. 58-4-23, Mexico 56; Kino, Relación de la Segunda Navegazión, Oct. 20.

ate died, perhaps? What reports from the Indian wars in the north? Any more news of the Pueblo Revolt? In the afternoon Atondo, Kino, Goñi, and four soldiers rode over the thorny ridge to the beach, where the Capitana had already cast anchor. From on board they received "many letters from the father missionaries of Hiaqui, Mayo, Cinaloa, and Mátape," principal mission centers of the mainland coast. What a joy to these men in the California exile! "There were also all the supplies which the Admiral had sent for, many wethers, some goats, much beef, fish, and shrimp, much maize and wheat flour, as well as horses and mules."

The voyage had been highly successful. The trip to Yaqui—more than a hundred miles north over the blue water of the Gulf—had been made in three and a half days, in spite of a severe hurricane, and the return had been accomplished in thirty hours. Among the most prized treasures brought in the Capitana, says Kino, were "grapevines and young pomegranates and quinces, which I had requested of Father Marquina," rector on the Yaqui. "And we planted them, trusting that in their time the Californias or Carolinas will produce wine for many masses." It is the hope planted with a seed that justifies the labor.

The anchorage at San Bruno was far from safe, and as soon as the Capitana was unloaded it was sent for shelter to the near-by island of Los Coronados, where it was to remain till Atondo and Kino should return from a projected exploration in the west. With it went Chief Dionisio and another Indian called Santiago. "Dionisio greatly enjoyed the trip, but Santiago got seasick and wept." We may laugh, but to Santiago it was not amusing. Two days later the crew of the Capitana returned to San Bruno, presumably in the launch, bringing back Dionisio and Santiago safe and sound, but not until their worried friends had gone in search of them.

A week later, on November 30, feast of the Apostle San Andrés, Atondo signalized what he had accomplished by a formal ceremony. "After Mass," says Kino, "possession was taken of this California and of this new province, which we called San Andrés, in the name of his Majesty, Carlos II, God spare him, with all solemnity, in the presence of many natives, with many volleys of arquebus shots and of the cannon." The result was more emphatic than had been intended. "The chamber burst and wounded the cannoneer, and it was a very special favor of Heaven that there was no damage except that an Indian was hurled to the ground, and that a few drops of blood were drawn from the face of a seaman, though without serious injury to the one or to the other." Kino now took spiritual possession, and the celebration was continued with horse races, sham battles, and the distribution of presents to the natives. Religious devotion and human enjoyment were not regarded as incompatible.[1]

XXXVIII

A JACK RABBIT JUMPS INTO HISTORY

Curiosity as well as duty led the Spaniards to make short excursions into the surrounding country during these early days. In most of them Kino took a prominent part. Everywhere he went he met new Indians, made new friends, found new water holes, new sites for missions. In the course of one of these early jaunts the men found a hot spring about two leagues from the settlement, "and although the water comes out close by another ordinary cool spring, it is so hot that one cannot put his hand in it." This was a phenomenon to talk about. Two men on horseback went four leagues inland to look for a river told of by the natives, but did not find it. Rivers are scarce in that desert. Four energetic fellows climbed some high mountains near by to look for mines. What if they really should discover one! They found no minerals but brought back some wild figs.

A week later a more extended journey was made into the interior. Indians had previously urged Atondo to go with them to punish their enemies, and to be sure to take his dogs, "for, according to the opinion of the Indians, these animals are more ferocious than any kind of fierce lion or tiger." Atondo put them off by saying "Not now," but "Más tarde."

---

[1] Atondo to the viceroy, November 24, 1683; Kino, Relazión de la Segunda Navegazión; Act of Possession, Nov. 30 (Autos sobre la Entrada Primera, A.G.I. 58–4–23, Mexico 56); Kino to the Duchess, San Bruno, December 15, 1683 (original Spanish manuscript in the Huntington Library; extract in the central archives of the Jesuit Order).

Directly responsible for setting Atondo in motion was Dionisio, The Sun. One day loud talking was heard in the Edu village. Dionisio was haranguing his people, telling them that their enemies, the Noys and the Didius, were threatening them. The Admiral now decided to go and investigate. For the foray he took twelve men, six on foot, and six on armored horses. Kino went as chaplain and map maker, and to see what he could see. Guided by Dionisio and five other Indians, on November 22 these knights of the cactus and their humbler footmen went inland toward the northwest. A strange sight the helmet-crested Spaniards, riding hide-covered horses, must have made as they flitted through the mesquite. The thrill of adventure which they felt was hardly stronger than that which I experienced when I re-explored their trail.

Three leagues from the camp the horsemen visited a fine water hole and named it San Vicente.[1] There in a grove they dismounted for a siesta. Suddenly Dionisio sounded an alarm. The enemy had come. The soldiers took their weapons, but the *enemigo* proved to be the foot soldiers, who had fallen behind and now came up. Everybody had a good laugh. Instead of by hostiles, Atondo was visited here by many friendly Indians. Says Kino, "one of them gave me a hare which he had killed with an arrow. I named this Indian Sebastián." The foot soldiers now turned back. The horsemen, continuing northwest, visited two more good water holes, naming them San Sebastián and San Pablo, one for the donor of the jack rabbit, the other for a Didiu chief. In this way both rabbit and chief got into history. It was now nearly five o'clock in the afternoon, and they were six leagues from San Bruno. "But we all had very good horses and so we arrived in good time." Several Indians accompanied them to camp, "running almost with the speed of the horses." Father Eusebio's smile had conquered all fear.

This *Primera Entrada,* or first expedition, as Kino calls it, had taken the explorers six leagues northwest from San Bruno. In the region shown on his contemporary map as Llanos de San Pablo there is today a place called Llano. It is a level, grassy, and slightly wooded plain several miles in extent. Between it and San Bruno is San Juan, which

---

[1] San Vicente was not identical with San Xavier, the same distance from San Bruno.

gets its name from the now ruined mission of San Juan Londó, founded there by Salvatierra a few years later.[1]

XXXIX

APOSTOLIC LABORS

These were red-letter days for Father Kino. With the geography somewhat changed, his dream had come true. He was now, indeed, a missionary *entre infieles,* on the rim of Christendom. A new world was unfolding before him. He was a born explorer, and every excursion into unknown places quickened his Latin pulse. But his heart was with his Indians. The pages of his letters are crowded with the flitting forms of the simple brown-skinned people, to teach whom he had crossed Europe, the wide Atlantic, and the continent of Middle America. His San Bruno diaries give us a vivid picture of a true missionary, devoted heart and soul to the one object of converting and civilizing the natives, and for whom no task was too mean, no incident too trivial, if it contributed to the main end. He was like the artist, or the scholar, much of whose labor would be unbearable drudgery to one not inspired with the zeal of a devotee.

Father Eusebio regarded the poor natives with a real affection, and he stood ever ready to minister to their bodily wants, or to defend them against false charges or harsh treatment. He took sincere delight in giving them instruction, and in satisfying their childish curiosity regarding such things as the compass, the sundial, the lens with which he started fires, and the meaning of the strange symbols used in his maps. Nothing gave him such true pleasure as some sign that an Indian was becoming interested in the Faith. He dwells at length and with evident delight on the story of a little native girl who knelt before a picture of the Virgin and begged permission to hold the Christ Child; on the progress made by his charges in repeating the prayers, singing the Salve and reciting the litanies; and on their zeal in

[1] Kino, Relación de la Segunda Navegazión; Atondo to the viceroy, November 24, 1683. Autos sobre la Entrada Primera, A.G.I. 58-4-23, Mexico 56. When they returned they learned that Father Goñi had baptized an infant.

helping to decorate the crude church for the celebration of feast days.

The natives were generally friendly, eager for gifts, and willing to help the Spaniards at their tasks. But they were veritable children. Fickle, crafty, prone to petty pilferings, quick to take offense, and easily frightened, they taxed the patience and wisdom of Atondo, and likewise of his soldiers, to whom, much as to the English frontiersman, the good Indians were all dead. Kino regarded the natives as his personal wards, and he deplored anything that would reduce their trust in him or in his Faith. Yet he had a clear appreciation of Atondo's position of responsibility, and showed a laudable patience in the kaleidoscopic shift of scenes from friendship to hostility, from mirth to tragedy, from the sublime to the ridiculous.

Father Eusebio's primary task was to induce the sons of the desert willingly to accept Christianity. To do this he had to make them his friends, dispel their shyness, and win their confidence. The best means by which to make a beginning were little presents,—sweetmeats, glass beads, bright ribbons, gewgaws, such as the king had provided with the gift of $6000. Clothing, except for ornament or as a protection from the cold, was regarded as an essential for the natives rather by the Spaniards than by the Indians themselves. Sometimes a garment bestowed as a gift was later found discarded by the roadside.

It was with the young that Kino, like every missionary, was especially concerned, and frequently when he made an excursion he found himself followed by a troop of Indian boys running by his side, trying to keep up, or crying if left behind. Often one or more urchins might be seen triumphantly mounted behind the Father on the haunches of his horse. He tells with zest how a young boy who was living at the mission resisted the efforts of his parents to take him away, calling for help on "Padre Eusebio."

Kino's visits to the village of San Bruno, in the flat below the mission, illustrate his gentle methods and his magnetic gift for winning hearts. "I went down to the near-by ranchería of San Bruno, accompanied by a little Indian called Dieguillo. As soon as they saw me the people of the village began to withdraw and flee into the woods, especially the women and children, but I called them back and gave them some little things to eat, and some gewgaws of the kinds they like; and I consoled a sick woman, calling her Isabel. When I returned to the camp I was accompanied by many Indians, men and women, big and little."

It was not the name Isabel, but Kino's smiles and his gewgaws, that won the day. The Indians were now ready to listen. "I taught them the prayers and regaled them, and four of them, two large boys, Ignacio and Francisco, and two small boys, Eusebio and Dieguillo, remained to sleep in our house." Two days later: "In the afternoon I went down with Father Goñi to the village of San Bruno, and returned accompanied once more by many Indians. Among them was the little boy Dieguillo, for although his people did not wish him to remain . . . with us, and took him away with them, about eight o'clock at night he fled from them and came to sleep in our house."

The difficulties of language, as always, were a stupendous obstacle to conversion. Infants and dying adults could properly be baptized without instruction. But healthy adults must be indoctrinated before baptism, and all children must be taught the Catechism. In order to give this instruction, either Kino must learn the Indian languages or the Indians must learn Spanish. Both processes were important. So Kino was a diligent student of the native tongues, and at the same time that he drilled them in the Catechism he taught his little neophytes Castilian. On the principle of division of labor, Father Eusebio devoted himself especially to learning the language of the Didius, the north people, Father Goñi that of the Edues, the south people. Two soldiers likewise became specialists and official interpreters in one language each, Contreras for the Didiu tongue, Díaz for the Edu.

Kino's ingenuity sometimes was put severely to the test to teach Christian concepts in the simple Indian speech. A classic example is his own story of how he explained the Resurrection by reviving some apparently lifeless flies. When the astonished Indians shouted *Ibimu huegite* they had given the Father the word he was seeking.

The edifying effect of an impressive sacrament was sometimes sadly spoiled by an absurd occurrence. Every veteran missionary had a bag full of amusing stories about such experiences. On Monday, October 11, many Indians attended Mass, knelt down, "and showed much humility." Suddenly a dog belonging to the Spaniards bit an Indian, and "they all made a hullabaloo." A riot ensued. Another Indian threw a stone at the boy who had caused the dog to go on a rampage. His aim was bad and he hit instead an Indian girl. The girl howled, the Indians fled, and began to fill up some wells which the Spaniards used. Soldiers seized their weapons, and only the Admiral's "pacific prudence" prevented a serious disturbance. Next day the Indians returned. To appease them, the boy who had caused the trouble was punished, "at which all of them were greatly pleased."

Through the childish simplicity of the Indians the symbolism employed to attract them sometimes miscarried. One day, said Kino, "we set up in our little church a large and pretty statue of the Holy Christ, but as soon as the Indians saw it they ran away, very much afraid of it. They hardly dared to talk with us, or among themselves except in very low tones or in whispers, asking who that person was and who had killed him, and if he were some cruel enemy of ours, for it worried them very greatly to think that we treated people so. There was no way to pacify them except to tell them that he was our friend. And when we explained to them that he had gone to Heaven, and that we too must go there, one of them said to me 'Let's go at once.' "

Kino was overjoyed at the first baptism of a native. At the same time he saw clearly that to baptize a dying Indian, infant or adult, was to risk one's reputation or even one's life. This was a danger which missionaries always had to face. On his return with good news from his expedition to San Pablo Kino wrote, "When we arrived at . . . San Bruno we found other and even better news, to the effect that a little before noon a moribund infant of the near-by village had been baptized. The rite was solemnized by Father Mathías Goñi. Because the little fellow, who was called Pedro, died a few hours after baptism, Father Goñi gained among the heathen the reputation for being a bad doctor, and next day they would not even permit him to come near their sick ones." More than one missionary was martyred under such circumstances.[1]

.[1] Kino, Relazión de la Segunda Navegazión; Kino, Segunda Entrada en la California, a 1° de Diz⁰ de 1683 (Spanish manuscripts in the central archives of the Jesuit Order). Kino, The San Bruno Diary, Dec. 21, 1683, to May 8, 1684. Known as the Tercera Entrada because it begins with this heading, which in fact covers only a small part of the diary; Kino to the Duchess of Aveiro y Arcos, San Bruno, December 15, 1683.

With all this zeal on the part of Fathers Kino and Goñi, and with all the evidences of tractability on the part of the natives, one might wonder why there were not more baptisms at San Bruno—only eleven in more than a year and a half. The answer is that Kino was reluctant to bring the natives into the Church until he was assured of the permanency of the mission, lest they be left without spiritual ministrations. Half a century before, in the days of Hurdaide, the Great Captain of Sinaloa, the Jesuits could report thousands of baptisms each year. The stability of Sinaloa was guaranteed. But it was not yet certain that California would not be abandoned.

Such were the apostolic labors of one of the world's greatest missionaries. If the picture is not typical it is because Atondo the soldier, and not Kino the missionary, was the responsible figure in the scene. Here at San Bruno Kino was trying to conduct a mission in the shadow of a presidio. Later in his career he found himself in a different situation.

Farther Afield

XL

THE FACE OF THE GIANTESS

THE SAN BRUNO SETTLEMENT HAD BEEN FOUNDED. The formal act of taking possession of the province of San Andrés on November 30 by Atondo for the Crown in the name of Carlos Segundo and by Kino for the Church in the name of Bishop Juan, put a period to this paragraph in the history of "the largest island in the world." The Admiral and the Rector were now free to undertake the more ambitious exploration into the interior which for many days they had been planning.

They sallied forth on December 1. For this longer journey they had more elaborate equipment than for the *Primera Entrada*. Besides the Admiral and Kino, head and soul of the enterprise, there were twenty-five soldiers, six Indians from Mayo, six of the Edu nation, Dionisio's people, and six Didius, Leopoldo's men. There were fourteen horses, five of them armor-covered and fierce-looking, and six pack mules carrying provisions for a twelve days' journey.[1] Camp was left in charge of Captain Guzmán and Father Goñi. On the Capitana at Coronados Island remained Alférez Lascano with ten sailors and deck hands.

The knights rode out, followed by the footmen. Three leagues northwestward took them to the fine water and pastures of San Isidro. This place, called Londó by the Edues and Cathemeneol by the Didius, was the spot where later was built the mission of San Juan Londó, whose picturesque ruins are still well preserved. Here they camped and were visited by natives. Five of them, all Didius, joined the expe-

---

[1] For this expedition we have two excellent manuscript diaries: Kino, Segunda Entrada en la California a 1° de Diz° de 1683. Contemporary Spanish manuscript in the central archives of the Jesuit Order. Atondo, Diary of the expedition to the Plains of San Xavier, Dec. 1–8, 1683. Autos sobre la Entrada Primera, A.G.I. 58–4–23, Mexico 56.

dition. They must have pronounceable names, so Kino called them Vicente, Santiago, Juan, Andrés, and Simón.

In the *Primera Entrada* Kino and Atondo had continued northwest up the level valley that led to the plains of San Pablo. This time the adventurers set for themselves a far more difficult task. They planned now to swing west and scale the precipitous sierra that hid from the narrow coast plain the mysterious region that lay beyond— a land of giants the natives said. Both the giants and the sierra gave zest to the exploit.

The way up the lofty wall of rock, that was the first question! The Indians said they could answer it. Guided by the five Didius, Atondo went four leagues to a fine spring which they named San Francisco Xavier, for it was the eve of the Feast of St. Francis. On the way the Indians gathered for the explorers luscious pitahayas, which were still in season there. The water at San Xavier was worthy of comment in that arid land, for it actually flowed. "We were very much pleased," wrote Kino, "to see the first running stream in this California, for this water hole"—he called it an *aguaje*—"had this quantity of water. We gave rewards and presents to the Indians who showed it to us"—and well they might, for such a rarity—"and they as well as we were very much pleased. We noticed and learned that many Indians lived here for some months of the year although there were none now. Kino saw in this fine water supply another mission site. Here at San Xavier siesta was taken, camp made for the night, and a great smoke sent up to let the people at the settlement know of their safe arrival. The place was near two conspicuous peaks which were in plain view from San Bruno, and indeed, from fifteen leagues out at sea. To dedicate the fine site to the spiritual conquest a large cross was erected.

The mountain wall was now towering close ahead, and in the afternoon five men went forward to find a trail between the two peaks for the next day's march. At night the scouts returned. After having advanced two leagues they had found water holes and a large carrizal or reed marsh, but they had encountered, just beyond, a mountain cliff so steep that horses and mules could not ascend. If Atondo could not go straight ahead he might go around. So next morning he approached the range by a different route. But it was of no use. After ascending the lower slopes for some two leagues, the same distance the explorers had covered, they reached cliffs and crags which the animals could not pass. The prospect was discouraging.

Scouts were again sent out, now in two parties, Contreras with five men and Itamarra with four. Contreras sent back a note to report that the ascent was impossible for horses and difficult for men. But the climb was worth it, for there, a league above the horsemen, a beautiful plain lay before them. It was now evident that the horses must be left below. This was tough on a race of men born to the saddle. But there was no help for it. So Atondo sent food up to the scouts, telling them to remain over night on the mountain top. He would follow on foot.

Next morning they made the plunge. Leaving the horses and mules in charge of six men, the rest set forth. Each one carried, besides his weapons, his own pack of supplies for three days. Kino's youthful prayer for a "difficult mission" was being answered. And what better sport could he wish? Twenty-nine men, besides five heathen Indians, made the start. For a league they scrambled like flies up the face of the bare mountain wall of living rock; in places even the nimble Indians had to crawl on all fours. Three or four spots, called the "Passes of Santa Bárbara," were so bad that it was necessary "to haul up by a lariat not only the munitions and provisions, but also the Admiral and others." I cannot believe that Kino was one of them. Each reader will have to rely on his own imagination for the picture presented by Atondo as he dangled from the cliffs.

The start had been early. The winter sun had barely showed its face when the puffing band reached the top. From a miraculous occurrence of the day before, the spot where they gained the summit was called Santa Cruz. The scouts had thrown down a dry cardón tree, a species of tall, straight cactus which flourishes there in veritable forests. "When it fell on the ground a limb was so imbedded that with the trunk it formed a cross, as if it had been made on purpose with the hands, and it was set up and venerated and left in that position."

It was now that the rugged sierra was given the name by which it still is known. "Because it is so very high," Kino writes, "for at sunset it can be seen from Hiaqui, and likewise because a few days ago some persons said and believed that in these lands of the Noys there were giants, we called the range La Giganta." And La Giganta it still is both in fact and in name. The Giantess rises six thousand feet almost sheer out of the Gulf.

XLI

THE GIFT OF SAN XAVIER

The view was worth the climb. The scouts had not exaggerated. Facing westward from Santa Cruz the exhilarated explorers looked out on the "beautiful and most pleasing plains," of which Contreras had told. These llanos, too, already had a name, for, says Kino, "since yesterday, because they were discovered on the day of the glorious Cherubim, they have been called the Gift of San Francisco Xavier"— Dádiva de San Francisco Xavier.

Westward Ho! They were now in the land of the Noys, country of the giants. What a thrill they would have if one should only appear! And how scared they would be! Eagerly Kino pushed forward, charmed by the scene, so sharply in contrast with the wooded mountains of his native Alps. The Admiral puffed along behind. "We traveled about four leagues through these spacious plains, the five friendly heathen Indians showing us the roads and several watering places. We found many tracks of Noys Indians, and finally saw three of them on top of the high, green hills. They shouted and yelled at us, but we could not make out what they were saying." In the distance they looked more like pygmies than men of Atlas proportions. Imagination created out of other realities sights only less interesting than giants. "At noon," says Kino, "we came to a pretty water hole close to a little hill which has the form of a sepulcher, and we called it the Sepulcher of San Clemente." If we knew what particular variety of sepulcher the explorers had in mind we would know what to look for in an attempt to identify the spot.

Taking siesta at the water by the Sepulcher, in the afternoon they went forward, weary but exuberant—Kino at least. "We traveled more than a league over the continuous and pretty plain of the Gift of San Xavier, which is about five leagues long, in places a league wide, and in others a little more or a little less." Still no giants. In fact, most of the inhabitants, more like rabbits, were fleeing in terror. "The road," says Kino, "was crossed by a great many trails and covered with footprints of children and adults, who had withdrawn from several villages which there are in these plains." At the end of the valley they found a lake of very fine water about three leagues in circumference. "And we called it the Laguna de Santa Bárbara, because it was her day." This honor, we trust, repaid the saint for being tagged the day before with the bad roads over which they had to drag Atondo with a lariat.

If there were no giants there was a cave. And what explorer, young or old, is not intrigued by a cave? "Near this laguna we planned to camp, but because it began to mist we decided to withdraw to a grotto which was in front of us, about two arquebus shots away. We sent three of the Mayo Indians to explore it." We must remember that since breakfast these horsemen had climbed up the face of La Giganta, and then walked five leagues, or some twelve or fifteen miles. So it is not strange that instead of going themselves they sent the Indians to explore. By this time they were quite willing to give the natives credit for anything they might discover. "On their return they told us it was clean and nice, and big enough to hold everybody, but because it stopped misting and the sky began to clear we did not go to it." The young fellows were doubtless disappointed at this decision. A night in a cave would have been great fun—and probably uncomfortable.

One wishes we might know what was being said by the timid natives as they scurried out of the valley and peered from the rocks and hillsides at the queer-looking visitors who carried strange weapons. If only the Indians could have written, what a different history we should have. Their breathless spies the day before no doubt had spread hair-raising tales of centaurs at the foot of the mountain and headed west. Kino merely remarks, "sixteen soldiers who ascended some hills saw many Indians who were fleeing into the interior of the country." [1]

Atondo's men had done a big day's work since they left camp at the foot of the cliff. In fact, the Admiral and two or three others were about played out and would have been glad to turn homeward. But Kino was curious to know what was beyond the mountains over which the natives had scampered. The result was a division of the party. Atondo decided to camp here beside the refreshing lake, while the strongest men went forward, equipped for two days' travel, one going and one returning.

XLII

THE STRONG GO FORWARD

Kino was one of the strongest, both in heart and limb. Leaving the Admiral with ten men in these plains of San Xavier beside the lake of Santa Bárbara, next day Father Eusebio set forth northwest with the remaining eighteen, to take a peep over the ridge. His effort was quickly repaid. "We had scarcely traveled half a league, ascending a piece of bad road, when we came to a pretty valley of good land which they call migajón, very level, well grown with purslane, pigweed, gourds, firewood and groves, with a large village, and with very fresh tracks of children and adults, all of whom had withdrawn to the more remote high hills and canyons of these lands." For this fine site Kino had a name already selected before seeing it. He explains how this came about. "In the morning when we set out from camp we had promised that the best place that we should find we would dedicate to the glorious patriarch San Joseph." Surely they would discover none finer than this one, "and so this valley, plain, watering place and ranchería we called San Joseph."

But they could not tarry to enjoy the scene. They were limited to two days, and there was more beyond. Three of the "strongest,"

[1] Kino, Segunda Entrada en la California (central archives of the Jesuit Order); Atondo. Diary of the expedition to the Plains of San Xavier (A.G.I. 58–4–23, Mexico 56).

Kino, Itamarra, and Bohórques, scaled a high cliff, and from it they saw, both with and without a telescope, "another pretty lake, and a large plain, and many other hills, sierras, and plains, stretching more than twenty leagues toward the north." Descending from the cliff and traveling northwest over the country at which they had gazed, all took siesta at the lake, "and drank from its most beautiful and crystalline water in the shade of some large fig trees and of a cliff." These fig trees were evidently tunas. The lake was five leagues northwest of the camp where Atondo had been left to sleep and rest. It was northeast of and not far from the present Comondú. Here as elsewhere the frightened natives had scampered into hiding. They had the advantage of having little baggage to carry. On the way, at recently abandoned village sites, Kino saw "fresh fires, many metates, arrows, and many pieces of mother of pearl and other shells, which without doubt must be from the Contra Costa"—that is, from the Pacific Ocean.[1]

When they came to giving this beautiful lake a name,—it was after they had traveled a league beyond it,—there was a disagreement, so Kino resorted once more to pious gambling. "Because there were different opinions regarding this name, for many wished to call it after their own saints, we wrote on some little papers the names of all nineteen who were on this expedition. We put the little papers in a hat"—as we still do—"and drew out the lots. Salvador was drawn, this being the name of the little Indian boy who was with me, a page of Father Goñi, brought by him from Yécora. . . . And so we called this lake the Laguna de San Salvador. In the same way we drew lots in order to give a name to the highest mountain which we had in sight. Eusebio was drawn and so we named it San Eusebio." Chance, friendly this time, thus conferred on Kino an honor which he would have been too modest to claim for himself.[2]

This day had other diverting encounters in store for the explorers. From San Salvador they swung three leagues southwest and south, "just as before noon we had traveled five leagues northwest." This

---

[1] Kino, Segunda Entrada en la California; Atondo, Diary of the expedition to the Plains of San Xavier.
[2] This drawing of lots was done in the afternoon, a league after leaving the lake. The mountain, San Eusebio, was one in sight from the lake. See Kino's map of 1683.

entry in Kino's diary gives us a good clue to his entire route that day. It is confirmed by his map. After going a league beyond the lake (at the place where they drew lots), they saw seventeen Indians coming with bows and arrows. "Behold, what a wondrous sight! A certain king of the Indians and sixteen of his followers were seen descending from the peak and coming toward us as we were walking along, clothed in the manner of his people," and armed with bows and arrows. "All the soldiers stood at arms and in good order, to be prepared if there should be a fight."

But it was Kino, not the soldiers, who had the best weapons. He resorted to a kind of diplomacy at which he was clever. "I brought forth some red bandannas (chomites) and some glass beads. The Indians came toward me, laid their weapons on the ground, and sat down as a sign of peace. When I reached them the chief, who was about fifty years old, very tall and gigantic [but not exactly a giant], arose, leaving his large and fine lance on the ground and making signs that we should go forward toward the north. But neither he nor those with him said a single word." This huge, solemn chief must have a pronounceable name, so Kino dubbed him Juan, and pursued his handkerchief diplomacy. "I gave him the chomites, putting them on the heads of himself and the rest, who still remained sitting, with their weapons on the ground. The strings of glass beads I put on their necks, giving them to understand that we were friends."

Imagination helps us to visualize those seventeen brown men sitting on the ground, erstwhile stark naked but now fully clothed with red handkerchiefs on their heads and strings of glass beads round their necks. "They were all pleased, and they told us that on the other side of the Cerro de San Eusebio there ran a river which went to the Contra Costa, something which the other Indians, the Edues and Didius, had also told us at the Real de San Bruno." This river was evidently the one now called La Purísima.

While here Kino learned new and interesting facts about the native speech. He was in the land of the Noys, those "bad men over yonder" of whom Dionisio had complained. "I talked to them in the two languages of the valley of Nuestra Señora de los Remedios,[1] al-

---

[1] The Valley of the Río Grande, or San Bruno.

though I had little hope that they would understand me, thinking that their language would be a third tongue and very different. But he replied to me in the Nebe language,[1] and we noticed that his speech was not very different from that of the Didius of the plains of San Pablo near the valley and Real de San Bruno." Kino's linguistic horizon had expanded by travel. Continuing south from Juan's village (a part of the three leagues traveled southwest and south) they passed another abandoned village site, and then moved eastward toward San Joseph, the pretty place they had discovered and so praised early in the morning.

Now occurred a little drama which helps us to understand the awe and terror with which the natives so often first beheld white men in their land. On the way a poor fellow, taken by surprise, was frightened nearly out of his wits. "We met a lone Indian who came running, and who to his complete surprise suddenly found himself among people so little known of and never before seen. Although he had his bow and arrows, he stood dumfounded, and not knowing what he was doing, especially when the dog which we had with us went out to meet him. I went up and drove the dog away, so that he did him no harm." We can see Kino's long robes flying in the breeze as he runs to rescue the poor Indian from the dog.

More handkerchief diplomacy. "I talked to him in the Nebe tongue, put a little red chomite on his head, encouraged him not to be afraid, since we were his friends, and asked him where there was water. And although he was very pale and trembling he told us that the watering place was a little farther ahead. We went forward, pleased with the report of the water, and at having had so good an opportunity to let the Indians know that we had not come to injure a single person, for we did not do so even when we had this poor lone fellow in our hands." The poor Indian doubtless was agreeably surprised.

The remainder of the story of the expedition can be quickly told, although it still cost the explorers many aches and blisters. Swinging east now over rough country, they arrived at San Joseph at night, "no less sweaty and tired than thirsty, after twelve leagues of travel on

[1] The Didiu.

foot during this day's journey." Thirty miles on foot through that country in one day would leave anybody tired, sweaty, and thirsty. Next morning (the 6th) they rejoined Atondo's party at Santa Bárbara. During Kino's absence the Admiral had erected a cross on the highest peak in the vicinity, and sent men to examine a large valley toward the south which they had descried from the heights. Before night they returned, reporting "a very large plain which had become lost to view, called by them San Juan Bautista." It was the great plain that stretches south and west of Comondú.

The explorers now headed homeward. On the way they camped at the Sepulcher of San Clemente, then continued to the passes of Santa Cruz and Santa Bárbara, down which they scrambled "with the difficulty customary in such cliffs, three or four persons holding with lassos and aiding the one who was descending." The Admiral heaved a sigh of relief; he was glad to be safe down. Siesta was taken at the camp of the six soldiers and the horses. Moving forward three leagues, they halted at the edge of the plains of San Pablo; at nine next day they reached San Isidro. Here Kino said Mass with vestments for which he had sent ahead to the settlement. At San Bruno, he says, "we arrived about four o'clock . . . finding a great many friendly Indians who like our own people welcomed us with very great joy, and there were many salvos of many arquebuses which they all fired off."

This *Segunda Entrada,* or second expedition, had been a real adventure and a pronounced success. In their explorations beyond the lake of Santa Bárbara they had been in the vicinity, though south, of old Comondú.

Kino and Atondo now prepared reports and wrote letters to their friends. Kino drew a plan of the fort, church, and barracks, and made a map of California, showing the settlements at La Paz and San Bruno, and all the principal explorations thus far accomplished.[1] It bears the date December 21, 1683. The original is still preserved and is one of the world's cartographical treasures. Atondo sent to the viceroy this map and the Act of Possession of the Province of San Andrés. Both Kino and the Admiral wrote full accounts of this expedition to the

---

[1] Kino, Delineación de la Nueva Provincia de S. Andrés, del Puerto de la Paz, y de las Islas circumvecinas de las Californias, ò Carolinas. Dec. 21, 1683.

plains of San Xavier. Kino's diary reads like an adventure story. His widened horizon gave him new visions of missionary expansion. Perhaps some of his old college mates would come to join him. To Father Paul Zingnis he wrote, "With the willing assistance of the heathen themselves, I have built a dwelling house even for those, whoever they may be, who may come from our beloved province of Upper Germany." [1]

With these precious documents on board the Capitana weighed anchor and sailed away.[2] Once more the colony was cut off from communication with the mainland. All three vessels were now on the coast of Mexico, and long before they returned anxious eyes many times scanned the southeastern horizon to catch a glimpse of a white sail.

XLIII

A PASS THROUGH THE SIERRA

Kino was soon again on the trail. The tall "king" Juan, in that chat by the roadside, had told him of a great river and a mighty ocean "just over yonder," beyond the mountain. He must see that river and that ocean and the people on its shores. So he buckled on his spurs once more. His particular aim now was to find a way for horses and pack mules through or around the Sierra Giganta. Then he would be ready for a great expedition to the sea.

On December 21, the very day when he finished his map, Kino set out northwest. He was accompanied by Nicolás Contreras, the scout who first had scaled La Sierra Giganta, eight mounted soldiers, and four natives, Vicente, Simón, Francisco, "and the boy Eusebio, ten or twelve years of age," with provisions for four days, two going and two returning. Atondo did not take part in this expedition. Per-

---

[1] Kino to the Duchess of Aveiro y Arcos, San Bruno, December 15, 1683. Original Spanish manuscript in the Huntington Collection; Kino to Zingnis (?), December 15, 1683. Original Latin manuscript in Bayerische Hauptstaatsarchiv, München, Jesuitica Nos. 293–294; Atondo to the viceroy, Dec. 20, 1683. Autos sobre la Entrada Primera A.G.I. 58–4–23, Mexico 56.

[2] I have not learned the precise day of the sailing of the Capitana, but I infer that it was the 21st.

haps his blisters were still tender. At San Isidro, three leagues out, they were joined by fifteen additional Indians. Three more leagues took them for siesta to the village site of San Pablo. It was unoccupied now, for its natives had recently moved to San Vicente. From here forward they were on new ground. When they mounted in the afternoon to push northward, none of the Indians continued with them, Kino tells us, "although Vicente and Eusebio followed behind, and also a crow, which two leagues back had begun to accompany us, sometimes with us, sometimes ahead, never getting farther than an arquebus shot away; and thus he continued with us." He was the mascot of the party.

Kino was looking for an opening in the sierra. "And traveling to the north all the afternoon for more than six leagues, with the mountain range or Sierra Giganta always to the west of us, or on our left, we arrived at a new river called Santo Tomás, it being the day of this glorious apostle of the Indies." It was Arroyo Bunmedejol, now Bombedor, phonetically the same. A true California stream, it sometimes flowed. "Although at that time the river was not running, it retained in several places a large quantity of very good water." At the same place I found tanks containing water in the summer of 1932. Here they camped "in the good company of Vicente and Eusebio." In spite of the long journey the horses "were not at all tired." How about little Eusebio? He, like Vicente, had walked—or trotted—twelve leagues that day, thirty miles or more. The little black mascot was still with them.

Just at sunset the explorers saw a canyon which seemed to offer a way through the sierra. So next morning when they mounted they turned west toward this opening, "ascending always along the sands and bed of the river Santo Tomás." At noon they took siesta at a grove of immense willows "and a most beautiful spring of very good water which was flowing in great abundance about half a league from the road."[1] Setting up a cross, they named the place Santo Tomás, "since this is the source of the river that we have named for that saint." They were on the right trail. It led through the sierra. Continuing almost due west, and climbing a slope "which was not very bad," they reached the summit where there was a dry arroyo running

[1] It was one of those springs characteristic of the arroyos formed at the foot of La Giganta.

westward. It was at the head waters of Arroyo Comondú, a branch of the Purísima River.

A way had been found through the Sierra Giganta and there was time to see a little of the country beyond. They now traveled six leagues downstream through a valley called San Flaviano "because it was his day," finding "well-trodden trails, good lands, metals, and indications of many people," though at first there were none in sight. At dark, guided by Vicente and little Eusebio, they came upon some fires. Here must be a village. Not to alarm the natives they turned back half a league and camped without water.

Next day they retraced the half league, and from a hill looked down on a large settlement. All of Kino's trouble was repaid. "It was a great ranchería filled with natives, most of them tall and of good figure." Frightened by the horses, the chief sent the rabble of women and children away. Kino called to the men but at first they would not come near. Finally, they sent an ambassador, whom Kino called Juan. This seems to have been the favorite name for Indians, like "George," for Pullman porters.

All ten horsemen now descended to the village, but Vicente and Eusebio stayed safely behind. These people were Didius, and when Kino spoke to Juan in the Nebe tongue he understood. Kino gave him chomites, pinole and panocha. Seeing the gifts, other Indians came up, and soon fifty had assembled. "Everything that we gave them, that is, small clasp-knives, scissors, petticoats, mirrors, coxcates or glass beads, etc., they gave to their chief." Kino named this potentate Nicolás and his village San Nicolás, in honor of both the saint and the good scout, Nicolás Contreras. The place was near present Arroyo Comondú.

Men and horses were now refreshed with fine water, and Kino had a good chat with his hosts. He knew he ought to hurry back, but perhaps he might see a little more of the country. "Notwithstanding it was the third day of our expedition, and our provisions and the approach of Christmas warned us to try to return as soon as possible to our Real de San Bruno," he says, "we tarried in conversation with these affable Indians until ten o'clock in the morning."

The child-like natives marveled at the white man's medicine. "I took the time by means of a little sundial, showing them the movements of the magnetic needle, and the lens by which the sun kindles a fire, thus making them friendly. They asked many questions and begged for various things. Some wanted my rosary, some my crucifix, and others my cloak; some were content to hear and know the names of these things, others inquired what they were for. They were interested when I told them that the cloak was a protection against cold and a cover at night when one is asleep." Kino had made new friends; perhaps they would visit him at San Bruno.

Turning back now, the explorers were accompanied by ten or twelve villagers, who led them southeast toward a shorter pass over the Sierra. The trail was too steep for the horses, and Kino feared he would be forced to swing back north six or seven leagues to the pass of Santo Tomás. But a prayer was followed by a new discovery. "It was doubtful whether we should reach our camp of San Bruno for Christmas. But after we had promised divers works of devotion to the blesséd souls in Purgatory and a prayer for each one, it pleased our Lord that no farther than two shots of an arquebus to the north of the summit where we were, we found another well-trodden trail which ascended the Sierra Giganta, and by it we easily went up." The descent of the eastern slope was difficult, but the trail was much shorter than that by Santo Tomás, and they were soon on the Plains of San Pablo.[1]

Next morning they passed the village of San Vicente,[2] and by ten o'clock they were back at San Bruno, in time to hang up their Christmas stockings, though probably these Latins did not observe this Nordic pagan custom. Their arrival at the settlement was hailed by volleys of musket shots. And Christmas eve was celebrated by "feasting and music, lights, and dancing in the church, and a little after midnight, three Masses." They had found not one but two passes for horses through the Sierra Giganta. The great expedition to the Contra Costa could be undertaken.

Three short excursions were now made up and down the coast. The second day after Christmas Kino and Goñi, accompanied part

[1] Kino, Tercera Entrada la Tierra Adentro hasta el Poniente con 10 Caballos. In the San Bruno Diary. Manuscript in the Archivo General y Público, Mexico, Historia, Tomo 17. Printed in *Documentos Para la Historia de México,* Cuarta Série, Tomo I (Mexico, 1857).
[2] Evidently they did not pass through San Isidro on the return.

way by Atondo, rode up the beach and near Punta Mercenarios discovered "a fine spring of good water" which Kino named San Juan. It was not the same as San Juan Londó, a place farther inland. From a hill Kino descried a bay sheltered from the north and east. It was the one under Point Púlpito, the towering rock which is so conspicuous from a steamer on the Gulf. When he and his party returned at night to San Bruno they found a savory dish awaiting them. One of the men at the settlement that day had killed a coyote and a deer.[1] "The Indians ate the coyote while the señores conquistadores ate the deer."

Kino next turned south. There were things in that direction which he wished to see, and New Year's was a day of good omen. Ibo, The Sun, had not visited San Bruno for many days, and Father Eusebio was anxious to see him. So on January 1 he set forth again. With the Admiral, Father Goñi, and five Indians he rode down the coast. After going two leagues they struck a bad road and turned to the sea. There they saw a gruesome memento of one of the misfortunes attending their La Paz episode. Scattered about lay "the bones of some of the horses and sheep which had been cast overboard from the Capitana at the time when, because of contrary south winds, the port of La Paz could not be made from Hyaqui with supplies." Guzmán's tragic story told at San Lucas was thus confirmed. The Capitana, Kino concluded, had been brought to this shore by divine will, in order that the gentle Didius might be discovered and converted.

Two days later Kino, Atondo, soldiers and Indians left San Bruno on another jaunt to the south. At four leagues the journey came to an end at a canyon which the horses could not cross. They were about halfway to the land of The Sun. Climbing a peak, with a field glass they viewed an inspiring panorama. To the north they could see the Real de San Bruno, in front the islands of Carmen and Las Pitahayas; to the south the bay of San Dionisio; and beyond it the Bay of Los Danzantes, or the Dancers. The vista called for a longer journey in that direction, but not now; the stock of provisions would not warrant it. Therefore, after distributing liberal presents to the natives, the explorers returned late at night to San Bruno.[2]

[1] The San Bruno Diary, entry for December 27, 1683.
[2] The San Bruno Diary, entries for January 1 and 3.

Pioneer Life

XLIV

DAYS GO BY

THE SPRING AND SUMMER OF 1684 were spent at San Bruno in the routine of life at fort and mission. Kino and Goñi labored with their spiritual charges, learning the native languages, winning and teaching the young, visiting rancherías, distributing presents. The soldiers cleared patches of ground and planted crops. The major tasks at the settlement were the making of adobes, quarrying stone, and completing the fort, barracks, church, and its residence. At all these labors the natives assisted with varying zeal and spirit. The Mayo Indians served as their leaders and teachers. Each jacal, or house, at the barracks had natives regularly assigned to it to carry water and fuel and to perform other menial labor. The chief return which the Indians got was food—to them the first consideration, for, in their native state, at some seasons of the year theirs was a pathetically bare cupboard. The Mayo women served as cooks for the officers, padres, and soldiers.[1]

The Indians still were generally friendly, but they were fickle and thievish. They stole not only trifles at the fort, but also sheep, goats, and even mules. When punished they took umbrage or fright and sometimes moved away. The barometer of their confidence was the stay of their boys at the mission with Kino and Goñi. When relations with the soldiers were satisfactory they freely turned their children over to the missionaries. At the least suspicion they took them to their native huts.

Life at San Bruno was far from monotonous. In fact it was kaleidoscopic, as will be seen from a few entries in Kino's diary, each one chosen from a different day:—The Admiral and Kino go to visit

[1] The San Bruno Diary, *passim.*

San Isidro. A cornfield is planted. An earthquake shakes the church and nearly rings the bell. The Didius flee from their village on the news that the Edues are coming. Another visit to San Isidro, where maize, wheat, and turnips are planted. Atondo has a Mayo Indian woman flogged and Kino protests. Goñi makes his retreat and the Admiral gives a party in honor of the occasion. Kino goes to the beach for shells with which to decorate a new retablo for the altar. He refuses to assist in distributing the royal alms to the Indians; it is none of his business. A soldier stones a native for a small offense and the Admiral gives him a caning. Indians steal a goat and are punished. Angered or frightened, the Didius move away, and extra guards are placed at night around settlement and stock for fear of an attack.

Crosses are set up for the *Via Sacra*. Mules are missing. Mayo Indians steal a raft in which to flee to the mainland. Three thousand adobes have been finished for the buildings. An Indian steals a sheep and is caned by the Admiral. The runaway Mayo Indians return, for the Gulf is pretty wide. Fish are bought from Indians. The Didius return, are again friendly, and building proceeds. The Admiral and soldiers make the Stations of the Cross. A novena is finished. On the anniversary of the canonization of San Ignacio and San Xavier, new frames are put on their pictures. Kino baptizes a Mayo boy. Eighteen Indians, big and little, sleep in Kino's quarters, "which would not hold any more." Father Eusebio must have disciplined his nose.

An alarm is spread that the Indians are stealing stock. There are many confessions, communions, a sermon, and catechism. A cross blows down and natives of their own accord replace it with a new one. The Indians aid greatly "in carrying stones and zoquite for the walls of the fortification." The natives make a successful fishing expedition. Swollen gums, a sign of scurvy, afflict the soldiers. The Indians of the village raise a hullabaloo at night. They carry up the mesa for Kino "very pretty and large stones for the altar." Palm Sunday is celebrated. There are thunder and rain in the Sierra Giganta.

Kino becomes mason and builds a "decent altar of pretty stone." The mission is visited by a woman "more than a hundred years old, perhaps even a hundred and fifteen or twenty." Father Goñi, feeling under the weather, is bled. Next day he is bled again. The Admiral and soldiers again make the Stations of the Cross. Some onions are missed from the Admiral's garden, they are found in the olla of a soldier, and it costs him "the whole afternoon in the stocks." A new frontal is placed on the altar. Father Goñi feels better. The Indians of the village hold another nocturnal powwow. A soldier is caned by the Admiral for complaining over short rations. The Indians watch Kino make a map and are greatly interested in his strange medicine. Water is brought in barrels from San Isidro three leagues away because that at San Bruno is salty. The third bastion of the fort is begun.

There is a report that a ship is in sight, but it is "only a little smoke." The Indian boys speak many Castilian words, like "ven acá," "ciéntate aqui," "válgame Dios," "uno, dos, tres, quatro." The Indians at night set up another great weeping and howling. A soldier throws a club at an Indian and is duly caned by the Admiral. On April 13 Kino eats California-grown melons. The Admiral's dog bites an Indian. Kino teaches the native boys their ABC's. Rations are getting short. Kino makes altar breads from Yaqui wheat. He goes again to San Isidro. A cross is set up on a bastion of the fort. Father Eusebio shows the Indian boys some pictures, and explains the Resurrection by reviving half-drowned flies.

A mother brings to Kino Baby Bunting "wrapped up in a jack rabbit skin." Padre Eusebio gives the Indian boys a rubber ball to play with. They think it is alive. The village of San Bruno, fearful of the Edues, moves across the "river" nearer to the camp. Kino again visits San Isidro. Some natives chase a soldier; the Admiral swaggers, says he alone "could kill a dozen or fifteen Indians," starts in pursuit, and slays an innocent native. Kino remarks, "The Admiral regarded what he had done as a courageous and manly deed." We do not have the Admiral's view of the case. Frightened or angry, the village moves to a place further from the fort, but Indians continue to aid with the building.

Four native boys bring Kino four iguanas and a bird. The Indians assist in bringing up to the fort some very heavy logs for the building. There is fear that the natives will set fire to the settlement, and as a precaution large cauldrons are kept full of water. San Isidro Indians urge Padre Eusebio to move to their village to live. Kino's boys give him lessons in the native tongue, and he again explains the Resurrection. On May 8 the Indians make a big catch of fish—and here Kino's diary abruptly ends.

XLV

BUILDING

A major interest during these months was the completion of the fort, storehouses, barracks, and church. Kino's diary is full of comments which reflect his sympathy for the hard-working Indians, his pride in their customary loyalty, his enthusiasm for the perfection of the mission plant. There seems to have been no resort to physical force in the employment of the natives; they came and went pretty much as they wished. The primary inducement to perform the laborious tasks was food, so scarce in that desert land. They worked for pay, the wages being sustenance. A few extracts from Kino's diary illustrate these building activities, and make it plain why so considerable a ruin of the fort and mission built by Atondo and Kino still stand at San Bruno.[1]

February 8. "The Indians were bringing for us and carrying up stones to make the walls of the fortification, and . . . for the same purpose our Mayo Indians were making adobes, which during all these days had turned out very well."—March 8. "They continued building with adobes both the fortification and two or three little houses, one for the sentinel with an earthen roof in which to keep the powder, shot, etc."

March 12. Shortage of rations now threatened to cripple building operations and to reduce the loyalty of the natives. "It is incredible how hard all these days the native Indians, women as well as men, worked in bringing and carrying up stones and zoquite [clay] for the walls of the fortification and of the bastions which they were

---

[1] The San Bruno Diary, *passim*.

building. It is true that they continued to give them their handfuls of maize for their labor, but the alms of the half almud of maize which during the past three, four, or five weeks, they had been giving them whenever they said the prayers in the church, ceased from this day forward, and the Admiral told me that he now had neither maize nor anything else to give them." Kino had his own stock of food, but it too was getting low. He writes: "On my part there was no other alleviation or attraction than a few beans, tortillas of wheat flour, a little pinole, maize, and wheat with which I had been aided by the great charity of the fathers of Hiaqui, Mátape, and Mayo."

March 28. "Today, since the Admiral and his men were occupied in the building of the stockade of the fortification, I with the heathen Indians erected in our little church a very decent altar of pretty stone." Next day "the door of the church was made, while the Admiral and his men were occupied in the building of the fortification."

April 7. "As usual many native Indians, both Edues and Didius, worked at carrying whatever was necessary, content to receive a few handfuls of maize for the three trips which they made. Some brought three large stones from the woods, others made three trips for clay or zoquite for the walls, and many times they themselves went to quarry the stones with the iron bars."

April 23. "It was noticed that there were very few or almost no native Indians to aid, according to custom, with the work of building, bringing grass, firewood, water, etc., and that those few seemed to work unwillingly. The cause may have been that the pay was very small and perhaps not very punctually given, for it consisted of two or three tortillas and some little handfuls of pozole distributed among thirty or forty or more persons. Indeed, from the ranchería of San Ysidro there were no Indians whatever, and it was suspected that they had withdrawn *in totum*. But the pay was now increased, and they began to give them a little more liberally the pozole especially, for we still had about seventy fanegas of maize." The strike now ended and the Indians returned to their tasks.

April 24. "Work was pushed on the building of the last bastion, and the beams and joists were laid, for within this bastion, as in the other two, there was a room like a spacious apartment in which might be put provisions and other things, and it was covered with a good roof." An Indian had been punished, and Kino feared the rest would abscond. Nevertheless, on May 2, "all the ranchería came as usual to aid greatly in the building of the fortification, carrying zoquite, stones, water, and firewood for the camp and grass for the horses, with great surprise on our part at the docility of the very good Indians."

Such is the vivid picture of the building of fort and mission left us by Kino's faithful pen. With these and numerous other entries in his diary, telling with explicit detail of the use of stone in the structures, when I set forth to visit the scene of Kino's labors I had little doubt that I should find unmistakable remains of the historic mission. And I was not disappointed. In the two and one half centuries that have elapsed since the stones were carried up the mesa with such toil, no one in that desert land has taken the trouble to carry them down. And why should they?

XLVI

PLANTING

It was understood that eventually the California missions must be at least in part self-supporting through agriculture. The king could not supply them indefinitely. The colonists came prepared with seeds, and planting was at once begun. When first they arrived, the country was green and prospects seemed good. We have seen with what optimism Kino set out the fruit trees brought in the first shipload of supplies from Yaqui. The hopes with which land was cleared and seeds committed to the soil, the rejoicing over "first fruits," the disillusionments which came from experience, the ravages of frosts and drought, and the rather pathetic results all told, are fully revealed by Father Eusebio's patient record.[1]

The first disappointment was the complete disappearance of all water into the sands of the Río Grande. Irrigation was out of the question. On the 5th of January there was a little rain. This was

[1] San Bruno Diary, *passim.*

encouraging and clearing went forth with renewed vigor. As with the building, let the diary tell the story.

January 10. "During these days the Admiral ordered a cornfield prepared and planted near the fort. Some of the nights were very cold, and some of the watermelons which previously had been planted were frosted. The wheat which I had sown in a few patches came up very nicely, giving us good hopes that with the first wheat which should be harvested, hosts might be made with which to celebrate the Holy Sacrifice of the Mass in these Californias or Carolinas."

January 14. "We ate the first roasting ears, beans, and turnips raised in these Californias or Carolinas. They were offered on the altar of Our Lady of Guadalupe, for the few patches which we planted in the middle of October did not fail to yield reasonably. But with the cold spells of December and January we learned by experience, and we hoped that by planting earlier, as soon as the river should go down at the end of the rains,"—they still believed in rains,—"we might have very good and fertile cornfields." Three days later Kino planted "a little maize, wheat, and turnips" at San Isidro.

February 13. "Señor Domingo Julián [de Sosa]"—he was the best farmer as well as a devout Christian—"offered and gave at the altar of Our Lady of Guadalupe, as first fruits of his new cornfield of these Californias, many very large ears of maize and some little calabashes."

March 12. The need of raising food for the Indian laborers was becoming more pressing. Of this urgency new hope was born. "Experience was teaching us that for the reduction of these people there were no alms or presents more suitable than the things necessary for their sustenance. . . . Neither is there any doubt that when the first rains come it will be possible to plant much seed, both of maize and of wheat, and of everything that is raised in Sonora, Hiaqui, Mayo, and Cinaloa, for the support both of them and of ourselves. In fact, we do not fail to be eating already some vegetables—onions, turnips, and radishes—which we planted and are growing in this California. Today they offered on the altar to Our Lady of Guadalupe some very fine chick peas, the first fruits of those raised in these lands."

For our information we are not reduced to reliance alone on Kino's superb diary. On June 6, 1684, Atondo signed a sworn statement summing up the agricultural efforts of the colony and his official part in them, supplementing the story told in fragments by Father Eusebio.[1] It recited that "in the middle of the month of October of the past year of 1683, Domingo Julián de Sosa, in a piece of land which to him appeared to be the most moist and suitable, planted some patches of maize, calabashes, and garbanzos, and although the season was not favorable, nevertheless they succeeded in growing and maturing, although not with perfection, on account of the frosts in the month of December, when they were injured."

Sosa's agriculture was a private venture. Encouraged by his success, Atondo planted a community field, and urged the rest of the soldiers to follow Sosa's example. "It appearing to me that this piece of land was suitable for planting all kinds of seeds and crops, according to the opinion of all the men most experienced in matters of cultivating the soil, with the labor of the infantry I had a reedmarsh in the bed of the river cleared of mesquites and other trees which were on its banks. The trees served to fence the field, which was planted with seven almuds of maize and three of frijol, the work being finished on the 8th of January of this present year of 1684."

Sad to say, Atondo's efforts went almost to naught. He continues: "But because the winds covered with sand all of what was planted in the bed of the river, it did not produce anything, except some sixty or seventy hills [*matas*] which happened to fall in the shelter of the fortification. For lack of moisture these hills did not come to complete maturity, but from them they gathered seven and a half sacks of roasting ears, some of them barren and without any kernels."

Others besides Sosa had private crops. "I having charged the soldiers to plant all kinds of seeds in the places which to them seemed best, they planted wheat, habas, garbanzos, and frijoles; and of vegetables, onions, turnips, radishes, melons, watermelons, and calabashes; and of fruits, grapes, quinces, pomegranates, oranges, and lemons." This is eloquent testimony to the wide variety of domestic plants carried with the Spanish pioneers wherever they went. "The wheat

---

[1] Deposition of Atondo, San Bruno, June 6, 1684, in Autos sobre Parajes A.G.I. 1-1-2/31, Patronato 31.

yielded well and had good kernels." Some of the men watered the crops by hand, with water laboriously drawn from wells dug in the sands of the Río Grande. "Others, who had some little pieces of land sufficiently moist, raised a crop without watering it, although the land suitable for this is so small in amount that it can serve only to show whether or not it is likely to bear fruit, for not more than two almuds can be planted all told. The habas, garbanzos, and frijoles grew and matured like those of New Spain, although the frijoles, because they were planted earlier, were taken by frost and killed in the pod. The garlic, onions, radishes, and turnips yielded as well as those of New Spain. . . . The lemons, watermelons, and calabashes dried up for lack of moisture. . . . The grapes, quinces, pomegranates, figs, oranges, and lemons were frosted and never took new root."

It was plain, therefore, that without irrigation not much could be expected from agriculture. And the water available in the Río Grande for irrigation was next to nothing. The successors of Kino and Atondo in the San Bruno Valley have all had the same experience.

XLVII

MAROONED

The ships did not come. Spring passed, the summer sun scorched the desert, and still no sail was in sight. The little colony was marooned on the Peninsula, facing starvation.

The delay was due to difficulties of administration at long range, and especially to the problem of assembling equipment from all parts of Mexico and transporting it to a remote harbor like Matanchel. Every important request by ship officers for funds, supplies, or laborers had to be carried by couriers on horseback to Guadalajara or Mexico City, considered by officials, and the decision returned over the same long trail by the same slow method. Timber for careening and repairs had to be cut in the forests; soldiers, ship stores, and provisions, must be gathered from widely separated points—Vera Cruz, Acapulco,

Aguascalientes, Guadalajara—and transported to the coast on the backs of mules.

The Almiranta had left San Bruno on October 16. Eight days later it reached Mazatlán. There Captain Pereda picked up the ruinous Balandra and conducted it to Matanchel, where he arrived about November 3. When the mail brought by the Almiranta reached Mexico the officials were still wrestling with the budgetary demands made by Atondo from San Lucas two months before. The viceroy granted most everything then requested. He ordered naval stores purchased in Vera Cruz and Mexico and sent at the earliest possible moment to Matanchel. The horses and mules asked for would be purchased in Sonora and held ready at Yaqui for one of the ships. Fresh provisions would be obtained from the Yaqui missions. Rice for San Bruno was purchased from Valladolid (now Morelia) and cheese from Aguascalientes, "the best in New Spain." Supplementary orders were hurried to Anguís, Atondo's lieutenant in Sinaloa, to have all these things ready at the Admiral's call. As for the anchor requested by Atondo, Bastida, the fiscal, noted that because of the difficult mountains west of Tepic, once it had cost $600.00 merely to send an anchor from Guadalajara to Chacala. So he recommended that the one now demanded be made at the mines of El Rosario, where there were excellent workmen.[1]

When Bastida reminded the viceroy that a third missionary was needed for California, he remarked, "Your Excellency might inform the Society of Jesus that the one selected for the enterprise must not be Father Suárez, for he has had some trouble with Diego de la Parra." As a consequence Father Juan Bautista Copart, a Belgian missionary from the Tarahumara, was chosen for the place.

Supplying California was like pouring water through a sieve. The viceroy had strained every resource to grant Atondo's requests sent from San Lucas. Now came the new ones brought in the Almiranta from San Bruno. Before these were disposed of the Capitana arrived at Matanchel, about New Year's Day, with letters from Atondo reporting another sheaf of wants. It was a continuous performance. Captains, pilots, and Zevallos, president of the Audiencia of Guadala-

[1] For this chapter see Autos sobre Parajes, and Autos sobre la Entrada Primera.

jara, incessantly bombarded the viceroy. He in turn kept Bastida and the junta busy discussing the requests. Men, anchors, armor, cannon, and provisions were liberally authorized, slowly assembled and with imponderable difficulty transported to Matanchel. Atondo had called for pearl divers. They were authorized and sought for but were not obtained in time to sail with the first ship.

One knotty problem was the careening of the vessels. Where should they be repaired and how pay for the work? Pereda reported that Matanchel was unsuitable for the purpose. It was so infested with mosquitoes that no one could work there. In fact, the seamen declared that "they would be hanged rather than remain." Permission had scarcely been given to do the careening at Chacala when the mosquitoes disappeared. Andrés, who now replaced Pereda in command, decided that Matanchel was preferable to Chacala. The sum of $3000 was appropriated for the careening, but before it became available Andrés was compelled to borrow money from Father Amézquita, of Compostela, the priest who had formerly helped Atondo out, and who had loaned Captain Parra $890 to equip the Balandra.[1] At last, near the end of July, the Almiranta was ready, raised anchor, and sailed for California. There were many official sighs of relief.

During the long summer months the men at San Bruno anxiously scanned the southeastern horizon, hoping to catch a glimpse of a white sail above the blue waters of the Gulf. Would no vessel ever come! For nearly eight months—since December—the pioneers had been isolated on the Peninsula with no breath of news from the mainland. The wait was nerve-wracking and tedious, but like most things it came to an end. On August 10 everybody at San Bruno who was able ran to the beach, for the Almiranta had anchored near the shore. She brought supplies and twenty additional men. There were official dispatches from the viceroy, and personal letters for the California exiles. On board also was Father Copart, who now joined the missionary force in place of Father Suárez, who never reached California. Five days later Kino made his final vows in the hands of his newly arrived brother.[2] He was now a "professed" Jesuit, bound by a special vow

---

[1] Moraza says that it left Matanchel "at the end of July." Letter to Atondo, December 6, 1684. Autos sobre Parajes, A.G.I. 1–1–2/31, Patronato 31.

[2] Kino, *Hist. Mem.*, I, 45.

from which only the Pope could release him. His "difficult mission" had not lessened his zeal. On the Almiranta also came Moraza, the royal veedor. Too ill to go to La Paz with Atondo, he had sailed for that port with Parra on the Balandra, but had abandoned the voyage at Mazatlán. He now reached California—a doomed invalid.

The Almiranta was none too soon, for supplies at San Bruno were nearly exhausted. On that day, says Atondo, "we found ourselves with the following provisions: 3 wethers, 2 ewes, 2 lambs, 33 goats, 8 hens, 2 roosters, 9 hampers of flour, 7 fanegas of maize, 2 fanegas of frijoles, 16 arrobas of butter in two botanas and some berigas, 25 small maggoty cheeses, an almud of garbanzos, half an almud of lentils, and 2 almuds of chile, there being in this settlement 61 persons." And this figure did not include the hundreds of hungry Indians roundabout. The twenty new men put an additional strain on the Admiral's commissary department. Nor did they add much strength to the colony, for they were a ragamuffin lot, with scarcely a shirt to their backs, and even less skill in the business of soldiery.

From one of the dispatches Atondo got a jolt. At the suggestion of Bastida, the viceroy ordered him to eliminate from his documents the word "conquest" and substitute "pacification and settlement." And he must not embroil himself in inter-tribal wars. The allusion was to his expedition to punish Chief Dionisio's enemies. He must be more gentle in his dealings with the Indians. The lesson of La Paz was not forgotten. And he had reported the killing of an Indian at San Bruno for some minor offense. He must remember that his was a missionary enterprise. With the admonition came copies of pertinent chapters from the *Recopilación* of the laws of the Indies regarding relations with the natives. That great code was not a dead letter. Atondo must study and observe the law.[1]

---

[1] Respuesta Fiscal, January 27, 1684; junta, February 1; junta, February 4 (Autos sobre la Entrada Primera, A.G.I. 58–4–23, Mexico 56).

Preparing for a Great Adventure

XLVIII

A HE-MULE FOR THE PADRE

EVER SINCE KINO'S DISCOVERY OF A PASS FOR HORSEMEN through the Sierra Giganta, he and Atondo had planned to follow up this triumph by making a grand expedition clear across the Peninsula to the South Sea. For so strenuous an exploit the summer was too hot. Besides, the expedition could not be made without more horses, mules, munitions, and provisions. These could not be had until one of the vessels should return. The Almiranta had now arrived. It brought no horses and mules, but it bore instructions for obtaining them at Yaqui. So the great task now set for the Almiranta was to bring from across the Gulf the horses, mules, and provisions necessary for the projected expedition. Right manfully the officers and crew did their part; right sturdily the little craft plied back and forth, plowing the waves and braving the winds of the Gulf to carry men and cargoes. The little *San José*—for that was the Almiranta's name—deserves remembrance in California annals.[1]

Nearly twenty days were needed to unload and repair the ship before it was ready for another voyage. Then Atondo ordered Captain Andrés to take on wood and water and speed away, "endeavoring to save all possible time in the voyage." At Yaqui he must promptly "embark the horses and mules, both pack and saddle animals," which Anguís might deliver to him, and "likewise all the other things which may be delivered to him by the Captain in the way of provisions, wine, shields, armor [*cueras*], and other munitions, as far as the tonnage of the vessel will permit." Having loaded his cargo, he must not delay his return an instant, for he had many voyages to make.

[1] Details regarding these voyages to Yaqui and other preparations for the expedition across the Peninsula are contained in the San Bruno Diary, *passim*. And see especially Autos sobre Parajes, original manuscripts, A.G.I. 1–1–2/31, Patronato 31.

The ship at last was ready. Next day—it was August 29—Andrés sailed. On board was Father Kino, who went to visit his brethren across the Gulf, view their missions, and enlist their aid. With him he took an Indian named Eusebio, not "little Eusebio," but a man some fifty years old. "He was the first to leave his home land within the memory of man." His going was a "surprise to many" and a great source of delight to himself. His impressions, Kino thought, would greatly benefit the California missions. It was lucky that Kino went to Yaqui, for when Andrés arrived there, Anguís was engaged in suppressing Indian troubles, and Father Eusebio was left to raise most of the supplies from the Jesuit missions. He was highly successful.

In less than a month the Almiranta was back. About ten o'clock on September 25 it cast anchor at San Bruno, carrying on board "ten horses, two pack mules, and forty-five wethers." Kino was one step nearer to his expedition to the South Sea. Besides, he returned "laden with many gifts useful in household affairs." He could now make more liberal gifts to the Indians.

Kino's hopes of good results from Eusebio's visit to Yaqui were fully realized. For now, "returning home, he tells of much that is to be admired and of the sights he has himself marveled at in the other regions; all of which is not to be scorned, nor will it be ineffective as a means of increasing the Faith. . . . Indeed, from the very time when these Californians learned that we had brought their own Eusebio safely back . . . and that our country had an abundant supply of food, flocks, and fruits of all kinds, they lost their suspicion . . . that we had come into their country for this purpose only—to carry off with us food, and the women and children whom we lacked in our own country."[1]

On the very day after its arrival the ship again turned its prow northward. The success of the first voyage had been imperiled by reason of Anguís's absence from Yaqui. In order that the next one might not

---

[1] Atondo to Andrés, San Bruno, August 28, 1684; Atondo, deposition, August 29, 1684; Atondo, certification, September 25, 1684 (Autos sobre Parajes, A.G.I. 1–1–2/31, Patronato 31); Kino to Scherer, on board ship, San Bruno, September 25, 1684. Original Latin manuscript in Bayerische Hauptstaatsarchiv, München. Jesuitica, Nos. 293–294; Kino to Paul Zingnis, San Bruno, October 6, 1684. Original Latin manuscript No. 14 Literae P. Francisci Eusebii Kinus ad P. Paulum Zignis ex Insulis Californiis Seu Carolinis. Bayerische Staatsbibliothek, München, Jesuitica, No. 282.

fail, Atondo borrowed money from his men at San Bruno and begged Kino to send one of his companions to act as agent to purchase supplies among the missions. Father Goñi undertook the voyage, accompanied by a soldier to help select horses and munitions. Encouraged by Eusebio's glowing reports, four adventurous Indians also went. On October 25, about ten o'clock in the morning, "poco más ó menos," the Almiranta again anchored at San Bruno, bringing "15 horses, 2 pack mules, and 150 arrobas of meat—all obtained at the Yaqui missions."

Hurry back, Captain Andrés! Within two days the Almiranta sailed on its third trip. This voyage was still shorter than the others. In less than three weeks the ship anchored once more at San Bruno bringing "15 mules, 2 horses, a he-mule for the Father Rector, 2 packloads of fish, 20 tierces of meat, 7 of cheese, 4 botanas of tannin, 12 fanegas of frijoles at the account of the Admiral, and shoe iron and bars."

More speed, Captain! The crew hastened the unloading, and two days later (November 16) the Almiranta again sailed for Yaqui. This voyage was surprisingly short. On December 2 the Almiranta returned with her sides bulging, for she brought "16 horses, a she-mule and a macho, pack animals, 55 wethers, 250 arrobas of meat, 61 arrobas of fish, 12 bottles of mescal wine, 20 fanegas of maize, and 12 arrobas of butter." [1] It will be remembered that an arroba is twenty-five pounds and a fanega nearly two bushels.

The Almiranta had bravely made its four voyages and done its bit. There were still twenty-five horses to bring from Yaqui, but the vessel needed repairs. From its last trip it had returned so lacking in cables that Andrés dared not cast anchor on any of the coasts. So the ship was now sent to Matanchel. Moraza wrote, "The Almiranta has made four voyages to Yaqui, and I hope to God it will make this one, for its own sake and for ours, for it goes lacking everything, and we remain with provisions for only three months." Captain Andrés carried other messages to Mexico. Atondo again appealed to the viceroy for pearl divers, by means of whom to repay some part of the expenses of California; and for the dispatch of the Capitana and the

---

[1] Atondo, Certifications, San Bruno, September 26, October 25, October 26, November 14, November 16, and December 2, 1684; Atondo to the viceroy c. December 13, 1684. Manuscripts in Autos sobre Parajes, A.G.I. 1–1–2/31, Patronato 31.

Balandra with much needed supplies, since there were enough for only three months. And he sent nineteen arquebuses to be repaired.[1]

Among the passengers went Father Copart, whom Kino was sending to Mexico to make a special appeal for his neophytes. His stay in California was brief. But he made good use of his time studying the Nebe tongue, in which he wrote a Catechism or manual of Christian instruction which later was Salvatierra's guide at Loreto. When he departed, Copart took with him three Indian boys as Exhibits A, B, and C, from the "Largest Island in the World." Atondo wrote, "Father Juan Bautista Copart, apostolic man, goes in the interest of this conversion, and if your Lordship promotes it with the zeal which all those of the enterprise profess and have demonstrated, I have no doubt you will interpose your authority . . . in order that they may not leave us to perish of hunger.[2]

On December 14 Captain Andrés weighed anchor and set sail for Matanchel, where he arrived on December 23. He lost no time in addressing the viceroy. Once more the little colony at San Bruno was left marooned.

XLIX

A HARVEST FESTIVAL AT SAN ISIDRO

Meanwhile San Isidro had come more and more into prominence as a center of interest. Here was an excellent water hole with a carrizal and a permanent pond in the bed of the arroyo. A short distance below the aguaje was the Indian village. The importance of the place was greatly enhanced with the coming of the new supply of horses and mules from Yaqui, and with preparations for the projected expedition to the Contra Costa. San Bruno had scant pasturage and poor water; both were excellent at San Isidro. This place was

[1] Moraza to the viceroy, San Bruno, December 11, 1684; Atondo to the viceroy, San Bruno, c. December 13, 1684; Andrés to the viceroy, Matanchel, December 23, 1684. Original manuscripts Autos sobre Parajes A.G.I. 1–1–2/31, Patronato 31.
[2] Atondo to the viceroy, c. December 13, 1684; Zevallos to the viceroy, January 1, 1685; same to same, January 25, 1685; Kino to Bishop Garabito, San Bruno, December 8, 1684. Autos sobre Parajes, A.G.I. 1–1–2/31, Patronato 31. For Copart's Catechism see also Salvatierra to Ugarte, Loreto, November 27, 1697. *Doc. Hist. Mex.,* Segunda Série, I, 109–154.

on the route which it was expected to take on the journey over the mountains. Consequently the Admiral sent the main horseherd to San Isidro, established a soldier guard there, built barracks, and a storehouse for the supplies for the expedition. Later a small chapel was erected.[1]

We have an official summary of what had been done at San Isidro before the year was out. On December 5, 1684, Atondo certified that a fortification of fascines, quarters for the guard, and a storehouse of xacal had been built there, and that a frame church was under construction, "all on the skirt of a little hill overlooking the water hole, which must be ten varas long and five varas wide, more or less." Although it had not rained for fourteen months, except for one little shower, this watering place had always been "permanent and abundant, enduring throughout the year, and it has been recognized to be water which descends in veins from the Sierra." So abundant was the water, indeed, that it had supplied fourteen soldiers, the horse and mule herd, and for a time a concourse of 2500 Indians, and yet was not exhausted or even diminished. Moreover, in spite of a fire, the pastures were still good. Such a pool and such pasturage in this desert country were indeed notable treasures.[2]

The concourse of Indians to which Atondo referred was a harvest festival held at San Isidro early in November, 1684. It was an interesting affair, and the circumstantial account of it which has come to us will be prized by ethnologists. Atondo looked upon it with some misgivings, and the padres were not sure that it was not the work of the Devil. In the guise of a pagan religious powwow, it might be preparation for a massacre. Possibly martyrdom was at hand. To participate in the ceremony hundreds of Indians descended from the Sierra to join with those of the valley. The central feature of the mitote was the worship of a statue or idol representing a god of the harvest. The principal medicine man or priest in the performance was Chief Leopoldo. When Nicolás Bohórques, corporal of the horse guard at San Isidro, wrote to Atondo about the curious spectacle, the Admiral sent at once for Soto-

[1] Kino, Relación de la Segunda Navegazión a las Californias, Dec. 1 to Dec. 8, 1684; San Bruno Diary, January 17, April 20, April 25, May 4, 1684; Salvatierra to Ugarte, April 1, 1699. In Salvatierra's day the place became the site of Mission San Juan Londó.

[2] Atondo, Certificación, December 5, 1684. Autos sobre Parajes, A.G.I. 1-1-2/31, Patronato, 31.

mayor and Rodríguez, the two soldiers who first saw the fiesta, in order that he might learn what it was about and give a faithful account to the viceroy. The witnesses having come to San Bruno, they were sworn to tell the truth regarding what they had seen. The story which they related was the following:

On Monday, the 6th of November, about noon, while they were guarding the horses which were pasturing round about San Isidro, "they saw how an Indian captain of the Didiu nation, whom we call Leopoldo,[1] although he is not baptized [he was little Eusebio's father], went up to the top of a hill dressed in a fiber net all covered with bunches of hair which covered him from his shoulders to his feet," like a Turk. On his head he had something like a toque or little cap, made of feathers of various colors, which fell over his shoulders. In his right hand he carried a white stick a yard long and having two square holes in it. In his left hand he carried a bow and arrow. Climbing upon a rock which was on top of the hill he gave loud shouts and made many gestures.

"After he had been on this rock for a time Leopoldo descended with such speed that he caused them surprise. Many Indians came out to receive him, and within an hour other heathen—there must have been about fourteen of them—went up the hill with the captain, dressed in the same way. Passing below the same rock, without stopping they descended to the ranchería."

Next day about noon Sotomayor and Rodríguez "saw a great procession set out from the ranchería, headed by Captain Leopoldo and others. Behind him was one of his wives; then followed an Indian and then another woman; and in this way they went intermixed, men and women, with canes in their hands and bunches of feathers on their heads, dancing and running, and paying homage to a statue of the size of a newborn child. Its face was painted black. It had long locks, and three bunches of white feathers on its head, the one in the middle standing up and the others hanging down a little." What kind of clothing it had they could not distinguish.

"This statue was carried by the last Indian in the procession, who went crouching with it till they came to a place where they had set

---

[1] He was the principal Didiu Chief in the vicinity of San Bruno.

up a pitahaya tree. On the tip of this tree were placed some wreaths, made of twigs of a tree which they call copale. Above them there were two wooden pennants woven of branches of the same tree and painted red, black, and white.

"They put the image underneath a brush shelter raised a little above the ground, and at the foot of a large pile of seed which they call *medesé*." These seeds were evidently mesquite beans. "As soon as they had placed it there the dance ceased for a spell. Afterward they resumed it and continued for two days and two nights in the following manner: In single file, men and women intermixed, they ran a long race. On coming to the end of the course the captain and all his men would stop near the image and begin to talk, at the same time bowing down and making obeisance. After this they would rest for about a quarter of an hour and then repeat the same race and the same ceremony.

"On the last day of the dance, a little before dawn, they gave such a loud whoop that they caused the infantry to seize their arms, thinking that they were coming to attack them. At the same time the witnesses heard a great wailing among the women. Shortly after this the Indians began to sing and continued all day, shouting and dancing, with pauses at intervals. At sunset they sat down in circles in various places and commenced to distribute the seed of the *medesé* which they had heaped up near the statue." The corporal ordered three horses armored and three light ones saddled. Mounting them, men went to see if they could count the great heathendom in attendance at this fiesta. They did not succeed in doing so, but all six thought there must be two thousand five hundred Indians, men, women, and children. They may have been seeing double that day.

"This same day Captain Leopoldo came to where the Real de San Isidro is fortified and asked the corporal if he might bathe where the horses drank. Permission having been granted, all the soldiers saw them bring another heathen who was badly used up. He appeared to be greatly emaciated and could hardly move. They put him in the pool and after he had bathed they placed him before the captain, who looked very attentively at him, bowed his head, began to weep, and then returned to the ranchería. The food which was left over they distributed among everybody, and then they went to their respective lands."

There was more to this story. A day or so after the festival was over, Leopoldo and another chief went to the garrison at San Isidro and asked Corporal Bohórques for food. When the Corporal asked him about the statue which his people had been worshipping, he replied that it was the god who gave them their food, coming down from heaven when it rained to give them pitahayas and *medesé*. Leopoldo added that he had now gone back to the sky. The Corporal, doing his Christian duty, told Leopoldo with emphasis that the statue was no good, "that it gave them nothing, and that the Holy Cross was better, because it gave us food and brought us the ships." "Well," Leopoldo replied, pointing with his finger, "tell this cross here to give us some food." Stumped for a minute, the Corporal hesitated, then replied, "We have it here in order that we may ask it for food. When our provisions are gone it will bring us more; for it sent us those which came in the ships and the clothing also." Father Kino had an ally in the Corporal. It is not recorded whether or not Leopoldo was convinced.

Other incidental items were learned about this native idol. The Indians said that he talked to them in their language, that he had one foot and two teeth, one below and one above. He was hardly a beauty, we conclude. Atondo was sure the idol was an imp of Satan. "Who can doubt," he wrote to the viceroy, "that the Devil must influence them against us, in so far as he thinks he can do us injury, trying to prevent us from succeeding in the conversion of these souls who are so near salvation?" Kino had a good ally in the Admiral also.[1]

L

OPTIMISTS AND PESSIMISTS

While the Almiranta was bringing horses and mules from Yaqui, Kino and Atondo were laying plans for their great adventure. The

---

[1] Atondo to the viceroy, San Bruno, December 13, 1684; depositions of Nicolás Bohórques and Manuel Valdés, San Bruno, December 16, 1684. Autos sobre Parajes, A.G.I. 1–1–2/31, Patronato 31.

South Sea and a river in the west were beckoning. Ever since their journey to the Plains of San Xavier they had heard rumors of great things on the Contra Costa. Optimists believed and pessimists discounted the stories. Some saw the doughnut, others the hole.

Foremost among the optimists, of course, was Kino. A Didiu named Francisco gave glowing reports of the country beyond La Giganta. "He told us of three rivers which unite and flow to the opposite coast. On one of these, in the country of the Edues, they plant beans; on the other . . . much maize . . . like that which we have planted and a few days ago gathered. They told us too of the manner of planting, how they take the kernels of maize and put them in little holes. Taking some reeds, they showed us by means of them how high the maize grows." This story was circumstantial, and had the earmarks of verisimilitude. Surely it could not be made out of clear cloth.

"Next he told us that near the river there is a very large population . . . and that the Edues and Didius are at war." All this fitted in with what naked King Juan had told Kino that day near Lake San Salvador. He conjectured that the great river must be the one called on the old maps Río de la Magdalena. Other reports filtered in, keeping Kino eager to put on his spurs and fare forth.

The River of the West and the South Sea now filled Father Eusebio's letters. In September he was hoping to start soon with fifty men. "What an abundant harvest of souls," he wrote his old teacher, Father Scherer. Kino the missionary was now speaking. Scherer was a geographer. So Father Eusebio sent him a map of the Jesuit missions in Sinaloa and Sonora. When he returned from the west, he would be able to add to this somewhat incomplete sketch "all the things which we are going to see and enjoy on this expedition of ours to the nearest western shores of Carolina . . . trying to note on it accurately all things which have not been mentioned in any geographical chart up to this time, since no map exists of the interior lands of California." Kino the cosmographer of New Carolina was now speaking.

Delays continued. December came and still the start had not been made. The plan now was to take thirty men. While they talked they made actual preparations. On December 8 Kino wrote the Duchess,

"With the favor of Heaven we shall soon be on the march . . . the Admiral, with thirty men-at-arms, ten or twelve servants, Christian Indians from Mayo, and more than thirty pack animals. Likewise we shall be accompanied by twenty or thirty friendly natives." Kino's heart swelled with exuberance. Missionary, cartographer, and explorer were now all speaking.[1]

Not everybody was so enthusiastic as Kino. Some of the officials at San Bruno saw more of the hole than of the doughnut. One such was Moraza, the recently arrived inspector and receiver for his Majesty at the settlement. The somber hues of what he saw were partly due to his chronic illness, for indeed the poor man was near to death's door.[2] At the very time when Kino was writing *cartas* bubbling with optimistic anticipation, Moraza was begging Atondo to delay the journey. The Indian powwow at San Isidro caused him, and many others, serious misgivings. Outwardly it had been conducted in friendly spirit. But who knew what diabolical plot Satan had hatched there in secret?

Atondo's valor and prudence were patent to everybody, said Moraza. The fortitude of the Admiral and his men "those who come after us will find it difficult to believe." And so they will. But the exploration of the interior ought to be deferred a few days. The safety of those to be left behind demanded it. The Almiranta was about to leave for Mexico. "We lack even the hope that the Capitana and the Balandra will ever come." Who then would succor the settlement in Atondo's absence? He was taking the thirty best men on the expedition, and this would leave San Bruno and San Isidro at the mercy of the natives. "Your Grace knows the quality of the men who will remain. For of those who came from Guadalajara some were mere boys and all were greenhorns, who even today do not know how to load or shoot a musket or handle a shield. . . . And I wish your Grace could see the soldiery which you might be pleased to order

---

[1] Kino, The San Bruno Diary, Feb. 21, 1684; Kino to Scherer, on board ship, San Bruno, September 25, 1684. Original Latin manuscript in Bayerische Staatsbibliothek, München, Jesuitica, Nos. 293–294; Kino to Zingnis, October 6, 1684. Original Latin manuscript, *ibid.*, No. 282; Kino to the viceroy, San Bruno, December 8, 1684. Autos sobre Parajes, A.G.I. 1–1–2/31, Patronato 31; Kino to the Duchess of Aveiro y Arcos, San Bruno, December 8, 1684. Original Spanish manuscript in the Huntington Library.

[2] Moraza had come with the Almiranta in August, having remained ill at Compostela when Atondo went to La Paz.

made of those who will remain." To begin with, they had no weapons
of any consequence; those sent to Guadalajara for repairs came back
in even worse condition than before.

It must be remembered, too, said Moraza, that because of the
drought the Indians were on the point of starvation, and therefore
could not be trusted. Without the restraint of the soldiery they would
kill and eat all the horses, "and us as well, I fear, if we are not very
careful and wide awake." And who would there be to restrain such
a multitude of savages? He visualized the mob of howling Indians
at San Isidro. The expedition might be cut to pieces on the way, and
then what? It was rumored that Dionisio the tall Edu, and Leopoldo,
the Didiu chief, were right now in the interior and up to some mischief, perhaps planning to attack the supply train. "God forbid," for
then everybody at San Bruno would starve! And why get so excited
about the expedition? Father Eusebio talked about a great river and
fertile lands in the west. But Moraza had been told a different story.
And if fertile lands should be found, of what use would they be, so far
away from a base on the Gulf? Finally, all the men should be allowed
to vote on the matter. Moraza was a democrat—and he was ill.

The Admiral stood midway between the optimists and the pessimists. He was keen to undertake the expedition to the South Sea,
but he was not happy with the conditions under which it would have
to be made. On the eve of starting he wrote to the viceroy a long
string of complaints. First there was the delay in starting; October
would have been a better season. Now the horses were lean and weak
and the men in rags. "Indeed they are so badly clothed that most of
those who came from Guadalajara, [the recent recruits], did not have
even a shirt."

Things had been sadly mismanaged in Mexico, said the Admiral.
He had requested coats of mail and none had been sent. He had
asked for helmets and none had come. He had ordered metal armor
for the horses and the factor at Guadalajara had sent him bull-hide
cueras. "One soldier on an armored horse is a tower," but what could
he do with only leather for protection? Somebody had bungled the
matter of horseshoes, and as a result the supply was inadequate. This
was a calamity. "How can we start without horseshoes? How can

the horses cross barrancas, climb steeps, and scale mountain ranges, when either they lose their shoes or break them," with none on hand for replacement?

And surely the men could not go on foot with the customary impedimenta, which indeed were really medieval. "For it is very clear that a poor soldier cannot travel a hundred and sixty leagues burdened with leather jacket, shield, arquebus, a pound of powder, a hundred balls, a hundred slugs, a calabash of water, and provisions for the eight or nine days in which he may be absent from camp. Finally, in a land filled with heathen it would be good luck to get back without experiencing disaster, because the Indians, seeing their opportunity, know how to take advantage of it. The soldiers being worn out, dead with hunger, and burdened by so heavy a load, might all be killed in ambush. These and many other evils follow from not having sent the horseshoes which I requested." With all his *ifs,* the Admiral, long ahead of Creasy, might well have written the *Fifteen Decisive Battles of the World.*

But in spite of the drawbacks and dangers enumerated, Atondo was going forward with a stout heart—so he said. "I trust in the Divine Majesty that although not more than thirty men at most will be able to go inland, and they not so well equipped as the situation demands, we are to have very good success, and to add"—here was the telling phrase—"and to add to the Crown in the time of your Excellency's administration a New World. Indeed, for this, for God, and for my King, I have made the efforts which I leave to the consideration of your Excellency, whose greatness I predicted would merit many honors. . . . On returning from the expedition I shall go to present myself at the feet of your Excellency . . . in conformity with my capitulation." This meant that Atondo would go to receive a hoped-for promotion. And again, "I trust in His Divine Majesty that I must experience very good success, discover a new kingdom, and make it a vassal to the Crown of Spain for the salvation of these souls, for the welfare of our monarchy, in the service of your Excellency." [1]

---

[1] Muñoz de Moraza, Representation to Atondo, San Bruno, December 6, 1684; Atondo to Moraza, San Bruno, December 9, 1684; Atondo to the viceroy, San Bruno, December 9, 1684; same to same, San Bruno, December 10, 1684; same to same, San Bruno, December 13, 1684. Autos sobre Parajes, A.G.I. 1–1–2/31, Patronato 31.

First Across the Peninsula

LI

THE RIVER OF SANTO TOMÁS

THE EXPEDITION WAS MADE AS PLANNED, in spite of all handicaps and doubts. On December 14 the Almiranta weighed anchor and sailed for Mexico. On the same day Atondo and Kino rode to San Isidro, the rendezvous where men, provisions, horses, and mules were assembled. Next day the start was made.

It was an interesting company that marched northward that mid-December day. Besides the Admiral, Father Kino, and Dr. Castro the surgeon, there were twenty-nine soldiers, two muleteers, and nine Christian Indians from the mainland, a total of forty-three persons. In addition there was a following of California natives to serve as guides. Kino with his astronomical instruments was prepared for his duty as cosmógrafo. He and Contreras were the principal interpreters. The soldiers wore cueras, or leather jackets—marvelous armor of bull hide. Each carried a shield, arquebus, a pound of powder, a hundred bullets, a hundred slugs and a calabash for a drinking cup—the cumbrous outfit of which the Admiral had complained.

There were five armored horses led *de diestro,* in good medieval style, for Atondo had brought from San Lucas that many suits of metal horse armor. There were thirty-two light-armored mounts in bull-hide cueras, thirty pack mules loaded with provisions, two mules ridden by the arrieros, and twenty-two relay animals, a total of ninety-one mounts and sumpters. No wonder the natives fled when they saw such a cavalcade coming. In the packs there was a goodly supply of little wares, especially cowhide moccasins, called catles or cacles, to serve as presents for the Indians.[1]

---

[1] Atondo to the viceroy, December 13, 1684. Autos sobre Parajes, A.G.I. 1–1–2/31, Patronato 31. Atondo says there were eighty-one horses and mules, but the items total ninety-one.

As they passed through each village Kino and Atondo made a distribution of these gewgaws, and the guides were encouraged to broadcast a story of Spanish generosity. Nearly every day after camp was made, a squad of soldiers and Indian laborers were sent ahead to explore the road for the next day's march. Frequently the going was so bad that these pioneers had to spend hours, and sometimes an entire day, in opening a trail, cutting down trees, prying rocks out of the way with crowbars, filling holes, or leveling steep pitches. Often Kino, accompanied by two or more soldiers, climbed some commanding peak, in order with his telescope to learn the nature of the country, look for smokes of Indian villages, and prospect for signs of precious metals. As they neared the western side of the Peninsula the chief aim of these observations was to catch a glimpse of the majestic South Sea.[1]

One of the greatest difficulties of the journey was that of the horses' feet. The Admiral's fears were justified. The road was rough and terribly stony, and the animals often went lame. Horseshoeing was an almost daily business, and more than once a whole day was spent in camp to rest the animals and repair their shoes. More than one poor mount played out and was abandoned by the wayside as food for the hungry natives, who left nothing for crows or buzzards. The caballos did their part in the expedition. Timid though they were, the Indians several times disputed the passage of the Spaniards, as Moraza had feared they would do, but with presents and "good talk" they were won over, and they performed incalculable service as guides. Frequently the Spaniards were followed by troops of natives from one village to the next. The women especially were friendly, and sometimes made trouble for the commander.

The itinerary and the incidents of the journey can merely be summarized here. Only the full diary which was kept can do the adventure justice. And only one who has retraced the expedition can read

---

[1] The story of the expedition is admirably told by Atondo in his Diary of the Expedition to the Contra Costa, December 14, 1684, to January 14, 1685. In Testimonio de Autos de la Ultima Entrada que hizo en las islas de la California el Almirante Don Ysidro de Atondo y Antillon y de lo que de ella Resultó, y la Resolución de Junta General en que consta la providencia y medios que se han elexido, A.G.I. 1–1–2/31, Patronato 31. Because there are two expedientes with almost identical titles, this one is cited as Autos de la Ultima Entrada (I). So far as I am aware, this diary has never been used before.

the historic journal with full measure of understanding. Till the explorers had crossed the Sierra Giganta they followed essentially the trail taken by Kino and Contreras the year before—when young Eusebio trotted behind and the little black crow was mascot.

Four days after leaving San Bruno the cavalcade arrived at Santo Tomás, the arroyo by which Kino and Contreras had crossed the mountains.[1] With the heavy pack train the traverse now was a more difficult undertaking than it had been before, and Atondo halted a day to prepare the road. Adjutant Chillerón with ten soldiers and four Sinaloa Indians performed the back-breaking task. Equipped with picks and axes, they went ahead and spent the day cutting trees, removing rocks, and filling bad holes. When they returned in the evening they were a tired band. That night Chief Leopoldo came to camp. Atondo gave him presents, and Kino urged him to send messages ahead, telling his people of Spanish friendship and especially of generous presents. Leopoldo complied and thus rendered useful service. Moraza had misjudged him.

Early next morning the explorers sallied forth up the steep. In spite of all the road building of the day before, the loaded pack animals had a hard pull, "and although each soldier went up on foot assisting a mule, some of the animals did not fail to fall down." La Cuesta Trabajosa—the difficult climb—they very appropriately named this acclivity. Six toilsome leagues were covered that day, to an arroyo which the natives called Comondé. It was the Comondú, an affluent of the present Arroyo Purísima. Camp was in the vicinity of San Nicolás, the village visited by Kino and Contreras the year before, for thus far they were on their former trail. Among the natives familiar faces were seen, and friendly smiles of recognition.

Three grueling days were now spent descending this arroyo to the forks of the Purísima. Whoever has been in that rough country will not find this difficult to believe. For two of these days the camp was followed by friendly Didius, including "five pretty young women" brought by the rascal Leopoldo, who thus raised a new problem of discipline for Atondo. It was the Admiral who thus described the damsels. On the subject Kino was discreetly silent. Camps were made at Santo

---

[1] The Indian name for it was Cupemeyení.

Domingo, Las Higueras (still on the map in the same vicinity) and La Thebaida—the Theban Desert. On this stretch they passed the canyon site of the later founded mission of Old Comondú. Here in this desolation began the territory of the Güimes, thirty of whom were met and given presents. In return their chief gave Atondo "a little toque of nacre which they use to bind up their hair." The Admiral probably did not wear it.

A pleasing sight now met their eyes. Two leagues down the arroyo on the third day took the explorers to "some springs of water which form a river. According to a report which the natives gave us, although it has not rained in fourteen months, it carries so much water that there is more than enough to run a mill." Man and beast alike now drank to satiety. The place was the one still called Ojo de Agua— the spring—at the forks of Arroyo de la Purísima. It is an unmistakable landmark in that unslaked desert, and an eternal joy to the thirsty.

Here Atondo's route swung sharply southward, down the river, and the country became rougher than before. Even yet no wagon road traverses it, and when in 1932 I told my local guide where I was bound, he looked dubious and shook his head. Three leagues farther on, fifty-four Güimes appeared on the trail and tried to turn the Spaniards back. The soldiers bristled, but Kino came to the fore. He had weapons more powerful than sword or blunderbuss. "With the good words which were spoken to them by the father superior . . . and by showing them catles and other wares" they were soon won over. By now the San Bruno natives were so afraid of the Güimes that in spite of all Atondo's coaxing they turned back "on the dead run," as he says, "leaving us without guides in the middle of the sierra." But the loss was not serious, for the now affable Güimes filled the breach. Directed by these new friends, Atondo continued two leagues downstream and halted at Ebocoó, naming his camp Río Deseado de Santo Tomás, or Santo Delfín Pamplona. The river had indeed been desired, but the country proved to be not highly desirable.

Next morning men and horses awoke with sore feet and aching muscles. It was the day before Christmas, the men were homesick, and the hardest part of the entire journey lay before them. The road ran in a canyon close to the stream bed.[1] Huge rocks lay hidden in the dense canebrakes through which they had to pass, and blocked the road. Five horses went down. "There was much danger of death to the horsemen, some by drowning and others from the boulders." Surgeon Castro was among those who came near drowning. Only two leagues were made, and camp was pitched in a little place called Noche Buena, "because we arrived on Christmas Eve."

"Here," says Atondo, "the heathen thought we were gods,"—rather ragged ones, to be sure—"and that we had the rain in our hands." But the Admiral was less moved by the flattery than by his sense of helplessness in that barren land. "When we asked them if it had rained, lamenting and with the appearance of sadness, they said that it had not, and that they had suffered much hunger . . . and that we must make it rain." They were indeed a poverty-stricken fragment of humanity. "We witnessed such need among them that we saw them eating the sprouts of the reeds and the roots of tule," says Kino, "and yet, when we gave them some of our food they were afraid to eat it, thinking that in it we were giving them some poison." By these barbarians all strangers were regarded with suspicion.

Next day was a gloomy Christmas for these boys from Spain and Mexico. To go forward seemed almost out of the question. Corporal Bohórques, who was sent out to reconnoiter, declared that the next two leagues were impassable for horses on account of the rocks. "Even for soldiers to go on foot with their arms it was necessary to give the weapons to someone who had gone up first and then for one to help another." Atondo sent men to try an opening seen in the mountain cliffs, "but such were the rocks, and the risks that the mules and even the armed men would go over the precipices," that the plan was given up. Another party of scouts tried still another way out through the cliffs, with no better results.

But Atondo was game. He would make the attempt right down the canyon in the bottom of the river, rocks or no rocks, for, he said, "although it might be at the risk of death we must go forward." So on the 26th they set forth down the middle of the stream. The men never forgot that day. It was not merely that canyon walls towered

---

[1] In some places the gorge of this stream is a thousand feet deep.

above them; the stream bed where they were forced to travel was a gray wilderness of boulders. The route lay "through rocks such that most of the men dismounted in order to pass. . . . Some fell on the boulders and others in the water, and most of the packs fell off. Nevertheless, those who went on foot filled up the holes with rocks and stones" so the horses could follow, until they came out to passable country. Here they met Indians who guided them, now over good terrain for three leagues, to camp at San Estevan. It was near the present Purísima, the first level spot in that vicinity big enough to stand on.[1]

Here a day was spent in camp to give the footsore animals a much needed rest and to repair their shoes. While the blacksmiths were paring hoofs and driving nails, Kino and two soldiers climbed a near-by peak to view the country. They strained their naked eyes and they squinted through the telescope. The soldiers thought they descried the sea; Kino, more cautious, "said that to him it appeared to be the sea, but he would not swear to it." They named this peak El Sombrerete for reason enough, "because it had the shape of a sombrero." Persons familiar with the country will recognize the aptness of the name.

The worst was over. In comparison with what had gone before, the rest of the way to the sea was like a boulevard. Next day Atondo descended the river five leagues to Los Inocentes, so named for a Church fiesta and not for the inhabitants. Because the animals were limping, he left most of them here, where pasturage was good, in charge of trustworthy Contreras.

LII

THE SOUTH SEA

Now for the climax of the adventure! Now for the South Sea! With Kino, eighteen soldiers, three Christian Indians, and two packs of provisions, on the 29th the Admiral continued seven leagues to Santo Tomás. Three leagues next day took them to the junction of the

---

[1] Scherer in his maps has San Estevan out of position.

stream with another which they called Río de Santiago, in honor of Spain's fighting saint. It was the present San Gregorio. Here they found good water and a village so recently abandoned that the fires were still burning. Two more leagues that day, over the narrow peninsula that lies north of the estuary, took the explorers to the shores of the Pacific Ocean. They were the first Europeans to cross California anywhere in all its vast stretch of a thousand and then another half a thousand miles. For this feat alone, if for no others, the names of Kino and Atondo would go together down the ages.

Each man felt like a Balboa. Near the ocean there were great sand dunes. Climbing over a low gap in one of them they descended to the beach. The tide was out. To the south about a league lay the opening through which the united rivers emptied into the sea. To it the eager explorers rode, part of the way among stones and rocks, on which they found "shells of rare and beautiful luster, of all colors of the rainbow, every one of them larger than the largest mother of pearl shells." Among them were blue abalone shells, so large that the natives used them as drinking cups.[1]

Father Eusebio never forgot those blue shells. Years later they became a central factor in another drama in which he played the leading part. "And we found various bones of whales, large, medium-sized, and small," says Atondo. "I ordered Corporal Gerónimo Valdés to measure the two largest jawbones, and he found that each one was thirty-one palms long. He tried to see if he could reach around one of them, but, although he is a good-sized man he was unable to do so." How human these fellows were!

They had now reached the estuary. Atondo sent Clemente García and Juan de Lara, who rode the tallest and most spirited horses, to see if they could cross its mouth, but the water was too deep. So they swung northeast, along the shore of the inlet as far as the Río Santiago, where they pitched camp.

Kino had a new thrill when some natives appeared on the top of a sand dune. He called to them and showed them some little presents. He shouted native words that he knew and waved his robes in pantomime. But they were afraid, and instead of descending to receive the

---

[1] From this incident Kino has been called the first conchologist of the West Coast.

gifts, they signaled him to come up. With two soldiers he complied. As he ascended the natives withdrew, but when he hung his presents on some bushes, immediately the Indians descended and took them. Soon fifty more came, in two bands. "The father again called to them in their idiom . . . and they replied that they feared lest we had come to make war on them. He told them not to be afraid, for we came only to give them presents." Atondo now joined Kino, "showing them what we were going to give them, calling them with tender words, and sitting down on the ground near where they were." This did the work. "Now four or five of them came down to receive from our hands hawks bells, scissors, knives, handkerchiefs, earrings, fillets, bracelets, and moccasins." Having accepted presents, they begged the Spaniards to go away from their water hole, in the desert their most precious possession. In spite of Kino's promise to regale them next day they departed and were seen no more. They would not trust the strangers.

Next day—it was Sunday, December 31—Atondo and Kino made a rapid excursion up the coast. They traveled six leagues, saw scampering Indians, discovered a saline of fine white salt and returned to camp at Santiago. Here the wayfarers watched the Old Year out and the New Year in—those who were not too sleepy.

Next morning, January 1, 1685, from the camp at the head of the bay, Atondo made a careful description of the harbor. This evidently is the reason why they called it Año Nuevo, although they had discovered it two days before New Year's. The description is accurate and graphic. Those Spanish pioneers were thorough. It all looks now just as they described it exactly two hundred and fifty years ago, so accurate were their observations.[1]

This work finished, the explorers started back for San Bruno. In the main they retraced their own trail, traveling a little faster than on going. At Santo Tomás Kino set up his sextant and took the latitude of the mouth of the harbor. Two days later an armored horse fell into the river and was drowned. He was spared many an ache climbing the

---

[1] This sentence was written in 1934. The Estuary which they called Puerto de Año Nuevo now bears the name of Laguna de San Gregorio. Some distance from the sea the Laguna receives the Arroyo de San Gregorio. The entrance to the estuary from the sea is called Boca de San Gregorio.

mountain steep up Arroyo Comondú. On the 13th—lucky this time—the explorers were given a hearty welcome at San Bruno.[1]

Kino and his associates had made history. But their bright dreams of a sparkling stream on the Contra Costa bordered by rich and cultivated vegas went a-glimmering. The day after his return to San Bruno Atondo certified that none of the lands discovered were suitable for planting. Kino was more optimistic, and he told of the exhilarating exploit in a letter to his old friend, Father Wolfgang Leinberer, in Germany. He was blessed with rose-colored glasses.[2]

LIII

THE GIANTESS BARS THE WAY

Atondo did not rest long from his journey to the South Sea. The river of Santo Tomás and the port of Año Nuevo were not what he had hoped for. He must have more glowing accounts to carry to the viceroy. So he was soon again on the move. The early sea explorers had given enthusiastic reports of Magdalena Bay,[3] near latitude 25°. There, perhaps, was better country, and perhaps the bay could be reached by crossing the Peninsula by a more southern route than the one just taken through the valley of Santo Tomás.

Therefore, on February 16, Atondo buckled on his armor once more

---

[1] Kino to Leinberer, San Bruno, April 9, 1685 (Latin manuscript, Bayerische Staatsbibliothek, München, No. 282); Kino to the Bishop of Guadalajara, October 10, 1685 (A.G.I. 1–1–2/31, Patronato 31). Also Kino, *Hist Mem.*, I, 215–221, 238; *Favores Celestiales,* corresponding sections.

[2] At least two or three Kino maps showing the results of this expedition to the South Sea were printed during Kino's day. See the Bibliography for a discussion of his maps. The above account is the first one to make known the facts about the crossing of California in 1684, a matter which has occasioned much pointless guessing. Venegas, when he wrote the Empressas Apostólicas in 1739 did not know about the expedition, and in discussing Kino's *Tabula Californiae* published in 1705 he declared there was no Río de Santo Tomás such as that map shows. Burriel, in his revision of the Venegas manuscript, confesses that he knows nothing of an expedition to the South Sea in 1684 or 1685, says that "Kino being extremely careful, . . . it does not seem credible that he would be in error regarding the fact of the discovery," but is unconvinced nevertheless. Stitz, not knowing of the diary of the Atondo-Kino expedition, enters into a long discussion as to whether the discovery was made in 1684 or 1685, and opines that the River of Santo Tomás was the Magdalena, which of course is far to the south of the region explored by Atondo and Kino (Peter Stitz, *Deutsche Jesuiten als Geographen.* Saarlouis, 1932).

[3] For early explorations on the outer coast of Baja California see the authoritative work of Henry R. Wagner entitled *Spanish Voyages to the Northwest Coast of America.*

and sallied forth "with the intention of going to the port and bay of Santa María Magdalena, on the Contra Costa, to see if perchance toward the southwest there might be found better lands for planting and for Spanish settlements." With him this time went Father Goñi, for it was he who had specialized in the Edu tongue. Diego Díaz, one of the soldiers, was also a competent interpreter. Atondo's outfit was much as before. There were twenty-one soldiers, a muleteer and blacksmith, a slave, four Christian Indians from the mainland, several friendly natives from San Bruno, and a mule train with provisions for twenty-five days. Five armored horses were led *de diestro* by the halter. In the packs there were little presents for the natives, furnished by the king. Kino did not go on this expedition, but he tells us the story, which he learned when the explorers returned. We have it in greater detail from the Admiral's excellent diary.[1]

Hopefully Atondo started down the superlatively rough Peninsula. He tried every opening that seemed to promise a way through the Sierra Giganta, but the ponderous monster merely frowned. Nearly every day scouts were sent ahead to explore the road and make friends with the Indians. Pioneers followed with crowbars and axes to remove rocks, cut trees, and open a path. Shoeing mules and horses was a major business in camp during the whole expedition. On the way they encountered numerous villages inhabited by people with good physique and gentle disposition. In friendly spirit they showed Atondo the trails and gave his men presents of fish and roasted mescal, "in this season their principal sustenance." Present giving was not one-sided. The explorers probed every promising canyon, but none deigned to offer a passage. Though Atondo craned his neck toward the right till his muscles were stiff, it was of no avail. So, says Kino, "they found themselves obliged to skirt only this eastern coast."

At the end of five arduous days of scrambling over rocks, barrancas, and cliffs, they were forced from the mountains to the shore at San Dionisio Bay. Here, at the village of Cumchó, they were visited

---

[1] Kino, Relación de la Segunda Entrada de las Californias, ó Carolinas, deste año de 1685 hazia al Sur. Begins February 16. Unsigned Spanish manuscript in the Huntington Library; Atondo, Diary of the Expedition to the South, February 16 to March 6, 1685. Testimonio de Autos d la Ultima Entrada (I), A.G.I. 1–1–2/31, Patronato 31. Stitz, who did not have the diary, erroneously states that Kino took part in the expedition. *Deutsche Jesuiten als Geographen*, 17.

by Ibo, The Sun, more familiarly known to them as Chief Dionisio. Ibo's friendship was as ever generous, but it did not prevent his hungry people from stealing a horse that night. Corporal Aragón, who went out to look for the animal, found it dashed to pieces in a barranca. The Indians had driven it over a cliff. As a gruesome proof Aragón brought back the horse's ears. After Atondo departed, Ibo sent him a dog which he had left behind at Cumchó.[1]

Three days later, a few leagues farther down the coast, the cavalcade filed up a steep point of land and descended on the other side to a narrow beach. Suddenly a musket shot rang out in the rear. Precisely at that moment, as luck would have it, the Admiral's mule mired in a bog. Scrambling off his mount, Atondo hurried on foot to see what had happened. Assuming that it was "some matter of war" he sent for the vanguard to fall back to help, and ordered that the five armored steeds be mounted for action. Before he arrived at the scene four more shots were fired. The soldier in him was stirred.

Corporal Aragón now explained what had happened. As the Spaniards had passed along the narrow way, forty Indians lay stretched out lazily on the beach. It was a trick. When they saw the Spaniards going single file down the cliff they suddenly sprang up, bent their bows, fired into the rear guard, and wounded two of the relay horses. In self-defense and as a lesson the soldiers shot and killed an Indian— the very one, it turned out, who had killed the horse the night before. The rest of the Indians now fled up among the rocks.

For four more days Atondo continued down the coast, reaching a place which he called San Agustín, in front of Isla del Carmen and thirty-five leagues from San Bruno. Seeing no prospect for crossing the mountains—for he had tested every canyon that led west—on the 28th he turned back. As far as San Dionisio he retraced his southbound steps. From there he took a new route, near the coast—evidently the one which Salvatierra followed so often in later years. San Bruno was reached on March 6th.

The Admiral had not attained his main objective—Magdalena Bay—but he had accomplished an important bit of exploration. The country traversed, like the Valley of Santo Tomás, a few years later

---

[1] Cumchó, or Conchó, in Salvatierra's day became the site of Loreto, capital of California.

became a favorite missionary field of the Jesuits. In the course of the thirty-five leagues traveled before they turned back—nearly a hundred miles—they visited and named fourteen villages. Some of them contained two, three, or even four hundred persons,—that is, they must have seen a population of two or three thousand people.[1]

Atondo, as before, was pessimistic at what he had found on his hard march. He declared that he had seen no piece of land worth considering for cultivation. There were no aguajes which would serve for irrigation, most of them being open pozos dug in the sands of the dry arroyos. He had seen no trees fit for building except now and then a mesquite. He had found no quadrupeds, and as to birds, only crows, ducks, cranes and sea fowls. As to the natives, they were corpulent, robust, good-looking, and more numerous than any before seen in California. It was notable that they had houses—little jacales of brush and reeds. This was a novelty.

Kino, thinking only of missions, and not having struggled with the cliffs and canyons which had beset the Admiral's path, was more enthusiastic, and on hearsay testimony he gives us interesting data concerning the culture of the Indians visited by Atondo and Goñi.

LIV

A SAIL

Since the middle of December the colonists at San Bruno and San Isidro had been again marooned on the Peninsula, without a vessel to connect them with the outer world. The Balandra had never yet appeared. The Capitana had gone to Matanchel for repairs and supplies more than a year ago, after her voyage to Yaqui, and had not returned.[2] Captain Andrés in the Almiranta had sailed for Matanchel on December 14, the very day when Atondo and Kino started for the South Sea. When it left, there were provisions for only three months. Ere another

---

[1] The villages named were the following: San Sereno, La Concepción, San Simeón, Los Mártyres del Japón, Santa Agata, San Pedro, San Mathías, San Ignacio, San Francisco Xavier, San Valerio, San Francisco Borja, San Augustín, San Nicolás de Tolentino, San Gerónimo (Kino, *Relación de la Segunda Entrada hazia al Sur*).

[2] December, 1683.

sail was seen there were hungry stomachs and anxious faces at San Bruno. But before March ended two of the vessels arrived. The Balandra, after its troubled voyage to La Paz, was put in command of Aberiaga, in place of Parra, who so gladly had resigned. The vessel was repaired, careened, and loaded with supplies. Early in 1685 it sailed from Matanchel and about March 6 entered the Bay of San Dionisio. This was just after Atondo had passed by on his return from his exploration to the south. Only ten or twelve days previously [1] the distressing slaughter of the Indian by Atondo's men had occurred in the same vicinity. Not knowing of the incident, and therefore without any fear, Aberiaga put a seaman ashore with letters for San Bruno.[2]

Then, says Kino, the Indians demonstrated their gentleness and their freedom from the spirit of revenge. They "not only did no harm whatever to the ship boy, but on the contrary, they came showing him the road, accompanying him the eight or nine leagues which intervened. And because he was fatigued with thirst they went ahead, came to this Real de San Bruno, and begged for water to carry to him, and then ran back to refresh him with this succor, all with great love and peacefulness, such as might be expected from the most friendly and Christian Indians." There were cheers when a few days later the Balandra anchored at San Bruno.

In the interim Captain Guzmán careened and repaired the Capitana at Matanchel and went to Guadalajara to confer with President Zevallos regarding supplies, pearl divers, and other things needed for California. Zevallos furnished Guzmán provisions, including fifty loads of flour, two hundred fanegas of maize and rice, forty fanegas of beans, and cheeses from Aguascalientes. Late in December Guzmán left Guadalajara with a pack train carrying these supplies, instructed by the president to hasten as soon as possible to California to succor the hollow-cheeked colonists.

Atondo had asked for pearl divers. Efforts to obtain them from Acapulco proved abortive. Zevallos then sent to La Purificación, where four were obtained at a salary of 350 pesos a year each and three reales

---

[1] February 23, 1685.
[2] Kino, Relación de la Segunda Entrada hazia al Sur. The Balandra arrived at San Bruno on March 12.

a day for rations—the same pay as that of the soldiers. When Zevallos wrote on January 1, 1685—the day when Kino was on the shore of the South Sea—they were still at Guadalajara. Of this the president had made certain. He understood their kind. "They will set forth within two or three days, for I have kept them in jail in this city in order that they might not flee, and they will be escorted to Matanchel under careful guard and custody, in order that they may be transported to those islands in the Capitana in the care of Don Blas de Guzmán." Evidently diving for pearls in California was not regarded as a holiday sport.[1]

The divers followed on the Captain's trail. On January 12 Guzmán was still in Matanchel; the divers had arrived there and, said the Captain, "with the divine favor we shall sail within ten or twelve days," determined to make "the greatest possible speed in our voyage." But it was March 25th before the Capitana arrived at San Bruno with the supplies and the pearl divers. Bastida, the fiscal, blamed Guzmán for a part of the delay, saying that he ought not to have wasted time by going to Guadalajara.

Both the supplies and the pearl divers were welcome. The latter especially pleased Father Kino; they might save an enterprise which was in danger of going on the rocks. He wrote to Father Leinberer in Germany on April 9. "Fifteen days ago four divers or pearl fishers, came to us, sent hither by his Excellency the Viceroy. Next week they . . . are to begin pearl fishing, under the supervision of the Lord General or Admiral himself. We are in good hopes that within the next two or three months pearls will be found in sufficient quantity to cause the king's ministers in Mexico to look with favor upon the much more important business" of soul saving.[2]

Meanwhile Father Copart was anxiously seeking aid in Mexico for the California missions. Zevallos reported to the viceroy that the Jesuit

---

[1] Zevallos to the viceroy, Guadalajara, January 1, 1685. Autos sobre Parajes, A.G.I. 1–1–2/31, Patronato 31. Zevallos procured also for Atondo a gunsmith at the same salary as the divers, "assuring your Excellency that it has cost me no little trouble, because there was no one in this city except a few unskilled laborers." Kino wrote on April 9 that the pearl divers had arrived fifteen days previously, which would be about March 25 (Kino to Leinberer, San Bruno, April 9, 1685). Latin manuscript in Bayerische Hauptstaatsarchiv, München, Jesuitica No. 282.

[2] Guzmán to Zevallos, January 12, 1685. Autos sobre Parages, A.G.I. 1–1–2/31, Patronato 31; Bastida, respuesta fiscal, January 26, 1685. *Ibid.*

had arrived in Guadalajara "with three little wild Indians (Chichi-mequillos) who are very intelligent." But when Paredes read Copart's earnest request for permission to go with his boys to the capital he advised him to forego the journey to avoid needless expense and hard-ship.[1]

[1] Zevallos to Paredes, January 25, 1685.

California in the Balance

LV

DROUGHT AND EPIDEMIC

WHEN GUZMÁN REACHED SAN BRUNO things were in a bad way, The drought had continued unbroken for eighteen months, except by one light shower, and only the slenderest crops had been raised. To this difficulty was added sickness among the men. Rations of stale and salty food, little relieved by fresh vegetables, had done their work. Their dire effects were accentuated by the saltiness of the water at San Bruno, which increased with the length of the drought. The combined result was an outbreak of scurvy which in April became an appalling epidemic. Some soldiers died, others were paralyzed, and the majority were on the sick list. Indian servants about the fort and mission had the same experience. Nothing weakens the wills of men so quickly as illness. So the settlers began to clamor to be taken away.

Atondo had his hands full. Three urgent questions presented themselves. (1) His contract provided that he must keep exploring till he had found a satisfactory site or exhausted all the possibilities of the "island." By his own rash act he had spoiled his chances at La Paz; San Bruno had proved unsatisfactory. Was it not time to look for a better location? (2) Divers had arrived and pearl fishing must be tried out. Where should the test be made? (3) The scurvy-inflicted men must not be left to die at San Bruno, but must be moved to the mainland for a change of climate and diet. To what place should they be taken?

To these three questions two more were now added. The viceroy was worried more than a little over the California enterprise. Very few baptisms had been performed, and San Bruno had shown slender prospects of self-support. Atondo's expedition had been undertaken primarily for missionary purposes. Solicitude for souls on the part of the government was genuine and sincere, yet it had always been hoped that agriculture or mines in California might be made to pay expenses. The experiment had already entailed a heavy burden on the treasury, now mounting well up toward a quarter of a million dollars. The cost of careening, repairing, and manning the vessels, and the support of a large garrison, had proved especially heavy. The situation could not go on indefinitely. The missions must be maintained, but costs must be reduced. Thus it was that by one of the vessels Atondo received from the viceroy an order[1] to report the best means for maintaining the California missions, consonant with the greatest possible saving to the royal treasury; and how best to reduce the size and cost of the vessels, after having transported the families and stock for the permanent colony still in contemplation. This order arrived just when things at San Bruno had reached a crisis.

To get advice on these urgent matters Atondo called a council. In it sat Kino, Goñi, Guzmán, Moraza, Lascano, and Contreras. With grave countenance the Admiral propounded five questions, including the two which the viceroy had raised:[2] How best and cheapest might the conversion be maintained? How best reduce the size and cost of the vessels? Whether the Capitana should sail to a higher latitude to look for a better site? In what direction should the projected pearl-fishing expedition be made? In case San Bruno were temporarily abandoned, to what place would it be best to take the sick to be cured, and the mules and horses to prevent their being killed and eaten by the San Bruno natives after the colonists had departed? To each member of the junta Atondo handed a sheet of paper containing these queries and requested a reply in writing.[3] To supplement the data thus obtained he held a muster of the soldiers and asked Castro the surgeon to report on the epidemic.

With the findings before him Atondo answered the viceroy's inquiries. If the government so ordered, he said, the California missions

---

[1] Dated October 17, 1684. Details regarding the situation at San Bruno are contained in Testimonio de Autos de la Ultima Entrada que hizo en las yslas de la California el Almirante Don Ysidro de Atondo (I), A.G.I. 1-1-2/31, Patronato 31.

[2] The order given here is not precisely the same as that of the questionnaire, the second and third questions being interchanged to correspond with Atondo's more logical order, as observed in his reply.

[3] Lascano reported on April 5, Guzmán on April 6, Moraza on the 9th. The replies of Kino and Contreras are undated. Autos de la Ultima Entrada (I), A.G.I. 1-1-2/31, Patronato 31.

might be maintained, at San Bruno and at San Dionisio, without further exploration; but preferably a new site should be sought. For either alternative he proposed plans for retrenchment. If economy was the order of the day he would gladly co-operate.

The other questions, those propounded by Atondo himself, had to do with immediate action. When the muster of soldiers was passed before the Admiral's moist eyes only fifteen men appeared in the ranks; thirty-nine were too ill to answer roll call, and four were reported as dead. Castro the surgeon solemnly testified that he had tried all remedies known to him but without avail; the men were becoming worse instead of better, and he recommended an immediate change of climate for the patients. The grim facts revealed by the muster were emphasized by a petition from the men. It recited that most of the soldiers were ill with scurvy, several of them paralyzed. There was no one to nurse them, because the slave women and other domestics were as prostrate as themselves. And they begged Atondo not to leave them at the mercy of the Indians, but to take them to some port on the mainland to be cured.

Atondo had seen enough. His answers to all three questions were clear cut. He decided to send the sick in the Capitana at once—*cuanto antes*—to the Yaqui missions, in the hope that with a change of climate and diet they might recover. With part of the able-bodied men for a crew, Guzmán and Kino in the Capitana would explore northward in the Gulf to find a better site for a settlement; with the rest, Atondo and Goñi in the Balandra would hunt for pearls.[1] For this venture the Admiral's presence was necessary, to look after the royal interests, because Moraza, the royal veedor, was so desperately ill that he had already been given the last sacraments. All were agreed that the best place for pearl fishing would be among the islands between San Bruno and Cape San Lucas.

In short, Atondo decided, for the time being, completely to abandon California, in the hope of returning to San Bruno when the sick had recovered, or preferably, of moving to a better site.

Kino dissented. To him the viceroy's questions and Atondo's de-

---

[1] Muster roll, April 9, 1685; Dr. Castro's statement; Petition of the soldiers, April 9, 1685; Atondo's decision; Decreto, April 11, 1685; Kino's opinion is given at length. Autos de la Ultima Entrada (I), A.G.I. 1-1-2/31, Patronato 31.

cision seemed ominous. He feared, with reason, that having once departed from San Bruno, the Spaniards would never return, and his precious Indian boys and girls would be left without the means of salvation, for which they were ready, as he eloquently asserted. Such a calamity he deplored. He, too, outlined a plan for retrenchment, which was not just like that of Atondo. He was not convinced that agriculture was impossible at San Bruno. He heartily favored looking for a better site, but to the abandonment of San Bruno even temporarily he he was emphatically opposed. He would gladly go with Guzmán to explore for a better location; let Atondo hunt for pearls; but at all hazards do not abandon San Bruno! So he wrote, "It seems best to care for and nurse the sick men here, for the season most favorable to health is just beginning." Let the Capitana bring from Yaqui "some cows and calves for the refreshment of the sick and of the well. . . . This is my opinion, *salvo meliori*—saving a better one." His appeal was in vain.[1]

LVI

PULLING UP STAKES

Early in May Atondo put the new plan into execution. We get the story from Kino's pen.[2] The fort was dismantled, household effects and mission treasures were packed for shipping. On the 6th most of the Spaniards' belongings were loaded on the vessels and the sick men carried aboard. Poor Moraza was near the end of his earthly career. While soldiers and sailors directed, friendly Indians trudged back and forth carrying bales, boxes, and bundles. Next afternoon the Admiral, Captain Guzmán, the Alférez, and Father Kino went to the landing. Kino embarked on the Capitana, with seven California boys, eager to accompany him and to climb around the ship, but five of them were put ashore next day amid tears "which caused surprise and compassion on the part of everybody." Atondo and Guzmán remained ashore that night, attending to the loading of the twenty best horses and mules. The rest were left for the natives, who said they would use

---

[1] Kino's protest against the abandonment of San Bruno, *circa* April 6, 1685. Kino to Lienberer, San Bruno, April 9, 1685.

[2] Kino to the Bishop of Guadalajara, Tórin, May 30, 1685. A.G.I. 67–3–28, Guadalajara 134.

them in gathering their pitahayas and other fruits. They more probably would eat them. This was an ignominious fate for the animals brought with such effort by the overworked Almiranta during those four historic voyages. The loading of the horses was an heroic task, but at last the kicking and squirming equines were stowed head to tail in the hold of the ship.

The sorrow shown by the natives for the departure of the Spaniards "was incredible," says Kino, and they were comforted only by the hope that in two months they would return. "Everybody . . . was very much grieved to see such gentle, affable, peaceful, extremely friendly, loving and lovable natives left deserted, when already many of them were begging for holy baptism. . . . And they confessed that it was not easy to find another heathendom so free as these people from the ugliest vices, such as drunkenness, homicide, etc."

Especially keen was the grief of Eusebio, the middle-aged Californian who had been with Kino to Yaqui and wanted to go again. Similarly disconsolate was a girl some fifteen years old, named Francisca. Her father had been killed by the Spaniards, leaving her an orphan. She spoke both Indian languages, was well versed in the Catechism, and for several months had been a servant in Atondo's household. Besides working in the kitchen she had been nurse for the infant daughter of a female slave of the Admiral. "But the poor orphan . . . neither by means of these arguments which she put forth, nor by the many tears which she shed, was able to get permission to embark." Reluctantly the Admiral permitted two of the boys to go with Kino to learn the Spanish language, and to keep him in practice in theirs, with the understanding that they should be brought back.

On May 8 Atondo embarked on the Balandra, with Father Goñi and the four divers, and Captain Guzmán boarded the Capitana. A troop of loyal natives brought to the ships a supply of fresh water from San Isidro, miles away in the interior. Others, thinking to be helpful, brought cast-off things purposely left behind by the Spaniards at the camp. A little before noon Guzmán and Kino visited the Admiral on board the Balandra. In return Atondo visited the Capitana to make a list of passengers and crew. All was ready now. About three o'clock a wind favorable for the Balandra arose, Atondo went aboard it, and set sail for Sinaloa to equip himself for his pearl-fishing voyage.

The Capitana was less favored by breezes, for she was northbound. The wind was in the prow, so she was not able to raise anchor till nightfall, when the wind shifted and a land breeze arose. With this aid she set sail. Crossing the Gulf at fair speed, on the 10th she anchored in the mouth of Río Yaqui.

There the horses were unloaded and couriers carried letters to the missions. Part of the sick men were hurried up stream to Tórin. Two days later word came that Moraza and two other soldiers had died there. The inspector had paid the full price in the service of the California Indians. On the 16th Guzmán and Kino reached Tórin with the rest of the sick men—there were nine now—"and everybody, healthy and infirm, was welcomed with great charity by Father Andrés Zerbantes." The thick-walled old church that still stands like a fortress on the hill at Tórin, overlooking the ruins of the once thriving town below it, if not the same is successor to the temple that was occupied by the Jesuits when Kino was there two and one half centuries ago.

From Tórin Kino went to near-by Raun to visit Father Marquina, the rector, whom he found engaged in building "a very pretty new church and house, and sustaining with maize and wheat many persons who on account of the drought of this year were suffering great hunger." His laborers were the then gentle and friendly Yaqui Indians. More than once in early days they had put to flight a no less doughty soldier than Captain Hurdaide. But kindness and fair dealing by Father Ribas and his successors had won them. Since Kino wrote, the scene has been desecrated. The Yaqui valley is less flourishing today than in the time of Fathers Marquina and Zerbantes.

LVII

GREENER PASTURES

Thirty-five summer days were spent at the Yaqui missions preparing the Capitana and the crew for the exploring voyage to the north. Guzmán's principal problem now was to get a supply of tasajo, or jerked meat. Some delay occurred and Kino returned to the anchorage.

There were cross currents in the community. "A certain person," unnamed, prevented giving the cattle which had been promised by Father Marquina. Clio has denied us the details of this promising bit of gossip. "And so it was planned to send the ship to Raun and Tórin for meat, and very quickly the one hundred arrobas were obtained." This was twenty-five hundredweight. Kino added cheerfully, "Within four or five days"—he was writing on May 30—"we shall set sail to go to a higher latitude to see if there are better lands for the settlement and conversion of those regions and of such lovable people. May our Lord be merciful to them in His infinite goodness." [1]

For the voyage to the north we have Guzmán's diary and his map —both now used for the first time, the former found in Sevilla, Spain, and the latter in Lima, Perú. Kino gives us additional details. These precious documents make plain a hitherto obscure episode, and explain a monument to Kino on the modern map.[2] The explorers left the mouth of Río Yaqui on June 13. Sailing west—for California was their objective—in the afternoon they caught sight of the Cape of the Fat Virgins (Punta de las Vírgenes Gordas), the point of land in front of the three great peaks now called Tres Vírgenes. For six days they zigzagged about, near the California coast, without gaining much latitude. The land "was extremely rough, and the least promising of all that had been seen in the Californias"; nor did they see "people or smokes." The prospect for a better mission site here was not encouraging.

Fearing the north-lying shoals of Salsipuedes—"Get Out If You Can"—called Los Dragones on Guzmán's map—they turned eastward to the Sonora mainland, and at night on the 19th they "anchored in the mouth of a bay or arm of the sea which we had discovered." Next day they sailed into the estuary. This body of water, named San Juan Bautista by Guzmán and Kino, is now most appropriately called Kino Bay.[3] Of the many places in America discovered or explored by Kino this is apparently the only one which bears his name.

[1] Kino to the Bishop of Guadalajara, Tórin, May 9, 1685, A.G.I. 67–3–28, Guadalajara 134.
[2] Guzmán, Diary of the Voyage up the Gulf, May–September, 1685. Autos de la Ultima Entrada (II), A.G.I. 58–4–23, Mexico 56. Shortly after discovering this diary in the archives of Sevilla I obtained from Perú a copy of Guzmán's map of the same voyage.
[3] Kino's map of 1696 shows it a little above the mouth of the Sonora River. From Guzmán's map and the fact that he called Tiburón Island a "point," I conclude that he applied the name San Juan Bautista to the wide strait between Tiburón Island and the mainland.

Leaving the Capitana at anchor in the bay, Guzmán went with ten men in the launch, "in order not to imperil the ship," to explore the Bocainas or narrow channels by which one must find his way through the shoals and up the Gulf. Kino remained with the Capitana. Guzmán went five leagues westward and camped that night on Tiburón Island, which he called Punta de Tiburones. That is to say, he regarded Tiburón Island as a peninsula, and the channel where he had left the Capitana as a closed bay. Next day, going two leagues westward, evidently along the southwest shore of the island, he landed on a beach which he called Playa de Balsas, or Beach of the Rafts. Climbing a high peak he viewed the Bocainas, and concluded that the channels were unsafe for a ship as large as the Capitana. The prospects for ascending the Gulf were not good, and the search in that direction was abandoned.

Next day they returned to the estuary, passed the anchored ship, and "in 29°" entered an arm of the sea, which they called El Sacramento. It was the inner stretch of Kino Bay which is now called Laguna de Santa Cruz. "It looks like a powerful river," says Guzmán. "It is soundable with six or seven fathoms. We did not see the end of it because it extends far inland"—twenty or thirty miles in fact. "It has on both banks rancherías of Indians, who, according to appearances, inhabit them. They say that in the rainy season the river of Los Ures and Cucurpe [the Sonora] enters this bay, and this is very probable, because we found outside on the seashore many canes and trees which the river ejects." This is correct. Two branches of the Sonora River join below Ures to flow toward the Gulf as one. Around the head of Kino Bay there is a large marsh into which the Sonora River drains in high water. Otherwise it is lost in the sands before reaching the bay. Guzmán continues, "Because we did not find water to drink we turned back to the ship."

The Capitana was obliged by southwest winds "to remain in that Ensenada de San Juan for fifty days,[1] and although it was in the shelter of a mountain, with the fury of the wind we dragged the anchor." The mountain behind which they were sheltered is on the south side of the bay near its mouth. Guzmán adds, "This place is the home of the

---

[1] Computation from the dates in the diary shows that it was only forty-five days.

A view of Kino Bay

Fol. D.C.D.

DELINEA
TIO
NOVA ET VERA
PARTIS AVSTRA
LIS
NOVI MEXICI,
CVM AVSTRALI
PARTE INSVLÆ
CALIFORNIÆ
SÆCVLO PRIORI
AB HISPANIS
DETECTÆ.

NO

SERIS

S.N.

P. de
S. Ioan

I. Casú

MAR   VER

O DE LA   CALIFOR

PARS   INSVLÆ

PROV.   PROV.   GVI.   Tortuga
Los Reyes   Ensenada de
Las Higueras   la Conception
La Trinida   S. Ildefonsi
S. Delfin   S. Domingo
DE   de Silos   S. Nicolas
CA   S. Leopoldo   S. Iosephs   MIES   S. Oderi   S. Iuan
S. Esteban   La Gigenta   S. Isidoro
S. Martyr   S. Barbara   I. de S. Bruno
Connocentur   Noche Buena   S. Salvador EDVES S. Dionisio
Natividad   P.   S. Agostino   N. S. del
S. Lago   Rio de la Madalena   S. Pedro   Carmes
AN   MOGIS   Monterey
S. Thom. Cant   S. Cruz
DRES.   P. de Danan   S. Diego
                                            tes   S. Ioseph
                          FOR   S. Agostino   S. Espiritu S.
                                GVAI   P. de S. Carlos
                                            P. de Matanza
B. de   CV.   B. del
Las Tetas   St.   P. CO
Madalena   P. del Marques   PAZ   RAS.
I. Zaqui   Tieraltana   NI_   ROS
Las Mesas   P. de la   P. de N. S. de
B. de S. Marta   Paz   Guadalupe
                          P.   DE LA S. TRI   Sierra de
                                            Æ.   NI   DA
LEVCAE.   Sierra del Enfado   P. de N. S. de
                                            P. de   Camoas

Germanicus.   5   10   15   20   25   30
Hispanicus.   5   10   15   20   25   30   35
Gallicus.   5   10   15   20   25   30   35   40

OCCASVS

30

29

28

27

26

25

24

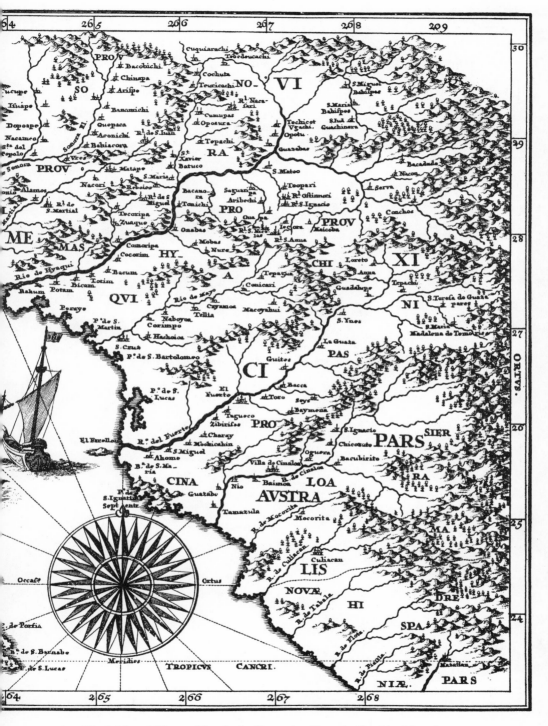

Kino's Map of Western New Spain. Drawn in 1685 and printed in Scherer's
Geographia Hierarchica, Munich, 1703

A present-day Seri family on Tiburón Island

Seri nation, heathen Indians on whom we wasted a box of goods in order to induce them to bring us water from their ranchos, which are distant a league and a half from the beach." These Seris were the gentle ancestors of the now fierce but sadly depleted tribe who have taken a last refuge on Tiburón Island.

While the ship was at anchor, waiting for favorable winds, Kino made good use of his time. He visited the Seris in their homes, and by his magnetic personality he quickly won their hearts. "They also are a very gentle people, as we saw and experienced," he writes. When the time came for the ship to sail they told him he must not leave. Today white men are not always welcome among them. "With very great insistency they begged me to remain with them and baptize them, saying they would give me horses, fish, and many products of the country, and that they would build me a house and a church, etc. On three different days I said Mass in their country." [1] He had made another conquest.

This visit by Kino to the Seri coast had a definite influence on his later career. His mind soon was soaring with new missionary air castles. But for the present duty called him south. The winds having subsided, on August 9 the explorers sailed for Yaqui, arriving on the 12th. In their absence the homesick soldiers, now convalescent, had begged their commander to take them overland, but he had refused. Getting a scant supply of meat and flour, and taking on board these now mutinous men, Guzmán and Kino started for Matanchel, via California. At San Bruno they stopped to leave the two boys whom Kino "had brought for practice in the language." There, to Kino's joy, they found the country green, for it had rained in his absence. He had a new argument for future use. The very poles of which the houses were built were burgeoning into foliage. This augured well for a return to take up the work of the mission. But not now. So the Capitana sailed away again, leaving the natives, some to weep, others to rejoice. [2]

[1] Kino said they were in 28½ degrees north latitude. Kino to Bishop Garabito, Guadalajara, October 10, 1685. El Obispo da quenta, A.G.I. 67-3-28, Guadalajara 134.

[2] Father Goñi tells us that the Capitana gave up its task of site hunting because of the severity of the climate. This we can well believe, for it was August. Goñi to the Bishop of Guadalajara, San Ignacio, September 22, 1685. El Obispo da quenta, A.G.I. 67-3-28, Guadalajara 134.

LVIII

TWO OUNCES OF PEARLS

Meanwhile Atondo with Father Goñi and the four divers went in the Balandra to the Sinaloa coast to prepare for his pearl-fishing venture. His diary, hitherto unused, is perhaps our most detailed account of pearl fishing in the Gulf during Spanish days. Through its pages pearl gathering is transformed from romance to reality. The adventure gave Father Goñi rather unclerical experiences and some clear-cut opinions about pearl fishing as a business.[1]

Leaving San Bruno on May 8, Atondo reached the port of San Ignacio on the 17th. Casting anchor, he sent a messenger to San Felipe, requesting tallow and pitch for his craft, and provisions for his crew, including "wine, and fowls for diet." In due time the supplies came down to the coast in a pack train, the Balandra was greased and caulked, and a ship boy was obtained to replace a Chino deck hand who was ill.

When Atondo was about ready to sail he got a letter from Yaqui reporting the death of Moraza. Now, Moraza had been keeper of one of the three keys of the sacred chest devoted to guarding the royal fifth of the pearls which might be gathered. So the Admiral in a formal decree reassigned the keys, one to himself, one to Aberiaga, and the third to Adjutant Chillerón, "they being the persons of highest rank who are going with me to the pearl diving." Soon came the news of the mutiny at Tórin. Atondo thereupon sent Chillerón to deal with the mutineers, and put Escalante in his place as keeper of a key. Atondo declared that he would put into the treasure chest everything obtained from the Indians in exchange for the "axes, machetes, and other merchandise belonging to the alms which his Majesty ordered given to me to distribute gratuitously to the natives of said kingdom." Evidently the word "gratuitously" had a flexible connotation.

The weather was so bad that Atondo did not finally get away till

[1] Atondo, Diary of his pearl fishing voyage, 1685. Spanish manuscript in Autos de la Ultima Entrada (II), A.G.I. 58–4–23, Mexico 56.

July 14. His intention was to go directly to Cape San Lucas, but circumstances changed his plans, and he steered toward the Bay of La Paz, scene of his troubles just two years before. Entering the bay on the 16th, the pearl fishers anchored at Kino's island of Santo Thomás, where the salt beds were.[1]

Here the Balandra remained for ten days, engaged in pearl fishing, whose technique the diary graphically discloses. Tropical moonlight, beautiful women, soft music, the sea hissing softly across the sands? No, it was none of these. It was a most monotonous and grimy job.[2] Each day a small crew in the launch, Atondo often at their head, took the divers to various places in the vicinity of the anchored Balandra and set them to diving for oyster shells. Each day's catch was taken to the ship, the shells were opened in the presence of all the crew, the pearls taken out and meticulously counted. The three official keepers then solemnly produced the clinking keys, opened the royal chest, and deposited the precious grains to the credit of his Majesty. Meanwhile the burning mid-summer sun beat down upon the patient servants of God and the King. The best pearls obtained were called *taladros,* the inferior ones *aljófares.* Still below these were the *berruecos.*

Only through details can we visualize the actualities of pearl gathering in the Gulf, a business already a century and a half old when Atondo made his venture. As with so many other things, acquaintance dispels the romance. The first day's fishing was at the port called San Xavier. Before night the divers, by dint of many leaps into the water, brought up two hundred oyster shells. On board the Balandra "the shells were opened in the presence of all the men of the fragata, and there were found twelve little grains of taladro and some aljófares, all of which were put in the royal chest with three keys." A start had been made.

At Las Gaviotas the catch was two hundred and fifty shells, yielding a few aljófares and fifteen grains of taladro, "among them one

[1] Atondo, Auto, San Ignacio, June 10, 1685; Atondo, Auto, San Ignacio, July 9, 1685. Autos de la Ultima Entrada, (II), A.G.I. 58–4–23, Mexico 56. Oya wrote on June 28th; Father Cerbantes wrote to the same effect on June 29th.

[2] Dr. Sanford Mosk wrote in 1931 at the University of California (Berkeley) an illuminating doctoral thesis on pearl fishing in the Gulf. Part of it was published as "The Cardona Company and the Pearl Fisheries of Lower California" (*Pacific Historical Review,* III, 50–61, Glendale, March, 1934).

of the size of a chick pea." On succeeding days this process was repeated at different places in the bay. On the 22d the catch was three
hundred shells, with thirteen grains; on the 24th two hundred and
fifty shells with eighteen grains, "one the size of an acorn"; on the
26th, six hundred shells, fourteen grains; on the 28th forty shells, two
grains. Nearly always besides the grains there were "some aljófares."
By this time if it were not for the element of chance the occupation
would have become tiresome routine. But it still was a gamble and
therefore intriguing. Perhaps the very next shell would yield a fortune. The lure was like that of prospecting for gold.

Atondo now raised anchor and descended the bay to La Paz to
get water—and to take another peep at the palm-fringed beach where
he had built his stockade two years before. Would Father Goñi's
old friends be there to greet him and to receive presents from his
gentle hands? Or would he be welcomed with a shower of arrows?
Landing in the launch, from the famous well on the shore Atondo
got a supply of the precious fluid. Twelve Indians put in an appearance and then fled. To prove his friendly intentions the Admiral left
them some sandals hanging on the trunks of the great palms. Two
days were thus spent at La Paz, then the visitors sailed north. They
had scarcely started when they were becalmed at Las Calaveras,
the caves of the skulls, where the divers brought up thirty shells which
yielded ten little aljófares. That night they anchored again at Santo
Thomás.

La Paz Bay had been given a trial. High south winds preventing
him from going to Cape San Lucas, Atondo next made Espíritu Santo
Island his base. The crew went north with the launch to that island
and brought back one hundred and fifty shells which yielded fourteen aljófares. On August 1 the Balandra moved up, and the same
day the divers gathered eighty shells with two grains of taladro, "flat
like two lentils." Next day they fished up forty shells called *crias*.
When opened they yielded "neither pearls nor aljófares."

The plan was to barter for pearls as well as dive for them. Let the
Indians help. A stock of trading goods had been brought for just
this purpose, and the opportunity now presented itself. While exploring in the launch the crew met four rafts of native fishermen,

and with one of the women they traded a knife for some fish. In the course of the dickering the Indians told them "by signs and some words which they understood, that farther on there were women who had pearls which they would exchange for knives." So Atondo moved the Balandra to the village indicated. It was on an estuary sheltered by mountains and three islands, apparently the Port Ballena of today. The Indians had spoken the truth. The Balandra having anchored, the natives swarmed around it on their rafts, "each one bringing a package the size of a nut, wrapped in rabbit skin." The packages contained little pearls. In exchange for knives the Admiral obtained fifteen grains of taladros, "among them being one of the size of a shot, and shaped like a pear."

Atondo's diary here contains ethnological pearls. He continues, "Close to the sea the natives have some huts made of branches, which can serve them only for shelter." This was news worth recording, because few Californians had houses of any sort. "The children of this island are fair and well featured, and so are the women. The latter wear grass skirts with which they cover their thighs, and the young women from fifteen to twenty cover their breasts with the skins of sea birds."

Next day the divers worked at Point San Simón y Judas without success. Here Atondo experienced Indian shrewdness at bargaining. In the afternoon natives of the island "came on board with five lead-colored berruecos, twenty-five grains of taladros of the same luster, and some pieces of polished shells," which they tried to palm off for pearls. "They showed us their good luster, but would not give them to us until we handed over the knives. In order that they might know that we considered them worthless, in their presence we threw them into the sea."

Atondo now turned to the *comederos*—those great and numerous shell heaps along the coast where the Indians fished and ate oysters. Presumably they would be near the best fishing grounds. Escalante and a crew were sent on this quest, instructed to employ the natives as before, "showing them that for their labor we would pay knives, machetes, and axes, and that they should begin by giving them presents of sandals, chomites, and hawks bells." Escalante went north to the channel between Espíritu Santo and Isla Partida. He met twelve natives there, but found no comederos. That afternoon the divers brought up three hundred shells, which yielded "nothing but six aljófares." Nor did the August sun relent.

The Admiral next resorted to using the natives as divers in his own company. There were rules regulating the matter, but Atondo knew the law and presumably observed it. At any rate, he paid the Indians liberally for their labor. "We gave them to understand that they should go in the launch . . . and that for each fifty of the large ones I would give them a knife." The bargain was struck. Guiding the crew to a place where Atondo's men had already fished, the natives set to work and brought up five hundred shells. Whatever chagrin Atondo's divers may have felt at being outclassed was dispelled when at night these five hundred shells yielded "only eight aljófares." The Indians could dive, but they could not guarantee pearls.

Espíritu Santo had been given a fair chance, so Atondo moved to San José, the island next north. At the beach he was met by the reception committee. They were not in formal attire. "About two in the afternoon some twenty Indians came and began to shout and make signs that we should land, for they were bringing *boxoo,* as they call pearls, and asking for knives." Escalante landed and bartered for six grains of taladro, "among them some of bad luster." Aboard the Balandra the Indians sold some more boxoo. "There were twenty-six grains of taladro, the smallest about the size of a coriander seed, the largest of the size of a chick pea and shaped like a little calabash." There were also thirteen lead-colored berruecos.

The Indians told Atondo of another landing where the women would sell pearls,—the women seem to have been the trading sex,— and next day he went to the place in the launch. Here the natives tried the trick of selling as pearls ground shells made up into balls and polished. The Indians must be humored or they would not help, so Atondo took the humbugs, gave sandals in return, and then threw the bogus pearls into the sea. Escalante explored the near-by island of San Judas Tadeo, but found no comederos and obtained no pearls.

The next stop was at Matanzas, the place which got its name and its fame from the massacre of Vizcaíno's men eight decades before.[1] Here Atondo described a remarkable farallón, or island of rock. It was pure white, as though the place had been cleansed of its bloody stain. Atondo's comment shows that he had imagination. "It looks like a ship with its sails unfurled, and from close by it resembles the saddle of a horse." But alas there were no pearls. At San Carlos Bay they discovered a saline from which they obtained four baskets of rock salt for the ship. But no pearls. The island of Pitahayas was explored. No pearls. At Isla del Carmen they found whale skeletons and a great comedero. But no pearls. At San Valerio they landed, cleaned out the pool which Atondo had used in February and obtained barrels of water. But no pearls. Quite as niggardly, the bay of San Ignacio yielded no pearls. During a storm four days were spent at San Xavier, which likewise yielded no pearls. A little better luck now. The launch was fitted out for another try at Isla del Carmen. At the end of four days the crew returned with four hundred and eleven shells, which yielded thirty-one grains of taladro, "the largest like a grain of pepper."

Two days later there was a sudden burst of cheers. The Capitana was in sight, having left San Bruno three days before. Guzmán told his story and showed the Admiral his diary and his map, which were examined with keen interest. But Atondo kept on with his pearl fishing. Indeed, the Capitana lent a hand. That day the crew of the Balandra with the four divers gathered one hundred and thirty shells. Atondo took four Indians in the Capitana's launch to the same place and they brought up two hundred. In honor of the occasion, the three hundred and thirty shells were taken to the Capitana to be assayed. The newcomers looked on with special interest. "I ordered the divers to open them in the presence of everybody," says Atondo, "and from them there came out a grain of the size of a pepper seed, and three much smaller, though of taladro, besides some aljofaritos." Gravely he adds, "and they were put in the royal chest."

Among the witnesses to this performance was the optimist Kino, and his eyes were opened. Atondo continues: "This scarcity surprised

[1] Atondo, Diary. For an account of the massacre of Vizcaíno's men see H. H. Bancroft, *History of the North Mexican States*, I, 150.

all the men of the Capitana, especially the Father Rector Eusevio Quino and the Captain [Guzmán], who, because they had never seen any opened, paid close attention." Perhaps Atondo enjoyed the humor of the scene.

The Capitana and the Balandra now prepared to go their separate ways, the former to Matanchel and the latter to Cape San Lucas to continue pearl diving. But the crew of the Balandra loudly protested. In a petition they urged that the vessels be kept together in so stormy a season; the pearl diving had been tested and failed, and both vessels might better go to Matanchel. Atondo would not give up, but he compromised by ordering Guzmán to follow him to Cape San Lucas. On September 1 they started south, but next day they were driven back by storm to anchor. On the 3d they took shelter at San Agustín, and on the 5th reached Monserrate. On the 7th Guzmán could not see the Balandra. Therefore, lacking provisions, and the weather still being stormy, he went on his way to Matanchel, where he arrived on September 17 "so needy that we did not have enough water for a ration that day."

Looking for the Capitana, the Balandra now followed to the mainland and put in at San Ignacio. Atondo sent a courier to San Felipe for mail, which was brought by Chillerón, who had returned from Yaqui. Another messenger was sent to the missions for supplies. Three days behind Chillerón a pack train brought two loads of salt meat, two fanegas of maize, thirty cheeses, and fifty squawking fowls. Atondo blessed the missionaries for their thrift and their generosity.

Thus equipped, the Admiral steered again for Cape San Lucas, determined to make another attempt at pearl fishing. Father Goñi did not accompany him. He was a poor sailor and he had already paid full tribute to the briny deep. He says, "since the sea handles me roughly, and because I am not needed at Matanchel, I am remaining in this province of Sinaloa."[1] Perhaps he longed for his mountain mission at Yécora. Atondo went on his way, but the weather was bad, Captain and pilot protested, and the Admiral, yielding to necessity, turned his prow toward Matanchel, where he arrived three weeks be-

---

[1] Goñi to Bishop Garabito, on board the Balandra, San Ignacio, September 22, 1685. El Obispo da quenta, A.G.I. 67-3-28, Guadalajara 134.

hind the Capitana." [1] In the harbor he found the Almiranta preparing to return to California with a cargo of supplies. Father Copart had gone to Guadalajara with his Indian boys to get help for the California missions.

Four days later Atondo called together the crew of the Balandra. From the chest of the three keys he took the pearls, showed them to divers and men, and asked if any were lacking. The answer, which contained more grains of humor than the chest held of pearls, was unanimously "No!" Next, in the presence of the same assemblage, he had them weighed. "And we found that the pearls and aljófares of good luster weighed two ounces and two drachms." The Admiral now solemnly declared that he would keep the pathetic "treasure" in his possession to give to the viceroy or his representatives.

Father Goñi briefly summarized his impression of pearl hunting. As he saw it, any dependence on pearl fishing for the support of California missions would be futile. Atondo had given it a fair trial. The trouble was simply that there were no pearls to be had. "All the pearls and aljófares which it has been possible to assemble are worth at most a hundred pesos, and the only reason for not having accomplished more is because there are no more. The shells that contain them are few, and all of us have experienced and seen that in four hundred shells, having chosen the largest and oldest, there was obtained from all of them only now and then a pearl or aljófar, and sometimes nothing at all." [2]

The story of Atondo's venture could have been reduced to a few lines, but from it the reader would have learned nothing about pearl fishing.

LIX

THE BEST PEARLS

From Matanchel Kino hastened to Guadalajara, and there to Bishop Juan he poured out his grief at the abandonment of California. An-

---

[1] October 8.
[2] Goñi to Bishop Garabito, on board the Balandra, San Ignacio, September 22, 1685.

guish of soul gave a keen edge to his powers of argumentation. He now set forth at length the views he had outlined in answer to Atondo's questionnaire before leaving San Bruno.

The point at issue was not a matter of cost, but of salvation. Hardship, discomfort, drought, hunger, expense, did not count so long as souls were saved. It was a shame to abandon California just when the natives were so eager for conversion. They had been pleading for baptism, and they had begged permission to embark with the departing Spaniards to seek the water of salvation on the mainland. Why leave them thus disconsolate and in fear of damnation? For, "since, thank God, many of them are already well instructed in the mysteries of our Holy Faith, and know very well that only good Christians and baptized persons are saved and go to heaven, while bad people go to hell and never-ending fire, and that all of us have both body and soul, and that the soul never dies, and that our souls must be resurrected, those of the good for glory and those of the bad for damnation, they have very great fear of the eternal fires of hell, and they very greatly wish to be our friends, and to obtain from us holy baptism and to be saved."

California, said Kino, had been abandoned on the ground that it was uninhabitable. This was a mistake. During the last year, it was true, the country had been excessively dry. But the drought was not confined to the "island." It was general on the mainland likewise. "It is known to us that the drought and sterility, the epidemics and the mortality, were very common in all the neighboring provinces of Hiaqui, Mayo, Sinaloa, Nueva Vizcaya, and Nueva Galicia. Indeed, from Mexico Dr. Don Martín de Solís wrote that the Lake of Texcuco had dried up, so that one could go on foot dry shod across it." In fact, the situation was worse on the mainland than in California.[1]

It must be remembered, too, that last year the California climate had been exceptional. It always is. Two years previously, when

---

[1] He added "sufficient evidence of the very great drought and general sterility of the [previous] year, it appears to me, are the many thousands of loaves of bread which your Illustrious and Most Reverend Lordship two or three times a week until now has ordered distributed among the many poor of this city of Guadalaxara." Here was an argument which Bishop Juan could comprehend. Evidently Mexico was on the Dole that year.

first the colonists reached San Bruno, they had found the country green and stock had thrived. Then had come the long drought. But just now, in August, when they returned from the voyage up the Gulf, the land was "very green and pretty, and all the water holes had an abundance of very good water." Indeed, the very timbers of the houses were sprouting. "We found the land so fertile and good that on the roads over which in past months the maize had been carried, and even in the houses of the camp, where the mist had entered, there was much maize growing, as well as beans, chick peas, lentils, and chile,—and the very poles of which the houses were built had put out branches and leaves."

True there had been some sickness. But there had been vastly more on the mainland, where in some places the graveyards would not hold all of the dead. The epidemic at San Bruno was not inherent in California's climate, but had come from a local cause. The water at San Bruno was salty, hence the scurvy. But better sites could be found. San Isidro to the north, San Dionisio to the south, and Santo Tomás in the west all had fine water.

Abandon California? No! Move to a better site—to San Dionisio with its three beautiful harbors, to San Isidro with its laguna and its wide plains, "very suitable for planting any year when rains do not fail entirely." And there were reports of still better places further north. It must be remembered that of all the vast island not one per cent had been explored. A man named Juan de Herrera, looking for Atondo, had reached latitude 32° or 33° in the Gulf. He had found level land, "and they say that there were watering places so very abundant that they could not see the bottom of them."

Kino turned to retrenchment. To desert California now would be all the greater pity, since the missions there could be maintained in future much more cheaply than in the past. Hitherto expenses had been excessive because large vessels had been used. They called for many officers, and for large crews with high wages. But small boats could be used instead. With one or two longboats, officered by two or three Spaniards and rowed by a few natives, all the supplies necessary could be carried over. The Gulf was only twenty-five leagues wide, and ordinarily a voyage lasted only twenty-four hours. Indeed, the crossing was often made in twelve hours. Men sometimes even made the voyage in pirogues.

Then there was the matter of pearl fishing. Atondo had hoped to help out with the costs by profits from this pursuit. He had not succeeded. But Kino knew what was the trouble. It was that the natives, who lived on oysters, kept the pearls from "growing." By feeding the Indians other rations, the pearl beds could be protected and future profits realized. This was a clinching argument. By founding missions and saving souls, profit in pearl hunting would be promoted. Surely the government ought to listen. So Kino proceeded to demonstrate. Atondo had hunted pearls all through August, along the whole California coast, and all he had got "was a matter of little moment." And "this was not because in these places there were lacking good and large comederos, but because the oysters in these shells, together with the other sea foods, are the daily menu and sustenance of the many coastwise natives, who dive for them. And they do not give the pearl a chance to grow. For the best and largest pearls are found only in the oldest shells." But, feed these oyster eaters, and tell them "they must not fish in the comederos for pearl shells, and they will leave them intact, and pearls will increase and grow. For most of them have no esteem for pearls, but only for the oyster inside." And then,—here was another way to save money,—"and then, when it is time to order the fishing made they will do it without the expense of divers, for the Indians are among the best divers to be found, and they will be very content with only the food of the oysters in the shells." It was almost a case of rats and catskins.

However, all these were merely incidental considerations. There were more precious pearls to think of. The Californians were ripe for Christianity. Through fear that they would be deserted, only a few had been baptized. But there were myriads ready for that sacrament. "Speaking of fishing for the best, the divine, the celestial pearls, which are souls," Kino continues, "I may say that up to now in California there have been only eleven baptisms, and these were of eleven moribund infants. Of these, eight died a few hours after holy baptism. The other three recovered and are now alive, and may His Divine Majesty not permit them to remain completely abandoned in their heathendom. For more than eight months now many natives have been begging for holy baptism, and although during that time many have been instructed in the mysteries of our Holy Faith, nevertheless, because over there the news has spread that the Californias are to be abandoned, a beginning of the baptisms has not been made. But if the Divine Majesty permits that we shall return thither, it all can be secured with the good dispatch of moderate funds."

Finally, as to immediate expenses, it must not be forgotten that the Almiranta was already equipped, provisioned and waiting to sail for California. Why, then, should it not go immediately, and begin fishing in earnest for the best, the divine, the celestial pearls?[1]

[1] Kino to the Bishop Garabito, Guadalajara, October 10, 1685. El Obispo da quenta, A.G.I. 67–3–28, Guadalajara 134. He had "just arrived."

The Balance Tips

LX

GOOD NEWS AND BAD

PART OF WHAT FATHER EUSEBIO ASKED FOR had already been granted, though he did not know it. When Viceroy Paredes received Atondo's reports of April and May, written on the eve of the departure of the colony from San Bruno, he was greatly troubled. He decided before making a final disposition of the California question to await the results of the voyages of the Balandra and the Capitana, the one to hunt for pearls, the other to seek better lands in which to found missions and make settlements.

So much for the more distant future. But there was the immediate question. Should Kino's already instructed neophytes be abandoned and left without hope of salvation? The answer was emphatically No! On the contrary, it was decided that the two posts of San Bruno and "Río Grande"—he probably meant San Bruno and San Isidro—should be maintained, with a force of twenty men and two missionaries, paid and supplied at royal expense.

This was not all. There were likewise the many Indians whom Kino and Atondo had met in their explorations. Should they be abandoned? Again, emphatically No! Paredes declared that he would maintain missions in any part of the "island" already explored "where there are heathen who wish to be converted, whether or not the island is suitable to begin the conquest, settlement, and reduction." Human souls must be put before profits. Paredes was four-square on the question. This decision was reported to Atondo on July 3.[1]

It was in the middle of September, while he was on the Sinaloa

---

[1] Junta General, June 19, 1685, and related documents. Autos de la Ultima Entrada (II), A.G.I. 58–4–23, Mexico 56; the viceroy to the king, Mexico, September 3, 1685. El virrey da quenta, A.G.I. 67–3–28, Guadalajara 134.

coast, that the Admiral received the dispatch. It presented a problem. It meant that he was to take or send back to San Bruno twenty men and the missionaries. But this he could not do at once, for the missionaries and most of the soldiers had gone to Matanchel. So thither he also went, as we have seen.

Early in November, when returning to the coast from Guadalajara, near Compostela Kino met Atondo bound for Mexico City. In his company went Rafael El Inglés. It was now that Kino learned of the decision of July 3. He was delighted, and his joy bubbled forth in a letter to Bishop Juan. "I have just arrived at this city of Compostela. Yesterday I met the Admiral, who had just left this city to go to Guadalajara and to Mexico, and he gave me the very good news of the great hopes entertained that the conversion of those very peaceful and vast lands of the Californias or Carolinas is to be continued." Bless the good viceroy! Kino adds a word about his own plans. He and Copart would return to California. "Tomorrow, if God be pleased, I shall go to the plantation of Santa Cathalina, and to the port of Matanchel, although most of the crew are in Guainamota, this city of Compostela, and Tepique"—all neighboring places.

Kino adds a zealous suggestion that El Inglés be converted. "Raphael the Englishman goes with the Admiral, and in Guadalajara or in Mexico, as your illustrious Lordship may think best, may you bring it about that he may be freed from heresy and be reconciled with the Holy Roman Catholic Church—*ut absolvatur ab hyresi et ut reconcilietur Santae Ecclesiae Catholicae Romanae.*"

The good news was soon confirmed. Kino reached Matanchel on November 12. There he received a sheaf of letters from a host of friends in Mexico. Among the communications was the viceroy's decision of July 3, that cheering document of which Atondo had told him when they met a few days before. It warmed Father Eusebio's heart. California would not be abandoned! It was "all so greatly in favor of that conversion that it seemed to me that nothing more could be said or desired, for he ordered that we continue it with twenty men and the two father missionaries. And he gives expressly to understand, with these words, that in California 'It is desirable to maintain the country already explored where there are heathen who may wish to be converted, whether or not the country is suitable.'"[1] Not San Bruno and San Isidro alone, but Santo Tomás and San Dionisio as well would come into the fold!

Then came a shock. All the good news was spoiled by another communication which arrived from Mexico at the same time.

LXI

KINO SAILS TO MEET THE PIRATES

Just when the California vessels arrived at Matanchel reports reached the viceroy that sea pirates—Pichilingues—were hovering round the West Coast and committing depredations again—or yet. Several buccaneering vessels were said to be in the harbor of La Navidad, lying in wait for the Manila Galleon, which was soon due to arrive on its annual voyage from the Philippines to Acapulco, a course which for a century had been run with great regularity. These freebooters would imitate their prototypes, Drake, Cavendish, and Spillberg, and fill their ships with spices and silks from the Orient, or overhaul the west-going galleon with its cargo of silver for the China trade. It is not surprising that such a report should cause the viceroy to worry, for in recent years English, Dutch, and French buccaneers alike had raised veritable hell on both sides of the Isthmus. A short time previously Panamá had been sacked and destroyed by these villains from the Atlantic.[2]

So the viceroy called on Atondo for help. The presence of his ships at Matanchel was a godsend. In a dispatch dated October 31st the Conde said: "Because yesterday a report arrived that the three vessels of the Armada de Californias were in the port of Matanchel, with nothing to do in the enterprise of the conquest for which the armada was constituted, having left those islands because they were un-

---

[1] Kino to Bishop Garabito, Compostela, Nov. 5, 1685. El obispo da quenta, A.G.I. 67–3–28, Guadalajara 134; Kino to Bishop Garabito, Matanchel, Nov. 15, 1685; *ibid.*

[2] These particular freebooters were part of the Grogniet band who had just raided Panamá and the western coast of Central America. See Marguerite Eyer Wilbur. *Ravenau de Lussan: Buccaneer of the Spanish Main* (Cleveland, 1930). In the archives of Parral there is a document which gives new data on the episode.

inhabitable, it is possible now to order that this little fleet may go to convoy the China Ship." And he did so order.

Kino was astounded at the news, so close on the heels of the other. So the vessels had "nothing to do with the enterprise . . . for which the armada was constituted?" California was to be deserted after all. He immediately wrote to Bishop Juan. "From this is seen the sad and unhappy abandonment of the Californias, and the great loss of so many expenditures and labors, and of so many souls, so gentle, so docile, so peaceful, catechized, instructed, and now so desirous to receive holy baptism, on the pretext that those lands are uninhabitable."

Bishop Juan must help save the situation! "And so on my knees (and Father Juan Baptista Copart[1] requests the same), I beg of your most illustrious Lordship by the most precious blood and death of our Redeemer, that you have pity on so many, so submissive and so docile souls whom, with all the sincerity of my heart, once and a thousand times, I commend to your very holy and divine zeal, because you are their legitimate and most vigilant pastor, whom they so much love and venerate!"[2]

Obedient, Atondo deferred his journey to Mexico, returned to Matanchel, rigged up the little fleet, and prepared to sail.[3] On November 29 he left the harbor and went out to warn the China Ship. The search was not long, for the very next day they fell in with the Galleon. Two days later, on board the Almiranta, Kino wrote to Bishop Juan, "and today, feast of the glorious death of San Francisco Xavier, the 2d of December, we are bringing it, thank God, safely toward the port of Chacala." From here the Admiral and Kino convoyed the Galleon safely to Acapulco, far down the coast. Putting well out from shore, they passed La Navidad unseen by the pirates. Kino sailed on the Galleon and learned much about the great profits made in the Manila trade. He did not go to the Orient, but he did sail in the China Ship.

---

[1] Copart had left Guadalajara and was on the coast planning to return to California in the Almiranta.

[2] Kino to Bishop Garabito, Matanchel, Nov. 15, 1685. A.G.I. 67–3–28, Guadalajara 134.

[3] Kino mentions the order on November 15. He does not mention Atondo's presence at Matanchel, but it is reasonable to suppose that the Admiral opened his own mail. Ten days later he and Kino were at Matanchel preparing for the voyage.

Father Eusebio was feeling better. The little fleet had saved a rich cargo from capture by the buccaneers. Surely this service must bring favor for the California missions. Now the vessels would not be junked. "We rejoice," he says, "that whereas the ships of the Californias have had the happiness to aid the China Ship to escape from its enemies, the result will be that they will all the more surely be retained for the continuation of the conversion of so many most amiable and docile and gentle souls of the Californias."

And, indeed, this was not a needless cruise on which Atondo and Kino were sent. Not long afterward the freebooters did no little damage all along the coast, at Colima, Petatlán, Mazatlán, and other places. But their mad career was soon checked. Captain Juan Redondo defeated five vessels at Santiepaque. Two of their craft were burned, "and they departed with a loss of fifty of their men," leaving "the seas of California free of corsairs." Some of the prisoners were taken to Mexico City.[1]

Kino was rather vain of his pirate chasing, for he was a man of action. Here was news for the Duchess. So he wrote her "how in the California ships we went to meet and warn the Galleon or ship of the Philippines against the pirate enemies who were on the coast of the South Sea and awaiting it in order to rob it; and that our Lord was pleased that we should bring the Galleon safely to the port of Acapulco, leaving tricked the four ships of the enemies." Atondo too was well pleased with his exploit. To Bishop Juan he wrote, "Everybody admits that if the frigates had not been in New Spain the Galleon would have been lost, a means of which our Lord took advantage in order that we might return to the aid of those miserable people." [2]

Years later Kino repeated the story in a higher tone of pride. The

---

[1] Kino to Bishop Garabito, Chacala, December 2, 1685. El Obispo da quenta, A.G.I. 67–3–28, Guadalajara 134. From Acapulco both Kino and Atondo wrote letters to Bishop Juan. See also Dunn, William Edward, *Spanish and French Rivalry in the Gulf Region, 1678–1702* (Austin, 1917) p. 41; Kino to the Duchess of Aveiro y Arcos, Mexico, July 19, 1686. Original Spanish manuscript in the Huntington Library. Neumann to Stowasser, citing a letter from Kino, Sisoguichic, July 29, 1686. Latin manuscript in the archives of Prague. Printed in Stöcklein, *Neue Welt-Bott,* I, No. 32. Kino's letter was evidently about March or April, 1686.

[2] Kino to the Duchess of Aveiro y Arcos, Mexico, Nov. 16, 1686, reviewing a letter written "about six months ago." Original Spanish manuscript in the Huntington Library; Atondo to Bishop Garabito, Mexico, February 16, 1686. El Obispo da quenta, A.G.I. 67–3–28, Guadalajara 134.

tale had mellowed with age and the value of the treasure saved had greatly risen. "We having come to the harbor of Matanchel . . . the viceroy sent us to meet and warn and rescue the China Ship, since at the same time the Pichilingue pirates were waiting for the ship in the port of La Navidad, in order to rob it. Meeting her within two days, thanks be to the Lord, and putting to sea with her, so that she might neither come to land nor be seen by the enemies who were in the port of La Navidad, we all arrived in safety at the port of Acapulco, leaving the pirates mocked, and our Lord having rescued four or five millions for the royal crown and his loyal vassals without loss." [1]

LXII

HOPES REVIVED, THEN SHATTERED

From Acapulco Kino and Atondo went to Mexico City, whither they had been ordered by the viceroy. The journey of more than two hundred miles on muleback took them over the historic trail which for a century had been used by travelers bound for Manila in the Galleon, and by pack trains carrying to Mexico and Vera Cruz the cargoes of silks, porcelain, and spices brought from China to sell at picturesque fairs in New and Old Spain. It was the same road over which Kino's friends had set out for the Orient after he bade them goodbye in Mexico City. As he made his way slowly along the narrow, crooked trail, he alternately gazed up at lofty peaks, or shrank from dizzy cliffs over which, with his heart in his mouth, he peered into horrifying canyons. Today one makes the same journey in a few hours in a comfortable high-power automobile. But the cliffs and hairpin curves still make one dizzy.[2]

Kino went to lodge in the Casa Profesa, where he had lived that first summer in America, nearly five years before, and where he had written his book on the comet. There were warm embraces by old friends, and a torrent of questions about the distant land where he

---

[1] Kino, *Hist. Mem.*, II, 237.
[2] The travelers were in the capital in the middle of January.

had participated in so many adventures. While in the city he helped to convert "twenty-one Englishmen," perhaps some of the fifty buccaneers captured on the west coast. Possibly Rafael El Inglés was among them. One wonders if Kino saw spectacled Sigüenza, and if so what they said. Of course, Sigüenza's book had not yet been published. Atondo rejoined his family, from which he had been parted nearly seven years. In due time he delivered to the royal treasury—with mock gravity we fancy—his pathetic little package containing "two ounces and two drachms of pearls and aljófares, and likewise two quartas of berruecos of bad luster," all formally certified on more than that many ounces of paper bearing the royal seal.[1]

Soon after reaching the city Kino had a conference with the viceroy. The cosmógrafo had already proved his mettle. Having heard by word of mouth his views on California, the Marqués asked him to put them in writing, and he made the same request of Atondo. Kino replied on January 21; Atondo ten days later. While they differed in some details the fellow laborers agreed in the essentials. Their suggestions regarding minor matters varied, but in spirit they were one. With equal earnestness they urged the reoccupation of California, with missions both at San Isidro and San Dionisio.

When on February 15 Kino wrote to Bishop Juan, he was hopeful. "Last week we made these reports and at once they were considered in council and sent to the fiscal, Don Pedro de la Bastida, and every hour now we are awaiting the reply and the final decision." He adds, "all these gentlemen, and their Excellencies likewise [the Conde and the Condesa] have assured me that without any doubt, by the divine grace, the conquest and conversion will be continued. And so it seems probable that a few weeks from now we, the twenty-five men and four missionary fathers, shall go to Acapulco to embark"—the Capitana was still there—"and it is very probable that we shall put in at Matanchel on the way to the Californias. May the Lord so order for His greater honor and glory."[2]

This optimism was justified by events immediately ensuing. On March 1 Bastida gave a favorable opinion regarding the reports of

---

[1] Autos de la Ultima Entrada, (I), A.G.I. 1-1-2/31, Patronato 31.
[2] Kino to Bishop Garabito, Mexico, Feb. 15, 1686. El Obispo da quenta, A.G.I. 67-3-28, Guadalajara 134; Atondo to Bishop Garabito, Mexico, Feb. 16, 1686, *ibid.*

Kino and Atondo. Ten days later a junta ordered him to confer again with these men. At the same time he was to request the Jesuit provincial, now Luís del Canto, to take full charge of the California missions, under guarantee of a government subsidy.[1] Perhaps with a free hand they could do for California what they had done for Paraguay. And the viceroy would be relieved of a White Elephant.

Father Canto at the time was out of the city on a tour of inspection, so the fiscal talked with Daniel Marras, the vice-provincial. Father Daniel replied that the Jesuits greatly appreciated the compliment, but felt it unwise to take upon themselves the temporal concerns of such a conquest, though they would be glad as always to supply the necessary missionaries.[2]

Bastida thereupon conferred again with Kino and Atondo. As a result he recommended the reoccupation of California under government control with four missionaries (three at royal expense), twenty-five soldiers, and eight Yaqui families as laborers. The Almiranta and the Balandra, he said, should be continued in the California service. For the support of the mission Indians there would be needed each year three hundred fanegas of maize and two hundred and fifty pesos with which to provide salt meat. To cover all costs Bastida recommended an annual appropriation of $30,000. A junta of the same date approved all of the fiscal's recommendations—"for the present" and until the king should give a final decision. The plan was authorized by the viceroy and reported by him next day to the king.

The decision had a big *if* in it. The California castle might tumble at a breath. The return to California was to be effected "when there should be found means from the Real Hacienda for the purpose"; this was uncertain "in view of the exhausted condition in which it finds itself at present." But luck was on Kino's side. Just then a trainload of silver came down from Zacatecas—$80,000 of it for the royal treasury,—and the *if* seemed to be erased. Plans were made for the return

---

[1] Junta, March 11, 1686 (Autos de la Ultima Entrada, (I), A.G.I. 1–1–2/31, Patronato 31); The Bishop of Guadalajara to the king, Guadalajara, February 18, 1686; El Obispo da quenta, A.G.I. 67–3–28, Guadalajara 134. In a postscript dated March 10, 1686, Bishop Juan said he was sending the two letters of Kino and Atondo written from Mexico, reporting the viceroy's decision to reoccupy California with a presidio and that the missionaries should return.
[2] Venegas, Miguel (Burriel), *Noticia de la California* I, 237, (Madrid, 1757), 3 vols.; *Natural and Civil History of California*, I, 212 (London, 1759), 2 vols.

to California. Father Eusebio would gladly have embraced every mule driver and every mule in the pack train.

Life looked cheerful now. It must have been right after hearing this good news that Kino wrote optimistically to his old traveling companion, Joseph Neumann, who was laboring in the Chihuahua mission bearing the wholly heathen name of Sisokitschick—or rather the Tarahumara name which Neumann gave a good German sound. To a friend Father Neumann wrote, "When I was just about to close this letter I received a very long one from the Venerable Father Eusebius Chinus"—the Venerable Kino was not yet forty-one—"missionary of our Society, and at present superior of the missions in California. Because of his mathematical knowledge as well as of his missionary endeavors, he has acquired such a reputation that, in spite of some opposition, the viceroy of Mexico has decided to follow his advice by building a presidio and establishing several missions in California. The money for the presidio has already been raised." Father Eusebio was becoming known to Fame.[1]

Then suddenly poor Kino's hopes were shattered. The king of France had Spain's monarch over his knee and his hand was poised in the air. The silver train had scarcely arrived from Zacatecas when from Spain there came an urgent appeal for half a million pesos "even though it might have to be borrowed, in order thereby to repay at once the damages done to a richly laden French ship which a few years previously had gone to the bottom of the Bay of Cádiz." France would not be put off any longer. At almost the same time—in April—there came from Spain a royal cédula ordering the viceroy to succor Nueva Vizcaya, Father Neumann's country, which threatened revolt, "even though it might be necessary to suspend the conversion of California." Thereupon the return to the Peninsula was indefinitely postponed.[2] With the French indemnity to pay and the Tarahumara war to finance, the California game was up. Another chapter in Kino's life was finished.

[1] The viceroy to the king, March 15, 1686, Autos de la Ultima Entrada, (II), A.G.I. 58-4-23, Mexico, 56; Kino, *Favores Celestiales*, Parte IV, Lib. i, Cap. 1; *Hist. Mem.*, II, 238.
[2] Kino, *Favores Celestiales*, Parte IV, Lib. i. Cap. 1; *Hist. Mem.*, II, 238; Venegas, *Noticia de la California*, I, 239. The order was dated December 22, 1685. See Dunn, *Spanish and French Rivalry in the Gulf Region*, 41.

LXIII

WHAT THEY HAD ACCOMPLISHED

There is a type of historian who might call the Atondo-Kino episode in California a failure. But what is failure? Often it is growth in wisdom. Civilization goes forward by a process of trial and error. We tend to profit by experience, and in proportion as we do this all experience may be regarded as gain. Baja California was a difficult region, as nearly devoid of means for sustaining civilization as almost any place in the world. Various attempts had been made to occupy the barren Peninsula. None had accomplished the specific thing intended, but each had made its contribution. Atondo and Kino by hard experience acquired an intimate acquaintance with two regions, La Paz and San Bruno, and explored two other important districts, the River of Santo Tomás and the Bay of San Dionisio. If these two pioneers had returned, the occupation of the latter was to be the next step.

They did not return, but their experience was utilized to advantage by their successors. When Salvatierra took up the work of Christianizing Baja California twelve years later, he began exactly where Kino left off. San Dionisio became his capital and the valley of San Bruno was reoccupied at San Isidro. The River of Santo Tomás, renamed La Purísima, became one of the important mission districts under Salvatierra and his associates. Kino while on the Peninsula compiled a vocabulary and arte or grammar of the Güimí (Cuchimí) language, spoken by the natives at San Bruno. Copart wrote a Catechism in the Edu or Monquí tongue, which Salvatierra used when he began his great work at Loreto. Kino, Copart, Goñi and the Admiral had shown the way.

Atondo's experience demonstrated that a large Spanish colony could not exist in sterile Baja California, under methods then known, without too great a drain on the royal treasury. The hope that colonization and missionary work might go hand in hand was abandoned as a consequence of Atondo's example, and the Peninsula was turned over to the Jesuits to be Christianized, with Spanish colonization left out of the scheme. Kino's proposal for a smaller garrison and smaller vessels was tried out by Salvatierra and proved to be sound. Kino suggested that for the support of the California missions, agricultural bases might be established on the mainland. Thus far the Yaqui missions had served this purpose. In keeping with this idea, Guaymas was founded by Salvatierra as a granary and stock ranch as well as a port for California.

In short, the work of Atondo and Kino was a success, in so far as it pointed the way to a better plan. Moreover, Kino was a distinct personal link between his period and the next. He never lost interest in the people whom he had left behind at San Bruno; he kept alive the project for re-establishing the California missions; and it was directly and personally from him that Salvatierra got his inspiration for his remarkable achievement. Finally, California had been for Kino himself a school of experience which prepared him to accomplish similarly remarkable things.

Secondary and unlooked-for results of human enterprise often outweigh those at the time regarded as primary. It was so in this case. Few if any missionary episodes are better illuminated by contemporary records than this one whose scenes were La Paz and San Bruno. Atondo and Kino were the first to cross the Peninsula. The diaries, maps, linguistic notes, and letters of Kino, Copart, Atondo, Guzmán, and others connected with the enterprise constitute a definite contribution to North American exploration, cartography, ethnology, and history, comparable, we might say, with the famous reports of Frémont, or of Lewis and Clark. The Atondo expedition cost in the neighborhood of a quarter of a million of pesos. This was a large sum. But more than one scientific expedition, fitted out in recent times at greater expense, has accomplished much less even for pure science than Kino and Atondo achieved and recorded.

APOSTLE TO THE PIMAS

A New World Calls

LXIV

SERIS AND GUAYMAS BECKON

WE HAVE IT ON OFFICIAL AUTHORITY that the abandonment of California was such a shock to Father Copart that he lost his reason, and that fifteen years later he had not recovered.[1] Not so Father Kino. He was a good fighter. And he was not a man to cry over spilled milk, or to beat his brains out against a stone wall. He had done his best. California was abandoned for the present and there was no help for it. So he now turned his thoughts to the Seris, those people on the mainland whom he had visited just a year before. "They also are a very gentle people," he had written to Bishop Juan. And they had begged him so earnestly to go and cast his lot with them. Near them lived the Guaymas, who likewise were asking for missionaries. He would be glad to serve these heathen. He broached the idea to the provincial.

"But there are no alms from his Majesty for the purpose," said Father Canto.

"Give me permission and I will request the necessary funds from his Excellency, the Viceroy," Kino replied.

"Write out your plan, and I will present it," said the provincial. This would be more seemly.

So Kino drew up another report,—he must have been weary of making reports—and Canto took it not only to the Count but to the Countess, as well—to her first in all probability, for she was an enthusiastic backer of the Jesuits. Bastida was consulted, he approved the plan, and funds were found to carry it out. For the Tarahumara trouble had subsided, and Kino's enterprise would cost much less than $30,000 a year, the sum proposed for California.

[1] A.G.I. 67–3–28; Kino, *Hist. Mem.*, I, 49.

So June 19 found Kino facing the future, courting Hope and not Despair. He was going to a new field, to achieve by indirect what he could not accomplish by direct means. On that day he wrote to the Duchess. In his missive rang that old-time jubilant tone. "The truth is that, thanks to His Divine Majesty, by means of a letter which I wrote to [Luís del Canto] the Father Provincial . . . , we have obtained three alms for three new missions, which, when the Flota and the new missionaries come, with divine grace, we shall go to begin in the heathendom of the Seris and Guaimas Indians, who also beg for holy baptism."

The prospect of a new field did not erase California from the picture. Quite the contrary. "The new mission will be in front of California and in sight of it, and so close that there are no more than fifteen leagues of sea between the two, and it will be a very great advantage for the one and the other that we undertake the conversion on both sides of this arm of the sea or Strait of California." This idea became a central theme and a guiding principle in Kino's life work. Let the fertile Sonora mainland foster the missions of sterile California.[1] He had struck his keynote.

In mid-November Kino was still in Mexico, but he was about ready to depart for his new field of labor. He did not wait for the Flota to bring a companion. Having spent nearly a year in the capital city, he was anxious to be on the move. He wrote again to the Duchess, recounting his hopes of March, and how they were dashed in April by the royal cédula suspending the California enterprise. But April showers had brought May flowers. His pack train was being made ready and he would soon be on his way.

"I shall leave this City of Mexico, God being pleased, two days

---

[1] Kino to the Duchess, July 19, 1686. Years later Kino summarized these events. "On the occasion of this suspension [of the California enterprise] I asked of the father provincial, who at the time was Father Luys del Canto, permission to come to the heathen people of these coasts nearest to the above mentioned California, and when his Reverence said to me that there were no alms from his Majesty for this purpose, I told him that if he would give me permission I would ask them of his Excellency. He replied that I should make a report, and with it and one of his own his Reverence asked and obtained two alms for two persons. With one I came to this Pimería, and with the other Father Adam Gil came later to the neighboring Seris. When these alms were conceded, the fiscal of his Majesty, Don Pedro de la Bastilla [Bastida], may God preserve him, insisted that these coasts would afford the best opportunity possible for continuing afterwards from here with the conquest and conversion of California." (Kino, *Favores Celestiales*, Parte I, Lib. i, Cap. 1; *Hist, Mem.*, I, 106. See also *ibid.*, II, 238–239.)

hence." He was going to the Seris and Guaymas, but his hopes were still in California. "The superiors here have promised me that when from Madrid shall come the decision in favor of the conversion of California, they will send me for the continuation of those missions.[1] Then I shall leave to another and better man the mission which I am going to found among the Seris and Guaymas, for, being supplied with bells, chalices, and ornaments for the altar, I am leaving Mexico two days from now."

This was Kino's goodbye to the Duchess on the eve of his departure for his new field. In closing he commended to the Lady "the twenty-one Englishmen whom we converted here a few days ago." By November 20 his outfit was ready, and on that day he fared forth.[2] He was again a globe trotter, and therefore in his element.

LXV

THEY SHALL NOT BE SLAVES!

Traveling once more the long road to Guadalajara, there Kino stopped to arm himself with an important weapon to be used in defense of his future neophytes. By now his prospective field of service had come to include the Pimas as well as the Seris and Guaymas.[3] Just before he left the capital Father Canto was succeeded as provincial by Father Bernabé de Soto, a veteran missionary from the Tarahumara country. Now, at the suggestion of both Canto and Soto,

---

[1] The dispatch which gave the alms for these two new missions said that "together they are to serve and aid to facilitate very greatly the continuation and conversion of near-by California." Kino asked the Duchess for her aid also in restoring the California missions.

[2] Kino to the Duchess, November 16, 1686. Original Spanish manuscript in the Huntington Library. Two weeks later Mansilla wrote to the Duchess: "Father Francisco Eusebio Kino assured me that he was reporting to your Excellency the condition of the Californias and of the three new missions which are at its ports, and for which the Father has just departed, assigned by the singular zeal of the Conde de Paredes and the pious urgings of my Lady the Condesa" (Mansilla to the Duchess of Aveiro y Arcos, Mexico, November 29, 1686. Original Spanish manuscript in the Huntington Library.)

[3] At a later date Kino wrote that his intention had been to begin with the Guaymas. "After I had lived in California and had come from there sometimes to Hiaqui, having very friendly relations with the neighboring heathen Guaimas, I very much desired and solicited their conversion, because I considered it very advantageous to the conversion of California. And in fact, when I came fifteen [seventeen] years ago from Mexico to these new conversions, the plan was to begin there among the Guaimas. Afterward there was so great a field here that only three years ago," etc. (Kino, *Favores Celestiales*, Parte III, Lib. iii, Cap. 6; *Hist. Mem.*, II, 92).

Kino presented a petition to the Royal Audiencia of Guadalajara. It recited that he had been appointed by the viceroy missionary to the Seris, Guaymas, and Pimas of Nueva Vizcaya; that "the alcaldes mayores and other officials of that province, under color of *repartimientos de sellos,* cause the Indians to be taken involuntarily for service in the mines, even before they are baptized, contrary to several cédulas of your royal person, by which violence they are terrorized and caused to flee from conversion to the Holy Gospel, and to refuse to accept the gentle rule of our Holy Faith, thereby imperiling not only the welfare of their souls but also the royal hacienda."

There was the abuse; now for the remedy. "And so, charitably, and with the Catholic zeal of your royal person for the reduction and conversion of the heathen to our Holy Faith, and in order that the Holy Gospel may be propagated in remote lands, your Highness will please order issued your royal provision to the effect that none of the alcaldes mayores, their lieutenants, or other ministers of justice, shall take or cause any Indian to be taken . . . under the title of seals, for service in the mines of that province, until five years have passed after their conversion"; that newly converted Indians who voluntarily work in the mines or in other occupations shall be paid a fair daily wage; "and that with respect to both one and the other grave penalties shall be imposed."

Kino presented this petition at a most opportune time, for there had just arrived from Spain a royal cédula which ordered that for twenty years new converts might not be taken away under seal. And President Zevallos, already Father Eusebio's firm supporter, was at Guadalajara to give him a favorable hearing. Consequently, without delay, the Audiencia issued an order that the royal cédula be enforced in Nueva Vizcaya and Sonora, and that new converts be not obliged "to go in any manner or under any pretext to serve in mines or on haciendas."[1] In other words, Kino got more than he asked for. He had sought protection for his natives for the term of five years. By the cédula they were now protected for twenty years after baptism. Such a weapon against abuse of the natives was sure to raise up enemies

[1] Kino to the Audiencia of Guadalajara, December 16, 1686. A.G.I. 67–1–36, Guadalajara, 69; Auto of the Audiencia of Guadalajara, December 16, 1686, *ibid.;* Cédula of May 14, 1686, printed in *Hist. Mem.,* I, 108–109.

for him, but for the sake of the cause he was willing to take his chances.

Thus armed, Kino lost no time; in fact, he worked at record speed. His petition was presented on December 16. The Audiencia met, granted his request, gave him his document, and before night he was on his way to his next field of adventure.[1]

LXVI

ON THE CAMINO REAL

We do not know the details of Kino's journey to Sonora. Some future biographer may discover them. We saw him leave Guadalajara for the north country. We next catch sight of him at Los Frayles on Mayo River in the vicinity of Alamos, and then at Conicari, the Jesuit mission in the same region, where three years previously Father Goñi had obtained supplies and laborers for California. No account of his long trek has come to us. But we do have the story of a similar missionary journey over almost precisely the same trail, the twelve hundred miles from the capital to the Mayo River. From this we are able to approximate the outlines of Kino's odyssey.

Years behind Kino, Father Jacob Baegert came to Mexico, went thence by land to Yaqui and from there crossed the Gulf to California.[2] As far as Conicari, places passed through and incidents of the trail were doubtless much the same for both travelers. Baegert's party was larger than Kino's and his pace was considerably slower. With nine other Jesuits Father Jacob left Mexico City on November 16. They had twelve servants and muleteers, mainly Indians, and twenty mules for mounts and to carry the baggage. Thus they made an impressive train. Passing through León, they reached Guadalajara

---

[1] Kino tells us that he left Guadalajara on December 16. *Favores Celestiales*, Parte I, Lib. i, Cap. 2; *Hist. Mem.*, I, 107. See Lesley Byrd Simpson, *The Encomienda in New Spain* (Berkeley, 1929); *Studies in the Administration of the Indians in New Spain* (Berkeley, 1934).
[2] It was in 1750. The story of Baegert's journey is told by himself in a letter to his brother, September 11, 1752. "Brief eines Elsasser aus Californien in Nord Amerika an seinen Bruder in Schlettstadt, 1752, von Pater Jacob Bägert, d.G.J." Aus dem *Patriotischen Elsasser*. Strassburg und Colmar, 1777.

and continued through Tepic, Rosario, Culiacán, and San Felipe, reaching "Los Alamos or Los Frayles" on March 19, more than four months after leaving Mexico. On the west coast both Kino and Baegert probably passed also through Compostela, Mazatlán, and Fuerte. Coming from Mexico City on a Southern Pacific train today the traveler is close to the trail as far as Culiacán. There he leaves it at his right, for the old towns along the camino real, Mocorito, Sinaloa, Fuerte, and Alamos, and all the rest nearly to the Arizona line, were in the foothills or the mountains. There, and not along the railroad, is the ancient Camino Real. There is Old Mexico.

Baegert traveled "soldier fashion," from four to six hours a day, though sometimes eight or ten hours "in order to reach an inn, which means water for man and beast." His party went thus slowly in order to spare their animals for the long, hard journey. Here and there they stopped a week or more at a place, for priests and other inhabitants generously offered the travelers their best hospitality. The visit broke the monotony of life for the hosts, who rarely saw newly arrived Europeans. And besides, during these stops the Jesuits held high-pressure revival meetings.

Outside of the cities and towns most of their camps were in the open, with an occasional stop at some hacienda. At first the Jesuits slept on their mattresses in two tents. Beyond Tepic, where the hot country began, for protection against insects, scorpions, and snakes, each one slept in his own little tent, "which, supported by poles, was hung up lengthwise of the mattress and tucked well under it" to keep out vermin. The roads were rough, stony, mountainous, unimproved, and in most places mere mule trails; in fact "just as they were a year after the creation of the World."

Baegert had recently come from verdant, timber covered, and thickly settled Alsace, and he was struck by the sterility of the country and the sparseness of population along his trail. His comments are colored by homesickness and his customary pessimism. "If all the cultivated land between Mexico and Hiaqui were put together," he said, "one could walk through it in an hour." Excepting the widely separated towns strung along the trail, from León forward the whole country was "a wilderness full of mountains but without forests, . . .

Photo by North

The Camino Real in Lower California

The Plaza of Fuerte, Sinaloa

The author building road in Guadalupe Canyon

God knows I never saw anything like the woods by the Ill or the forest of Hagenau." Poor homesick Nordic.

The aridity of the terrain depressed him. Often they had to carry water from one camp to the next. "All the streams and stagnant water in the same stretch of country would not fill a river half the size of the Rhine. . . . Several times we drank from a hole which we dug in the sand of a river bed. . . . Often we drank from a ditch, or a cavity in a rock a yard and a half in width, where some of the previous year's rain still remained for the consolation of travelers, insects, and beasts. This was not to everyone's taste, but we managed to drink it and thanked Heaven for it." At another season, of course, where he now saw the dry sand of the stream bed, Baegert would have found roaring torrents. And perhaps he would have complained at that.

For food Father Jacob had mostly sun-dried beef (tasajo or jerky) and tortillas, which he described for his German friends as "cakes made of Indian corn and warmed on a little piece of iron. . . . The so-called tamales are miserable stuff. . . . They are nothing but Indian corn dampened and grated, then rolled up again like an unshucked ear of corn, wrapped in some of the corn husks and eventually eaten. During our journey I was once obliged from stern necessity to eat this stuff for ten days." It is too bad for Baegert that he did not have rose-hued glasses such as Kino always wore. The two men represented diametrically opposite types.

"Throughout the whole dreadful journey," he continued, "Guadalajara is the best city after Mexico, and outside of these two cities and two others there is no attempt at architecture beyond one story of unbaked brick." The tree-grown plazas and the arched and columned portales of the little pueblos do not seem to have interested him. The missionary at Mocorito had recently roofed his new church with cedar. This, said Baegert, "is the only church from Tepique forward which is built of stone and mortar." "The streets and the floors of the houses differ in no way from the open fields. For windows they have only light holes, with a few bars across them as a protection against thieves and murderers but not against bats. . . . Nothing better than this is to be seen. It is not surprising to find such great and general poverty, for the whole country has absolutely nothing to offer but a few unfortunate gold and silver mines."

After thus decrying the poverty he saw, Baegert was just as crochety at signs of wealth. "I have seen everywhere, but especially in Culiacán and Los Alamos, even during times of fasting, and when they came to us to confession as we passed through, such finery among the women as I scarcely ever saw in Mexico, not to speak of Alsace. For with astonishment and pity I have seen many a woman dressed in velvet cloth of gold, while in Alsace many hundreds of horses and cows are far better housed than these vain and pitiable children of Adam." Alsace always has taken good care of its horses and cows. Father Jacob was scandalized, too, by the gay dress of some of the Mexican clergy, "yellow stockings, brown knee breeches, a white waistcoat, a red silk scarf, a brown cloak, a battered little peaked hat, with a green and gold ribbon! In this costume one of them met us one Sunday and accompanied us through the village. It is true that this dress is not prescribed for the clergy, but it is the custom of the country."

And so poor Baegert thought it a hard trail which he had traveled. But Father Jacob was a pessimist. He wrote like a man with chronic dyspepsia. These things which to him looked so bad or so worthless, to optimistic Kino no doubt were matters of interest and delighted wonderment. One was perhaps as far from literal reality as the other. But what is reality? Is it what one sees, or what he thinks he sees?

LXVII

GOD REPAYS WITH LIBERAL INTEREST

Kino was at Los Frayles on February 13, 1687, and he wrote from Conicari two days later. Los Frayles was a rich silver region in the vicinity of the modern Alamos. The mines got their name from some columns of white rocks resembling hooded friars, or frayles, which one sees perched high up in a mountain near that city. The silver deposits had been discovered at the very time when Atondo and Kino were struggling to Christianize California. The coincidence was regarded as a divine disposition and a most favorable omen.[1] The rush was still going strong, and Father Eusebio responded to its Western spirit.

At Conicari Kino met the southbound mail, and in order not to lose the opportunity he sat down on February 15 and wrote to Father Juan Marín and to the Duchess. The new mines at Los Frayles were now the talk of the whole frontier, and they filled Kino's two letters. On the way from Mexico he had heard a variety of opinions as to their value. "Some whom I have met have related prodigies of their plentiful and rich metals, and others, though they are in the minority, have said that they are of small moment, only surface deposits, and without sufficient depth."

Kino as usual was among the chief optimists. "Yesterday and the day before yesterday, in order to reach this holy mission of Conicari, I passed through the mines of Los Frayles themselves . . . and I have just seen and recognized most palpably how very clearly and certainly are verified the words of the new and very Catholic royal cédula of his Majesty, God spare him," namely, that for every peso spent from the real hacienda in conversions, God "always repays . . . with liberal increase." Now, indeed, "it is very well seen that our Lord is repaying liberally all the costs which . . . may be entailed in promoting the conversion of the Californias and in the near-by Guaimas, Seris, and Pimas and other heathendoms. And it cannot have happened without particular disposition of the sovereign Lord that, at the same time that, with so Catholic funds, his Majesty during these four or five years has sent us to the conquest and conversion of the Californias,

---

[1] Father Joseph Neumann, learning from Kino of the decision made in March to reoccupy California, wrote from the Tarahumar country: "It is surprising that immediately after this decision had been reached, rich silver mines were discovered in Sinaloa, just opposite California, which will give to the royal exchequer a much larger income than the presidio and the missions will require." (Neumann to Stowasser, Sisoguichic, July 29, 1686. Latin manuscript in the City archive of Prague. Printed in Stöcklein, *Neue Welt-Bott*, I, No. 32). At a later time Kino wrote: "We have seen and we now see how at this very time and in the very years and months of the expenditures for this above-mentioned enterprise of the Californias, God our Lord granted the discovery of the very rich mines of the camps which they call Los Frailes, Los Alamos, and Guadalupe. These posts are opposite, near to, and on the same parallels of twenty-five and twenty-six degrees as California, which through these Catholic expenditures it was the intention to conquer . . . for our holy Catholic faith." (Kino, *Favores Celestiales*, Parte V, Lib. ii, Cap. 2; *Hist. Mem.*, II, 237–238.)

here in the very sight of the same Californias there should be discovered such wealth that many prudent men unanimously acknowledge and confess that they have not seen such treasure anywhere in the country thus far discovered." Among the personages met by Kino here and who entered into his subsequent life was General Domingo de Terán (or Therán), who with "wealthy gentlemen and merchants of the vicinity" was building at the scene of the rush a real or mining town, with casas reales, church, and residences ranged round a plaza.

That the diggings were rich Kino was convinced. Of forty-three mines explored each one was sufficient to establish a new camp. "The poorest are of four marks per quintal and the best of forty, fifty, or sixty marks per quintal, when tested by fire, and by quicksilver from twenty-four to seventy marks. . . . Many more mines can be opened, . . . and if they establish the royal quicksilver depots at this new camp the royal fifths will be greatly increased." In short, the generosity of God in making known these rich mines at this very time was "enough to edify one and to surprise the Universal Orb." [1]

The mines did indeed prove to be fabulously rich, a branch of the mint was established there, Alamos became a beautiful city, and the wives of the mine owners were enabled to wear the velvet cloth of gold and the dazzling jewelry which so scandalized Baegert a few years later.

[1] Kino to Father Juan Marín, Conicari, February 15, 1687. Kino to the Duchess, same place and date. Original Spanish manuscript in the central archives of the Jesuit Order.

In Pima Land

LXVIII

THE WELCOME

ROM CONICARI OUR BLACKROBE CONTINUED NORTHWARD, arriving in Sonora at the end of February. Without loss of time he proceeded to Oposura,[1] now Moctezuma, there to confer with Manuel González, the father visitor of Sonora. The importance of Oposura as a religious center in the olden days is reflected by the truly monumental church still facing south on the plaza and which, viewed from an angle as the traveler tops the ridge forming the northern rim of the town, looks like some ponderous Roman fortress of ancient days. Once seen it is never to be forgotten. The visitador of the Sonora missions occupied an important place. Customarily the provincial of a Jesuit province made an annual tour of his jurisdiction. But in the Province of New Spain, embracing so vast a district, this was impossible, and only rarely did a provincial reach the remote district of Sonora. Consequently the visitador was essentially a vice-provincial. So to González Kino went for orders. On the day of his arrival began that close association which ended fifteen years later only with the death of González on a desert trail which the two apostolic men were traveling together.

Here at Oposura was made the decision by which Father Eusebio was sent to his permanent destination. His hope had been to go to the Seris, renew his friendship with them, and from their country soon return to California. But other heathen called. At Cucurpe, the last mission on the upper San Miguel River, Father Aguilar was stationed, on the outer edge of Christendom. He had been asking González for a Jesuit to carry the Gospel a step further into the Pima

---

[1] On Río Moctezuma, a branch of the Río Yaqui. In his Inocente, Apostólica, y Gloriosa Muerte, Kino says he went to Cumpas to see González. This is not a contradiction, as Cumpas and Oposura were close together.

heathendom, just beyond. In fact he was at Oposura at the same time as Kino. There was another consideration. Some of the Pimas were restless, and were threatening adjacent Spanish settlements.[1] Missionaries could help tame them. So to Cucurpe, fifty leagues to the northwest, González and Aguilar escorted the new reaper in the missionary harvest.[2] From there he would push forward to a new outpost.

En route Kino saw several persons of importance, some of them destined to be his neighbors and fellow laborers to the end of his days. At San Juan, the military and political capital, he talked with Castillo, alcalde mayor of Sonora, "who with the great respectfulness which characterizes him, gave obedience to the royal cédula and the royal provision." These were the documents by which Kino was promised protection for his Indians against slavery in the mines and on haciendas. Castillo kissed the papers, placed them above his head, and murmured, "los beso, los obedesco, y los pongo sobre mi cabeza."[3] Swinging westward now, Kino went to Valle de Sonora, the historic spot made famous by Cabeza de Vaca, Coronado, and Ibarra, when Europeans first came upon the scene. Here, at Guépaca,[4] he saw Father Juan Muñoz de Burgos, rector of the district to which Cucurpe belonged. Father Muñoz would be Kino's immediate religious superior, as Castillo was his political chief. The padlocked, dilapidated old church now facing the plaza of Guépaca from the northwest corner and still bearing on its façade the symbol JHS sadly reflects the change which has overcome the land since that day when Kino and Muñoz there first met.

Crossing the next range westward now, the travelers entered the valley of San Miguel River, and ascended its banks through the old mission towns of Opodepe and Tuape, to Cucurpe, all three under the charge of Father Aguilar. The church at Cucurpe—"en donde cantó la paloma—the place where the dove sang"—perched high on a bluff above the San Miguel, was the last Christian temple on that fron-

[1] Chief Oôcagui, dubbed "Canito" or "Grayhead," "governor and captain general" of the heathen Pima villages near the Spanish border, had just been sentenced to hanging for conspiracy with hostile tribes (Causa Criminal Contra Canito. MS in the Parral Archives. By mistake a modern label on the expediente calls the chief "Canuto").
[2] Kino, Favores Celestiales, Parte III, Lib. iv, Cap. 8; Hist. Mem., II, 109.
[3] "I kiss them, I obey them, I place them above my head."
[4] Now called Guépac, or Huépac.

tier. Its picturesque ruins, eloquent of the past, can still be seen on the same spot, looking down on the modern village in the flat beside the river far below. The man from Segno was at the very portal of the heathendom which he had come to conquer with gentleness and the Faith.[1]

LXIX

THE SONORA FRINGE

Behind Kino as he faced north and west from Cucurpe lay Sonora, the Christendom which would serve as his base and support, and whose boundaries he hoped to extend. Sonora was old. It had a considerable Spanish population, devoted mainly to mining and cattle raising, but in the wider valleys also to agriculture. Because European influence had progressed from south to north, the southern Spanish settlements were more ancient and the towns larger than those in the north. The bulk of the inhabitants were of native stock—Opatas in the upper Sonora and Yaqui valleys, and south of them Lower Pimas, Yaquis, and Mayos. In most of the Indian towns the Jesuits had worked for half a century or more. The province already had a tradition of apostolic labors and missionary heroes, and was dotted with church towers whose bells daily called the people to worship and toil. Some of the oldest missions had already been secularized—that is, turned over to the parish clergy—and the erstwhile neophytes were being absorbed into the racial mixture that goes to make up the present day Sonora population.[2]

Cucurpe was near the outer edge of the mountain country. To the west, beyond low sierras, was the wide coastal plain, broken by still smaller ridges. Eastward, Sonora presented a series of rugged mountain chains. The region, indeed, is a vast physiographic washboard,

---

[1] Kino, *Favores Celestiales,* Parte I, Lib. i, Cap. 3; *Hist. Mem.*, I, 109–110; II, 239. Opodepe at this time was a mining town as well as the seat of a Jesuit mission.

[2] Precious details regarding many of the ranches, mining camps, and missions of Sonora are contained in the record of the official tour of inspection made by General Isturiz a few months before Kino arrived on the scene (Visita que practicó el Gral. Gabriel de Isturiz en la Provincia de Sonora. 1685. Original manuscript in the Parral Archives).

with its corrugations running north and south. A journey across it from west to east is like a trip in a roller coaster—shown on a slow screen. The valleys between the sierras are sometimes mere canyons, but in spots are wide and very fertile. Over the first range to the east lay the inexpressibly beautiful valley of Sonora River, the original core of the province, where Spanish settlements had grown up around the native towns of Banámichi, Aconchi, Guépaca, Arizpe, Bacanuche, Bacoachi, and others—all still there today. Beyond the next range eastward—a very high one—in the valley of Moctezuma River, lay Cumpas, Oposura, Batuco, and settlements farther south; across the next sierra on Río Bavispe were Oputo, Guasabas, and Bacadéguachi; further east, over another great range, passable only by the dizziest of mule trails, on the north-flowing arm of Bavispe River, were Guachinera, Bazeraca, and Bavispe. Spiritual lord of the Bavispe Valley was veteran Father Polici, who had founded and now literally held the fort at the mission of Bazeraca.[1] Still beyond, Sonora was separated from Chihuahua by the yet greater Sierra Madre. Over all this rugged country Kino was destined to ride back and forth innumerable times in succeeding years, until he knews its trails as few others knew them.

Northeast of the Sonora settlements lived the Apaches and their allies, ruthless enemies of the Spaniards in the south and of the Pima Indians in the west. The Apaches occupied the country that is now southeastern Arizona, living notably on the upper Gila River and in the Chiricahua Mountains—the region of the Apache reservations today. The most troublesome bands were the Chiricahuas. Intermingled with them were the Jocomes, a broken-down tribe which lost its identity in the eighteenth century. Frequently associated with the Apaches and Jocomes were the Sumas and Janos, who lived farther eastward in and beyond the Sierra Madre, mainly in Chihuahua.

These hostile tribes, whose very names became a doleful refrain in Sonora history, were a constant scourge to the Spanish settlements. Their rôle on the border was a logical corollary to the northward advance of the Spanish frontier in the seventeenth century. When first heard of, the Apaches, though warlike, covered a narrow range and were devoted somewhat to agriculture. But the Spaniards brought

---

[1] Now spelled Bazerac.

Ruin of Mission Church at Cucurpe

Valle de Sonora, view from below Aconchi

Jesuit Church at Aconchi

A general view of Arizpe, from the east

The Valley at Fronteras

Church at Bazerac. Side view.

horses to the frontier, the Apaches acquired them, and their range widened. The Spaniards had also vast herds of cattle which the Apaches came to prize as food. In other words, the Spaniards raised stock and at the same time gave the Apaches the means of stealing it. As the 17th century waned, the raids became longer and longer, until by Kino's day the Apaches not only ravaged border missions and outlying ranches, but penetrated the very heart of Sonora, supplementing theft with fire and murder. The blame was not one-sided. Spanish soldiery pursued the invaders, slew the warriors when they could catch them, captured women and children and kept them as slaves. The Spanish-American soldiery were as ruthless as the Anglo-Americans who a century and a half later inherited the hatred of the children of these same sons of the desert.

The Apache has left his mark on the map. His resistance stopped the Spanish advance about where the line was finally fixed between two nations. A boundary drawn by the treaty of Guadalupe Hidalgo [1] cut the Apache tribe in two, leaving part of them on each side. The mistake was corrected six years later by the Gadsden Purchase, which recognized a frontier dating from the seventeenth century. It was already marked out when Kino came upon the scene. When he arrived, the northern line of Sonora settlements ran roughly through Bacanuche and Bacoachi on the upper Sonora, Cuquiárichi and Fronteras on north-flowing Río Fronteras, and Batepito on the same stream. Just south of Fronteras flourished the mission of Cuchuta. From Batepito the frontier swung southward up Bavispe River to Bavispe and Bazeraca. In Chihuahua the presidio of Janos was a bulwark against the Janos, Sumas and adjacent tribes. The garrisons of Fronteras and Janos, some two hundred miles apart, co-operated to watch all that long border, assisted by the citizen soldiery of the interior. Between the two presidios lay the Sierra Madre, through which the troops made their difficult way by Guadalupe, Púlpito, or Bavispe Pass. Favorite watering places along the way were Agua Prieta and San Bernardino, points now square on the international boundary. Both garrisons were almost constantly on the move, patrolling that infested line, driving marauders from ranches, missions, and towns,

[1] At the Gila River.

pursuing them into the mountains, winning or losing battles. The return of the soldiery with a band of captives was a signal for bell ringing and public thanksgiving. It is easy to understand why in Sonora even today it is common for an irate parent to call a difficult child "un puro Apache—a regular Apache!" The lore of the Apache frontier yields nothing in romance to that of the Scottish Border, and for the writer who has equal gift to gather and portray it there awaits a renown not excelled by that achieved by Sir Walter Scott. In both cases it is partly true that the "romance is crime in the past tense."

LXX

PIMERÍA ALTA

Sonora was at Kino's back. In front of him lay Pimería Alta, the vast, unsubdued and little known Indian country to which he had been assigned. It was the land of the Upper Pimas, as its name signifies. Usually known in Kino's day as the Pimería, it was sometimes called Pimería Alta to distinguish it from Pimería Baja, land of the Lower Pimas. The real name of the Pima tribe is Ootam, but they were nicknamed Pimas from *pim,* their word of negation. Pimería Alta included the area now embraced in northwestern Sonora and southwestern Arizona, districts lying on opposite sides of an international boundary line. But there was no such boundary in Kino's day. North and south, Pimería Alta extended from the San Ignacio River to the Gila, and east and west from San Pedro River to the Gulf. It was then included in the province of Sonora, itself a division of the kingdom of Nueva Vizcaya, whose capital was Parral. It continued to be a part of Sonora till the middle of the nineteenth century, when the northern portion was cut off by the Gadsden Purchase and became a part of the United States. But that was more than a century and a half after Kino entered Pima Land. In his day there was no United States, nor was there any thought of such an entity. All America was a colony of Europe, and Pima Land was a part of New Spain.

Kino found Pimería Alta occupied by different divisions of the great Pima nation, most of which have representatives in the same region today. Like so many other North American tribes, they have never left their homelands since the Europeans first visited them. In the southeastern portion of the area, nearest the Spanish settlements, were the people then regarded as the Pimas proper. They lived on all the slopes of the watershed which zigzags roughly westward from Huachuca Mountain to Nogales, having villages on the upper waters of the south-flowing Sonora, San Miguel, and Cocóspora rivers, on the west-flowing San Ignacio and Altar, and on the north-flowing San Pedro and Santa Cruz.[1] These are the modern names of the streams. This area was like a relatively flat and very irregular cone, with its apex in Huachuca Mountain. Its whorl of streams made something like a geographical cowlick, with Huachuca Mountain as the bald spot. Westward the people called Pimas extended down the Altar Valley to and including Oquitoa, and down the San Ignacio some distance below the modern city of the same name. Beyond them the Piman people called Sobas ranged along the lower San Ignacio and Altar rivers, and along the Gulf Coast farther west. Caborca was a principal town of the Soba tribe.[2]

North of the Pimas proper lived the Sobaípuris (Sobajípuris). A line drawn eastward from Tubac through Fairbank approximates the old boundary between the two peoples. Of the Sobaípuris there were three groups: one living all down the San Pedro River northward from the vicinity of Fairbank;[3] another on the middle Santa Cruz between San Xavier del Bac and Picacho; a third on the Gila River from the Casa Grande westward nearly to the Bend of Gila River. These last, then called the Gila Pimas, occupied a region corresponding to the present day Pima Reservation. In the eighteenth century, after Kino departed, the eastern Sobaípuris were destroyed or driven from San Pedro River by the Apaches. Their descendants today, and the descendants of the Santa Cruz River group, are to be found mainly on the Pima and San Xavier reservations.

---

[1] A few lived as far east as Teuricachi Valley, in the vicinity of Cuquiárichi (Causa Criminal Contra Canito, Parral Archives).

[2] The other Pimas sometimes called these coast-dwellers "Desnudos" or "Naked People."

[3] Shortly before Kino arrived, Captain Pacheco Zevallos broke up a threatened alliance between the border heathen Pimas and the Jocomes, Janos, and Sumas. At this time Quíburi was a settlement of Jocomes and Pimas intermingled (Causa Criminal Contra Canito, Parral Archives).

West of Santa Cruz River were the Pápagos, the name meaning "The Bean Eaters." They lived in scattered villages and occupied a wide range. Some of the Pápago settlements south of the Arizona line have been abandoned. North of that line the Pápagos still live in the same general area and to a great extent on the very sites they occupied in Kino's day. They are among the tribes which have been least disturbed by the white man.

Pimas, Sobas, Sobaípuris, and Pápagos were all of Piman stock and all spoke the same tongue. All were Upper Pimas. On the northwest Pima Land was fringed by Yuman tribes—Opas and Cocomaricopas on the lower Gila; Yumas, Quíquimas, Cócopas and others on the lower Colorado. These people spoke and still speak a language altogether distinct from that of the Pimas. On the west coast, below the Sobas, were the wild Tepocas and Seris, who, like the Upper Pimas, offered a wide-open field for missionaries.

Pimería Alta in Kino's day had a population of perhaps 30,000.[1] They were an agricultural people in the main. When Kino first visited them the Indians of the Altar, the San Pedro, and the Santa Cruz valleys all raised crops by irrigation,—cotton for clothing, and maize, beans, calabashes, melons, and wheat for food. The Pápagos were somewhat less advanced in this respect, but they were conspicuous for their extensive bean patches, and at Sonóita, at least, they had acéquias, or irrigating ditches. The Yumas and Cocomaricopas raised large crops but without artificial watering. Much more notable than the acéquias in use at the coming of the Spaniards, were the remains of many miles of aqueducts and the huge ruins of cities which had long before been abandoned, structures which are attributed by scholars to the ancestors of the Pimas.[2]

---

[1] See Carl Sauer, *Aboriginal Population of Northwestern Mexico* (Berkeley, 1935); Kino, *Hist. Mem.*; Manje, *Luz de Tierra Incógnita*.

[2] Velarde, Luís, "Descripción particular de las naciones . . . de la Provincia de Sonora," in Manje (Mange), *Luz de Tierra Incógnita*, 333–342 (Mexico, 1925); Russell, Frank, *The Pima Indians* (Washington, 1908); *Rudo Ensayo . . . de la Provincia de Sonora*, edited by Buckingham Smith (San Augustín de la Florida, 1863).

On the San Pedro the Pimas proper, as they were then considered, ended with the village of Huachuca (on the site of Babacómari Ranch), and on the Santa Cruz with Tumacácori. The railroad from Tumacácori on the Santa Cruz to Fairbank on the San Pedro approximates the northern row of their settlements. According to Kino, the Sobaípuris began with Gaybanipitea near Fairbank on the San Pedro and with Bac on the Santa Cruz. The author of the *Rudo Ensayo*, writing half a century later, included in the Sobaípuris only the Pimas of San Pedro River. The Gila Pimas, because they are the ones best known to modern ethnologists, are

Such were the people in whose midst Kino soon found himself. The general facts above set forth were known imperfectly or not at all when Kino came. It was he who first made them patent. To learn them cost him the toil incident to thousands of miles in the saddle. Pima Land was the stage for the new drama which now began, and in which the man from Segno played the leading part.

LXXI

PROSPECTING

Kino lost no time at Cucurpe. He was eager to visit the people among whom he was to work, and he anticipated the outdoor joy of exploring their country. So in spite of their long ride from Oposura, on the very day after their arrival at Aguilar's mission the three fathers set forth for the new field of labor. This was March 13, 1687. It was in the very month when La Salle, the great French explorer, was assassinated in the wilds of Texas.

Five leagues up the valley of the San Miguel River they came to the village of Bamotze, or Cosari, home of Chief Coxi. On the way they passed El Pintor, the cliff with the mysterious carved symbols, and El Soldado, where red canyon walls overhang the midstream trail. Coxi was absent when Kino arrived, but his people were assembled and waiting, for Aguilar had notified them the day before; and they gave the visitors an affectionate welcome, "for, months and years before, they had asked for fathers and holy baptism." Father González baptized a dying headman at the heathen's own request. This was a good omen, notwithstanding the day was the 13th. Cosari was now given a new name, and we are told the reason for the choice. "On account of the noble picture of Nuestra Señora de los Dolores, which some months previously, in May, with his very Christian piety was given me by the excellent painter, Juan Correa, we named as advocate of this place Neustra Señora de los Dolores."[1] In this way

now designated as the "Pimas proper." But in Kino's day they were frequently listed as Sobaípuris, or Soba y Jípuris.

[1] Kino to the procurator of Mexico, Cucurpe, March 13, 1687. Quoted by Father Adam Gilg in a letter dated at Mexico, October 8, 1687. Printed in German in Stöcklein, *Neue Welt-Bott,*

Dolores became associated with one of Mexico's most famous artists. Kino brought more than one painting to the wilderness.

How they camped that night and succeeding nights Father Eusebio does not tell us. He was more interested in seeing the country than in details of eating and sleeping. His work would embrace more than one village, and he was eager to learn what was farther on.

Next morning González turned back to Oposura. He had introduced to Pimería Alta its most remarkable Black Robe. "Girdle Fathers" the Pápagos now call the Jesuits, to distinguish them from the gray-robed sons of Saint Francis. As soon as he had gone, Kino and Aguilar saddled up and set forth westward over the sierra to visit the Pima villages in the valley of the San Ignacio River. For Kino this was the first of many horseback rides over that mountain range.

At every turn in the road there was something new. For several miles their trail ran westward over a grassy plateau covered with mesquite. As they advanced they ascended the slope of Sierra de Comedio, or del Torreón. At the top they threaded a narrow, tortuous pass through a deep notch in the mountain. As they descended the other side Kino saw at his left, high up on the rocky shoulder of the pass, the Torreón, or huge black, tower-shaped cliff which gives the Sierra its alternative name. Down the western slope they wound their way over flower-strewn and mesquite-covered hills, then descended to an arroyo. Crossing it, guiding northwestward, and skirting the Sierra, after a ride of ten leagues from Dolores they arrived at the San Ignacio River. At the point where they reached the stream, near a grove of great cottonwoods, they entered the village of Cabórica,[1] "whose inhabitants, with their chief," says Kino, "met us carrying bows and arrows, and to our great pleasure welcomed us kindly. We named the place San Ignacio," and San Ignacio it still is today. The camino real from San Francisco to Mexico City until recently passed right down the middle of the village.

Next day, swinging north up the fertile valley, skirting the sparkling

---

I, No. 33; Kino, Inocente, Apostólica, y Gloriosa Muerte del V. Pe. Francisco Xavier Saeta, VII, 189. Original manuscript in the Biblioteca Nacional, Mexico. Evidently Correa gave Kino a picture of Nuestra Señora de los Remedios also. See the journey of Kino and Salvatierra to Santa Clara Mountain in 1701.

[1] Also spelled Quibori. Today one reaches Dolores more easily from Magdalena than from San Ignacio.

Photo by Bolton

The pass through Sierra del Torreón

Photo by Bolton

Site of Mission Dolores, on the hill

Photo by Bolton

On Cocóspora River, near Remedios

river and its continuous groves of great alamos, or cottonwoods, at a distance of three leagues [1] they reached the village of Imuris, perched high on the bluffs at the right, between the forks of San Ignacio and Cocóspora rivers, and looking westward across the former stream. Here the cottonwoods were even larger than at San Ignacio. The scene presented a sharp contrast with arid California. They named this place San José. Unlike San Ignacio, here in modern times the native name has prevailed over that of the saint. It is still generally called Imuris. Near by was, and is, the peak of Ubúriqui (Cabórica), or "Castle of the Wind" concerning which the natives told superstitious tales.[2]

After a short chat with the villagers, Kino swung eastward up the pleasant alameda of Cocóspora River. For a few miles he traversed a gradually ascending plain, then near Babasaqui he entered the canyon. Here the gorge of the river is deep, narrow, and picturesque, and the swift stream winds in and out among the cottonwoods. Kino's horse no doubt in gratitude drank and pawed the cool sparkling water, and the pack mules brayed their thankfulness. If Kino's eyes were sharp he saw at the left the caves round which romantic legends now hover. Emerging from the canyon he reached the mouth of another stream. Swinging to the right and up this branch, he crossed the valley of Aquituni, then entered a gorge where the tributary breaks through rocky red hills.[3] This canyon passed, a mile or so farther up the valley he reached a large Indian village which thrived on the lands watered by the little river. Coágibubig the Indians called it. Here, on a commanding hill, on the left bank of the stream, he selected a site for a mission to be called Nuestra Señora de los Remedios. The village, the river, and the ruins of the mission he later built there still bear the names which Kino gave them.

Saddling up next day, he ascended the river over rolling country to Ojo de Agua, the fine spring which still feeds the stream. Then he climbed the grass-covered divide between Remedios River and the

[1] By speedometer it is seven miles.
[2] Ubúrique is evidently the same word as Caborca, or Cabórica. See Manje and Velarde for folk-tales of this region.
[3] The wagon road today leaves the stream, turns to the right, winds over red hills, and drops down to the stream again at Remedios. Men on horseback follow the stream-bed up the canyon.

San Miguel. Close by on his left loomed cone-shaped Sierra Azul,[1] "half revealed, half concealed" behind her veil of dark-blue haze. Finally, descending the southward slope, he followed a poplar-fringed and sandy bottomed arroyo (not favorable to automobile travel, as experience has shown me) and on through open country dotted with live oak to Dolores.

The new padre had ridden his first circuit in the Pimería, a jaunt of some seventy-five miles. The little quadrangle between the San Miguel and the San Ignacio rivers, embracing the four native villages, Dolores, San Ignacio, Imuris, and Remedios, was the nucleus and base of the vast region which in years to come Kino made his missionary realm. For his abode and headquarters he chose Cosari. The welcome everywhere given him by the natives had warmed the missionary's heart. "In all places they received with love the word of God for the sake of their eternal salvation. We returned, thanks to the Lord, safe and rejoicing, to . . . Dolores. Father Aguilar went on to Cucurpe, and I began to catechize the people and to baptize the children."[2]

LXXII

DOLORES

The place chosen by Kino for his hearth site was one of peculiar fitness and beauty. It is a commonplace to say that the missionaries usually selected the most fertile spots for their temples. This is true. But it is instructive to give the reason. They ordinarily founded their missions near the villages of the Indians for whom they were designed. And these were usually placed at the most fertile spots along the rich valleys of the streams. The natives were the engineers. And so it was with the village where Kino founded Dolores.

Near where Cosari stood the little San Miguel breaks through a narrow canyon whose sheer western walls rise several hundred feet

---

[1] Blue Mountain, sometimes called Cerro de los Remedios.
[2] Kino to the procurator, May 13, 1687, *loc. cit.* Kino, *Favores Celestiales*, Parte I, Lib. i, Cap. 4; *Hist. Mem.*, I, 111–112.

in height. Above and below the canyon the river broadens out into rich vegas of irrigable bottom lands, half a mile or more in width and several miles in length. On the east the vale is hemmed in by near-by Sierra de Santa Teresa, on the west by more distant Sierra del Torreón. Closing the lower valley and hiding Cucurpe stands Cerro Prieto; and cutting off the observer's view toward the north rises grand and rugged Sierra Azul. At the canyon where the river breaks through, the western mesa juts out and forms a cliff, approachable only from the west.

On this promontory, protected on three sides from attack, and affording a magnificent view, Kino placed the mission of Dolores. Here till recently stood its ruins, in full view of the valley above and below, of the mountain walls on the east and the west, the north and the south, and within the sound of the rushing cataract of the San Miguel as it courses through the gorge. This meager ruin on the cliff, consisting in 1911 of a mere fragment of an adobe wall and saddening piles of debris [1] was the most venerable of the many mission remains in all Arizona and northern Sonora, for Our Lady of Sorrows was mother of them all, and for nearly a quarter of a century was the home of the remarkable missionary who built them.

Cosari was not only a beautiful site; it was also a strategic location. Chief Coxi, when Kino arrived, was not merely a village headman, but was also cacique or captain-general of many settlements toward the west. This gave Kino a peculiar hold on the Pimas over a wide stretch of country. When Father Eusebio first visited Dolores Coxi was absent, but he soon returned and their joint work among the Pimas began. Through the captain-general Kino at once sent friendly messages to remote villages, telling them that he had come as a friend.

In his first work of conversion Kino was greatly assisted by the older missions to the south and east. This was a typical procedure. By their help, he wrote two months after his arrival, "I am able to

---

[1] It was in 1911 that I first visited the site of Dolores. Since then even the fragment of a wall has disappeared. The above description, published by me in 1919, has subsequently been copied or paraphrased by several writers. Along the ridge west of the spot here indicated there are archeological vestiges of an extensive mission plant, such as Kino frequently described.

maintain myself in this newly discovered corner of the world." Father Roxas of Ures gave him provisions, horses, "and some silver." Most useful of all the aids were Francisco Cantor, an able interpreter in the Pima tongue, and Francisco's brother, a blind temastián or native teacher, both of whom also Kino obtained from Father Roxas. "Although blind as to corporeal sight," the temastián was "an apostolic Indian very well instructed in the things of our Holy Faith," and "with notable care and solicitude he instructed all the Indians of El Bamotze and other neighboring pueblos." [1]

Kino had scarcely started his work when Holy Week arrived—the last week in March that year. Dolores was not yet equipped for so important an occasion, so his neighbors helped him out. He, Aguilar, and Roxas arranged jointly to celebrate Easter at Tuape, a central place downstream with a spacious church. As the festal day approached, cavalcades of Spaniards on horseback and bands of Indians on foot moved toward the appointed rendezvous. Kino took with him more than a hundred Pimas from Dolores, forming a procession as they descended the sandy river trail. What a picture they made! In the ceremonies some forty recently baptized Indian children occupied the center of the stage. In their childish innocence they warmed the hearts of the spectators, especially of the señoras. "The Spanish ladies of the mining town of Opodepe," says Kino, "dressed them richly and adorned them with their best jewels, like new Christians, for the Procession of the Blessed Sacrament, to the delight of all."

Building a mission was not all a matter of pious emotions. There was hard work to do. The missionary often wielded ax, spade, or trowel, swung the lasso, applied the branding iron, or cinched the girth of a groaning mule. Back at Dolores Kino pushed forward his material tasks. Before the end of April, with the aid of the willing natives, he had built on the commanding hill a chapel for services and a simple house for himself. In this time he had baptized thirty

---

[1] Kino to the procurator, March 13, 1687, *loc. cit.;* Roxas to the provincial, Ures, March 31, 1688. Spanish manuscript in the central archives of the Jesuit Order; Velarde, in Manje (Mange), *Luz de Tierra Incógnita,* p. 319 (Mexico, 1926). Gilg was near Dolores early in March, 1688, at which time he brought Kino a package of welcome letters from Freiburg. Kino to ——, Dolores, March 15, 1688. Latin manuscript, Preussische Staatsbibliothek, Berlin.

children, "among them being two sons of the chief." This was a triumph. Influential people were coming into the fold; others would follow. And the natives were tractable. "These Indians are willing to learn, especially the young people," Kino writes, "and they assemble frequently for Christian instruction."

Near the end of April Father Eusebio again made the circuit of San Ignacio, Imuris, and Remedios. In the first two places "things were going well, in spiritual and temporal matters, in Christian teachings, beginnings of baptisms, buildings, planting of crops, etc." [1] In Remedios conditions were less favorable; there someone had sown seeds of opposition. But in spite of this note of discord, Kino's enthusiasm grew with each passing week. At the end of June he reported in his three missions "more than sixty baptisms of infants and some of adults. And the natives of the pueblo of . . . Dolores, thank God, already repeat and chant the prayers and the Christian doctrine, the *Benedicto*, the *Alabado*, and perform the acts of contrition in the same manner as in the pueblos of Christians of long standing."

By this time numerous Indians had moved to Dolores from the country round about. The place now presented a busy building scene, where the natives were making "adobes, doors, windows, etc., for a very good house and church" to replace the temporary structure. And, said Kino, "by the divine grace, very soon the same will be done likewise in the two other pueblos [of San Ignacio and Imuris], for the people are very industrious in such tasks, as well as in raising wheat, maize, and beans." The natives of Remedios were still discontented.

The bells for Dolores arrived from Mexico, an event which the Indians had awaited. "And now," wrote Kino, "they are placed on the little church which we built during the first days. The natives are very fond of listening to their peals, never before heard in these lands. And they are immensely pleased also by the pictures and other ornaments of the Church, and they have very great esteem for the things touching their eternal salvation."

[1] Kino, *Favores Celestiales*, Parte I, Lib. i, Cap. 6; *Hist. Mem.*, I, 113; Kino to the procurator, March 13, 1687, *loc. cit.*

But Kino had still greater news to impart to his friend Mansilla, to whom he was writing. Chief Coxi, himself, and his wife as well, were coming into the fold! They had followed in the footsteps of their two sons. A big event was in store. "The solemn baptism of the governor of this pueblo of . . . Dolores, who likewise is captain-general of the rest of the Pimas as far as the Sea of California," wrote Kino, "is awaited with more interest than the coming of his god-father, who, it appears, will be Captain Josef Romo de Vivar." Captain Josef was an influential citizen at Bacanuche, a mining town fifty miles over the mountains to the east.

The much-heralded affair occurred just a month later, July 31. It was the most notable gathering at Dolores thus far. "We celebrated the feast of our Father San Ignacio with the baptism of our governor and his wife, and more than forty of the adults and children." Coxi was christened Don Carlos, in honor of the king. The occasion was more than a local affair. To it came "some Spanish gentlemen from Bacanuche, and Father . . . Aguilar and his choir from Cucurpe. There were solemn vespers, a sung Mass, a procession, etc." Most important of all, "there came also to attend the same function and fiesta five chiefs from the principal villages of the interior." The result was most cheering. "Although hitherto some of them had been little attached to our Holy Catholic Faith, since the fiesta and the ceremony of the baptisms they have been so content and consoled that they are requesting father missionaries for themselves and for their countrymen."

Kino's tact now manifested itself. Before him was a great missionary harvest already white. He needed all the aid he could get. There were so many things that he lacked—wax for candles, beads for presents, clothing for his naked neophytes, not that they cared so much, but they must be civilized. Alms for the spread of the Faith were the fashion of the day. Mansilla had asked permission to help. It would be unkind not to give him a chance. Kino was not unkind.

"And since your Reverence says that you wish to succor this new mission with some little alms, I do not wish to prevent you from being the co-founder of it and of many others. And so I say that if you should have a very good opportunity and should be pleased to send a little wax, a little sayal, some little chomites, some glass beads, a little Ruan de China, some little blankets, or any of these trifles, they may be delivered . . . to Father Juan Bautista de Ancieta and to Miguel de Espinosa, the muleteer from Mátape, who is a very reliable person. All these things will greatly promote and advance the spiritual and material foundation of these new conversions." [1] Kino was giving Father Mansilla such a fine opportunity!

Six months later Kino's exuberance had not abated one whit. He had been in Dolores just a year. In that brief time, he wrote, "in this vast and very fertile vineyard of the Indian tribes which they call the Pimas, . . . I have been able, through the celestial favors of the heavenly saints, to wash about three hundred Indians in the holy water of baptism. . . . God willing, hundreds, and later, thousands will be gathered into the bosom of our sweet, most holy Mother Church, for about five thousand of the neighboring Indians have come asking at this time with most ardent pleading for holy baptism." This would be an average of more than a dozen visitors a day. They must have been a heavy strain on Kino's larder, and sometimes on his patience. "They envy the happy lot of those in the three new settlements or congregations whose care I have undertaken. In this charge where I am working, a mission having been established, and many very suitable rooms of a house having been built, we are now occupied in the erection of a new church, with the help of some soldiers, and its walls have very happily arisen to a height of several feet."

This success was praised by the visitor, Father González. Early in January, 1689, he inspected Kino's missions, riding with him to San Ignacio, Imuris, and Remedios, and also to Cocóspora, "whither up to this time no father had ever entered." At Dolores "he was so pleased with the structure of the church and the house which had been begun, the Christian teaching, the devotion at prayers, the book of baptisms, the singing school, the rich lands and fine crops," that he "said and wrote that he had not seen a new mission which enjoyed in so short a time so many conveniences and such progress in

[1] Kino to Mansilla, Dolores, June 30, 1687; same to same, Dolores, August 6, 1687. Original Spanish manuscripts in the Huntington Library.

spiritual and temporal matters." Kino's heart swelled with justifiable pride. Six months later he was able to write, "Already the baptisms exceed six hundred . . . and we are continuing with the building of houses and churches." He refers to those in his circuit as well as at Dolores.[1]

LXXIII

THE GOSSIPS CAUSE TROUBLE

It was not all a bed of roses, however. The joys of working with the affable Indians at Dolores were offset by troubles arising elsewhere. Kino at first had found the natives everywhere friendly, willing to work, and attentive to his teachings. But somebody soon began to spread malicious rumors. Father Eusebio does not tell us who the gossips were, but he does record the nature of the tales. He had hardly arrived at Dolores when "a false report was dispatched to the alcalde mayor of . . . San Juan"—this was Castillo—"that these natives, on the coming of the father missionary, had moved away." There was no truth in it. The rumors reached the ears of González and worried him sorely, and to learn the facts he wrote to Tuape, at the time when Kino, Aguilar, and Roxas were celebrating Holy Week there. In reply they wrote a joint letter completely discrediting the rumors. Castillo was convinced.

What Kino called the "Second Opposition" he encountered at Remedios, when he made the second tour of his circuit in April and May, 1687. At San Ignacio and Imuris he found the natives well disposed. But in Remedios they were surly. Satan had been busy there. The Indians told him that they did not wish to be Christians nor have a missionary. "Why?" said Kino. In reply they gave five reasons, prob-

---

[1] Kino to ——, Dolores, March 15, 1688, *loc. cit.;* Kino to De Soto, Dolores, June 15, 1689. Original Spanish manuscript in the central archives of the Jesuit Order; Kino, *Hist. Mem.,* I, 115–116; see also Kino, Inocente, Apostólica, y Gloriosa Muerte del V. Pe. Francisco Xavier Saeta, Libro VII, Cap. iii. In spite of vigorous work on the permanent church of Dolores, it was not ready for dedication till April 26, 1693. The ceremony at that time was a notable event, attended by neighbor Jesuits and by Pimas from long distances (Kino, *Favores Celestiales,* Parte I, Lib. ii, Cap. 6; *Hist. Mem.,* I, 125).

ably not so logically as Kino reviewed them: First, they had heard it said that the fathers had natives hanged. In the second place, "they required so much labor and planting for their churches that no opportunity was left the Indians to plant for themselves." Third, "they pastured so many cattle that the watering places were drying up." Fourth, "they killed the people with the holy oils." Fifth, "they deceived the Indians with false promises and words. I had falsely said that I had a letter or royal cédula of the king our sovereign [protecting them from forced labor in the mines], whereas I had no such letter, for if I had I would have shown it to the Señor lieutenant of Bacanuche."

"These chimeras, discords, and altercations disturbed me greatly," says Kino, "but I recognized at once whence they might have come." The historian here wishes that he had spoken more plainly, naming the offenders. The inference is that his opponents were men who desired a free hand in using the Indians for work in the mines or on their haciendas. The first four complaints of the Indians at Remedios were general and impersonal. Some of them were reflections of a chronic difficulty on missionary frontiers. But the fifth charge was specific and personal. Kino could nail it and he proceeded characteristically to do so.[1]

Two days after returning to Dolores, accompanied by his Indian officials, he set forth east over the mountains twenty leagues to Bacanuche. His reception there was most cordial. "I showed the royal provision and royal cédula to the Señor lieutenant, Captain Francisco Pacheco Zevallos, in whom I found all kindness, and told him of what had happened in . . . Remedios because of the untruths which had been spread so falsely during the preceding days against the fathers. Gradually things were remedied and the calumnies of the malicious and of the Common Enemy were hushed. And although there was no lack of tales and of pretended dangers from persons of little loyalty, the natives of this Pimería became so inclined to our Holy Faith that from places further inland . . . they asked for fathers

[1] Kino's position was made more difficult by the ruthless destruction of the heathen Pima pueblo of Mototicachi, north of Arizpe. Higuera, the soldier who perpetrated the outrage, was condemned to death but escaped and fled. (Autos fhos. sobre . . . la desolación del pueblo de Mototicachi, 1688. Parral Archives.)

and holy baptism."[1] This was not the last time that Kino felt called upon to deal vigorously with calumnies.

[1] Kino, *Favores Celestiales,* Parte I, Lib. i, Caps. 5–7; *Hist. Mem.,* I, 112–115. Venegas, Miguel (Burriel), *Noticia de la California,* II, 89. See also Venegas, *Natural and Civil History of California,* I, 295. "But the hardships which this worthy man suffered from the Indians were the least, or rather not to be compared to those he met with from some Spaniards, against whose violences he was a wall of brass, in favor of his converts. They obstructed his enterprises and prevented his being assisted by others, it being their interest, that the poor Pimas should be branded with the name of rebels and enemies, that they might commit depredations among them, and force the Indians to serve them as slaves." This probably refers especially to a later period.

Wider Horizons

LXXIV

MÁS ALLÁ

WHILE HE WORKED AT DOLORES and rode his seventy-five mile circuit, Kino constantly cast his eyes farther afield. Through Chief Coxi he sent friendly messages to people beyond the range of his own quadrangle, "inviting them likewise to become Christians, saying that for them would be the advantage, for I had come that they might be eternally saved." He did not forget the Seris and Guaymas among whom he had hoped to work, and who were still asking for missionaries. "May the Divine Mother not permit that there be any such delays and waiting for the salvation of so many souls as is usually the case," he wrote to Mansilla.

News from the west and northwest was more intriguing. Five chiefs from the interior had attended the baptism of Chief Coxi. Some of them came from the Altar Valley, near the Sea of California. They asked for missionaries, and they told of populous regions beyond—*más allá*. "God our Lord knows that I should like to go with them at once," Kino wrote Viceroy Monclova. His geographical outlook was expanding, and his feet were beginning to tingle with the lust of the trail. But he could not go yet. He must first put Dolores on a solid foundation.[1]

With the press of tasks in his own pueblos, and the new opportunities beyond the border, Kino asked for two assistants. Fathers Adam Gilg and Marcos Kappus came a year behind him, but Kappus took the place of Aguilar at Cucurpe, and Gilg, though sent to assist

[1] Kino, *Favores Celestiales,* Parte I, Lib. i, Cap. 5; *Hist. Mem.,* I, 112; Kino to Mansilla, Dolores, June 30, 1687, *loc. cit.;* Kino to Mansilla, Dolores, August 6, 1687, *loc. cit.;* Kino to Viceroy Monclova, Dolores, August 30, 1687. Original Spanish manuscript in the Biblioteca Nacional, Lima, Perú.

Kino, went to work among the Seris. So they did not help in the northwestern field now unfolding, and Kino again called for more missionaries. He was partial to North Europeans. "All of us feel a thousand million desires to have news of the coming of some new workers. And if they could be . . . from the North, because these climates are somewhat cold"—he was writing in Sonora on June 15! —"it will be a matter of much consolation, and the harvest will be very great." And when he said "great" he meant it. "Not of thirty or forty souls . . . but of a thousand and more souls for each missionary who may come." It was difficult to resist Kino's salesmanship, and his requests were seconded by González and Castillo.[1]

The appeal bore fruit, four new Jesuits were appointed, Kino was relieved of part of his charges, missionary work was extended into the Altar and upper Cocóspora valleys, and plans were made for the upper Santa Cruz. New names now enter the roll of honor. Father Luís Pineli was assigned to San Ignacio, with near-by Magdalena and El Tupo as visitas or sub-stations; Antonio Arias to Tubutama and Oquitoa, two large villages on the Altar River; Pedro de Sandoval to Sáric and Tucubavia, higher up on the Altar; and Father Juan del Castillejo to Cocóspora. When these Jesuits arrived the proposed distribution was somewhat modified. Early in 1691 Pineli was at San Ignacio, Sandoval at Imuris, and Arias at Tubutama. Castillejo did not come, or soon departed, and Sandoval was assigned to Cocóspora. Remedios also seems to have been entrusted for a time to Sandoval.

These new toilers did not remain long in the vineyard. Kino intimates the reason. "They came in and accomplished some good in this Pimería, but the opposition, obstacles, and false reports to the effect that so many fathers were not needed, since the people were very few, greatly retarded and almost entirely put a stop to matters."[2]

---

[1] Gilg to the procurator, Mexico, October 8, 1687. Printed in German in Stöcklein, *Neue Welt-Bott*, I, No. 33; Roxas to the provincial, Ures, March 31, 1688, *loc. cit.*; Kino to De Soto, Dolores, June 15, 1689, *loc. cit.*; Kino, *Hist. Mem.*, I, 115–116; *Favores Celestiales*, corresponding chapter. Venegas tells us that Father Gilg had to give up his work among the Seris because he could not master their language. Other missionaries had similar difficulties. Venegas, *Noticia de la California*, II, 211; *Natural and Civil History of California*, I, 410.

[2] Kino, *Favores Celestiales*, Parte I, Lib. ii, Caps. 1, 2, 6; *Hist. Mem.*, I, 116, 118–120, 126; Kino, Inocente, Apostólica, y Gloriosa Muerte, Lib. III, Cap. v; Lib. VII, Cap. vi. Some of the new missionaries came from the Tarahumar country, driven out by the revolt of 1690. Neumann tells us that they were American-born and lacked the staying qualities of Jesuits directly from Europe (Neumann, Letter of Sept. 2, 1693, MS.).

Once more we wish that Father Eusebio had been a little more explicit. But he was not writing for gossips, nor for historians.

LXXV

A JAUNT WITH SALVATIERRA

A mighty stimulus was given to Kino's work by the visit of square-jawed, hawk-nosed, and clear-headed Juan María de Salvatierra. Father Ambrosio Oddón had become provincial of New Spain for a Triennium.[1] As visitor of Sinaloa and Sonora he appointed Salvatierra, who was still missionary at Chínipas, in the rugged mountains east of Alamos. At the same time Kino was made rector of his district, as successor to Father Muñoz. Father Oddón had heard many conflicting reports regarding Pimería Alta, so he sent Salvatierra to learn the truth. He was just the kind of man to find it. He had been for ten years missionary in a most difficult field. He was a man of nerve equal to that of Kino. Before coming to Pima Land he made a perilous visit to war-torn Tarahumara where Fathers Foronda and Sánchez had recently been martyred. It was Christmas Eve when Father Juan rode up the hill from the south and dismounted at Dolores, just in time for the holidays, and he delighted Kino and his neophytes by conducting the Christmas services in the "new and spacious church," not yet completed.

This function over, Kino and Salvatierra set forth on a tour which occupied a month, and carried them into lands which neither one had ever seen.[2] In the course of it they made plans which proved vital to both the Pimería and California, and determined Salvatierra's career. The travelers were equipped with pack mules, extra riding animals, and the necessary servants. First they went north to Remedios, which Kino was again taking under his personal care, "for the people were still much deceived because of the discord that had been sown against the fathers." Descending the canyon westward, they visited Father Sando-

---

[1] Oddón became Provincial in November, 1689. Kino, *Hist. Mem.*, I. 89.
[2] The story of the journey is told by Kino in *Favores Celestiales*, Parte I, Lib. II, Caps. 1–5; *Hist. Mem.*, I, 117–124.

val at Imuris, and continued thence down the river. Beyond San Ignacio Kino was on new ground, and his eyes were wide open. We too are intrigued by these first glimpses of a new land.

They visited Magdalena, on the river, and El Tupo a little to the west, both in charge of Father Pineli. Swinging northwest now, they went ten leagues to Tubutama, on Altar River, where Father Arias was stationed. Here they found more than five hundred Pimas assembled, for Salvatierra's coming had been heralded. Among the throng were headmen from Chief Soba's tribe, that numerous people downstream to the west. While here the Feast of the Kings was celebrated and Kino preached from the text "Kings come from Saba"—*Reges de Saba veniunt*—a neat play on Chief Soba's name. We trust that Kino smiled at his own pun. With Soba's wise men— from the West—Kino discussed the conversion of their people and promised to visit them later—*más tarde*. Continuing up the Altar, the travelers visited Sáric and Tucubavia, where they counted more than seven hundred natives who, says Kino, "welcomed us everywhere with great pleasure to themselves and to us. Almost everywhere they gave the father visitor infants to baptize, and presented us with many supplies."

It was their intention to turn back now to Dolores by way of Cocóspora, but a special circumstance changed their plans. At Tucubavia they were met by messengers from the north. In their hands they bore crosses. Kneeling before the Black Robes in humble veneration, they begged them to visit their villages also. Here was an appeal that could not be resisted. Salvatierra remarked to Kino that "those crosses which they carried were tongues that spoke volumes and with great force, and that we could not fail to go where by means of them they called us." So to the north the apostles reined their horses. Surmounting the divide in the vicinity of Nogales, guided by the messengers they descended to Santa Cruz River and there visited Tumacácori, a large Pima town nestling among the huge cottonwoods whose giant successors—or the same ones—still dispense welcome shade. The villagers had prepared three arbors or brush shelters for the visitors, "one in which to say Mass, another in which to sleep, and a third for a kitchen. There were more than forty houses close together." Some infants were baptized, and Salvatierra promised fathers for the assembled natives.

Opponents had said that the new missionaries were not needed. But Salvatierra was convinced. "When his Reverence saw so many people, so docile and so affable, with such beautiful, fertile, and pleasant valleys, inhabited by industrious Indians," he said to Kino, "My Father Rector, not only shall the removal from this Pimería of any of the four fathers assigned to it not be considered, but four more shall come, and by the divine grace I shall try to be one of them." After the craggy mountains of Chínipas, the cottonwood groves of Arizona looked good to Salvatierra, and the gentle Pimas lost nothing by comparison with the lean-limbed and sensitive Tarahumares.

And now new evidence was added. Out of the north a band of warriors appeared at Tumacácori in full regalia. They were chiefs and headmen from the great Sobaípuri settlement of Bac, some forty miles beyond. They had come to urge the Black Robes to visit their people also. Bac was a metropolis; Tumacácori a mere village. But duty called Kino home, and Bac had to bide its time. So the apostolic pair swung sharply south up the Santa Cruz River to Guébavi, through the fine bottom lands of Bacoancos, now appropriately called Buena Vista, and around the great bend of the river, through San Lázaro to Santa María,[1] a ride of fifteen leagues from Tumacácori, all the way through shady cottonwoods and beside a sparkling stream.

At Santa María Kino and Salvatierra spent five days baptizing infants and catechizing adults. Then they packed up their vestments and portable altar, promised to come again, and continued south over the live-oak hills and down the fertile river valley to Cocóspora. Here at the end of January they spent another five days catechizing, baptizing, and preparing a report to Father Oddón. It was now that the high-perched mission at Cocóspora was turned over to Father Sandoval. These things done, Kino and Salvatierra continued through Remedios to Dolores. This enlarged circuit—over two hundred miles —had taken Kino and his companion from the valley of the San

---

[1] The river and the settlement now called Santa Cruz, in Kino's day were both called Santa María. The native settlement of Santa María was also called Suamca or Bugata. Buena Vista is just south of the international line.

Miguel to the upper waters of the San Ignacio, Altar, Santa Cruz, and
Cocóspora rivers, all the way among gentle Pimas.

Salvatierra was deeply impressed with Pima Land. But something
else impressed him still more deeply. As they rode side by side, up
hill and down dale, Father Eusebio inspired his strong-jawed companion with a new and consuming ambition. "In all these journeys,"
Kino writes, "the father visitor and I talked together of suspended
California, saying that these very fertile lands and valleys of this
Pimería would be the support of the scantier and more sterile lands
of California." The seed thus planted in Salvatierra's breast took firm
root and grew to be a tremendous tree. Before saying goodbye, Father
Juan urged Kino to undertake the conversion of both the Sobaípuris
of the north and the Sobas of the west, "and with respect to California, even the building of a small bark in which to go there." [1]

LXXVI

THE SOBAÍPURIS

The journey with Salvatierra was for Kino the prelude to a remarkable series of travels. Indeed, from now forward he became quite
as much explorer as missionary. At equipping a pack train or cinch-
ing a saddle girth the padre became an expert. He had served his
apprenticeship with Atondo in the exploration of the Peninsula. He
now found a wider field for his skill on the trail.

When at Tumacácori, Kino had promised the messengers from
Bac that he would soon return. A year later his interest was greatly
quickened by a border incident. Indians stole a horse herd from a
mission far to the east of Dolores. Suspicion fell on the Sobaípuris of
Quíburi River (San Pedro), who for several years had been charged
with depredations. Captain Ramírez with soldiers followed the trail
which led to a village on that stream well north of the present Benson.[2] Ramírez was a level-headed soldier. He made peace with the

---

[1] His visitation finished, Salvatierra left the active mission field to become rector of the
Jesuit College at Guadalajara. The frontier thus temporarily lost an able man.
[2] Baicatcan, just south of El Embudo.

people, and conducted à band of chiefs to Dolores to see the already famous Black Robe. From him they begged for missionaries. "And thus," wrote Kino, "all this Pimería is now reduced and is asking for the blessing of eternal salvation. For all this, much will always be owed to Captain Francisco Ramírez." To Ramírez's report, it may be added, we owe a good part of all that we know of the Pimas of San Pedro River down to the date when it was written.[1]

These new people were calling Kino. It was a summons he could not disregard, so he took the trail once more. He gives us a glimpse of his traveling outfit, which was elaborate and attested his efficiency. "In spite of the obstacles which were present," he says, "and seeing that the whole of Pimería was quiet, during the last part of August and the first part of September [2] I went in with fifty pack animals, my servants, and some justices"—meaning native officials—"to the Sobaí-puris, both of the north and of the northeast." What a dust he must have kicked up! "The former are in the valley and river of Santa María, to the west, the latter in the valley of the river of Quíburi, to the east. The journey to the former was more than eighty leagues by very level road."

And it was a most interesting road. As far as Tumacácori Kino retraced the trail he had traveled southward with Salvatierra. We now have the details of the route. From Dolores he went to Remedios. Thence his trail lay down the river to the narrow gorge between its high red walls, and to the valley of Aquituni, at the junction. Here he swung to the right up Río de Cocóspora, ascended the narrow canyon, winding along the river, crossing and recrossing, stopping to rest and drink under the great cottonwoods, till he emerged on the plain above. Before him now lay a broad expanse—rich meadows along the stream, low mountains on either side. A few miles further up he entered the village of Cocóspora, climbed the high hill at the left where stood the rudimentary mission, and gazed up and down the valley at the lush meadows and verdant cottonwoods along the river.

---

[1] Testimonio de Autos de Guerra Tocantes al Capitan Francisco Ramírez de Salazar. A.G.I. Sevilla, 67–4–11, Audiencia de Guadalajara. Manje tells us that Escalante, who was with Ramírez in 1692, was also with the 1697 expedition. He tells where Ramírez turned back, and that he had been farthest north in these parts (Manje, *Luz de Tierra Incógnita*, 249). See Velarde's eulogy of Ramírez for this work.

[2] 1692.

Chief Cola de Pato (Duck Tail) and his people did him reverence and rendered willing aid.

Into the saddle, "Adiós," and Kino continued up the valley. Ahead, on his right, lay Sierra del Cabrito, which more resembles a reclining elephant than a goat. Three miles above the mission the river swings sharply east toward Cananea. But Kino's road kept northward up a dry sandy arroyo past the site of the ranch now called La Paz, through marvelous grassy oak groves where mission cattle were already grazing, over low hills, and down the wide gentle slope to San Lázaro at the bend of the Santa Cruz River. The name of the place at the bend has been retained to this day.

Swinging left, Kino now traveled down stream through splendid cottonwoods, with El Picacho ahead. Passing just to the right of this fantastic peak, he jogged down the oak-covered valley, past Capazura, later called Santa Bárbara,[1] to San Luís Bacoancos, a village amid the huge cottonwoods—now Buena Vista, almost on the international border. Still descending the river, Kino was soon at Guébavi and at Tumacácori, where the natives gave him an affectionate welcome. The great padre had returned! He had kept his promise. His packs were filled with little presents. He said kind words. He told beautiful stories and baptized the newborn babes. He was a Magic Man.

From here forward Kino traversed a region for which his precious record is our earliest, as is true of so many other regions that he explored. Continuing north down the river, between lofty Santa Rita on the right and lesser ranges on the left, after traveling some forty miles he entered the famous town of Bac, or Batki,—"The Place near the Well,"—named by him San Xavier after his own patron saint. San Xavier del Bac it still is called, and it is still famous. The village contained at the time more than eight hundred people.

Kino now gave the wide-eyed natives a lesson in history and geography. "I spoke to them the Word of God, and on the map of the world I showed them the lands, the rivers, and the seas over which we fathers had come from afar to bring them the saving knowledge

---

[1] For an account of this expedition see Kino, *Hist. Mem.*, I, 122–123. His map of 1696 (Teatro de los Trabajos) shows Capazura about where Santa Bárbara now is.

of our Holy Faith." We can see the simple folk marvel at the white man's paper which told the wonderful story. What medicine he had! "I told them also how in ancient times the Spaniards were not Christians, how Santiago came to teach them the Faith, and how the first fourteen years he was able to baptize only a few, because of which the Holy Apostle was discouraged, but that the Holy Virgin appeared to him and consoled him, promising that the Spaniards would convert the rest of the people of the world.

"And I showed them on the map of the world how the Spaniards and the Faith had come by sea to Vera Cruz and had gone into Puebla and to Mexico, Guadalaxara, Sinaloa, Sonora, and now to . . . Dolores del Cosari, in the land of the Pimas, where there were already many persons baptized, a house, a church, bells, images of saints, plentiful supplies, wheat, maize, and many cattle and horses; that they could go and see it all, and even ask at once their relatives, my servants, who were with me. They listened with pleasure"—Kino may have enjoyed a professorial illusion here—"to these and other talks concerning God, heaven, and hell, told me that they wished to be Christians, and gave me some infants to baptize." He had fairly hypnotized his hosts.

From Bac Kino went to visit "the other Sobaípuris, of the east, on the Río de San Joseph de Terrenate, or de Quíburi, who in their chief ranchería, that of San Salvador del Baicatcan, are thirty leagues distant." It was here at El Embudo that Ramírez had made peace with the Sobaípuris a few months before. Evidently Kino did not go to Baicatcan, notwithstanding the implication of his language here.[1] He more likely reached the San Pedro at Benson. Turning upstream, at the mouth of Babacómari Creek, just across the river from Fairbank he visited Chief Coro's famous town of Quíburi. "Captain Coro and the rest of them received me with all kindness," says Kino. "It is true that I found them somewhat less docile than the foregoing people, of the west." From here the way home led westward to Huachuca,[2] village of El Taravilla or "The Prattler," thence south through Bacadéguache, Santa María, San Lázaro, and home over the Cocó-

---

[1] See note above, p. 267.
[2] At the site of Babocómari Ranch.

spora road. Kino had rolled back the curtain and opened to us another vista. His trail was a thread binding the Sobaípuris to him with a tie of affection which they never lost.

One must not think that Father Eusebio did nothing but explore. His main employment was the routine of teaching and mission building. Next year (1693) a new corps of workers arrived in the Pimería, and Kino was kept busy equipping and installing them. To San Ignacio and its sub-stations, where Pineli had toiled, Father George Hostinski came for a brief period. He was from the Tarahumar missions, and to them he soon returned. Before the end of the year his place was taken by Agustín de Campos, next to Kino the most important missionary in Pimería Alta in the seventeenth century. He took over the work of Pineli in the San Ignacio Valley. The place of Arias at Tubutama was filled by Father Daniel Januske (Janusque) also from rebellious Tarahumara.[1] Father Barli succeeded Sandoval at Imuris and Cocóspora. His stay there was brief, for on January 3, 1694, he died at Cucurpe and was buried there.[2]

Meanwhile Kino and his Pimas toiled diligently on the material plant at Dolores. Early in 1693 the new church was completed and ready for dedication. The ceremony took place on April 26. It was an event for all the Pimería, Christian and heathen. To it came important personages from all the country round. Father Juan Muñoz de Burgos, then visitor, was there in his official robes and said Mass, and he declared the church to be one of the best in Sonora. From Mátape came the rector, Father Marcos de Loyola; Father Hostinski rode over the mountain from San Ignacio and preached the dedication sermon. "Likewise there came very many Pimas from the north and west." In their feathered headdress, bright-colored blankets, strings of beads, gaudy bracelets, enormous ear pendants, and bizarre face paints, they lent to the occasion a touch to be seen only in such a frontier laboratory of human civilization.[3]

---

[1] In 1690 the Tarahumares martyred Fathers Foronda and Sánchez, with the result that some of the Jesuits went to other missionary fields.

[2] Barli was succeeded at Cocóspora in 1695 by Fernando Bayerca, also a bird of passage. A report dated Dec. 13, 1692, states that four Jesuits were then at Parral ready to go to the Pima missions in accordance with the order of 1689. (Relación de las Misiones Nuebas y Religiosos Misioneros del tiempo de Govierno del Excmo. Señor Conde de Galve, December 12, 1692. Original Spanish manuscript, Maggs Collection, No. 52.)

[3] Kino, *Hist. Mem.*, I, p. 125.

LXXVII

CHIEF SOBA'S PEOPLE

Late in 1693 Kino made his promised visit to the Pimas of the lower Altar Valley. These people, called the Sobas, were so-named for their cacique, "head and captain of more than four thousand Indians." El Soba had a reputation as a great fighter, and long had been at war with the eastern Pimas. His home was at Unuicut, in the vicinity of Caborca. Ten or twelve years previously the Sobas had killed El Podenco (The Hound), chief of Cosari, and since that time the two Pima groups had been mutually hostile. So Kino conceived the plan of making peace between them. This would be merciful, and it would facilitate his work. And Kino was eager to look once more across the Gulf of California.

With Father Campos, Captain Romero, servants, and suitable pack train, Kino set forth on December 11, 1693, on the first recorded visit to the lower Altar River. He again rolled back the scroll of the unknown. His journey was made without mishap. At Caborca, just beyond Soba's home, he found the people affable "except that in some places they appeared afraid, wondering at new and white faces, which they had never seen before." From Caborca he continued west, over a wide sandy waste, but his trouble was rewarded. From a little range which he called El Nazareno—the name of the ship in which he was wrecked in the harbor at Cádiz some fifteen years before—he looked out across the Gulf to California, "for," he writes, "it is not more than fifteen or eighteen leagues wide." [1]

Kino returned to Dolores with visions of a great missionary field among the Sobas. But he needed official co-operation; so he rode over the mountains to San Juan to see General Domingo Jironza Cruzat, a veteran from troubled New Mexico, and now alcalde mayor of Sonora and commander of a new Flying Company, designed to check the Apaches. Kino told Jironza of his plans, and requested him to furnish a representative of the civil and military authority who

---

[1] Kino, *Favores Celestiales*, Parte I, Lib. ii, Caps. 5–6; *Hist. Mem.*, I, 123–125.

should accompany him to appoint native officers in the villages which he might visit, and to report on the country and its inhabitants. In other words, Kino's project involved the extension of both the spiritual and the political realm for Spain. This was a typical procedure. Church and State went hand in hand.

Jironza gladly complied, for he took the measure of the missionary, and the two became fast friends. To fill the office he selected his own nephew, Juan Matheo Manje, a youth who now began to occupy an important place on the Sonora frontier, and who for many years was Kino's closest associate in exploration. Manje was made of good stuff. He had come from Spain in 1692, reached Sonora in 1693, and was soon made alférez of his uncle's Flying Company at San Juan. For Kino's purposes he was now promoted to be lieutenant alcalde mayor. Though only a lad, he was mature for his years, intelligent, and a most excellent diarist. He became one of Sonora's notable men.[1]

On February 1 Kino and Manje rode west from the capital on the first of their many jaunts together. Kindred spirits, their hearts beat in unison. Before night of the third day they reached Dolores. On his former journey to the Sobas Kino had taken Father Campos. For the present excursion he invited another tenderfoot, Father Kappus, now neighbor at Cucurpe. While Kappus was getting ready at his mission, Kino and Manje made similar preparations at Dolores. They assembled saddle and pack animals, prepared loads of provisions, and equipment with which to say Mass. "This done, carrying as a strong defense for the journey a picture of the Celestial Pilgrim Apostle, San Francisco Xavier," they set forth west on February 7. Chief Coxi rode proudly at the head of a band of loyal servants.

As they entered the villages on the way the Indians generally welcomed the visitors with arches and crosses placed along the trails, and lodged them in ramadas made for the purpose. Manje distributed presents and gave to chiefs and headmen canes of office decorated with ribbons. Kino instructed the natives in the Faith and baptized infants and sick adults. As spokesman for Manje, who did not yet know the Pima tongue, he admonished the natives to obey the king, and to keep the peace with their neighbors. The Indians

---

[1] Manje, *Luz de Tierra Incógnita*, 211–214.

were everywhere friendly and gave the visitors presents of maize or whatever else they had. These were typical scenes in all of Kino's tours among the Indians henceforth.[1]

Crossing the range to Magdalena, where Campos was in charge, there they were met by Kappus, two Spaniards, and twenty Indians, to serve as guides and in case of need as defenders. Now leaving the river behind, they made their way to Caborca by a new route. Again Kino was pathfinder. Four leagues west they visited El Tupo, a village of two hundred natives near a marsh or ciénega which soon became famous—or perhaps it would be better to say infamous. Eight leagues northwest of here, over a mountain, they were welcomed at El Bosna by a hundred natives "on their knees."

They now swung down the San Ignacio valley. Five leagues south over dry level country they passed the village and lake of Oacuc, now called Ocuca. Six leagues west over a mesquite plain, at El Comac they passed a poverty-stricken village of a hundred and twenty naked Indians whose women were scantily clad in rabbit and deerskins. In compassion for their poverty Kino distributed among them a packload of pinole and meat. Seven leagues west and northwest they threaded the mountain gap now called La Ventana (The Window) at the forks of San Ignacio and Altar rivers, through which the combined streams run—underground. At the Ojo de Agua, or Spring, where the river again bursts forth, they were refreshed "with cold, crystalline water." Two leagues down stream through irrigated fields to Pitquín, and three more through shady cottonwood groves, brought them to Caborca, where they were welcomed by a hundred and sixty Indians with crosses and arches, roads swept, and with "dances and jubilation."

Some of these people had traveled fifty leagues from the north to meet the visitors, for their coming had been heralded. Beribboned canes of office were bestowed; the Indians asked for a missionary to teach them, "and rendered vassalage to our King and natural Lord." They were told of God and His holy law, says Manje, "and how He rewards good people and Christians with glory, and bad people with the blazing and eternal fire of Hell, to which He condemns the miser-

[1] Kino, *Hist. Mem.*, I, 123–127. For details see Manje, *Luz de Tierra Incógnita*, 214–215.

able souls who do not love, serve, and reverence Him—and they were horrified at the burning." At this very time Puritan divines were preaching the same doctrines in Boston.

Young Manje describes Caborca for us. "This place is commodious and pleasant for a mission. It has fertile and rich lands, all under irrigation, with acéquias, where they harvest plentiful maize, beans, and calabashes, and if they only had axes, which they lack, they could cut down many groves, and there would be a superabundance of lands for three thousand Indians who might be assembled of those who now wander naked to the north and to the west on the coast of the sea, and to found a rich mission and a flourishing Christendom. Their country is temperate, has fine pasture lands, and salt beds for the raising of cattle and horses."

Caborca henceforth was a marked spot on the map. But for the present Kino did not stop to enjoy it. He would climb the Cerro del Nazareno once more, and would try to reach the Gulf. So next day with his cavalcade he proceeded down stream. At the end of two leagues the river disappeared in the sand, and water was obtained only from rainwater pools or by digging pozos or wells. Here they left the baggage train and continued with only one load of provisions.

As they crossed El Nazareno, Kino and Manje climbed its highest peak, whence they had a magnificent panorama. Beyond the sand dunes they gazed on the blue waters of the Gulf. Still beyond, on the California side, they saw four high peaks, which they called the Four Evangelists. Three of them they named Matthew, Mark, and John, with Spanish spellings, of course. The fourth they called San Antonio, "since the name of San Lucas is already given to the Cape of California." [1] Thrilled by the view, next day they pushed eagerly forward.

Though the land was a barren desert, the journey had its diversions. Descending the Sierra by a barranca, at three leagues they found Indian women dipping water with ollas or jugs from a pool. The frightened women fled, leaving their pottery behind. Manje sped after them and soon was at their heels. Don Matheo was young

[1] Kino, *Favores Celestiales*, Parte I, Lib. ii, Cap. 7; *Hist. Mem.*, I, 126. See also Manje, *Luz de Tierra Incógnita*, 216–222.

and good-looking, and he gave the women presents, so they followed him back to the pool and helped him water the thirsty horses. From the diverting incident the site was called the Place of the Ollas. Manje's lady friends were nearly naked, with only a slender covering of jack-rabbit skin. And not all of them were in the bloom of youth. "One of them was so aged that from her looks she must have been about a hundred and twenty years old." But that was just young Manje's guess. To one of his age fifty years and a hundred look about the same.

At the sand dunes Kappus was left behind with the horses. Kino, Manje, Coxi, and native guides pushed forward two leagues to the very Gulf shore "to which in the sixty years since the province of Sonora was settled, no one had arrived before, and we were the first," says exultant Manje. The event would go down in history! And it did. Kappus and the rest followed to the beach, took a sniff at the fresh salt air, gathered sea shells, and next day retraced their steps.

A day and a half were spent at Caborca, during which time Kino told the assembled natives one of the most celebrated stories in all literature. There was but one God. He created the heavens, light, the land, birds, animals, the fish of the sea, the water, trees, plants, and fruits for the use and sustenance of the man Adam. He made Adam from the earth and gave him a soul. His wife, named Eve, He made of Adam's own rib. He promised them the reward of glory if they would serve Him, love Him, and obey all His precepts, and the everlasting fire of Hell if they should offend Him and break His commandments. Kino told his listeners how all humankind, descended from Adam and Eve, fell under God's displeasure through original sin. But with infinite mercy and pity, in His good time, He sent His Son to save mankind from the blazing fire of Hell. He explained to them the Flood, from which only eight persons were saved, all the rest perishing in the waters. He told them of Christ's birth, suffering, death, resurrection and ascent to Heaven, whence at the end of the world He would come to awaken everybody, to judge them with His upright justice, reward good Christians with eternal glory, and condemn bad people *and heathen* to the eternal fires of Hell. Kino taught them how to make the sign of the Cross, say Our

Father, the Ave María, the Credo, and the commandments, and he explained the saving grace of the sacraments. Of course this was all in the simplest of language.

As the Magic Man talked, the eyes of the natives opened wide. The sermon had its effect. "With evangelical urgency" they then and there begged the missionaries to baptize eighteen infants, "and that Father Kino should come again to see them." Meat, pinole and other presents were given the Indians, and they were entrusted with two pack loads of biscuits and flour to keep till Father Eusebio should return, which would be soon.

From Caborca Kino retraced his steps as far as El Comac. Swinging now to the right of his former trail he continued southeast to the San Ignacio River. Here he met forty unarmed Indians led by no less a personage than Chief Soba himself, coming to render obedience. Disillusionment was both sudden and complete. Soba was "as poor as he was naked, without other ornament than innocence." Manje must have laughed, whether Kino did or not. In order to accept a pack load of pinole given him by Kino, the Cacique required his wife and another woman to "divest themselves of the two deerskins with which they covered their modesty. In these they put the pinole while the women hid themselves naked behind a clump of bushes." And this, says Manje, "is all the greatness of the so-called Gran Soba. . . . It is true that he is a valiant Indian, as are all his people, and that for many years he waged wars against other bands and rancherías, until these two expeditions, when with our communication they have become reconciled." Kino brought peace, not a sword.

Another thrill of discovery was just ahead. A few leagues farther up the river they passed "a round hill where there are a hundred trenches, with a stone wall around it in the shape of a snail shell or spiral, clear to the top." This is our earliest account of these famous Trincheras.[1] "And they say that on top there is a plaza de armas where, in the wars which they have had, if the enemy gained the first one they went round the second and so on to the end, until the enemy had used up all their arrows, when they came down from the moun-

---

[1] See Sauer and Brand, *Prehistoric Settlements of Sonora with Special Reference to Cerros de Trincheras* (Berkeley, 1931).

tain and killed them." Continuing up the river to Magdalena, the travelers recrossed the Sierra del Comedio to Dolores.

The expedition was a memorable achievement. "These," wrote Manje, "are the results of the exploration of the lands of El Soba, in which, going as far as the Sea of Californias and returning, we traveled one hundred and fifty leagues. We counted nine hundred and fifty heathen Indians. Fifty children and sick adults were baptized. They were given some knowledge of God and instructed in the principal mysteries of our holy Faith as far as the brief time permitted. The nation is now peaceful, desirous of receiving evangelists and holy baptism, resigned to serve God, with vassalage to his Majesty. For the founding of missions there are, all along its river, fertile lands for agriculture, which, if the woods are cut down, can sustain with abundance more than three thousand souls, who can be congregated from the villages of the surrounding country, which we did not see in order not to stray from the road." But he would see them later.

LXXVIII

BOAT BUILDING IN THE DESERT

As he traveled homeward, Kino planned for another journey to the west. His expressed purposes were to seek out other villages, discover a saline near the coast of which they had been told by the Indians, build a bark at Caborca, "carry it in pieces with oxen and mules, and put it together on the shores of the Gulf of California." Thus did his imagination soar. The central feature of the program was the building of the boat. He would carry forward the exploration of the Gulf which with Guzmán he had ended at Tiburón Island nearly nine years before. Manje entered into his plans with all the enthusiasm of youth.

These pioneers set to work immediately and with a will. "At the mission of Dolores," says Manje, "we made futtocks and timber-heads to carry in packs on the journey, with the idea of making keel, mast, and other appropriate accessories at Caborca, so that if we came out well with the building (although without ship carpenter who understood the business, and with only the Indian carpenters of Father Kino who followed the instructions of his Reverence as to size and shape) we might embark for California . . . as well as to discover toward the northwest the course of the arm of the sea, its ports, bays, islands, nations and everything else that we could about the disposition of the land, rivers, sierras, trees, and plants of this unknown North America." This was an ambitious program for two men who knew nothing about practical boat building or navigation![1]

Preparations were quickly made, and on March 16 Kino and Manje set forth from Dolores equipped with provisions, altar and vestments for saying Mass, hewn timbers, saws, axes, and other tools, and twenty Indian carpenters and servants. That night they stopped at Magdalena, and lodged in the adobe house. Taking the road northwest, next day they passed El Tupo, quaffed a refreshing drink at the lagoon and springs a league beyond, drove their animals hard, and in spite of the heavy loads, by night covered the eighteen leagues to Tubutama, where Father Daniel Janusque for a year had been ministering to four hundred natives. This was a day's work to be remembered.

Next day the cavalcade turned southwest down the Tubutama River, swung round the little mountain of the same name, skirted shady alamedas along the stream, and admired fields of maize and other crops well cultivated with irrigation by the Pimas. In succession they passed through the villages of Santa Teresa, Ati, and Oquitoa, welcomed as usual by smiling Indians who had erected crosses and arches along the road. Kino preached and baptized infants; Manje counted the natives and gave canes of office. The stops were brief. Continuing two leagues to a place which Manje called El Altar, where the river sinks into the sand, they camped for the night. The name Altar has tenaciously clung to the site, to the river, to the valley, and to the district.

To Oquitoa four Indians had come to ask Kino to go northwest off the road to baptize some sick persons. The call could not be denied. Next day, sending the pack train to Caborca down the Camino Real, as it was already called, he and Manje, guided by the four messengers,

---

[1] Kino, *Hist. Mem.*, I, 123–127; Manje, *Luz de Tierra Incógnita*, 222–223.

rode rapidly northwest eight leagues over dry plains and baptized three sick persons at a village called Quisoli, near the mountains where there were some small springs. It was worth the trouble, but the day's work was not yet over. Traveling west twelve leagues, at night they reached another village, called Vacpia, on a small stream where there were reeds and tanks of rainwater. This was the later well-known village of Arivaipa, to the north of Caborca. In the dark the village and its excited inhabitants made a weird picture. Kino and his companions were welcomed by "heathen natives who with songs and dances celebrated our arrival all night long." Next day the hardy travelers rode southeast some fifty miles over sterile country to Caborca, stopping at two poverty-stricken villages on the way.

Kino now proceeded at once to the main business. It was coats off for everybody. "To make a beginning of the building of the bark a large and thick cottonwood was cut, because in this country there is no other kind of tree or timber." They dug around its roots so that the planks would be longer. They cut at the roots but the tree refused to fall. Manje was nimble and resourceful. He says: "I climbed the tree to tie reatas and ropes so that the men could pull from below." They pulled all too well. "While I was tying them to the tip end of the tree it came down, I clutching the trunk, but, although with the fall and the crash many of its branches were broken, I escaped without any injury or scratch whatsoever." Such is the luck of youth. The Indians laughed and the work went on. "Father Kino went at once to give thanks to God because no accident had happened." The trunk was cut thirty-eight feet long "to give a clean keel from stern to prow, not counting the bows and stern posts, which would be eighteen cubits." This would make a boat some sixty feet long.[1]

Manje now set forth on a new adventure. Leaving Kino to direct the axmen and carpenters who were preparing timbers for the bark, he traveled south, west, and southwest to discover new villages and learn more about that salt bed. In the course of a week he visited Soba's village of Unuicut, scaled El Nazareno, again visited his lady friends at Las Ollas, there climbed a peak and descried the salt bed, rode nine leagues southwest across playas and sand dunes to reach it,

---

[1] Kino, *Hist. Mem.*, I, 123–127; Manje, *Luz de Tierra Incógnita*, 224–225.

and near by discovered "a little port . . . shaped like a sack" inhabited by "an infinity of fish, large and medium, and of many kinds." This bag-shaped port, which Manje named Santa Albina, is now called Libertad, and is a paradise for fishermen, easily reached by automobile from Caborca. Retracing his route Manje arrived at Caborca on April 1, finding Kino waiting to go home, "because it was not possible to continue with the building of the bark until another time, after the timbers for making it, which were already cut, should be seasoned or dried." That night Kino baptized six natives for whom young Manje became godfather.

Next day by a stiff jaunt they ascended the river twenty-one leagues to Tubutama where Father Daniel entertained them with all hospitality and benevolence. The following night they reached Magdalena and lodged in the casa de adobe there. On the 4th they arrived at Mission Dolores, whose temple, says Manje, "we entered to give thanks to God and to the Sorrowing Mother for bringing us home safe, having traveled going and coming about two hundred and twenty leagues, listed nine hundred and eighty heathen Indians whom we had not previously seen, and baptized eighty children and adults, sick and well. All the nation remains domestic, peaceful, and desirous of missionary fathers to instruct them in the mysteries of our Holy Faith and to communicate to them the waters of grace." Another significant exploration had been accomplished.[1]

LXXIX

MANJE TAKES THE WATER CURE

Thinking that the timbers at Caborca would now be seasoned, early in June Kino and Manje went once more to Caborca to continue with the boat building. Equipped with packloads of provisions, tools, and servants, they retraced the trail to Tubutama, where they were again welcomed by Father Daniel. Here they separated. Kino with the servants and axmen went down stream directly to Caborca. Manje

[1] Manje, *Luz de Tierra Incógnita*, 226–228; Kino, *Hist. Mem.*, I, 126.

made an excursion to the north and west to visit villages of which they had heard but had not seen. Kino furnished him provisions and presents for the Indians.

Manje first ascended the Altar River to Búsanic, with its beautiful springs, and to Tucubavia, where he found four hundred natives.[1] All the way he saw well-cultivated fields, part at least without irrigation. He counted the people, gave canes of office, accepted vassalage in the name of the king, and talked of Christianity. At Tucubavia he was welcomed with "jubilee, fiesta and dancing." He says, "Most of the night I talked to them, through the interpreter, of God and His holy law and of obedience to his Majesty, gave them canes of office and little gifts, and they were well pleased." Manje carried great dignity on his young shoulders.

Thus far he had been on ground covered by Kino and Salvatierra during their historic jaunt three years before. He now entered new country, of which his account is our earliest. He was once more a pathfinder. Saying Adiós, he went northwest to Gubo Verde (now Pozo Verde, home of myth, near the international line), a village of ninety impoverished people who obtained water from "a tank of greenish color," hence the name Gubo Verde.[2] Striking north now fourteen leagues, he visited a village named Cups in Pápago Land, north of towering Baboquívari Range.[3] Here the natives told him of some casas grandes, or large houses, five days north on a west-flowing stream where there were cannibals.

Frightened, the guides refused to continue north, so Manje turned back. Traveling thirty leagues southwest through Pápago country, he visited Moicaqui, "close to a high peaked mountain at whose foot were some springs of water and some lakes." The description is unmistakable. Moicaqui was the village later called Bacapa, now Quitobac, where peak, springs, and lakes are still in juxtaposition exactly as Manje describes them, and as they could occur only once in nature.[4] Manje hurried on. Next day he traveled south twenty-five

---

[1] Tucubavia was north of Sáric, in the vicinity of present Esteritos.

[2] Just west of Sásabe.

[3] Cups was evidently at Nootai Wafya (San Lorenzo) at the north end of North Comobabi Mountains.

[4] Moicaqui figured prominently in the uprising of 1695 in the Altar Valley, and is frequently mentioned in the La Fuente–Terán Diary.

leagues—the actual distance is more than eighty miles by speedometer —"over plains and mountains of malpais and cactus, suffering extreme thirst and need of water," reaching at night a village two leagues from Caborca, where he and his men drank so much water that all became ill. The youth had made an historic tour through Pápago Land.

Manje's arrival at Caborca was anything but joyful. He was sick nearly unto death. And Kino had bad news for him. The boat building for which they had come was suspended. He had received by special messenger from the visitor, Father Muñoz, "a letter ordering him to cease the building of the vessel. And although he had a letter from the Father Provincial ordering him to build it, being a religious as humble as he was obedient to his immediate superiors, he at once gave up the plan until he might anew consult the superiors of the Province." Someone was interfering.

Kino was anxious to return to Dolores at once, but Manje's fever became so bad that he was confessed and given the last sacraments. So they did not start for four days, the patient's fever raging the while. He wanted to go home. He says, "I begged them to carry me out of that country with such hot and burning sun, and, traveling part way held on horseback and part way carried on the shoulders of Indians, after six days, tasting nothing but atole or gruel, and this not more than three times, and having covered forty-five leagues, on June 26 I arrived at the mission of San Ignacio." Perhaps he had typhoid fever.

Kino left next day for Dolores. Manje remained at San Ignacio in the care of Father Campos. By now he was afraid he wouldn't die. He had a horrible taste in his mouth. Campos nursed him as best he could, but he had old-fashioned notions about fever. "And," says Manje, "while the Father ordered made for me quintessences of stews of eggs, pullets, and others of all kinds, in order that I might not lose everything I swallowed, on account of my grave illness, during which everything I of necessity ate tasted salty, he prevented me from drinking water, which was my sole desire and craving, by hanging the tinaja high up so that I might not reach it." But not even this precaution sufficed, for Manje's fever drove him almost mad. Water he would have, and he got it. He tells us how. "In the silence of the night I dragged myself, weak though I was, and climbed high up to the shelf

where the olla was standing. When I took hold of it the thing cap-
sized, and the water spilled over me from head to foot, giving me a
complete bath. But I did not get my drink, for with the noise and com-
motion and my shouting I awoke the Father." And now all of
Campos's medical notions about fevers were flouted. For, says Manje,
"with my fright, from this minute my illness, which was such that
for twelve days the fever had not abated one jot, now left me completely." And still for two more centuries doctors adhered to the
notion that a fever-tortured patient must not drink cold water.

After nine days Manje, now recovered, went to Dolores, and
thence to San Juan, where he reported to Jironza. He had again made
history. Summarizing his excursion into Pápago Land he wrote: "And
thus in this journey and exploration, going and coming, suffering
hunger, danger, thirst, grievous sickness, and many other hardships,
I traveled two hundred and ten leagues, listed nine hundred persons
in villages which I discovered and which had not been seen in the
preceding journeys, all domestic, peaceful, gentle, and desirous to
obtain father workers to instruct and baptize them. They rendered
vassalage to our king and natural lord, voluntarily and without bribe.
By means of these discoveries, talks, gifts and coaxings (for with kindness even wild beasts become tame) we hope with the help of' the
most Excellent Señor Viceroy and the Reverend Father Provincial of
Mexico with alms and evangelists, to achieve in this Pima nation
a Christendom as flourishing as it is extensive, for which there are
rich and fertile valleys, rivers, arroyos, lands for agriculture, and
thousands of souls without the light of the Holy Gospel; and that
the royal dominions of his Majesty and the law of Jesus Christ may
be extended, for as lord of the Western Indies his Majesty orders this
promotion, and he relieves his conscience by entrusting so pious a
cause to his Most Excellent Viceroys. And for any omission which
may be made by his royal ministers God will ask for a strict accounting
in the solemn personal and final judgment of souls which may be
damned through their fault." [1]

For a youth this was sage talk.

[1] *Manje, Luz de Tierra Incógnita,* 228–232; Kino, *Hist. Mem.,* I, 123–127. Soon after his
recovery young Manje became entirely bald.

LXXX

THE GREAT HOUSE ON THE GILA

The order to suspend work at Caborca on the bark dampened Kino's ardor for the Soba country, and he turned his attention north once more. Stories of a Casa Grande on a west flowing river beyond Bac stimulated his curiosity. What could it be? When Manje told him the tale "his Reverence was incredulous for some time." Later, when at Dolores, Kino asked some native visitors from Bac about the story and they confirmed it. So it was true after all! He was all on fire again. Would they guide him to the great wonder? They would. Agreed. And so they started.

With pack train, servants, and his visitors as guides, Kino set forth.[1] Going to Bac by the now familiar trail, he continued forty-three leagues from there to the Casa Grande near the Gila River. He discovered the Great House on November 27th. His was the first recorded visit to that famous ruin, and for this reason his own account of it, although written several years after the event, deserves insertion here entire. It is unique.

"In November, 1694, I went inland with my servants and some justices of this Pimería as far as the casa grande, as these Pimas call it, which is on the large River of Hila, that flows out of New Mexico and has its source near Acoma. This river, this large house, and the neighboring houses are forty-three leagues beyond and to the northwest of the Sobaípuris of San Francisco Xavier del Bac. The first village, that of El Tusónimo, we named La Encarnación, as we arrived there to say Mass on the First Sunday of Advent; and because many other Indians came to see us from the village of El Coatóydag, four leagues farther on,[2] we named the latter San Andrés, as the following day was the feast of that holy apostle.

---

[1] "They accompanied him as guides to go to see them and discover them, counting many people on the road he traveled, which going and coming was more than two hundred leagues, and he made a sketch of it because I did not go on this expedition." Manje, *Luz de Tierra Incógnita*, 235.

[2] Tusónimo was near Sacatón. Kino's map shows "Soacson" next below San Andrés. Anza calls it "Sudacson." In 1694 the First Sunday of Advent fell on the 29th. On Kino's map El Coatóydag is the third village below San Andrés.

"All were affable and docile people. They told us of two friendly nations living further on, all down the river to the west, and to the northwest on the Río Azul, and still further, on the Río Colorado.[1] These nations are the Opas and Cocomaricopas. They speak a language very different [from that of the Pimas],[2] though it is very clear, and as there were some who knew both languages very well, I at once and with ease made a vocabulary of the tongue, and also a map of those lands, measuring the sun with the astrolabe." Scholars would like to discover that vocabulary and that map. Rare treasures they would be.

Now follow a precious description of the venerable ruin as Kino saw it, and his ideas about its origin. "The casa grande is a four story building, as large as a castle and equal to the largest church in these lands of Sonora. It is said that the ancestors of Montezuma deserted and depopulated it, and, beset by the neighboring Apaches, left for the east or Casas Grandes [of Chihuahua], and that from there they turned toward the south and southwest, finally founding the great city and court of Mexico. Close to this casa grande there are thirteen smaller houses, somewhat more dilapidated, and the ruins of many others, which make it evident that in ancient times there was a city here.

"On this occasion and on later ones"—he was writing some time after this first visit—"I have learned and heard, and at times have seen, that further to the east, north, and west there are seven or eight more of these large ancient houses and the ruins of whole cities, with many broken metates and jars, charcoal, etc. These certainly must be the Seven Cities mentioned by the holy man Fray Marcos de Niza, who in his long pilgrimage came clear to the Bacapa ranchería of these coasts, which is about sixty leagues southwest from this casa grande and about twenty leagues from the Sea of California.[3] The guides or interpreters must have given his Reverence the informa-

[1] Kino's notion of the Río Colorado at this time was wholly erroneous. His map of 1696 represents it as a very small stream west of Río Azul (the Verde) flowing into the Gila from the northeast.

[2] They spoke the Yuma tongue.

[3] He refers to San Luís Bacapa (Moicaqui), now Quitobac. Here Kino was in error. Niza did not travel so far west as Bacapa (Quitobac). See Sauer, *The Road to Cíbola*. Kino wrote this account some years after his first visit to the Casa Grande. Meanwhile he had been several times on the Gila River and had greatly modified his geographical notions. Two years after this first visit he made his map of Pimería Alta called *Teatro de los Trabajos Apostólicos*.

tion which he had in his book concerning these Seven Cities, although certainly at that time and for a long while before they must have been deserted."

The Pimas had many superstitions regarding the Casa Grande as well as a variety of legends of its origin. They were afraid to burn any of the timbers of the structure. In the casa there was a room devoted to religious offerings, in which the Pimas placed gourds, feathers, arrows and other valuables. They believed that near by was buried a large olla or jar full of chalchiguites, precious stones resembling emeralds, and said that anybody who tried to steal it would go to the bottom of the hole where it was buried. Close by the great house the natives pointed out a little hill sliced in two, whose parts closed up and swallowed anybody who dared go between them. These and other dire performances they attributed to the witchcraft of Montezuma.

Kino was silent on such matters. But Campos, who in later years several times visited the ruins and said Mass in them, strove to relieve the natives of their fears. Challenging Montezuma, he burned timbers from the ruins for firewood, and had his servants remove and throw away the native offerings. But when he begged the Pimas to show him the olla with the chalchiguites they refused. In all probability the treasure has never been removed. Here is another chance for someone to make his fortune.[1]

Mission Dolores now gave its name to a new administrative district, so important had it become. At first it had been included in the rectorate of San Francisco Xavier. As new Pima missions were founded, the need of a separate unit was recognized, and in November, 1694, just when Kino visited the Casa Grande, the rectorate of

which represents his ideas at that time. It shows the Gulf of California as a strait continuing north as far as Cape Blanco. The upper branch of the Gila, above Casa Grande, is called "Río Sonaca ó de Hila." The lower reaches of the Gila are called Río Grande del Corral. What is evidently Salt River is called Río Azul. The Río Grande del Corral empties into a small bay in the Gulf. Farther north the Río del Tizón empties separately into the same bay. Cocomaricopas are shown along the Río del Tizón. On the Gila below San Andrés the map names a score of villages which Kino had never seen. He probably got the names from the Pimas during this visit.

[1] For an account of Campos's visits to Casas Grandes, see Velarde, in Manje, *Luz de Tierra Incógnita*, 311–312.

Dolores [1] was founded. It included Cucurpe, Dolores, and all the Pima missions lying beyond—Remedios, San Ignacio, Imuris, Magdalena and Tubutama. In all there were now six missionaries in the district. The first rector was Father Kappus, of Cucurpe, Kino's nearest neighbor.

[1] Nuestra Señora de los Dolores, of course.

Rebellion in the Valley of the Altar

LXXXI

BULLETS FLY

ROM THE WAY IN WHICH KINO WANDERED AMONG THE INDIANS without military escort, one might imagine that he was laboring in a land of peace and quiet. Far from it. While he was thus occupied in the West, the Tarahumares martyred Fathers Foronda and Sánchez in Chihuahua, and the Sonora soldiery were busy defending the northeastern frontier against hostile Apaches.

A multitude of episodes illustrate the almost incessant game of give-and-take between red man and white, and the constant peril in which the missionaries spent their days on remote frontiers. It would be difficult to say who was most to blame for the chronic troubles which impeded their labors. A prairie fire once started is hard to check; so are hostilities between contiguous peoples. On the Sonora border Spaniard and Indian frequently outraged one another. Under these circumstances, Jironza, La Fuente, Manje, Solís, Medrano, Terán, and other men-at-arms were kept constantly on the move. A regular military highway ran from Caborca through Fronteras, San Bernardino, and Guadalupe Pass to Janos and El Paso. The Apache wars did not begin with Cochise and Gerónimo. Nor were these the only valorous chiefs who resisted the white man. Gerónimo came late.

This year of 1694 was disturbed by raids and alarms which sorely worried Kino. A few examples are illuminating. From them we learn the occasions and nature of the raids and the make-up of the frontier forces engaged. Almost any other year would serve as well for purposes of illustration, for the situation was chronic. In March several horse-herds were stolen from the Sonora missions. The theft was charged to the Sobaípuris. To verify the suspicions, Lieutenant Antonio Solís made an excursion through the villages on San Pedro

River, then swung west to Bac. At one place he thought he had the damaging evidence he was looking for. He came so suddenly upon a village that the inhabitants fled in terror. Seeing a tasajera or frame of drying meat, he assumed that it was horseflesh, and without investigation he killed three Indians and captured two. When it was too late it was learned that the meat was venison. The Sobaípuris were exonerated, but the three dead men remained quite dead. It is gratifying to know that Solís's rash act was condemned even by his own soldiers.[1]

In May Jironza again sent Solís out against marauders with sixty soldiers and citizens from Sonora, thirty soldiers from Janos, and one hundred and fifty Indian allies, Pimas and Opatas. In a campaign lasting a little over a month they won a "happy victory" over the enemies in their own country. That is to say, they killed about sixty gandules or braves, and captured thirty Indians, big and little. There were more slaves for mines, haciendas, and house servants. As to the glory, opinions will differ.

In military circles hard-fisted Solís was the hero of the hour. He had scarcely returned to his post when Jironza received a hurry-up call for help from Father Janusque, of Tubutama, alone in the Altar Valley. His Indians were discontented, two of them were giving tlatoles or harangues to the rest, and his life was in danger. Solís was dispatched to the scene with thirty men. "Having arrived and done what he was ordered to do, God was pleased that the heads and disturbers should be captured,"—God perhaps was not so pleased as Jironza thought,—"and the punishment which they merited being inflicted in sight of the rest, the other rancherías remained quiet and the father missionary very well content." Jironza does not tell us what the merited punishment was, but the offenders were probably hanged.

This episode had scarcely passed into history when Jironza got an urgent letter from Father Carranco, missionary at Nácori, complaining that Conchos Indians were molesting his neophytes. Re-

---

[1] A letter written by Jironza to the viceroy reflects the troubles of the Sonora frontier. He wrote from his capital at San Juan Bautista on October 18, 1694, reviewing the last half year. Autos de guerra tocantes al Capitán Ramírez de Salazar. A.G.I. 67–4–11, Audiencia de Guadalajara. See also Manje, *Luz de Tierra Incógnita*, 232–235.

sponding, Jironza hurried Adjutant Madrid with a squadron to the scene. At the end of five days he found the marauders, engaged them in battle, killed five, and captured six. An interrogation showed that they had been implicated in a raid on Nácori three years before. Jironza had them catechized and baptized by Father Carranco and executed "á usanza de guerra." Jironza thus kept his conscience clear by sending the culprits to Heaven, where he presumably expected to dwell with them in eternal bliss.

Water dammed here broke out yonder. In August, nine or ten hostile bands held a council near Janos, away to the east in Chihuahua. Fearing an attack, Captain La Fuente appealed to Jironza for help. Alférez Acuña was rushed to the scene with twenty-five Spaniards and fifty Indian allies. That very day there was another emergency call. Hostiles descended upon Bavispe, destroying grain fields and killing several old men and women. The little pueblo nestling beneath the towering Sierra Madre was chilled with terror. Veteran Father Polici, neighbor missionary at Bazeraca, appealed to La Fuente, who hurried to the spot and attacked the enemy as they retreated. Four days later Jironza was called from bed at midnight by a breathless rider. He was a messenger from Corporal Medrano, who reported a vast gathering of enemies near Batepito. Solís, who had been enjoying a short breathing spell, was sent with twenty-five soldiers and a large force of allies. Joining Medrano they pursued the enemy twenty-eight days in the mountains but failed to overtake them, "for," says Jironza, "I need not tell your Excellency how rough these sierras are." If the viceroy had seen them he certainly would not need to be told.

September brought no surcease. On the 5th a courier came from Father Polici to report an attack on his mission at Bazeraca. La Fuente hurried from Janos. Jironza answered the call in person, and arrived just after the enemy had withdrawn badly worsted, for the place was well fortified and entrenched, as were so many of these missions. While at Bazeraca Jironza and La Fuente agreed to start on a joint campaign in October, after the horses had recuperated. Jironza then returned to his post to assemble supplies.

Before his back was turned there was another excitement. Solís had summoned the Pimas to Batepito to unite with a Spanish force.

After they arrived he sent Acuña out to reconnoiter. This was September 29. That very day he captured five Indian women. The captives reported that all the enemies were coming in a body to attack the mission of Cuchuta, over the mountains near Fronteras. With the captive women clinging to the haunches of their horses, Acuña and his men galloped back to Batepito and gave the alarm. Solís hastened with his Pima and Opata allies to Cuchuta, arrived at midnight, and fortified himself at the mission, whose ruins still overlook the rich valley that lay in front of it.

The women had told the literal truth. Next morning six hundred enemies—cut off a cipher?—attacked the place, and killed a soldier. But the battle had only begun. Solís now gave the war cry. "Santiago!" Spaniards, Pimas, and Opatas together rushed from their ambush and with the first volley of lead and arrows killed twenty-five gandules, routing the rest. The Spaniards lost one soldier killed and eight injured. It was learned afterward that many of the assailants who had been wounded in the fray died from the poisoned arrows used by the Pimas. Jironza wrote to the viceroy, "That great victory, your Excellency can well understand, was a very severe punishment for such a number of enemies." [1] Solís was once more the military hero. The Battle of Cuchuta was long remembered.

The Pimas had again demonstrated their loyalty, and they soon gave still another proof. The joint campaign set for October got under way in November. Manje took part in it, now fully recovered from his illness, "although without any hair, for it had all fallen out" in spite of the water cure which he had taken. We are not told whether or not it grew in again, and are forced to leave the matter to the imagination. Two hundred Pimas joined the expedition, "as punctual as they were loyal," and together red men and white scoured the wild sierras round about Batepito. One day when scouting single file in a sheer-walled, funnel-shaped canyon, with no outlet but a narrow ledge, thirty-six Spaniards and the Pima allies were attacked "by more than seven hundred enemies, Apaches, Jocomes, and Janos" —cut off another cipher? Says Manje, "As we rushed like blind men with arquebuses and swords, in order not to lose to them the sixty

[1] Jironza to the viceroy, San Juan Bautista, Sonora, October 18, 1694, *loc cit.*

extra horses with which we had entered, they must have thought we were in their hands." One valiant Spaniard was killed, one wounded, and ten allies put out of commission. The enemy suffered a much heavier loss. At night the returning warriors reached Jironza's camp, where he was guarding the horseherd and baggage.

Two days later La Fuente arrived on the scene and went with men to recover the dead soldier and give him Christian burial. The enemy had fled. When La Fuente saw the asperity of the canyon "he said he would have hesitated to enter it, and that not even three hundred soldiers were enough for so many enemies in such rugged cliffs." The campaign was now closed and all returned to their posts. "And from that time the Pima nation remained more avowed and sworn enemies of the Apaches, Jocomes and Janos, and firmer friends of the Spaniards."

It is an ill wind that blows nobody good. These wars made "business" for a few profiteers, as wars always do. In this case Francisco Salgado came in for a share. He was a pack-train owner and provision merchant, and it was he who supplied Jironza's commissary department with food for these military expeditions. From prosaic looking bills presented to the government for payment we get intimate data regarding these matters. The provisions for the soldiery were mainly carne seca (dried beef), pinole or corn meal, and biscocho (hardtack). Most of these supplies were delivered at the presidio of Fronteras by Joseph López, Salgado's mayordomo de recua or pack-train master. The carne seca was billed at 2 cents a pound, the pinole at nearly 3 cents a pound (250 pounds for 7 pesos) and the hard tack at 6 cents a pound. Freight charges were 50 cents an arroba, or 2 cents a pound. For the six campaigns of the last half of 1694 Jironza presented to the government vouchers showing that for food and freighting incident to these skirmishes he had spent 2086 pesos, not counting costs which he had personally borne.[1]

---

[1] Jironza to the viceroy, October 18, 1694, *loc. cit.* Affairs at this time on the Indian frontier east of the Sierra Madre, in northern Chihuahua, then within Nueva Vizcaya, are vividly illustrated by an expedient, or file of documents, in the archives of the city of Parral entitled: [Causa] Criminal en averiguación de la sublevación de Indios Zumas, 1685. Ajusticiados 77 indios. The last phrase makes all too plain the seriousness of the situation.

LXXXII

AN ARROW FALLS AT CABORCA

Favorable reports of the Sobas and Sobaípuris were sent by Kino to the provincial and by Jironza to the viceroy. They tallied on the main point: the harvest was great and the laborers were few. Impressed by the evidence, the viceroy provided funds for two new missionaries, and the provincial sent for the work Fathers Fernando Bayerca and Francisco Xavier Saeta. Bayerca was assigned to Cocóspora.

Saeta was a young scion "of the best blood of Sicily," who had recently come to America. In fact, he had crossed the Atlantic from Cádiz with Campos. Having finished his studies in Mexico, he was sent to the Pimas for his first charge. He arrived at Mátape in the middle of October, just when Father Muñoz, the visitor, was on the way to inspect the Pima missions and install Bayerca.[1] Hurrying up, Saeta overtook the visitor at Dolores. His exact destination was not yet determined. Should he be sent to Tumacácori, to Caborca, or to Tucubavia? After some deliberation, for each place had its claims, he was assigned to Caborca, where he would found a mission to be called Concepción. He would be a neighbor of his friend Campos, only a hundred miles away.

Kino was instructed by Muñoz to install Saeta in his new mission and to do all in his power to equip it. He did not shirk. He agreed to send him a hundred head of cattle, a hundred sheep and goats, saddle and pack animals, a drove of twenty mares with their colts, sixty fanegas of wheat and maize, "together with household effects," all of which he would deliver at Caborca a little at a time. Thus did Dolores become the Mother of Missions.

Father Muñoz went to visit San Ignacio and Tubutama, and to conduct Bayerca to Cocóspora. Two days later (October 19) Kino and Saeta set out with their pack train of equipment for Caborca.

---

[1] Bayerca was assigned to Cocóspora in 1694. Manje says that Saeta arrived in Sonora at the end of 1694 and went to Caborca in January. Manje, *Luz de Tierra Incógnita,* 237. This is incorrect. Saeta returned to Sonora in January, 1695, after his begging trip, and it is this visit there which Manje confuses with his first arrival.

Going to Magdalena, from there they continued to their destination by the shortest route, down the San Ignacio River. With Kino to introduce him, young Saeta everywhere met a warm welcome. On the road he was given eight or nine infants to baptize, "which caused the venerable father great surprise, pleasure and consolation." It was for this that he had come from far distant Europe. At Pitquín they were met by a delegation of natives, and all the way thence to Caborca they found crosses and arches erected along the road.[1] Kino spent one day with Saeta instructing the Indians and advising the new missionary; then he returned to Dolores by way of Tubutama. Father Janusque was delighted when told that he had a neighbor "only fifty miles away." His ideas of neighborhood were not unlike those of Daniel Boone a century later on another American borderland.

As interpreter Saeta had brought from Dolores Francisco Pintor, the Ures Indian who had assisted Kino when he first began his work seven years before, and who had accompanied Manje on his jaunt through Pápago Land. Francisco must have felt a proprietary interest in the whole frontier. Saeta found a little house already built, the one erected by the Caborcans during Kino's previous journeys. He set to work building a chapel, laboring with his own hands—*laborantis manibus nostris*. Within a week after his arrival he wrote Kino that his neophytes had already made five hundred adobes.

Everything progressed famously and Saeta glowed with his success. In November he went east to collect among the old missions of Sonora alms to aid him in building the church, which, to meet his wishes, must be a fine one. His tour was typical of the way in which new missions asked aid of those already established. A good missionary had to be a sturdy beggar. Of first importance was food—beef, maize, and wheat—with which to feed the mob of natives who worked at the building, making adobes, quarrying and carrying stone, cutting timbers, and putting them in their places.

Saeta's youth was engaging, his enthusiasm contagious, and the response liberal. Kino started off the subscription list with a promise

---

[1] Kino, Inocente, Apostólica, y Gloriosa Muerte del V. Pe. Francisco Xavier Saeta, Lib. I, Cap. i.

of sixty additional head of cattle, sixty sheep and goats, sixty fanegas of wheat and maize, and a drove of mares for breeding purposes, and he promptly sent by his pack train and herdsmen all this and more.

Work on the church, fields, and gardens now boomed. Pitquín and other villages became visitas of Caborca, among them being Unuicut, home of Chief Soba. In spite of the hard work Saeta's spirits were in the clouds. He was too busy to think of his troubles or to rest. In March he wrote to Kino, "My children . . . attend Mass every morning and Catechism twice a day, large as well as small. They work with all love. . . . I have planted a very pretty garden plot in which the little trees are set out"—a gift from Kino—"and the vegetable seeds planted for the refreshment of the sailors from California."

Yes, Saeta had caught Kino's vision. "How much the venerable father desired and solicited even the new transmarine conversions of California may be judged from the two following letters." They show also how intimately Kino helped with the new mission. Saeta had received from him one hundred and fifteen sheep and goats. "The fifteen will be for our dear California, as your Reverence suggests." A hundred cattle also had come from Dolores. "As your Reverence suggests to me, the five spotted cows, with your Reverence's brand—[if we only knew the mark we would reproduce it here] —are assigned, as is your wish, to our most beloved hermitess, Rosalía de las Californias, to whom I am constantly praying '*Sit portus et aura suis*—May she be a port of safety and a breeze to her clients,' in order that some day we may go to set up with our own hands her image, and in time her own statue, on that innocent and happy little peak dedicated to her."

Kino invited Saeta to visit him at Dolores during Holy Week. To one exiled, like the young Sicilian, among naked heathen, the temptation was great. But he was too busy and was happy. Vacations are chiefly for persons who do not find joy in their work. "I greatly appreciate your Reverence's noble attention . . . but I must say, my father, that I shall not be able to enjoy your Reverence's favor, for I am already very much engrossed, both in spiritual and temporal matters." He was building a town, farming, and ranching. The present city of Caborca is his monument. Later he yielded partially to pressure and suggested to Kino that they meet at half-way Magdalena, "for, although I am very busy, I will steal that short bit of time and, like fleet Saeta"—a play on his own name[1]—"will fly to place myself at the feet of your Reverence, to receive your commands, and to discuss many things. . . . Here work proceeds with vigor—*fervet opus.*" Except for two postscripts to the same letter this was Saeta's farewell to Kino. The proposed chat "about many things" was never held. The letter was written on April 1. The very next day Saeta won the martyr's crown and thereby was exalted to enduring fame.

The trouble started at Tubutama. Solís's punishment of disturbers there a few months before had not ended difficulties. It may have enhanced them. The Pimas resented having an Opata overseer. It was customary when a new mission was founded to employ Christianized Indians from the old establishments to serve as teachers of the neophytes at the new ones. This had been the practice ever since Cortés's Tlascalan allies were used to help Christianize the wilder tribes north of Mexico City. It was a part of the genius of the Spanish régime. But the plan had its drawbacks. Sometimes it worked badly, especially when the teachers and the taught were of different languages.

So it was at Tubutama. Father Daniel at this time employed as chief herdsman an Opata named Antonio. Like so many inconsequential men when clothed with authority, Antonio became harsh and arbitrary. He bellowed out commands lest he be thought unimportant. He kicked helpless people about to bolster up his self-esteem. At heart he was doubtless a coward. He had one of his outbursts of temper on March 29, shortly after Father Daniel had started for Tuape to observe Holy Week. Perhaps it was Father Daniel's absence that gave him the courage to go on a rampage. He knocked down and kicked with his spurred boot the Pima overseer of the farm. The Pima called to his friends, "This Opata is killing me!" Pimas within hearing hurried to the rescue, pierced Antonio with arrows, pursued him when he fled on horseback and did him to death. They did not

[1] Saeta means arrow.

stop here. A smouldering fire of revolt now burst forth into a flame. They plundered and killed two other Opatas, Martín and Fernando, who happened to be there at the moment, burned the mission residence and church, desecrated sacred articles, and slaughtered mission cattle.

While some of the Indians were wreaking this destruction, others pursued Father Daniel, but were detained by one of the old men. Campos had heard rumors of impending trouble at Tubutama and had sent a warning to Janusque, but it was not delivered. Father Daniel failing to appear at San Ignacio, Campos set forth with mission Indians to rescue him. By a strange coincidence, or "by the special providence of our Lord" as Velarde put it, both took the same bypath, off the camino real, and therefore met on the way. Returning to San Ignacio, they went together to Tuape.

The fire of rebellion now blazed still higher. The Opatas were slain, the Spaniards had fled; but down the river there were other imported Indians and another padre. Death to the foreigners! Out with them all! The rebels knew they would have to pay, but they might as well pay for sheep as for lambs. So down the river they started.

Saeta got wind of what had happened at Tubutama, but he thought the assailants were Jocomes. His letter above quoted was written on April 1. That day he added two postscripts. "P.S. I. Through lack of vinegar I have not yet sampled my pretty garden." Before night he got a letter from Kino, and to his own missive he added another postscript. "P.S. II. The bearer of your Reverence's letter," an Indian runner, "has grieved me unspeakably by the news he has brought me, to the effect that the Hocomes attacked San Pedro del Tubutama the other day and killed poor Martín and the boy Fernando, who were returning from bringing me the cattle. In God's name, your Reverence, tell me what happened, as well as about Father Daniel!" On the outside of the letter after it was sealed he added a third postscript: "The news of the deaths of Martín and the boy is confirmed. Let your Reverence not lose sight of me." Evidently he still thought the murderers were the Jocomes. We do not know what misgivings he may have had during that long uncertain night.

Next morning his uncertainty was ended. At Oquitoa the rebels enlarged their gang to forty. Others joined them at Pitquín. On April 2, Saturday of the Gloria, they reached Caborca, and went to the missionary's quarters in the guise of peace. After a friendly talk Saeta bade them goodbye and accompanied them to the hall outside—the room then used as a church. Suddenly they drew their bows and disclosed their horrible intent. Saeta called for aid but no help came. Kneeling, he received two arrow shots. Then, rising, with the weapons still piercing his body, he ran back to his room, embraced a crucifix, fell bleeding on his bed, and there expired. The agony, it is a mercy, was not prolonged. To make sure of their work the assassins filled his poor body with arrows till he resembled Saint Sebastian.

The murderers now turned on Saeta's assistants. Chief of these was Francisco Pintor, the famous interpreter and temastián from Ures, he who had been a mainstay while Saeta was learning the native language. Him the assassins ruthlessly dispatched. Then they killed José, the herdsman, an outsider from Chinapa, and Francisco the sabanero, from Cumpas. These lives taken, the rebels plundered Saeta's house, slaughtered and stampeded cattle, sheep, goats, and the horse herd, and then returned upstream. The valley was cleared of foreigners.[1]

In the Church the term martyr has a technical significance, and not all missionaries killed while on duty are given that distinction. Father Saeta met the conditions. "I call the Venerable Father . . . Saeta a martyr," wrote Velarde, "in the sense permitted by the decrees of our very holy Father Urban . . . because . . . judging by what they did with the sacred ornaments, holy oils, arras, chalices, and patens, which were the same excesses as those committed in Tubutama, I am convinced that they killed him *in odium fidei*—through hatred of the Faith. . . . Happy death and fortunate father, for he merited the honor of dying for Christ, which is won only by outstanding virtues and an innocent life."

---

[1] Kino, *Favores Celestiales,* Parte II, Lib. iii, Cap. 10; *Hist. Mem.,* I, 142–143; Inocente, Apostólica, y Gloriosa Muerte, Lib. I–III. Manje says that Francisco was killed before Saeta, who received twenty-one arrow wounds (*Luz de Tierra Incógnita,* 237, 321). His account was written several years after the event.

LXXXIII

A SOLEMN PROCESSION

Father Eusebio learned of Saeta's death at nine o'clock next day, Sunday. The news was carried to Dolores by a faithful Caborca Indian in twenty-seven hours, a distance of more than a hundred miles. Did the messenger ride a horse, or was he on foot? History does not tell us. Two hours later Kino received Saeta's last letter. It seemed to contradict the tale of disaster, but only for the moment. Coming on the heels of reports of the Tubutama uprising, carried to San Ignacio and Cucurpe by Father Janusque, the news of the massacre was alarming. It was made doubly so by simultaneous rumors that a vast horde of enemies were coming to attack the other Pima missions. At the very same time hostile Jocomes and Janos were pressing the northeastern frontier of Sonora with unusual fury. The Tarahumares, over the Sierra, were conspiring. Was the tragedy of New Mexico to be repeated?

Kino and Kappus hurried the alarm to Jironza at San Juan. Kino sent Chief Felipe, the Indian governor of El Bosna, to Caborca to find out more in detail what had happened.[1] Father Muñoz and the citizens of San Juan wrote appeals for help to Janos and Parral. Jironza did not delay. In spite of conditions on the northeastern border he quickly mustered the soldiers of his presidio, citizens of that vicinity and of Opodepe, and a band of Tepoca Indians who had already been assembled for another purpose. To these were added Manje, Fathers Campos and Bayerca as chaplains, and many Pima Indians of Dolores, San Ignacio, Cocóspora, El Tupo and other places. It was a typical frontier army, white and red men mixed, such as could be seen at this time almost anywhere from Chile to the St. Lawrence. Indeed, Frontenac at the very same moment was preparing just such a contingent in Canada to lead it against the Iroquois of New York.

With his following Jironza proceeded first to Tubutama. The

---

[1] Kino, Inocente, Apostólica, y Gloriosa Muerte, Lib. I, Cap. iv; Kino, *Favores Celestiales,* Parte I, Lib. iii, Caps. 8–10; *Hist. Mem.,* I, 139–143; Manje, *Luz de Tierra Incógnita,* 236–246. See Francis Parkman, *Count Frontenac and New France Under Louis XIV,* Chap. XVIII.

people of that pueblo and of others near by had fled through fear to the mountains. A sick woman who was discovered was killed by the Tepoca Indians, contrary to orders. After vain efforts to find other natives of the vicinity, Jironza led his forces down stream. Above Pitquín they met Chief Felipe returning from his reconnaissance. He had found Caborca deserted. Finding the dead bodies decomposing he had burned them, according to native custom. He brought with him, carefully encased, the crucifix which Saeta had embraced in his last moments, and as the army approached he devoutly knelt and presented the box to Father Campos. There was a miraculous touch to the incident. The texture of the statue "was so soft that it appeared to be living flesh, showing the veins, nerves, and arteries. Father Agustín gave it as an exquisite relic to Lieutenant Antonio de Solís, and now it is placed in the mission of Arispe, with great veneration, in a splendid golden sepulcher with six glass lunas, which serves as a coffin in the procession and in the burial during Holy Week." So Manje wrote a few years later. Where is the statue now? Very probably on some altar in Sonora, or perhaps in a private home. Someone doubtless has a tale to tell.

At Pitquín Jironza's men captured a native woman and two little girls. As they neared Caborca, Manje, who knew the country, went ahead to reconnoiter, accompanied by a body guard of Seri Indians. Suddenly they came upon a man and two boys in a mesquite grove. The Seris shot one of the boys, whom Father Bayerca baptized before he expired. The man escaped. The other boy, called Antonio, clung to Manje, and thus was saved. With the exception of these three natives, Caborca was deserted.

In an effort to learn who were the perpetrators of the massacre— for this was still a matter of uncertainty—Jironza interrogated the captives, who agreed that the malefactors were not Caborcans, but Indians from Tubutama, Oquitoa and Pitquín. That is to say, the trouble had arisen at Tubutama. "Whence it is concluded," wrote Manje, "that it ought not to be permitted that a few Indians of a different tribe should be allowed to dominate hostile and populous nations such as the Pimería."[1] Other incidents in mission history pointed

[1] Manje, *Luz de Tierra Incógnita*, 236–246, 319–325.

Pencil sketch by Pinart, 1879

Mission at San Ignacio

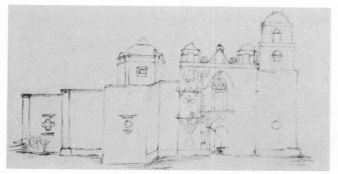

Pencil sketch by Pinart, 1879

Mission at Tubutama

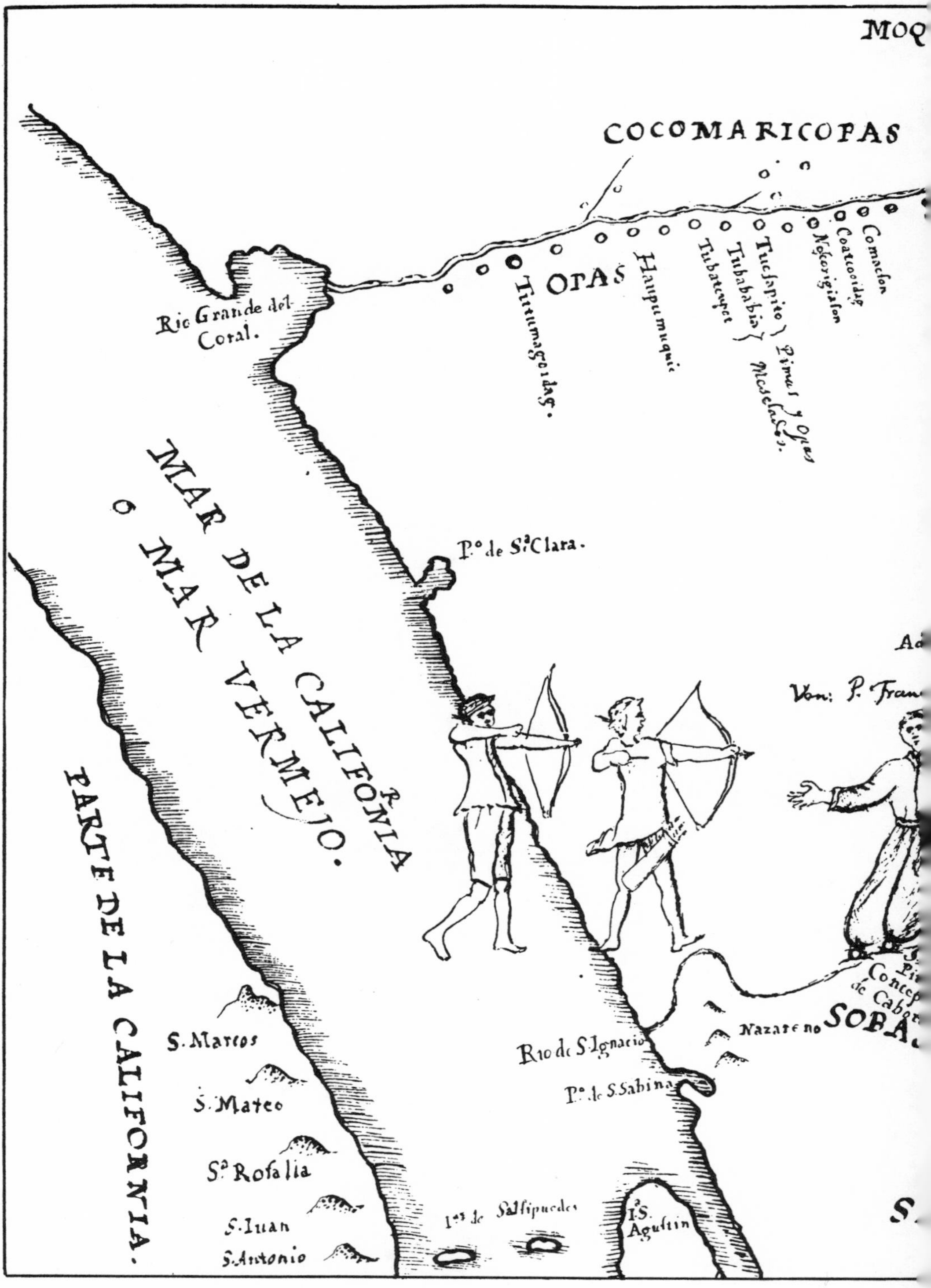

MOQ

COCOMARICOPAS

Rio Grande del Coral.

OPAS

Titumagoilas.

Haupumuqui

Tucipito) Pimas y Opas
Tubabaia) Mesolaso.
Tubateype

Comacon
Coaticorido
Mecorgidon

P.º de S.ª Clara.

MAR DE LA CALIFORNIA
O MAR VERMEIO.

Von: P. Fran

PARTE DE LA CALIFORNIA.

S. Marcos

S. Mateo

S.ª Rofalia

S. Iuan
S. Antonio

Rio de S. Ignacio

P.º de S. Sabina.

Nazateno

Pi
Concep
de Cabe
SOBA

I.S.
Aguftin

I.ª de Salfipuedes

S.

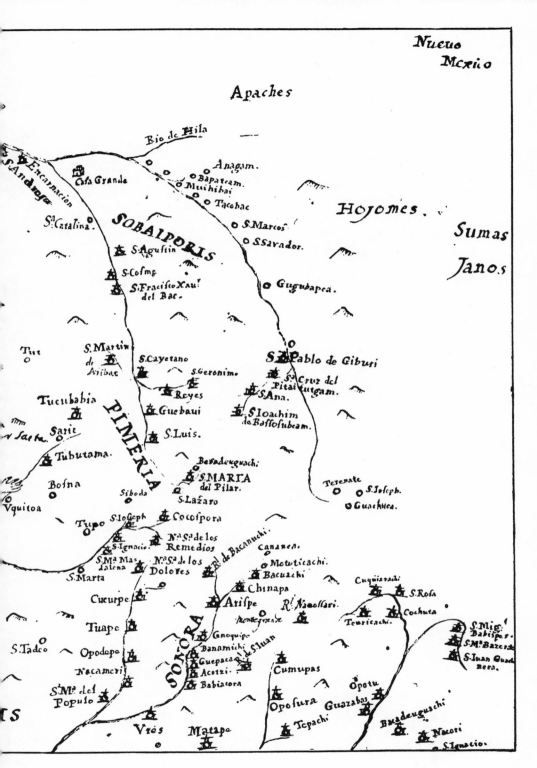

Kino's Map of Pimería Alta showing the Martyrdom of Father Saeta in 1695

(From the original manuscript)

Mission Santa Cruz

Mission at Pitiquito

to the same moral. After the Pitquín woman was questioned she was baptized and executed, since her village had participated in the attack. The process by which she was dispatched was less refined and ceremonious than the execution of Joan of Arc. But the two were perhaps equally blameless; and after execution they were equally dead.

Jironza and Manje gathered up the bones, ashes, and even the dried blood of Father Saeta, "and placed them with decency and veneration in a box." They found various papers, books, and pictures, but the vestments and altar ornaments had been carried off by the malefactors. Manje gives us the details. "I had the happiness to aid in gathering up the bones, ashes, and head, which we found with the hair of the deceased father still attached. We locked them in a medium-sized box. Near these things I also found on parchment a picture of a nun. Judging from the grey and black habit, she was a Benedictine or a Franciscan. The picture bore the name of Santa Coleta, and showed an angel fitting an arrow to a bow, while another arrow already pierced the saint's heart and a third was visible in the space between her and the angel.

"They also pulled twenty-two arrows from the ground in the deceased father's bedroom, and much dried blood, and with these arrows it appears they finished killing him. Missals, books, pictures, and sacred vessels were gathered, but all were ruined. Only the field of wheat was intact, and it was high enough to cover a man, had large heads and was filled, whereas the fields which we had left in Sonora were only beginning to head, evident proof of the richness of this land." Manje saved the broken cross on which the statue of Christ was nailed. "And I carried it to the Reverend Father Eusebio Francisco Kino, who placed it on the altar of his mission of Nuestra Señora de los Dolores." The picture of Santa Coleta which Manje found he also took to Kino, who put it in his Breviary, beside the one given him by the Duchess.

Before turning back Jironza's men ruthlessly destroyed the wheat and maize fields of the Caborcans, turning into them their drove of three hundred horses, as they did with the fields of all the villages in the valley, "in order that those who took no part in the murder and rebellion might deliver the instigators and make peace." [1]

Carrying the precious relics on a mule, Jironza and his cavalcade returned in solemn march over the long trail to Dolores, where they arrived on May 2, just a month after the massacre. Saeta was the first missionary martyr of the Pimería, and his burial was conducted with pomp. At Dolores, next day, the Feast of the Invention of the Cross was celebrated with great solemnity, Jironza confessing and receiving communion, to the great edification of everybody present. In the afternoon the funeral procession, headed by Jironza, Kino, Bayerca, and Manje, proceeded south to Cucurpe, five leagues distant, for the burial. Saeta's remains were carried "with all the veneration possible . . . between two files, composed of soldiers and citizens and many Indians . . . amid salvos of arquebuses and other demonstrations." Jironza, "to the great satisfaction of all, deigned to lead by the bridle the mule which bore the little box containing the bones of the venerable father." As they neared Cucurpe the chaplains went ahead, put on their vestments, and with Father Kappus came out to welcome the procession. Arrived at the cross near the foot of the hill on top of which stood the temple—the ruins are still there—the mourners lifted the box of relics from the mule, and Jironza carried it reverently on his shoulders up the steep to the beautifully arched church that looked down on the pueblo and the river.

Next day Saeta's remains were laid to rest. Kappus, the rector, sang the Requiem Mass, in the presence of a great concourse, including all the officials, soldiers, and citizens of Opodepe and San Juan, as well as Jironza's soldiers and Indians. Repeated volleys of musketry were fired. A part of the ceremony was the installing on the altar of a new retablo which had recently come from Mexico. "The burial of the holy body was on the Epistle side of the main altar of the church of Cucurpe," because on the Gospel side Father Barli, of Cocóspora and Imuris, had been buried a few months before.

Manje adds, "All these demonstrations were decided upon by the reverend fathers and General Jironza both on account of the merits of the angelic life and other virtues of the deceased father, and to furnish an example to the many Pima and Seri Indians who accom-

[1] Manje, *Luz de Tierra Incógnita*, 239.

panied the army, of the veneration which is shown even to the ashes of the dead priests, in order that they may understand the high appreciation of the ministers of God and the teachers of His Law." [1]

LXXXIV

LA MATANZA

While at Dolores Jironza agreed with Kino to request the Pimas not implicated in the uprising to bring the ringleaders to justice, as a basis for making peace. The loyal pueblos gladly entered into the arrangement, and proceeded to carry it out. Pursuant to the plan, in the middle of May the governor of El Bosna took to Kino two vestments brought to him from Tubutama. They were wrapped in a neatly tanned lion's skin,[2] and on his knees the chief delivered them to Father Eusebio. One of the vestments was red. Robed in the other, which was white, Kino chanted Mass on the feast of San Isidro, Sunday, May 15. Things were being arranged for the return of whatever else was held by the Tubutamas, and for the delivery of the chief malefactors, especially through the governor of Dolores. By word of mouth and by writing, Almazán, now alcalde mayor of Sonora, assured Kino of his approval, and by Almazán's order and in his name, Kino promised peace and general pardon for all who might assist in delivering up the delinquents. This should be kept in mind as the story proceeds.

But secular counsels were divided. When Jironza returned to San Juan he encountered opposition. Some officials maintained that the rebellious Indians should be soundly chastised. Jironza was persuaded, and a second expedition was arranged. With a larger force than before—soldiers, citizens, Indian allies, supplies, and cavallada—the army marched over the mountains to San Ignacio. Antonio Solís was in command.

---

[1] Kino, *Inocente, Apostólica, y Gloriosa Muerte*, Lib. III, Caps. iv–v; Kino, *Favores Celestiales*, Parte I, Lib. iii, Cap. 11; *Hist. Mem.*, I, 144; Manje, *Luz de Tierra Incógnita*, 240. Manje also emphatically says that Saeta was buried on the Epistle side.

[2] Doubtless the skin of a cougar or mountain lion.

Under these circumstances the Indians were puzzled, and in doubt whether or not to believe the promises that had been made. When at the end of May the governor of Dolores went to summon the people of Tubutama and vicinity to come in peace and without weapons to meet the army, under promise that only the ringleaders would be punished, they replied that they were afraid of treachery. Even the loyal governor of Bosna hesitated. Hearing of the difficulty, Kino went in person to San Ignacio, and from there sent a message to the alcalde of El Tupo, telling him to summon the people to meet the army at La Ciénega, the marsh near his village. The alcalde, the governor, and the governor's brother now went inland and soon brought to La Ciénega more than a hundred Indians from Tubutama and other places. They came humbly, carrying crosses and unarmed, the innocent bringing the guilty. Things were moving forward. As a reward for this service the alcalde of El Tupo was promoted to be governor of his village.

This diplomacy had not been accomplished without the use of force.[1] According to Manje, Solís went to Tubutama and Oquitoa, and killed several Indians in surprise attacks, with the result that others sued for peace, which was granted on condition that they should deliver the heads of the revolt, dissemblingly bringing them in with the innocent. Whatever the facts in this particular, Kino and Manje agree in their accounts that the Pimas came to El Tupo and delivered up the delinquents. There they were surrendered to the soldiers to await their fate. Thus, said Kino, "it seemed that with much skill a just and very good punishment of the culprits had been achieved, and that the innocent and all the Pimería would remain content and quiet."

A stratagem was now devised for arresting also the accomplices of the captive ringleaders. But there was a mishap. "It seems that there was still lacking this misfortune or very heavy cross, or last fury and effort of the Common Enemy," says Kino. The army under Captain Solís arrived at El Tupo, and there on the 9th of June it met the assembled natives. Manje describes the scene. "On the third day fifty Indians came, and when they reached the camp of the sol-

---

[1] Kino, *Inocente, Apostólica, y Glorioso Muerte,* Lib. V, Cap. i; Kino, *Hist. Mem.,* I. 144–145.

diers at El Tupo, which was pitched at some springs in an open plain cleared of woods, they left their bows and arrows close to a little grove of mesquite, distant about four arquebus shots, and according to agreement went unarmed to the camp.

"The soldiers, mounted on horseback, now formed a circle, with dissimulation putting the Indians in the center. Then the four Indians who had promised peace"—the three governors and the alcalde —"pointed out those who had accompanied the ringleaders who had stirred them up for the rebellion and murder (for the ringleaders were prevented by their capital crime from appearing). Three Indians were bound. Seeing that they were proceeding to bind others who were pointed out, all became excited and began to bolt." Kino here puts in a touch which Manje omits. The governor of Dolores now played the part of assistant verdugo, or executioner. Grasping a chief offender by the hair of the head he said to Solís, "This is one of the murderers." Thereupon Solís with a cutlass struck off the victim's head.

Instead of a peace talk the scene now became a hell of carnage. Frightened, guilty and innocent alike started to break through the circle of horsemen. Obeying previous orders for such a contingency, in a flash soldiers and Tepoca allies shot down forty-eight terrified Indians, including eighteen charged as guilty and thirty regarded by Kino as innocent. Very appropriately the place where it occurred became known as La Matanza—The Slaughter. And no wonder Solís acquired a reputation for bloodthirstiness.

Among the killed were the new governor of El Tupo, and the captain of El Bosna, both of whom had done such fine service for the Spaniards—or had so betrayed their own people. Even bloody Solís was shocked. He was compadre of the captain of El Bosna, having been godfather of his son baptized that very day. "In fact everybody, the palefaces, and even those who killed the victims, and especially all the Pima nation, were very deeply grieved." But the Indians remained dead, guilty and innocent alike.[1] Harsh as he was, Solís

---

[1] Manje, *Luz de Tierra Incógnita*, 240–241; Kino, Inocente, Apostólica, y Gloriosa Muerte, Lib. V, Caps. i-ii. Solís was soon afterward discharged from the army and publicly disgraced in Mexico. Velarde erroneously puts the Matanza after the Indian attack on San Ignacio and Imuris. Manje, *Luz de Tierra Incógnita*, 325.

was sick of his job, and well he might be. Kino was prostrated with grief. But "there was no lack of persons who thought a very good stroke . . . had been achieved." The Matanza was a sad example of the brutality often experienced by the natives at the hands of Europeans in most parts of colonial America.

LXXXV

REAPING THE WHIRLWIND

After the slaughter of so many Pimas, innocent as well as guilty, Jironza assumed that the tribe were thoroughly frightened into submission, so he prepared to go east with his soldiery to join La Fuente and Terán in another one of those frequent campaigns against the "common enemy of the North, the Apaches, Jocomes, and Janos." He was to meet them in the vicinity of Cuchuta. Leaving Corporal Escalante with three soldiers at San Ignacio to guard and escort Father Campos in his travels, and Manje with three armed civilians from Bacanuche to protect and assist Kino at Dolores, the army started north under Solís. On June 19 it was in camp at Cocóspora. Jironza went south to Opodepe to continue preparations.[1]

The Pimas were cowed for the moment, but anger burned in their breasts. The backs of the soldiers were scarcely turned when they saw their chance for revenge. Not only the relatives of the slaughtered, but many former neutrals as well, joined in the resentment. In large bands they went to Tubutama and Caborca and burned the buildings of these missions, which thus far they had left standing. Then some three hundred warriors assembled preparatory to destroying Campos's missions at Imuris and San Ignacio. Among their weapons they had the very bows and arrows returned to them by Solís after the matanza at El Tupo.

The Spaniards still had friends among the Pimas. One of these was the chief of El Síboda, north of Imuris, now a station in a beautiful vale on the Southern Pacific Railroad. Though a heathen, he

---

[1] Manje, *Luz de Tierra Incógnita,* 241.

went down the valley to San Ignacio to notify Campos of the impending blow and to warn the neophytes of both Imuris and San Ignacio to withdraw.

As soon as Campos learned of the danger he hurried Cosme, a Christianized Yaqui Indian living at the San Ignacio mission, to Cocóspora to call the soldiers back to the rescue. Cosme, thinking to improve upon his orders, took matters into his own hands. At Imuris he engaged a mission Indian to carry the message to Cocóspora. While his substitute ascended the canyon, Cosme himself stopped at Imuris to round up the horses of the mission, so that when the soldiers should arrive on winded and tired animals they would have fresh remounts ready at hand. This done he hurried back to San Ignacio.

From the time when the Síboda chief brought the warning, Father Agustín and his four guardsmen kept their horses saddled and in readiness. They did not have long to wait. About eight o'clock next morning, when they were eating breakfast, the enemy came with ear-splitting yells and began their work of devastation. Corporal Escalante and two soldiers sallied out and bravely held them back. The fourth soldier waited while Campos put on his spurs and mounted. All being ready they rode full speed eastward over the mountains, through the pass at El Torreón, "the padre in the middle and two soldiers on each side restraining the fury and fighting the whole two leagues which the enemy pursued." [1]

Cosme's improvement upon his orders was a fine idea, but it did not work to perfection. The Pima messenger was lazy or sleepy, and he did not arrive at Cocóspora till daylight on the 20th, the day of the attack. The news he bore startled the camp, and the soldiers crawled out of their tents staring and rubbing their eyes. Then, quickly mounting, they raced the fourteen leagues down the red-walled canyon past Babasaqui to Imuris and to San Ignacio. But they were just too late. They found burned to ashes and desolated the pueblos, houses, and chapels of Father Campos at Imuris, San Ignacio, and Magdalena. Nobody was killed. At San Ignacio the vestments

[1] Manje, *Luz de Tierra Incógnita,* 242; Kino, Inocente, Apostólica, y Gloriosa Muerte, Lib. V, Cap. ii.

were burned. The raiders slaughtered a few sheep and goats and ran off horses, but left most of the cattle unmolested. The soldiers pursued the enemy into the mountains, overtaking and killing some of them.[1]

A different scene was enacted at Dolores, where Manje was on guard. The news of the attack on San Ignacio was brought by Cosme, the same Yaqui who had carried the alarm to Imuris. Hurrying back from there to his mission, he took his station on a peak to watch for the enemy. Not seeing Campos and the soldiers leave, as soon as he saw the dense smoke of the conflagration at San Ignacio he crossed the Sierra, spurring his horse the whole ten leagues to Dolores. This time he did not entrust the errand to a lazy Pima.

As Kino and Manje were eating, sometime in the forenoon, Cosme entered the comedor. Breaking down and weeping, he told them between sobs that the Pimas had burned alive Padre Agustín and the soldiers, together with the house and everything else. Manje now seized Cosme's rôle of Paul Revere. "Instantly I mounted a good horse," he tells us, "and rode *á rompe-cinchas*—at breakneck speed— the sixteen leagues to the pueblo of Opodepe, where I arrived at three o'clock in the afternoon, finding the Reverend Father . . . Kappus and General Jironza drinking chocolate." The next cup was left for a later time.

Manje told his astounded listeners the distressing news, ate a bite, went to the cavallada and got a new mount. All three saddled up and in a few minutes were raising a dust on the northbound trail, and making the canyon walls ring with hoofbeats. That afternoon they rode twelve leagues, arriving by nightfall at Cucurpe. Manje had ridden that day twenty-eight leagues or some seventy-five miles. At Cucurpe they found Father Campos and the four soldiers "who had come out of it safely, seeing which we were relieved somewhat of our anxiety." He adds, "and they recounted at length what had occurred at the burning of the pueblo," as no doubt they many times recounted it to the end of their days.[2] The question arises why Manje did not see Campos at Cucurpe on the way south? Clearly they were not

---

[1] Kino, Inocente, Apostólica, y Gloriosa Muerte, Lib. V, Cap. i; Kino, *Favores Celestiales*, Parte I, Lib. iii, Cap. 12; *Hist. Mem.*, I, 145.

[2] Manje, *Luz de Tierra Incógnita*, 242. As a result of this attack some of the neophytes of Imuris and San Ignacio went over the hills to live at Dolores.

there, so Cosme and Manje must have made better time than Campos and his four soldiers, missing them somewhere on the way. We may be sure they did not stop to decipher the inscriptions on the rock at El Pintor—if the inscriptions were there at the time.

Meanwhile Kino was waiting at Dolores, anxiously looking in all directions from the vantage point afforded him by his high-perched mission. Early next day Manje hurried on from Cucurpe with two soldiers, fearing that Dolores would be attacked next. When he arrived there he found that the three citizen soldiers had already departed for Bacanuche, "leaving Father Kino alone," and for himself a letter explaining that they must hasten home to look after their families. This was no trivial excuse.

The news got worse instead of better. That same day a warning came saying the rebels were indeed on the way to destroy the mission of Dolores. Kino's first thought was for his church ornaments, and Manje helped him secrete them. "We stole forth in the silence of the night," says Matheo, "to hide in a cave a league away the boxes of ornaments, vessels, books, missals, and other treasures of the church and of the padre. But although I protested to him that we ought not to return to the pueblo, he assured me that nothing would happen, and setting out to return we arrived at daybreak." That was an anxious night for young Manje. "I confessed myself as for death on account of what might happen, in order not to desert the minister of the pueblo." There was heroism.

Not only Dolores but also Remedios and Cocóspora, all three under the personal charge of Kino, escaped destruction in the general holocaust. And Manje firmly believed this escape due to the profound influence of Kino. "From the conspiracy and the burning, if not from the fear, only the pueblos of . . . Dolores were exempt. This I attribute to the virtue and the continuous and fervent prayers of Father Eusebio Kino, first missionary of that revolted nation, for, since he had been their spiritual father and had wiped their tears in their times of need, affliction, and trouble, defending them always, gratitude perhaps kept them from burning and destroying his mission and his spacious painted and adorned church." Kino himself modestly wrote a few years later, "We were all in great straits, but I sent such quieting messages as I could to all parts, and by Divine Grace the trouble went no further."[1]

LXXXVI

ARMIES GATHER

Jironza was alarmed. Fearing now that the uprising would not be confined to the Pimas, but would spread to other tribes, Christian as well as heathen, and embrace the whole province in the flames of rebellion, as had happened in New Mexico fifteen years previously, he hurriedly called for help. He sent messengers at breakneck speed to La Fuente and Terán to hurry west to help save Sonora. For him to meet these generals on the Apache border, as had been planned, would now be out of the question. Instead, they were urgently needed in Pima Land. Other couriers rode in other directions. Nameless Paul Reveres made long rides in the hot July sun to summon assistance for the threatened province. These hard-riding couriers played their part in history.

When Jironza sent his SOS, La Fuente and Terán were already on their way.[2] They left Janos on June 15, with seventy-five soldiers and some sixty Concho and Opata allies. Crossing the wide Chihuahua plains and threading precipitous Guadalupe Pass, on June 25 they camped at the fine waters of San Bernardino. Two days later they received Jironza's appeal, carried by a mulatto courier. Letters from Muñoz and Kappus told of the Matanza and of the vengeful destruc-

---

[1] Manje, *Luz de Tierra Incógnita,* 241–243; Kino, *Favores Celestiales,* Parte I, Lib. iii, Cap. 12; *Hist. Mem.,* I, 145. Velarde tells us that Campos escaped martyrdom a second time that day by fleeing to Cucurpe instead of to Dolores, the road to which the rebel Indians were watching. "Although sorrowfully, because now on two occasions the palm of martyrdom had slipped through his fingers, he thanked Our Lord, who doubtless spared him from such danger in order that with his zeal and his holy industry he might remain in this Pimería." (Velarde, in *Luz de Tierra Incógnita,* 325.)

[2] Besides the writings of Kino and Manje, we have for this chapter the hitherto unknown manuscript diary of La Fuente and Terán, who led the army from Janos to Pimería Alta. It is entitled Testtimonio de Auttos de Guerra fechos por los Capitanes Juan Fernández de la Fuentte, Don Domingo Therán de los Rios, y Don Domingo Gironza Petris de Cruzati. Sobre las Guerras de las Nassiones Janos, Jocomes, Sumas, Chinarras, Mansos, y Apaches, y la pasificazn. de los Pimas. Año de 1695. Original Spanish manuscript in the Municipal Archives of Parral, Chihuahua, 202 folios. See also Autos de Guerra Tocantes al Capitán Ramírez, A.G.I. 67–4–11. Audiencia de Guadalajara.

tion of Imuris and San Ignacio. Campos had fled to Tuape. Of Kino's fate they knew nothing. Perhaps he, too, had been killed.

La Fuente's impulse was to push forward at once. But to prevent a raid on Sonora behind their backs, he and Terán turned aside to break up an assembly of Apaches in the Chiricahua Mountains, made peace with them, recovered captives and stolen goods. The side trip was a brilliant success. Then they hurried on to join Jironza. Their route was along the military trail to Arroyo Cabullona, up that stream through the mountains to San Pedro River, to Santa María (now Santa Cruz), and to Cocóspora, where they arrived on July 13. There they found Solís with his troops awaiting a hundred Yaqui allies. Kino and Campos were also there. Next day Jironza came from Dolores, and Higuera arrived with eighteen Sinaloa soldiers. It was a gathering of the hosts.

Here at Cocóspora La Fuente, Terán, and Jironza planned a campaign to the country of the rebellious Pimas. "Good talks" were sent to the hostile villages, urging them to deliver up the ringleaders of the revolt, promising pardon if they complied, fire and sword if they refused. Through interpreters La Fuente harangued the allies, exhorting them to assemble their warriors. At first it was proposed to send fifty men to Tumacácori thence southwest over the mountains to attack Tucubavia by surprise, but this plan was soon given up. It was decided that Jironza should not go with the army, but should remain behind to gather up and forward the provisions—a hundred loads—donated by the missionaries. They furnished the sinews of war.

A muster of the army was then held, each division separately. The Spanish warriors presented themselves on horseback. La Fuente had thirty-seven soldiers from Janos, Terán fifty-six from El Gallo, Higuera twenty-two from Sinaloa, and Jironza forty-eight soldiers and citizens of Sonora. There were more than a hundred native allies, armed with bow and arrow. Chief Corma lined up with thirty Conchos from Chihuahua who had come with La Fuente and Terán;[1] Juan María Salvatierra, chief of Cocóspora, with ten Pimas; Eusebio Kino, chief of Santa María, ten; Coro, pagan chief of the Sobaípuris,

---

[1] The Christianized chiefs were listed under their baptismal names. Two of them, it will be noted, were named for Salvatierra and Kino.

ten; Jironza, chief of Huachuca, eight. This made forty-two Pimas. Pablo Banico presented twelve men from Ures; Isidro Sauri, eight Opatas from Arizpe; Juan de María, eleven Opatas from Banámichi, Aconchi, Guépaca, and Sinoquipe. Useless horses were cut out of the herd and left behind; excess baggage was deposited for safekeeping at the mission house under guard of twelve soldiers.

On July 20 Kino said early Mass, and the army started south, Campos going as chaplain. Two leagues down the valley, at the estancia or ranch, halt was made to round up eighty cattle donated by Kino to feed the army. While in camp a soldier and his horse were killed by lightning. In the afternoon Kino and Jironza left the army and went to Dolores to forward supplies.

Next day, driving the cattle ahead, the march of the army was continued. At Imuris they found church, mission house, and Indian huts all burned and dead cattle lying around. La Fuente pushed ahead with sixty men. At San Ignacio he found church, house, and huts in ashes. Next morning at daybreak he reached Magdalena, where church and pueblo had been destroyed by fire. Terán overtook La Fuente here, and in the afternoon he in turn went ahead. He found El Tupo deserted, captured an Indian at Ciénega de la Matanza, and went forward to Búsanic. Next day (the 23d) La Fuente followed and camped at La Matanza. Moving their men like cautious chess players, the generals were taking no chances.

The rebels, through their spies, learned that the Spaniards were coming. Frightened, from Tubutama they sent messengers to meet the army, begging that the chaplain be sent ahead without the soldiers to talk things over, for with reason they were afraid of the troops. But the request was not granted. Instead Terán entered Tubutama by night, took the inhabitants by surprise and killed twenty-one Indians. Terrified now, the Tubutamas and their neighbors fled into the mountains, "so far away that for many days it was not possible to do a thing of consequence." The garrisons went up from Tubutama to Sáric, and "completely laid waste their fields and provisions, punishing some accomplices." [1] War is always savage.

---

[1] La Fuente and Therán, *Testtimonio de Auttos de Guerra*, for the corresponding dates; Manje, *Luz de Tierra Incógnita*, 243–244; Kino, Inocente, Apostólica, y Gloriosa Muerte, Lib. V, Cap. iii; Kino, *Favores Celestiales*, Parte I, Lib. iii, Cap. 13; *Hist. Mem.*, I, 145–146.

For several days La Fuente despaired of getting in touch with the fugitives, then difficulties began to clear up. The General moved his camp up to the Estancia (Ranch) of Tubutama, still so-called, where there was pasturage for his horses and mules, and from there sent friendly talks to the frightened refugees. One of his messengers, a man whom he had captured and reassured, was particularly successful. On the night of August 6 he brought into camp the chief of Tucubavia and three other Pimas. All came "without weapons and with crosses, apparently very repentant for what they had done." All night long there were tlatoles between the chief and La Fuente. The General was encouraged. "All will be arranged very satisfactorily, and more quickly than we expected," he wrote to Kino next day.

Things did, indeed, move rapidly now. A few days later there were more than fifty Indians in camp. Confidence was being restored. The General appointed new Indian officials in the once rebellious towns, the efficient peace messenger being made governor of Tubutama. The title of captain-general of the Pimas was conferred on the chief of Tucubavia, the large town upstream. The repentant people of the district laid the principal blame for the trouble on the *mador* and *caporal* of Tubutama, and promised to bring them or their heads to the Spaniards. La Fuente now regarded peace "as good as made," said he would "give his head" for any misdeed which henceforward the Pimas might commit, and urged that the missionaries return to their former posts.[1]

Caborca and the villages near El Tupo, scene of the horrifying Matanza, were the slowest to regain confidence, and to these districts La Fuente now turned his attention. In a letter written on August 17 he reviewed what he had done and begged Father Eusebio's assistance. The garrison was now returning to El Tupo, while he, next day, with five principal Indians, was starting down the river to Caborca to pacify the Pimas there. Father Eusebio could help.

Saeta's death and the aftermath told on Kino's rugged constitution. Muñoz wrote on May 11, "Your Reverence's health has caused me a great deal of worry, for they have reported to me that they had seen

[1] La Fuente and Therán, *Testtimonio de Auttos de Guerra*, for the corresponding dates; Kino, *Inocente, Apostólica, y Gloriosa Muerte*, Lib. V, Caps. iii-iv; La Fuente to Kino, August 17, 1695, *ibid.*

you looking very ill. But I am inclined to think that in the present case the heart and spirit of your Reverence will be suffering even more, on account of the uprising of this new Christendom." This illness may explain why Kino did not go to the scene of the revolt with the army. Two months later he was still under the weather. He tells us that he received a letter on July 25, at the time when he was suffering from fever. But now, in August he responded to La Fuente's appeal.[1]

LXXXVII

DOVE OF PEACE

Once more Kino became peacemaker in the districts of El Tupo and Caborca. This time he was more fortunate than before. In the work he was greatly assisted by two influential natives. These were the captain of Dolores, and the new governor of El Bosna, successor of the unfortunate Pima who had met death in the Matanza.

Kino writes of the diplomatic mission which he now undertook. It meant another long jaunt over mountains and deserts at a time when he was far from well. "Because by several letters it had been intimated that I should go if I could to see the army, and likewise the children, for they also greatly desired it, on the 21st of August I went to El Tupo and to the near-by Ciénega, where the camp was stationed. I sent ahead the captain of this pueblo of . . . Dolores and of these conversions. And because of his going and mine there came to see me and the Real de la Ciénega [that is, the army], . . . a great number of natives of six or seven principal rancherías, El Tupo, El Bosna, El Araupo, Santa Marta, Tucucot, Arituba, Doagsoma, etc., all of whom had withdrawn through fear. The governor of El Bosna also came to see me, for without his coming they considered that the peace treaties would be of little satisfaction." This chief was an important man.

Long talks were held. While Kino was in the midst of these conferences a sergeant came from La Fuente ordering the army at La

---

[1] Kino, *Inocente, Apostólica, y Gloriosa Muerte*, prefatory statement and Lib. IV, Cap. i.

Ciénega to escort the native delegates to Caborca for a conference. Kino argued that the military escort of the natives was unnecessary, would merely increase their fear, and that he himself would conduct them. He adds, "And I having offered to take them down in peace, which was the only thing the generals were aiming at, the garrison remained [at La Ciénega] and I went down with the sergeant [and the Indians] to the camp of La Concepción." There they met La Fuente and Terán at the head of their eighty soldiers.

Kino now took charge of negotiations. When he arrived at Caborca two Indians had already been killed, and two women and three little girls had been captured. Kino had one of the women released and sent her out to summon her people to see their old friend, the Boat Man. The name was still magic. Next day the woman came bringing seven or eight Indians. Two days later she and these others brought in several more "bearing the crosses of peace." They came from seven different rancherías, "that is, from La Concepción del Cabotca, San Diego del Uquitoa, El Actun, El Moicaqui, etc." For Kino and many of the visitors it was a renewal of old friendships. There were embraces and talks about the "good old days."

Meanwhile La Fuente's soldiers were scouring the country. On the 25th twenty men sent out by him encountered a lone Indian. He tried to escape, they shot him with a musket, and broke one of his thighbones. When they took him to camp Kino baptized him with the name of Luís, because it was the day of this saint.[1] Kino tells us that "he got better and told his relatives many good things about the soldiers, saying that they had warned him many times in a friendly way to give up his arms, and that he was to blame for not surrendering and for being wounded in that way." This was unusual charity for a man in his predicament. Investigation confirmed the conclusion that the Caborcans were not responsible for the murder of Father Saeta, and that the assault was perpetrated by men from Tubutama and Oquitoa. Not even Pitquín was involved.[2]

Things being thus satisfactorily arranged at Caborca, La Fuente,

[1] Saint Louis, King Louis IX of France.
[2] Kino, *Innocente, Apostólica, y Gloriosa Muerte*, Lib. V, Cap. iv. Manje places this incident in the first expedition to Caborca after the revolt, but he is clearly wrong, for the story is given circumstantially in the diary of La Fuente and Terán. (Manje, *Luz de Tierra Incógnita*, 239.)

Terán, Kino, Campos and all the soldiers went up to Tubutama, and next day rejoined the main camp at La Ciénega. There on August 30, Feast of Santa Rosa, patroness of the Indies, the final peace agreements were celebrated. We have Kino's graphic account of the picturesque conference.

For several days the soldiery and a large delegation of Indian ambassadors had been waiting. There were the captain general of Dolores, the governors of El Bosna, El Tupo, and El Doagsoma, "and many other natives of all the villages of these environs." In the camp now were Generals La Fuente and Terán, Fathers Kino and Campos, and all the soldiery and the native allies comprising the army of pacification.

In the morning Father Kino said Mass in the village of El Tupo, and Father Campos at the military camp. Long speeches followed. The Indians deplored the death of Father Saeta and the seven Christian Indians killed during the first uprising; they condemned the war of revenge in which the missions of San Ignacio and Imuris had been destroyed; they grieved for the deaths of some eighty of their kinsmen who in consequence of these outrages had met death during the Matanza and in the subsequent campaigns; they protested that all these tragedies had resulted from the homicides committed by the handful of recalcitrants at Tubutama and Oquitoa.

At the end of all this oratory—we learn little of what the Spaniards said, but we can guess—general and special peace agreements were made. The chiefs pledged themselves "to seek out and deliver alive the persons, or if dead, the heads of the principal malefactors who were still at large . . . , namely the mador and the caporal of San Pedro del Tubutama." They went further and at their own suggestion pledged themselves to "add the heads of the alcalde of San Ambrosio, and others whom they knew to have aided him and co-operated in the murder of Father Saeta." Lastly—and here was Kino's special triumph—the missions would be restored. The chiefs declared that they were very desirous of having the padres return to them. They would receive them with all love and affection; and immediately they would rebuild the churches and houses which had been destroyed.

The drama in the desert ended in a love feast. The pleasure at the conclusion of the peace pact was expressed "by the many and very friendly embraces which were given mutually by the Spanish generals and captains and the Pima captains and governors, all the natives being very grateful for the Christian charity of the generals, of whom they had heard it said that the royal arms were designed only to kill and molest good people and not to aid and defend them. . . . And they now said goodbye with fine expressions of warmest friendship." Of course, this is the white man's version.[1]

For General Terán the Pima campaign had a most regrettable sequel. As soon as the treaties were made at El Tupo, the three companies went to Cocóspora and thence on a war against the Apaches, Janos, and Jocomes—the campaign which had been interrupted in July by the Pima raid. Jironza had again joined his company and he now led it to the foray. Father Campos went as chaplain, for which service he could be spared, because his mission was destroyed. The diary gives us new details regarding the trail from Santa María to Quíburi, whence the army continued east. From the white man's viewpoint the campaign was a success, for they surprised the enemy in the Chiricahua Mountains, killed sixty Indians, in battle or by clubbing or hanging them after capture, and brought back seventy women and children as prisoners, whom they distributed among the soldiers as prizes of war. But the enemy had a means of revenge—or perhaps Fate was on their side. Most of the soldiers and Father Campos returned ill, due, it was thought, to quenching their thirst at a pool which the enemy had poisoned. During part of the march Campos was borne by Indians on a stretcher.

To General Terán the illness was fatal. He died in camp at midnight September 29–30. In order not to leave his friend in the wilderness, La Fuente at once had the body securely wrapped from head to foot, and summoned seven hardy soldiers equipped with remounts. Loading the gruesome cargo on the back of a mule, at one A.M. they set forth with orders to cover the fifty leagues of mountain and plain to Janos within twenty-four hours, and bearing a letter begging the curate there to bury the corpse near the main altar of the parish church.

[1] Kino, *Inocente, Apostólica, y Gloriosa Muerte*, Lib. V, Cap. iv.

The couriers arrived on schedule time and on October 1 the General was laid to rest near the altar mayor,[1] as La Fuente desired.

Thus ended the life of a soldier who had served over a wide stretch of the American frontier. Kino had met him in 1687 on Mayo River, where he played an important part in developing the Los Frayles mines. Four years later he was made governor of Texas and in that capacity he led an expedition from Coahuila to Red River to ward off danger from the French of Louisiana. Before rushing to the scene of the Pima disturbances of 1695 he was commander of the garrison of El Gallo, in Chihuahua. And now he responded to the last reveille in the eternal war against the Apaches of Arizona. Terán's career was a typical one—characteristic perhaps of military service at that date in the whole Western Hemisphere.

[1] La Fuente and Therán, Testtimonia de Auttos de Guerra; Kino; Inocente, Apostólica, y Gloriosa Muerte, Lib. V, Cap. iv; Manje, *Luz de Tierra Incógnita,* 243–244.

Account Rendered

LXXXVIII

SEED OF CHRISTENDOM

THE BLOOD OF THE MARTYRS IS THE SEED OF CHRISTENDOM. This patristic text was popular doctrine among seventeenth century missionaries. The death of Father Tapia, first Jesuit martyr on the Pacific Coast of North America, struck off a new spark of missionary zeal. The murder of seven Jesuit teachers by the Tepehuanes in the mountains of Durango fanned the spark into a flame. Fresh fuel was added when Pascual and Martínez met the death of martyrs in the wild sierras of Chínipas. The massacre of four Jesuits by the Tarahumares of Chihuahua caused the blaze to leap higher. And now, from the cruel death of Father Saeta, Jesuits and seculars alike predicted that missionary zeal would burn still more brightly, and they promised a bountiful harvest of souls in the Pimería.

The news of the martyrdom spread over New Spain as if by telepathy. Every courier proclaimed the message. Indian runners spread it from tribe to tribe. Another Black Robe had fallen. Kino in many letters to friends told of his personal sorrow at the blow. In reply a score of religious and seculars wrote him words of sympathy, and prophecies of new triumphs of the Faith through the shedding of the blood of this first martyr of Pima Land.

To understand how these men looked upon the matter one must read their letters. Fortunately many of them have been preserved. Father Kappus, now rector at Cucurpe, wrote to Kino five days after the tragedy, "Every moment, imperceptibly—*sensim sine sensu*,—I am experiencing a greater and greater veneration for this glorious new protomartyr. I trust in the Divine Goodness that Our Lord will use this innocent victim for the benefit of the conversion, through the winning of a great many souls . . . and I have confident hopes that all these evils must fructify very, very great blessings." Father Muñoz, the visitor, wrote immediately from San Juan, "Be of good spirits, your Reverence, for I hope in the Lord that all this must redound to the greater glory of God." In another letter he asked, "In what new conversions have we not seen the spilling of the blood of apostolic men whose watering has fertilized the harvest of many souls?" Manuel González, rector at Oposura, wrote, "Be of good cheer, my beloved father, for out of evil God our Lord is able to bring much good."

Jesuits from a greater distance sent similar words of encouragement and prophecy. "How could such happiness fail to arouse envy?" wrote Father Antonio Leal from Durango, "and how could the Devil permit to escape so many souls whom he regarded as his own, without doing his utmost to put obstacles in their way? . . . When has not the Faith of God had such setbacks? But not for this has it been stamped out even though apostles and disciples of Christ and all their successors in all the centuries have died. And though the flesh be weak the spirit is willing—*Et si caro infirma, spiritus promptus;* the fire of the Spirit has been lighted once more, arising from the ashes of the martyrs. Your Reverence, whose part it is not to despair—for the blood of our brother is to be the watering whereby these new plants shall wax greater, and in Heaven he will be the advocate of those poor souls,—your Reverence has been and must be their apostle." The provincial wrote from Mexico, "The fathers will have a thousand desires to achieve with their fervors a fate like that of their holy companion. But the Lord, being content with Father Saeta, wishes the rest for the instruction of these people, and that their martyrdom, being bloodless, may be more prolonged in the constant danger of death."

Seculars as well as clergy predicted great results from Saeta's fall. It was easy for them to cheer, for they would never be missionary martyrs themselves. But they were wholly devout and sincere. "I regard the death of the Venerable Father Francisco Saeta as one of the greatest glories which could be desired," said Captain Picondo. "Many have wished to die for Jesus Christ in such a ministry but have not succeeded. Fortunate one and a thousand times is the Venerable Father Francisco Xavier Saeta, to whom it was permitted by our Lord that his stole should be bathed in blood. Now I consider all that Pimería as flourishing, and that it must yield very ripe fruit for the army of the Holy Church; and the reverend fathers of the Pimería should rejoice, and should be congratulated that they have a martyr companion in Heaven who is and will be their advocate before our Lord Jesus Christ."

Manje, Kino's protégé and dearest soldier friend, was equally optimistic. "By virtue of the blood of the most zealous father martyr, Francisco Xavier Saeta, that harvest of souls is being fertilized, and in time it must become most flourishing. . . . And may the innocent blood of our venerable father martyr not be like that of Abel, which begged for vengeance, but be a well of prayers and petitions for the conversion of these heathendoms."[1]

Kino saw the use to which Saeta's martyrdom could be put. For eight years, while he had been working to plant Christianity among the Pimas and defending them from their detractors, he had been appealing for more workers for the harvest already white. Now a new argument had been provided for him. Pima Land had a martyr. The death of his friend was a hard personal blow, but his own feelings were of no consequence. Saeta's death must be made to serve the cause. God had given him an unexpected weapon for the warfare against heathendom and the forces of the Common Enemy. For him to fail to use it would be to shirk his duty. Kino did not shirk; instead, he seized the weapon and wielded it with all his power. And here was a case where the pen was mightier than the sword. To capitalize the tragedy Kino immediately wrote a history of the event, in order to make known to all the world the missionary field which Saeta had watered with his blood.

He called his book "Innocent, Apostolic, and Glorious Death of the Venerable Father Francisco Xavier Saeta, of the Company of Jesus, Missionary of the new Mission of La Concepción de Nuestra Señora del Cabotca, of the Pimería in the Province of Sonora; with Apostolic Opinions of the Same Venerable Father in Regard to Making New Conquests and Conversions of Souls. Also the Present State of These New Nations and Conversions; together with a General Map

[1] Kino, Inocente, Apostólica, y Gloriosa Muerte, Lib. IV, Caps. i–iii.

of All the Missions, entitled 'Theater of the Apostolic Labors of the Company of Jesus in North America, 1695.' By Father Eusebio Francisco Kino of the Company of Jesus."

The book, the original manuscript of which is still preserved in Kino's own handwriting, was just what its title indicated. It was dedicated to the provincial, Father Almonacír, for whose eyes especially it was intended. Then, in over a hundred large pages, Kino wrote as an eyewitness and with the zeal of a devotee the story which we have briefly set forth above. He told of Saeta's coming to the Pimería, the founding of the mission of Concepción at Caborca, Saeta's journey in Sonora to solicit alms, his return to Caborca, his last zealous letters, his cruel martyrdom, the pious journey of Jironza and Manje, Campos and Bayerca to recover his ashes, the impressive return procession to Dolores, and the solemn burial at Cucurpe. Then followed the history of the aftermath—the unfortunate massacre of the Pimas at El Tupo, the retaliatory attack on Imuris, San Ignacio, and Magdalena, the assembling of the army, the march of La Fuente and Terán to Tubutama and Caborca, the oratory and the peace agreements at El Tupo.

Kino quoted at length the letters written to him by friends prophesying richer harvests in the missionary field watered by Saeta's martyr blood. These prophesies he supplemented by a history of the martyrdoms of Jesuits in all New Spain from the time of Tapia's death in Sinaloa. He set forth Saeta's views on missions, which one suspects were largely Kino's own opinions put into Saeta's mouth, for they condemned many of the things which had occurred in the Pimería.

To all this Kino added an account of the Pima missions since his own arrival, a description of their promising condition at the time he wrote, in the fall of 1695, a statement of the obstacles in the way of their prosperity, the need of more missionaries, and the qualities of the model worker—typified by the protomartyr, Father Saeta. Finally, this really first-rate history of the exciting episode of which Saeta was the center, was illustrated by a large and detailed historical map of Jesuit New Spain—a map which in itself was a landmark in American cartography.

LXXXIX

MOTHER OF MISSIONS

It was now eight years since Kino had arrived at Dolores. He felt like a veteran. He had traveled much during this time. But his chief labor had been that of a missionary, occupied in the daily grind: saying Mass, teaching the Catechism, healing the sick, farming, branding cattle, equipping pack trains for market, building, entertaining Indian delegations from afar, visiting his sub-stations, assisting neighbor missionaries, and preparing the way for new missions farther and farther in the interior.

Father Eusebio devoted one section of his book to a description of the Pima missions at the time when he wrote, that is to say, in the latter part of 1695. It is the record of his own achievements during these eight years. Dolores was the prize jewel of the Pimería, the masterpiece of its greatest missionary. It then had more than ninety families, and the books showed that since the beginning more than four hundred persons had been baptized. Many of these of course had died. The mission had a fine church, a good and spacious residence, farm buildings and workshops, a pack train, productive fields, flourishing gardens and orchards, and well-stocked ranches. It was in reality a substantial village, a complete frontier unit of mission culture and of agricultural exploitation. Kino describes his cherished establishment with pardonable pride. It is only too bad that his word picture was not supplemented by the brush. Perhaps some day a painting or a drawing made by a contemporary will even yet emerge from its hiding place in some archive, attic or library.

"This mission has its church adequately furnished with ornaments, chalices, cups of gold, bells, and choir chapel; likewise a great many large and small cattle, oxen, fields, a garden with various kinds of garden crops, Castilian fruit trees, grapes, peaches, quinces, figs, pomegranates, pears, and clingstones. It has a forge for blacksmiths, a carpenter shop, a pack train, water mill, many kinds of grain, provisions from rich and abundant harvests of wheat and maize, and other things, including horse and mule herds; all of which serve and are greatly needed both for domestic use as well as for expeditions, and for new conquests and conversions, and to purchase a few gifts and attractions, with which, together with the Word of God, it is customary to contrive to win the minds and the souls of the natives."

All these multitudinous activities and establishments were conducted by a well-organized and numerous corps of native officials, functionaries, and craftsmen, trained by the master. Kino continues: "Likewise in this new mission of . . . Dolores, besides the justices, captain, governor, alcaldes, fiscal mayor, alguacil, topil, and other fiscals, there are masters of chapel and school, mayordomos of the house, and other servants whom they call cowboys, muleteers, ox drivers, bakers, rope-makers, gardeners and painters [vaqueros, arrieros, boyeros, panaderos, bolineros, hortelanos, and pintores]." It is evident that specialization was practiced in the training of the Indians, who worked better this way than as "all-round hands."[1]

Each head mission, or residence, where the missionary lived, had one or more sub-stations or visitas. The rule in the Pimería was two. Besides Dolores, Kino now had Remedios and Cocóspora directly in his charge. Remedios was located on Remedios River, a few leagues north of Dolores, in a narrow but fertile valley, the site chosen by Kino during that first jaunt in the Pimería eight years previously. The church, whose ruins are still to be seen, was perched high on the hills west of the river and half a mile or more south of the present village of Remedios. From this temple Kino and his neophytes had a superb view of the river valley and of near-by Cerro Azul.

Kino continues his description: "To this district or mission of . . . Dolores belongs its second pueblo of . . . Remedios, distant seven leagues to the north. It was begun a few years ago on the occasion when the two other pueblos of San Ignacio and San Joseph de los Hymeres . . . were given to the new fathers when they entered.[2] It has more than thirty families already assembled, and as many more

---

[1] Kino, Inocente, Apostólica, y Gloriosa Muerte, Lib. VI, Caps. i–iv.

[2] Kino refers to those who came in 1691. In that year he was taking over Remedios when Salvatierra inspected the mission. I infer that Sandoval, from his mission at Imuris, had previously administered Remedios. Kino, *Favores Celestiales*, Parte I, Lib. ii, Cap. 1; *Hist. Mem.*, I, 118.

will settle here, by bringing them from other places less abundant and less convenient than these more beautiful ones. It has, already begun, a church, a large house, with adequate living quarters, likewise large and small cattle, a horse herd, and fields of wheat and maize. A hundred souls have been baptized."

Kino prided himself on making Dolores the Mother of Missions. He would carry the Gospel to all the Pimas and to sterile California. It was for this that he had worked so hard, assisted by his neophyte laborers, to lengthen the irrigating ditches at Dolores, broaden its fields, increase their yield, enlarge its herds, and establish new ones in villages farther and farther inland as nuclei for new missions when more missionaries might come. Dolores, he now wrote, "aids . . . three other missions, for as was said by Father George Hostinski in the sermon of the dedication of this church, this mission from that time forward would be the mother of four other new missions. Indeed, subsequently, even last year and in this year of 1695, it has given for the founding of the new mission of . . . Cabotca, the value of more than a thousand pesos in large and small cattle, droves of mares and horses, provisions, clothing, house furniture, etc. For it has an abundance of all these, and to that end it was established in such a manner that it might be able, as the oldest, to aid many others which afterward might be founded, especially because it has been seen both in California and in other parts that for the lack or shortage of these temporal means, so many spiritual goods such as conversions and the salvation of so many souls are neglected and lost."

So Kino included in his report a description of the daughters of Dolores.[1] He began with San Ignacio, the mission over the sierra, founded amid the shady cottonwoods beside the musical waters of San Ignacio River. The completed church still stands near the Camino Real, on the edge of the little pueblo of San Ignacio which has grown up beside it, first an Indian village, now a settlement of Mexicans. Kino continues: "The second mission or district of this Pimería is San Ignacio del Caborica. It is distant from Nuestra Señora de los Dolores ten leagues toward the west. It has more than forty families assembled, besides as many more in its environs which can be assem-

---

[1] Other than those administered directly by himself.

bled as time goes on. It has the church and house half finished, with plentiful large cattle and horses, and although during this uprising the roof, etc., were burned, now they are rebuilding everything anew and better than before. It has a very fine location, an admirable and pleasing plain and meadow, among the most beautiful to be found in all these provinces, close to a very good river with a very large growth of trees and with plentiful lands. This year if the uprising had not retarded and hindered everything they would have harvested more than three hundred fanegas of wheat." [1]

San Ignacio now had three visitas, Imuris, Magdalena, and El Tupo. Imuris, a few leagues up the San Ignacio River, overlooked the shady alameda from a high bluff between the forks of San Ignacio and Cocóspora rivers. Magdalena was four leagues below San Ignacio on the same stream. All three settlements still stand today where Kino and his associates placed them. Imuris is now a fair-sized pueblo, Magdalena a flourishing city and the metropolis of its district. El Tupo was the village where the terrible Matanza had recently occurred. Let Kino describe them as they were in 1695.

"The second district belonging to San Ignacio is San Joseph de los Hymeres, which is three leagues to the north of San Ignacio. It enjoys equal conveniences and amenities by way of land, rivers, plains, groves, very extensive alamedas, near-by pineries for its buildings, etc. In the visitation of the father visitor Juan María Salvatierra,[2] it was found with more than sixty houses or families of natives. It has already begun a good and spacious church, with a transept. They have rebuilt the house which was burned on the same day that they burned San Ignacio. It already has had and it now has bountiful harvests of wheat and maize in its very large and very pretty plains, with most abundant pasturage and three good rivers.[3] The large and the small cattle become so fat here that every year even the bulls afford a supply of lard and tallow.

"Likewise up to now there has belonged to San Ignacio the third district, called Santa María Madalena, which is on the same river as San Ignacio, four leagues farther south. Very near by is the large village of more than two hundred souls called San Miguel del Tupo,

---

[1] Kino, Inocente, Apostólica, y Gloriosa Muerte, Lib. VI, Cap. iv.
[2] In January, 1691.
[3] Three branches of the river come together at Imuris.

which also belongs to Santa María Madalena. And in all parts there are many natives baptized."[1]

In the valley of the San Pedro del Tubutama River, now called the Altar, there was the mission of Tubutama with its visita of Oquitoa. Though damaged and abandoned during the uprising, the buildings were being repaired. It is not clear whether Father Janusque had returned or not. Caborca was not yet reoccupied. Tubutama, standing on a high mesa, overlooking the Altar River and its fertile fields, is one of the picturesque places in the Altar Valley today. Oquitoa. farther down the same valley, occupies a similarly favored location on the opposite bank of the river. Like most of the other missions, they have become Mexican towns, monuments to Arias, Janusque, Kino, and Campos, and to the industrious Pimas who were there when these Jesuits arrived.

Kino continues: "The third district or mission is San Pedro del Tubutama. It was begun and founded by Father Antonio Arias, aided by the religious generosity and charity of Father Pedro Castellanos, missionary of the two districts of Acotzi and Babiácora of the valley of Sonora. This pueblo of San Pedro del Tubutama is distant twenty-five leagues from . . . Dolores, and about ten from San Miguel del Tupo. . . . This pueblo . . . has had on several occasions more than four hundred souls. Last year we counted one hundred and sixteen boys and girls under instruction. It has a house with three or four good rooms which they are rebuilding, extensive and very fertile lands, a garden, fields of wheat and maize, beans, etc., with many rancherías of numerous people in its environs, who could and ought to be assembled in good pueblos on the same river. . . . In that pueblo there must have been about two hundred baptisms.

"Its second pueblo is San Antonio del Uquitoa, seven leagues lower down on the same river. Four years ago it had more than eighty baptisms, most of them of infants, among them being the little son of [Soba], the principal chief of all the nation. Both pueblos were left badly ravaged by these uprisings and wars of 1695, although now thank God they are being rebuilt."[2]

[1] Kino, Inocente, Apostólica, y, Gloriosa Muerte, Lib. VI, Cap. v.
[2] This comment seems to imply that this paragraph was written in Mexico in 1696. Aconchi and Babiácora are below Guépac. See Mora Contra Kino, Arizpe, May 28, 1698, paragraph 59. Original Spanish manuscript in the Biblioteca Nacional, México, Californias, legajo 53.

To the north of Remedios was Cocóspora, in one of the most attractive sites of all. Here, since the uprising, Kino himself was in charge. High up on a hill on the right bank of Cocóspora River, the ruins of a once beautiful and richly decorated church today look down upon one of the most prosperous haciendas in northern Sonora. Beyond Cocóspora in 1695 lay the Pima villages strung like beads on Santa Cruz River, ready and awaiting missionaries. Kino continues: "The fourth district begun was Santiago del Cocóspora, which is fourteen leagues north of . . . Dolores. It has more than two hundred persons attached, a house and a little church already built and now being roofed. The pueblo has ornaments, a bell, large and small cattle, fields of wheat and maize, and it must have about a hundred natives baptized. It has extensive lands and a most beautiful valley with large alamedas, pine forests, and many other groves. Its second pueblo might be that of San Lázaro, by attaching to it the numerous people in its district, or Santa María del Pilar, where already there is a house, with fields of wheat, maize, etc., and many baptisms."

Kino's next paragraph sums up beginnings already made in numerous outlying villages which he had visited. "In the following posts likewise there are earth-roofed houses of adobe, many baptisms already performed, and fields of wheat and maize for the fathers for whom they have asked us so urgently and whom the father visitors and other fathers, and various royal justices, alcaldes mayores, generals, captains and lieutenants for so many years have promised them, but whom we have never given them: In San Cayetano del Tumagácoric and San Gabriel de Guebavi, which are about thirty leagues to the north of . . . Dolores; and in San Francisco Xavier del Bac, of the Sobaípuris, which is distant about sixty leagues to the north of this district. All these posts named are on the river of Santa María del Pilar [now the Santa Cruz], and have very numerous people in their districts, especially toward the west and the Sea of the Californias." Kino means the Pápagos. He now returns to the San Ignacio and Altar Rivers. "Likewise in Santa Marta, farther down than Santa María de Madalena, and in San Ambrosio del Tucubabia, there are beginnings of houses which they are building for the fathers whom they have requested and who have been promised them, for they already have many infants and some adults baptized."

Among all the missions Kino gave the place of honor to the one where the protomartyr of Pima Land had shed his blood. "The fifth district or mission of this Pimería is that of La Concepción del Cabotca, the last in point of foundation but the first and chief one in the glories of the precious watering by the apostolic blood of its holy minister, the Venerable Father Francisco Xavier Saeta, whom I have many times heard say, 'He has placed me as a chosen arrow— *Posuit me ut sagittam electam,'* alluding saint-like to his surname, Saeta, which in Latin signifies arrow, for he was so chosen that with his precious and apostolic blood he must soften the resentment which during these last years they have felt because the necessary fathers have not come. And with grief will be verified the words: 'The children asked for bread and there was no one to break it unto them [1]—*Parvuli petierunt panem et non erat qui frangeret eis.'*"

XC

IN THE CAPITAL ONCE MORE

His book finished, Kino started for Mexico posthaste, to request more missionaries for his Pima Land and to report the abuses which hindered his work. His long ride to the capital and his fervent appeal to the authorities constitute the next chapter in the story. The decision to make the journey was no sudden event. Soon after he and Manje in February 1694 caught sight of California from the mountain of El Nazareno, Kino had written to the provincial asking permission to go to the capital to discuss the extension of missions into the explored mainlands, and the renewal of efforts in California. The permission was granted, but his going at this time was prevented by the protests of soldiers, officials, citizens, and missionaries, who reported to Mexico that Kino was needed in the Pimería, where he was "accomplishing more than a well-governed presidio." The Pima uprising of 1695, last-

---

[1] Kino, Inocente, Apostólica, y Gloriosa Muerte, Lib. VI, Cap. v.

ing from April to the end of August, together with Kino's illness, still further delayed his going.

Now there were added reasons for the journey. It was rumored that Solís had made pernicious reports to Mexico regarding the Pimas. Complaints had been made of Kino's own methods, and he wished to answer them face to face with the authorities. And he had business with Salvatierra. So, when the peace agreements of August 30 relieved the pressure of home affairs, he decided to avail himself of the license, "almost an order, . . . from the father provincial, and go to Mexico for the good of so many souls in need." As a preparation he wrote his book on the martyrdom of Father Saeta. To care for Dolores in his absence, Campos was called from San Ignacio.

"And so," he says, "setting out from these missions of Sonora on the sixteenth of November, 1695, in seven weeks, and after a journey of five hundred leagues, I arrived in Mexico on January 8, 1696." He had retraced his northward route traveled eight years before, when first he came to Pima Land. A fifteen-hundred-mile horseback ride was no small undertaking.[1] He adds, "It was God's will that I should be able to say Mass every day of this journey; and the three masses of the Feast of the Nativity I said in the new church of Nuestra Señora de Loreto of Guadalaxara. The same day on which I arrived at Mexico Father Juan María Salvatierra arrived by another route,[2] while that morning the new government was being installed, Father Juan de Palacios having entered as provincial."

Kino took with him to Mexico some Indian boys, among them the son of the captain general of the Pimería (head Indian of mission Dolores), as samples of the people for whom he went to plead. And they "received the utmost kindness and favors from the new father provincial and his predecessor, from his Excellency the Conde de Galve, and even from her Ladyship, the viceroy's wife, who were delighted at seeing new people who came from parts and lands so remote."

It was now fifteen years since Father Eusebio had first arrived in Mexico City from Europe, and nine since he had left there for Pima Land. A decade and a half on the frontier doubtless had left their

[1] Kino had just passed his fiftieth birthday.
[2] Salvatierra at this time was serving at the novitiate of Tepotzotlán.

marks on his face and hands as well as on his outlook upon the world. Then he was ready to go with the ship, now he was steering it. He had become a man of affairs. Many of his old friends of first days had departed, some to their final reward, but a few were left to welcome him and listen to his tales of the border. Sigüenza was still in the capital, and Kino tells us that he was still nursing an imaginary grievance. Whether or not they met does not appear. In the interim Don Carlos, too, had been a pioneer, having taken part in the exploration of Pensacola Bay. He, as well as Father Eusebio, had become a royal cosmógrafo and thus found practical use for his mathematics.

While in the capital Kino showed his usual vigor, and succeeded with some of his purposes. He had long sessions with Father Palacios, the new provincial, and conferred personally with the viceroy and members of the Royal Audiencia. He made a heavy assault upon the false charges against and the grave abuses heaped upon his Pimas. As Alegre tells us, "He showed that in the recent uprising the guilty parties were some captains of the presidios who were excessively arrogant." Solís of course was one of them. "He demonstrated clearly the iniquity with which they had outraged the inhabitants of Moto-ticatzi," obtained a decision in their favor, "and an order that they should be restored to their lands." Finally, he accomplished the primary object of his journey, for the provincial assured him that he should have five new missionaries for Pima Land. If the gossips spoke the truth, this friendly act did not prevent Palacios from admonishing Father Eusebio to avoid irritating his colleagues. While in the capital Kino and Salvatierra jointly urged the resumption of missions in California, now ten years abandoned, but at the time they did not succeed.[1]

On February 8 Kino set out for the Pimería, accompanied for a distance by Father Antonio Benavides, who turned aside to Durango to prepare himself for work in Pima Land.[2] At Conicari Father

---

[1] Kino, *Favores Celestiales*, Parte I, Lib. v, Cap. 1–2; *Hist. Mem.*, I, 158–160. Astrain, P. Antonio, *Historia de la Compañía de Jesús en la Asistencia de España*, Tomo VI, 493–494. (Madrid, 1920.)

[2] See note on Benavides in Mora Contra Kino, May 28, 1698 (*loc. cit.*). Alegre, followed by Astrain, says that Kino left Mexico accompanied by Father Gaspar Barillas, but Kino mentions only Benavides. Alegre is certainly in error when he says that Kino returned to Sonora by way of

Eusebio stopped to observe Holy Week. From there he forwarded mail to Horacio Polici, including the dispatch appointing Polici visitor for the new triennium. Somewhat more slowly Kino followed, going to Bazeraca, far over the mountains near the Chihuahua border, to consult the new visitor about plans for the future. Henceforth the relations of these two Black Robes were intimate, if not always placid.

On his way from Bazeraca to Dolores Kino had a narrow escape from death, an incident which he passes by with casual comment. The Jocomes were again on a rampage. By good luck Kino got safely through, but his escort was not so fortunate. "I had to return in the company of Captain Christóbal de León, his son, and his men, for the greater security of my person; but his Divine Majesty saved me from the great misfortune into which his Grace fell, for the hostile Jocomes killed him and all his people on the road not very far from Oputo, while I went to say goodbye to father rector Francisco Carranco and Father Pedro del Marmol." In the middle of May Kino arrived at Dolores after an absence of half a year. Father Campos now returned to San Ignacio.[1]

With Padre Eusebio on the job, the border awoke from a six month's sleep. His return was the occasion for a grand assemblage of Pima chiefs. While on his way to Bazeraca he had sent a messenger to Dolores to order the Indian officials there to go to all parts of the Pimería telling the people that Padre Eusebio was on his way home. They promptly complied, visited the villages, and invited governors, al- caldes, capitanes, fiscales, and caciques to come to welcome Kino and hear his messages from the great men in Mexico. In June, at the ap- pointed time, the chiefs arrived at Dolores from all the country round. What happened there should be carefully noted. It appears like a simple matter of course, but it had an echo later.

Kino assembled the visitors in the church and addressed them in the Pima tongue. He told them how glad he was to be back, and delivered to them greetings from the viceroy; from Juan de Palacios, the new

the Tarahumara country, for Kino gives circumstantial data regarding his return through Guadalajara and Conicari (Alegre, III, 12; Astrain, VI, 493).

[1] Kino, *Favores Celestiales*, Parte I, Lib. v, Cap. 1–2; *Hist. Mem.*, I, 158–161. See the San Ignacio Mission Register, where Campos says the Indians did not return till 1698. Father Carranco was apparently at Nácori when Kino turned aside to visit him.

provincial; and from Polici, the new visitor. "And these captains and governors and their families, having understood them all, unanimously gave signs of great gratitude for such friendly remembrances." As a more substantial way of showing their gratitude, the chiefs all turned in and helped Kino harvest his wheat, as they customarily did every year. For several days the sickles sang through the yellow grain in the valley below the church. While they were at Dolores some of the visitors were catechized and baptized; others who asked for baptism were denied it on the ground that they had not been sufficiently instructed. Under circumstances which will appear, this was a detail worth mentioning. As a record of this gathering and as evidence of Pima loyalty, a formal report of the assembly was sent to Mexico, including a list of all the Indians who took part in it.[1]

[1] See Kino, *Favores Celestiales*, Parte I, Lib. v, Cap. 2; *Hist. Mem.*, I, 161; Mora Contra Kino, May 28, 1698. The list and report were sent in by a friend named Estrada.

Storm Center of Pima Land

XCI

TWO PIMAS EAT CALABASH

D ID EVERYBODY APPLAUD KINO? Not by any means. He was too able for that. Lesser men were jealous of him. Formalists could not comprehend him. Before going to Mexico he had aroused opposition. In fact, charges against him had already been sent to the capital; when he returned to Dolores they multiplied. Most of them were trivial and inspired by envy of a man who could accomplish things. One of the complaints was that he knew the Pima language only imperfectly; another that he baptized *trochemoche,* pellmell, without proper instruction. Even disobedience was included among the charges. Part of the trouble, one suspects, was hostility toward North Europeans on the part of Spanish and Mexican born Jesuits. Though a native of Italy, by his neighbors Kino was often called a German.

The man who seemed to know the most and to be most heavily conscience-burdened about Kino's short-comings was Father Mora, of Arizpe, who now became rector, and therefore was Kino's superior for a triennium. Mora had come to Arizpe in 1694 at the age of thirty-two. He soon established a reputation for strict discipline of his neophytes in matters of catechism, ceremonies, and respectful manners. His office of rector bore heavily on his young shoulders, for he was seventeen years Kino's junior.[1] For such a man Father Eusebio was doubtless a most uncomfortable subordinate. He was unconventional, he was running away with the show, and the rector's only recourse was an appeal to the rules. By his jealousy Mora encouraged gossip and talebearing among Kino's neighbors, and by his complaints to Father

---

[1] Mora was a native of Puebla, Mexico. In his obituary he was called "a baron full of God, full of letters, full of charity." He died at Arizpe on January 6, 1720, after serving there twenty-six years (Carlos de Roxas, Historical sketch of the Arizpe mission, July 28, 1744, MS.).

Polici he temporarily shook the confidence of the visitor and even of Kino's old friend Manuel González. Polici, in an attempt to pour oil on troubled waters—or perhaps to carry water on both shoulders —soon found himself in an awkward position. In the end he swung back and frankly recognized and employed Kino's matchless abilities.

Polici had scarcely become visitor when Mora lodged complaints against Father Eusebio. "What can I do now," the visitor replied, "entering the government at this time, when his Reverence is already in the land with full support?" At Bazeraca Kino and Polici had talked of new missions on the northern frontier. Father Eusebio was pleased with the conference. "I found in his Reverence all affection, and a very great and fatherly love for these new conversions." Polici's comment on the visit was quite different. He wrote to Mora, "Father Eusebio Francisco Kino is going to his mission, and I trust that it may be for the service of our Lord, for the superiors emphatically [*impense*] command him to adjust himself to the wishes of the superiors and of your Reverence. He leaves this house knowing exactly what I wish and how he ought to comport himself with the superiors, brothers, and neophytes." Mora regarded this as a good scolding for Father Eusebio. On the other hand, Polici exhorted Mora so to proceed "that the other fathers may not listen to stories about Father Kino." Life in the missions was not without its savor.[1]

The welcome given to Kino by the Pima chiefs on his return to Dolores started a whispering campaign. Kappus, of Cucurpe, took part in the talebearing. In a little note, which Mora burned "because the father himself asked him to do so," he told Mora of the assemblage of Indians. Why did Kappus wish his note destroyed? And did he not know that Mora would tattle on him as well as on Kino? Mora was greatly wrought up over the event. It was increasing Kino's fame. The assemblage, the list of visiting Indians, the baptisms, and the report that Kino spoke to the chiefs in Pima, he said, were an attempt to demonstrate his power over the Indians and "to undo or disprove in Mexico . . . what had been written there" against him, namely that he baptized pellmell, and that he did not know the Pima language.

[1] Polici to Mora, May 6, 1696, quoted in Mora Contra Kino, May 28, 1698, par. 25; same to same, May 29, 1696, *ibid.*, par. 3; same to same, May 24, 1696, *ibid.*, 74.

Moreover, he said, Kino probably called the chiefs to help him harvest his vast wheat fields, "as was customary every year."

Kino's message to the Pimas from the officials in Mexico Mora found highly diverting. "To those of us who view things from here, this . . . was very amusing, especially to persons who know the Indians . . . for even of those who live among Spaniards not the smallest part have any knowledge of who the viceroy is, or the father provincial, or that the father visitor is called the Padre Grande." Palacios, the provincial, to whom Mora was writing, could hardly have felt flattered by Mora's words.

Alms for mission San Ignacio caused irritation, and Mora exaggerated the incident. It arose in this fashion. During Kino's absence in Mexico Campos was in charge of Dolores. When Kino returned Campos talked of leaving the Pimería, for his mission of San Ignacio had been wrecked in the recent uprising. Kino begged him to remain, promising him all aid possible in restoring it. Mora asked Campos what he needed, had the list approved by Polici, and sent it to Kino. Then, said Mora, the adjustment of this transaction took more than a year and a half, and it was not entirely settled when it was dropped because of weariness. "What he gave cost much ill feeling." This often happens.

Mora complained that Kino evaded with frivolous excuses his many exhortations to "keep his word and obey what they ordered him." He gives an example. Kino was preparing to take a pack train load of flour to Los Frayles, with which to buy clothing for his neophytes. He was ordered first to give the promised alms to Campos. Kino replied that the sale of the flour was urgent, for if the Pimas did not get the clothing they might complain and make trouble. Mora regarded this as a frivolous excuse. But the pack train went on its way.[1]

The merriest gossip was caused by Kino's arrest of two Pima chiefs and jailing them in his own house. The incident was an aftermath of the martyrdom of Father Saeta. The Pimas had promised to deliver the mador and the caporal of Tubutama or their heads. When Kino returned from Mexico they had not been delivered. Moreover, he was convinced that these two Indians were not the guilty ones. He named those he considered the real offenders and proceeded to arrest them,

---

[1] Mora Contra Kino, May 28, 1698, pars. 4–6.

because no one else would do so. In fact, General La Fuente had approved this plan. Kino several times invited them to go to Dolores, but they did not respond. Well, he knew how to bring them, and he had willing agents. The chiefs of the villages agreed to deliver up the suspects at a specified place, and Indian justices from Dolores were sent by Kino to receive them. When they passed through San Ignacio and reported their errand Campos was scandalized. Kino was meddling in secular affairs. Campos sent the justices back to Dolores "with a very plain and significant letter to Father Kino." Father Eusebio was incensed at the interference. Campos was a young upstart whom he had initiated! To Mora Kino wrote, "By this time the punishment of . . . the sacrilegious homicide of Father Saeta might be accomplished if a *quidam casi blanco* . . . had not prevented it." To an English ear this sounds like an awful name to call a brother Jesuit!

Mora admonished Kino not to mix in secular affairs. But the Master of Dolores was determined that the guilty men should be brought to justice. So he sent his agents out again. "There was no one to stop him now," says Mora, "because on this second occasion Father Campos was not at his mission." He continues with the story. "They seized the Indians, brought them to Father Kino's pueblo and put them in jail, in the very house of the father, in the room next to the church, they say because there was no suitable room in the pueblo. There they locked them up." To his rôle of missionary Kino had added those of sheriff and jailer. The kettle now boiled.

Kino was not trying to conceal anything. He was open as day. He promptly wrote to Mora that the prisoners were there, at the disposition of the rector, the visitor, or the royal officials, and he sent a notice over the mountains to Lieutenant Peralta, Mora's neighbor. Meanwhile Father Ruíz, a new missionary, arrived at Dolores, on his way to San Ignacio. He ran into a hornet's nest the very first day. Kino requested him to baptize the prisoners preparatory to meeting their fate. Ruíz demurred on the ground that he could not properly catechize them because he did not know the Pima language. Kino assured him that they were already thoroughly instructed; so they were taken from the prison to the church, the baptism was performed, and they were returned to the jail to await the next move.

The question of Church immunity now arose, as it frequently did on the missionary frontier. When Kino told Ruíz that he expected Peralta to come for the prisoners, Ruíz asked him how they could be taken out of jail by the royal officials, the church being a sanctuary? Kino replied that it would not be difficult to have them invited to eat calabash at the Captain's house. This is Mora's story. As soon as Peralta got the news he rode posthaste from San Juan to Dolores, thirty leagues in one day. Mora was now in another pickle. He too feared that Church immunity would be violated, and he wrote to Kino to be careful on this point. But his letter was too late, for the Lieutenant reached Dolores a day ahead of it.

Peralta and Kino talked the matter over and very amicably arrived at a plan. It was the one hinted at by Kino in his alleged conversation with Ruíz. The prisoners were led out of the house unbound and unguarded. In the yard Peralta met them. He, too, was anxious to clear his skirts on the question of sanctuary, so he took written testimony then and there, "to the effect that the Indians were . . . outside of the asylum." Thereupon he arrested them and took them away. Kino now coolly wrote to Mora, "I am reporting to your Reverence that Lieutenant Pedro de Peralta came to take away the malefactors. I think they left this house of their own free will and went to the house of the Captain to eat calabash." Of course he smiled as he wrote.

Mora, now frightened or scandalized, asked Kino for a fuller statement of what had happened, "since otherwise I could not defend him." Kino replied rather casuistically: "As to the matter of the removal of the Indians, it is certain that their first plan, which was to take them out without my knowledge [*me inscio*] while I was saying Mass, was very wrong. But since I emphatically showed them and told them how bad this plan was, they decided to order them to eat calabash at the house of the Captain. Thereupon they went out unbound and of their own free will, and they took them away." [1]

Mora thought this defense a little specious, but his own suggestion was scarcely more convincing. "How much better it would have been," he said, "if they had taken them at the time when his Reverence

---

[1] Mora Contra Kino, May 28, 1698, pars. 7–14.

was saying Mass, in order that he might have some excuse, to the effect that he could not prevent them. But since his Reverence says that this plan, unknown to him [*illo inscio*] was very wrong, we must assume that the fact that they took them with his knowledge [*illo sciente*] was very proper. Well, what shall we say? The invitation to eat calabash, according to what Father Kino said to Father Ruíz . . . was in his sight, by his consent, and probably even by his advice—*illo vidente et consentiente immo et probabiliter consúlente.*" It does look that way.[1]

Kino had come to a turn in the road. He had aroused more opposition than he could withstand. Polici ordered him to liberate the prisoners, though it was after they had already been released to Peralta. Knowing he was beaten, Kino climbed on the band wagon. He wrote to Mora, "Will your Reverence please advise me what we can do in order to have them set free? And if your Reverence pleases, it appears that the two of us, your Reverence, I, and some other fathers, may be able to effect their liberation and insure the complete quietude of this nation."

But Kino's aid in the matter was not asked. Polici ordered the rector to see if he could get the prisoners freed. Mora complied, obtained their liberation, and was well pleased with himself. "Although the order was so difficult," he wrote, "I took every means within my power to attain this end, and, without anyone else intervening in the matter, aided by God, who was everything, and by a good stroke, within two days after receiving the order I took them from the Lieutenant and brought them unbound to this mission [of Arizpe], where I kept them until I negotiated their complete pardon in writing." The pardon would at least seem to be an admission that Kino was right on the question of their guilt. Mora now conducted the Indians to Dolores, and from there sent them with an escort of soldiers to their own lands. "I did not dare to leave them at Father Kino's mission

[1] Kino at this time evidently expected the culprits to be executed, and that he would be called upon to prepare them for their final journey. "So desirous was he for the execution," says Mora, that he continued his letter saying, "Lieutenant Pedro Peralta said that . . . he would summon the Captain from here and the alcalde and some more justices, to examine the case of the prisoners, and that perhaps they would summon me to prepare them for the execution." Velarde writes, "The two old leaders of the sedition and those who first wounded Father Saeta were pardoned through the intercession of the Fathers, and even more, I believe, through the blood which flowed from the blessed martyr." Velarde, in Manje, *Luz de Tierra Incógnita*, 325.

. . . because I thought they were not safe." What he feared is not stated.

Mora now wrote Kino "a serious letter setting before him all the things in which he had been at fault." But Father Eusebio had been scolded enough, and he had a comeback. He was admonitor, with the right to censure his own rector, and he exercised it with vigor. Mora squirmed. "Now taking advantage of his office of admonitor," says the rector, "he discharged upon me that which I shall not even discuss, but your Reverence will see that it is good evidence of the respect which the father has for his superiors and of his great virtue and humility."

The story spread. Mora sent Kino's offensive epistle to Father Polici, who was duly shocked. "The letter of Father Kino is for Rome," he said. "A ream of paper will not suffice now to undo the letter of Father Eusebio with arguments, however convincing. But we tire ourselves; he does not read letters, but merely emits generalities in order to continue with his rôle." Polici instructed Mora, as rector, to administer to Kino a severe rebuke. But Mora was cautious now. "I excused myself," he writes, "saying that I feared that Father Kino would decide on a worse one for me. For the blow which his Reverence had given me was very stinging." Kino was *l'enfant terrible* of the Pima border.

Others were brought into the comedy. Father Manuel González, who had "always defended Father Kino, both here and in Mexico," took Mora's side. "I think that now he is wrong, and your Reverence should console yourself that you have done your duty,"—as one hit by an automobile might console himself for having had the right of way. "The letter of your Reverence to Father Kino is very good. That of Father Kino is as equivocal as what he wrote about Sigüenza." Evidently the Sigüenza story had reached the border. "Who has said that the fathers are alguaciles to arrest anybody? Who has said that the house of the father ought to serve not as a church and a refuge to the afflicted but as a jail for the gibbet?"

Jesuits farther from the scene regarded the matter as a good joke. Mora wrote Marmol "that Father Kino was hastening to erect a gibbet in the corridor of his house to hang the Indians whom he had imprisoned inside." With Marmol at the time was Father Kappus. "One of them made a jest of it and the other broke out laughing." They sent the letter to Father Carranco, and he laughed. Mora himself laughed after it was all over. "I, even now, every time I think of it, although I may be alone, can never help laughing. They were in the church *materialiter* and in the prison for hanging *formaliter*." If he had laughed good-humoredly at first there probably would have been no trouble.

Father Muñoz was puzzled. "One thing leaves my mind upset, or else I have no mind. It is that Father Kino keeps all of us in hot water while he is entirely serene." Perhaps Kino saw the joke, too. Mora adds, "In this serenity all this affair was left, for they did nothing to the father." And here was where Mora's shoe pinched. They did nothing to Kino. The superiors, too, perhaps smiled.

During the summer the tide had run strongly against Kino. But it soon turned. No matter what his neighbors thought of him or said about him, his ability nobody denied. Kino and Polici had planned for missions among the Sobaípuris of San Pedro River. Polici ordered Mora to draw up a report of the affair of the Pima chiefs, to be sent to Rome. Mora, nothing loath, proceeded to put it in shape. A week later he got a shock. Polici now wrote him that he was planning three or four missions among the Sobaípuris, and ordered Mora to entrust this work to Kino, as an enterprise "of very great service to God and the king." Mora was completely nonplussed. He had considered Father Eusebio nearly done for. And now Kino was to be magnified by a new venture. "Seeing this," Mora writes, "and knowing the doings of Father Kino, and that he had just come out of the foregoing affair unscathed, I said to myself, *inde mayorem gloriam resurgendo mani-festabit*—rising again, by virtue of this he will win greater fame." Just that happened.

Mora protested. To entrust these new missions to Kino would be very embarrassing, "because it will be said that they could neither live with him nor without him—*nec tecum possum vivere nec sine te.*" And how Kino's stocks would rise! "To put him in charge of these missions will enable him to write prodigies and marvels, and his fame will go on increasing at such a rate that every day it will be more difficult to believe anything to the contrary." This, too, happened.

Mora was puzzled on another ground. On the very same day (November 1) when Polici by letter ordered Mora to entrust the new missions to Kino, by word of mouth he ordered Campos to take charge of them. Campos reported this to Mora, who was again at a loss what to do. This is Mora's story. "Since Father Campos knows the [Pima] language very well and Father Kino does not, the latter ought to remain in his Cotzari, and Father Campos should go to this enterprise." But Mora had his orders, and he obeyed them. With ill grace and jealous fears he instructed Kino to take charge of the Sobaípuris missions.

The rector had been preparing his report against Kino, but he now hesitated. He was at sea. Polici had disappointed him. "All this took from my hand the pen with which to continue the report, and up to the present I have not had the spirit for it, seeing that with one hand the father visitor writes me against Father Kino, while with the other hand he supports him."

Polici was indeed between two fires. Half innocently he had lent himself to the attack on Kino. But he needed him; and he could not stop him. Better go with than against him. So while he supported Kino he tried to pacify Mora, compromising himself in the effort, and increasing poor Mora's bewilderment. Kino would soon be confined to Dolores, said Polici. "I regard him as an old and twisted prop"— Kino was fifty-one—"but until we have new props it is necessary to make use of him."[1]

XCII

KINO ASSIGNED TO CALIFORNIA

Mora was cheered by a new ray of hope. Father Eusebio might be sent elsewhere. Soon after Kino returned from Mexico City Salvatierra succeeded in attaining the object toward which they had jointly worked ever since they had made that memorable journey together

[1] Mora Contra Kino, May 28, 1698, pars. 15, 16, 18, 24.

five years before. During all this time Father Juan María had constantly urged the claims of the poor California natives. He had met objections on every hand. Provincial, audiencia, viceroy, and king had all opposed the plan on practical grounds. But the long road had a turning. The new Father General of the Jesuits, Thirso González, Kino's friend of Sevilla days, openly espoused the cause. Palacios, the new provincial, was won over and the audiencia fell in line. The result was that in 1697 Salvatierra and Kino were assigned to California to take up the work where Father Eusebio had left it twelve years before. It being understood that no funds could be expected from the impoverished government, Salvatierra was released from other duties to seek private donations. In Mexico City he was aided by Father Juan de Ugarte, "a man of giant size, as shrewd as he was pious."

The two men were immediately successful. They had the golden touch. A count and a marquis together headed the list of donors with a subscription of $2000. Others soon raised the total to $15,000. The Congregation of Dolores added $8000. Juan Caballero subscribed $20,000, with which to establish and support two missions, and promised to honor all drafts signed by Salvatierra. Pedro Gil de la Sierpe, treasurer at Acapulco, gave Salvatierra a launch, and promised to lend a galliot in which to cross the Gulf. Thus was begun the famous Pious Fund of the Californias, which still exists.

To crown all, the viceroy issued a license granting approval of the plan. It bore the date February 5, 1697. "It empowered Salvatierra and Kino to undertake the conversion of the Californias on two conditions: first, that it should be at their own expense, and second that the country should be taken possession of in the name of the king." This the two Italians were most willing to do. No Spaniard could have been more patriotic. They were given extraordinary powers. "They might enlist and pay soldiers, appoint and remove officials; indeed the whole affair was left in their hands." The terms were very similar to those under which the Jesuits had so long and so successfully operated their great missions in Paraguay. It is to be remarked that the Black Robes now undertook at their own expense a task for which eleven years previously they had been offered an annual subsidy of $30,000. But the conditions were different.

"Thus," says Bancroft, "the boon so long and patiently sought was obtained—permission to enter at their own risk and cost a poor and unattractive country for the purpose of converting the heathen; . . . It has been the fashion to see sinister and selfish designs in all Jesuit undertakings; but . . . no just person will suspect that the founders of California were actuated by any but the purest motives." And no one who has studied the matter can doubt the justice of this eulogy.

Leaving Ugarte to collect and invest the funds, Salvatierra hastened to Sinaloa and Sonora to prepare for his voyage. He spent some time searching in vain for the two boys taken from California when Atondo withdrew from the Peninsula.[1] They would be useful as interpreters, but they "were concealed by their masters lest their services as slaves might be lost." While waiting for the vessels promised by Sierpe, Salvatierra visited his old friends high up in the mountains of Chínipas, where he had labored for a decade as missionary. A new revolt in the Tarahumara Alta kept him there longer than he had anticipated. When he returned to Yaqui in August the vessels had already arrived from the south in command of Romero, after a terrible voyage. It was still some time before Salvatierra sailed.

XCIII

NEITHER WITH NOR WITHOUT YOU

It now became indeed a case of *nec tecum nec sine te*. Mora could not be happy in the same rectorate with Father Eusebio; the higher officials could not spare him. The news of Kino's assignment to California reached Pima Land by early May. Mora was delighted, and as rector he made plans to put Campos in charge of Dolores, where he had previously labored for a half a year. Kino, obedient and not wholly displeased, prepared to join Salvatierra at Yaqui. The two men for once were agreed. Kino was willing to go to California;

---

[1] Bancroft, H. H., *North Mexican States and Texas,* I, 278–281, and authorities therein cited; Venegas, *Noticia de la California,* II, 1–22.

Mora hoped he would. But Campos begged to be excused from his part in the program, preferring to remain at San Ignacio.

Polici opposed Kino's departure, for he was needed for the projected enterprise in the north. Father Eusebio, too, must beg to be excused, Polici wrote the rector. "I have ordered Father Kino under precept of holy obedience to propose the incompatibility of [going to] California with the status of the Pimería and with what is planned with respect to the Sobaípuris." When Father Eusebio was preparing to start for California—as Palacios had ordered—Mora asked Polici what was to be done about it. Should he be urged to stay or not? "To stay," Polici replied. "Your Reverence must give no other opinion to the father than that he must remain, for within a few days the father provincial will write *ad instantiam* of the generals and captains who have written to his Excellency, to urge that he be not sent to California. I have seen letters of the governor of Parral concerning this matter, and this is my opinion."

Kino was between two superiors who did not jibe. So he shrewdly suggested a way out. He was needed by both Pima Land and California. For both fields he had a deep affection. Here was a chance to serve them both and make one contribute to the other. The Pimería could help California. For eleven years this had been his dream. Why not compromise and thus solve a delicate problem for his superiors? So on June 3 he wrote to his old friend Thirso González, now the exalted General of the Order, proposing that he be given permission to spend half his time in Pima Land and half in California. Perhaps in this way he could best serve God. This done, he closed out affairs at Dolores, said goodbye to friends and neophytes, loaded his baggage on mules and started for Yaqui.

Meanwhile the higher-ups of the province were moving heaven and earth to keep Kino in the Pimería. Polici wrote to Rome that Father Eusebio could not be spared. Jironza, the governor at Parral, and other influential seculars, hurried petitions to Mexico urging that Kino be allowed to remain in Sonora, where he was needed to defend the province from the Indians. More than one hard-ridden horse contributed his breath and his muscle in order that the messages might not arrive too late. Mora spread the story that Kino inspired these requests that he remain in Pima Land, but he apparently convinced nobody but himself.

The petitions succeeded. While Salvatierra was waiting at Yaqui, the provincial's order came to Polici that Kino must remain in the Pimería, and was relayed over the sierras to Dolores by special courier. Palacios wrote to Kino, "The Señor Viceroy has requested me to leave your Reverence with your dear Pimas, and so you must care for them, because in other places they fear a general uprising." When this order reached Kino he was already on his way, but obediently he turned back. Salvatierra was getting anxious. "We were only waiting by the hour for Father Francisco Kino when we received a letter saying that because of the danger which Sonora would run if he were absent they would not let him go." On this turn of affairs Kino later commented, "Although I was going most gladly they detained me as being necessary over here, as the father visitor, Horacio Polise, then the Señor military commander and alcalde mayor of this province of Sonora, Don Domingo Xironza . . . wrote me by messenger." Mora subsided.[1]

XCIV

SALVATIERRA IN KINO'S FOOTSTEPS

Early in October Salvatierra was ready to sail from Yaqui to California. The plan was to go directly to San Bruno and begin where Kino had left off. Father Francisco Picolo,[2] famous church builder of Carichic in the Tarahumara, had been appointed in Kino's place but he had not yet arrived, so Salvatierra went without a missionary companion. The Jesuits at Yaqui had generously supplied Atondo and Kino; they now contributed liberally to Salvatierra's outfit. Father Ribas's labors there were still bearing fruit. Besides provisions they

---

[1] Polici to Mora, March 24, 1697, cited in Mora Contra Kino, May 28, 1698, par. 28; Palacios to Mora, April (?), 1697, *ibid.*, par. 1; Polici to Mora, May 6, 1697, *ibid.*, par. 28, Sept. 24, 1697, *ibid.*, par. 30; Bayerca to Mora, July 7, 1697, *ibid.*, par. 31. See also Kino, *Hist. Mem.*, I, 158–159, II, 158, 240–243.

[2] Father Francisco usually wrote his name Piccolo, but his associates in America generally used only one *c*, and I have conformed.

donated live stock with which to start ranches—thirty cattle, one horse, ten sheep and four pigs.

With Salvatierra went sixteen men. Alférez Tortolero commanded five soldiers; Romero, master of the little galliot, had six sailors. In addition there were three Christianized Indians from the mainland. Such was the slender colony which at last put Baja California on the map to stay. Romero had previously been on the coast, and was thus a link between the old and the new. As patroness of the enterprise Salvatierra took a statue of Our Lady of Loreto, a work of religious art which became famous in California annals. To give him a start in the Edu language he had a copy of Copart's carefully compiled notes. They served as another nexus.

On the evening of October 10 they set sail, anchoring that night outside the Yaqui harbor. Next morning the galliot was grounded in a squall, but they managed to get away. After a two days' voyage they safely reached the other side, and on the 16th they anchored at San Bruno Bay, whose story is now picked up where Kino had left it twelve years before. What would they find at the old mission site? Landing, with several companions Salvatierra crossed the ridge that lay between the coast and the abandoned settlement. What he saw was most depressing. "At sunset," he says, "we arrived very tired at the old Real de San Bruno, built on a mesa. . . . There was nothing but fallen stones," the ones so laboriously assembled by Kino's Indian wards, "all tumbled down among cactus and thorns, except a piece of one curtain which was still standing about a vara high, and facing the plain above." This is just about what I found there in 1932. The place has been little disturbed in the last two hundred and thirty-five years.

Salvatierra learned from the natives and wrote to Ugarte what had happened at San Bruno. Some of the Californians had wept at the departure of Kino and his companions twelve years before. But not all of them. Some were only too glad to see the Spaniards go, for they had entertained a smoldering hostility from the first. Their dissatisfaction was increased by the fact that two boys taken when Atondo's colony left were never returned. The outcome was a reaction at San Bruno as soon as Kino and Atondo sailed away. Native Hispanophiles now recanted or became outcasts. "The poor people who in that entrada showed themselves to be partisans of the Spaniards, when deserted were made to pay for it by those disaffected," says Salvatierra. "As soon as Don Isidro withdrew they fell upon the friends of the Spaniards, killed many of them, and finally all joined together and burned all the buildings, houses, and the presidio which Don Isidro had built." [1]

A few Indians now visited Salvatierra at San Bruno and were friendly though timid. The aguaje had not improved. "Twice they brought us water, each supply worse than the other from saltiness." Next morning Salvatierra and his band returned to the galliot, accompanied by a handful of natives. One of them, "now a man grown, said he was called Francisco. He spoke a few words of Castilian, but he was destitute of the language of God's heaven." Evidently he was the Francisco who had been such a favorite with Kino.

Salvatierra was discouraged by what he had seen, and at the ship he held a council. What should be done? The water at San Bruno was salty, and the site in other particulars was unsatisfactory. Romero had a suggestion. Once he had taken water on board ship at the Bay of San Dionisio. There the water was fine and the whole country green and promising. Why not settle there, at the place which Kino and Atondo had so highly commended? Father Juan was disposed to be convinced but he wished to be sure, so he left the decision to the Virgin. He as well as Kino was a pious gambler. "We chose the Madonna as patroness that she might show us the way," says Father Juan. "We cast lots in her name and the slip of paper containing the name of San Dionisio was drawn." He naïvely adds, "and to tell the truth, I had felt that the choice would fall that way, being inclined to this belief by my desire to avoid another trip to San Bruno." So they sailed south some ten leagues to San Dionisio Bay and there founded the mission of Loreto. The first Indian baptized by Salvatierra was named in honor of Juan Caballero, the generous donor. "Now that we are here in California," he wrote, "and little Juan, the first Juan that this fragment of the New World has had, is now with me,

[1] Salvatierra to Ugarte, Nov. 27, 1697; same to same, July 3, 1698. Several of Salvatierra's letters written from California at this time are printed in *Doc. Hist. Mex.;* Segunda Série, Tomos I and IV.

The Bells of Loreto

Jesuit Church at San Juan Londó (San Isidro)

the rosary about his neck, the Faith is already established in California on a firm footing." Little Juan probably did not realize his own importance.

There were other links with the old days. Salvatierra built on the foundations laid by Kino. At Loreto he was soon visited by a personage no other than Chief Dionisio—Ibo, The Sun, so prominent in Kino's time—now grown older and nearly dead with a horrible cancer. What he had learned at San Bruno about clothing he had lost, for he was stark naked like the rest of the natives. But he had not forgotten Kino's religious teachings. Indeed, he now asked for baptism, was given it, and became Salvatierra's warmest supporter. Father Juan quaintly tells us that Ibo and his followers from San Bruno still remembered a few words of Spanish, such as "Santa María," "Mantequilla," "Perro," and "Señor." Some of them could say "Ora pro nobis." Ibo asked for the "Almilante," Padre Eusebio, Padre Matías, and Padre Juan.[1]

Loreto thus became Salvatierra's capital. But as soon as he could get matters well settled there, he went to San Isidro to restore the Faith where Kino had planted it. Andrés, another old friend of Kino, furnished an occasion. He was one of the Indians who went to Yaqui in the Almiranta during the memorable supply voyages. He too remembered the Spaniards kindly, and sent word that he desired baptism. Delighted, Salvatierra sent messengers to bring Andrés to Loreto, but they returned reporting that he was sick at San Isidro, having been bitten by a rattlesnake. Fearing that Andrés would die a heathen, Father Juan, with Tortolero and six other men, set forth á caballo, a dozen Indians going on foot to carry maize and water. Thus was Atondo's difficult trail reopened. It is now an automobile road, though hardly a boulevard.

After a hard journey of eleven leagues they reached San Isidro by moonlight, halting on a little mesa near the aguaje "at the site of Atondo's ranch," says Salvatierra. He adds that by the Loreto people (the Edues or Monquís) the place was called Londó. And so the identity of Salvatierra's San Juan Londó with Kino's San Isidro is firmly established at the outset. None of the buildings remained

---

[1] Salvatierra to Ugarte, Nov. 27, 1697.

standing. But certainly the stones assembled must have been in evidence, as indeed they were in 1932.

Next morning Salvatierra's men made a ramada and he said Mass. In the top of a large mesquite tree they carved a cross, "whose memory will remain many years," says Salvatierra. He was a true prophet; its memory he preserved. But no Andrés nor any other Indian was in sight. The tale about the rattlesnake had been a hoax, or perhaps Andrés had recovered. Soon a messenger arrived and reported that part of the people of the village had gone to the beach to fish, and the rest to gather mesquite beans on the slopes of La Giganta. So Salvatierra returned to Loreto without accomplishing his purpose.[1]

But he did not forget Andrés, and soon afterward he again sent for him to come to Loreto. In due time Andrés and other Cuchimíes from Londó and San Bruno arrived. Andrés said they wished to be baptized and build in his country a ramada or a church for Christian doctrine "which he knows very well." So Salvatierra prepared to go once more to San Isidro. It rained most of January, thus confirming Kino's view of California climate. When the weather improved, Andrés started home, expecting Salvatierra to follow, but on the way he was killed by hostile Monquís. Five Cuchimíes had remained at Loreto, and shortly after the death of Andrés, Tortolero and eight soldiers embarked in the launch to return them to San Bruno. Arriving at night, they found people awaiting them on the shore, but were prevented by contrary winds from anchoring, so they returned to Loreto. Three visits had now been made to Kino's country.

Soon after this, Salvatierra definitely founded the mission of San Juan Londó on the site of San Isidro, where he had carved the cross in the mesquite tree. In March the launch sailed again for San Bruno. At the same time Father Juan, Tortolero and eight soldiers went overland on horseback. They arrived on March 14 at midday, and halted at Londó "on the little elevation where Don Isidro de Atondo had established his ranch." Aided by Indians they now built a rude temple. Says Salvatierra, "We raised the poles and planted the forks, then the frame of the first ramada and church." Tortolero made a cross and set it up. In the next two days thirty persons were

[1] Salvatierra to Ugarte, April 1, 1699.

baptized, one adult, called Isidro, and "twenty-nine angels from two to eight years old." Isidro died and was given Christian burial, the first in the campo santo.[1]

Salvatierra tells us explicitly of the changing of the name San Isidro to San Juan. One of the neophytes was named Juan, "and the church where the pueblo is now being founded, and to which will be reduced little by little the rancherías of San Bruno, San Juan, and those of the Sierra de San Isidro was called San Juan de Londó, being given this name in honor of our first benefactor Don Juan Caballero." [2]

Thus the mission of San Juan was built by Salvatierra on the site of Kino's San Isidro, and to it were attached the Indians of San Bruno. Father Juan had picked up the work in the San Bruno Valley where Kino had left it. He traveled in Kino's footsteps. Salvatierra, too, came and went. Each left his mark. The remains of San Bruno are now a sad pile of ruins. But the tiny church of San Juan Londó, which when finished was built of stone, is still in a fair state of preservation. It is still another link between two great California pioneers.

[1] Salvatierra to Ugarte, July 1, 1699.
[2] Salvatierra to Ugarte, July 9, 1699.

ON THE TRAIL

The North People

XCV

A PAGEANT AT BAZERACA

WHILE THE QUESTION OF CALIFORNIA WAS PENDING, Kino threw himself whole-heartedly into plans for missions among the Sobaípuris. Here too, he encountered opposition and discouragement. Somebody had an ax to grind. It was again noised abroad that these people were allied with the Apaches and other enemies of Sonora. It was said "that they were cannibals, that they roasted and ate people," and that for this reason one could not go among them. Mora's jealous criticism of Kino caused Polici to waver, and for a moment he thought of entrusting the work to Campos. But the plan was Kino's, and Kino was the one man to put it through. So Polici told him to go ahead.

And Kino went ahead. Little men made trouble for the man from Segno, but they did not stop him. On December 10, 1696, he set forth from Dolores for Río de Quíburi to visit Chief Coro, to see if the adverse reports were true. Couriers went in advance to tell of his coming. His route was the now familiar one, past Cocóspora and Santa María, over Canelo Hills, and down Babocómari Creek to the San Pedro. On December 15 he halted his cavalcade at Quíburi. There were handshakings and embraces. This place, said Kino, was the "principal and great ranchería; for it has more than four hundred souls assembled together, and a fortification or earthern enclosure, since it is on the frontier of the hostile Hocomes." The chiefs here were evidently dubbed for their musical qualities, the head cacique being called El Coro (the Chorus), and a lesser one El Bajón (the Bassoon).

Kino gave talks on doctrine and on civilized living. As a result, he tells us, "the principal captain, called El Coro, gave me his little son to baptize, and he was named Oracio Polise; and the governor called

355

El Bajón and others gave me their little ones to christen. We began a little house of adobe for the [awaited] father, within the fortification, and immediately afterward I put in a few cattle and a small drove of mares for the beginning of a little ranch."

Back from this successful expedition, Kino prepared to set forth immediately to the western Sobaípuris, in the Santa Cruz Valley. This time he took with him a large drove of stock with which to found ranches for new missions. On January 13 he started. To the bend of the Santa Cruz his route was the same as before. Swinging left at San Lázaro and descending the river, he stopped at Bacoancos, to leave there a herd of cattle for a new ranch. At Tumacácori there were already sheep and goats, "which the loyal children of the venerable Father Francisco Xavier Saeta had taken thither, having gathered them in Consepción at the time of the disturbances of 1695." At San Xavier del Bac Kino was "received with all love by the many inhabitants of the great ranchería, and by many other principal men, who had gathered from various parts adjacent. The Word of God was spoken to them, there were baptisms of little ones, and beginnings of good sowings and harvests of wheat for the father minister whom they asked for and hoped to receive."

In March Kino made a third expedition to the north. Setting out from Dolores on St. Patrick's Day, he went again to Quíburi. It was evidently at this time that he "put in a few cattle and a small drove of mares for the beginning of a little ranch." He returned by way of Tumacácori and Bacoancos, "looking in all places after the spiritual welfare of the natives, baptizing some infants and sick persons, and consoling all with very fatherly messages from the father visitor, and even from the Señor alcalde mayor and military commander."

Kino's missionary business had a secular accompaniment. At the same time that he baptized and preached, he notified the natives "to be ready to go with the soldiers on the expedition against the enemies of the province, the Hocomes, Xanos, Sumas and Apaches." This statement illustrates the part which virile missionaries like Kino played in the defense of the frontier. "With the same intent and purpose" —that is, to summon the Indians to the campaign—Kino set out once more for Quíburi on the 17th of April. At this time he gave over the pueblos of Cocóspora and Suamca (Santa María) to Father Pedro Ruíz de Contreras, "with complete vestments or supplies for saying mass, good beginnings of a church and a house [at Cocóspora], partly furnished, five hundred head of cattle, two droves of mares, a drove of horses, oxen, crops, etc." The work of these four months represents a very distinct advance of the permanent mission frontier.

Kino was always a good showman. He now staged another pageant. Mission ranches had been established over the divide, but there were no missionaries. There must be a demonstration, and Kino provided one. The results of the four expeditions to the Sobaípuris were signalized and capitalized by organizing a pilgrimage of Pima chiefs to distant Bazeraca to see Father Polici and ask for padres. "So great were the desires of these natives of this Pimería to obtain missionary fathers that they determined to go to Santa María de Bazeraca to ask them of the father visitor." Kino managed the affair.

The natives met by appointment at Dolores toward the end of September, 1697. "Some had come fifty, sixty, eighty, ninety, one hundred and more leagues' journey to reach . . . Dolores, and as they had never gone so many leagues away from their country, I went with them through Sonora." One wonders what Mora said as he heard of the colorful company marching by with triumphant Kino at their head. They threaded the narrow canyons, scrambled up and slid down the steep mountains, crossed the narrow valleys, and forded the then rushing streams that cut the long rough trail which led to Polici's mission. "In the Real de San Juan, in Oposura, in Guasavas, through which we passed," says Kino, "both the seculars and the fathers received us with all kindness. On the sixth of October, feast of Our Lady of the Rosary, we reached Santa María de Bazeraca."

If Polici still had any lurking doubt, he was now convinced. The Pimas were welcomed "with a thousand tendernesses and with such joy by the father visitor, . . . that his Reverence on the following day chanted a solemn Mass to the Three Holy Kings, the first gentiles who came to adore the Messiah—*Primitiae Gentium*. And his Reverence, through various inquiries, even secret, which he made and ordered made, was so well satisfied with the great loyalty of these Pimas that he wrote a very fine letter to the Señor military commander

[Jironza], requesting that the Pimería be favored; that efforts be made to obtain for it the fathers it needed and deserved, since thereby the province would be quieted and made rid of the hostile Jocomes and Janos, who would retreat to the east; . . . and that some soldiers should come into this Pimería, at least as far as Quíburi, to see with their own eyes the good state of affairs and the ripeness of the very plentiful harvest of souls." [1]

This triumph was a partial offset for Father Eusebio's failure to go with Salvatierra.

XCVI

A SCALP DANCE WITH CHIEF CORO

Kino thus gives Polici credit for suggesting an expedition to the Sobaípuris in the fall of 1697. Manje takes the credit to himself and at the same time explains one of the causes of Spanish suspicion of the Sobaípuris. Some of them rode horses, and the Spaniards took this as evidence that they stole them. Manje explained it otherwise. After the destruction of the village of Mototicachi some ten years previously, several stock ranches near the Pima border had been abandoned.[2] Some of the stock was left unclaimed and soon became mesteña, or in English, mustang. The neighboring Indians captured the unbranded colts and soon were going about on horseback. When Solís went inland in 1694 he found the Indians riding these mustangs, but saw no horses with Spanish brands, so criticism subsided for a time. Nevertheless, suspicion soon showed its head once more. Therefore, says Manje, "to extinguish the bad opinion with which they were retarding the coming of missionary workers, . . . secretly I begged the General, my uncle, that a squadron of soldiers be sent on this expedition with Father Kino and me, which he granted me in order to set right the soldiers who entertained the current bad opinion." [3]

---

[1] Kino, *Favores Celestiales*, Parte I, Lib. v, Caps. 4–5; *Hist. Mem.*, I, 164–167; Alegre, Francisco Javier, *Historia de la Compañia de Jesús en Nueva-España*, III, 101.

[2] One of these was San Lázaro, the property of Romo de Vivar, of Bacanuche.

[3] Kino, *Favores Celestiales*, Parte I, Lib. v, Caps. 4–5; *Hist. Mem.*, I, 168; Manje, *Luz de Tierra Incógnita*, 246–247.

In response to these requests of both Polici and Manje, who really spoke for Kino, Jironza sent fair-haired Cristóbal Bernal with twenty-two soldiers, "valorous men," from Fronteras, to join Kino and Manje at Quíburi and make the investigation.[1]

This was a significant expedition. It was the first recorded exploration of San Pedro River to its mouth. It gives us our first close-up picture of the Sobaípuris Indians who then lived all down its banks. The records kept were remarkably accurate, as we learn by retracing the trail of the explorers with the diaries in hand. With them we, too, become explorers.

Kino and Manje left Dolores on November 2, 1697, just when Salvatierra was getting started at Loreto. They were equipped with three packloads of provisions, equipment for saying Mass, ten Indian servants, more than sixty horses and mules,[2] and some presents "by means of which to regale and tame with generosity the Sobaípuri Pima nation, for among these people benevolence is the best lodestone." From Dolores Kino followed the familiar trail through Remedios, Cocóspora, and San Lázaro, to Santa María. The diaries give intimate glimpses of the settlements on the way and reconstruct for us with surprising vividness that new missionary frontier.

Santa María was the last village with a padre. From here to San Pedro River the way was known to Kino, for he had been over it several times; but we now get new light on what was already an old Pima highway, doubtless with well-beaten trails. Saying Adiós at Santa María, Kino and Manje continued up the narrow vale which ten miles north widens out into beautiful San Rafael Valley, lying between Huachuca Mountains on the east and Patagonia Range on the west, then the site of the Pima village of Bacadéguache, and now occupied by prosperous ranch homes. The month was November, the grass was green, and the vista enchanting.

Now crossing Canelo Hills, much as the road runs today, they swung northeastward, and at the end of fourteen leagues or some

---

[1] Of the expedition we have four accounts: a brief one by Kino in his *Favores Celestiales,* Parte I, Lib. v, Caps. 6–7; *Hist. Mem.,* I, 168–174; a briefer one by Bernal, countersigned by Kino, Acuña, Escalante, Barcelona, and Barios, written at Dolores, December 3–4, 1697, and addressed to Father Polici; a diary by Bernal, Kino, Acuña, Escalante, Barcelona, and Barios; and a diary by Manje, in *Luz de Tierra Incógnita,* 246–259. (Also in MS.)

[2] Manje says thirty horses; Kino says more than sixty horses and mules.

thirty-five miles from Santa María they halted for the night at Huachuca, the village where ruled Chief Taravilla, "The Prattler." Here
the travelers were welcomed by eighty persons and lodged in an
adobe house with beams and an earthen roof. Huachuca was situated
in a moist, fertile valley, with carrizales or reed marshes, where plentiful crops were raised. The spot was manifestly La Ciénega—"The
Marsh"—now the site of Babocómari Ranch.[1] The name of the village
is still preserved in Huachuca Mountains and Fort Huachuca near by.
Huachuca was the last village of the people whom the Spaniards
called Pimas proper. Those beyond were Sobaípuris.

Next day the travelers rode eastward, down Babocómari Creek,
to San Pedro River, and halted at Santa Cruz de Gaybanipitea—the
natives are responsible for the hard name—a town of about one hundred inhabitants living in twenty-five houses. The visitors were lodged
in "the adobe house which previously they were ordered to build for
the missionary father for whom they came to ask; and they care for
about one hundred cows given them for this purpose by Father
Kino." Santa Cruz was at the mouth of Babocómari Creek directly
across San Pedro River from the site of Fairbank.

Next day Kino and Manje were joined by Bernal. The blond Captain had left Fronteras on the 5th with twenty-two soldiers and a pack
train. Among his officers were Alférez Acuña, famous interpreter,
and Sergeant Escalante, the doughty soldier who had defended Campos
so gallantly in the raid on San Ignacio, and who had been with Ramírez
on his expedition down the San Pedro in 1692. All three were frontier figures. Bernal's men were "well armed and equipped with all
the usual weapons, both offensive and defensive, and with sufficient
horses"—perhaps five per man. While this was a diplomatic mission,
Bernal was prepared for contingencies of war. From Fronteras he had
marched westward to Santa María, where he learned from Father Ruíz
that Kino had passed through two days before. So he followed over
the padre's trail to Santa Cruz.[2]

---

[1] Kino, *Favores Celestiales*, Parte I, Lib. v, Cap. 5; Bernal, Diary for corresponding dates.

[2] Kino says he received the letter and waited for Bernal at Quíburi, but his statement is
general, whereas the diaries of Manje and Bernal, which give explicit details, make it clear that
the halt was at Santa Cruz. Kino, *Favores Celestiales*, Parte I, Lib. v, Cap. 6; *Hist. Mem.*, I, 168.
From Fronteras Bernal went northwestward to Santa María, evidently expecting to join Kino
there. His marches were eight leagues to Suratpani de Guachi, north of Fronteras in the vicinity

After embraces and handshakings the combined party proceeded downstream a league to the great ranchería of Quíburi, then the largest on the river, and the home of Captain Coro, head chief of the Sobaípuris—Manje says "head chief of all the Pimas." The site of Quíburi is clearly marked today by extensive ruins two miles north of Fairbank. It was on a dangerous Apache frontier, and was placed in a commanding position on a high bluff overlooking all the country round. At this time it was fortified.[1] Here Manje counted five hundred persons living in one hundred houses. The natives raised by irrigation plentiful maize and beans, besides cotton, which they wove, dyed, and wore for clothing. There is not so much agriculture or so large a population in the same district today.

Coro gave his visitors "a splendid welcome," entertaining them in an earth-covered adobe house "with presents in their style." Indeed, the arrival of Kino and Bernal was at an opportune time for Kino's purposes, for Coro was commemorating a recent victory over Apaches. "He celebrated our arrival all day with an exquisite dance in a circle in whose center there was a tall pole from which hung thirteen scalps, bows and arrows, and other spoils of as many Apache enemies whom they had killed. And in all the rancherías they were dancing over the same victory, whereby we verified how friendly this nation is to the Spaniards. . . . And the very soldiers took part in the dance, joyous at being undeceived." What better demonstration for Bernal's benefit?

Kino tells the story more briefly. "We found the Pima natives of Quíburi very jovial and friendly. They were dancing over the scalps and the spoils of fifteen enemies, Hocomes and Janos, whom they had killed a few days before. This was so pleasing to us that Captain . . . Bernal, the Alférez, the Sergeant and many others entered the circle and danced merrily in company with the natives." Bernal was convinced.[2]

of the railroad station of Cima; twelve to Terrenate, another place with a border-town history that would furnish a theme for a great novel; then twelve leagues to Santa María. See diaries of Manje and Bernal. See also the account of Ramírez's expedition of 1692, and that of La Fuente and Terán in 1695, over the same route.

[1] In the eighteenth century a Spanish presidio called Santa Cruz was established here, and the present day ruins on the site are no doubt mainly those of the presidio rather than of the Indian fortification. In this way the name Santa Cruz was transferred to Quíburi.

[2] Kino, *Favores Celestiales*, Parte I, Lib. v, Cap. 6; *Hist. Mem.*, I, 168–169.

That night and next day were spent at Quíburi, during which time Kino and Manje gave talks on the mysteries of the Faith, and Bernal concerning matters of state and war.

XCVII

SENTINELS OF THE APACHE BORDER

Kino had planned to go to the northernmost Sobaípuris to visit Humari, head chief of the lower San Pedro Valley. The Black Robe and the Cacique were already friends, for a few months previously Humari and his two sons had visited Dolores. Kino baptized all three, christening the old chief Francisco Eusebio, and promising missionaries for his people. Bernal at first was hesitant about going further, having been told that for such a venture he would need two hundred soldiers. "To this I replied," says Kino, "that one could penetrate to the last Sobaípuris as safely as one could go to Sonora." With this assurance Bernal decided to accompany the fearless missionary, and Chief Coro offered to join the expedition with ten of his gandules. He could spare no more because Quíburi was on a dangerous frontier and must not be left unguarded; he had other enemies than the Apaches, for there was bad blood between his villages and those downstream under Humari.

So Kino and his companions set forth on a new adventure. On the 11th after Mass everybody packed up and prepared to mount. Before starting Bernal and Manje confessed and received communion, for the Apaches were good shots. At the last moment Coro decided to take thirty men instead of the ten he had promised. He felt safer that way. Another geography lesson was in store for Father Eusebio. It gave him—and us—our first clear view of the Pima people of the lower San Pedro Valley. For some distance downstream they were on Coronado's trail to the Seven Cities of Cíbola.

As the explorers marched northward they traveled cautiously with scouts ahead, for on the right was Apache Land, and Coro was not sure of his reception by Humari's people. Messengers went forward to notify the villages that the great Black Robe was coming, and every-where the Spaniards met a ceremonious welcome and generous hospitality. Kino and the officers were lodged in houses built by the natives especially for the occasion. As they entered the settlements they found roads cleared and arches and crosses erected. Kino, aided by Manje and Acuña, dispensed Christian instruction and baptized children. Bernal appointed native officers, gave them canes with flut-tering ribbons, accepted homage in the name of the king, and harangued the villagers about loyalty, duty, and particularly about war on the Apaches.

The terrain over which the explorers traveled north from Quíburi is arid and rough, so difficult indeed that much of it has been set aside in recent years as forest reserves, because it is unfit for cultivation. San Pedro River, whose banks or bed they followed, runs through a narrow valley with mountains on each side, sometimes near, some-times more remote. In places the canyon of the river is deep and at times it is precipitous; but there are frequent patches of bottom lands with fertile soil. In these flats the Indians had their irrigated fields. They are now occupied by ranchers, some of Mexican and some of Anglo-American stock. But the road in 1934 was still about as brush-grown as in 1697.

For sixty miles north of Quíburi Kino and his companions found the country uninhabited, because of the trouble between Coro and Humari, and on that stretch several sites of recently abandoned villages were noted. But between El Embudo, just south of Redington, and the mouth of Aravaipa Creek, a stretch of some thirty-five miles, there were no less than ten villages. The most thickly settled stretch was between El Embudo and 111 Ranch, a distance of about twenty miles, with eight villages. The population today and the areas under cultivation are probably smaller than when Kino descended the val-ley two hundred and thirty-nine years ago. To the historian who now travels down this brush-grown river road with the diaries in hand, it is a rare experience to be able to determine the site of prac-tically every village visited by Kino on that historic journey. The diaries are the peepstones, the Urim and Thummim, by which we still can see through Kino's eyes.

Every detail is precious, but we have room for only a few. The first day they traveled ten leagues downstream through level plains, where St. David and Benson now stand, and camped at Los Alamos, a spot so-named from its large and shady cottonwoods. It was at or near the place now called Tres Alamos,[1] a few miles north of Benson. Next day they rode thirteen leagues, passing the sites of several recently abandoned villages, and camped at Baicatcan, another abandoned site in a fertile plain. Five years previously Kino had called this place the principal village of all the eastern Sobaípuris. It was some five miles north of Cascabel, about at Sosa's Ranch, where there is a fertile river bottom now under cultivation. Just beyond was El Embudo, or the Narrows, where the river runs through a canyon. On the authority of Escalante, who had been with Ramírez in 1692 and was now in Bernal's company, it was here that they had turned back, fearing to thread the narrows, lest they be ambushed by Apaches. And Ramírez, said Manje, "was the one who had been farthest inland in these parts."[2] So Baicatcan was a landmark.

Next day, having passed El Embudo, which proved to be no great affair, they entered a wide, open plain, and at the end of two leagues came to Cusac, a village of seventy persons living in twenty houses. This plain, which is easily identified, is beautified now, as then, by a fine growth of cottonwoods and mesquite along the river. Thus Cusac was the first inhabited place in a stretch of nearly sixty miles below Quíburi. Here the Spaniards were welcomed and given great jícaras or baskets of cooked calabash, beans, and pinole. In return they gave the natives presents, with "good talks" thrown in.

Two leagues beyond Cusac they reached Jiaspi,[3] or El Rosario, a town of one hundred and forty-four persons living in twenty-three houses. Half way on the road the local chief and several headmen

---

[1] Kino, *Favores Celestiales,* Parte I, Lib. v, Cap. 6; *Hist. Mem.,* I, 169, 170; Bernal, Diary, p. 4; Manje, *Luz de Tierra Incógnita,* 249–250. Down the river from Quíburi to the site of Benson it is about fifteen miles. Tres Alamos is some ten miles further north.

[2] On this stretch they passed through the present Apodaca Valley. Kino in 1692 went from Bac to the San Pedro River to visit the eastern Sobaípuris, "who in their chief ranchería, that of San Salvador del Baicatcan, are thirty leagues distant" from Bac. He visited head chief Coro, the implication being that he visited him at Baicatcan. That being the case, Coro had moved south since 1692. But Manje's statement about Ramírez makes it practically certain that Kino had never previously been at Baicatcan. See Kino, *Favores Celestiales,* Parte I, Lib. ii, Cap. 4; *Hist. Mem.,* I, 123.

[3] Bernal gave the distance from Baicatcan to Jiaspi as three leagues, Manje as four.

El Embudo, from the south

Site of Quiburi, on the bluff at the left

came out to welcome and escort the visitors to the village. Bernal in one stroke drew for us the picture which greeted their eyes: "We found all the people, men, women, and children, drawn up in two files and unarmed, waiting to render obedience to me, and greatly pleased to see me and Captain Choro." Jiaspi was in the same wide valley as Cusac, right at Redington, which stands on a mesa facing south and looking up the valley. Here there are fertile fields and many evidences of Indian occupation. A great fireplace in the home of a leading citizen is partly built of rare metates or grinding stones picked up in the vicinity.

There was a stir in the Spanish camp. Just when Kino was in the act of baptizing four infants, Chief Humari, with numerous followers, hove in sight from the north, dressed in all his regalia. He had come to bid Kino welcome. At the same time that he embraced the Black Robe he chided him because the promised missionaries had not come to his people. "This Francisco Jumari," says Captain Bernal, "is an old man with a large following, and is a principal chief of all the rancherías." [1]

Here Bernal was more than ever convinced of Pima loyalty. The evidence was unimpeachable. He saw six recently taken Apache scalps, still red, and two Apache boys who had been captured by warriors of Bac. The soldiers, too, were now certain that these Pimas had been falsely accused of horse-stealing, "for they did not see or find any sign, indication, or vestige of a single horse whatsoever. On the contrary, they were afraid of those which we had with us." Kino had won a victory for his Pima friends. His journey proved to be a successful peace mission, also, for next morning after Mass, while soldiers, gandules, and the native rabble looked on, Humari and Coro embraced in public and were reconciled. Coro now felt more at ease—and so did Kino.

This ceremony over, the march was continued with exalted spirits. A league or less downstream they stopped for a brief talk at Muyva, a village near the present Markham. Within the next six leagues they passed through four more villages strung along the river, having a

---

[1] The previous Easter Humari had gone clear to Dolores, at least a hundred leagues, to be baptized. Kino instructed him and christened him Francisco Eusebio (Manje, *Luz de Tierra Incógnita*, 250–251).

total of five hundred persons living in one hundred and thirty houses made of reed mats in the form of "nave and gallery." Near the north end of this stretch is Sacatón Ranch, on which one or more of the first three villages must have stood.

The fourth village was Arivavia, which they named San Pantaleón. Some three miles beyond Sacatón Ranch, over low hills, and just north of where the road turns west to Oracle, another valley opens out. Here, apparently, Arivavia was situated. It was one of the principal settlements on the river, it had bountiful crops, and its dwellers "gave the soldiers so much maize flour that they did not have enough bags . . . in which to put it. . . . The Indians were repaid with knives, ribbons, and other little gifts which they greatly esteemed." Just beyond Arivavia, a league or less, they came to Tutóyda, a village of a hundred souls near the site of 111 Ranch house, and two or three leagues farther downstream, about at Mammoth, they camped at Comarsuta, a settlement of eighty persons.

The next was a red-letter day. Three or four leagues beyond Comarsuta the explorers reached Ojío, home of Chief Humari. Right proudly the old cacique led the procession through the settlement, and right joyful was the welcome. "Here the people exceeded all the other villages in demonstration of jubilee, with dances, arches, and roads swept. They entertained us in a house of poles and mats so spacious that it held all the soldiers, the padre, and the men, in the center there being a little chapel in which to say Mass." To celebrate their triumph, the Spaniards named the place La Victoria—the Victory! They had safely penetrated the dreaded land. They had come as Humari's guests, and he was not a cannibal after all. Kino's words had proved to be true.

Next to Quíburi, Ojío was the largest settlement on the San Pedro. It contained three hundred and eighty persons, living in seventy houses. Being on the frontier, and the home of the great chief, it was a bulwark against the near-by Apaches. It was situated just south of the mouth of Arivaipa Creek, and extended perhaps all down the fertile bottom-lands from Zapata's Ranch (Norton's) to Beard's. At the latter place, right by the roadside—crossing the road, indeed—there are still plainly to be seen ruins of a large fortification, evidently of Indian origin, and doubtless built for defense against the Apaches. It is not mentioned in the diaries and may be of a later date.

At Ojío the Spaniards were visited by chiefs from Busac and Tubo, villages comprising eighty-five men and situated to the eastward on an arroyo called Babiteóida. This was Arivaipa Creek, which has fine lands for some twelve miles upstream, where it emerges from a deep canyon. These people, who lived nearest the Apache border, were especially admonished to observe loyalty. Captain Bernal gave canes of office to Humari and his sons and threw in for full measure "a very good talk." Captain Coro also "made them a talk, and they were very friendly. Likewise the governor of Los Dolores, called Francisco, whom Father Kino has with him, made another talk, giving them to understand how important it is for our souls to receive holy baptism. . . . This function over, they embraced me and all the companions, and I bade them goodbye." [1]

Thus, in the San Pedro Valley below Fairbank there lived more than two thousand people in. fifteen villages, chief of which were Quíburi and Ojío. Everywhere they raised with irrigation plentiful crops of calabashes, frijoles, maize, and cotton, a fiber which was dexterously woven, dyed, and used for clothing. Of these people and their country Manje wrote, "The whole valley is wide, long, and very fertile. Their fields are irrigated with acéquias, and the Indians are dressed and adorned with colored mantas, belts, and strings of beads around the neck." And thus did the superb reporters, Kino, Manje, and Bernal, record for us their visit to these interesting folk. It is a chronicle which never since has been and never can be equaled, for the people of chiefs Coro and Humari no longer dwell on their native stream.

XCVIII

A BETTER VIEW OF THE CASA GRANDE

Things having gone so well thus far, Kino decided to continue to the Gila Pimas and visit his old friends there. Coro consented to

[1] Diaries of Manje and Bernal.

accompany him. Bidding goodbye to Humari and his people, and led now by new guides, next day (November 16), the cavalcade moved north down the river six leagues, to the junction of the San Pedro with "the great Río de Jila." The town of Winkelman is now almost on the spot. Taking refreshments of "sweetmeats" here,—in celebration perhaps,—they swung northwestward down the left bank of Gila River, and at three leagues camped about at Crescent Ranch, above Branaman, where the valley opens out into a wide flat. From some unrecorded incident the camp site was called Manje's Place—Paraje de Manje. The name should be restored. The wayfarers were a little nervous now, for they were in Apache country, so they observed formal military order. At camp they were told by the guides of ancient edifices across the river, "casas grandes which it was conjectured were made by the Mexican nation when it set out from the north." The conjectures were doubtless made by the Spaniards, not by the guides.

Next day they climbed Tortilla Range on the left and skirted the river to avoid the marshes of the vega, and, it is suspected, to be farther from the Apaches. As they rode along the ridge they could see to the east the Sierra Florida, "where the hostile Apaches are accustomed to live and where on one occasion a battle was fought with them." Toward the sunset, Manje tells us, they "saw the casas grandes which, although they were at a distance of seventeen leagues, looked like castles." Here one may be disposed to be skeptical. But if they had a telescope they could see a long distance from a peak. At the site of Kelvin they swung west, traveling still on the mountain, to avoid the narrow canyon just beyond. The highway from Kelvin to Florence now swings well to the south; Kino kept closer to the river.

Having traveled eight leagues for the day—they were long ones—they camped at a "round, green little hill which looked like a flower garden and a crag, with a cold, crystalline spring high up, which gushed forth near the top and watered all the skirts." This spring, which they named San Gregorio, is at Donnelly's Ranch, three or four miles south of Cochran, a railroad station on the Gila River. Fine as it was, there was not enough water for all the horses, so they descended to the vega of the river, traveled two leagues downstream, and camped about opposite Price. They had left the mountains behind.

Continuing next day through an extended, sterile plain, after going five leagues they saw across the river ruins of old edifices. Acuña, Escalante, Barrios, and Truxillo, full of vigor and of curiosity, swam across to examine them, not knowing, perhaps, that they were the first in all written history to put them on record. We hereby acknowledge the debt. "They said that the walls were two varas thick, like a castle, and that there were other ruins near them, all of ancient construction." These are the ruins a mile or more west of Florence, north of the river, and locally known as Manje's House. Acuña's House would be a more appropriate name, and the great interpreter deserves a monument. Continuing four leagues west amid wind and rain, they arrived at noon at the more famous Casa Grande, where, indeed, there were several casas, with one overtowering all the rest. Kino left us a description of them based on his visit three years before. Manje and Bernal now give us better ones.

"We arrived at noon at the Casas Grandes, within which Father Kino said Mass, for to this place he had traveled without breakfast," Manje writes. It has been sentimentally assumed by modern writers that Kino did this purposely in order to say Mass in the remarkable ruin of which he had been the proud discoverer. But no, sad to say, the documents discredit this pretty tale. It was because in the morning it had been too stormy to permit a stop for breakfast. Manje continues: "One of them is a large edifice whose principal room in the middle is four storeys high, those adjacent on its four sides being three storeys. The walls are two varas thick and made of strong argamasa and clay. They are so smooth inside that they appear like planed plank, and so burnished that they shine like Puebla pottery." They still glisten. "The corners of the windows, which are square, are very rectangular, and without hinges or cross-pieces of wood by which to make them with mold or frame. The same is true of the doors, although they are narrow, which shows that this is a work of Indians. The house is thirty-six paces long, twenty-one wide, and of good architecture, with its foundations as is shown by the drawing in the margin." [1]

----

[1] The drawing is reproduced by Fernández del Castillo in his edition of *Luz de Tierra Incógnita*, p. 365. It shows no great artistic skill on Manje's part.

But this large edifice was only one of many in the group. "At a distance of an arquebus shot twelve other houses are seen, half fallen down, likewise with thick walls, the roofs all burned, except that of a low room of one house, which has some round beams, smooth and slender, which appear to be of cedar or savin. On top of these beams there are reeds very evenly laid, and on top of these a mass of argamasa and hard clay, and it has a high ceiling very carefully made. In the vicinity there are evidences of many other ruins and rubbish-heaps from earthquakes [1] for two leagues around, with much broken colored pottery, plates, and ollas of fine clay of various hues and resembling the jars of Guadalajara in this New Spain."

Manje's observations are interesting and sensible. "From this it is inferred that the settlement or city was very large, and of people with civilization and government. This is proved by a mother ditch which runs from the river through the plain, making a circle three leagues in circumference with the settlement in the center. It is ten varas wide and about four deep, whereby they drew off perhaps half of the river, both to serve as a defensive fosse as well as to supply water to its districts and to irrigate their fields in the vicinity. The guides said that at a distance of a day's journey toward the north and on the other side of the river there are other edifices of the same structure, on an arroyo called the Verde, which joins this one." He refers to the later-discovered ruins near Phoenix.

Manje now throws in a little Pima folk lore, and gives his own theory of the origin of the casas grandes. "They said that they were built by a people who came from the north country, whose chief is called El Siba, who, according to the definition in their language is The Bitter Man or The Cruel Man, and that on account of the bloody wars made on them by the Apaches and twenty nations confederated with them, many dying on both sides, they migrated. Part of them, because of disagreements, separated and returned to the north, whence they had come years before. Those farthest east and south, we judge from the accounts, and it is reasonable, are the ancestors of the Mexican nation." Nearly eighty years later the Pimas at Casa Grande told Father Font the diverting legend of The Bitter Man.

---

[1] *Altos de terremotos.*

Kino adds other details: "The soldiers were much delighted to see the Casa Grande. We marveled at seeing that it was about a league from the river and without water; but afterward we saw that it had a large aqueduct with a very great embankment, which must have been three varas high and six or seven wide—wider than the causeway of Guadalupe at Mexico. This very great aqueduct, as is still seen, not only conducted the water from the river to the Casa Grande, but at the same time, making a great turn, it watered and enclosed a plain many leagues in length and breadth and of very level and very rich land. With ease, also, one could now restore and roof the house and repair the great aqueduct for a very good pueblo, for near by there are six or seven villages of Pimas Sobaípuris." [1]

XCIX

QUICKSILVER AND BLOND WOMEN

Kino continued west to see the Gila Pimas, those interesting people who still occupy essentially the same lands on which they then lived. He calls them Pimas Sobaípuris, the same as those on San Pedro River and at Bac. He had visited them three years before, and he now met old friends, several of whom had been with him to see Father Polici at Bazeraca.

While they were at the Casa Grande three headmen of a village on the Gila a league away came and embraced Kino and all the company, inviting them to their home. All set forth, and at the village they found the people waiting in two files to welcome them. They rendered obedience to Bernal and brought for the visitors water, and bread made of mesquite beans, because the maize harvest had failed that year. This village had one hundred and thirty persons.[2] Kino preached and baptized nine children, "although at first they were afraid of the horses and soldiers, because they had never seen any before." This would seem to mean that Kino did not visit this

[1] Diaries of Manje and Bernal; Kino, *Favores Celestiales,* Parte I, Lib. v. Cap. 7; *Hist. Mem.,* I, 172–173; Manje, *Luz de Tierra Incógnita,* 251–253.
[2] Manje, *Luz de Tierra Incógnita,* 253.

village on his former journey. These ceremonies concluded, the Spaniards went to camp on the river at a place near by where there was no pasturage.

Next day they proceeded westward down the Gila, accompanied by the three headmen and all the people, and went four leagues through lands without pasturage to the village called Tusónimo "on account of a great pile of horns of wild sheep which looks like a mountain. Because of its abundance this animal constitutes their ordinary food. Indeed, from the way the heap overtops the highest of their houses, there would seem to be more than a hundred thousand antlers." An actual count perhaps would not have made so good a story. This village, called by Kino La Encarnación, became a landmark on the Gila. It was in the vicinity of Blackwater. Kino's coming had been heralded. The natives had built a house for him and they welcomed him with arches and crosses. The Magic Man had come again. "The heathen Indians welcomed us with jubilee," Manje writes, "and we counted two hundred affable and docile souls." They were easier to count than the antlers. "We spent the night here, and the father and I spent the time instructing them through the interpreters in the knowledge of God and the mysteries of our Holy Faith, with the result that they begged us to baptize for them fifteen children and seven sick adults." The petition was granted.[1]

Leaving the horses with a guard, in order that they might recuperate with the fair pasturage found near by,[2] next day they continued with twelve soldiers—Coro was in the party—down the river westward and traveled seven leagues to Tudacson,[3] called by Kino San Andrés when he had visited it three years before. It was near the river in the vicinity of Vah Ki. Three leagues before arriving the visitors were welcomed by Palacios, the chief who had gone to Dolores, where he was baptized and named for the father provincial, and thence with Kino to Bazeraca to see Polici. He was now overjoyed to see the great padre, for they had been companions on a long,

---

[1] Bernal says sixteen infants and four large boys were baptized. "Then four captains were christened, among them the captain of the ranchería of the eastern frontier, who was given the name Juan Francisco de Acuña," named, of course, for the famous interpreter.

[2] By Bernal the place where the cavalcade was left was called Santa Isabel, but it was close to Tusónimo.

[3] Also called Sudacson and Sutaquison, corrupted on modern maps into Sacatón.

long trail. Continuing to the village, the visitors found crosses and arches erected along the way, and the roads cleared and swept. The soldiers were entertained in a house of poles covered with reeds, and for Kino a house of mats had been especially prepared. Palacios supplied the visitors with pinole, mesquite beans, and calabashes "which were reciprocated with little gifts." Four hundred persons were counted.

At San Andrés Bernal and Manje were attracted by a very special circumstance, more notable than the sheep horns. A young man appeared all streaked with what seemed to be vermilion or red hematite. He was asked where he got the paint. "Five days' journey toward the northwest and the Río Colorado," he replied. Then he brought forth a ball of it wrapped up in a buckskin. It was red, very heavy, and so liquid and oily that it seeped through the buckskins in which it was enveloped. "And from what I have read of philosophy in Agricola's *De Re Metallica,* it appeared to me to be quicksilver," says our learned Don Matheo, citing this ponderous Latin tome. "Therefore, Alférez Francisco de Acuña asked and repeated very careful questions"— Acuña was the star interpreter—"and the Indian told him that on breaking the red metal which they bring to paint themselves with, drops come out like thick water and of the color of a lead ball; that he cut it with a knife; that on taking hold of it it slips through the fingers because of its subtility; that they make little pools of it in the ground; and that taking what will fill the crown of a hat one cannot lift it because it is so heavy." [1]

The visitors were excited, for nothing stirred a Spaniard like "una mina." And quicksilver was so important that it had been made a royal monopoly. Visions of wealth and of kingly favor passed before their eyes. "All these are signs and marks of quicksilver," said Manje, "And if perchance it is this, it would be of great service to his Majesty

[1] Manje, *Luz de Tierra Incógnita,* 253–254; Kino, *Favores Celestiales,* Parte I, Lib. v. Cap. 7; *Hist. Mem.,* I, 183. "Barica" in the manuscript, rendered "Barúa" in the printed text of Manje's book, p. 254, is evidently a copyist's error for "Agricola." The first complete edition of the great work, *De Re Metallica, by* Georgius Agricola, was published in Latin in 1556. It remained the standard textbook and guide for miners and metallurgists for one hundred and eighty years, until the publication of Schlüter's work in 1738. Young Manje had evidently studied the ponderous treatise while a collegian in Spain, and now, on the outer edge of civilization, he was citing it as an authority. How many men who since have mined in the same region could read the book? Agricola's treatise was published in a superb English edition by Herbert Clark Hoover and Lou Henry Hoover (London, 1912).

and useful to the mines of New Spain if such a treasure were discovered, for there being in the world no other quicksilver mines than those of Almadén in Spain, Cuancabelica in Perú, and Carintia in Germany, when our output fell off it cost his Majesty heavily to obtain and transport it so that the mines of silver and gold in the Indies might not shut down." Don Matheo knew his history. This story of quicksilver would be real news in Sonora, and eager questions would be asked there. Why did they not go to see the mine? Manje tells us. It was because "the horses were in bad shape and the soldiers too few to resist the hostile Apaches who are in its vicinity. But we agreed to return with more supplies and a larger force to discover it." There could be no better testimony to their respect for the Apaches.[1]

The Indians told another tale almost as interesting as the one about quicksilver, and potentially as important for the Empire. It was about white strangers in the West. "They reported also that at times white people came to the Río Colorado on horseback with shields, swords, and arquebuses, though they do not discharge them. And although we thought they might be the apostate Moquis who revolted in the year 1680, and who not having powder did not shoot the people, on the other hand, since it is added that they are white, it may be that they are Englishmen who live toward the coast of the Gulf of California, or Spaniards who have been lost in various vessels which in times past have been wrecked near the coast, and coming out by floating on planks have settled, but lack powder, and who may have domesticated the horse-like deer which they say there are toward the north." The "horse-like deer" were probably elk. Why may not these strangers have been Frenchmen from the Mississippi Valley? Or was the tale just a hoax?

Bernal's account gives an added touch of human interest.[2] "Like-

---

[1] Manje, *Luz de Tierra Incógnita,* 254–255. He added: "But several wars with the hostile Apaches occurring soon afterward, and Don Jacinto de Fuensaldaña becoming Capitán Volante, with his omissions, lawsuit, and removal, this discovery remained in silence."

[2] Bernal, Diary, Nov. 21, Manje, *Luz de Tierra Incógnita,* 255. Bernal's account of the quicksilver is as follows: "A heathen Indian whom our Father [Kino] appointed fiscal told me and Alférez Francisco de Acuña that in the interior toward the west there is a vein which, according to what he told us, is of red metal. When a rock is broken it comes out of the holes, and according to what is given to understand and from what he wears smeared over his face, it is seen to be quicksilver. In order that he might explain it, a bullet was shown him. Taking it, he said that what came out of the holes was of the same color, and that when it fell on the ground

wise the Indian said that white men come on horseback on saddles, with their blond women, and that they make war upon the people farther inland. When he was asked how white these strangers were, he replied, pointing to Juan Bernal, that their color and hair were like his." This story gave the fellows something to talk about for days to come, for in Mexico even today the sight of a fair-haired woman—una huera—sets all the male sex a-flutter.

C

THE SANTA CRUZ TRAIL

Retracing their steps to Tusónimo, and swinging southeast, Kino and his party now followed the trail up the Santa Cruz River to Tucsón and Tumacácori, a highway which is still used with slight modifications. The Indian laid it out long before the white man came. Kino had opened it to Europeans three years previously, but of that journey we have few details. This expedition gives us our first intimate data. With Kino we are again pathfinders.

From Tusónimo the travelers went three leagues southeast and camped without water in the vicinity of Casa Grande, but west of it. Next day they continued in the same direction four or five leagues to a water tank or aljibe which attracted attention as a prehistoric work of man. It was northward of Picacho. The natives told Bernal that the reservoir was made by the same people who built the Casa Grande. It was in the shape of a parallelogram sixty by forty varas (165 by 110 feet) in dimensions, with walls of argamasa or stone and mortar, judging from the hardness of the material. The reservoir was fed with rainwater by intakes at the four corners. At this time the aljibe had water, and the jaded animals slaked their thirst, which was great, for they had been three days without a drink.[1]

he could not get hold of it because it slipped through his fingers, and that although with some labor he had made a medium-sized buckskin bag, indicating the size of a sleeveful, and even though it was much less, he could not raise it from the ground. He asserted that its color was whiter than the bullet which we showed him. He said that to go to the vein they traveled four days, and that there was another of the same material near by, but that it was distant a two days' journey without water."

[1] Bernal tells us that "the tank is in a flat close to a little arroyo, and so arranged that the

Continuing the same day ten leagues south (Bernal says fifteen), they halted long after dark near the river bed at Santa Catarina de Cuituabagu, a village of two hundred persons and forty houses southeast of the Picacho.[1] This place became another station on the Spanish trail. There were fields near by, but at this season the site was dry and the natives obtained their water from springs far to the west. The visitors were welcomed with torchlights, arches, and crosses. A house of mats was ready for Kino, and everybody was supplied with baskets of calabashes and beans, and with jars of water which the native women had patiently carried on their heads across the plain.[2] Kino was especially impressed by one of the crosses which the natives had erected in honor of his visit. At its foot there were seven little carved wooden daggers, painted blue. He was greatly edified "because they represented to him the Seven Sorrows of Holy Mary," and when he departed he carried the cross to his mission as a relic. Where is it now?

Traveling on the 23d nine leagues up the dry river bed, they halted at a village of a hundred persons in Valle de Correa, another landmark. It was in the vicinity of Rillito, at the end of Tucsón Range.[3] Crops here were dependent on seasonal rainfall, and the natives drank from a deep well dug in the sand. Six leagues more on the same day took the cavalcade to San Agustín de Oiaur, near the site of Tucsón.[4] The chief, dubbed Romo de Vivar, for his godfather, the Bacanuche miner, came out to welcome them, and had his people lined up in two files. The visitors were lodged in a specially prepared house of mats, large enough for all. Here at San Agustín the river was running "with some volume," and the stretch from here to Bac was the most populous and most fertile spot in the whole valley. The natives had extensive fields under irrigation, raised large crops of maize, frijoles, cotton, calabashes, watermelons and cantaloupes, wove

water enters it. The rim is of the same earth, and it has a circumference of about two hundred varas [550 feet]" (Bernal, Diary, Nov. 22). This aljibe must have been in the plain northward of El Picacho. On the Mallery map of Arizona Territory, San Francisco, 1887, "Blue Water" is noted in that vicinity at the place where the road forks to run straight north to Casa Grande. See Manje, *Luz de Tierra Incógnita*, 255–256.

[1] It is in the vicinity of the Oitpar mentioned by the Anza expedition.

[2] Bernal says there were one hundred persons and twenty-five houses.

[3] Bernal says it is "where the Valle de Correa begins." Was the valley named, perhaps, for Kino's artist friend in Mexico?

[4] Evidently north of it.

the cotton, and wore it for clothing. Manje counted eight hundred persons in one hundred and eighty-six houses. Here a chief from San Pedro River arrived bringing a sword lost by one of the soldiers on the way north. The loyal deed was rewarded by the gift of a knife.

From Oiaur to Bac, or Bacóida,—the place near the well—a distance of six leagues, the settlements were nearly continuous. At Bac the natives, headed by Chief Eusebio, outdid themselves in hospitality. They lodged the travelers "in an earth-covered adobe house with beams, which they had built for the father missionary who has been promised them, and they care for a drove of mares and cattle which Father Kino gave them for the mission, and a field of wheat from which they had kneaded bread made for us, an Indian having brought a sieve from Dolores." The bread was baked in an oven made at Kino's order.[1] The utensils of European civilization were thus creeping in. In the vicinity nine hundred persons were counted, and the Spaniards were given ore from the west which appeared to be silver. Two Jocome captives were purchased, a girl of twelve by Bernal and a boy of ten by Acuña. Here Coro, who had made the grand circuit, said goodbye and went eastward to his home at Quíburi, mounted on a horse given him as a reward for his services in the expedition. We can see his feet swing "Indian fashion" as he beats time with the motion of the horse, for red men all ride alike. From Bac the route was over the already familiar trail upstream to Cocóspora. Two days were spent at Remedios, "to work with the Indians in the building of a large church." On December 2 they reached Dolores.

Manje thus sums up the journey. It "was two hundred and sixty leagues going and coming"—about 650 miles —"through lands mostly unknown, though without any embudos [canyons] such as were expected, but of extended plains, and pleasing and delightful valleys with fertile lands abundant with crops, all the people affable, friendly and desirous to be Christians. We counted 920 houses and 4700 persons, and baptized 80 children and some adults who were catechized as well as the time would permit." They urgently requested mission-

---

[1] "We found and killed cattle, sheep and goats, and found even bread, fresh and very good, which they baked for us in the new oven which I had ordered" (Kino, *Hist. Mem.*, I, 173).

aries, "and, if they were granted it would not only be a flourishing Christendom, but by means of it, as a step on the way, the rest of the nations of North America would be reduced. It would be discovered whether the mine is of quicksilver, or the Sierra Azul rich in silver and gold ore, like the rich kingdoms of Teguayo and Quivira according to reports of the ancients. And by way of the Colorado, with a vessel, there would follow commerce with New Mexico"—the Grand Canyon was overlooked—"the reduction of the apostate Moqui Indians, and with small expense [it would be possible] to extend the dominions and attract to his Majesty and regenerate the people in the Catholic Church, even with some profit to the royal treasury. May God grant that this be achieved by His grace, and that so many souls redeemed by His blood may not be lost."[1] Tantalus was still up to his tricks.

Kino wrote of his triumphant journey to the Father General: "By means of it we have discovered plainly and patently that the Pimería not only is not bad, as for the last ten years some have falsely declared and reported, but is so fine and friendly to us and to our Holy Faith, that with two blows which on the 15th of September and the 26th of October of this present year of '97 they have given to our enemies the Hojomes, all this province of Sonora and its confines remains, as we hope in Our Lord, already with the desired peace and quietude, and free from its most pestiferous enemies."

---

[1] Manje continues with geographical notions which seem to represent a later date, when he wrote his book. Manje, *Luz de Tierra Incógnita,* 258. Kino reported to Thirso González late in December, 1697, enclosing Bernal's letter to Polici (Ex. Arch. Procuratoris Generalis, S. J. Collegia Mexicana, N. 97a. Romae). "It . . . will serve until I am able with divine favor to make a fair copy of my diary which, together with other notices, I shall entitle "Manifest Disillusionment" (Manifiesto Desengaño), and with its maps I shall send it to your Reverence as soon as possible." I have not seen this diary or the maps. Possibly Kino never finished them.

Kino is Vindicated

CI

CHIEF CORO WINS A VICTORY

THE JOURNEY TO THE GILA gave convincing testimony to the loyalty of the Sobaípuris and it had its effect. "This entry," wrote Kino, "was well received by all good men, because of the abundant and clear evidence which was thereby obtained as to whether the farthest Sobaípuris were good or bad, friends or enemies, implicated and culpable, or innocent of the robberies and hostilities of the province. The father provincial wrote a very fine letter and promised fathers for this Pimería and sent them."

Of the missionaries sent one was Gaspar de las Barillas, who arrived at Dolores at the end of January, on his way to re-establish the missions on the Altar. Kino and Manje accompanied the new worker to his destination. Barillas was to choose between Tucubavia, Tubutama, and Caborca. Kino evidently had not been among the Sobas since Saeta's death two years before. But in all places he was well received by his old friends. While at Caborca he set the natives at work again on the building of a bark in which he hoped to go to California. He had appealed from Muñoz to the provincial and obtained a new permission. Barillas chose Caborca for his headquarters, and returned to Arizpe for his baggage. He went again to his mission in June, but left in July,[1] "because of certain pretended dangers." So Caborca was once more deserted.

The evidence of Pima loyalty obtained in the last expedition to the Gila was soon supplemented by their valiant defense of the province on the field of battle. They were now doubly vindicated. The new year opened with two savage attacks from the northeast. Kino

[1] Kino. *Hist Mem.*, I, 174–175. Barillas, by the way, was another Black Robe from Tarahumara.

had scarcely returned from Caborca when he heard bad news from Cocóspora. On February 25, 1698, Jocomes, Sumas, and Apaches swooped down on that mission three hundred strong, at a time when it was almost without men, for they had gone to the frontier villages to purchase maize. Father Ruíz, aided by a few neophytes, and shielded by a bull-hide barricade, defended himself manfully. There was a stiff fight in which one of the enemy was slain. Two women of the mission were killed, the village, the church, and the father's residence were sacked and burned. The enemy ran off some of the mission horses and all the small stock. A few Cocóspora natives pursued them, but they were ambushed and nine more of their men bit the dust. Father Ruíz, who by no means lacked courage, fled to the interior missions for safety.[1]

Excitement now shook the frontier. Couriers carried the news to San Juan. The Sonora garrison there prepared to pursue the marauders; Kino summoned the Pima allies to join the campaign, and they loyally responded. The combined force pursued the enemy to Sierra de Chiricahua, killed thirty, captured sixteen, and recovered horses and other stolen property. It was a signal victory.[2] But a more notable one followed in which Chief Coro was the hero. While the Apaches were thus being despoiled of the plunder taken at Cocóspora, another large band attacked Quíburi. Kino's account of the exciting event cannot be improved upon.

"The avowed enemies, the Hocomes, Sumas, Mansos, and Apaches, who between great and small numbered about six hundred, persuading themselves that they could accomplish in Santa Cruz on Río de Quíburi what they had done the month before in the pueblo of Cocóspora, showed their arrogance by attacking the village at daybreak on the morning of March 30. They killed its captain [3] and two or three others, and forced them to retreat to their fortification, which consisted of a house of adobe and earth with embrasures. But the enemy,

---

[1] Mora says that Ruíz "miraculously defended himself within the little patio of his house, aided by two Indians and with a bull-hide for a fortification." Mora Contra Kino, 60; Kino, *Favores Celestiales*, Parte I, Lib. v, Cap. 9; *Hist. Mem.*, I, 176; Manje, *Luz de Tierra Incógnita*, 258–259.

[2] Kino, *Favores Celestiales*, Parte I, Lib. vi, Cap. 4; *Hist. Mem.*, I, lii; Manje, *Luz de Tierra Incógnita*, 258.

[3] I assume that this was El Bajón.

defending themselves and covering themselves with many buckskins, approached the fortification, climbed upon its roof, destroyed and burned it, and with a shot killed one man, for they had one of the arquebuses which on other occasions they had taken from the soldiers. They sacked and burned the village, killed three mares of the ranch which I had here, and began to roast and stew meat and beans, and to parch and grind maize for their pinole, both the men and the women, who had all fought as equals, considering themselves as already quite victorious." By standing at Fairbank and looking west across the river one can in imagination easily reconstruct this stirring affray, for just there the scene was laid.

"But meantime the news reached the neighboring village of Quíburi, which is a league and a half from Santa Cruz, and immediately its captain, called El Coro, came to the rescue with his brave people, together with other Pimas who had come from the west to barter for maize, and who contributed to the fortunate outcome of the event, for they were supplied with the arms which we had ordered them to provide to go on the expedition with the soldiers of the presidio."

A most unusual scene was now enacted. The desert men gave a good example of the institution of championship by which medieval people often settled their differences. "The captain of the enemy, called El Capotcari, proposed—for with Captain Coro came many Pimas [1]—that they should fight ten on one side and ten on the other. Captain Coro accepted the challenge and selected ten Pimas, while Captain Capotcari selected ten others, the most valiant of all he had. Five were Apaches, as was also one of the other five." That is to say, they fought in two phalanxes, five against five in each case. The show was worthy of a Roman arena.

The battle was now on. "They began firing their arrows, and, as the Pimas were very dexterous in shooting and also in parrying the arrows of their adversaries, and as the Apaches, although expert in shooting arrows and with the lance, are not dexterous in parrying the arrows, five Pimas soon wounded the five Apaches who were their antagonists, as did four other Pimas their adversaries, the Hocomes

---

[1] El Capotcari was a predecessor of the more famous Gerónimo. Manje and Jironza give slightly different details. Manje says there were five hundred Pimas. Capotcari evidently saw himself outnumbered.

and Xanos." It was now a battle between Capotcari and his personal *vis-à-vis*. "Capotcari was very skillful in catching the arrows, but his opponent, a valiant Pima, grappled with him, . . . threw him to the ground and beat his head with stones."

The god of victory crowned Coro and his Pima braves. "Thereupon all the rest of the enemy began to flee, and the Pimas followed them through all those woods and hills for more than four leagues, killing and wounding more than three hundred. Fifty-odd remained dead and stretched out near by, and the rest, as they were wounded with the poisonous herb, died along the trails. The remainder, about three hundred, went, after this ill fortune and from fear of the Pimas, as they confessed, to ask and to offer peace" at Janos, El Paso, and New Mexico.

Coro's victory was a triumph long remembered and talked about. The Apaches had met their match. Chief Coro, by a special messenger, rushed the news to Kino, sending the "count of the dead on a notched stick." By another courier Kino hurried the report to Jironza at San Juan, and to the Jesuits in various places. There was great rejoicing. Jironza declared "that this victory would serve for the complete relief of all the province." Polici the visitor gave "a thousand thanks to His Divine Majesty for the very fortunate event." The rector of Mátape dedicated a Mass and a solemn feast to the Most Holy Trinity. At San Juan all the church bells were rung, and Morales, lieutenant there, wrote Kino "hearty congratulations for so happy a victory." Captain Almazán gave thanks on behalf of the citizens of San Juan and Nacozari:[1] "and he offered and gave presents for those Pimas, as did also the father rector of Mátape." In the minds of most persons Kino's Pimas were fully vindicated.

But there were still doubting Thomases. Some pessimists refused to believe the Pimas were friends of the Spaniards. "Whereupon," says Kino, "I called the Señor lieutenant of this Pimería [Antonio Morales] to draw up the certificate and legalized report of what had happened." The energetic Kino did not stop here. He would go in person to help gather the evidence. His fifty-three years did not check him. The din of battle merely quickened his pulse and lim-

[1] Kino, *Favores Celestiales*, Parte I, Lib. vi. Caps. 2–3; *Hist. Mem.*, I, 177–182.

bered his stiffening joints. Mounting his best horse, he took his servants, pack mules and extra cavallada and rode north the hundred-odd miles to the scene of the remarkable combat.[1]

"I went in the fifty leagues to Santa Cruz de Quíburi, and on the twenty-third of April we viewed the dead bodies of the enemy. There we encountered the twenty-two soldiers who also, because of the incredulous, had come in, by way of Terrenate, and who were actually investigating the above-mentioned and contradicted deaths." Sent by Jironza, they were led by Escalante and Manje. It was a gruesome sight which met the missionary's eyes. "We saw and counted fifty-four corpses near by, thirty-one of men and twenty-three of women. The natives gave us various spoils, which we brought away with us, among them an arquebus, powder and balls, a leathern jacket, buffalo and deerskins, bows and arrows, and scalps of the above-mentioned enemies. Of the Pima natives of the ranchería of Santa Cruz five died and nine were wounded but recovered."

Kino was jubilant. He no sooner returned to Dolores than he sat down and wrote an account of "the signal victory," as evidence of "the fine loyalty" of the Pimas. He quoted from letters written by many sorts of people in Sonora, offering congratulations and thanks. And of course he turned the good fortune to account. The Pimas must have more missionaries. "Now nothing is lacking except that those who can . . . should succor this extensive Pimería, which has more than ten thousand souls, with the ten or twelve suitable father missionaries which it needs. And would that they might be somewhat like the two who so gloriously . . . are laboring actually in California"—Salvatierra and Picolo—"and giving the lie to those little favorable to this Pimería." [2]

Jironza, too, was rejoiced over the victory, and he capitalized it as one of the signal events of his own administration. Chief Coro thus did more than one Spaniard a good turn. To the viceroy Jironza reported "a fortunate victory over the Hocomes, Apaches, and other nations in rebellion against the royal crown." Before the event he had promised the Pimas $1000 in clothing for a good stroke, "in order to

---

[1] Kino went twice to Quíburi in April. See Mora Contra Kino, May 28, 1698.
[2] Kino, Breve Relación de la Insigne Victoria, Dolores, May 3, 1698. Postscript, October 25. Original manuscript, Biblioteca Nacional, Mexico. Manje, *Luz de Tierra Incógnita*, 259.

encourage them, animate them, and keep them grateful in the service of the two Majesties." And when he wrote on May 16 he was waiting for Coro and his headmen to appear at San Juan to claim the reward. He closed by asking the viceroy that "in order to keep this Sobaípuris nation more grateful they be given the consolation of ministers of the gospel."[1] Kino and Coro had scored.

CII

MORA BLOWS UP

All this praise for Kino was more than poor Mora could stand. He had planned for many months to report to Father Palacios the grave shortcomings of Father Eusebio, but had refrained. Now he could contain himself no longer. On May 28 he finished a seventy-nine-page report, in which Polici shared honors with Father Eusebio. The visitor, who had seemed so hostile to Kino, had now gone over to him soul and body. It was Kino this and Kino that! "Everything the father visitor has done in the Pimería is because of what Father Kino has told him. Father Kino has been charged with the new missions. Father Kino has been granted a license for his continuous excursions, with great damage to his missions."

The particular damage to which Mora alluded was Father Eusebio's neglect of his neophytes while exploring. "Well, how much time would he have to stay at home and think of the instruction of the Indians? Between the month of September of last year, '97, and this month of May '98, the following journeys by the father have been noted, all recorded in letters of his, which, to avoid prolixity, I shall not cite. In September to Santa María Vasseraca, two hundred leagues there and back; in October to Quíburi, a hundred leagues there and back; in November more than two hundred leagues going to and coming from Casa Grande; in December to the west ninety leagues; in Janu-

---

[1] Jironza to the viceroy, San Juan Bautista, May 16, 1698. Original Spanish manuscript, A.G.I. 67–3,28, Guadalajara 134. Terrenate is north of Cananea. The stream then called Río de Terrenate is now San Pedro River.

ary to the Real de San Juan, Sonora, Oposura, etc, a hundred leagues; in February to the west ninety leagues; in March to Quíburi, a hundred leagues; in April twice to Quíburi, two hundred leagues; in May, when this report is made, to Sonora, San Juan, and Oposura, a hundred leagues. Anyone who hears tells of so many leagues must say this is a lot of traveling, and must take much time and many days." Yes indeed.

Kino hid behind the vow of obedience, said Mora. "I imagine that he is very well satisfied and serene with saying that the higher superiors charge and command him to make these journeys, and that he is merely obeying them. Who will pretend that the superiors order him to do what he likes to do? He deceives himself if with vain flattery he talks of and praises obedience, because in this matter he does not obey the prelate but the prelate obeys him." The prelate, of course, was Polici.

Father Eusebio's motives were not becoming to a religious, Mora declared. He had secular ambitions. He wished to be considered the defender of the province. "One of the principal reasons for these excursions has been.in order that Father Kino might find himself made convoker and co-operator, to the end that the Pimas might make themselves capital enemies of the Jocomes, Janos, Apaches, and other nations who invade this province. For it appears that the father visitor has had the idea that in this way everything would be composed; in the first place, in order that the Pimas, . . . might not join the enemies; in the second place, in order that the enemies, being diverted with wars against the Pimas, might do no damage here. . . . And I ask, is it for this purpose that we come to the missions?"

And Mora was sarcastic about Coro's victory over the enemies. It was not so much to brag about. "That which is appropriate to this paper is to say that the Pimas, having come out victorious, have remained so frightened that they moved at once from where they were living and established themselves farther inland, for fear that the enemy should destroy them."[1] This was true. After the battle Coro moved at once with his people from Quíburi to Sonóita Creek, where, in the vicinity of Patagonia, he established a settlement called by the

---

[1] Mora Contra Kino, May 28, 1698, par. 46.

Jesuits Los Reyes. Coro had valor; better than that, he had discretion.

Father Eusebio had resumed his boat building at Caborca, and this worried Mora. "Such has been the occasion of the excursions of Father Kino to the north. The motive for those to the west has been an enterprise of which I have never seen the like." With his fault-finding Mora mixed a hearty laugh. He regarded Kino's maritime project as a huge joke. Perhaps it was. "Even since he has been ordered to remain in the Pimería and drop California, he is saying that he is going to embark for California by way of the Pimería and is building a bark. And this building is completely upsetting him. What he is attempting to do is an impossibility, but no argument will convince him. The bark is to be constructed from a canoe made from a cottonwood. This I have heard said by Father Kino, and by others who have already seen something of what has been done. The poop is the root of a cottonwood tree. Above this canoe they are to put ribs of mesquite. This will constitute and form the bark. The carpenters doing this work are the Indians who do not even know how to hew a tree. The master builder is Father Kino, who, every time he goes, shows them by means of little models what they have to do. A witness of this is Father Gaspar de las Varillas, who saw it." [1]

As Mora viewed it the whole idea was quixotic. The bark was too costly ever to be finished. Even if completed it could not be launched "since they are building it about thirty leagues from the coast. River by which to go there is none. If they wish to carry it, how many oxen, or mules, or men, will be necessary? What water will they drink on the road? Even when going light to the sea, water is carried in calabashes for the men to drink, and the animals suffer greatly."

Kino had "made so much noise over this bark" that he had raised false hopes, said Mora. In an emergency they sent from Yaqui asking Kino to loan his boat to transport goods to California, "but they found him *minus habens.*" And Kino had other designs than to serve California. In his bark he planned to ship produce to the mines at

---

[1] Kino resumed his work on the bark when he escorted Barillas to Caborca, and he was there again in February, 1698.

Alamos, or Real de los Frayles. This, said Mora, was ridiculous. Perhaps he, as rector, would have to destroy the bark to stop the crazy man who was building it. If so, he hoped he would not be misunderstood. "Rumors against me may come to the ears of your Reverence, charging that I have ordered it burned. I swear before God that it will be in order that the father may have some quiet, and to avoid the labors and hunger which are being suffered by the Indians whom the father has at work,"—evidently they were still at it—"to avoid for his district many profitless expenditures which he might employ in other things and to put an end to the continual murmurings which are going on concerning this matter, which is regarded as a chimerical affair." Apparently the gossips were buzzing in the rector's receptive ears.

Having once uncorked his bottle of grievances, Mora's complaints gushed forth. He had been ordered to guard against irregularities in his rectorate. All the irregularities that he knew were "those of Father Kino." Father Eusebio had encouraged hostilities between Sobas and Tepoquis. He had been charged with beating one of his own neophytes. "This story is current among these Indians; whether it is the truth or a lie I do not know." The chief witness in the case had contradicted himself, it may be said, leaving Mora's charge rather flat. Rumor had it that one of Kino's mission Indian women had miscarried "as a result of the ill treatment which she received at the hands of the same Father Kino," because she did not make some clay *caxetes* to his liking or as rapidly as he wished. The principal witness in this case played safe by hedging. "All this is what I have heard and not what I have seen." It was just some more gossip. On hearsay testimony the same witness told Mora that another Indian had died two days after a beating by Father Kino. Another informant told the rector that many times at Kino's mission he had heard children crying, "and on asking who they were and why they were crying he had been told that they were little pages of the father who had received some punishment at his hand." This looks bad, for everybody's heart goes out to a child. But it might be worse. In more recent times school children and even sons and daughters have had their ears boxed, and have howled more loudly than the pain has warranted. Even dullards quickly learn this trick. Besides, the story was confessedly hearsay gossip.

Mora returned to the evil consequences of Kino's explorations. "From this charity with bodies follows charity with souls. . . . The principal thing for each one of us to consider in this matter is scrupulous care in the administration of the sacraments and the teaching of the doctrine to persons who are immediately in our charge. Well, how can this be done by Father Kino, who is always on the go, and does not stay in his district a whole week at a time? Montenegro charges with mortal sin anyone who is absent from his mission a single day." Someone had just written Mora that Kino never stayed at Dolores, "and since he is not there no Indian does a thing or remains there. And if in pueblos which are very carefully attended and well administered it very frequently happens that Indians die without confession, merely because the father is absent ministering to some other pueblo . . . how often will this happen if one is absent more than he is present? How many children will remain without baptism? How many feast days without Mass? How many neophytes without instruction?"

Kino was a bad disciplinarian, said Mora. It was common opinion that of all the neophytes at the missions, "the Indians of Father Kino are the least well bred and trained. All this was reported by Father Campos, who administered the district of Father Kino for seven months," while Kino was in Mexico. Campos had indeed written that "The Indians of Cotzari . . . are so insulting, so malevolent, so ill-bred, so obnoxious, that I become greatly vexed by merely thinking of them. . . . How shall one comport oneself with Indians who go and come every minute? How undo and dismantle that great Rochelle of villains?" But Campos was young, and Kino's Indians perhaps viewed him as school children regard a substitute teacher. Besides, when Campos wrote this criticism he was begging permission to stay at San Ignacio. He may have overstated the case.

"There might be some excuse," Mora continued, if Kino had a substitute during his absence, but he had none, so the Indians were left alone. Was it right to accept royal alms without giving due spiritual return? "With what conscience is it possible to make the Indians work to support the minister who assists them in nothing, especially if the labor is excessive, such as is the sowing of the wheat which the father sows in Dolores? For this is positively the largest amount sown in all the missions of Sonora"; and if this should appear to be an exaggeration, "just ask those who have seen it." Mora was of course merely advertising Kino's ability. It was like General Grant's whiskey. Palacios may well have remarked "Find me some more Kinos."

Reports had come to Mora of Father Eusebio's carelessness in baptisms, performed without due instruction. Having no time to give the matter personal attention, he often depended on native teachers, it was complained. This was bad enough at the missions. How much worse must it be when he christened Indians during his excursions? He baptized them in the mesquite brush and then left them without ministers. "When they live in those distant lands without a teacher, I say, what kind of Christian life will they practice?" And Polici, the visitor, was partly to blame, for he too had bizarre notions. When he sent Kino to found missions for the Sobaípuris, he ordered "that while they cultivate the soil and labor, his Reverence, with a temastián, shall teach them how to pray, explaining to them the principal articles; and when he sees that the wall is twenty-five adobes high, if they wish to become Christians he shall baptize them. . . . And so the measure of instruction is the height of the wall? . . . and what will twenty-five adobes of height avail to relieve them of twenty-five thousand bricks of incapacity?" We must admit that Mora wielded a vigorous pen.

There were even worse charges. It was rumored that Kino approved of using information obtained in confessions for purposes of "external government." If true this was bad; fortunately it was only hearsay. "Whether or not Father Kino follows this rule in practice I do not know," said Mora. "What I do know is that if he does practice it in confessing the Indians, and they learn of it, he will cause a very great scandal, just as he has done among our people who have heard that he holds this opinion." Palacios, to whom he was writing, no doubt noticed the *if*. Worse than this, Kino talked uncharitably about his brother Jesuits, even to seculars. What opinion would laymen have of the Black Robes?

In short, for the good of the province, said Mora, Kino ought to be removed from it. No Jesuit could remain in the Pimería who did not agree with him in everything. Nearly every missionary who had been in the district had criticized his methods, but nobody had been able to restrain or reform him. "And since up to now the father has always come out on top, it follows that he does not permit those who enter to remain." There had been twelve fathers in the Pimería in nine years.[1] "Among them there have been men of all ages, of all natures, of all nations, and with all of them there have been discords." The case of Campos was cited as an example. The trouble, Mora said, usually came over Kino's gifts to the new missions. He "tells all the world that whatever he has, whatever he does, whatever he acquires, is for the new missions, and yet when the time comes much unpleasantness is caused by what he gives, which ordinarily is nothing.

"Let it be asked of all, or most all, of the fathers who have been in the Pimería, why they left it, and you will see what they reply." Ask Barillas. In short, said Mora, "one cannot escape one of two extremes." Anyone coming must oppose Kino and so be driven out by him, or agree with him and be allowed to remain. "And in order that in this particular no one of them may outshine him, his Reverence tries to discredit them all so that he alone may have apostolic fame."

Just here was where Mora's shoe pinched. So he begged that Kino be removed. Father Eusebio may have had some of the faults catalogued. But it is plain that Mora was blindly jealous of his subordinate, who had run away with the show.

CIII

A STATUE IS INSTALLED

If Kino was crushed by Mora's diatribe, assuming that he heard of it, he soon found solace in a notable celebration at Remedios, an

[1] Arias, Barli, Barillas, Bayerca, Campos, Castillejo, Hostinski (Ostine), Janusque, Pincli, Ruíz, Saeta, Salvo, Sandoval.

affair which attracted attention all the country round. Indeed, the occasion was at once an act of devout worship and a victory celebration. Kino's fame had not suffered by opposition.

In the alms from Mexico that year there came a fine statue of Nuestra Señora de los Remedios, a gift for the mission bearing that saint's name. While Kino and his laborers were finishing her "good, neat, and prettily painted chapel," the treasure was carefully guarded at Dolores. The installation of the statue was planned for September 15, feast of the patroness—and, militant Kino adds, "anniversary of the day when last year of '97 the neophytes and the Pimas Sobaípuris made the first attack on the hostile Jocomes." The event was made the occasion for "a little fiesta for this great Lady and Sovereign Queen of the Angels," and at the same time a celebration of the victory.[1] On the day before the ceremony the Lady was gently carried by the natives up the sandy, mesquite-bordered, twenty-mile trail from Dolores to Remedios, "where she was welcomed with capa de coro, peal of bells, chirimías, harp and guitar, Salve and chanted litany."

We have a graphic description of this festivity written by Kino himself on the day after it occurred. He makes us spectators with reserved seats. The account reflects the conspicuous place occupied by a frontier mission. "For this fiesta there were assembled some Spanish gentlemen of the mining camp of Bacanuche, the principal caciques and headmen of all this Pimería, and from the most remote parts of it ten captains, twenty governors, and twenty-six other justices, alcaldes, topiles, fiscales-mayores, alguaciles, and fiscales ordinarios, all of whom welcomed Our Lady on their knees." It was an impressive spectacle, with a strong appeal to both white man and red. "Many of these captains and governors came from the north and northeast and from the west. Captain Humari came from the Río de Jila and the governor of La Encarnación from the Río and Casa Grande, more than one hundred leagues away; the captain of Santa Catalina came eighty leagues; Captain Coro sixty leagues; the captain of Sova, fifty-six leagues; the captain and governor of San Xavier del Bac,

---

[1] The story is told in Kino, Colocasión de Nuestra Sa. de los Remedios en su nueva Capilla de su nuevo pueblo de las nuevas conversiones de la Pimería en 15 de Setiembre de [16] 98 Años. Original Spanish manuscript, A.G.P.M. Misiones, Tomo 26. Printed under a wrong title in *Doc. Hist Mex*. Tercera Série, 814–816.

sixty leagues." What greater testimony could be had of Kino's influence over the Indians? Coro, now a hero, received many handshakings and embraces from Spaniards.

On the 15th there was a procession, "in which the Virgin was carried under the baldaquin, borne by the Spanish gentlemen, and her solemn Mass was chanted in the church, which is not yet completed, although the chancel and the choir are now more than three yards high, which made it possible that with ramadas Mass could be chanted with decency for the great concourse. Afterward there was a talk in the language of the natives [1] about the great blessing which was coming to these their lands, through most holy baptism and through the Catholic Faith, for the salvation of their souls."

Kino did not forget that he was a soldier of the King as well as of the Cross, and he continued with conscious pride in his valorous Pimas. "Likewise they were told of the good manner in which they must join with the Spanish arms against the enemies of this province of Sonora, as was desired by the military commander, and as he requested of me, and as they had done on other occasions, in particular on the 30th of March of this present year of '98, when they joined in the good blow struck at the Jocomes, Janos, Sumas, Mansos, and Apaches; for in this way with divine favor they would obtain the fathers whom with such anxiety they are requesting and so greatly need."

Sermons were relieved with material cheer. "We killed some beeves for these our natives, gave chocolate to some of them, and bade them goodbye very well content and very well pleased with the well-founded hopes that they would obtain fathers, in spite of such hindrance by so many and such false reports. Likewise, when I said goodbye to these Pimas of the north and northwest, I told them that within eight or ten days I must go to the Río Grande and Sea of California, . . . and that of this they should inform those new people of the coast. They promised that they would do so promptly and the principal men of that region wished to go with me as guides and companions." They kept their promise.

---

[1] Father Eusebio was still tender on this point.

The Northwest People

CIV

THE MYSTERY OF THE RÍO GRANDE

KINO WAS SOON AGAIN ON THE MOVE, eager to see what was farther on—*más allá*. In the Pima towns on the Gila he had met Opas and Cocomaricopas, who lived farther down the stream. They had told him of their villages; he wished in turn to visit them and tell them more about Christianity. Then there was the quicksilver mine of which they had heard during the last expedition. In this Jironza was particularly interested. A great discovery was possible, perhaps a new mining rush. And there was California. Kino still nursed this dream. Salvatierra was on the Peninsula now, in need of help, and Kino wished to lend a hand across the Sea. In order to do this the coastlands must be explored. All these things pointed northwest, so a new expedition was organized.[1] The idea was Kino's; Polici and Jironza co-operated; even Mora said a faint "Amen."

In August Polici wrote Mora, who was still rector, saying that Father Eusebio was to "undertake the exploration of the Río Grande as far as the sea, in order to report to the father provincial and to his Excellency, who commands that the new conversions be promoted and that a hand be given to Father Juan María by way of the northwest." Mora gasped and dutifully transmitted the letter (Kino already had the order directly from Polici), adding, "in this evangeli-

[1] The principal authorities for this first exploration of Pápago Land are Kino, Relasión Diaria de la Entrada al Nortueste (Sept. 21–Oct. 18, 1698). Original Spanish manuscript, A.G.P.M. Historia, Tomo 393; Kino, Carta del Padre Eusevio Kino al Padre Visitador Horacio Polici acerca de una entrada al Noroeste, A.G.P.M., Tomo 16. This letter is almost identical with one incorporated by Kino in his *Hist. Mem.*, I, 184–189; Carrasco, Diario fho . . . desde el dia 22 de Septiembre hasta el dia 18 de Octubre; Jironza, Instructions to Carrasco, San Juan Bautista, September 15, 1698; Carrasco to Jironza, Dolores, October 18, 1698; Jironza to the viceroy, San Juan Bautista, March 8, 1699; Baltazar de Tobar, dictamen fiscal, Mexico, October 16, 1699 (A.G.I. 67–3–28, Guadalajara 134).

cal enterprise I shall be hoping against hope—*in spem contra spem.*" [1]
Not enthusiastic.

Jironza lent a hand by sending with Kino an escort of soldiers
under Captain Diego Carrasco, whose appointment as lieutenant of
the Pimería Kino had just obtained. Carrasco went as royal agent,
the position Manje had formerly occupied in Kino's explorations. He
was instructed to regale the Indians, "win them with presents, and
give them good talks, to attract them to the fold of our holy Catholic
faith in order that they may give obedience to his Majesty." He was
to keep a diary, give saints' names to the Indian villages, count the
people, "explore their lands, springs and water holes," record distances traveled, appoint governors, and give them canes of office. "And
I especially order him to make careful inquiry of the Indians of the
Yubaxípuris nation concerning the quicksilver mine which they say
exists, where, how, and in what place." There was a final admonition,
an index of Jironza's personal regard for the Master of Dolores. "And
he shall not desert or leave the reverend father until he has restored
him to his mission, for this is important to the service of both majesties." [2]

For some months Kino had been in poor health and was still very
weak. Nevertheless, as soon as he received Polici's order he assembled
the necessary provisions and some little gifts for the natives, and on
September 22 he set forth. He took with him besides Carrasco, the
governor of Dolores, seven other servants, and twenty-five pack
animals. There is no mention of soldiers other than Carrasco. Kino
was proving his faith in Pima friendship. He trusted them. His instructions provided that he take Father Gilg or Father Campos, but
neither one went, so Kino and Carrasco were the only white men in
the party. Forty animals Father Eusebio had sent ahead five days
previously to await him at Bac. Twenty others were to leave Dolores
ten days later and meet him in Caborca.

Kino went north by the already familiar route through Tumacácori
and Bac to the Gila, attending to a multitude of things on the way,
giving encouragement here and admonition there. At San Lázaro

[1] Kino, Relasión Diaria, quoting Mora's letter.
[2] Jironza to Carrasco, San Juan Bautista, Sept. 15, 1698.

he left orders for the building of the new church. At San Luís del Bacoancos a governor was appointed, a calf killed for food, and infants baptized. Canes of office were given at Guébavi. At Bac they found the relay animals, killed two beeves, baptized some children, and sent messages ahead. Here, too, Kino was visited by Chief Coro, "who, since the attack on the 30th of March in Quíburi he had made on the Jocomes, had come with his people to live here in the interior." Coro knew that henceforth he would be a target for Apache arrows, so, as already has been stated, he had moved to Los Reyes, on Sonóita Creek, in the vicinity of Patagonia.

Passing Tucsón, Santa Catalina and Montezuma's Tank,[1] and leaving the Casa Grande at the right, on the 29th the explorers reached La Encarnación. Next day a messenger from Caborca arrived bearing a cross, and reporting that the chief of that pueblo was on his way to meet and guide the party. In the afternoon canes of office were given and Kino went down to San Andrés, near where Vah Ki now stands. There they were welcomed by more than five hundred natives, "with the same hospitality as that shown by the previous people, with arches and crosses erected, with many provisions, foods and houses prepared and with great appreciation for the Word of God."

Next day, with three servants Kino rode west down the river, "anxious to ascend a mountain which was in sight"—it was Sierra la Estrella— "to see if from its summit could be seen the lands and villages round about, and if it were possible to descry the very sea coast, and the best road to go out to view the disemboguement of the Río Grande"—he means the Gila—"into the Sea of California." It must be remembered that Kino at this time supposed that the Gulf of California extended indefinitely north, perhaps to Puget Sound, and that the Gila and the Colorado had separate mouths. His map of 1696 represents his notions on these points.

On the way Kino passed some villages and "two other casas grandes of the Montezumas." One of them was the ruin near Vah Ki now called Casa Blanca. But he did not reach the mountain, for his illness returned to trouble him. "I was taken with such a fever that after traveling five leagues I was obliged to halt under some cot-

---

[1] The Aljibe discovered and described by Kino on the former journey. See page 375.

tonwoods near the Río Grande, and in the afternoon I had to return with much difficulty to San Andrés." This was a new note for the veteran trail maker, who seldom admitted any physical weakness or offered an excuse.

The Cocomaricopas had already arrived at San Andrés. Kino observed that their language and dress were very different from those of the Pimas, but that they were affable, well-featured, closely interrelated with the latter, and like them desirous of Christianity. Down stream, on the inter-tribal border, there were three or four villages where nearly everybody knew both tongues. This day and the next Kino talked with the visitors about the Faith and gave them presents. "To a very tall Indian" was given the governor's cane. The fiscal[1] was promoted to the rank of captain and another was made fiscal mayor. Kino "sent them away very well content with very good talks for all of their extensive nation." He had sealed another tribe unto himself. But he had not yet solved the mystery of the Río Grande.[2]

CV

THROUGH PÁPAGO LAND

On October 2 Kino made a new start. Heralds went before him. He had learned that the Gila swung north around the mountains, and understood that its junction with the Gulf was to the southwest. This was a modification of his former notion. His map would have to be changed. He had learned, too, of large villages to the south. So he left the Gila and entered the Pápago country, hoping by that route to reach the river's mouth, at the same time that he made new friends. Thus far, except for the last day's travel down the Gila, he had been on a familiar trail.[3] When he now set forth from San Andrés he was on new ground. His diary and that of Carrasco from here to Quitobac give us our first knowledge of a two hundred mile stretch

---

[1] Appointed at the time of Kino's previous visit.
[2] Kino Relación Diaria; Carrasco, Diario fho.
[3] Kino had been as far as San Andrés the previous year.

across Pápago Land. As we ride with him we too become explorers of a new region. The most remarkable thing about the journey is that Kino found the Pápago villages exactly or nearly where they are today, and bearing the same names, to which he and Carrasco added the names of saints.

Striking nearly south from San Andrés, they traveled across a desert plain. But they were not unprepared, for they carried a small supply of water in gourds and at noon took a frugal drink. At the end of twelve leagues they beheld a pleasing sight—messengers carrying four ollas or jars of water, so that not only Kino's men but some of the animals also were able to moisten their lips. Guided by their new friends, who spoke the Pima tongue, they soon reached their village of San Angelo del Bótum. It is still in the same place and still bears the same name, Vótum.[1] Americans, with their genius for the commonplace, call it Cocklebur. Here they were welcomed by more than sixty persons, "with arches and crosses placed, and with many of their foods from their fields—maize, beans, and watermelons, although never in that village or in the others of this vicinity and coast had there entered another white face or Spaniard." This reception in the desert attests the manner in which Kino's name went before him. On this whole journey among complete strangers he found the same hearty welcome. Here at San Angelo five infants and one sick adult were baptized.

Next day in the forenoon they went eight leagues southward to San Bonifacio, the name given by Kino to the two villages of El Coati and El Sibuóidag.[2] Two leagues before they arrived a headman came out to welcome them, bringing water. Half a league farther on eight others came running, then eight more, and a little later still eight more. It was a perfect example of hospitality in the desert, where, next to life, water is of all things the most precious. At San Bonifacio Kino found more than three hundred natives assembled, with crosses and arches placed, roads cleared, and houses and food prepared. His journey was like a triumphal march. He gave the vil-

---

[1] Vótum (Cocklebur) is about thirty miles almost due south from Vah Ki and fifteen miles southwest from Casa Grande station.

[2] Now Coat and Sivoidag. They are still regarded as one village, though some five or six miles apart. They are east and south of Kwahate (Quajate) Mountains.

lagers a long talk and baptized four infants, while Carrasco distributed canes of office. It was learned with satisfaction that some of these people had taken part in Coro's victory at Santa Cruz, for this was another evidence of Pima loyalty. The head chief, "who must have been a hundred years old," gave the Spaniards a "very pretty talk" and urged them to remain till next day.

But Kino could not accept the invitation. He had sent word to another place that he would arrive that night. So he pushed south, accompanied by the aged chief and twenty of his men. All the afternoon the horses' hoofs clicked against the stones. How far the old chief was able to keep up is not recorded. A journey of eight leagues took Kino to "the great ranchería of Adid," which he named San Francisco. As before, the wayfarers were met by runners with ollas of water on their heads. Adid is still in the same place and still bears the same native name, though devoted to a different saint. It is the modern Santa Rosa del Achi, now as then a great Pápago center.[1]

All this country was populous. At Adid they were welcomed by more than seven hundred people in two files, "just as in pueblos of Christians," with crosses, arches, a house, roads cleared, foods prepared, and many torchlights, for they arrived after Vespers. "The file of men was a hundred and fifty varas long"—a block and a half —"and that of the women more than ninety, the one and the other swarming with boys, girls, and infants." What a scene it presented in the chill October evening! And how good the fire felt!

That night Kino talked to the attentive natives about God. Next morning he baptized one hundred and two children, "for most of whom here as on other occasions Lieutenant Diego Carrasco was godfather." Don Diego now had plenty of spiritual responsibilities. Some of the people assembled had come from neighboring villages, and here eight canes of office were given—"those of governor, fiscal mayor, and alguacil of San Francisco del Adid, and likewise those of governor to the chiefs of Anagam, El Cubit Tubig, and El Gaga." Anagam, still there, is three miles north of Santa Rosa, and El Gaga,

---

[1] Like all these Pápago settlements, which are farming communities, Santa Rosa spreads over several miles. Achi means pointed, and refers to a peak west of the village.

now Kaka, is twenty miles northwest of Santa Rosa.[1] In the afternoon the travelers went three leagues to San Serafín, where they were welcomed by four hundred people. Kino preached, and baptized sixty-one children. This village, later called San Serafín del Actúm Chico, was modern Akchín, six miles southeast of Santa Rosa.[2]

Next day Kino's cavalcade made a long march, passing through three villages, in one of which he baptized four infants, naming them for the four Evangelists, Matthew, Mark, Luke, and John—which, of course, he pronounced Mateo, Marcos, Lucas, and Juan. After traveling sixteen leagues, at four in the afternoon he reached a large settlement which he called Nuestra Señora de la Merced del Batki. It was the place now called by the natives Vachtk, or the Pool, two miles east of the base of South Mountain of Quijotoa Range. The pool is still there, but the village has moved southeast six miles to Big Fields. By air-line Batki was only twenty-four miles from Adid, which means that the three villages visited on the way were off the direct line.[8]

At Merced Kino was welcomed by more than two hundred people, and he baptized thirty-three infants. Soon after he arrived, three hundred visitors came from near-by villages.[1] These figures did not include the large and not very distant ranchería of Baggíburi buta, which was reported to have more than five hundred souls. Baggíburi buta was southeast of Batki, underneath Baboquívari Mountain, as its name implies, and in the same direction was Ootcam. "There were long talks, and we consoled them that on another occasion we would try to come to baptize the rest of the infants, especially those of Baggíburi buta and Ootcam," says Kino.

Here at Merced Kino got encouragement for his efforts to reach the outlet of the Río Grande de Gila into the Gulf. It came especially from an Indian woman who trudged into town from the west with a pack on her back. Kino needed her help. "During these days there had been no lack of arguments and objections which some [of the Indians], even those whom they call domestic, raised about trying

---

[1] Cubit Tubig was perhaps Kukómelik, or Kómelik, now twelve miles north of Anagam, but then in a different place. Phonetically the names are manifestly identical.
[2] Called Aktin by Lumholtz, *New Trails in Mexico*.
[8] Father Bonaventure thinks they were the Ati field villages of Kölipadva, Sikulhimat, and a village near Iron Pump belonging to Batki.

to reach the sea and the mouth of the desired Río Grande." But Kino's brave spirit would not be crushed, and he met every argument with a practical program. "The first objection which they raised was that there would be a lack of water in those sand dunes, to which I replied that a mule would go loaded with gourds and ollas, and I ordered crates prepared for that purpose. The second objection was that there would be no grass; and I replied that an extra mule would carry grass. The third objection was that the heat would be greater on the sea coast [it was October], and I replied that we would travel by night. And now, today, we found people who offered to go as guides; and there was even an Indian woman who had come loaded with snails and little shells from the sea, which she herself had brought from there." If the woman could make the trip, surely they could. All objectors were now silenced. Who could withstand the dauntless man?

So now they traveled with firmer step. On the 6th they turned sharply southwest thirteen leagues to San Rafael del Actúm Grande,[1] near the break between Ajo Range and Sierra del Nariz. On the way, swinging south of Mesquite Mountains, they found a good watering place. Four leagues before reaching San Rafael they were welcomed by chiefs and headmen, and at the village by four hundred persons. Great quantities of pitahayas—a delectable food—were among the gifts this day. Kino preached and baptized eighty-five children; later in the day more than a hundred Indians came from a near-by village bringing a present of white salt.[2] Here, too, they were met by residents of Sonóita, a village to the west, on the road to the Gulf. Next morning Kino baptized eleven more children, and took the latitude with an astrolabe, concluding that he was in 32° 30′. This was much too high. Accompanied by the chief of Sonóita, that day they reached his village after traveling eleven leagues westward. Sonóita still exists in essentially the same place where it then stood.

At Adid and Actúm Grande Kino had found abundant crops of

---

[1] The place is still called Akchín. It is three miles north of Menager's Dam, which is three miles from the Mexican border. It is the parent village of Kerwo (Gue Va), several miles further north, to which the successors of the people whom Kino saw have moved. Their places at Akchín have recently been taken by Pápagos from Nariz, across the line in Mexico (Father Bonaventure).

[2] These visitors may have come from Quitobac, whose people were salt merchants, obtaining their supply from the Gulf.

maize, calabashes, beans, and watermelons, but here at Sonóita, although there were acéquias, on account of the drought this year they had planted only calabashes. These were plentiful. This march through the Papaguería, land of the Bean Eaters, was epochal. None who have come after Kino and Carrasco have deserved quite the thrill to which they were entitled, and no record of exploration of that country can stand beside their precious diaries.

CVI

GEOGRAPHY GETS ANOTHER JOLT

Here at Sonóita the trail for Caborca turned sharply south. But Kino was headed for the Sea, to find the mouth of the Gila River. So he baptized twenty-four children, then continued west to "a good place called San Serguio, four more leagues along the arroyo which runs clear to the sea and has flowing water in many places." This arroyo was Sonóita River; San Serguio was the place now called Quitovaquita, ten miles west of Sonóita, a pretty spot with a fine cool spring and a little pond, beside which lived a prosperous Pápago family when a few years ago I retraced the historic trail.

Kino had come prepared with his crates, gourds, and ollas, in which to carry grass and water to the Sea, but the precaution proved to be unnecessary. His new guides told him that the Sea was near, and that there were water and grass on the way, so he left his pack mules and crates here at San Serguio, a welcome relief for both mules and muleteers.[1]

The adventure on which Kino now embarked requires a man of mettle today. But the seasoned Black Robe recorded it as a mere matter of course. Accompanied by the governor and fiscal of Sonóita, he set forth from San Serguio. "Traveling eighteen leagues over a very good road with plentiful running water, grass, carrizales, and tulares," they reached "the ranchería of the sea," which they named Santa Brígida in honor of St. Bridget's Day. It was a village west of Pinacate Moun-

[1] Kino, Relación Diaria; Carrasco, Diario fho.

tain, around whose southern end they had swung. They were welcomed by twenty friendly natives, who prepared for them calabash and other food, most acceptable after a ride of over forty miles. In reply to his eager questions, the natives told Kino that from the near-by mountain they could see the mouth of the Río Grande; that it was not far away; and that beyond it, on the very large Río Colorado, lived tribes who cultivated maize, beans, calabashes, and cotton. Kino proposed to go to see these people, but his companions objected on the ground that they had no relay animals.

If he could not go to the Río Grande, he would view it from the Sierra. So next day he rode with guides seven leagues eastward up a rough trail to the summit of the mountain. It was worth the hard climb. Below him he saw the Gulf, with a good inlet (Adair Bay) close by, which he called Santa Clara and whose landmarks he carefully noted. He observed the desolation of lava on the mountain top and marveled at the great sand dunes near the Gulf. And he learned a new fact about the Gila and Colorado rivers. The guide pointed out to him the place where they united, far to the north, and "about a day's journey before they together enter the Sea of California." [1]

This information completely upset one of Kino's geographical notions, and he now must have smiled—or blushed—at the map he had drawn three years before to insert in his book on the death of Father Saeta. On that map the Río del Tizón lay north of the Gila, ran west parallel with it, and both emptied independently into the Gulf, which continued another thousand miles or more northward. The Colorado River, on the other hand, was shown as a very small tributary of the Gila, half way between the Casa Grande and the Gulf. The new discovery pleased Father Eusebio, but in one matter he was disappointed. He had hoped to descry California, but he did not succeed, because the atmosphere was so hazy that day.

Returning to Santa Brígida in the afternoon, next day they retraced their steps to Sonóita, finding there the caballada, which had been brought forward from San Rafael. With the animals came the chief of that village "who in everything showed himself so loyal that he was given the cane of captain-general of these coasts, and was

---

[1] As a matter of fact, the junction is some seventy miles from the Gulf, airline.

charged to carry very good talks to his relatives, the people of the Río Colorado." How the chief must have swelled with importance when he returned to San Rafael!

Kino had made the first recorded crossing of the heart of Pápago Land. He first had climbed Santa Clara Mountain. He now opened the trail from Sonóita to Caborca, building on what Manje had done. Swinging southeast, he traveled fifteen leagues to Bacapa, guided by the chief of the place, who had met him at San Rafael. Bacapa, now called Quitobac, where they arrived at sunset, nestled beneath the conspicuous conical mountain where Manje had visited it four years before. A hundred and sixty natives welcomed Kino with great quantities of pitahayas. "This ranchería has very good water holes," says Kino. In fact, there are several springs here, from which a pleasant lake has been formed. Kino assumed that Bacapa was the Vacapa of Friar Marcos de Niza. It is plain that he had read history, though few modern scholars will agree with his conclusion. But writing history was not his chief concern. He was making it. And there were souls to save.

Next day Kino baptized sixteen infants, then traveled twenty-two leagues to Arivaipa, arriving by moonlight. Having no automobile, he did not bog down in the arroyo as I did when following his trail. Here he was welcomed by more than five hundred natives in two files, "with many torches, with arches and crosses erected, and with a house and food prepared." The natives still cultivate the Arivaipa fields, and the name persists, to remind one of Kino's remarkable travels. Next morning he baptized thirty-four infants, rode fifteen leagues, and after Vespers reached Caborca, where he found fifteen pack animals awaiting him, as he had ordered. His trails now completely circumscribed the Pimería.

From Caborca the homeward route of the travelers was the familiar one through Tubutama. The road is the same today. Everywhere the natives were preparing fields, stock, and buildings for expected missionaries, with such zeal that Carrasco was greatly edified. On the way Kino baptized newborn infants, branded cattle, and sent ahead a load of fresh pitahayas, "a rare fruit for this season." Then, passing through Magdalena, he arrived at his mission on the 18th in time to say the Mass of the glorious Evangelist, San Lucas, as an act of thanksgiving.[1]

CVII

SINGULAR CONSOLATION

If Kino had wished to pose as a hero he might have recited a story of hardship and tribulations on such a trail. But he told only of blessings and opportunity. "In this expedition," he says, "we have felt singular consolation and alleviation. 1. For having been able to say Mass every day. 2. For the baptism of so many infants, and the great affability with which the natives accompanied us on the roads from one village to another, and came out to welcome us with refreshments of many jars of water and pitahayas, and with fiestas, dancing, and singing by day and by night. 3. For the very good pack animals, not one of which ever became footsore or lame or fell behind, although in the space of twenty-five days going and coming we traveled more than three hundred leagues, and there were days' marches of twenty-one or twenty-two leagues. 4. For the very good roads, water holes and firewood, good pastures, and a superabundance of provisions. 5. For the uniformly good health and cheerfulness of everybody, and for the well-founded hopes of other and even better successes in the future, for the Californias as well as for us and for these coasts. May God grant them in the peregrination of this life and in the glorious eternity of the Celestial Fatherland. Amen."[2]

Father Eusebio had traveled eight hundred miles on horseback in twenty-five days. He had baptized some four hundred Indians, chiefly infants. He had met and dealt with Cocomaricopa visitors at San Andrés. He had learned that the Gila and the Colorado joined before entering the Gulf.[3] But there is nothing in his reports to indicate that

---

[1] Kino, Relación Diaria; Carrasco, Diario fho.; Kino to Polici, Dolores, October 20, 1698 (in Kino, *Favores Celestiales*, Parte I, Lib. vi, Cap. 4; *Hist. Mem.*, I, 184–189).

[2] Kino, Del Estado, grasias al Señor, Pasifico y quieto de esta dilatada Pimería y de la Provia. de Sonora, Dolores, October 18, 1698. Original manuscript, A.G.P.M., Historia, Tomo 393. This is a continuation of Kino's Relación Diaria of the same date.

[3] Oñate had learned this in 1605, but like so many other things, it had to be "discovered" again. Most Anglo-American geographical discoveries between the Alleghanies and the Pacific Ocean were of regions long known to Spaniards, to Frenchmen, or to British from Canada.

he had any inkling that California was not an island, extending well toward Alaska, as shown on his earlier map. The distinguishing feature of this great exploration was the first known crossing of Pápago Land from the Gila to Caborca, and the first reconnaissance of Pinacate Mountain. He found that Pápago Land contained more than forty villages, most of which practiced agriculture. Carrasco counted more than four thousand people between the Gila and Caborca. He and Kino gave more than forty canes of office to captains, governors, alcaldes, fiscales, and topiles.[1]

In another way the journey was an immense triumph for Kino. Pimas, Cocomaricopas, and Pápagos were everywhere friendly. There was not the slightest indication of hostility, or one iota of evidence that any of them were allied with the Jocomes and Apaches. Their detractors should have been silenced. Carrasco had been sent as a secular eyewitness. His report to Jironza was enthusiastic, and he warmly seconded Kino's request for missionaries.

This epochal exploration Kino recorded in one of the very best of his diaries. Carrasco also kept a journal. It is very similar to Father Eusebio's, but it has a significance all its own. Carrasco was the king's agent. He first appointed royal representatives in central Papaguería, and these official acts may today be regarded as basic titles of the Indians to their lands.

When Kino got back to Dolores he found that gossips had been tongue-wagging. It was even reported that he and his companions had been killed by the Indians. Consequently, at the end of his diary he added a demonstration "Of the Peaceful and Quiet State, Thank the Lord, of this Extensive Pimería and of the Province of Sonora." This vigorous paper is another proof of the fighting qualities of the Padre on Horseback. Gentle as he was, when aroused he could strike straight from the shoulder. He declared that all the charges of Pima attacks during the last fifteen years had been false. All the killings and hangings of Pimas had not ended the raids, because the Pimas did not perpetrate them. The stories of stolen horses among the Sobaípuris had all been proved to be calumnies. The Sobaípuris had demonstrated their friendship by Coro's victory at Quíburi. The reports made in

---

[1] Carrasco, Diario fho.; Carrasco to Jironza, Dolores, October 18, 1698, *loc. cit.*

1697 that Kino feared for his life, and in 1698 that the Altar Valley was again in revolt, he branded as lies. Rumors recently circulated that he and his men had been killed by the Indians were "manifestly rash opinion or false testimony." It had been declared that the Pimas, being few, did not need many missionaries. "But on various occasions I have said that there were more than ten thousand souls. And now, after this expedition which we have just made, I assert with proof that the natives of this Pimería number more than 16,000." This figure he proceeds to demonstrate, closing with a vigorous appeal for more missionaries.

When Kino had finished his diary he wrote out a fair copy and dedicated it to Jironza in flowery language which should have made the soldier blush. But if it was a little Gongoristic, like the dedication to the viceroy of his book on the Comet, it was a sincere effort to show his appreciation. It is a generous summary of what Jironza had accomplished for the protection, peace, prosperity and conversion of Pima Land and the rest of Sonora. If Jironza has descendants they doubtless treasure this great tribute to their distinguished ancestor.[1]

---

[1] Kino to Polici, Dolores, October 18, 1698 (A.G.P.M. Historia, Tomo 16); Kino, Dedicatory to Jironza, Dolores, December 8, 1698 (Bibliothèque Nationale, Paris, Mexicain, 174); Jironza to the Viceroy, March 8, 1699 (A.G.I. 67-3-28, Guadalajara, 134).

The Camino del Diablo

CVIII

THE OGRESS OF POZO VERDE

K INO'S CROSSING OF THE PAPAGUERÍA aroused great enthusiasm among his friends. Polici and Jironza congratulated him and in letters to the provincial and the viceroy they urged missionary expansion. Especially interested were Salvatierra and Picolo, who at once began to talk of a joint expedition with Kino to a higher latitude in the Gulf.[1]

Nevertheless, opponents or doubters wrote adverse reports to Mexico. Kino had nailed the lies about the Pimas and Pápagos, so the slanders were now focused on the tribes beyond, whom he had never visited. These tales "were to the effect that the Cocomaricopas and other new nations of the Río Grande, to the westward of La Encarnación and San Andrés, and on the Río Colorado, to the northwest, whither we did not penetrate, were so barbarous and such cannibals that they roasted and ate people, and they added other unheard of chimeras."

Kino proceeded in characteristic fashion to scotch the yarns. He would go and see the Cocomaricopas in their own lands. Let them eat him if they liked him that well. And he would learn more about the Yumas living north of Sierra de Santa Clara of whom he had heard during his last expedition. So he mounted his horse, rode to San Juan, and got permission from Jironza to take Manje with him as a secular witness. Carrasco had done admirably, but Manje was to Father Eusebio like a son. As a missionary companion Kino enlisted Father Adam Gilg. For equipment he took servants and ninety pack animals. He assembled eight loads of provisions, eighty horses, and

[1] Kino, *Favores Celestiales*, Parte I, Lib. vi, Cap. 5; *Hist. Mem.*, I, 189–191. Kino here quotes letters by Salvatierra and Picolo.

ornaments for saying Mass. Vaqueros went ahead driving thirty-six cattle with which to establish a new ranch at Sonóita as a base for northwestward explorations. Of the great tour now made Kino wrote a short account and Manje kept a detailed diary.[1]

Leaving Dolores on February 7, 1699, Kino and his party crossed the sierra to San Ignacio, where he obtained more provisions and horses from Father Campos. Going forward, he took the usual trail through Magdalena to Tubutama. Turning upstream now he revisited Sáric, Búsanic, and Tucubavia, in whose vicinity Manje estimated two thousand Indians. To here the inhabitants had been counted in a previous entry. Setting forth on the 11th, they followed Manje's former road ten leagues to Gubo Verde,[2] "so-called because of a tank of rainwater where the Indians drank."

They now struck westward through the Papaguería to Sonóita. They were in a new wonderland, and the record which they left is the first we have. Five leagues northwestward took them to a crystalline spring named Santa Eulalia, where there was a village of sixty poverty-stricken persons. This place is almost on the international boundary at the foot of Baboquívari Range, and is now called Pozo Verde.

More interesting to Manje than the people here was the folk-tale which they told him. Near the spring, he says, "we found a corral or patio, square in form, with walls of stone without mortar and as high as a man. Asking the natives what that large corral signified, they replied that a long, long time ago, in their heathendom, according to the story which had come down from father to son, a woman or monster of gigantic size had descended from the north. She was about three yards tall, with a snout like a hog and claws so long that they looked like eagle's talons, and she ate human flesh. On account of her atrocities and the deaths of Indians whom she swallowed at one gulp, although they gave her food, she was a terror to everybody. So they

[1] Kino, *Favores Celestiales*, Parte I, Lib. vi, Cap. 6; *Hist. Mem.*, I, 193–199; Manje, Relación Ytineraria del Nuevo Descubrimiemto, February–March, 1699 (Biblioteca Nacional, Madrid); Manje, Epitome en qe. se compendian las Materias y Médula de la Relación del descubrimiento, Feb.–March, 1699 (Biblioteca Nacional, Madrid); Manje, Relación diaria que hice con los R. Padres Eusebio Franco. Kino y Adamo Gilg (in *Luz de Tierra Incógnita*, Libro ii, Cap. 6). Brief accounts are in Bancroft, *North Mexican States and Texas*, I, 269–271; Ortega, *Apostólicos Afanes*, 282–285; Alegre, *Historia de la Compañia de Jesús*, III, 117–118.
[2] Later called San Estanislao del Ootcam.

tried to hunt deer and other game for her, on account of the fear which they felt lest she should destroy the people."

Meanwhile they plotted her destruction. "In common accord the heathen of the vicinity made that corral and invited the giantess, providing her much game, and wine with which to make her drunk. Then they held a dance within the corral, which lasted for some time, until the monster asked them to carry her to a large cave in a rock which they showed us close by, which was all wet and was her continuous habitation. She being seated in the cave and overcome with the drink and sleepiness, the many people who had assembled for this purpose piled up a great heap or mountain of firewood, covering the door with it, and then set it on fire. The combustible material burned up the monster, and so they freed themselves from her molestation. This is the substance of what they told us. The truth God only knows. What is certain is that this corral and the cave are plainly to be seen, and also that there have been giants in this country." [1]

This is the tale which Manje told in his original diary. A few years later, when he incorporated it in his book called *Luz de Tierra Incógnita,* the ogress had become an ogre. In this version, to appease the giant the natives "sacrificed to him two captive Indians whom they had brought from their enemies." To what better use could captives be put?

The legend of the Ogress of Pozo Verde, thus recorded in writing by Manje during this journey with Kino more than two centuries ago, is still told by the Pápagos, with some touches which Manje did not record. The ogress was Haw-auk-Aux, the Cruel-Old-Woman. As the story now goes, she lived in Baboquívari Mountains, at whose base Pozo Verde stands. Her buckskin dress was decked with lions' teeth and the claws of wild animals. The mountains shook at the sound of her voice, and when she combed her hair it obscured the sun, like a thunder cloud. Having killed and eaten all the animals, she began to devour human beings. On the advice of Eé-a-toy, Spirit of Goodness, the Pápagos arranged for a big dance and invited Cruel-Old-Woman. She came, danced four continuous days, and then fell asleep.

---

[1] Manje here tells of giant's bones at Oposura, now Moctezuma (Sonora), and in Perú. *Luz de Tierra Incógnita,* 261–262. Manje, Relación Ytineraria; Manje, Epitome (MSS. Biblioteca Nacional, Madrid).

Spirit of Goodness now threw her over his shoulders, took her to the cave where she lived, the Pápagos carried firewood, piled it in front of the cave, and set it on fire. When Cruel-Old-Woman awoke and jumped up she caused an earthquake which cracked the mountain. She would have crawled out, but Spirit of Goodness put his foot over the hole. And today, at Pozo Verde, right where Manje heard the story, you can see the footprint of Spirit of Goodness, the cave where the ogress was burned—and the pozo where Kino and Manje drank.[1]

CIX

NOAH'S ARK AND THE DEVIL'S HIGHWAY

Leaving Santa Eulalia, the rock corral, the cave, and the story tellers behind, the pathfinders traveled five leagues westward and camped at a pozo so deep that the horses had to be watered with jícaras or baskets. Five more leagues northward took them to the small running stream now called Fresnal Creek. "Near here," says Manje, "there is a high, square rock which, during eighteen leagues that we have traveled, looks like a tall castle, situated on the top of a high peak, for which reason we called it Noah's Ark." It was Baboquívari Peak.[2]

Turning their backs now on Noah's Ark, they swung west, camped on the 13th near Topawa (now Franciscan headquarters in Pápago Land), and next night at the distant marshes of Camotes, near the Mexican border. Swinging northwest next day, they struck their former trail at Actúm Grande, threaded the stony gap now called Menager's Pass—the only place to get through the mountains in this vicinity—and camped at some rainwater lakes in Nariz Flats.[3] On the 16th they reached Sonóita, four leagues beyond.

Here Kino found the cattle which his vaqueros had driven from

---

[1] Harold Bell Wright, *Long Ago Told*, 89–95 (London and New York, 1929).

[2] Father Bonaventure thinks the water hole of the previous camp was at the headwaters of Sonóita River, right on the boundary line, at Pozo Verde Fields, called by the natives Siggosik, or "Lots of Dogs." San Miguel, just across the line, is part of the same series of fields, both sites belonging to Tecolote.

[3] I am guided by Father Bonaventure in the identification of sites on this stretch.

Baboquivari Mountains, from the west

Mission San Miguel, in Pápago Land

Photo by Bolton, Jr.

Aguaje de la Luna (Heart Tank)

Dolores with which to establish a ranch at Sonóita, "as a convenient post, in order that some might serve for beef in continuation of these explorations of lands and nations of the North, as well as to succor the fathers of California if perchance they should sail to this latitude." The Indians welcomed the visitors, but the only food they could spare was beans, "for although they have a fair-sized arroyo, with permanent water, rich lands, and acéquias with which to irrigate them, they are not very industrious, and they do not harvest enough maize to last the year through." Inquiries were made regarding the trail beyond, the head chief and several others volunteered to go as guides, and with them in his train the Black Robe moved west down the river to El Carrizal, through which he had passed the year before.[1]

Kino now set forth to visit the people to the northwest, of whom he had heard at Sierra de Santa Clara—those tribes who lived near the junction of the Gila and Colorado Rivers. In this pursuit he opened a new trail—one of the hardest in all the Southwest; so difficult that it came to be called the Camino del Diablo, or the Devil's Highway. Kino and Manje on this historic journey were its first historians. To one who has been over the almost waterless route every item in the diaries has interest and meaning.

Leaving the river, on the 18th Kino swung northwest six leagues over dry rough country, but failed to find the water which the guides had promised. This was a bad situation, for the next aguaje was far ahead, so they drove their mounts hard. Pushing fourteen leagues further northwest, and skirting the west side of Sierra Pinta, after midnight they halted at the mouth of a deep gorge in that range. Here the guides showed them "a watering place high up in the rocks and barrancas, where, after climbing up with difficulty, we drank, but not the animals, which were in great need, because of the rough and precipitous climb." The description is accurate. The tinaja is a quarter of a mile or more up a rocky canyon, and high up on the mountain side. On account of their arrival by moonlight, they called the eerie tank the Aguaje de la Luna—Moonlight Tank.

Two and a third centuries behind Kino, I too, with my companions,

[1] Manje, *Luz de Tierra Incógnita,* 262; Manje Relacíon Ytineraria; Manje. Epitome. Anza in 1774 went over the same route. See Bolton, H. E., *Outpost of Empire.*

arrived by moonlight, the most brilliant I have ever seen. Nearly the whole night through it was light enough to read large print, and just before sunrise we took a picture of the full moon across the plain to the westward. So we got the full meaning of the name which Kino gave to the historic Tinaja. Before morning we had several touches of desert life, and I do not refer merely to cactus thorns. Soon after arrival I sat down to read the diaries on the spot where Kino camped, but I had scarcely started when a snake sought aslyum under my blanket. This caused a little stir, and a slight break in the reading. Just before daylight I heard sharp hoofbeats in the rocks some fifty yards away. Looking up I saw a massive-horned mountain sheep leaping up the cliffs, soon to disappear behind a boulder. These mountains are of solid rock, with scarcely a handful of soil. They are bare of trees, but choyas are plentiful, each of which, some three feet high, has a million needles. Father Baegert counted them, so we know. When the sun rose we ascended the canyon, climbed over huge boulders, then crawled up the white surface of the water-polished barranca for some two hundred feet. Anza, just seventy-five years behind Kino and sixteen decades ahead of me, says he reached the aguaje "more on hands than on feet." So did I. The tank did not fail us. In fact, it is seldom if ever dry, hence the sheep hover near. It is now called Heart Tank (Tinaja del Corazón) because when full the surface of the water makes a figure somewhat resembling a heart, but in reality more like a kidney.

Kino's weary horses were now suffering from thirst, and early next morning he hurried forward. As he jogged along at a swinging gait, white mule rabbits leaped across the trails, droves of truculent wild hogs (jabalíes) bristled their way to cover, and bighorns gazed placidly down at the travelers from their eerie crags. Going three leagues northwest across the plain, missing the remarkable Cabeza Prieta Tanks at his left, he continued west nine leagues, through Cabeza Prieta Range and across another desert plain, and camped at a small native village beneath the tanks which he called Agua Escondida— Hidden Water. These vast reservoirs, now called Tinajas Altas (High Tanks), placed in a series of levels far up the eastern face of the mountain, are one of the wonders of the Camino del Diablo. Here Manje counted "thirty naked and poverty-stricken Indians who lived solely on roots, lizards, and other wild foods." [1] They were Pápagos.

The Tinajas Altas are still important in that arid land. Kino's diary was the first guide to travelers there and it served for many decades. Kirk Bryan, a century and a half later, gives a fuller description in his *Guide to Desert Watering Places*. "Water will be found in a series of tanks in a very steep stream channel or dry falls 500 feet west of sign. The lowest tank is commonly full of sand, and water will be found by digging in the sand. The lowest tanks are best reached by turning to left (south), where a steel cable will be found, up which it is easy to climb the smooth rock face." Kino, less soft, needed no signboard and no cable. "The upper tanks are difficult to reach, and it can perhaps best be done by taking trail to right and climbing to 'window' and then going down to canyon above the falls. The water lasts all year, but the lower tanks are sometimes exhausted by travelers. If so, climb to upper tanks and pour water down channel to fill lower ones." Anza did just this when he watered his horses and cattle at Cabeza Prieta Tanks in 1774. "The water is palatable, but there are usually dead bees in it. Occasionally mountain sheep slip and fall into the tanks and contaminate the water," a circumstance which desert wayfarers usually disregard.

Going forward next day, the explorers traveled northwest, skirting Gila Range, "over extremely sterile plains, lacking pasturage for the animals, which were now all in." At the end of fifteen hard leagues they swung west into the mountains and camped at a dry arroyo, "and among the rocks of its bed . . . found some fonts of water in the form of tanks." So they called the place Las Tinajas. They are some fifteen miles southwest of Wellton, and are now known as Dripping Springs. Kino called them pilas, or baptismal fonts, a name suggested not only by the shape, but likewise by the marble colored rock in which the basins have been formed by running water through the ages. Here, too, mountain sheep hover about the life-giving tinajas.

One more thrust took the wayfarers to their goal. Next day, going

---

[1] Kino, *Favores Celestiales*, Parte II, Lib. i, Cap. 9; *Hist. Mem.*, I, 253; Manje, *Luz de Tierra Incógnita*, 263–264; Manje, Relación Ytineraria; Manje, Epitome. See Kirk Bryan, *Guide to Desert Watering Places* (Washington, 1922).

six leagues northwest, they reached the Río Grande or Gila River at a place which they called San Pedro. It was west of Wellton, about where the river swings northward before cutting the Gila Range. They had made the first recorded journey over the Camino del Diablo. It takes nerve and good equipment to follow their trail even today.

Traveling in February, Kino had found this vast desert dreary and forbidding. If he had made the journey in April instead, he would have beheld the same country decked out in its cheerful spring garb. At that season the most beautiful feature of desert plant life is furnished by the ocotillos. Slender, reed-like stems, they grow in clusters and spread out gracefully at the top. In the spring their sparse foliage is a bright, parrot green. But their distinguishing feature is their flowers. Each stalk, ten or fifteen feet high, ends in a brilliant scarlet blossom, at a distance resembling a gorgeous bird. And there are thousands of these ocotillo clusters scattered all over the desert. Then, too, the sahuaros are just budding, and soon will be decorated with little blossoms something like morning glories, which at a distance look like owls peeping out of holes at the tops of the great cactus giants.

CX

A MOJAVE MUNCHAUSEN

At the Gila River Kino found a large gathering of heathen Indians, a few of them Pimas,[1] but mostly Yumas, "who spoke languages entirely different." Manje now wrote our first eyewitness description of the Yumas after the time of Oñate nearly a century earlier. "They are a well-featured and large people," he tells us. "The women are pretty, and much whiter than those of any other nation of Indians known in New Spain." He describes their dress, or lack of it, their coiffure, ornaments, weapons, fishing nets, games, houses, and foods. Through a Pima who knew both tongues Kino told them of the Faith; Manje

---

[1] Kino says "more than fifty natives, Pimas, Yumas, and Cocomaricopas"; Manje says "six hundred."

enrolled them among the vassals of the king and distributed canes of office.

Next morning a hundred Yumas came to camp from the river junction beyond the range, "but not a woman among them." They brought great baskets of food for the strangers and were given gewgaws in return. Kino inquired how far it was to the sea. Some said it was three days, others six, "but all agreed that the nations on its banks were their enemies and that they could not escort us there" because of danger. Manje was for going to the Gulf, notwithstanding. Kino, more cautious, feared this would displease the Yumas, but promised to come again, visit the people in their homes, and perhaps "take siesta with the padres" in California.

Manje was not satisfied. He was determined to see what was beyond, so he went on horseback with guides to the top of a peak in Gila Range, whence he viewed the junction. "Farther to the west," he tells us, "they pointed out to me the beginnings of the arm of the sea, which, because of its greater distance and smoky atmosphere I was not able to descry." Manje still assumed that the Gulf ran indefinitely north. He was told, to his surprise, that the Colorado, which he now saw near by, was four times as large as the stream where they were camped, "indicating what would appear to be a league in width." The Colorado instead of the Gila now became the "Río Grande."

Curiosity was whetted by the familiar tales of the Oñate expedition to the Colorado ninety-five years previously, since which no recorded visit had been made to the locality. In 1604 Oñate left New Mexico with thirty men to explore the west. Passing through Zuñi and the Moqui pueblos, he struck southwest across Arizona, descended Bill Williams Fork, explored the Colorado, and followed it to the Gulf. The tribes which he encountered on the lower Colorado were essentially the same ones who dwell there now. With Oñate went Father Escobar as chronicler, and he told a most engaging tale.[1] Manje had with him a copy of Vetancurt's account based on Escobar's *Relación*. No wonder he was curious.

[1] See Bolton, Herbert Eugene, "Father Escobar's Relation of the Oñate Expedition to California," *Catholic Historical Review*, Vol. V (Washington, 1919), 19–41. Father Zárate Salmerón apparently had access to Escobar's account when he wrote his "Relaciones de Todas las cosas que en el Nuevo Mexico se han visto y savido." Printed in *Doc. Hist. Mex.*, Tercera Série, Tomo (Mexico, 1856).

Oñate visited and Escobar described the Mojaves who lived near the place today bearing their name. Just below them were the Bahace-cha tribe. Here Oñate met a chief, called Otata, who was a high-grade wag. He quickly learned that Oñate was looking for coral, silver, gold, and fabulous lands, and he proceeded to string him in good style. Coral, silver, gold, and fabulous lands were right in his line.

Chief Otata described the peoples living between the Colorado and the sea, "making a drawing of the country on a piece of paper, on which he indicated many nations of people so monstrous," said Escobar, "that I will make bold to affirm them with no little fear of being discredited." From what followed it would seem that Otata—or perhaps Escobar—had read Pliny. Otata told "of a nation of people who had ears so large that they dragged on the ground and big enough to shelter five or six persons under each one." Near them "there was another nation with only one foot," and "who lived on the banks of a lake in which they slept every night, entirely under the water. These people were the ones who wore handcuffs and bracelets of the yellow metal." Close by there was a nation who always slept in trees. "The reason why, we could not ascertain, whether it was for fear of wild beasts or insects, or from some natural characteristic or custom of theirs."

"The monstrosities of another nation . . . did not stop here, for they sustained themselves solely on the odor of their food, prepared for this purpose, not eating it at all." Then came a tribe "which did not lie down to sleep, but always slept standing up, bearing some burden on the head." Then there was the Queen of the Island of California, a veritable Amazon. "The principal person obeyed by the people who lived on the island was a woman called Ciñaca Cohota, which signifies principal woman or chieftainess. From all these people we learned that she was a giantess, and that on the island she had only a sister and no other person of her race, which must have died out with them." Finally, "we learned that the men of this island were bald, and that with them the monstrosities ended." Bald heads were the limit.

Father Escobar realized that these were tall yarns, and we cannot blame him for hedging a little. "It appears to me doubtful," he says, "that there should be so many monstrosities in so short a distance, and so near us. . . . But even though there might be still greater doubt of all these matters, it seems yet more doubtful to remain silent about things which, if discovered, would result, I believe, in glory to God and in service to the King our Lord. Moreover, although the things in themselves may be so rare and may never before have been seen, to anyone who will consider the wonders which God constantly performs in the world, it will be easy to believe that since He is able to create them He may have done so." This logic seems irrefutable.

Consulting their copy of Vetancurt, Kino and Manje proceeded to test some of Otata's tales. "We asked the oldest Indians if they had heard their ancestors say that they had seen a Spanish captain pass by with horses and soldiers. They replied that the old people had told of him, and that the Captain talked with the old people now dead, and went as far as the sea with armed white men and returned to the east, whence they had come." [1]

The inquiries about precious metals were less fruitful. "We did not learn about nor did they tell of the coral, silver, and gold which they possess within the sea, on the Isla Giganta, and among the nations of the north, of which they told Don Juan de Oñate. . . . Perhaps since he went to the sea beach by way of the Río Colorado and others more distant from this one, those nations told him of things unknown to these people." Manje's geography here was a little hazy.

The natives told another interesting tale. As Manje understood it, it was the ancient story of The Woman in Blue, here somewhat corrupted and coarsened. The old men "said that when they were boys, a beautiful white woman carrying a cross came to their lands dressed in white, gray, and blue, clear to her feet, her head covered with a cloth or veil. She spoke to them, shouted, and harangued them in a language which they did not understand. The tribes of the Río Colorado shot her with arrows and twice left her for dead. But, coming to life, she left by the air. . . . A few days later she returned many times to harangue them." The Woman in Blue had met better treatment in New Mexico and Texas. Five days previously Kino and

---

[1] In the printed text of Manje's *Luz de Tierra Incógnita*, 266, "se volvió para el oriente de asia donde habia venido" has been misread as "se volvió para el Oriente de Asia," something quite different.

Manje had heard the same tale in the village of Sonóita, but did not believe it. But now, says Manje, "since these people repeat the same story, and the places are so far apart, we surmised that perhaps the visitor was the Venerable María de Jesús de Agreda. It says in the account of her life that about the year 1630 she preached to the heathen Indians of this North America and the borders of New Mexico. And sixty-eight years having passed since then, to the present year in which we are told this story by the old men, who from their countenances appear to be about eighty years old, it would be possible for them to remember it." So the tale seemed plausible.[1]

One point in the story required a comment. "We only note the addition that they did not understand her. Now God, who performed the greater miracle by which she was conducted to these regions from Spain, and who does not do things imperfectly, would have given her the gift of tongues so that she might be understood. But as the accessory follows the principal, it must have been she. And . . . since they then were boys, they would have little understanding of what she was teaching them. Or else Satan, chaos of confusion, afterward confounded them, erasing it from their memories." So that was settled.[2]

Kino and Manje inquired likewise regarding the white people— "gente blanca"—in the interior, about whom the Pimas had told during a previous expedition. Yes, the Yumas had heard of them. They said that "toward the north and the seacoast lived clothed white men who sometimes come armed to the Río Colorado and trade a few goods for buckskins. . . . We do not know whether or not they may be the Spaniards from the ships which in the time of the first viceroys of Mexico were sent to discover lands and nations and who never returned, but being wrecked near land, with planks and by swimming came out and settled; or whether they are Japanese or Chinese; . . . or whether they are foreign heretics who may be settled among and living with Indian women. . . . These are matters worthy of investigation."

---

[1] This story is included in the *Memorial of Fray Alonso de Benavides, 1630,* Translated by Mrs. Edward E. Ayer. Annotated by Frederick Webb Hodge and Charles Fletcher Lummis (Chicago, 1916).

[2] Manje, *Luz de Tierra Incógnita,* 266–267; Manje, Relación Ytineraria; Manje, Epitome.

The items given the big headlines in the daily news are not always the important ones. So it was here. Kino in his account of this conference tells of another incident, of which little notice was taken at the moment, but which came to have a determining influence on his later career. "The natives at San Pedro in the two days when we were with them gave us various presents of the usual sorts which they have there. Among them were some curious and beautiful blue shells, which, so far as I know, are found only on the opposite or western coast of California. Afterward it occurred to me that not very far distant there must be a passage by land to near-by California; and shortly, by Divine Grace, we shall try to find out and see it with all exactness." [1] Father Eusebio little knew what travel—and travail—those blue shells were destined to cost him.

CXI

THE RIVER OF THE APOSTLES

Kino was sorry not to go forward to the Colorado River, but he considered it wise to await another time. So he decided to ascend the Gila River to see the people living on its banks—those Cocomaricopas who had visited him near the Casa Grande. This done, he would have two roads open to the Colorado. Five years previously, after his first visit to Casa Grande, he had drawn a map showing Indian villages all the way down the Gila to its mouth. At that time he had never descended the stream below San Andrés, and his map was based on hearsay. He now had a chance to revise it on the basis of first-hand knowledge.

Saying Adiós to the Yumas at San Pedro, on February 23 he set forth upstream on the first recorded exploration between Gila Range and Sierra la Estrella, the mountain he had wished to climb during his last expedition to the Gila. With Father Eusebio we again share the thrill of first discovery. The journey to Gila Bend, well over a hundred miles, lasted six days. Kino traveled all the way on the south side of the river, generally close to its banks and in sight of its shady

[1] Kino, *Favores Celestiales*, Parte I, Lib. vi, Cap. 6; *Hist. Mem.*, I, 195–196.

cottonwood groves. Most of the way to Sierra Pinta [1] he found the lands sterile and pasturage short, but he always had the water of the river at hand.

For some fifty miles above San Pedro the banks were uninhabited, for the people upstream were hostile to the Yumas. The natives encountered from here to Gila Bend Kino called Opas and Cocomaricopas,[2] now Maricopas. The villages were small. In most cases only the men appeared, the women and children hiding through fear of the strange men and their stranger animals.

These Indians were fine-looking people, fairer than the Yumas, but had similar customs and spoke the same language. Like the Yumas, the men went stark naked, but the women wore skirts made of willow bark fiber. They practiced some agriculture, without irrigation, planting little patches of ground fertilized by the freshets of the river. They raised maize, beans, and calabashes, and used the fruit of the screw bean for making bread or atole. Among the beans Manje noted white ones obtained by these natives from the Río Colorado, and since they were not raised in Sonora he took some home to plant. Culture borrowing was not one-sided. A principal article of native diet was fish, which was very plentiful in the Gila. "They fish," says Manje, "with large and nicely made nets, like those of Europe, and another contrivance with which they take out the catch. It is shaped like a little boat, is two varas long and about one wide, is woven from poles very carefully bent like ribs, all coming together as in the prows, others crossing them and tied, as is shown by the drawing in the margin."[3] The jícaras or baskets likewise attracted attention. Some of them held a fanega or more of maize. Larger ones, water-tight, were used for boats, in which two men paddled back and forth across the river, using their hands for oars. And at that time the Gila was a real river, with water in it.

As Kino and his party traveled they found the Cocomaricopas friendly, though timid. They welcomed the visitors with *Usu,* and used the same word to say goodbye. They furnished guides, and were

---

[1] Now Painted Rock Range.
[2] Manje called them Yumas, or Cócopas, whose language they spoke.
[3] The drawing on the margin of the manuscript conveys Manje's idea quite clearly, but does not show any great artistic skill.

generous with their provisions. At most of the villages long tlatoles or talks were made by Kino and Gilg about the Faith, and by Manje about the king. Possession was taken at each village in the name of his Majesty, and canes of office were bestowed upon the chiefs. The Cocomaricopas were especially admonished to make peace with the Yumas, for Kino came to bring good will among men.

The first village passed through was Tutum, or Tutumóydag, a village of a hundred men, in the vicinity of the present Palomas, but south of the stream. Kino named it San Matías. With no interpreter, communication here had to be by signs and gestures. Four leagues above San Matías was San Mateo Coat,[1] opposite or a little below Agua Caliente, where a hundred and twenty men were counted. Here "by good fortune" they found a blind man who knew both Pima and Yuma, and who served as interpreter. Conversation was easier now. A short distance above San Mateo they met fifty men from a village off the road. Then followed a long uninhabited stretch till they came to San Tadeo del Batqui. It was just west of Sierra Pinta, at a place with the first good pasturage above San Pedro.

Swinging to the right and away from the river now, they crossed Sierra Pinta—the Overland Mail of the California Gold Days followed the same route, leaving ruts still visible,—and at the end of three leagues returned to the river at San Simón del Tucsani. About halfway between Sierra Pinta and Gila Bend they camped at a village where fifty men showed themselves, though the women and children remained in hiding. At this place the land was fertile and Kino remarked it as a good site for a mission.

From here forward to Gila Bend the river bottom was thickly peopled, and they now found among the Cocomaricopas a large in-filtration of Pimas. Eastward of Tucsani they passed five villages a league apart, from two of which the people had fled. In the other three they counted seventy Cocomaricopa men. Three leagues beyond, at the Bend, they camped at San Felipe y Santiago de Oydabuise, in-habited by one hundred and fifty men, all Pimas. Here, for the first time on the march upstream, they were welcomed with crosses and triumphal arches. Kino noted it as a good place for another mission.

[1] On Kino's 1701 map called San Mateo del Sicoroidag.

Here on March 1 with new guides they left the river and took the cut-off from Gila Bend to the Pima settlements above Sierra la Estrella. This trail, then traveled for the first time in recorded history, has remained a highway to the present. Eleven leagues east that day through rocky and sterile hills took them to camp at a scant well in a plain with good pasturage. Going forward next day, they climbed a pass through Sierra la Estrella, from the top of which their eyes met a welcome view. There before them was the familiar valley of the Gila, and the guides pointed out to them Río Verde and Río Salado, which, united, flowed west and joined the Gila a short distance north of where they stood. "They say they call it the Río Verde because it flows through a sierra of many veins of green, blue, and otherwise colored stones. We do not know whether or not this is the Sierra Azul where, according to tradition, there has been seen an infinity of gold and silver." Here was another tale to investigate.[1]

At the suggestion of Father Gilg, Kino called the Gila the River of the Apostles, whose names he had sprinkled liberally along its banks. To complete the Twelve he now suggested that the rivers which we call Salado, Verde, Santa Cruz, and San Pedro might be named for the four Evangelists, Matthew, Mark, Luke, and John—in Spanish form of course.

Descending the sierra to the river, three leagues from the junction of the Gila with the Salado they camped at a village of two hundred friendly Pimas called San Bartolomé del Comac; then, ten leagues upstream over sterile plains, they reached San Andrés de Coata. Kino felt at home here, for he had already visited the place three times, and the Indians welcomed him with affection. Here he found the cross and the letter which on a former occasion he had sent to the Moquis, for no messenger had dared carry them through the Apache country. Undiscouraged, Kino now dispatched another message with better success.

To this place Manje had counted during the journey 1990 Indians never before seen or listed. Father Eusebio now had many changes to make in his map of 1696, based on information gained at the cost of his long hard ride over the Camino del Diablo and up the brush-

---

[1] Manje, *Luz de Tierra Incógnita,* 269–270; Manje, Relación Ytineraria; Manje, Epitome.

grown and sandy banks of the Gila River. Thus slowly and at the cost of much sweat was the map of Pima Land unfolded.

From San Andrés the way home was over familiar ground, through San Xavier del Bac. In his book written several years later, Manje tells us that two leagues after leaving Bac "there arose such a furious hurricane of wind and rain that, the horses bogging down, unable to travel, we were obliged to halt. That night Father Kino fell ill, for from the severe wetting his feet and legs became swollen. But in spite of the gravity of his malady, next day he insisted that we should go on. But having traveled three leagues south in a continuous rain, he began to vomit so from cholera that, seeing him debilitated and played out . . . , we halted under most trying circumstances." Kino improved somewhat, and two days later they continued to Tumacácori. When they arrived the river was too high to cross it to the pueblo, so the natives brought over a sheep to provide broth for Father Eusebio, "and they were very sorry for his illness and debility."

This paragraph presents Kino to us in an heroic light. But Manje has left a puzzle here. His manuscript diary and his book do not correspond as to dates, nor do they tell the same story after leaving Bac. In his diary he says nothing of Kino's illness or of the hurricane, but says that Father Gilg played out. "Today [the 8th] Father Adamo Gil became fatigued, both because of so long a journey today and because of the long expedition and his great age, from which is recognized his fervent zeal for the conversion of these heathendoms, for although he was sixty years old he undertook this exploration." [1] So wide a discrepancy is difficult to explain. Was Gilg the hero this time? Or were both padres ill?

---

[1] Manje, *Luz de Tierra Incógnita*, 271; Manje, Relación Ytineraria; Manje, Epitome.

The Blue Shells

CXII

THE PADRE GRANDE VISITS BAC
AND THE PÁPAGOS

GEOGRAPHY ASIDE, KINO GOT GOOD RETURNS from his last two expeditions. Soon after his arrival at Dolores the Cocomaricopas and the Gila Pimas sent him four buckskins and requested him to come again to talk of missions. Both the buckskins and the invitation were welcome. Moreover, "various new nations and rancherías" even from beyond the Yumas, sent word asking him to go to see them. And most surprising of all, the northern Apaches professed to be friendly. Chief Humari was proud to be the harbinger of the good news. He and the Gila chiefs sent Kino a report to the effect that by means of "the cross, letter, gifts and messages" which early in March were sent from San Andrés to the Moquis "the Apaches nearest the Colorado were won over to our friendship, for the messages, letter, and cross . . . the Apaches had received and applied to themselves, making peace with the rest." These people were evidently the Yavapais, of Río Verde, often called Mohave Apaches, though of Yuman stock. The good reports were confirmed by Chief Humari and the Gileño chiefs when on October 1 they arrived in person at Dolores. The welcome they met was suitable to the good tidings they bore.

With the new prospects Father Antonio Leal, now visitor, became enthusiastic. As a means of enlisting aid, he encouraged Kino to write a history of his work in the Pimería, whereupon Father Eusebio began his now famous *Favores Celestiales*. If he had done nothing but this Leal would deserve a place in history. And when Father Eusebio proposed another journey to the northwest to answer all these friendly calls, Leal decided to go with him to see the new peoples with his own eyes. When Kino asked what provision he should make for the visitor's comfort on the journey, Leal in true apostolic spirit replied: "Of me or for me take no thought. . . . I can eat a piece of jerked beef, and it tastes very good and suffices me. What I really desire is that the journey may be accomplished whereby the wish of those poor people may be realized."

Manje tells us there was a very special reason for the new expedition. Kino's opponents were conducting a whispering campaign against him. By manipulating mirrors and prisms, says the learned Don Matheo, tricksters could make even the fairest woman look like an ugly monster. In the same way hostile persons distorted Kino's glowing reports of the new tribes visited. They said that the land was barren and the Indians savages, who had no interest in missions; that "Father Kino's zeal for souls, coupled with a lack of prudence and judgment, had caused him to burst forth in hyperboles and superlatives in favor of the Pimas and other nations; and that like these exaggerating mirrors he had made a tiny insect look like an elephant, painting grandeurs in Pima Land which did not exist there."

And so the journey was undertaken to learn the truth.[1] Leal arrived at Dolores on October 21 (1699) bringing with him Father Francisco Gonzalvo, a young Jesuit from Sonora who had crossed the Atlantic with Campos. Three days later the three, accompanied by Manje, set forth for Remedios with servants and fifty saddle and pack animals, sixty-six more having already been sent ahead to Bac. It was another Kino cavalcade. From Remedios they continued over the regular trail through Tumacácori to Bac, where it was expected that Bernal the Blonde would join them with soldiers.

At Bac more than a thousand natives were counted, and Leal enthusiastically declared that its fertile lands would support "another city like Mexico." From here they continued north past San Cosme del Tucsón to San Agustín, where the journey was interrupted. The plan had been to go "to the Río Grande, the Río Azul, and the Río Colorado, to the Opas and the Cocomaricopas," to follow up Kino's last exploration on the Gila. But conditions changed. Two of Leal's

---

[1] For this chapter see Kino, *Favores Celestiales*, Lib. VII, Caps. i–iv; *Hist. Mem.*, I, 200–211; Manje, *Luz de Tierra Incógnita*, 273–281.

servants fell sick, and Bernal had not yet arrived, so Leal waited two days in camp. Meanwhile Kino and Manje went north to visit Santa Catalina. When they returned Kino got a letter from Bernal saying that he was joining Chief Coro in a new campaign against the Jocomes. These pests were again disturbing the border.

For Kino's adventurous program a military escort was desirable, especially since the distinguished visitor, the Padre Grande, was in the party. But there were no soldiers to be had. So the expedition to the Colorado was given up and instead they made an excursion into Pápago Land. This was Kino's second and Manje's third intimate contact with the gentle farmers whose descendants still dwell on the same sites. Retracing their steps to Bac, they sent Leal's sick servants to Dolores, and then turned west, over the time-old trail to Actúm, now called Santa Rosa. As one drives today over the highway from Bac to Sells, one is close to their route for a part of the way. Traveling twenty-eight leagues in three days, and passing two friendly villages, they reached San Serafín del Actúm, where Kino was given a heart-warming reception.[1]

The scene deserves a painter. "There came out to welcome us more than twenty justices who had assembled, and about twenty boys, who received us on their knees, with crosses in their hands, that they might give them to the Father Visitor; and afterward we were welcomed by more than four hundred men and women drawn up in a very long line with their little ones already baptized two years before.[2] They comprised about twelve hundred souls." The children were thriving, and the mothers, their faces broad with smiles and their white teeth gleaming, proudly exhibited their offspring to Father Eusebio, pronouncing perhaps the Christian names he had given them and forgotten. The Padre Grande was pleased and young Gonzalvo edified by the hypnotic genius of the Master of Dolores.

In the afternoon Kino and his train continued north to the near-by village of San Francisco del Adid, where they "were welcomed by two hundred men and about eight hundred souls," among them being

---

[1] On the 6th they camped at Bowles's Wash. Between there and Santa Rosa they passed through Tupo, at Coyote Field, and through Cups, at San Lorenzo, which lies at the north end of North Comobabi Mountains (Father Bonaventure).

[2] Kino made a slip here. It was only one year before. *Hist. Mem.*, I, 208.

many of the one hundred and two children whom Father Eusebio had baptized that memorable October 4th of the previous year.

Now another scene demands a painter—or perhaps a flash-light would serve. "All were much pleased to hear the Word of God," says Kino; "and at night there was formed a circle of twenty-five governors, among them being the principal one of the four Coco-maricopas who had come to see us. He with the governor of . . . Dolores spoke with fervor of their eternal salvation, and the Father Visitor for the first time heard that new language. And the Coco-maricopas with very rare courtesy and loyalty brought me a very fat and pretty horse"—a pinto, perhaps—"which we had lost and left behind the year before." Who said these new people were savages? Leal himself could now answer the gossips!

That night the visitors were lodged in a house built of poles and rushes. Next morning, after dispatching messages and gifts to the Gila tribes, the Apaches, and the Moquis, Kino swung south with his train to Merced del Batki where eight hundred people were assembled and the scenes of welcome were repeated. Here at Merced one of the servants fell ill, and Fathers Leal and Gonzalvo stayed in camp to care for him, then to proceed with the invalid slowly to Tubu-tama. Meanwhile, Kino and Manje made one of their most remarkable rides, a feat worthy of remembrance in all the lore of the saddle.[1]

On the 8th the hardy pair set forth *a la ligera*—traveling light—toward the west, to baptize any sick people who might be found in other villages. Leal and Gonzalvo did not belong in such fast company. Follow them who can. It was a breathless ride. That day they traveled thirteen leagues westward "to San Raphael of the other Actúm," where they baptized two infants and two sick adults. On the 9th they swung nine leagues north over sterile plains to Bagui-burisac, in the vicinity of Komaki, where they counted four hundred souls. Sixteen leagues further northeastward, after nightfall of the same day, they reached the villages of Coati and Sibagoyda, which Kino had visited the previous year. Like the rest they had assembled joy-ously to welcome him. The reception served as a salve for blisters

---

[1] Manje and Kino do not agree as to the details of this journey. Manje does not tell of going to Merced, and Kino says nothing of the long jaunt northeast from San Rafael to Coati and back to Sonóita. But there is nothing contradictory in the two accounts.

and a lotion for sore muscles acquired during the twenty-five league ride that day.

Next morning, after counting three hundred persons, preaching, baptizing three sick persons and distributing presents, the hard riders swung southwest, crossed a pass in a range, and having traveled thirty-three leagues reached Sonóita, passing two villages on the way. In the three they counted a thousand persons and baptized ten. Again weariness was assuaged by the smiles of villagers and the winning of the heathen souls.

Saying Adiós to the natives, on the 11th the iron men made a still more grueling ride. "By long marches and traveling day and night . . . and having covered fifty leagues," Manje tells us, they overtook Leal and Gonzalvo at Búsanic, and slept four hours. Next morning they butchered two cows and two sheep, distributed presents, preached and gave canes of office. The most surprising thing about this astounding tour is the fact that Kino records it as a matter of course, without a single exclamation point or a superlative adjective. They are reserved for us. Going forward next day to Tubutama, they arrived on the 18th at Dolores.

CXIII

MIDNIGHT TALKS

Kino now became absorbed in what proved to be a capital problem —whether California was not after all a peninsula, not an island. Gradually his geographical notions had taken on a new orientation. They were brought to a focus by the huge blue abalone shells given him by the tall Yumas on the Gila River in his last expedition. The genesis of the idea in his mind, as he remembered it, is explained by himself. "When, ten years ago, setting out from . . . Dolores for the west, and passing through the lands of El Soba, I arrived after a sixty leagues' journey, on three different occasions with different persons, at the coast of the Sea of California, we saw plainly that the arm of the sea kept getting narrower, for in this latitude of thirty-three degrees we already saw on the other side more than twenty-five leagues of California land in a stretch, so distinctly that we estimated the distance across or the width of that arm of the sea to be no more than fifteen or eighteen or twenty leagues. From this arose the desire to ascertain the width higher up; and in the year 1698, at thirty-two degrees of latitude, and at one hundred and five leagues by a northwest course from . . . Dolores, from the very high hill or ancient volcano of Santa Clara I descried most plainly both with and without a telescope the junction of these lands of New Spain with those of California, the head of this Sea of California, and the land passage which was in thirty-two degrees [1] latitude." This was when he crossed Pápago Land southwestward from the Gila to Sonóita and Caborca with Carrasco. He continues:

"At that time, however, I did not recognize it as such, and I persuaded myself that farther on and more to the west the Sea of California must extend to a higher latitude and communicate with the North Sea or Strait of Anian, and must leave or make California an island." His idea at this time was that shown by his map of 1696. "And it was with me as with the brethren of Joseph, who ate with him, and made merry with him, and talked with him, but knew him not until his time."

"A year afterward, at the suggestion of the father visitor, Oracio Police, I penetrated one hundred and seventy leagues to the northwest with Father Adamo Gilg and Captain Juan Mateo Manje, going beyond thirty-two [2] degrees north latitude, and almost reaching the confluence of the Río Grande de Hila and the Colorado, where the natives gave us some blue shells." This was at San Pedro, just east of Gila Range, on the Gila River, where he investigated Chief Otata's yarns. "And still it did not occur to us that by that way there was

[1] Kino, *Favores Celestiales,* Parte II, Lib. i, Cap. 2; *Hist. Mem.,* I, 229. For some strange reason Kino in this paragraph has twice substituted 35 for 32. The passage in the original is in his well-known hand, and is plainly written, so there is no question as to the correct reading of the manuscript, but he clearly means 32. In his correspondence, diaries, and maps, clear down to 1707 at least, Kino consistently puts the head of the Gulf near 32°. I therefore conclude that the changes in the *Favores Celestiales* were made at a later date, under circumstances which I cannot explain. The restoration of 32° here correctly represents his opinion and the results of his actual observations to the end of the period of his explorations. To retain his changes would do him an injustice.

[2] Kino, *Favores Celestiales,* Parte II, Lib. i, Cap. 2; *Hist. Mem.,* I, 230. Another slip for 32. Indeed, Kino here first wrote 32 and then changed it to 35. This passage in the manuscript is in his own hand.

a land passage to California, or to the head of its sea; and not until we were on the road returning to . . . Dolores did it occur to me that those blue shells must be from the opposite coast of California and the South Sea, and that by that route by which they had come . . . we could pass . . . to California."

Right then, on the trail from the Gila to Dolores, the great idea was born! Joseph's time had come. "And from that time forward I ceased work on the bark, twelve varas long and four wide, which we were building at . . . Cabotca . . . and here at . . . Dolores, intending to carry it afterward, entire, to the sea." [1] Evidently Mora had neither burned Kino's bark nor stopped his work upon it. [2]

Salvatierra saw the point. Three weeks after Kino reached Dolores with his blue shells—that is to say, on March 28, 1699,—Father Juan wrote: *"Quod felix faustum fortunatumque sit.* May it be happy, auspicious, and fortunate. Much have I rejoiced, and much has Father Francisco María Picolo rejoiced in the new, glorious entry to the Río Grande; and we are desirous of knowing whether from that new coast which Your Reverence traversed, California may be seen and what sign there is on that side whether this narrow sea is landlocked." This letter was written in reply to Kino's report of his expedition to Cerro de Santa Clara (Pinacate Mountain) in 1698. That report raised in Father Juan's mind the same question that was suggested to Kino by the blue shells. To both the idea occurred at nearly the same time; to both it resulted from Kino's tireless explorations.

The best way to find out was to go and see. So Salvatierra planned a voyage for that summer as far as latitude thirty-six degrees or even higher and asked Kino to join him. "I should greatly rejoice if your Reverence would come on the voyage of discovery, coming here after the harvest and the ingathering of the wheat, for thus you could disembark on the Río Grande. Your Reverence might embark at Hyaqui and upon your arrival here we should all set sail, your Reverence, Sebastián Romero, and one of us, with twelve soldiers, and

---

[1] Kino, *Favores Celestiales,* Parte II, Lib. i, Cap. 2; *Hist. Mem.,* I, 229–230. For more about the boat building see Mora Contra Kino, May 28, 1698. Elsewhere Kino makes other statements about the genesis of his ideas. See *Hist. Mem.,* II, index.

[2] In his letter of December 3, 1697, he wrote that he hoped to complete his bark "this Spring."

we should sail well up this coast, after going up to thirty-six degrees [1] on the coast of the Pimería." Instead of accepting Salvatierra's invitation to sail up the Gulf, Kino and Leal went through Pápago Land, as we have seen. At Sonóita, Kino tells us, his special errand was to inquire "about the land passage to California . . . and the blue shells of the opposite coast."

Another gift of blue shells drove the idea home. This time the Indians brought them to Kino's mission. "Being in the pueblo of . . . Remedios on the twentieth of March [1700], a governor from the Río Grande,[2] and other Pima natives, brought me a holy cross, with a string of twenty blue shells, sent me by the principal governor of the Cocomaricopas, who lives in the great ranchería of Dacóydag,[3] with a very friendly response to some messages which I had sent him. . . . And again reflecting that those shells were from the opposite coast, as I had seen them when I was in California, I informed several fathers of them, sending them afterward, together with the holy cross, to the Father Visitor Antonio Leal."

Kino's friends now became excited. Leal replied: "The cross and the shells came with your Reverence's letter to Arispe, and I greatly rejoice at seeing them, because of the distance whence they sent them, which is an indication of friendliness." "God bless me!" wrote Kappus, "And what great news and how rare is that which your Reverence imparts to me, . . . to the effect that it is possible to pass overland to California, news truly the greatest, if it is verified, but which, although desired so long it has never been possible to confirm." Evidently the idea had been discussed. "May our Lord grant that the news may be verified, since for Father . . . Salvatierra it will be most gratifying." Gilg, now rector of the district of San Francisco Xavier, declared that the question of the land-passage should be investigated. Jironza wrote that he was eager to know the facts. We have no comment by Mora.

To cap the climax, just at this time Kino got permission from Thirso González, now Father General, to spend half the year in the

[1] The thirty-sixth parallel cuts across the lower tip of Nevada and runs close to the Grand Canyon.
[2] This was a year after his return from the Gila with the blue shells and several months after his journey with Leal.
[3] Evidently San Matías Tutumacóidog.

Pimería and half in California. "For this reason," says Kino, "and in order at the same time to cast a glance at the spiritual and temporal condition of the three newly begun missions of the north and the northwest, I determined to go inland for a few days to find out and obtain all possible information in regard to these matters." So he started northward to take a look at his new missions and to learn more about the blue shells. On April 21 (1700) he set forth with ten Dolores Indians and fifty-three horses and mules. Passing through Cocóspora (deserted now for three years), and through Tumacácori, on the 28th he reached San Xavier del Bac.

Suddenly plans were changed, as they had been changed when at Bac with Leal. On the way Kino learned that Escalante had gone with soldiers to the Soba country. Perhaps there was trouble. This, together with the request of the natives of Bac that he stay with them, decided Kino not to continue at this time to the Gila.

But he did not give up his purpose. Quite the contrary. Instead he called a great conference of chiefs to talk about the Faith—and the blue shells. "And from this great valley of San Xavier, by way of the Río Grande westward as far as the Cocomaricopas and Yumas, and even to the Río Colorado, as I desired, I tried . . . to find out whether the blue shells came from any other region than the opposite coast of California. To that end I dispatched various messengers in all directions; some east to summon Captain Humaric; others north to call those of Santa Catalina, and those of La Encarnación and San Andrés of the Río Grande; . . . and especially others to the west and northwest, to summon various Pima, Opa, and Cocomaricopa governors from near the Río Colorado, to learn with all possible exactness in regard to the blue shells and the passage by land to California." While he waited for the Indians to assemble, Kino catechized and baptized natives at Bac, and laid the foundations for a church.

Soon the Indians began to pour in to see the great Black Robe. Chief Humari and his son came from the northeast, then delegates arrived from the Gila. On the 30th came the governor of La Encarnación. That night "in long talks" Kino told the visitors about the Faith. "At the same time I made further and further inquiries as to whence came the blue shells, and all asserted that there were none in this nearest sea of California, but that they came from other lands more remote."

Next day delegates came from the west. "We talked with them a great part of the night, as we had done the night before, in regard to the eternal salvation of all those nations of the west and the northwest, at the same time continuing various inquiries in regard to the blue shells which were brought from the northwest and from the Yumas and Cutganes. They admittedly came from the opposite coast of California and from the sea which is ten or twelve days' journey farther than this other Sea of California, on which there are pearl and white shells and many others, but none of those blue ones which they gave us among the Yumas and sent me with the holy cross to . . . Remedios."

On May 2 Kino set out southward for Dolores, where he arrived on the 6th after an exciting detour to San Ignacio. The new report which he now made regarding the blue shells aroused fresh enthusiasm. Kappus wrote from Mátape: "I thank your Reverence for your most delightful letter, and also for sending the blue shells; and I shall welcome most heartily the announcement of those discoveries. I am very strongly of the opinion that this land which we are in is mainland and joins that of California. May our Lord grant that there be a road as royal as we think and desire, for thereby the labor as well as the care of California will be lessened." That is to say, stock and supplies could be sent by land on foot or by pack train around the Gulf. Later Kappus wrote: "If your Reverence accomplishes the entry by land into California we shall celebrate with great applause so happy a journey, whereby the world will be enlightened as to whether it is an island or a peninsula, which to this day is unknown. May it redound . . . to the glory of God, thrice holy and mighty."

"I greatly desire that your Reverence may finally make this most desired expedition by land into the Californias," wrote Father Manuel González, now rector at Oposura. "If you accomplish this we must erect to you a costly and famous statue. And if the way is short there will be two statues. May God give your Reverence health and strength for this and many other equally good things." Kino replied that the two statues should be of Jesus of Nazareth and Our Lady of Los Dolores. He wanted none for himself.[1]

CXIV

NEW PÁPAGO FRIENDS

With the new yeast of adventure in his soul, Kino once more took the long trail. He would find the land passage to California if one there was. Then all the old geographers would see the error of their ways. And he would indeed "lend a hand" to Salvatierra. His vaqueros would drive cattle around the head of the Gulf to Salvatierra's very dooryard at Loreto! Incidentally, there were Pápagos whom he had not seen, and he had promised the Cocomaricopas another visit. And he tingled with the lust of the trail.

On September 24 Father Eusebio left Dolores with ten servants and sixty horses and mules. He does not mention any companions other than these Indian servants. Manje was missed, but Kino himself kept an excellent diary. The journey lasted just five weeks. The round trip covered three hundred and eighty leagues or nearly a thousand miles.

Going to Remedios, Kino descended the river, threaded the canyon, and turned north to Síboda. Here he had a new ranch with a thousand head of cattle and four droves of mares.[2] A fifteen leagues' journey over the range—where even now there is no wheel track—took him to Búsanic and Tucubavia. From here he sent a message to the Caborcans to meet him at Sonóita within twelve or fifteen days, when he expected to pass through that place on his way home. By a short cut he now journeyed to Pozo Verde, escorted by the chief of that village, who had met him at Búsanic. He says nothing about the ogress who had so intrigued young Manje.

Instead of continuing west to Sonóita, Kino now opened a new trail across Pápago Land, his route forming a slightly bent bow of

---

[1] Kino, *Favores Celestiales*, Parte II, Lib. i, Caps. 3–6; *Hist. Mem.*, I, 231–242.
[2] Kino, *Favores Celestiales*, Parte II, Lib. i, Cap. 7; *Hist. Mem.*, I, 243.

which the string was a straight line from Pozo Verde to Gila Bend. To Merced the same route had been traveled in the return Leal journey. From here Kino sent half of his servants and most of his horses to Sonóita to await him there. He then continued north a short distance, swung west through Quijotoa Range past Covered Wells to El Comac,[1] then northwest to a large settlement called San Gerónimo. It was the present-day Perigua, or a place in its vicinity.

Kino's diary gives us our first glimpse of this country. It was thickly settled and the Indians raised maize and calabashes. "They welcomed us with crosses and arches erected, with a little house, and with provisions prepared, two hundred and eighty Indians (for we counted them) being drawn up in a line, as in the Christian pueblos. An hour after nightfall a hundred and fifty other Indians of another village came to see us and extend to us a welcome. Because it was night neither the women nor the children had come. Upon inquiry we learned that in this vicinity, into which we had never before entered, there were more than a thousand persons, who had never seen a father or any Spaniards."[2] Again he was a trail maker. Next day native officials were appointed. Kino does not mention any military or secular official with him. In that case, he was acting for the king. Seven infants and three sick adults were christened, "and if we had stayed a day, as they requested, they would have given us more than one hundred infants to baptize."

Escorted by the chief of El Comac and other native dignitaries, Kino continued north six leagues to "a very good watering place," probably Toapit, at the foot of a range; then twelve more leagues between Sauceda and Sand Tank Mountains, on the skirts of one of which they climbed "to another aguaje among inaccessible rocks, which the pack animals could not reach to drink, although the guides brought us enough water for ourselves." In difficulty of access it was another Moonlight Water.[3]

---

[1] Now Komaki, northwest of Pozo Blanco and west of Sierra Blanca.

[2] This statement throws Perigua out of the itinerary of the previous journey of Kino and Manje, through Pápago Land.

[3] Between 1740 and 1750 Father Jacob Sedelmayr three times crossed Pápago Land by essentially the same trail. In October, 1781, Fages went north over the route on his way to Yuma. He mentions in his diary the village called Tachitoa or Cerro de la Pirigua. The people of the vicinity lived in houses of half-orange shape.

CXV

WHERE THE RIVERS MEET

Continuing north to Gila Bend, Kino descended the river through the Cocomaricopa villages he had visited the year before, welcomed everywhere with smiles and hospitality. The Black Robe had kept his promise. On October 6th he reached the village of San Pedro, at the bend of the Gila west of Wellton. This place was memorable for the gift, in February of the year before, of the blue shells which had set him to thinking. "They welcomed us now very affectionately, even giving the dog which was with us water and pinole in a little basket, with all kindness, as if he were a person, wondering that he was so tame and faithful, a thing never before seen by them. In this respect they were like the Californians when we went to see them the first time fifteen years before." As a matter of fact it was seventeen years before.

One is apt to find what one is looking for. Kino was now seeking evidence that California and the mainland were one and continuous. He found it. "In three other respects, we . . . learned during these days, these natives and their country are like the Californians: first, in the dress of the men and the women; second, in that the men cut their hair in one way and the boys in another; third, in that here there are various trees native to California, such as the incense tree and the tree bearing the fruit which they called *medessé*." This was the mesquite, whose fruit had played so prominent a part in the native harvest festival at San Bruno.

Kino and his band continued down the Gila River, now with Yuma guides. He was again on new ground. "Here the river runs about eight leagues to the north and afterward turns again to the west. On the way they gave us great quantities of fish, both raw and cooked; for, although they had their little fields of maize, beans, calabashes, and watermelons, the beans and maize were not yet ripe. We spent the night at a very good stopping place, which we called the Camp of Las Sandías, because there were watermelons in a very rich sandy beach at the foot of a hill, from the top of which California is plainly visible; and this day was the Feast of San Bruno, patron of California." It was the anniversary of his arrival at San Bruno seventeen years before. Camp was evidently a little west of Dome.

The 7th of October was a red-letter day. With his own eyes Kino saw California and the Pimería as a continuous land. We have his own words: "Setting out downstream, after going four leagues we halted near a village which . . . was on the other side of the river." It must have been about halfway between Dome and Yuma, not far from the old ruin known as Hacienda Redonda. "And while I dispatched some friendly messages to the villages round about, with the governor, the alcalde, and my mayordomo of . . . Dolores, and the four best pack mules that we had, I ascended a hill to the westward,[1] where we thought we should be able to descry the Sea of California. But, looking and sighting toward the south, the west, and the southwest, both with and without a long range telescope, we saw more than thirty leagues of level country, without any sea, and the junction of the Río Colorado with this Río Grande . . . , and their many groves and plains."

They were above the head of the Gulf, and a celebration was in order. "Returning to our stopping place, we ate lunch, adding some sweetmeats for joy that now, thank the Lord, we had seen the lands pertaining to California, without any sea between and separating those lands from it!" Kino had confirmed his opinion concerning the land passage. He had seen California with no Gulf in the way. Some day he would go down the Peninsula to visit Salvatierra at Loreto.

But he must turn back now. The guides were uncomfortable in Yuma territory, and duty called Kino home. "Because our Pima guides, the captain and the governor of El Comac, the son of the captain of San Raphael, and the captain of Actúm, named Miguel, were becoming weary, and because the time for collecting the alms of cattle which the fathers of these missions of Sonora were giving for California was pressing upon me, I decided to return to . . . Dolores."[2]

Then he changed his mind. About four in the afternoon he was

---

[1] The hill which he climbed was evidently the mesa north of the river. Indeed he may have ascended one of the two peaks called Los Cerrillos or Las Tetas.
[2] Kino, *Favores Celestiales*, Parte II, Lib. i, Caps. 7–8; *Hist. Mem.*, I, 242–250.

just starting east, to camp at Las Sandías, when the chief of the Yumas hove in sight from the junction—the tall chief to whom the cane of governor had been given the previous year at San Pedro. With ready tears he urged Kino to turn back, saying that his people were begging that he go to see them. The mules were already setting out with the baggage and the paraphernalia for saying Mass. "But I let them go," says Kino, remaining to speak very leisurely with this governor, who knew very well both the Pima and the Yuma language. "And having inquired carefully that afternoon and part of the night in regard to the Gulf of California, the surrounding new nations, and especially the large population of the great-volumed Río Colorado near by, it seemed to me a matter of conscience not to go to see those numerous natives."

Conscience and inclination were in full accord. Next morning Kino arose very early, rode east with flying robe, and overtook his servants at Las Sandías in time to say Mass there at dawn. This done, he faced about, leaving the pack train in camp, and started downstream. Having gone only two leagues he met more than forty Yumas. They had traveled all night, fearing that the Black Robe would leave without visiting them. When they learned of his decision to turn back they were greatly rejoiced, and smiles wreathed their faces.

Down the Gila Kino continued with his new friends, the crowd increasing as they traveled. Hearing that most of the Yumas near the junction lived north of the Gila, Kino asked the chief to send messengers to notify them to cross over to the south side. To this the chief demurred. The Yumas were too numerous to make this practicable; besides, hospitality dictated otherwise; they must entertain the padre in their own homes.

So Father Eusebio yielded and the throng moved on. Two leagues from the junction carriers met him with provisions. Nearing the chief's home he was led to a ford where the Gila divided into three branches. It was just northeast of the present city of Yuma. "And crossing it, after eight leagues of very good road [from Las Sandías], I arrived at the first Yumas of the very large-volumed Río Colorado." He had again unrolled the map. At the great Yuma town near the junction, which Kino called San Dionisio, he was welcomed by more than a thousand people; soon more than two hundred others arrived, and next day more than three hundred. These last came from the other side of the Colorado, "the true and real Río del Norte of the ancients, swimming across it," for the Yumas, especially their women, were expert swimmers. California mermaids are by no means of recent origin.

Kino talked with the assembled natives about the Faith, and they replied with long harangues. "These talks, ours and theirs, lasted almost the whole afternoon and afterward till midnight, with very great pleasure to all." They begged Kino to stay with them at least two days, saying that many people were coming from up the Colorado where dwelt the Alchédomas, and from down the river where lived the Quíquimas, Bagiopas, and Hoabonomas. "But I dared not linger, lest I fail in coming to collect the cattle for California, as I had been charged, and as the branding time was at hand." Explorer must yield to ranchman.

Next day, after Mass, the Yumas brought Kino two sick adults to baptize. One he named Dionisio, "because it was the day of this glorious, holy martyr; likewise, because the Mass of this saint had been said here, the village and very good post, close to the junction of the river, was called San Dionisio." Most of the Indians who arrived that morning, from across the river, were of very lofty stature, "and the principal one of them was of gigantic size and the largest Indian that we had ever seen." Even today the Yumas are a large and powerful race. This giant and two others were given canes of office. By his personal charm, the Master of Dolores had conquered another tribe. When he took leave of his new friends they were disconsolate, but he promised to return and they were consoled.

Kino now had a new notion of the Río Colorado, quite different from that of his map of 1696. Hitherto the Gila had been the Río Grande; now it faded into insignificance beside the Colorado. "This very large-volumed, populous, and fertile Colorado River, which without exception is the largest in all New Spain, is the one which the ancient cosmographers by antonomasia called Río del Norte. It very probably comes from Gran Quivira; and it is certain that by the fertile and pleasant lands of this great river one can penetrate to the

Moquis, since it flows ten leagues west of those pueblos, and since the village of San Dionisio, as I have found by measuring the height of the sun with the astrolabe, is in thirty-three and one half degrees of latitude." Kino was too high.[1] "Ascending this river, which comes almost uniformly from the northeast, another degree and a half,[2] which in this latitude makes a journey of thirty-six leagues, one reaches thirty-five degrees, which is the latitude of the Moquis, missions pertaining to New Mexico; and there is probably no danger in this region that the Apaches would impede the entry."

Saying goodbye to the throng of Yumas and the visitors who had come from all the country round, Kino retraced his steps to Las Sandías, there overtook pack train and caballada, continued two leagues to a village, and camped. The place was near Dome. While the others rested, he ascended another and higher peak, "whence at sunset"—it was an October sunset—he "plainly descried a large stretch of country in California, and saw that the two rivers, below the confluence, ran united about ten leagues to the west"—the distance is in fact only about eight miles, but he was viewing it from afar—"and then, turning southward, about twenty leagues farther on emptied into the head of the Sea of California." Evidently Kino had a sufficiently powerful telescope and was at an elevation sufficient to enable him to see the Gulf at a distance of some seventy-five miles to the southwest. There before him was the head of the Sea of California. There beyond it were the California mountains running indefinitely southward. Father Eusebio's triumph seemed complete. California was indeed not an island.

CXVI

DESERT TANKS

With exuberant spirits Kino now started home by the shortest route, one of many that he himself had opened. Swinging around

---

[1] Kino's map, *Paso por Tierra,* made in 1701–1702 and printed in 1705, shows the junction at about 33°. The actual latitude of the Yuma junction is a little below 33°.

[2] Kino first wrote "another two degrees and a half," changed the text to "another degree and a half," and neglected to change "thirty-six" to "thirty-five." I have made the correction.

Photo by Bolton

Las Tinajas, in Gila Range

PASSO POR TIERRA
A LA CALIFORNIA
y sus Confinantes Nue,
vas Naciones, y Nuevas
Missiones de la Comp.ª
de IESUS,
EN LA AMERICA SEPTEN,
TRIONAL.

Leguas Castellanas

APACHES

SOBA IPORIS

Rio Salado

Sierra Grande demsfada
desde el Rio de Hila
1699

Cala Grande

S.Bartolome
S.Andres
Encarnacion

Rio Azul

MAICOPAS

S.Angelo
S.Bonifacio
S.Catalina

S.Agustin
S.Cosme

S.Reginaldo deſPac
Seraſin
S.Francisco

La Merced
S.Rafael
S.Marcelo
S.Eulalia

S.Luis
del Bacapa

S.Felipe y
Santiago
S.Simon
S.Tadeo
S.Mateo del
S.Matias del
La Yeta

De Guadalupe
Del Tucſani
Del Batqui
Sicaroidag
Tutomagoidag

COCO
1699 1700

S.Pedro
S.Pablo

Aguaje de la
Luna

Agua Escondida

Caris

Medanos
de Arena

Rio Colorado
S.Dionisio
1700

YUMAS

Cutganes

Hoabonomas

1701

Alchodomas

Del Norte

Baqiopas

Quiquima

Sierra

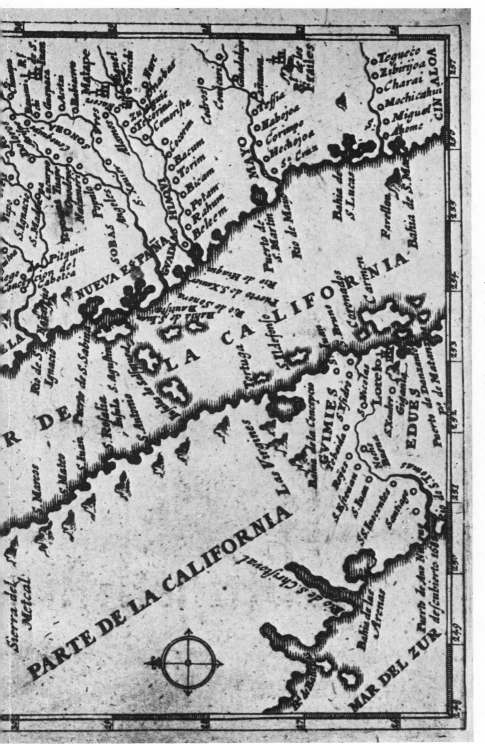

Kino's Map showing California as a Peninsula, 1701

(From the original manuscript)

Cerro del Cozón, on the Trail of Kino and Salvatierra

Quitobac, on the Trail of Kino and Salvatierra

the end of Gila Range, he left the river at San Pedro and set forth on the Camino del Diablo, retracing his path of February, 1699. His record gives us new light on this most interesting trail. He arrived at La Tinaja, the tank in Gila Range at the site now called Dripping Springs, in time to take siesta. Twelve leagues in the afternoon, skirting the range, took him at nightfall to "the watering-place which also the past year we had called El Agua Escondida"—Hidden Water— "because it was among the rocks." It was the now famous Tinajas Altas. The climb to the tanks was stiff and rough, but Kino's old muscles were limbered by the joy of his recent discovery.[1]

He wished to take another look at California. So, dispatching most of his servants with the caballada, to go ahead and wait for him wherever they might find good pasturage—the guides knew the trail —Kino ascended a peak above the tanks and unslung his telescope. What he saw confirmed his observations made from the lookout near the Gila. "I saw nothing more than the continuation of these lands with those of California and the sands of the California Sea"—those great sand dunes which rim the Gulf on its western shore. He was reassured. The Gulf did not continue indefinitely north. The old maps were wrong.

Scrambling amid rocks and cactus down the mountain, whose descent was quicker than the ascent, Kino took another refreshing drink, put foot in stirrup, struck eastward across the plain, overtook his pack train, threaded the trail through Cabeza Prieta Mountains,[2] crossed another plain, and arrived before sunset at the tank of La Luna, so named the previous year by him and Manje "because we had arrived there at night by moonlight." But, says Kino, "because this watering place is among rocks so high that the pack animals cannot ascend to drink, we determined to eat a morsel of supper there and then travel, and we did travel, three hours more by night, in order to reach the watering place of El Carrizal with more ease the next day."

Another strenuous ride followed. "Arising more than two hours before dawn, and setting out from the stopping place at the rising

---

[1] Kino, *Hist. Mem.*, I, p. 253, note 351.

[2] This identification of the trail is partly inferential. It is the most direct route between Tinajas Altas and Tinaja de la Luna. Another route passes an excellent tank called Tule Well, which he probably would have mentioned had he gone that way.

of the morning star" they continued down the western skirt of Sierra Pinta, swung eastward across the brushy plain, and after thirteen leagues of what Kino called "very good roads"—a modern motorist would dissent—they arrived at ten o'clock at El Carrizal, on Sonóita River. There Kino said Mass, ate breakfast, and took a "very good siesta," which men and animals sorely needed. He had climbed a mountain and traveled some sixty or more miles in a little over a day. But the iron man was soon on his way again. In the afternoon he continued eight leagues to Sonóita, where he found the relay which he had sent by way of Caborca to meet him. His word was law in that desert land.

Sonóita, from its relation to California, had taken on new importance to Kino. It would be a halfway station on the road to the Colorado. "This post and ranchería of San Marcelo is the best there is on this coast. It has fertile land, with irrigation ditches for good crops," all made by the natives, of course, "water which runs all the year, good pasture for cattle, and everything necessary for a good settlement, for it has very near at hand more than a thousand souls, and many more in its environs, while there is a notable lack of water on the rest of this coast, which extends fifty leagues south to La Concepción del Cabotca, fifty north to the Río Grande, fifty east to the valley of San Xavier del Baac, and fifty or more west to the confines of the Quíquimas and the mouth of the Río Colorado." In short, Sonóita was the very hub of the Pápago wheel. And Kino's estimate of distances was highly accurate.

One day was spent here to rest the horses, instruct and baptize Indians, count the cattle, and butcher. He called this "resting." Then, accompanied by the governor and other officials of the place, Kino swung into the homeward trail through Quitobac and Arivaipa. At Caborca he was edified by a most unusual welcome. Of the many natives who came forth more than a league to meet him, one greeted him with the words "Blessed and exalted be the Most Holy Sacrament of the altar and the immaculate conception of Most Holy Mary," which, says Kino, "among new people was a source of great pleasure and of some wonder to us." This Caborca Indian apparently had learned a good deal of the Spanish language as well as of the Catechism.

The rest of the way was over the familiar road through Tubutama. Here, to Kino's delight, "at the ringing of the bell they recited the prayers and the Christian doctrine, as in the pueblos of Sonora." At San Ignacio they found Campos shaking with tertian ague, that scourge of American frontiers. Passing through Imuris and Remedios, they reached Dolores on October 20th, "having traveled in going and returning three hundred and eighty-four leagues in twenty-six days, without our pack animals becoming weary and without any mishap, which we attributed to the celestial favors of our Lord, having happily caught sight of California and the passage to it by land, having solemnized forty-two baptisms, and discovered four other new nations and the great Río Colorado, or Río del Norte.[1] And we reported this news to the lovers of new conversions, as previously they had asked me to do."

CXVII

AND WE REPORTED THIS NEWS

Of course Kino reported the news. He was bursting with it. He had confirmed his geographical opinion. The Gulf was landlocked. Now he could realize his dream of California. His friends responded generously.

"I am greatly rejoiced," wrote Leal, "over the return of your Reverence from your journey, about which the father rector Juan María de Salvatierra had written me to ask your Reverence, because of the importance of its being mainland. Very good news also is that of the Río Colorado and of the other nations. But the laborers are few— *Operarii autem pauci.* That is the pity of it, for God now offers so rich a harvest in so great a field.[2] May He recompense your Reverence for such toil in discovering so many sheep, redeemed by the blood of Christ, but separated from His fold." Gilg, now rector in place of Mora, was equally pleased. "A hearty welcome to your Reverence

---

[1] Kino, *Favores Celestiales*, Parte II, Lib. i, Caps. 10–11; *Hist. Mem.*, I, 253–258.
[2] Kino, *Favores Celestiales*, Parte II, Lib. i, Cap. 12; *Hist. Mem.*, I, 259.

from your long apostolic excursion. It is now well established that the Sea of California does not reach to thirty-four degrees of latitude."

To Kappus, now rector of the College of Mátape, Kino sent some of the blue shells which he had obtained on the Gila. Kappus replied, "I esteem the blue shells above my eyes, especially the large one, which is truly a rare piece. May your Reverence live a thousand years. Yesterday Father . . . Salvatierra sent me four shells from the opposite coast,[1] and these are neither more nor less than of the same sort and source." General Jironza thanked Father Eusebio in the name of the king. "Certainly delightful news," wrote General La Fuente. And so Kino had everybody committed to the Blue Shells Theory.

Most concerned of all, and with best reason, was Salvatierra. Ten days after Kino returned to Dolores he received from Father Juan a letter written at Loreto in August, shortly before Kino started on his last journey. It therefore reflects Salvatierra's reaction to what Kino had previously done. "We have rejoiced to know the almost certainty that this land is a part of the continent and joins New Spain; the only thing lacking is to know in what latitude this Gulf ends. And we are all hoping your Reverence will write us after the rains, for next year, if they succor us, it will not be difficult to compass the hundred leagues, even though they may be a hundred and fifty, so as to meet. We are in great want, what with having had no supplies from Mexico in fourteen months. . . . But God's will be done, for I hope the gates of Hell will not prevail against the great little house of Loreto. . . . Accept, your Reverence, warm greetings from Father Francisco María Picolo, and from all the people of this Loreto, who have rejoiced in the hopes of the continental connection and who anxiously await the last news."

This letter reached Kino just as he was writing "the last news." He now told Salvatierra approximately where the Gulf ended.[2] In reply to this communication Father Juan joined him in the next expedition.

[1] That is, they had arrived the previous day.
[2] At this time Kino made a "little map" to illustrate his conclusions.

Kino and Salvatierra Join Hands

CXVIII

CATTLE FOR CALIFORNIA

FATHER EUSEBIO FULFILLED HIS PROMISE to send cattle and supplies to California. Indeed, without them Father Juan's neophytes would have suffered. Early in 1700, before Kino made his two great expeditions of that year, Salvatierra had crossed over to Sinaloa to attend to the careening and loading of the *San Firmín,* the ship which carried supplies from the mainland to Loreto. At that time arose the question of the gift of cattle which the Sonora missions were to contribute to poor California. From San Felipe Salvatierra wrote to Father Eusebio a letter which illustrates the close relations of these two men and the importance of Kino's thrift.[1]

"On Wednesday I shall take the road for Onabas, and if I am not prevented by ill health, or by some sudden call from . . . California, I shall go on to Mátape. . . . And because of the hope of happily seeing your Reverence there, I do not answer the points of your letter, so loving, which have caused my heart to swell. I have just received a letter from the father rector of Mátape in which he informs me that he has already received the ten loads of provisions which your Reverence sends for the missions of Loreto . . . , for which I thank your Reverence, and which I esteem above my eyes. And I thank you for the three hundred beeves which you offer for California."

But Salvatierra was forced to change his plans, and did not get to see Kino. "I thought to be able to reach Mátape, but the heat of the sun, the development of an eye trouble by the natives, the sudden return of the launch to California, and the necessity of my presence on the other side, because the people are alone, . . . has forced me to return from here. I greatly regret the ill fortune of not having been

[1] May 9, after Kino returned from founding San Xavier del Bac.

445

able to see your Reverence." So Salvatierra expressed his gratitude—and California's need. "In regard to the three hundred beeves which your Reverence wishes to give to California, I fear they will occasion want or damage in the missions of the Pimas, for, as I have heard, your Reverence is asking for new fathers to place in the Pimería. And so, for the present, let me say that your Reverence may keep one hundred for Pima Land, but the two hundred I need immediately for California, delivered at the port of Hyaqui, which the father provincial has assigned to me for cattle, and which is near Loreto Conchó, of California, a Christendom in which we have set foot, which is already established, and which is being fostered, conserved, and advanced. It has cost sweat, and blood, and great treasure, but through the patronage of Most Holy Mary the gospel is being spread from sea to sea, the villages intervening being now subdued from coast to coast." [1]

The appeal wrung Kino's heart and served as a challenge. Californians were hungry, those people among whom he worked with Atondo. He would feed them. So, in spite of the summer heat and of other occupations, he at once set about driving to Yaqui, by way of Mátape and Tecoripa, the two hundred head of cattle which he contributed in the name of Dolores. In June he personally accompanied them as far as Tuape. His trusty Pima vaqueros drove them the rest of the way.

His generosity did not end here. In October the urgency of branding and the plan to send more cattle to California had been among the reasons for hurrying home from Yuma. In November, after his return, the other missions offered goodly numbers of cattle for Salvatierra. Kino attended to assembling and sending them. For this purpose he went in person to Mátape "a fifty leagues' journey, to send them to the new ranch of Hyaqui, so that from that ranch the fathers of California might obtain the meat, tallow, and lard which might be needed, sending cattle alive to California also, as they might be needed and as occasion might demand."

Other Sonora missions besides Dolores were generous in their gifts

---

[1] Kino, *Favores Celestiales*, Parte II, Lib. i, Caps. 13–14; *Hist. Mem.*, I, 261–263. Salvatierra and Picolo had indeed been making great progress in California during these first years.

of cattle. "The district of Oposura gave one hundred, and a thousand head of sheep and goats, which were bought in Hyaqui in exchange for cattle. The district of Ures gave ten beeves more, and the district of Cucurpe one hundred; the district of Mátape gave sixty beeves besides some horses; the district of Guépaca seventy, the district of Arispe fifty, and other missions other numbers." And thus the mainland succored the starveling infant California. In this work of charity Kino took the lead.[1]

CXIX

FATHER JUAN GOES TO DOLORES

Salvatierra was as enthusiastic as Kino over the land route to California. To him it was a practical matter, a question of food for his neophytes and the direst necessities for his associates in that barren land. Kino loved the trail for the trail's sake, and he had ambitions as an explorer and map maker, as well as to spread the Faith. Salvatierra needed supplies for his California missions. Gulf transportation was slow, expensive, uncertain, and even perilous. The transport *San Firmín* had recently been wrecked. To ship twenty cattle across the Gulf had cost him $6000, or $300 a head. He estimated, optimistically, that 6000 cattle could be driven around the Gulf by land, granting the peninsular theory, for $600, or ten cents a head. No wonder Father Juan was more than anxious to verify Kino's discoveries. In fact, he would be glad to help.

Kino's report, made after his return from Yuma, increased Salvatierra's enthusiasm, and a joint expedition on the mainland to the head of the Gulf resulted. Kino was glad to get the testimony of another eyewitness, and the support of so important a man for his explorations. Late in December Salvatierra crossed the Gulf "with firm and well-founded hopes of returning by land in latitude thirty-one or thirty-two degrees" to his mission of Loreto Conchó. "I was spurred to this journey," he testifies, "by seeing the great expense, impossible

[1] Kino, *Favores Celestiales*, Parte II, Lib. i, Cap. 14; *Hist. Mem.*, I, 263–264.

to bear, of maintaining forever a large vessel for the transportation of cattle, and the present lack of vessels through the loss of the *San Firmín* and the bad condition of the frigate *San José*."

Salvatierra had other business on the mainland. He went first by ship to Sinaloa to arrange for a new cargo of provisions, then by land, early in January, 1701, to Sonora, to found a mission at Guaymas, for this post had been assigned to the California Jesuits in order that they might have a good mainland harbor and a supply base, at the same time that they spread the Faith among the Guaymas natives.[1] The mission project was impeded for the moment by floods. So, leaving affairs at Guaymas for a later time, Father Juan continued north, accompanied by a band of California neophytes, to join Father Eusebio and arrange for the expedition. As he journeyed he wrote Kino numerous letters on the subject of supplies—flour, biscuits, cattle, and pack animals—the sinews of exploration.[2]

In Mátape Salvatierra found every encouragement for making the journey, and new indications of land connection between California and the main. Kappus, rector of the college, showed him the three "God bless me" shells which Kino had sent him, "together with some skeins of thread and some black balls, very round and made of materials unknown to them." Salvatierra was delighted, for he recognized the shells. They were the same as those found on the Contra Costa and nowhere else. The natives there used them as cups for drinking. Salvatierra's California Indians were interested in the fiber of the skeins or belts, recognizing it as the same as that used by the women of the natives to the north of Loreto. They also recognized the material of which the black balls were made. These sons of California gave still another clue. They told of knives that used to come as trophies from the north with a progressive dance called the *Mico*. That is to say, the northern people carried knives

---

[1] In the development of California, Guaymas would now take the place which Yaqui had so long occupied.

[2] The above is Kino's version of the genesis of the expedition. He makes it appear that Salvatierra came to the mainland for the express purpose of exploring the road to California. Salvatierra, in his report to the provincial, gives the impression that the exploration was impromptu, and that it was suggested by the Mátape fathers after the Guaymas project had been set aside. But I think this due merely to his modest way of telling his part in arranging the plan (Salvatierra to the provincial, after May, 1701. *Doc. Hist. Mex.*, Cuarta Série, V, 105–156; Kino, *Favores Celestiales*, Parte II, Lib. ii, Cap. 1; *Hist. Mem.*, I, 266–267).

to their near neighbors on the south, and danced with them. The village receiving the trophy in turn passed it south, and so it went clear to Cape San Lucas. This is a precious ethnological item. Salvatierra conjectured that the knives must have come from New Mexico, hence there must be continuous lands between that province and Lower California.[1]

Another tale heard at Mátape strengthened Father Juan's belief in the land route. Indians of Magdalena and San Ignacio, Campos's people, reported that years previously other Indians had brought them for barter some clothing which had been cast up on the beach by the sea. "This story did not fail to arrest my attention," says Salvatierra, "and, considering that within the strait [Gulf] no bark had been lost, I surmised that this could not have been on the beach of the strait, but on the beach of the other sea . . . commonly called the Western Sea, . . . and that it might be the lost Philippine ship called the *Santo Cristo de Burgos;* and that if this were true, it was a sign that the strait was closed completely, and that there was no other sea than the great Sea of the South by whose shores this clothing would come, passing from hand to hand to the Pimas of Magdalena."

Not everybody was an optimist. "One person tried to upset it all with unfounded arguments," charging that the expedition was planned to find favor with the king, "since it would fall right in with one of his own ambitions. . . . Be that as it may," said Salvatierra, "I note it down merely to show how astute Satan is at interfering with everything."[2] The enthusiasts prevailed, the old missions were generous with supplies and servants, and Salvatierra continued north. At San Juan he obtained a military escort of a dozen soldiers and citizen volunteers, led by Nicolás Bohórques. Manje joined the expedition as diarist. Father Bartíromo, missionary at Tuape, in keeping with his generous practice, contributed liberally of provisions and

---

[1] Salvatierra to the provincial, *loc. cit.* Salvatierra's interest in the shells, the ball, and the fabric is reflected in the letter which Kappus wrote to Kino at this time: "Very greatly has the father rector Juan de Salvatierra rejoiced to see the blue shells, in particular the large one with which your Reverence favored me, and the two balls and the belt ("texido de la faxa"); and his Reverence no longer doubts that this land has connection with that of California" (Kino, *Hist. Mem.,* I, 271–272).

[2] Put in more modern phrase, "somebody is always taking the joy out of life."

pack animals. But the bulk of the outfit was provided, of course, by thrifty Kino.

Plans were momentarily upset by an Apache raid on Saracachi, right on Salvatierra's path—such were the hazards of travel even in the old settlements. The marauders killed six persons, wounded seven, sacked houses, "carried off horses and mares, we know not how many, and all the sheep and goats." Manje sallied forth to the defense. Escalante defeated the enemy and recovered some of the horses. For this victory Salvatierra congratulated Kino, saying it was a direct reward for his generosity in preparing for the expedition. California's patroness had smiled upon him. "Because your Reverence was occupied in giving mules and horses in honor of the Madonna of Loreto, and succor for her California mission, the Lady has looked upon her benefactor. Viva Jesús! Viva María! . . . Tomorrow or the day after I go on to Cucurpe."

On February 21 Salvatierra and Manje reached Dolores. There were hearty embraces, for Salvatierra and Kino had not met since they were together in Mexico, five years before. "Many salutes were fired," says Father Juan, "everybody rejoicing, especially Father . . . Kino and all the Pima Indians, who immediately recognized me." Of course the Pimas recognized him. He had a face which nobody forgot.[1] Before sunset this day messengers came from Cucurpe saying that the Apaches were again threatening. Immediately Manje and most of the soldiers, swearing as they went, rode south to give aid.

CXX

SINGING ON THE TRAIL

From Dolores to Caborca Kino and Salvatierra went by different routes. Father Juan set out westward with his California Indians and the pack train, escorted by only two soldiers, for the rest had gone with Manje to the relief of Saracachi. Salvatierra carried a picture of Our Lady of Loreto, a vara long and two-thirds of a vara

---

[1] Kino, *Favores Celestiales*, Parte II, Lib. ii, Caps. 2–3; *Hist. Mem.*, I, 268–270; Salvatierra to the provincial, *loc. cit.*

wide, painted by the famous artist, Juan Correa.[1] Crossing the Sierra to San Ignacio he was welcomed by Campos, "great master of the languages of all this nation." Father Agustín had come to the Pimería while still young enough to learn a new tongue. Two days were spent here waiting for Manje, and Salvatierra improved the time testing the story of the clothing cast up by the sea—the tale he had heard at Mátape. Campos furnished for the expedition additional supplies, and when they set forth again they had twenty mule loads of provisions and one hundred and fifty saddle and pack animals. It was an impressive train.

Manje arrived and they proceeded to Tubutama. From there Salvatierra slowly descended the Altar River, making friends with the Indians, preaching, and baptizing. All down the valley he found the natives suffering from an epidemic of pitiflor. At Caborca he waited three days for Kino, lodging in the house which Saeta had built. To assemble the people for Christian teaching he went about ringing a little bell and distributing presents.[2] Attendance at instruction was greatly increased by the death of a woman who had died while hiding from him. Father Juan drew a moral from the case and now the natives flocked to hear his talks, bringing their children for baptism.

Meanwhile Kino arrived. A week behind Salvatierra he had left Dolores with ten servants. On the way he stopped to fortify the missions of Remedios and Cocóspora with towers, for the Apaches were still on a rampage. Going thence by way of Síboda and Sáric, he descended the Altar Valley, gathering additional supplies and baptizing children. At Caborca he was welcomed at the door of the church by Salvatierra, the soldiers, and "more than four hundred Indians placed in a line, very much as in old Christian pueblos."[3] This form of reception of the Black Robes at the villages had become an established institution throughout the Pacific Coast.

---

[1] It will be remembered that Kino brought to Pima Land one or more pictures painted by this noted artist.

[2] Caborca as yet had no resident missionary, but Manje tells us that Father Barillas, who was old, visited it from time to time. Manje, *Luz de Tierra Incógnita*, 284; Manje, Relación Ytineraria, 1701. MS.

[3] Salvatierra to the provincial, *loc. cit.;* Manje, *Luz de Tierra Incógnita*, 446; Manje, Relación Ytineraria, 1701. MS.; Kino, *Favores Celestiales*, Parte II, Lib. ii, Cap. 6; *Hist. Mem.*, I, 278–279.

The first stage of the journey had been compassed. The next one was the long stretch of more than a hundred miles from Caborca to Sonóita. The road lay over dry and sometimes stony plains, half of the way being grown with cactus. Kino and Manje had been over it several times, but to Salvatierra and his Californians the trail was new. To escort the expedition over this difficult terrain, four Indians came from San Rafael. The Master of Dolores had but to beckon and all Pima Land responded. On March 9 in the afternoon the pack train set forth carrying forty loads of provisions and divided into sections because of the scarcity of water on the way. Early next morning the rest of the caravan started. That night they camped at Arivaipa, where the poor animals drank scantily from pools and pozos. Next day the whole party, united, set out for Quitobac. As they traveled, whenever Mass was said Our Lady occupied a place on the portable altar. Kino and Salvatierra shared honors, one caring for the painting in the forenoon, and the other in the afternoon.

This was the most glorious time of the year, and Kino was jubilant. "Various parts of this road," he says, "were made so pleasant and beautiful by roses and flowers of different colors, that it seemed as if nature had placed them there to welcome Our Lady of Loreto." Never before nor since, I venture, has so learned a band of pilgrims traveled that desert trail, and I do not except a party known to me which included two college boys, a university professor, and a dean. "Almost all day," Kino writes, "we were saying and chanting various prayers and praises of Our Lady in different languages—in Castilian, in Latin, in Italian"—both Kino and Salvatierra were from Italy—"and also in the Californian tongue; for the six natives of California, four large and two small, were so well indoctrinated and instructed in everything that they sang the prayers, which the father rector had already arranged for them in pretty couplets, in this Californian language. And we said with the Holy Psalmist, 'Thy justifications were the subject of my song in the place of my pilgrimage.'[1]—*Cantabiles mihi erant justificaciones tuae in loco peregrinacionis meae.'*"

This is one side of the picture. The missionaries and the Cali-

---

[1] Kino, *Favores Celestiales*, Parte II, Lib. ii, Cap. 6; Manje, *Luz de Tierra Incógnita*, 285; Manje, Relación Ytineraria, 1701. MS.; Salvatierra to the provincial, *loc. cit.*

fornia neophytes might sing their way through the flower-strewn plain, but it was a tough pull for the pack animals. Traveling all day with great hardship over the desert, they failed to reach Quitobac, and when they camped at Texubabia at ten o'clock at night, the natives concealed the watering place. "This day," says Manje, "was one of the greatest travail, anguish, and affliction, for now the animals played out on us for the great lack of water." In the night nine or ten animals fled, crazed with thirst.

Next morning Salvatierra by a trick discovered the aguaje. The natives brought a little water for the men, but said the spring was far, far away. He would see. "And so I secretly gave an Indian a handsome present, telling him to bring me a little water, and that if he brought it quickly I would give him the rest of the glass beads which I had in my hands. The Indian went, not seeing through my ruse, and I noted carefully that in going and coming he spent only about three quarters of an hour." The secret was out. The hidden water was not so far away after all. Salvatierra ordered his mule saddled and the mayordomo to follow with a large kettle. The spring, called Suaracán, was soon found, and there was plentiful water. It was on a hillside, only half a league from camp. All the animals were now taken to the spring and Kino celebrated a Mass of thanksgiving.

Quitobac, reached next morning, was an oasis in the desert, and here the expedition rested for a day. The animals fed on the good pasturage round about, and drank from the six plentiful springs which then as now formed a pretty lake. Salvatierra preached to the Spaniards in Castilian and to the Pimas in their own tongue, "which he had learned many years before." This must have been when he was in the Chínipas mission. He was a picturesque figure, and the natives watched him with interest. "He went in person to the wood near by and cut with an ax a large tree with which we set up a holy cross, the natives aiding." The cross was explained to the Indians, "who in imitation of the Christians all knelt down at the time when it was elevated."[1] In the folk lore of Quitobac hawk-nosed Salvatierra will not be forgotten.

This was a pleasant place in which to loiter, but the travelers had

[1] Kino, *Favores Celestiales*, Parte II, Lib. ii, Cap. 6; Manje, *Luz de Tierra Incógnita*, 285; Manje, Relación Ytineraria, 1701. MS.; Salvatierra to the provincial, *loc. cit.*

to move forward. On the 14th they reached Sonóita, where they were given a pious welcome by the natives, "for in all this they had been instructed by Father Kino."

CXXI

BEYOND SANTA CLARA

The significant part of the journey was now before them. Thus far they had been merely getting to the scene of their geographical problem. They now faced it. From Sonóita they sent for natives from the coast to serve as guides. As interpreter they took from Sonóita a half-witted topil who knew both Pima and Quíquima. Advancing to El Carrizal, they waited here a day for the guides, and sent a messenger to the Quíquimas announcing their coming. While in camp a debate was held as to which road to take around Pinacate Mountain. Kino on a previous journey had swung south of it, ascended it from the west, and looked into the yawning crater of the ancient volcano. Manje favored continuing to the Yumas over the Camino del Diablo. Salvatierra proposed a route past the north side of the mountain, but the Indians objected. They also vetoed a proposal to descend Sonóita River to the coast. Salvatierra, convinced that the Indians were lying about the difficulties of the journey, by means of presents obtained a more favorable opinion. Discussion ended when the guides came from the coast reporting that the Quíquimas were anxiously awaiting the visitors and that the road was passable. It was now decided to swing around the south end of Pinacate Mountain, as Kino had done.[1]

On the 18th the expedition went forward to undertake one of the hardest explorations in all North American history. Having traveled ten leagues down Sonóita River over a stony plain, they halted at a poverty-stricken village of two hundred souls with water so scant that both fathers had to lend a hand digging wells in the sand.[2]

---

[1] Kino, *Favores Celestiales*, Parte II, Lib. ii, Cap. 7; *Hist. Mem.*, I, 281; Salvatierra to the provincial, after May, 1701, *loc. cit.*; Manje, *Luz de Tierra Incógnita*; Manje, Relación Ytineraria, 1701.
[2] Salvatierra calls this place Totonat; Kino calls it Sucoybutobabia.

Near by they found in a cave an old woman who was "the very picture of senility." She was "so decrepit," says Salvatierra, "that she was all skin and bones, and everybody declared that she must be more than a hundred years old." Kino guessed her age at a hundred and twenty years; Manje put her at a hundred and thirty. "It was now found that the halt in a bad place was not an error of the half-witted Indian, but a merciful disposition of the hand of God, for the old woman, being catechized, signified a desire to be baptized, and she received the water of holy baptism, being called Mary, since through Mary the great happiness came to her." Three days later she died. This, said Manje, "appears to be a sign of predestination, the route having been changed in order that we might come here and win such a trophy."

Every day's march now was memorable. Everyone was strenuous, almost beyond endurance. In years to come everybody in the party had a tale to tell. On the 19th, led by the half-wit guide, the explorers traveled southwest five leagues through level, ash-covered malpais and sand to a village and a great tank called El Basoitutcan.[1] Here the horses drank their first water in forty-eight hours. The spot was south of the Cerro de Santa Clara and on its skirts. The villagers were naked and poor, living on roots, locusts, some sea food, and lizards which the travelers called Iguanas. They were probably chuck-wallas. At first, in spite of coaxing, the natives revealed only one tank, which was so scanty that scarcely a fourth of the animals could drink. "And since they had now been two days without water, it seemed necessary to turn back lest they should perish."

But they did not turn back. Salvatierra was again resourceful. Perhaps the Indians were lying again. "And so, the men being so fatigued, while they were resting I set out with a soldier called Tomás García, as if we were going out for a walk, and the soldier came upon a tank so abundant that four hundred animals all at once might drink at it for a long time." Hurrying back to tell the men at the camp,

---

[1] Manje calls it Basotutcan; Salvatierra writes Ayodsudao. All three names are phonetically similar. At the village there were cañadas thickly strewn with rocks "which from time to time form wells of stone, like natural aljibes." Salvatierra tells us that Ayodsudao lay "at the foot of the Serro de Santa Clara, which was now to the east." Manje says it was south of Santa Clara, and on its skirts. That is to say, it was near the southwestern base of the mountain.

he found that they too had discovered a tank. Here it was Kino's diplomacy that won. Two old Indians loaded with salt had passed by on the way to Sonóita. When asked about a water hole, they said they did not know of any, "but being presented by Father Kino with a cowhide and promised others if they showed us the aguaje, they were moved to point out another water hole. This incident was a matter of joy to everybody, seeing that we were favored by the holy spouse of María with two water holes." It was the Feast of San José. "For this reason we called the place San José de Ramos."

Next day was Palm Sunday, and palms were blessed in spite of the desolate surroundings and the task ahead. Then the explorers plunged forward. Guided now by the salt merchants, they continued westward along the skirts of the volcano, over malpais, brambly crags, and lava beds. The horses were crucified at every step, and the country presented a scene of incomparable desolation. As they ascended a grade along the foot of Cerro de Santa Clara, they saw "a horrible country, which looked more like ashes than earth, all peppered with boulders and . . . entirely black, all of which formed figures, because the lava which flows down solidifies, stops, and assumes shapes. And so in ancient times a horrible volcano must have issued from the Cerro de Santa Clara, . . . Indeed I do not know that there can be any place which better represents the condition of the world in the general conflagration." This is Salvatierra speaking, not Kino. After traveling six leagues, leaving Cerro de Santa Clara behind, they halted at El Tupo, a tank of rainwater in an arroyo filled with boulders and lava. Kino ascended a near-by hill and "descried California very plainly, to the west and southwest."

Monday the 21st dawned. Great sand dunes lay ahead. Fearing that the pack animals could not get through this "ashy cordillera," and not being sure of water, the pack train was left at El Tupo, with a few soldiers and muleteers to guard it. The main body set forth, traveling light, to cross the billows of sand. Not all, however, for some poor fellows, afraid they would die of thirst on the trail, hid and were left behind. Do not judge them too harshly till you yourself have faced those sand dunes.

The start was made at daylight. Nearly all day they crawled over sandy wastes and playas without pasturage. Part of the way was across huge dunes heaped up like mountains, into which the horses sank halfway to the knees. At the end of eight leagues—which to some seemed a thousand—they camped near the shore at three springs called by the natives Cuboquasivavia, and situated in an alkaline plain where there was some pasturage. There was an estuary near by. The three springs figure in the diaries as Tres Ojitos. They were so abundant that Kino sent back for the pack train and the caballada.[1]

Now came the climax of the day's experiences. "Since there was still some light," says Salvatierra, "without dismounting I went toward the sea as far as half a league from this place, where before sunset we distinctly and with great clarity saw California and the cordillera, and still more clearly after sunset, when it appeared to us that the sierra must be distant from us about ten or twelve leagues, and that the land on this side of the sierra must be even closer than that."

How about the blue shells? As was expected, there were none. To have found one would have been a sore disappointment. "We explored the beach, which has a good estuary," says Salvatierra, "but we did not find a trace either of blue shells or of mother of pearl shells, and the Indians said that the blue shells came from the other side, further on, and not from this sea." Kino noted with pleasure that in the north the mountains of the two sides of the Gulf curved toward each other, seeming to meet. But the evidence was not conclusive. A spur from the mainland range cut off the view and they could not see whether or not the arc was complete. It was therefore decided to ascend the coast ten leagues in an attempt to get an unobstructed view.

But this, unfortunately, did not prove feasible. Next day, when the pack train and the horses arrived, it was found that the springs were lower than the day before, with the result that only thirty or forty animals could drink. This disappointment was soon followed by another. While most of the men disported themselves on the beach, bathing and gathering shells to carry home, others were sent up the coast to examine a water hole reported by the Indians. Sad to say, it was found to be insufficient for all the animals.

---

[1] The distance to the beach is given by Kino as half a league and by Manje as two leagues. Manje says that the Tres Ojitos were in latitude 32° (Manje, *Luz de Tierra Incógnita,* 288; Manje, Relación Ytineraria, 1701).

"So the road that way was blocked," says Salvatierra, "and it was decided to turn back next day," in order that the horses and mules might not perish. They could not go ahead and they could not remain at Tres Ojitos. Retreat was imperative. One may say that part of the animals might have been sent back, the rest going forward to the aguaje up the coast. But we who were not present do not know all the circumstances.

Notwithstanding this set-back, Kino and Salvatierra were confirmed in their belief in the land passage. Not so Manje.[1] "We had a friendly argument," he said, "I alleging that in these matters one must record as certain what is certain and as doubtful what is doubtful." To clear up these doubts he proposed a bold plan. The guides said it was four days' journey to the Colorado. Let Salvatierra go back with the train. Kino, Manje, and two others would ride light, pass the playa in a day and a night, and reach the Colorado's mouth. From there they could answer the question at issue. But this plan was too risky and it was vetoed. So they hurried back lest the horses all perish and they with them. But first they took the latitude. Kino with the astrolabe "found that this Gulf of California ended in thirty-one degrees." This was a little too low. Where he stood it was near $31\frac{1}{2}°$. This, indeed, is the latitude reported by Manje in his diary.

Next day (the 23d) after Mass the caravan struggled back over the sand dunes to El Tupo, where they found the men who had fled through fear.[2] Arriving at sunset, they found so little water that they were obliged to continue on the back track to Basoitutcan, which they reached after midnight, leaving nine pack animals worn out on the way. At Basoitutcan the expedition halted a day to let the horses drink and feed, and to await the lagging pack animals. Here an interesting conference took place, and from it Salvatierra got new confirmation of his views. A party of strange Indians arrived, led by two caciques. "Sitting down according to the custom of the Californians who come from a long distance, they drank so many ollas of water that only a mule could equal them." They told of their relatives the Yumyums [Yumas] a day's journey distant, and of the Quíquimas a day beyond

---

[1] Manje, *Luz de Tierra Incógnita*, 288–289; Manje, Relación Ytineraria, 1701.
[2] The day's march was from fifteen to eighteen leagues.

the Yumyums. The Black Robes explained their errand, the guests were pleased, and sent a messenger to bring some friends to see them.

Next day a Yumyum arrived. "In every way, in his carriage, the expression of his eyes, and his entire body, he was like a Californian. I was especially pleased at hearing him speak, to see that now and then a word in his language was just like the language of the Cuchimí, a California nation which extends to the north of the site of Loreto Conchó we do not know how far." Salvatierra adds, "The ambassadors from Yumyum showed such affection that I risked losing a sheet of paper by writing a letter to Father Francisco María Picolo and entrusting it to the good fortune of reaching there." He lost.

The letter written, the conference over, "the sun being already high," the Yumyums departed and the Spaniards started east, traveling seventeen or eighteen leagues that day over their outward trail to El Carrizal. Here they halted, thirty-eight persons in all.[1]

CXXII

A FLANK MOVEMENT

Several days were spent at El Carrizal to recuperate the animals, await promised delegations of Indians from the west, and observe the Easter season. The pack animals were so worn out that the first of them arrived at El Carrizal two days behind the rest of the expedition. While camped here Kino took the latitude and made a sketch of "this extremity of California." A ramada was fashioned in which to celebrate Easter, the soldiers confessed, and Salvatierra preached a sermon. Men were sent to Sonóita with pack mules to get a supply of fresh beef.

Although the explorers remained in camp a day longer than the time agreed upon, the ambassadors did not come. The Jesuits got tired of waiting and decided that if the delegation did not arrive next day they would take a barrel of water, travel light northwestward fifteen or more leagues, climb a peak, and see where ended the half

---

[1] Manje, *Luz de Tierra Incógnita;* Manje, Relación Ytineraria, 1701; Salvatierra to the provincial, *loc. cit.;* Kino, *Favores Celestiales,* Parte II, Lib. ii, Cap. 7; *Hist. Mem.,* I, 281.

arch of the Cordillera of California which they saw on the Gulf shore but whose terminus was cut off from view by a spur of mountain. The Pimas tried to prevent the expedition, saying that the Quíquimas intended to kill them. But Indians finally came from the west and reported a good water hole one day's travel in that direction. So the journey was made.

Sending the rest of the caravan to Sonóita, on March 31 the party set forth northwest with six Pimas as guides, six loads of provisions, eighteen mules, and three horses, "traveling light, but carrying as a standard Our Lady the Madonna." Their route, which lay between Pinacate Mountain and the Camino del Diablo, was close to the present day stage road from Sonóita to San Luís. Kino records the journey. "Having marched a little more than thirteen leagues and leaving far behind the Cerro de Santa Clara, which was now to the south of us and hidden by other peaks, the Indians told us that we were near the camping place. Although the sun was about to set, and we were tired, in order to save distance we decided before going to the camp site to ascend a very high peak which is there to the west. It is very difficult and we went up rather on all fours than on foot, but in spite of this trouble we carried up the standard." Our Lady both guided and shared the honors of the scramble.

What they saw confirmed their former conclusion. "The sun set, and from the peak we saw with all clarity all the sea below, toward the south, and the place on the beach to which we had descended. We saw that the half arch of sierras of California whose end had been concealed from us by the spur of the mountains kept getting constantly closer together and joining with other hills and peaks of New Spain." Salvatierra was reminded of his native Italy. "The view from a distance is neither more nor less than that of the Tyrrhenian and Ligurian Sea, with the crown of mountains which enclose that strait joining the two shores of Genoa from the west and the east, with this difference, that this enclosure which we saw from the little peak, in the last angle at the west and all the north rose up not with mountains but with low hills, so that we descried clearly as many as three ranges of hills." A chief who ascended the peak with the Black Robes showed them where the Quíquimas lived, and explained that the blue shells came from the sea beyond the one lying in front of them. They saw that the mainland range ended in "these high white hills of sand and horrible sand dunes." From the mountain Kino clearly saw that the preceding October when he reached the Yuma junction he had gone far beyond the head of the Gulf. California was indeed a peninsula.

The fathers celebrated their achievement. "With this view of the strait we sang the Lauretanian Litanies to Our Lady as a sign of thanksgiving, and then we descended from the peak to the village called Pitaqui." Here there were three tanks of rainwater, a most essential feature of the situation.

Next day they proposed to go forward eight or ten leagues further, to climb another peak and get a clearer view. "But the Indians, instigated by the Pimas, boldly refused to go toward that sierra more than one day's journey," the one already covered, "alleging that the Yumyums were ill, scattered and hungry. We tried to remove all difficulties, especially that of hunger, which for them was real, saying that we would give them much flour, for we still had plenty. . . . But even this . . . did not avail, and they flatly refused to let us go forward." Guides were indispensable. So the explorers reluctantly turned back.

"Nevertheless," Salvatierra adds, "I felt sufficiently satisfied, with what I had seen with my own eyes, and with the reports drawn from the Indians near the closing of the strait, . . . that we would be able to advance further in order in a few years to succeed in opening communication by land between New Spain and California and these missions of the great Lady of Loreto."

Then and there Kino and Salvatierra agreed to come again in October, the best time for the water holes, "to journey far beyond until we should leave the sea entirely to the south, make a turn and leave it to the east, as we have it in California. While we were in this place the sun set on the peak from which was seen the closing, and it was found that we were in $31\frac{1}{2}°$." They were above that latitude. "Since we saw the closing to the north of us, we concluded that it must be as high as $33°$ at least. Since the conquest in California Lauretania and the known lands extends beyond $27°$, we hope that within a few years there will be communication between these two kingdoms of California and New Spain. Thus our King Don Felipe may achieve what all his predecessors were not able to accomplish, although they made the attempt. And his royal Majesty will owe this new kingdom to the patronage of the Lady of Loreto. And although during these first years he may spend treasure from his chest, in the name of her Son, in His good time Our Lady will know how to repay a hundredfold."

Returning now to Sonóita, they found many letters. It is a marvel how well the mail service worked. On April 3 Salvatierra with the ten soldiers started home by way of Caborca; Kino returned through the Papaguería and Bac. Before they separated Kino piously gambled once more. The disputed prize was the banner. The question arose, says Kino, "as to whether the father rector or I should carry the beloved picture of Our Lady of Loreto, and although I should have been content to have the father rector carry that great consolation with him, his Reverence decided that we should draw lots by writing on two little papers 'north' and 'south'; and since on drawing them the one for the north fell to me, to me fell the joy of carrying this great Lady of Loreto in the north of this Pimería of the Sobaípuris, she being our North Star." Kino remained at Sonóita several days building a church, and receiving delegations of Indians from the Río Colorado, with more blue shells. On April 6 he set out east through Pápago Land to Bac, and nine days later reached Dolores.[1]

Just the day before this (April 14) Salvatierra wrote Kino from Cucurpe, thanking him for his help. In another letter he asked Kino for a different kind of assistance—a good consignment of flour, tallow, and suet, shipped in skins. A few days later he was at Guaymas, where he founded the mission of San José de la Laguna, leaving Father Manuel Díaz in charge. The place, now called San José de Guaymas, is a short distance north of the city of the same name. Salvatierra found the transport *San José* awaiting him, embarked on the 9th of May, and was soon at Loreto. He had performed two major services for California: he had assisted in exploring the land route,

---

[1] Kino returned through Merced, San Serafín del Actúm and El Tupo to Bac. On the way they obtained red guacamaya feathers (Manje, *Relación Ytineraria*, 1701).

and he had founded Guaymas as a California base. While doing so he had enjoyed a great outing with the zealous optimist of Pima Land.

CXXIII

AWAY WITH BRITISH TEMERITY!

Kino received many congratulations for the new exploration. Ruíz, the alcalde mayor, wrote "I have been told that the journey . . . has been one of great satisfaction and pleasure, because the purpose in mind, of discovering a land route to California, has been accomplished. This news has been a source of very great pleasure to me; and therefore I shall appreciate it if your Reverence will inform me if it is true."

Salvatierra affectionately wrote from California, "Your Reverence has a thousand benedictions from all the fathers and seculars for your journey and for the discovery, from the peak, at a distance, of the joining of New California and New Spain." The implication was generous. "And much greater has been the rejoicing to know that your Reverence has the means and the desire to examine close at hand that which a distant vision might misrepresent." He alluded to their plans for another expedition.

Picolo wrote, "I give your Reverence a thousand congratulations for your discovery. May our Lord grant us the boon of seeing California carry on trade with New Spain by land for the relief of these missions and the salvation of so many souls." Leal, the visitor, was enthusiastic. "I have rejoiced greatly that your Reverence has now returned from your journey, which has been made with hopes so well founded as to constitute certainty of the continuity by land." Father Marcos Loyola, rector at Mátape, gave a word of praise: "The father visitor has just informed me . . . that you have succeeded in finding the way to California. I do not know how to tell your Reverence how much I have rejoiced on this account. . . . The great success of the journey is due to you." Of course this letter was not for Salvatierra's eyes.

Polici, "great encourager and promoter of the new conversions," wrote a letter of like tenor. Said Jironza, "I am still waiting for the blue shells which came from California by a continental route, discovered by the good endeavors of your Reverence, who are worthy of receiving repeated thanks from the superiors for undertakings so heroic." Father Wenceslaus Eymer, visitor of the Tarahumara, made short work of Queen Elizabeth's great admiral. "Away now with British temerity, with her English Drake, and let him keep silent who boasts that he has circumnavigated California, as if, by a foolish fiction, California were the Atlantis of the West."

While others applauded, Kino drew a map which made him famous. He called it the "Land Passage to California and its neighboring New Nations and New Missions of the Company of Jesus in North America. 1701." It exhibited the results of all of his explorations since his map made in 1696, but it was designed especially to show that California was a peninsula. In detail the map is surprisingly good, the latitudes and the configuration of the head of the Gulf, the Gila and the Colorado River being essentially correct. A copy of the map was sent to Father Kappus, at Mátape, who in turn sent it to a friend in Austria (June 8, 1701). Kappus, to whom Salvatierra had talked enthusiastically on his way back to California, was fully converted to the peninsular theory. "When in the future students of geography publish maps and indicate the tracks of early explorers, they will represent California not as an island—unless they choose to be inaccurate—but as a peninsula. That this information may be the more intelligible to persons interested in the subject, of whom there are many in Austria, I include a small map which was sent to me by the reverend Father Eusebio Francisco Kino for that purpose." [1] The map was printed in Europe and became the standard for many decades.

[1] Kino, *Favores Celestiales,* Parte II, Lib. ii, Caps. 10–11; *Hist. Mem.,* I, 293–302; Kappus to a friend in Austria, Mátape, June 8, 1701. In *Nova Litteraria Germaniae Aliorumque Europae Regnorum Anni MDCCVII. Collecta Hamburgi Lipsiae et Francofurti Apud Christianum Liebezeit.*

California No Es Isla

ACROSS THE COLORADO IN A BASKET

S ALVATIERRA AND KINO HAD AGREED, when on the last day in March they stood on the peak at Pitaqui, to go in October to put to practical test their certainty now that California was an island. Kino would ascend the east and Salvatierra the west side of the Gulf. At its head they would meet. Jironza offered to furnish Kino with a soldier escort, and Manje intended to join the expedition. Jironza had a double object. He hoped not only to settle the California question for good and all, but also to find the place from which the Indians obtained the elusive red substance which Kino and Manje had seen in the hands of the Indians on the Gila in 1697, and determine whether or not it was indeed quicksilver, that metal so important in mining.

There were changes in the plans for various reasons. Salvatierra was unable to join the expedition, for which he felt sincere regret. On September 10 he wrote Kino from Loreto, expressing his disappointment. Alluding to Drake, he perpetrated a pun. "God grant your Reverence all the strength which I wish you, and that with the patronage of the Madonna you may trample under foot the lion and the dragon—*Conculcabit Leonem et Draconem.*" Let us hope that punning was then considered good form. "We cannot go from here to meet your Reverence because we are without the necessary mounts, through lack of a suitable bark" with which to transport them from the mainland.

The soldiers promised by Jironza were not sent, because just before starting time a change was made in the military hierarchy, General Fuensaldaña becoming commander of the Flying Company in place of Jironza. There was bad blood between the two, and a new administration, of course, must have a "new policy." So the soldiers were not provided. Manje could not go because he was called out to punish some native witch doctors "who with malevolent and diabolical machinations were killing people." Certainly these frontier officials did not lack exercise.

Kino himself was delayed several days. This gave him time to get Salvatierra's letter with the disappointing news (October 18). On that very day he wrote to Father Thirso González telling of his hopes and his dreams. His letter is a good summary of his own understanding of the geographical problem and of his plans. He might go even to the Pacific Ocean. "Three years ago I discovered the terminus of the California Sea, although with some obscurity. Two years ago I discovered more clearly that passage by land to California. One year ago I saw it very distinctly, and on the Feast of San Dionisio, the 9th of October, I said Mass at the junction of the two very large rivers . . . and 1550 persons came to see me in that place, which I named San Dionisio (enclosed is a little map). I informed the reverend Father Juan María Salvatierra, and his Reverence came in March of this year and saw it with his own eyes. At present I am equipping myself to enter, with divine favor, this October and November, very far into California, until I get sight of or until I reach the very South Sea . . . and in order to go as far as possible . . . toward the mission of Loreto Conchó, where lives the reverend Father Salvatierra." [1] In the next paragraph he begged of González permission to found missions on the Colorado at the land passage in 32°, in order "to lend a hand" to sterile California. "And I should be very much pleased if for this purpose distinguished fathers might come from Europe." Pima Land could equip them.

Undaunted by the bad news from Salvatierra and Manje, Kino set forth on November 3 with only one companion besides his Indian servants—proof of his confidence in himself and in the natives among whom he traveled. He again took a partially new route, impossible as that might seem, since he had already made so many tracks across the map. Going north through Cocóspora to Guébavi, he swung south over the Nogales divide to Síboda, thence west through Búsanic, and

---

[1] Kino, *Favores Celestiales*, Parte II, Lib. iii, Cap. 1; *Hist. Mem.*, I, 306; Manje, *Luz de Tierra Incógnita*, 293; Kino to González, October 18, 1701.

across the Papaguería. With him he took a drove of mares for the ranch at Sonóita; cattle he already had there. On the way across the desert the Indians tried to frighten him out by telling him there was no water ahead. But Kino's diplomacy prevailed. "A good Indian stranger," he says, "whom we made a fiscal and gave some little presents, said he would take us to a good water hole, although we should arrive at nightfall or a little after, as we did arrive in the moonlight." The water hole had plentiful and good rainwater for man and beast. It was hard to bluff Kino out.

Father Eusebio's route this time took him through Ootcam, Anamic, Santa Sabina, and San Martín. At Sonóita he received friendly messages from Yumas and Quíquimas, and likewise presents "consisting of seven curious balls, and blue shells from the opposite coast of California." Apparently the balls were of the sort Salvatierra had told about. As usual Kino sent a courier ahead to report his coming. From Sonóita he continued over the Camino del Diablo. By now the jabalíes, mule rabbits, and bighorns must have almost ceased to be disturbed by this frequent traveler on that desert trail. Passing through El Carrizal, Aguaje de la Luna, Agua Escondida, and La Tinaja, he reached the Gila at San Pedro, where he found his courier and was given a hearty welcome.

This was November 16, only four days after leaving Sonóita. He had pushed his animals hard. Next day he continued around the bend to the Yuma junction, "and having crossed the Río Grande on horseback by the only ford it had in that vicinity, with a following of more than two hundred Yumas and Pimas from San Pedro, at nightfall we arrived in safety at San Dionysio, where also they received us with great affection." The Magic Man had come again! San Dionisio was between the forks of the Gila and the Colorado, and just across the Gila from the site on which the City of Yuma now stands. It was the strategic settlement of all the area.

Now began the significant part of the journey—the new part. Again Kino was pathfinder and apostle to new peoples. On November 18 he recrossed the Gila and started southwest down the Colorado —"a road which up to this time we had never traveled," with the purpose of visiting "the Quíquimas of California Alta" and rounding the head of the Gulf. Only two expeditions, those of Coronado (1540) [1] and Oñate (1605) are known previously to have traversed any part of this stretch of country. As he traveled Kino was accompanied by three hundred Yuma and Pima Indians, great and small, from San Pedro and San Dionisio. There was a special reason for this crowd. The crops of the Yumas had been poor this season. Kino tells us, "They went in these great numbers on this occasion because, they having told me that the Quíquimas had an abundance of provisions, maize, beans, pumpkins, etc., and they being that year very short of provisions, I said to them that I was now going to the Quíquimas, and would barter for, and buy, and give them provisions, beans, maize, etc., as I did." Kino was both medicine man and Father Bountiful.

Thirteen leagues down stream that day over level country past the site of Gadsden. On the right the Colorado River. On the left a great brush-covered flat, today become fertile fields. At sunset they arrived at a village of Yumas which they called Santa Isabel. It was near the present town of San Luís, close to the international line, which then of course did not exist. "All the people, although they were rather poor, welcomed us with all friendship and affability, and even late at night we sent messengers to report our coming to the Quíquimas, now near by." This gave time for the reception committee to make preparations.

At noon next day Kino's party reached the first village of the Quíquimas, where they met a hearty welcome and found abundant food —"maize, beans, various kinds of pumpkins, etc.,—things which in the six preceding days we had not been able to procure. So great was the affection of these natives that with these provisions they came more than two leagues to meet and welcome us." Kino named this village San Feliz de Valois, on whose feast day it was discovered. It was apparently in the vicinity of Lagunitas and of the Lugo Ranch.

They had scarcely arrived when a disturbing incident occurred. Kino's only white companion lost his nerve and ran away. "While we dismounted to receive the food, and to reciprocate with some little gifts and trifles, and to make them a talk on Christian doctrine, and

---

[1] Two divisions of the Coronado expeditions reached the lower Colorado River, one by water under Alarcón, the other by land under Díaz.

on the purposes of our coming, etc., the only Spanish servant who came in our company, on seeing so great a number of . . . new people, was so terrified that, without our noticing it until a quarter of an hour after mounting our horses again, he fled from us to the rear through fright, leaving us very disconsolate, and very apprehensive lest he should go and give some false bad news to the effect that some great disaster had happened to us."

Kino was sorely worried. This timid fellow would make trouble by spreading false reports. Timid fellows often do. Kino put two Indian boys on the best horses and sent them in pursuit, but they could not overtake him. He had too long a start. "This caused me to send letters by couriers by other and shorter roads, as had happened on other occasions, when they took us for dead, though the celestial favors of our Lord preserved us in a pleasant life of prosperous successes in these new conversions."

The natives of San Feliz were most friendly, for on various occasions they had received Kino's messages and gifts. Many people had assembled from all the country round. They had heard of the great Black Robe and now he was here. Yielding to an urgent invitation, the explorers remained in camp that day and half of the next. Kino talked about the Faith and gave canes of office. For his lodgings the Indians "made a decent little house or bower in a pleasant field of maize, which they had just gathered, for here begin very fertile and well-cultivated lands and very good pasturage."[1]

Father Eusebio tells us with what childish curiosity he and his companions were inspected by their hosts. They were captivated especially by the Jesuit's gorgeous regalia. "The natives greatly wondered at many of our things, for they had never seen or heard of them. They marveled much at the vestment in which Mass is said, and at its fine embroidery representing Spring, and its skillfully woven flowers of different beautiful colors; and they would ask us to keep it on so that those who continually came to visit us might have the pleasure of seeing it. Also, it was a matter of much astonishment to see our pack animals and mounts, for they had never seen or heard of horses or mules." One would question the last assertion. For a

[1] Kino, *Favores Celestiales*, Parte II, Lib. iii, Cap. 4; *Hist. Mem.*, I, 312–313.

century and a half they must have been hearing of white men to the south and east who rode around on strange beasts. Certainly the story of Oñate's march down the Colorado must have become folklore. But that was in the "Long, Long Ago."

At any rate, the horses provided a little diversion. "When the Yumas and Pimas who came with us said to them that our horses could run faster than the most fleet-footed natives they did not believe it, and it was necessary to put it to the test." Kino took the bet. A little respect for the white men would do no harm. "Thereupon a cowboy from . . . Dolores saddled a horse and seven or eight of the most fleet-footed Quíquima runners started, and although the cowboy at first purposely let them get a little ahead, and they were very gleeful thereat, he afterwards left them far behind and very much astonished and amazed." Translated into modern slang, the cowboy told the runners they were nothing to brag about.

Accompanied now by a mob of more than five hundred Quíquimas, Yumas, and Pimas, Kino next day continued southwest down the river, planning to cross it. The trail which they followed from San Feliz was several miles east of the present Colorado River, which changed its course in 1906. The river bottom was heavily grown with thickets, but the Quíquimas, led by their chief, cut "good, and straight, and short roads" for the horses. Five leagues from camp they reached the crossing. It was apparently about at Old Colonia Lerdo, near the abandoned railroad station named Ramón Ross. Both banks of the river were crowded with people, bearing presents of food for the great Medicine Man, and they built for him "a decent little house" in which to pass the night. The Californians swam over to the east bank, towing their presents in great coritas, or baskets, each holding a bushel or more of maize or beans. "They made them float on the water of the quiet, gentle river after the fashion . . . of little canoes."

Next morning occurred an historic voyage across the Colorado. Aided personally by the Quíquima chief and his following, Kino's men assembled long, dry timbers from the near-by woods, lashed them securely together with ropes brought for the purpose, and made a raft. Kino had intended to take two or three horses across, but the first one mired and he gave it up. The raft appeared a little shaky, and

Kino looked at his boots. The Indians caught the point and offered a solution. "In order that I might not wet my feet," he says, "I accepted the large basket in which they wished me to cross, and placing it and fastening it upon the raft, I seated myself in it and crossed very comfortably and pleasantly, without the least risk, taking with me only my Breviary, some trifles, and a blanket in which to sleep, afterwards wrapping up some branches of broom weed in my bandanna to serve me as a pillow." The head Quíquima chief and many of his followers pushed the raft and kept it afloat. On the other side the reception committee was right on hand. A great crowd assembled from all the country round, "and there were dances and entertainments after their fashion." The picture conjured up by this description is not precisely that of "Washington Crossing the Delaware." But the incident was memorable.

Kino now made a short excursion into Quíquima Land. In the afternoon he went some three leagues westward, crossing a fertile and thickly settled country. "All the road was full of small but very continuous villages, with very many people, very affable, very well featured, and somewhat whiter than the rest of the Indians. All this road was through a veritable champaign of most fertile lands, of most beautiful cornfields very well cultivated with abundant crops of maize, beans, and pumpkins, and with very large drying places for the curing of pumpkins, for this kind lasts them all the year." The "continuous, pleasant champaigns" which they were now crossing Kino called La Presentación, "because of having discovered them the day of the Presentation of Our Lady." Through changes in the course of the river the pleasant champaigns have recently given way to desolation.

Two hours before sunset they reached the chief's village and house. It was near the course of the present Colorado River, in the vicinity of the railroad station of Abelardo. Soon a chief of the Cutgan tribe arrived from the north with a large following to visit the strangers, bringing gifts. And they knew what would be most welcome. They brought "in particular many blue shells from . . . the other or South Sea, giving us very detailed information in regard to them, and saying that they were not more than eight or ten days' journey to the westward, and that the Sea of California ended a day's journey farther south . . . , this very large volumed Río Colorado and two others emptying at its head." The two other streams referred to were evidently those now called the Pescadero and the Paredones.[1]

What about the country beyond? To give expert information on this point the chief introduced a Hogiopa (Cócopa), who came from the south. He told about the road to Loreto "and of some stopping places," or camp sites, and by him Kino sent friendly messages and a promise to visit them. He urged the natives to cease their wars, and "left established some general peace agreements among the Yumas, Pimas, Quíquimas, Cutganes, Hogiopas, and other nations, in order that all in their time might be very friendly and good Christians." Ever an optimist! He adds, "I slept in a little house which they had made for me, and almost all night they kept talking among themselves in regard to their very earnest desire to embrace our friendship and our holy faith." This was a memorable experience which not everyone would appreciate so well as Father Eusebio.

Kino had crossed the Colorado. He had reached California by a land route. The head of the Gulf was south of him. To the west, hardly a stone's throw, lay Cócopah Range, and just beyond it the Sierra Madre of California. Still beyond was the South Sea, source of the blue shells. The map had unfolded. Next day Father Eusebio gave all sorts of good advice to his hosts, and wrote a letter for Father Salvatierra, which the Quíquima chief promised personally to carry as far south as he could—but there were enemies down there.

This done, Kino decided to return to Dolores. We wish he had continued south. He tells us just what considerations moved him to take this step: "First, so as not to be lacking in administration." Father Mora was still alive and his tongue perhaps still wagging. "Secondly, because I was uneasy about the Spaniard who had turned back on the way." Who could tell what mischief he might do? "Thirdly, because now, thanks to our Lord, already this much disputed but now very certain land route to California had been discovered, for the sea did not ascend to this latitude of thirty-two degrees, and its head ended ten leagues farther south and southwest." Kino was correct. La Presenta-

[1] See Coues, Elliott, *On the Trail of a Spanish Pioneer* (New York, 1900); George Kennan, *The Salton Sea* (New York, 1917); H. T. Cory, *The Imperial Valley and the Salton Sink* (San Francisco, 1924).

ción was about latitude 32° 20'. The head of the Gulf lay nearly south of him, just under 32°, as he said.

So Kino returned to the river. On the way he baptized two sick infants, one of whom he named Francisco Xavier, for his patron saint, the other Thirso González, in honor of his old friend. The counter march to the Colorado was a triumph. Everywhere the people were celebrating the visit of the great Black Robe who had sent them so many friendly messages, the man who was so fond of blue shells from the Other Sea. "In all these pleasant and continuous rancherías all this morning there were many parties and dances, and songs and feasts, with a representation or dialogue, and as it were, a little comedy, by the very friendly natives, to the great joy of all. In these festivities we spent all the morning."

Kino recrossed the river on the raft used the day before, swimming chiefs and tribesmen towing it over. He was like a feudal lord crossing a river within his own domain, personally rowed by his retainers. Few men of his day were held in higher honor or warmer affection among the natives of the Western Hemisphere. Frontenac, his Canadian contemporary, burned more gunpowder, but he exercised no more authority. But Kino was not thinking of temporal honor. His journey meant to him another triumph for the Faith. "I came in time to say Mass at our booth, as a thank offering for so many celestial favors of our Lord, of Most Holy Mary, and of San Francisco Xavier."

In the afternoon Kino returned to San Feliz, an army of Indians in his train, loaded with presents. "So abundant were the maize, the beans, and the pumpkins, dried and fresh, which the very friendly Quíquimas gave us, that the more than two hundred Pimas and Yumas could not load and carry it all." If Kino had been a feudal prince, like those of medieval Europe, he would have passed slowly through the country with his retainers, consuming this tribute as he went. But his was a different kind of suzerainty. So he gave most of the provisions to the needy Yumas, whose crops had suffered drought that season.[1]

[1] Kino, *Favores Celestiales,* Parte II, Lib. iii, Caps. 5–6; *Hist. Mem.,* I, 317–320.

CXXV

FELIX OMEN

The return journey was over the Camino del Diablo, through San Dionisio (Yuma), San Pedro, and Tinajas Altas. It was not without incident. At noon, on the 26th, they reached Aguaje de la Luna, the reservoir now called Heart Tank, high up on the slopes of Sierra Pinta. Here Kino performed a feat which should be commemorated by a monument. He made a path for horses and mules up the mountain side to the precious water tank. "All the afternoon we opened an impossible road through the very sharp stones and rocks where animals had never been able to ascend . . . , so that today all went up to drink." If any young athlete wishes to know what a feat this was for a fifty-six-year-old padre, let him scramble up the boulder-filled arroyo and finish the climb up the last slippery stretch on hands and knees as Anza did seven decades behind Kino. The last climb of two hundred feet is up a steep rock surface as smooth as glass. The mules could not make it. But along the north edge there was a seamlike crevice leading up to the tank. By filling this crack with stones a trail was formed by which the animals were able to ascend. The stones are still there, and thirsty mules and weary prospectors still profit by Father Eusebio's road building.

Next day they reached Sonóita, "where," says Kino, "we found our relay of horses, and the lost Spaniard, who confessed that he had turned back and fled for fear of so many new and unknown people, who had come to meet us among the Quíquimas, for he was afraid that, being so numerous, they would do us some harm." For his cowardice he thus atoned by honest confession. Kino continued east across Pápago Land by the most direct route, through Búsanic, Síboda, and Remedios, reaching Dolores on December 8.[1] Arrived there he sat down and drew a map, combining the results of all his explorations to the north, and showing California as a peninsula. It was a new draft of the *Paso por Tierra,* his most famous contribution to cartography.

On the very day when he reached Dolores, Kino reported his jour-

---

[1] Kino, *Favores Celestiales,* Parte II, Lib. iii, Cap. 6; *Hist. Mem.,* I, 320–322.

ney to Father Leal. His tone was triumphant. Great things were now possible.

"I have just arrived in safety, thanks be to the Lord, from my peregrination or expedition by terra firma to California. . . . I have traveled four hundred-odd leagues . . . and crossed . . . the very large Río Colorado, or Río del Norte, on a raft, at latitude, thirty-two degrees." Through this expedition and his previous gifts and messages the Quíquimas, Cutganes and other tribes, "more than ten thousand souls" had been made friends of the Spaniards and desirous of conversion. Their lands were rich and fertile. The head Quíquima chief had promised to carry a letter to Salvatierra at Loreto. What a feat that would be! What a thrill Father Juan María would get! And then the Blue Shells! "I bring with me not a few *conchas azules* from the opposite coast of California," declared by the Indians to be "not more than seven or eight days distant."

The commercial implications of his discovery stirred the imagination. This was the same South Sea by which the Manila Galleon came every year on its long voyage to Acapulco. With this land route now discovered, a new port could be opened in California for the China Ship, "to avoid the very circuitous and costly transportation of the very many goods which it carries by sea to Acapulco and by land from Acapulco to Mexico, and from Mexico to this Nueva Biscaya and the provinces of Sonora and Cinaloa, etc., matters concerning which there has been a discussion in the Royal Council." Kino thus visualized a port on the Pacific Coast, at San Diego Bay for example, with a direct overland supply route from there to Sonora. Here was a temporal service which would reduce the cost of transportation and bring favor to the Jesuits who had performed it. The king would reward them.

This was not all. The discovery would be a Godsend to travelers on the ocean. "At the same time through this port . . . the lives of so many of its sailors who every year are accustomed to fall sick and die from the painful disease of scurvy can be saved, since with fresh food they are easily cured and freed from this evil, for the disease originates from dried and salty foods, which are . . . stale from the long voyage." The suggestion was sound.

The way to Loreto by land was now plain. Below the Quíquimas lived the Hogiopa nation, more commonly called Cócopas. "Now that some of them have come to see me, although they speak a different language . . . on the next occasion, with the favor of the Lord, I shall have the road and way to them wide open, and, through them, very far inland, and toward Loreto Conchó, where live Father . . . Salvatierra and the two other fathers [Picolo and Ugarte], with the sixteen soldiers. For I consider that I was not more than one hundred and twenty-five leagues, more or less, from their Reverences"—a mere matter of three or four hundred miles! This was not a bad estimate. "And since from these things might result the conversion and salvation of very many souls, and important service to both Majesties, I commend it all strongly to the holy sacrifices of your Reverence."

Another shower of congratulations now rained on Kino's head— just what Mora had predicted. Father Gilg wrote with Scriptural allusion, *"Ex transitu felici Maris Rubri, felix omen pro Terra Promissionis Patrum Californiensium*— The successful passage of the Red Sea we consider a happy omen for the Promised Land of the California fathers." Salvatierra was delighted. He thanked Kino for his prodigious labors, called them "glorious," and promised to report them to Rome. General Fuensaldaña, even though he had not provided Kino with soldiers, now congratulated the great traveler, and promised "to co-operate in discoveries so blessed." General La Fuente, of Janos, joined in the chorus of praise.[1]

Most excited over the news was Kino's earliest Sonora friend, Father Manuel González, of Oposura. He had been visitor when Kino arrived in 1687, had escorted him to his new field of labor, and had always been one of his best backers. He now wrote in buoyant tone, proposing another expedition beyond the Colorado, in which he would gladly join, to go "even to where the California fathers were, in Loreto Conchó." He would like to be among the first to ride from the north triumphantly into Salvatierra's mission. Father Leal was consulted, he was favorable, and a new expedition was arranged for at once.

Just before he started Kino wrote again to Father Thirso González,

---

[1] Kino to Leal, Dec. 8, 1701, in Kino, *Favores Celestiales,* Parte II, Lib. iii, Caps. 7–8; *Hist. Mem.,* I, 323–326.

in Rome.[1] His letter painted a soaring vision which leaped from Pima Land to the ends of the earth. "I have written several letters to your Reverence, and I hope that they have reached your holy hands. In one of them went the new map of the passage by mainland to the Californias in the latitude of 32°. Now I am sending this one." The map here mentioned was evidently the second version of the *Paso por Tierra*.[2] The California dream would soon be realized. "In a short time, with the favor of Heaven, we shall send cattle by land, and shall have ranches in California itself near the land passage, for already on this side near the passage, in San Marcelo [Sonóita], there is a ranch with large and small cattle, horses, fields of maize, etc., and a decent little church."

The new lands must be named. Why not call them Upper California? "The father visitor . . . and I, and others, are of the opinion that this California near the new land passage recently discovered might be called California Alta, just as the preceding region where the three fathers are already established, as far as 30° of north latitude, might be called California Baxa." The suggestion caught the imagination and these names became official designations. Kino went on to say that he had written on California Baja a little treatise in Latin entitled *Novae Carolinae,* and that with the approval of the Father General he would write a similar one on California Alta "from 30° north latitude up to 40° or more." This new treatise, he said, might be called *Novae Philipinae seu California Superior,* naming Upper California for Philip just as Lower California had been named for Carlos. We have not seen either of these treatises. Their discovery would be most welcome. Where are they?

And there was more beyond. California was but a step to greater triumphs and more distant lands. "For with the favor of Heaven, if your Reverence and his Majesty, Philip V, God spare him, will give us workers and missionaries, all in good time they must go forward until they reach perhaps as far as Gran China, and nearly to Japan." Yea, more! "And perhaps to the north of these our lands we may be able to find a shorter road to Europe, partly through these lands and

[1] Kino to Thirso González, Feb. 2, 1702. Original Spanish manuscript in the central archives of the Jesuit Order.
[2] The one printed as *Tabula Californiae, Anno 1702.*

partly by way of the North Sea." [1] Northwest to Asia, northeast to Europe! Pima Land the base of advance!

CXXVI

SUNRISE ACROSS THE GULF

González arrived from Oposura at Dolores on the last days of January, 1702, with servants, fifty mules, and provisions, ready for the new expedition. To this equipment Kino added twelve servants, a few more loads of provisions, and eighty horses and mules. It was another Kino cavalcade. Manje was invited to join the expedition, but was prevented by Indian troubles. Kino awaited him several days and then went without him, to the loss of history, for Don Matheo was a superb diarist. [2]

"Hoping to catch sight of the Contra Costa and the South Sea," on February 5 they set forth. From Dolores they went by way of Remedios to Síboda, where now there were "more than a thousand cattle and seven droves of mares belonging to the new conversions." At Santa Bárbara, a short distance beyond, Kino left stock for "another little ranch . . . for these roads to the land passage to California." Continuing to Búsanic, he crossed Pápago Land by yet another route to Sonóita, and from there followed the Camino del Diablo to La Tinaja, the tank in Gila Range. [3]

Here they were detained two days by a terrific cloudburst, which sent the water roaring and tumbling down the narrow canyon and greatly swelled the stream that supplied the basin. "We saw that it passed over some very sightly rocks which looked like very fine tanks made by hand with very great art, and it seemed to the father rector that this tank with much reason might be named Aguaje de los

---

[1] Kino to Thirso González, Feb. 2, 1702.

[2] On the basis of Kino's reports Manje wrote an account of this expedition called Epitome ó Resunta del descubrimiento, 1702. Manuscript in the Biblioteca Nacional, Madrid.

[3] From Búsanic Kino went through San Estanislao del Ootcam, Santa Eulalia, the tank of San Vicente, the tank and well of Santa Sabina, the tank of San Martín, San Rafael del Actúm, thence to Sonóita. From here they passed through El Carrizal, Aguaje de la Luna, and Agua Escondida, or Tinajas Altas. Kino, *Favores Celestiales*, Parte II, Lib. iv, Caps. 2–3; *Hist. Mem.,* I, 336–339.

Alquives." Americans now call it Dripping Springs. The spot is memorable for another incident. While in camp here Kino observed a comet "in the Constellation of Aquarius." According to the astronomer Galle, there were two comets in 1702, the first in February and March, the second discovered on April 20. The former is evidently the one seen by Kino.[1] But with Father Eusebio comets had by now yielded to terrestrial themes.

Proceeding to San Pedro on the Gila, they followed its course northward downstream. "After going four leagues," says Kino, "we arrived at the opening where it may be said that California Alta begins, because its meridian passes through the middle of the head of the Sea of California." They were now about at Dome, where the river cuts through Gila Range. Kino's assertion regarding the meridian is essentially correct. He thus put the Colorado River within California. Next day they reached San Dionisio, head village of the tall Yumas. González was delighted with the place. "Well might one come all the way from Mexico to see it, on account of its very sightly groves, its copious and peaceful water, its fertile lands."

They were ready now for the main problem. Starting downstream on March 1 with a great following, they visited Santa Isabel, passed San Feliz and the November crossing, and continued to San Rodesindo. Here in the midst of a great assemblage of natives they arranged "for the descent to the very disemboguement of these rivers in the sea."

While Kino was camped here on the 3rd, natives kept coming in from all directions, invited by the Quíquima and Cutgan chiefs. Here the modest padre found himself popular with the women. "Because the sick infant, called Thirso González, whom I had baptized in the preceding November, was now very well, fine, and fat, his mother, and very many other mothers also, brought me their infants . . . begging me to baptize them too, but I put them off for a better season." This baptized child had thrived, and Kino was a favorite. It was different when one died. Father González, too, was popular. With his great charity he gave to the friendly natives "even his own

---

[1] This comet was seen by numerous navigators in the Southern Hemisphere between February 20 and March 1, always in the evening after sunset (Geo. F. Chambers, *A Handbook of Descriptive and Practical Astronomy*, I, 585).

shirts, white handkerchiefs, generous handfuls of chocolate, and the very shoes which he wore." [1]

Here at San Rodesindo Kino took the latitude and found it to be in 31½ degrees,—that is, half a degree below his November crossing. It was in fact above 32°. Next day they continued down the river to San Casimiro. This place was evidently at the sharp westward turn of the old river bed, at Marrón Coral.[2] about a quarter of a mile south of Monument No. 20, near the head of tidewater and a little below 32°. On the 5th they went straight south to the bayous of the Gulf, accompanied by Quíquimas, Cutganes, and Cócopas, the last-named people having come across the river from both west and south-west.

Kino now made a minute inquiry about tribes, mountains, and rivers to the west. He learned accurately that the Colorado emptied into the Sea of California "on the west side." It enters the Gulf, in fact, at its very northwestern corner. He was told, as in November, of two other streams entering the Gulf in the same vicinity, "the Río Azul, which comes from the north, and the Río Amarillo, which comes from the northwest, as the Río Colorado comes from the north-east, and the Río Grande, or Río de Hila, comes from the east." [3] The Río Azul is now the Pescadero, in whose channel the Colorado River has run since 1906. Kino's Río Amarillo is now the Paredones.

A day was spent teaching the Faith and giving canes of office to the Indians from the west. On the 6th, Kino made all possible efforts to cross the Colorado, but the bogs prevented "because it had rained these days." On the 7th, González "descended to the very mouth and to the sea by a westward course, and I, having collected information for us concerning all these natives of the west, and sent my messengers ahead to those on the other bank of the river, descended in the after-noon, having been detained by the continuous messages which they were sending me." As he traveled Kino's fame spread. Next day more than three hundred Indians, great and small, swam across the Colorado to see him, bringing "blue shells from the opposite coast,"

[1] Kino, *Favores Celestiales*, Parte II, Lib. iv, Caps. 3, 7; *Hist. Mem.*, I, 338–339, 350; Manje, Epitome ó Resunta.

[2] I camped there on the night of March 26, 1934, when retracing Kino's trail.

[3] Kino adds, "as may be seen in the maps of this treatise" (*Favores Celestiales*, Parte II, Lib. iv, Cap. 4; *Hist. Mem.*, I, 342). I have not seen these maps, if ever he made them.

Photo by Bolton

Junction of Gila and Colorado Rivers, at Yuma

Photo by Bolton

Where Kino saw the sun rise over the Gulf. The line in the distance is a mirage, not land.

The desert which Kino tried to cross, east of lower Colorado River

and towing great baskets of provisions, to urge him to cross the river to visit them. But Father González was now very ill—had been, indeed, during the whole expedition—so they decided not to cross over, promised to come again, and returned to San Casimiro.

But Kino could not make this decision stick. "On the ninth," he tells us, "so much were we moved by the petitions and desires of the natives on the other bank of the river, and so great was our desire to cross and see the Río Amarillo, and even to cross to the Sea of the West, or sea of the opposite coast, or South Sea [the Pacific Ocean], since we were assured that it was not more than eight or nine days distant, and since they brought us some little pots and other gifts which previously had been brought from the opposite coast, I decided to descend once more to the mouth and with the natives to cross the Río Colorado, and for this purpose we equipped ourselves with the necessary provisions and the best horses."

So next day they went again down to the mouth, "taking and joining many dry poles to make a very great raft on which to cross the very large volumed and very wide Río Colorado, Río Grande de Hila, and Río Azul, which all combined in the estuary made a body of peaceful waters." From this it is inferred that he was below the junction of the rivers.

Now again plans were changed. González's ailment became worse. "And as we found very difficult the crossing of the horses, because of the enormous bogs on the banks of the very large volumed river, we determined to defer this crossing for another and more opportune occasion, and again we consoled the natives as best we could, passing the night with them at the estuary, where the open sea came very near to our beds." That night González's saddle horse strayed away, but the Indians found and returned it.

Now came the final triumph! Next morning, the 11th, "the sun rose over the head of the Sea of California, proof most evident that we were now in California." This statement tells us where they were. The tidewater ascends nearly to the latitude of San Casimiro (Marrón Corral). At daybreak on March 27, 1934, I drove by automobile five or six miles south of that point, most of the way over the tide flats, and saw the sun rise over a vast expanse of tidewater. It was in the same vicinity—possibly a little farther southwest—that Kino saw the sun rise over the Gulf in 1702. "And besides," says Kino, returning to his proofs, "we saw most plainly more than thirty leagues of continuous land to the south, and many more to the west, and as many more to the north, without the least sign of any sea except that which lay to the eastward of us." This, too, is correct. South of them, looking down the west shore of the Gulf, there was a continuous stretch of land, extending west from the Gulf to the California mountains.

Kino had been cheated out of complete triumph by circumstances —the illness of a friend. Writing in 1935 we feel like saying that González should never have attempted the strenuous journey, fit only for such as Kino. But Father Eusebio did not complain. Besides, no more evidence seemed necessary. He had seen the sun rise over the Gulf.

CXXVII

A TRAGEDY ON THE TRAIL

Next day it was decided to return home by going straight east to Sonóita, across the sand dunes. Some declared that this would be impossible for lack of water and pasturage. These pessimists were reminded that the previous year Pimas from Sonóita had met Quíquimas on this road and entered into peace agreements. Some of the natives told of a canebrake on the route with plentiful water and feed. It was a forbidding prospect, but Kino had the nerve to try it. So he set forth east, "over most difficult sand dunes, and with continuous, violent, and most pestiferous wind." They were evidently headed toward Pitaqui, on the northern skirts of the Pinacate Mountain. During the entire day they found neither a drop of water nor a spear of pasturage. In the afternoon they encountered some natives, but "they themselves were going about as if lost and seeking water." That day the Black Robes traveled eighteen leagues, covering perhaps half the distance to the mountain.

But they were forced to give it up. The pessimists were right. So they retraced the eighteen awful leagues. "After passing a very toilsome night," says Kino, "we found ourselves obliged, with much more trouble, to return the following day, March 13, to San Casimiro." The pack train and relay did not arrive till the next day. This was one of the hardest and most dangerous marches imaginable, and they were lucky to get out alive. If they had known the way they might perhaps have gone forward as easily as back. But they had no guide who knew the road. They had made a noble endeavor, and few white men have ever traversed the route which they attempted.

Now retracing their steps to the Yuma junction, they returned by their old trail up the Gila to San Pedro, thence to Tinajas Altas and Moonlight Tank, reaching El Carrizal on the 21st. That night Father González had a dream. He told Kino that "although it was not well to believe in dreams, he could not deny that a dream, or what was apparently a dream which he had that night, had kept him very much consoled in the midst of his ills, attacks, pains, and fatigues. It was that . . . he and I, although with very great toil yet with equal joy, were crossing, at the mouth of the Colorado River, some very extensive and beautiful plains, one of which was called San Joachín."

Poor Father González was now a desperately sick man. Three days were spent at Sonóita to permit him to rest, but he got worse instead of better, and when they set forth across Pápago Land he had to be carried in a litter on the shoulders of the devoted natives. Runners were sent ahead from village to village to summon the strongest men to perform this task of mercy. "They did it with great care and with much charity and love, as if they were all old Christians."

Rumors of disaster to Kino's party had preceded them. At Ootcam he received a letter from Father Iturmendi, now missionary at Tubutama, saying that it had been reported that he, González, and all their people had been drowned in the Río Grande, and that in the missions the Masses and suffrages had already been said for them. Kino was disgusted with the tale. At Santa Sabina Father González was so nearly unconscious that Kino administered to him the last sacraments. Near Tubutama they were met by Iturmendi, with natives carrying refreshments for the travelers and delicacies for the patient. From Tubutama runners were hurried to Dolores, Cucurpe, Valle de Sonora, even to Oposura, two hundred miles away, to bring "persons skilled in curing with all possible remedies for so painful an illness." They were all in vain. Kino left González with Iturmendi hoping he would recover, but a few days later he closed his earthly career. For his zeal in saving souls Father Manuel had paid the supreme price.

Just fifteen years previously González had escorted Kino on his first ride to Pima Land. Kino had now escorted González on his last earthly tour. Iturmendi laid him to rest at beautiful Tubutama mission, on the hill overlooking the River of the Altar.[1] A decade later his remains were removed to Magdalena.

CXXVIII

CALIFORNIA NO ES ISLA, SINO PENISLA

From Dolores Kino promptly wrote Father Leal a long report, summarizing the events of the journey and in some places supplementing his diary.[2] In the main, however, it was a demonstration of the peninsularity of California. The old maps were correct, Father Aygenler's teaching had been sound, recent geographers had been led astray. Kino proceeded in categorical fashion. "In case there should be some incredulous persons or someone ignorant of it, the continuity of these lands would be rendered certain by the seven following convincing reasons or arguments":

1. Twice, in 1698 and again in 1701, he had seen the head of the Gulf from Cerro de Santa Clara. 2. Traveling forty leagues down the Colorado River from Yuma junction to its mouth, "no Sea of California has been found or seen, for it does not rise higher than barely to the latitude of thirty-two degrees." This is exactly correct. "Hence it is plainly to be inferred that Drake, besides many other

---

[1] Kino, *Favores Celestiales*, Parte II, Lib. iv, Caps. 4–7; *Hist. Mem.*, I, 342–348; Manje, Epitome ó Resunta.
[2] Kino to Leal, Dolores, April 8, 1702 (*Favores Celestiales*, Parte II, Lib. iv, Caps. 8–11; *Hist. Mem.*, I, 351–354).

modern cosmographers, in their various printed maps, with notable discredit to cosmography, deceive themselves as well as others, by extending this sea, or arm, or strait of the Sea of California from thirty-two to forty-six degrees, making it thereby an island, and the largest island in the world, whereas it is not an island but a peninsula." 3. On March 11 at the mouth of the Colorado Kino had seen the sun rise over the head of the Gulf across more than thirty leagues of sea. At the same time he saw continuous land west, south, southwest, north, northwest, and northeast. "Therefore, this sea does not extend to the north." 4. The natives at the mouth of the Colorado gave him blue shells and pots brought from the South Sea, a ten days' journey. 5. Indians from the southwest, seen at the mouth of the Colorado, told of the Jesuits in California and described their vestments. When Kino quizzed them about their foods they emphatically said that the natives at the California missions did not raise crops. This was essentially true. 6. On this journey and others he had gathered shrubs, fruit, and incense "peculiar to California alone." Near the head of the Gulf he had heard some words of the language of the California Guimíes. 7. The old maps showed California as a peninsula, not as an island; likewise some modern ones, among them that of his old professor, Father Aygenler.

Finally, for good measure, "if some hostile and obstinate persons should maintain that some Quíquima Indians say that further west the sea extends to the northwest, these Quíquimas speak of the other sea, on the opposite coast [the Pacific Ocean], and not of this our Sea of California, of which, since some call it the Red Sea, we may say, because we have found this passage,—"Dry land appeared, and in the Red Sea a way without hindrance—*Aparuit terra arida, et in Mari Rubro via sine impedimento.*" [1] All doubts settled, Father Eusebio turned to visions of vast missionary fields and boundless temporal triumphs now made possible.

To give weight to his report Kino obtained a certificate from Manje, then at the mines of Quisuani. Don Matheo was noncommittal on the question of the land passage. He certified that the report and

[1] Kino, *Favores Celestiales*, Parte II, Lib. iv, Cap. 8; *Hist. Mem.*, I, 354. He devotes a chapter to "Temporal means . . . for the total reduction of this North America." *Ibid.*, 357–362.

the signature were Kino's; that Kino had brought about the conversion of the Pima nation and founded many ranches; and that the Gulf west of Santa Clara Mountain was only twelve leagues wide.[1] "As to the rest . . . I have not witnessed them . . . but I do assert confidently that the relation is by a zealous minister to whom entire credit has been given." This was rather lukewarm. In fact, Manje did not accept Kino's conclusions, and said so in other writings.

Letters of congratulation poured in upon Kino as before. But Manje's skepticism caused some to doubt. Salvatierra told Kino that still another journey would be necessary before objectors would be silenced, and the expedition must be properly equipped. He wrote: "I received your Reverence's letter, accompanied by the map of the discovery of the landlocked gulf, which has been so much disputed that I have been no little depressed. There is no reason to be discouraged, but rather to try well to arrange with the superiors for another journey, by which this truth shall be ascertained, this time with evidence." He meant sworn testimony. "Your Reverence has already gone far. But in order now, once and for all, to remove this doubt from everybody, you still have to plan for the rest, and for all the means and proper arrangements to go provided with flour, maize, pinole, and all the other little regalements which you know to be conducive to success, in order to succeed once for all with God's work, and not be compelled to return only to argue more and more. Finally, your Reverence sees how important it is that you consult . . . with some person informed relative to the desirability of taking some armed men, so as to be able to stay with them one or two months at a place where the animals may recuperate, without fear that the Indians will make away with the food. This done, the host of new map makers will be silenced. But they are not going to be silenced until they are completely done for." Salvatierra was right. Father Eusebio had challenged a traditional view, which was heresy.

---

[1] Dated May 2, 1702 (Kino, *Favores Celestiales,* Parte II, Lib. iv, Cap. 12; *Hist. Mem.,* I, 363–365). Soon after Kino returned Manje wrote, evidently for his book, the "Epitome ó Resunta" of Kino's expedition. He added, "I am caused to believe this matter indeterminate by the fact that Father Manuel González returned with a contrary opinion as to the continuation of this coast-land with that of California, for both being learned and trustworthy I hesitate to approve the opinion of one and reject that of the other." But he admits that González lacked training in cosmography, in which Kino excelled. Manje must have obtained his information regarding the expedition from Kino or Iturmendi.

Kino talked of another expedition in the autumn of 1702 and the spring of 1703, but was prevented from undertaking it. On the receipt of Salvatierra's letter just quoted, he again proposed the matter, but was told that he was needed at his mission, so he applied himself to building new churches at Remedios and Cocóspora.[1]

[1] Kino, *Favores Celestiales,* Parte II, Lib. iv, Cap. 13; *Hist. Mem.,* I, 364–369; Salvatierra to Kino, March 3, 1703 (*ibid.,* I, 366–367).

PIONEER OF CIVILIZATION

New Ranches and Temples

CXXIX

MISSION BUILDING

WHILE HE EXPLORED, Kino was busy with the more immediate tasks of spiritual administration and mission building. In the six years following the Caborca uprising and the martyrdom of Father Saeta the formal founding of new missions did not proceed at a mushroom rate, in spite of enthusiastic predictions that Saeta's blood would fructify the soil of Christendom. There was a dearth of missionaries. Bands of gayly bedecked heathen chiefs went repeatedly to Dolores to beg for fathers to go to live with them and teach their people. From the west and the north there was an almost constant procession on the trails that led to Kino's door. Some came on horseback. Most of them trudged pigeon-toed on foot, carrying their bows and arrows. They brought presents for the Black Robe—curiosities, the fruits of their lands, and especially blue shells. Sometimes whole families came scores or hundreds of miles, the women carrying their infants slung on their backs.

"Padres y Españoles" was a constant refrain on the Pima tongue. Kino forwarded the appeals, and more than once he escorted the petitioners over distant and rugged mountains to the superiors that they might tell their story in person. The visitors, first Polici then Leal, promised aid and earnestly pleaded the cause of the natives with the authorities in Mexico. Kino with characteristic energy bombarded the provincials with word pictures of eager heathen on the verge of eternal perdition through lack of someone to show the way.

But the response was slow. Missions cost money; there was a shortage of funds in the royal chest and a depression in Mexico. The War of the Spanish Succession made ocean travel unsafe, absorbed royal attention and exhausted the treasury. Pious donors just now were devoting their gifts to Salvatierra and his companions for the conversion of California. Other frontiers demanded royal attention. Ever since the New Mexico uprising in 1680 the Indians of Chihuahua had been troublesome. Vargas had spent large sums for the government in the reconquest of the Pueblos, and in these very years was just bringing that episode to a successful conclusion.

There was still another obstacle. On the Sonora border—typical of all these frontiers—there were objectors to Kino's program. It was the same old story. They denied the need for more missionaries, said the Pimas were not numerous, maintained that they could not be trusted, and that consequently it was unsafe for the Jesuits to go among them. Some of the dissent came from seculars who wished freedom to exploit the labor of the heathen Pimas. Some sincere persons were unconvinced. These adverse views made the authorities falter—for one ignorant or jealous objector can shake the confidence of almost any administrator. And so more missionaries for Pima Land were difficult to obtain.

Meanwhile Kino toiled up to the last ounce of his more than ordinary strength to keep alive the sparks of Christianity and civilization in the Altar Valley where the rebellion had occurred, to prepare new missionary fields for the awaited harvesters of souls, and to furnish evidence with which to shut the mouths of misinformed or malicious detractors of his Pimas. Particularly did he gather with tireless zeal information to prove that the Pimas were numerous, friendly, loyal defenders of the Spaniards, and anxious for missionaries.

In each of the exploring expeditions recounted in the foregoing chapters, as he passed through the villages, Kino gave Christian instruction, baptized infants and moribund adults, encouraged agriculture, and directed building operations, with a view to the return of the missionaries to their old posts and to the founding of new ones. Each important village on the borders of Christendom was urged to build and keep in order an adobe house in which to lodge Kino when he made his visits, and for the promised resident missionary. The building of these adobe houses at the outlying villages was an extension of the system of requiring the Indians to construct at their pueblos and keep in order community houses (*casas de comunidad*) for the comfort of Spanish travelers. Some of the houses now erected in the villages under Kino's guidance were well-built structures of adobe with timber cross beams and earth-covered roofs. In many cases they were the first step in building a permanent missionary plant. Some of these structures in the Altar Valley were standing and in use half a century later when Father Pfefferkorn was baptizing the grandchildren of Father Eusebio's neophytes.

Kino did not stop here. A mission could not flourish without a stable food supply, enabling the neophytes to stay in one place to be instructed. If they wandered about, living by the chase, they could not be disciplined. So in these years Kino was active in the establishment of new stock ranches beyond the old border. They were placed not only at the sites chosen for new missions, but also at other places where grass and water were plentiful, and where stock could be raised for the support of missions at villages which lacked the necessary pasturage. Thus, through Kino's driving energy, old sites and new were prepared for the anxiously awaited missionaries. He kept alive the smouldering embers in the West, and he started new fires in the North. He was indeed the "Father of Missions."[1]

CXXX

IN THE WEST

In the West the principal old centers were Tubutama and Caborca. New centers were now promoted. San Ambrosio was developed to serve Tucubavia, Sáric and Búsanic. At Síboda, Santa Bárbara and Aquimuri stock ranches were established. Preparation was made for pushing into Pápago Land at Gubo Verde, Santa Eulalia, and Ootcam.

[1] Data regarding mission building during this period are scattered through Kino's *Hist. Mem.*, I, 159–379, and the diaries of expeditions kept by Kino, Manje, Carrasco, and Salvatierra, cited above. See especially Kino, *Hist. Mem.*, I, 189, 193–194, 200–201, 209, 243, 255–258, 275–280, 303, 346; *Favores Celestiales*, corresponding passages; Manje's diaries for the period as printed in *Luz de Tierra Incógnita;* Manje's manuscript diaries for the period; Bernal, Diario y Relación de la Pimería, Nov.–Dec., 1697; Kino, Relasión Diaria, Sept.–Oct., 1698; Kino, Del Estado . . . de esta dilatada Pimería, October 18, 1698; Carrasco, Diario fho., Sept.–Oct., 1698; Carrasco to Jironza, Oct. 18, 1698; Kino to Polici, Oct. 18, 1698; Kino to González, Oct. 18, 1701; Kino to Leal, Dec. 8, 1701; Kino to González, Feb. 2, 1702.

At distant Sonóita a mission ranch and a church were begun as a base for advance to California and the Colorado River. How and when these things were done will now be briefly told.

For nearly two years after Kino's return from Mexico in 1696 we have no record of a visit by him to the Altar Valley. In the interim Campos kept his eye on that outpost. Nearly three years after the martyrdom of Saeta there, Caborca was given a new minister. One of the fathers sent to the Pimería at this time was Gaspar de las Barillas, a man already burdened with the weight of years. It fell to Kino to install him in his post and set him up in business. At the end of January, 1698, Barillas arrived at Dolores, on the way to the Altar Valley. His precise assignment had not been made. He was to choose between Caborca, Tubutama, and Tucubavia. In February Kino escorted him to the valley. The natives were friendly and more than a thousand persons were counted. Barillas chose Caborca for his residence, and returned to Arizpe for his baggage and supplies. In June he went again to Caborca to take up his ministry, but because of "certain pretended dangers," as Kino somewhat contemptuously calls them, in July he departed.

So it was again left to Kino and Campos to keep the fires burning. Campos, being the nearest, went at least once a year to the valley to give instruction and baptize newborn babes. In his absence native temastianes periodically assembled the Indians and drilled them in the Catechism. Kino, on his way to and from the northwest, frequently passed up and down the valley, baptized, cared for the sick, preached, looked after stock, crops, and building.

The diaries of these expeditions give glimpses of this itinerant missionary work in the Altar Valley while resident fathers were awaited. Some of the entries are drawn upon here. They are only occasional flashes, but they suggest the complete picture. In October, 1698, when Kino passed through Tubutama and Caborca for the northwest, at each place there were cattle, sheep, goats, wheat, maize, and an adobe mission residence. Barillas had already departed.[1] On the way back, at Caborca Kino said Mass in the chapel which Saeta had begun. It was now completed, for, says Kino, "the neophytes finished erecting

---

[1] Kino, *Favores Celestiales*, Parte I, Lib. v, Cap. 8; *Hist. Mem.*, I, 174–175, 189.

the walls and roofed it." While here he branded fifteen cattle, killed a sheep and a beef, one of forty head at the place.

Kino continued up the river. At Atí he found the natives harvesting thirty fanegas of wheat for the awaited father. At Tubutama he branded thirty-six head of cattle. At the same place there were fifty sheep and goats, a little drove of mares, wheat, maize, beans, "and a three-room house built of adobe and earth-covered." One room served as a church; apart there were a kitchen, bakery, and oven. Father Eusebio instructed the children in the Catechism. From Tubutama he sent "talks" to Sáric, Búsanic, and Tucubavia, where also the Indians were caring for large and small stock, a drove of mares, wheat, maize, beans, "and a little earth-covered adobe church which they have prepared." This prospective mission at Tucubavia was called San Ambrosio.

We get another glimpse of the Valley a few months later. In February and March (1699), Kino, Gilg, and Manje went through the Soba country on the way to the northwest. At Tubutama they were welcomed by the natives drawn up in two files, and Kino and Gilg sat up all night giving Christian instruction to the assembled people. Francisco Pintor, native governor of Dolores, "refreshed their memories of the prayers and the mysteries of our Holy Faith, because since the uprising of 1695 and the burning of the churches they had lacked a minister." However, says Manje, "Father Agustín de Campos does not fail to visit, instruct, and confess them at least once a year." Manje noted that at Sáric, Búsanic, and Tucubavia there were "two thousand Indians for a good mission."

From Tucubavia Kino crossed Pápago Land to Sonóita. This visit was significant, for it marked the founding of a mission there. As he traveled west Kino's vaqueros drove from Dolores a herd of thirty-six cattle. These were now left at Sonóita for the beginning of a mission ranch, convenient for supporting northwestern explorations and to succor the padres of California, "if perchance they should sail to this latitude." There were talks about the Faith and vassalage. Manje counted eighty natives and was impressed by the lands, the river, and the acéquias with which the inhabitants irrigated their crops.

A step forward in the West was the founding by Kino of the ranch at Síboda, in the beautiful valley now called Cíbuta, through which one passes on the Southern Pacific Railway between Nogales and Imuris. Kino mentions it in September, 1700, when the ranch had "about a thousand cattle and four droves of mares for the new conversions which were being founded." The pastures of Síboda were especially rich, and Kino's men killed for the road "a fat beef, which had more than four arrobas of suet and tallow." Cíbuta still raises fat cattle.

San Ambrosio was now a promising "incipient pueblo" with a church. Here, says Kino, "they were tending for me seventy cattle, as many head of sheep and goats, and five droves of mares, besides wheat, maize and beans, together with their medium-sized church." When at this time Kino passed through Santa Eulalia, on the edge of Pápago Land, the natives there agreed to go to settle at Tucubavia if a missionary should come.

At Sonóita, as he went north in March, 1701, Kino found the roads cleared, crosses and arches erected, and a ramada prepared for his lodging. He preached, rounded up the sixty-three head of cattle and had two beeves killed for his retinue. On his return he stopped here four days and began the building of a church for the mission of San Marcelo. He gives us interesting details. On the 4th of April twelve small beams were cut and the altar was made. Next day the first Mass was said in the church, with the picture of Our Lady resting on the altar. When he departed eight packloads of provisions were left to be used by the natives while they finished roofing the church, and he gave orders for planting goodly fields of maize.[1]

CXXXI

IN THE NORTH

The most significant advance of the permanent missionary frontier during these six years was in the valleys of the upper San Pedro and

---

[1] Kino, *Hist. Mem.*, I, 193, 209, 243; Manje, *Luz de Tierra Incógnita*, 262–263, 278–279; Kino, Relasión Diaria, quoting Bernal's letter of August 10, 1698.

Santa Cruz rivers.[1] This work of Kino's was admirably supported by the efforts of Jironza, Manje, Bernal, Carrasco, and other seculars. Visitors Polici and Leal co-operated. But Kino furnished the initiative and the driving force. To accomplish his work he became diplomat, military agent, cattleman, and commissary as well as priest. To prepare the way among the Sobaípuris for the awaited Black Robes he rode up and down the valleys, tiring out saddle horses, driving herds of unruly stock, supervising building and the planting of fields, preparatory to the coming of the fathers, summoning native warriors when the Pima frontier was in danger. He was both Christian missionary and pioneer of civilization.

Only a few of the details of all this activity of "The Padre on Horseback" can find space here. A few are necessary, however, to reveal the tireless energy of the man, and to show how the missionary frontier was being pushed north as well as west. We have seen that in December, 1696, Kino visited Quíburi, on San Pedro River, near the site of present-day Fairbank, and made preparations for a mission there. At his suggestion the natives then began a house for a promised missionary, inside the fortification which they had built to withstand the attacks of the Apaches. Immediately afterward he sent to Quíburi "a few cattle and a small drove of mares for the beginning of a little ranch."[2]

This was but the beginning of the arduous task which Kino had set himself in that direction. He had scarcely returned to Dolores before he was again raising a dust on the northbound trail. Early next year he founded several ranches on the Santa Cruz River. This involved more round-ups, more pack trains, more soul-trying patience with careless vaqueros and wrong-headed cattle, more tolerance for the whims of his desert children, more weary horseback journeys, more coarse fare and comfortless nights in camp, more hours of utter discouragement, more temptations to sit comfortably down at Dolores, drink chocolate, and let the world wag on,—all outweighed by his joy in the salvation of souls.

In January, 1697, Kino again went north from Dolores with his

---

[1] As distinguished from missionary explorations beyond the borders.
[2] Kino, *Favores Celestiales*, Parte I, Lib. v, Cap. 4; *Hist. Mem.*, I, 165.

Indian helpers, driving a herd of cattle, a flock of sheep and goats, and a manada of mares. He presented a truly patriarchal picture, reminiscent of the fathers of Israel, driving their flocks and herds over the deserts of the Holy Land. As he proceeded on his way he distributed the stock at chosen sites for missions. Some of the cattle he left at the beautiful meadows among the giant cottonwoods of Bacoancos, right at the present international boundary line. No mention is made of leaving stock at Guébavi at this time. At Tumacácori there were already sheep and goats, which the loyal neophytes of Father Saeta had taken there, "having gathered them in Concepción at the time of the disturbances of 1695."[1]

From Tumacácori Kino continued north to Bac and founded a cattle ranch there. Besides the natives of the great settlement, the largest in all the Pimería, he met there many chiefs and headmen of the surrounding country, who had assembled to see the magnetic Black Robe. Kino improved the occasion to draw the friendly people more closely to him and prepare the way for a permanent mission. "The Word of God was spoken to them, there were baptisms of little ones, and beginnings of good sowings and harvests of wheat for the father minister whom they asked for and hoped to receive." This may be regarded as the definite beginning of the famous mission of San Xavier del Bac.[2] In fact, this "long drive" of stock by the great Jesuit in January, 1697, was an epoch in the history of the advance of European civilization northward down the Santa Cruz Valley.

In March Kino went again to Quíburi. His errand was a double one, to confirm the Faith and to summon the Faithful for the defense of Christendom. On his way back he visited San Gerónimo, Tumacácori, and Bacoancos, "looking in all places after the spiritual welfare of the natives, baptizing some infants and sick persons, and consoling them all with very fatherly messages from the father visitor, and even from the Señor alcalde mayor and military commander,[3] notifying

---

[1] Kino, *Favores Celestiales*, Parte I, Lib. v, Cap. 4; *Hist. Mem.*, I, 165. Years before this there had been a large ranch at San Lázaro, but "from here the Spaniards removed the cattle and horses when this nation became restless," evidently at the time of the destruction of Mototicachi (Manje, *Luz de Tierra Incógnita*, 247).

[2] It was evidently at this time, too, that the cattle and horses were sent to Quíburi, probably driven from San Lázaro by vaqueros when Kino made his way north (Kino, *Favores Celestiales*, Parte I, Lib. v, Cap. 4; *Hist. Mem.*, I, 164–166).

[3] Polici and Jironza.

them at the same time to go with the soldiers on the expedition against the enemies of the province." With the same double intent Kino again visited Quíburi in April. This place was a danger point on the Apache frontier and it needed his especial care.

Father Ruíz now arrived in the Pimería and for a time relieved Kino of one of his many charges. Father Eusebio at this time (March, 1697) turned over to him the mission of Cocóspora, with Santa María and San Lázaro as visitas. Cocóspora was delivered "with complete vestments for saying Mass, good beginnings of a church and house, partly furnished, five hundred head of cattle, almost as many sheep and goats, two droves of mares, a drove of horses, oxen, etc." The mission had prospered under Kino's watchful eye.[1]

The plants thus started in the north were carefully nursed and tended by the eager gardener. In the course of the next three years Kino and his companions went back and forth time after time between Dolores and the new posts on the Santa Cruz and the San Pedro, holding on until more missionaries should come. Their diaries give us intimate glimpses of mission beginnings in these stations where Kino had planted the seeds of Christianity and material civilization. Everywhere the flocks and herds which he had brought in were faithfully tended by the natives. Like the Pimas of Altar Valley, at his suggestion they built adobe houses in which to lodge him when he arrived, and for resident fathers when they should come. Proud was the village where he camped for the night and spent it in long "talks" about God and blue shells. Each time as he passed through he distributed little gifts, said Mass, gave religious instruction, baptized infants and sick adults, and encouraged the Pimas to hold back the terrifying Apaches. "Be brave, my children, defend the Faith, and God will send you bounteous harvests." Manje, Bernal, and Carrasco, when they accompanied Father Eusebio, made impressive discourses in the name of the king, reinforced Christian teachings, and bestowed canes of office on chiefs and headmen. Outstanding among all these caciques was Coro. The ranches founded by Kino, intended for the support of the projected missions, served also to supply him on his

[1] Kino, *Hist. Mem.*, I, 166. For comments on this point see Mora Contra Kino, May 28, 1698.

exploring expeditions, and likewise to equip soldiers and Indians for their campaigns against the Apaches.

There is space here for only a few individual glimpses of Kino's missionary labors in the upper Santa Cruz and San Pedro valleys during these three years, and of each of the young mission plants which he was cultivating there. Only a kaleidoscopic view can be given.

When in November, 1697, Kino, Bernal, and Manje went from Dolores to Quíburi, on their way to the Gila River, runners went ahead to herald their coming. When their dust was seen in the distance, villagers washed their children's faces and prepared them to stand in line when the padre arrived. At Remedios they obtained fresh beef for the journey. At Cocóspora Father Ruíz welcomed and lodged them hospitably. At San Lázaro they saw flourishing crops, and seventy people were counted. Santa María had two hundred inhabitants, who cultivated not only maize and beans, but also cotton, which they spun and wove for clothing. Bacadéguache, now San Rafael Valley, just west of Canelo Hills, was a flourishing heathen village. Huachuca, now Babocómari Ranch, was preparing for a missionary, and Kino was lodged there in an adobe house with beams and an earthen roof. At Santa Cruz Gaybanipitea, opposite the site of Fairbank, the Indians had finished the house built at Kino's request and the ranch now had about a hundred cattle. A league below, at San Pablo de Quíburi, there was likewise an adobe house built for the awaited missionary.[1]

The return journey was up the Santa Cruz Valley. At Tumacácori Bernal counted twenty-three houses and one hundred and forty-seven persons. "They have made a house with a hall and a bedroom for Father Kino." At Guébavi Manje noted a cattle ranch south of the pueblo. At Bacoancos there was an adobe house. Here fresh beef was obtained from the herd of eighty cattle, and ninety natives were counted.[2]

Ten months later Kino and Carrasco went north over the divide and down the Santa Cruz Valley. Everywhere, as usual, they were

---

[1] In another place the glimpses of Bac afforded by the diaries of the different journeys are brought together in one picture. See pp. 502–510.
[2] Kino, *Hist. Mem.*, I, 248; Manje and Bernal, diaries.

welcomed with arches and crosses, roads swept, and merrymaking. Carrasco, as representative of the Crown, gave canes of office and made good talks to the Indians. Kino looked after both spiritualities and temporalities. Cocóspora was deserted, padre and neophytes having fled after the Apache raid in March. At San Lázaro Kino charged the natives with "building the new church." [1] Bacoancos had a house of adobe and the natives were caring for sixty cattle, ninety-two sheep and goats, and a drove of thirty mares. Kino baptized, Carrasco appointed governors, and a beef was killed for the journey. Guébavi gave the travelers a welcome that was especially impressive. The nàtives, in order to properly clear the roads for Padre Eusebio had even cut down large trees. Canes of office were given to chiefs here and from Los Reyes (Sonóidag), Coro's village three or four leagues to the east, who had come to see the Great Man. Tumacácori now had seventy-four cattle, an adobe house, and a maize field promising forty fanegas.

In March, 1699, Kino, Gilg, and Manje ascended Santa Cruz Valley on their return from Gila River. This was the time when Kino (or Gilg?) was ill at Tumacácori. At Bacoancos they were lodged in the adobe guest house and they killed for food one of the hundred cattle on the ranch. In the autumn of the same year (October–November, 1699) Kino and Manje went north again down the Santa Cruz. With them they conducted Father Leal, who came to see the great missionary field which Kino had opened there, and Father Gonzalvo, from Sonora, who evidently came with a view to taking up his abode in Pima Land. Cocóspora was still deserted. At San Lázaro they found an assemblage of natives from Santa María, who came to welcome the Padre Grande as he passed. At Bacoancos Manje counted forty natives houses and Kino baptized the governor's son. There was a casa de adobe, a ranch with two hundred sheep and goats, seven cattle, two small droves of mares, eleven young colts, and good crops of wheat, maize, and beans. One beef and two sheep were killed for the road. A few days later the ranch of Bacoancos supplied Bernal with ten beeves for a campaign against the Apaches; he took them in passing and settled with Kino afterward. At Guébavi Manje counted ninety natives and remarked that there was a larger population at

[1] This was after the Cocóspora church had been burned in March, 1698.

Los Reyes four leagues to the east. At Tumacácori the distinguished guests were lodged in the casa de adobe, in which Kino said Mass. The fathers baptized here the governor's son and other children.

The next April (1700) Kino went north to inquire about the blue shells and at the same time "to cast a glance at the spiritual and temporal condition of the three newly begun missions of the north and the northwest." As he journeyed he jotted down notes. Cocóspora had just been reoccupied. At Bacoancos the ranch contained one hundred and fifty cattle, a drove of mares, one hundred and seventeen sheep and goats, an adobe house, and good fields of wheat, maize, and beans. Siesta was taken at Guébavi, where there were eighty-four sheep and goats, an adobe house, and good fields of wheat, maize and beans. Kino camped at Tumacácori. At Los Reyes, off the road to the east, Chief Coro, who had recently been baptized at Dolores with the name of Antonio Leal, now had a village of more than five hundred people. Kino tells us that "In all places there were many more people and more houses" than when he had been here six months before. The mission plants were growing. In April of the next year (1701) Kino on his way south spent the night at Tumacácori and passed through Guébavi. At Bacoancos he counted three hundred and forty head of cattle on the ranch, where, a week previously, soldiers and Indian allies had obtained a supply of beef for a campaign.[1]

CXXXII

SAN XAVIER DEL BAC

Of all the settlements in the country of the Sobaípuris, San Xavier del Bac—Bacóida, the Place near the Spring—was the largest and most promising, and the one which at this time most warmed Kino's missionary heart. Not only was Bac itself a large settlement, with fine land and plentiful water; it was part of a much larger population. Down the river toward the north for a distance of some twelve or

---

[1] Kino, *Favores Celestiales*, Parte II, Lib. i, Cap. 3; *Hist. Mem.*, I, 233–234, 292.

Mission Tumacácori

Ruins of Mission San Luis Bacoancos

The main gate at Mission San Xavier del Bac

fifteen miles the chain of ranches and irrigated fields was almost continuous. Eight miles north of Bac was San Cosme del Tucsón, or Tupsón, at the foot of the truncated peak now with collegiate touch called "A" Mountain—"A" for Arizona. The city of Tuscón embraces the site of the native village and preserves its historic name. Three or four miles north of San Cosme, on the northern outskirts of the present city, was the large village of San Agustín del Oyaur. In this stretch of a dozen or so miles there was a population of two or three thousand Pimas, living largely by agriculture, with fine irrigated fields of maize, beans, calabashes, melons, and cotton.

The Bac-Tucsón Valley was an oasis in a vast desert. Neighbors were distant, and to reach them couriers had to make long jaunts. To the west were the Pápagos, to the east the Pima villages strung along San Pedro River. Forty miles southward, up the Santa Cruz, Pima settlements began again at Tumacácori. Downstream north of San Agustín there were San Clemente, near the present Rillito, and Santa Catarina de Cuituabagum, near the Picacho. These two were the only villages on the Santa Cruz River between San Agustín and the Gila.

In each of his journeys up and down the Santa Cruz Valley Kino paid special attention to Bac and its people. His diaries give us a vivid picture of this great Pima settlement in the last years of the seventeenth century. His visits in 1697 have already been recounted. Next year he and Carrasco were welcomed there with crosses and arches placed along the road, lodged in a good house of mats, and given food, water and presents. Carrasco counted in the settlement one hundred and sixteen houses and more than eight hundred persons. In the pastures there were twenty cattle and thirty mares, which Kino had brought in the previous year. From Bac Kino made a short excursion to visit the populous villages down the river to the northwest.[1]

A few months later Kino, Gilg, and Manje returned from the Gila by the way of the Santa Cruz River. At Bac they spent two days on account of hard rains, for it does rain in season, even in this arid country. Then the land bursts forth in raiment of glory. They found

[1] Kino and Carrasco, diaries, 1698.

here thirteen hundred persons assembled to celebrate their arrival with dancing, singing, and general merrymaking, and Manje estimated three thousand persons in the vicinity. The Indians showed Kino one hundred fanegas of wheat which they had harvested and were keeping under lock and key in his casa de adobe. They "pointed with pride" in good American fashion to the herd of cattle which, along with the wheat, they were guarding for the awaited missionary, and to the drove of mares, with their recent increase, part of which had long ears but were no less loved by their dams. Kino and Manje gave the customary talks and religious instruction.[1]

In October of the same year Kino and Manje and Fathers Leal and Gonzalvo visited Bac. Leal came to see the great missionary field which Kino had opened. Gonzalvo was the young Valenciano, then only twenty-six years old, who had sailed from Spain with Campos, six or seven years previously. He had now come from his station in southern Sonora, with a view to moving to Pimería Alta.[2] Runners went ahead and at Bac the guests were given an impressive reception, for not since the visit of Salvatierra eight years before had a Padre Grande graced their town with his distinguished presence. "More than forty boys came forth to welcome us with their crosses in their hands," says Kino, "and there were more than three hundred Indians drawn up in a line, just as in the pueblos of the ancient Christians. Afterward we counted more than a thousand souls." The Faith and civilization were taking root. "There were an earth-roofed adobe house, cattle, sheep and goats, wheat and maize. . . . We killed three beeves and two sheep. The fields and lands for sowing were so extensive and supplied with so many irrigation ditches running along the ground that the father visitor said they were sufficient for another city like Mexico."

Leal was greatly impressed by what he saw, and his visit was decisive in the plan to found a mission here. Manje tells of his enthusiasm: "The father visitor having traveled through the whole valley, the fields and the agricultural lands, and seeing them so rich and fertile and irrigated by many acéquias, it seemed to him sufficient not

---

[1] Manje, *Luz de Tierra Incógnita*, 271.
[2] Record of the burial of Gonzalvo (Original MS. in the Bancroft Library).

only for a mission of three thousand Indians, but for a city of thirty thousand persons." [1] The prophecy has more than come true.

While Kino went north to visit again the villages beyond Tucsón, Leal and Gonzalvo remained in the vicinity of Bac. There Leal counted three thousand souls, "who, by their affability and the insistence with which they urged him to give them as a minister Father Francisco Gonzalvo, touched his heart." The youthful Valenciano's smile had won the Pima children. Leal granted the request and Gonzalvo promised to come, "telling them that he would return as soon as he was relieved of the mission . . . which he was administering, and that it was necessary to return to equip himself and bring his ornaments and books." [2] Kino too had a dream of Bac with himself in the picture.

Manje had a taste for adventure, and he recorded an exciting event which occurred here at this time. It is a gem of Southwestern folklore—the tale of the House of the Wind. "I and the soldiers accompanying him, the reverend father visitor went on foot to a little hill close by, the only one there is in these extended champaigns, which look in all directions." It was perhaps the once fortified flat-topped peak three quarters of a mile southwest of Mission San Xavier del Bac, which gives a commanding view of the surrounding country. "We climbed to the top to view the vast plains, and found running around the summit a fortification, consisting of a stone wall, with a plaza in the middle, in whose center there was a white stone like a pyre or a sugar loaf, half a vara high and stuck in the ground." It was a typical cerro de trincheras like the one formerly seen by Kino and Manje in the Altar Valley. "Conjecturing that it might be some idol which the heathen Indians worshiped, we used force and pulled up the stone, which was imbedded in the soil a third of a vara, leaving a round hole."

Then they got a surprise. "Not noticing anything at the time, we descended from the hill. But before we reached the village there arose a great and furious wind and hurricane which hurled us down

---

[1] Manje, *Luz de Tierra Incógnita*, 277; Kino, *Favores Celestiales*, Parte I, Lib. vii, Cap. 3; *Hist. Mem.*, I, 205.

[2] "In this way he consoled them with hopes, but although he came much later to the administration of this pueblo of San Javier and reaped a great harvest of baptisms and reductions, he did not remain longer than till the year 1702, when the rancherías of Juaxona and Tunortaca perverted two near-by rancherías, which began to kill the drove of mares and the cattle herd" (Manje, *Luz de Tierra Incógnita*, 277).

on the ground, making it impossible to walk on account of the fury and the force with which it blew. When the terrific wind arose, the Indians, none of whom had ascended with us, began to yell and make a hullabaloo, saying *Úbirique cúpioca,* meaning that we had opened the House of the Wind. This in fact was rebellion."

The Spaniards were not a little worried, as can readily be guessed. "The sun set, and all night long the wind blew so hard that we could not sleep, because it seemed about to blow down the house and pull the trees up by the roots." But the natives knew how to manage. Making the proper prayer to the Wind Spirit, toward morning they climbed the hill and closed the orifice. Thereupon "the furious hurricane ceased completely and the day was serene and peaceful." Manje continues, "It seems to be some volcano of air, and it is surprising that the region is not subject to earthquakes, for there never are any, according to what the Indians say." Whatever anger the natives may have felt over this disturbance of the House of the Wind, it did not mar Kino's relations with them. But the incident revealed another dark force for the missionary to combat.[1]

Things came to a head at Bac six months later. In April, 1700, Kino returned and with his own hands laid the foundations of the mission church. For so interesting an event details arrest our attention. It will be remembered that on April 21 he left Dolores to inquire about the blue shells and "to cast a glance at the spiritual and temporal condition of the three newly begun missions of the north and the northwest." He had with him three Indian officials of Dolores, seven servants and fifty-three horses and mules. Apparently there was no other white man in the party. He and his Indians unattended could carry the Gospel to the borders. At nightfall, on April 25, he arrived at Bac, was given a hearty welcome, and in return delivered greetings sent by the Padre Grande, Father Leal, whom they had so greatly impressed. That night he spoke the Word of God.

Kino had intended to continue his journey to the Gila and the Colorado, but he now changed his mind. He learned that soldiers had gone to the Soba country, which might mean that there was trouble there that would make an excursion to the Colorado unwise.

---

[1] Manje, *Luz de Tierra Incógnita,* 276. His manuscript diary gives additional details.

So, he says, finding himself with so many Indians in the great valley, "who were close to three thousand," and in view of the many prayers of the natives that he should stay with them, he decided to remain here, summon Indians from all directions and from them inquire about the blue shells.

While the chiefs were assembling he proceeded with founding the church for a great mission. The best account of what he did is the one which he himself wrote in his diary. "During the seven days that we were here, while most of those whom I had sent with the invitations were on the way, we catechized the people and taught them the Christian doctrine every day, morning and afternoon. We killed six beeves of the three hundred which they were tending for me here, with forty head of sheep and goats, and a small drove of mares. They also had a good field of wheat which was beginning to head; and during the following days they planted with maize for the Church a large field which they had previously cleared." On the 27th Father Eusebio baptized five Indian children.

Next day Kino wrote in his diary the entry which should set at rest forever the perennial conjectures regarding the date of the formal founding of the celebrated mission of San Xavier. It no longer avails to say "authorities differ." Here it is: "On the twenty-eighth we began the foundations of a very large and spacious church and house of San Xavier del Bac, all the many people working with much pleasure and zeal, some in excavating for the foundations, others in hauling many and very good stones of tezontle from a little hill which was about a quarter of a league away." The identity of this "little hill" has recently been discussed by Arizona historians. "For the mortar for these foundations it was not necessary to carry water, because by means of irrigation ditches we very easily conducted the water where we wished. And that house, with its great court and garden near by, will be able to have throughout the year all the water it may need, running to any place or workroom one may please, and one of the greatest and best fields in all Nueva Biscaya"—which with a jolt reminds us that Arizona was at that time indeed a part of New Biscay.[1] "On the twenty-ninth we continued laying the foundations of the

[1] Sonora, including Pimería Alta, at this time was an alcaldía mayor of Nueva Vizcaya.

church and of the house." The most famous structure in all that region had been begun.

Next day Kino went down the river to San Cosme and San Agustín, returning at night to Bac. The summoned Indians had begun to assemble from all the country round, and now the *Credo,* distant peoples, and blue shells became an engaging blend. That night, Kino tells us, "we had long talks, in the first place in regard to our Holy Faith, and in regard to the peace, and quietude, and love, and happiness of Christians, and they promised, as we requested of them, to carry these good news and teachings to other rancherías and nations much farther on, to the Cocomaricopas, Yumas, etc. . . . We discussed also what means there might be whereby to penetrate to the Moquis of New Mexico, and we found that by going straight north the entry would be very difficult, since these Pimas were on very unfriendly terms with the Apaches who lived between." Eight decades later the intrepid Garcés solved the Apache trouble by going round them—as stubborn people and stubborn mules are usually circumvented. Next day more delegates arrived, and again Kino talked with them nearly all night, in regard to the eternal salvation of all the nations to the west and northwest, and likewise "in regard to the blue shells." [1]

Such is the first hand story of the laying of the foundations of the first church at Mission San Xavier del Bac. It is a priceless record. It establishes, regarding a precious monument, an historical fact which will always be treasured.

Urgent tasks called, and at the end of seven days Kino turned his face southward, taking with him a pledge of loyalty. The farewell was touching. "On May 2, having solemnized three other baptisms and two marriages *in facie Ecclesiae,* and bidding goodbye to those captains and governors, we set out for . . . Dolores. All the children gave me many messages for the father visitor, the Señor military commander,[2] and all the Spaniards: and the captain of San Xavier del Bac gave me his son, who was probably about twelve years old, to come and he did come with me the sixty leagues' journey to . . . Dolores to be taught the prayers and the Christian doctrine and to assist at

---

[1] Kino, *Hist. Mem.,* I, 230–238; *Favores Celestiales,* corresponding passage.
[2] Leal and Jironza.

Mass." In other words, the boy was to serve as acolyte in the church at Dolores. The chief's confidence in Kino and his teaching was complete. Who can tell just what was the secret of this Jesuit's unexcelled gift?

This historic event at Bac closed with a dramatic incident which illustrates the quality of the man from Segno. Gentle as a child, and endowed with Christ-like compassion, he was as hardy as the toughest frontiersman. On May 2 camp was made at Tumacácori. Next morning as Kino was going at sunrise to say Mass he received a hurried appeal from Father Campos at San Ignacio. The soldiers there had arrested a poor Indian on some charge and were about to put him to death on the 4th. Father Eusebio must hasten to help save the prisoner! He did not hesitate. He said Mass and wrote a note to Escalante about affairs in the Altar Valley. Then, mounting his horse he sped south with his priestly robes flying. He does not brag about it, but merely states the bare facts. "Traveling that day more than twenty-five leagues," he writes, "I arrived almost at midnight at San Joseph de Hymeres, and the next day very early, in time to say Mass, at San Ygnacio, and we succeeded in rescuing the prisoner from death." By the railroad from Tumacácori to San Ignacio it is seventy-five miles. If Kino went by the then usual route through Cocóspora, the distance was considerably more. Yet next day he rode to Remedios, and the next to Dolores.

Here Kino found pleasing news. While at Bac, in his enthusiasm for the place, he had written to Father Leal, "pleading" to be missionary there, and asking for a successor at Dolores. He and the visitor had discussed the matter before, and now, on his arrival, he found a letter from Leal granting his request. The news was almost too good to be true! "Let me say, my father," the visitor wrote, "that, in regard to what your Reverence writes about the founding of San Xavier del Bac, what has been said has been said—*lo dicho, dicho*—and that your Reverence may look upon it as your mission, because it appears to me very expedient for progress in the future; for your Reverence being so far this way at Dolores, it is not easy to see and to go frequently to the people of the Río Grande. And so, when your Reverence may think best and may please, it shall be arranged, and your Reverence may go thither, as we agreed when we discussed it there."[1] Kino and Leal had made this plan several months before, after Leal had visited Bac. And the central reason for the proposal was that Kino might be on the frontier where things were doing, and nearer to the Promised Lands of the Colorado and of California.

Father Eusebio prepared at once for the change. He writes, "Here at . . . Dolores I ordered rounded up the fourteen hundred-odd cattle which were here, and told the overseer to divide them in two equal parts and take, as he did take, one part to San Francisco Xavier del Bac, and they made the necessary corrals, etc." The sorrow at the thought of leaving Dolores was mingled with the joy of moving on to a new and larger field.[2]

CXXXIII

BIRDS OF PASSAGE

In spite of his zeal for Bac, his permission to go there, and his actual preparations, Kino did not after all become its missionary. No Jesuit came to relieve him at Dolores, and so another was sent in his place to San Xavier. This was one of the great sorrows of his optimistic life.

Appeals for more workers, nevertheless, had at last proved partially effective. As a result of Kino's continual bombardment, Leal's wide-eyed journey through the Pimería, and his emphatic reports to Mexico, four missionaries arrived in 1701. Father Eusebio's personal disappointment now gave way to joy for Pima Land. His new missions would have resident pastors. More souls would be saved. Two of the new-comers were sent to the Altar Valley and two to the Santa Cruz. Quíburi did not get one, for Chief Coro had withdrawn with his people to Los Reyes. Father Ignacio Iturmendi was put in charge of Tubutama, and aged Father Barillas was reassigned to Caborca, which

---

[1] Kino, *Hist. Mem.*, I, 238–240.
[2] Kino adds: "But never did a father come to succeed me in Nuestra Señora de los Dolores, nor could I go permanently to San Xavier del Bac" (*Favores Celestiales,* Parte II, Lib. i, Cap. 6; *Hist. Mem.* I, 241). Yet Father Velarde says he was Kino's companion for eight years.

he had occasionally visited since 1698. Each of the missions, of course, had several visitas, or substations. To the Santa Cruz Valley came Father Juan de San Martín, to found a mission at Guébavi, with Tumacácori and Bacoancos as visitas. Youthful Gonzalvo came to San Xavier, and so kept his promise made to the admiring natives there the previous year.

The coming of the four new Black Robes was an event for the border, the topic of the day in the refectories of the missions and in the huts of the native villages. They arrived in hot mid summer, and Leal assigned them to their posts. "They found the many docile people," Kino wrote, "and cattle, crops, and harvests, and the beginnings of houses and churches which his Reverence had seen with his own eyes. And they remained very well content, with great hopes of establishing there in the interior some very flourishing missions, as they said and wrote to me and to other persons on different occasions." [1]

Kino gave the newcomers his customary generous help, assisting them with stock for their ranches. He had already sent seven hundred head of cattle from Dolores to Bac in addition to the original herds which he had driven in himself. His aid to the other newcomers is reflected in letters written by them and by Father Leal. On the last day in June Father San Martín, weary and sweaty, was at San Ignacio on the way to his new destination. His baggage train had preceded him. On that day he wrote to Kino in reply to a friendly note of welcome and an offer of assistance: "Yesterday afternoon, on account of the rain, which was heavy, we did not set out from San Ignacio for Imuris, although the loads and packs had already gone." But the delay had its reward. "As nothing happens by chance, so far as God is concerned, His Majesty disposed my detention in order that I might receive your Reverence's letter and learn from it the very great charity which your Reverence does me, offering to assist me with all that is necessary for the new pueblos where holy duty assigns me."

Iturmendi likewise thanked Kino for generous assistance. From Tubutama he wrote on July 8 acknowledging the favor. "God will

---

[1] Kino, *Favores Celestiales*, Parte II, Lib. ii, Cap. 13; *Hist. Mem.*, I, 303; Manje, *Luz de Tierra Incógnita*, 284. Manje wrote in his diary, March 6, 1701, that the former missionary at Caborca, "Father Gaspar de las Barillas, occasionally enters, but leaves because he is so old and [Caborca] is so remote from the rest of the fathers and missions" (*ibid.*, 284).

reward your Reverence for the gift of cattle, sheep, goats, etc; the reward you will receive in the next life, for you show yourself a father to us poor fathers. I have been very grateful for the many favors of your Reverence." Leal also expressed his appreciation. "Much comfort have I had in your Reverence's letter, and because of those which the fathers have written to your Reverence. Now God is moving against the hindrances of the enemy; so I trust in His Majesty that He wills these provocations for your Reverence for your greater reward." [1]

Kino assisted with the mission plants as well as with the ranches. "In all places," he says, "buildings were constructed, and very good beginnings were made in spiritual and temporal matters. In Guébavi in a few months we finished a house and a church, small but neat, and we laid the foundations of a [permanent] church and large house." The ruins of this church or a later one are still to be seen on the bank of the Santa Cruz River. Some of these structures must have been substantial. Over half a century later Pfefferkorn became missionary at Atí, in Kino's time a visita of Tubutama. He tells us, "In 1756 I went to the place of my mission, where I found still standing the church which Father Kino had built for his future missionaries, and which was left undamaged in the revolt of the Pimas in 1751." Tradition thus gave Kino credit for these buildings, and whether well-founded or not it illustrates the name which he left in the land.

The new laborers, like so many of their predecessors, proved to be birds of passage. Two returned to other fields, and two were quickly removed by death. Aged Barillas was too frail for so thorny a vineyard as Caborca and he soon departed. San Martín's stay at Guébavi was likewise short, and we soon find him back in the vicinity of Hermosillo. [2] Father Gonzalvo remained at Bac for a year and won the hearts of the natives. Manje tells us, "Although he came . . . to the administration of San Javier and reaped a great harvest of baptisms and reductions, he did not remain longer than till the year 1702, when the two near-by villages of Juaxona and Tunortaca revolted and began to

---

[1] San Martín to Kino, June 30, 1701; Iturmendi to Kino, July 8, 1701; Leal to Kino, July 21, 1701 (all quoted in Kino, *Favores Celestiales*, Parte II, Lib. ii, Cap. 13; *Hist. Mem.*, I, 302–304).

[2] Kino, *Favores Celestiales*, Parte II, Lib. ii, Cap. 13; *Hist. Mem.*, I, 303, II, 93–94; Pfefferkorn, *Beschreibung der Landschaft Sonora*. In March, 1704, Father San Martín was at Pitquín, now Hermosillo (*Favores Celestiales*, Parte III, Lib. iii, Cap. 7; *Hist. Mem.*, II, 93–94).

kill the drove of mares and the cattle herd." [1] The Pimas were not all as gentle as Leal had thought—and Gonzalvo was not Kino.

But Manje did not tell—perhaps he did not know—the whole story. We get a flash of light on the closing of Gonzalvo's brief career at Bac from the pen of his fellow voyager to America. In the summer of 1702 Gonzalvo rode down the valley to the mission of San Ignacio sick unto death. The end soon came, Campos laid him to rest, and wrote the following entry in the *Libro de Entierros,* or burial register, of his mission of San Ignacio—the original of which lies before me: "On the 10th of said month of August, Feast of San Lorenzo, about four o'clock in the morning, Father Francisco Gonzalvo, having received all the Holy Sacraments, died at the age of twenty-nine years. He was by nation a Valenciano, for we came together from Spain. Being missionary at San Xavier del Bac, he came to this my house already ill and died of pneumonia, performing up to the last instant continual acts of Faith, Hope, and Charity, with all his faculties and in full conformity with the will of God our Lord. And he is buried in the chancel of Santa Ygnacia on the Gospel side.[2]

AGUSTIN DE CAMPOS, J.H.S."

Iturmendi, as we have seen, went out in March, 1702, to meet González on his return with Kino from the Colorado River, escorted him to Tubutama, nursed him in his last days, and laid him to rest there. Not long behind González, Iturmendi likewise went to his final sleep. Thus three Black Robes died on this frontier between April and August—González, Iturmendi, and Gonzalvo. Theirs was a life more hazardous than warfare. Father Eusebio had indeed found a "difficult mission." Ten years later Father Campos went to Tubutama, removed the remains of both Jesuits to Magdalena, and recorded the event in his own hand: "At the end of January [1712], having brought from Tubutama the bones of Father Manuel González, missionary for many years at Oposura, ex-visitor, who died at Tubutama on his return from the Río Colorado, whither he had gone with Father

---

[1] I conjecture that these names are varied spellings of Tucsón and Tututac. Possibly the Tunortaca is the same as Tumamac, the name of a site near the Desert Laboratory.
[2] *Libro de Entierros.* Mission San Ignacio. Original manuscript in the Bancroft Library. The record says he died of *un resfrío.*

Kino in the year 1702, and those of Father Ygnacio Yturmendi, missionary of Tubutama, who died there on June 4, 1702, within a year of his coming, we placed the remains solemnly in this chapel, those of Father Manuel in a little box on the Gospel side, and those of Father Ygnacio in another on the Epistle side.[1]

AGUSTIN DE CAMPOS."

So Kino was left to carry on, discouraged though he must have been. In the fall of 1702 he made the round of the visitas in the west and the north, helping personally with the development of the mission plants. "It had been some time since I had seen the children of the west and of the Soba nation, or the Sovaípuris of the north and of San Xavier del Bac; therefore I went in to work on the two churches of San Ambrocio del Búsanic and Santa Gertrudis del Sáric, and began the large church of La Concepción del Caborca, to the westward; and to look after the cattle, crops, and harvests of wheat and maize which they were tending for the fathers whom they hoped to receive."

Kino did not forget Sonóita and the far northwest. "I went in as far as San Marzelo, whence, by the captain of El Comac, I sent wheat to sow at the Colorado River and in the Yuma and Quíquima nations, grain and seed which had never been seen or known there, to see if it would yield there as well as in those other fertile new lands; and it did yield and does yield very well." This one deed extended wheat culture more than a hundred miles farther into the wilderness. Thus was Kino a pioneer of material civilization.

Of course he did not forget Bac. "Afterwards," he says, "I began also the very large church of San Xavier del Bac, among the Sovaípuris." The inference is that he went to Bac and continued the church whose foundations he had laid in April, 1700, and that this new activity was after Gonzalvo had departed. So Bac did fall once more to Father Eusebio's care. "And in all places there was a very rich harvest of souls, so ripe that I as well as some other persons, zealous for the advancement of these new conquests and conversions, was of the

---

[1] *Libro de Entierros,* 1703–1816. Mission Magdalena. Original manuscript in the Bancroft Library.

opinion that it would be well if I should go to Mexico to try to obtain the fathers necessary for the salvation of so many souls."

Leal again wrote words of encouragement and appreciation. "I thank your Reverence heartily for the great work which you are doing for the welfare of those poor souls. God will repay it. For the report of the supplies, crops, churches, sick people, etc., for everything, your Reverence will receive your reward in heaven." [1]

CXXXIV

PATRON OF ART

Kino in his thrift had been able not only to produce a surplus for new missions, but also at times to makes gifts to the Jesuit Province of New Spain, or for the Holy Sepulcher of San Ignacio, or for the cult of the Holy Patriarch. His competence was notable and doubtless was noted. In this generosity the native chiefs had direct participation. Late in 1697 Kino wrote to the Father General, "This year with Divine favor I shall send to Mexico goodly alms for the Holy Sepulcher of our Holy Father in Rome.[2] My intent and that of the three principal captains or *regulos* of this Pimería"—too bad he does not name them, but we may be sure that Coro was one—"is that in these two or three years we shall send for that Holy Sepulcher a thousand pesos for four statues of silver or marble, or for paintings, as your Reverence may decide and prefer." These were the statues proposed: "One of Nuestra Señora

---

[1] Kino, *Favores Celestiales*, Parte II, Lib. v, Cap. 3; *Hist. Mem.*, I, 373–374. This is the last actual glimpse we have of Kino at Bac, although presumably he was there more than once during the next nine years. About 1703 Velarde joined Kino at Dolores and left him freer to travel. In 1704 Father Gilg hoped to be assigned to Bac. In October he wrote from Mátape, "Now my Father Kino, good courage, for my great desire, intention and design is to go to San Jabier del Gran Bac of the Pimas, setting out shortly from Mátape. *Faxint Superi et Superiores*— May the gods and the superiors grant it" (Kino, *Favores Celestiales*, Parte III, Lib. iv, Cap. 6; *Hist. Mem.*, II, 106). In his report signed February 2, 1710, Kino mentioned San Xavier del Bac as one of the interior mission stations with *"temastianes,* or teachers of the doctrine, . . . many infants and some adults baptized, . . . cabildos of justices, governors, captains, alcaldes, fiscales, . . . topiles, alguaciles, good beginnings of houses for the . . . fathers . . . churches, fields of wheat, maize, and beans, cattle, sheep and goats, horses and mules, droves of mares, and beginnings of gardens, all of which the very domestic and loyal natives tend, just as if the fathers whom they pray and beg for . . . were actually living there" (*Hist. Mem.*, II, 270–274).

[2] Kino to Thirso González, Dolores, late in December, 1697. Original Spanish manuscript, Ex. Arch. Procuratoris Generalis, S.J. Collegia Mexicana n. 97a. Printed by Tacchi-Venturi in *Archivum Historicum Societatis Jesu*, III (Rome, 1934), 251–254.

de los Dolores, another of our Father San Ignacio, the third of San Francisco Xavier, and the fourth of San Francisco de Borja, these being the principal patrons of the chief pueblos of this Pimería, and the names of the principal captains and governors."

Kino understood the mechanism of credit, interest, and exchange. "Another hundred pesos I shall send for the expenses which my letters may cause in Rome. And if your Reverence approves, this eleven hundred pesos may be borrowed in Rome. For this district of Our Lady, which is already worth more than forty thousand pesos and gives four or five or more thousand pesos each year [to the new missions], will pay not only the principal but also the interest, as they call it,[1] of five, or six, or seven per cent, which may be used in Rome or in Spain. I say this in order that your Reverence may decide immediately, or so much the more quickly, whether this little aid by these good children may be made use of in a work so holy that all the children of so holy, yea! a most holy Father, desire it, and their children's children, and those yet unborn—*Et nati natorum et qui nascentur ab illis.*"[2]

Regarding these statues the distinguished Father Tacchi Venturi just now tells us: "When Chino made these suggestions, the design for the new altar and tomb of the Founder of the Society, in the Gesù, a work which is the masterpiece of Brother Andrea Pozza, had already been approved. As is well known, only one of the four statues which Chino would have liked to see included in the design actually found a place there. This is the statue of San Ignacio, an admirable work by the sculptor Le Gros."[3] This work of art, then, was in part made possible by Kino and his Indians of Pima Land.

There were other contributions. Four years later Kino sent to Mexico ninety-seven marks of silver (about seven hundred pesos) for the Holy Sepulcher, "and on other occasions other amounts." He had promised two thousand pesos for this purpose, but customary difficulties in sending the silver from Mexico occurred. But he suggested a

---

[1] "Ut vocant."

[2] This is perhaps an echo of Vergil, *Georgic* I. 434; *Totus et ille dies et qui nascentur ab illo:* "Both that whole day and those that shall be born thereof."

[3] Father Pietro Tacchi Venturi, "Nuove Lettere Inédite del P. Eusebio Francesco Chino, d.C.d.G." in *Archivum Historicum Societatis Jesu,* III, pp. 248–264.

way out. Why ship silver for pirates to capture? Why not balance credits across the Atlantic? So he wrote to González that if he could find someone in Europe to give a thousand pesos for a mission, it could be used over there for the Sepulcher, and he in turn would endow a new mission, thus making unnecessary the shipment of coin or bullion. In fact he would give not only the thousand pesos, "but fifteen hundred or two thousand pesos in the goods of these new, rich districts," the choice of mission founded to be determined by the European donor and the Father General.[1] This was a clever way to suggest an endowment for a new mission. It is like the fifty-fifty gifts to modern universities —which trustees have come to handle with gloves.

Through difficulties of trans-Atlantic shipment, or through indifference to his requests, silver sent by Kino to Rome for these pious purposes did not always reach its destination. A few months later he wrote to González again about his gift for the Sepulcher of San Ignacio. "For although we have sent to Mexico several amounts of silver for that purpose (on one occasion there were ninety-seven marks, which amount to more than seven hundred pesos)[2] I have had no news that they have gone over; and much of this they have sent to us invested in goods from Mexico which we did not request." So he again asked the Father General to find a donor to give $2000 for a mission; or if preferred, one thousand of it could be spent in Rome for the Holy Sepulcher or for the cult of the Holy Patriarch. In return Kino would give two thousand dollars for a new mission.

To dispense all this generosity Kino insisted that he was able; no need to worry about that. "For besides the stock above mentioned, I have here in this district of . . . Dolores and its vicinity more than two thousand more cattle, many sheep, goats, many horses, wheat, maize, etc. And I shall not die happy without first keeping this promise, which is of such consolation to me, *et promisum cadit in debitum.*"[3]

---

[1] "If perchance in Europe there were some pious persons who would be pleased to give as alms one thousand pesos to the new conquests and new conversions and missions of California and of this region, I would be pleased to have your Reverence use there that one thousand pesos, and I would give here in exchange not only an equal sum, but fifteen hundred or two thousand pesos." Kino to Thirso González, October 18, 1701.

[2] Therefore a mark was worth about seven pesos.

[3] "And the promise becomes an obligation." Kino to Thirso González, February 2, 1702. Original Spanish manuscript in the central archives of the Jesuit Order.

CXXXV

REMEDIOS AND COCÓSPORA IN NEW ARRAY

After Kino returned from his journey to the Colorado in 1702 he
hoped to follow up the triumph by another expedition, one which
would take him clear around the head of the Gulf and down the
California coast to Loreto. In imagination he saw himself embracing
Salvatierra, Picolo, and Ugarte there and telling of his adventure. At
the same time, his visits to the industrious Yumas and Quíquimas inspired him with the idea of going to Mexico to appeal for more missionaries, as he had done after the martyrdom of Saeta. The plan to
go to the capital seemed timely just now. The king had granted alms
for eight new missionaries for the Pimería. Procurators were in Europe,
and it was hoped they would return in the autumn with a large contingent of young and enthusiastic Jesuits. Now would be the time to
strike.

This would mean another long horseback ride to Mexico City,
but little cared Kino for bodily aches. Time enough to rest when he
became old—he was only fifty-seven now. To present his project to
Father Leal he saddled up and rode again over the familiar mountains
to Guépaca. Leal was convinced. He not only thanked Kino by word
of mouth, but wrote him a long letter to show to the new visitor, who
was expected soon, urging him to send Father Eusebio to the capital "to
speak face to face" with the provincial and the viceroy, in an appeal
for more workers.

Prospects seemed good. But an unforeseen circumstance caused a
change of plans. Mars thrust in his gory hand. Just now all Europe,
and many parts of America as well, were ablaze with the War of the
Spanish Succession. The annual fleet could not sail from Cádiz to
Vera Cruz. Consequently the new Jesuit provincial could not come
on time, nor the procurators who had gone to Rome, nor the eight
missionaries who already had been granted and even equipped at
Sevilla. War raises various kinds of hell; this was a new brand, Kino
thought. It left his pagan friends still in the toils of Satan. The upshot
of the situation was that he concluded that the proposed journey to

Mexico would be untimely. Other considerations prevented him from making his projected expedition around the head of the Gulf. So he concentrated his efforts on things nearer home. "The heaven-appointed time must not have arrived," says Kino, "for my going or expedition by land to California, Upper and Lower, was prevented, and I therefore tried to apply myself to other ministries."[1] The particular ministry to which he now devoted himself was the completion of the churches at Remedios and Cocóspora.

What with Kino's many occupations and the Apache attacks, building had gone slowly at these places, though he had under way two fine churches, each with a transept, which was not common in Sonora. It is interesting to follow their varied fortunes, for they illuminate the daily life of the great missionary.

When he went north in February, 1699, Kino left the walls of the church at Remedios "nine varas high and ready to be roofed." In his absence there were heavy rains, and on his return he found that the edifice had suffered greatly. "The conduits were now clogged and the water, collecting in a great pond, soaked the foundations so that the presbytery fell down, which it was a great pity to see." When he saw the havoc his heart sank, but he set about repairing the damage. A year later the work was still in progress and Manje noted that the temple when finished would have "the best nave and transept of all those in the province of New Spain."[2]

Building operations at Cocóspora were even slower than at Remedios, for they suffered a still greater disaster. When in March, 1697, Kino turned Cocóspora over to Father Ruíz, there were "complete vestments or ornaments for saying Mass, good beginnings of a church and a house, partly furnished, five hundred head of cattle, almost as many sheep and goats, two droves of mares, a drove of horses, oxen, crops, etc." Kino had been active there.

Ruíz remained at Cocóspora only a year, when he was driven out by an Indian attack. On February 25, 1698, the Jocomes, Sumas, and

---

[1] Kino, *Favores Celestiales*, Parte II, Lib. v, Cap. 3; *Hist. Mem.*, I, 373–377. The procurators were Rolandegui and Vera.

[2] Kino, Colocasión de Nuestra Sa. de los Remedios en su Neuva Capilla, Sept. 15, 1698. Original Spanish manuscript, Archivo General y Público, Mexico, Misiones Tomo 26. Manje, *Luz de Tierra Incógnita*, 272, 275, 279; Kino, *Hist. Mem.*, I, 243.

Apaches swooped down on the place at a time when most of the men were away. Ruíz and a handful of defenders put up a good but a losing fight. The enemy killed a number of neophytes, sacked the pueblo, and burned it. When they pursued the marauders, the defenders were ambushed and nine of their number killed. Father Ruíz, having lost everything, even to his clothes, fled to the interior. The natives, too, deserted, and for two years Cocóspora was without missionary or inhabitants.

But confidence was gradually restored, and in April, 1700, Kino found at Cocóspora one hundred and fifty natives "who had just returned to settle this pueblo, and had just rebuilt and roofed a hall and a lodge for the father's house, with orders soon to roof the little church also." [1] The rebuilding and the administration of the mission were now in Kino's personal charge. A year later he fortified the pueblo with towers. [2]

Now, at the end of 1702, his projected journeys to the Colorado and to Mexico having been prevented, Kino turned as a major interest to the completion of the churches at Remedios and Cocóspora. In a little more than a year they were finished, and were objects of pride and personal satisfaction to their builder. Of his work on these temples he wrote with enthusiasm, and his own words will be more interesting than mine. "Because my going to Mexico, as well as to California, had been prevented, I applied myself to building with all possible vigor and speed, so as to have this work more advanced, the two churches in my second and third pueblos, on which small beginnings had been made." He had set himself a standard and now he rose above it. "When the Father Visitor, Antonio Leal, saw this church of . . . Dolores, he said it was one of the best he had seen in all the missions. Nevertheless, the new ones which I undertook in the following months turned out even better, for they have transepts."

For this work of building Kino had thriftily prepared the means. "After having commended all things to His Divine Majesty and to our great patron of the new conversions, the glorious apostle of the Indies,

---

[1] Kino, *Hist. Mem.*, I, 115, 119–120, 166, 174–177, 232–233, 274–275, 292. Manje, *Luz de Tierra Incógnita*, 247.
[2] Kino, *Hist. Mem.*, I, 274.

Pencil sketch by Pinart, 1879

Mission Cocóspora

Interior view of ruins of Mission Cocóspora

San Francisco Xavier . . . I have tried to have in the three pueblos of my administration . . . sufficient supplies of maize, wheat, cattle, and clothing, or merchandise, such as cloth, sayal, blankets, and other fabrics, which are the currency that best serves in these new lands for the laborers, master carpenters, constables, military commanders, captains, and fiscals." These last were the native functionaries who kept the crews at work.

From the produce of his stock ranches and farms Kino could feed and clothe the workers, and purchase all necessary materials from the outside. He asked for little in the way of alms; he was a self-sustaining frontiersman. Near-by forests furnished timber. The neophytes were willing workers, and distant chiefs vied with each other in the number of gandules they could contribute for the enterprise. Sometimes they came with their entire families, and then Cocóspora looked like an Indian camp. Spanish neighbors, soldiers and citizens, contributed advice and skill.

"In these and the following months," Kino continues, "I ordered the necessary timber cut for the pine framework, sills, flooring, etc. I went into the interior and brought more than seven hundred dollars worth of clothing, tools, and heavy ware, and from other places I obtained more than three thousand dollars' worth, which shortly and with ease were paid for with the goods, provisions, and cattle of the three rich districts." [1]

To assemble laborers, messages were sent far and wide. Bac especially responded. "I invited some men from the frontier for the work on these buildings, and there came far and away more than I had asked for; and very especially, for entire months, the many inhabitants of the great new pueblo of San Francisco Xavier del Bac, which is sixty leagues distant to the north, worked and built on the three pueblos of this place and of my administration." Captain Coro came with his men. Other chiefs and their subjects rallied "from the west, the south-west, and the north . . . with their whole families." Thousands of adobes were made, "and high and strong walls were erected for two large and good churches, with their two spacious chapels, which form transepts, with good and pleasing arches. The timbers were brought

[1] Kino, *Hist. Mem.*, I, 379.

from the pineries of the neighboring mountains, and the two good buildings were roofed, and provided with cupolas, small lanterns, etc."

All this work Kino personally superintended, continually riding back and forth from one mission to another. He tells us, "I managed almost all the year to go nearly every week through the three pueblos, looking after both spiritual and temporal things, and the rebuilding of the two above-mentioned new churches." The round trip was nearly a hundred miles.

Of the new edifices Kino was pardonably proud. In the midst of his building a letter came from China saying that there Father Castner had built a fine sepulcher in honor of the Jesuit apostle San Xavier, costing about one hundred and seventy patacones or pesos. Well, said Kino, this was a trifle! Remedios and Cocóspora each had a transept and two chapels, "and each chapel would have cost more than five hundred . . . patacones. And the two churches would have cost about ten thousand pesos were it not for the fact that, thank the Lord and His celestial favors, through the fertility of the land of these new conversions, without the districts being pledged to a hundred pesos, the expenditures were reduced to five hundred beeves for consumption during the construction of these two buildings, five hundred fanegas of maize, and about three thousand pesos in clothing, which is the money used and current among the natives of these new conversions." China could not be mentioned in the same breath with Pima Land! Father Eusebio's dream of the Orient had been completely dispelled.

Here Kino throws light on his marketing activities. Surplus ranch products were sold for merchandise at towns and mines. "These goods are acquired in the many places where there are traders, all over the province of Sonora, not to mention the many mining camps old and new, which there are in all these mission districts, in exchange for provisions, flour, maize, meat, lard, tallow, candles, etc., which the districts produce, as well as for the silver which some, or most, give for these provisions."[1] Kino was a business man.

[1] Kino, *Favores Celestiales,* Parte II, Lib. v, Cap. 7; Parte III, Lib. ii, Cap. 15; *Hist. Mem.,* I, 378; II, 80–81, 86–88.

CXXXVI

DEDICATION CEREMONIES

At last the two beautiful churches were finished. The dedication was a great event for all the Pimería. It was planned for December 3, Feast of San Xavier, but there was delay and the time was set for January. Invitations were sent in all directions to Indians and Spaniards. Couriers rode east over the mountains to the Sonora settlements, and Indian runners sped west, northwest, and north to summon brown-bodied guests from distant tribes. From his neighbors Kino received gracious and encouraging replies, whose sweetness must have gone far to offset the wormwood with which the charges of his enemies were seasoned. "Your labor has been very great, and our Lord will repay you," wrote Leal. Manje, now alcalde mayor of the province, and General Ruíz, his predecessor, sent kindly messages. Captain Almeida hoped that Kino would "live to build twenty temples."

The season was inclement, and some of the Jesuit neighbors were kept at home by colds. Among those present was Father Gilg. Indian friends responded from far and wide. "Many natives from the interior, from the north, west, and especially the northwest, attended the two dedications, greatly to our pleasure. Many of them came more than one hundred leagues, as did the captain of the Yumas, with many of his people." They had trudged three hundred and fifty miles to see the spectacle to which the Master of Dolores had invited them.

The dedication of Remedios occurred on January 15 and 16. Next day a procession wound its way northward twenty miles to Cocóspora, where the ceremony was repeated on the 18th, 19th, and 20th. In it Father Gilg took a prominent part. The celebration was conducted "with all the ceremonies and benedictions which our Holy Mother Church commands, according to the holy Roman ritual. His Reverence chanted the two principal solemn Masses, aided by the good choir of . . . Remedios, and the father rector Adamo Gilg preached very well in the Pima language." So Father Adamo, who had struggled hard to learn the Seri speech, now commanded the Pima tongue also.

No better linguists than these Jesuits ever labored among the American Indians.

The installation of the statue of our Lady of Remedios four years previously had resolved itself into a paean of praise to Chief Coro and his gandules for their brave defense of Christian Sonora. Now, in the dedications, Kino found encouragement for his California dream. The Indians from the Colorado did not come empty-handed, but brought what they knew Father Eusebio most prized. They came with "gifts of shells from the head of the Sea of California, and with very good messages from the . . . Quíquimas, Cutganes, Coanopas, etc., nations on the land route to California. They sent their blue shells from the opposite coast and from the Sea of the South, where every year the China ship, or Manila galleon, is accustomed to come, and summoned me and other fathers to go to see them and to treat of their baptism and of their reduction to Our Holy Catholic Faith.

"And the blue shells from the opposite coast were a new argument for the passage by land to California, which was at thirty-two degrees of latitude, in spite of the contradiction of obstinate persons little inclined to these new conversions. For it was contended that these natives were unable to cross a great arm of the sea which the opponents placed there instead of the land, over which they bring us the shells which are produced only on the opposite coast of California. There, clearly, we have the land route to California."

So in the sermons delivered during the dedication, the Blue Shells and the Land Passage got inextricably mixed with Scriptural teachings.[1]

---

[1] "So sure were we of the singular celestial favors which we experienced in the two dedications of these two new churches," says Kino, "that with great satisfaction to ourselves and to all the amiable guests the three following admirable sacred texts were confirmed: 1. 'Say ye among the Gentiles that the Lord has reigned, for he hath corrected the world' (*Dicite in gentibus quia Dominus regnavit etenim correxitt orbem terrae*. Psalm XCV), for many with great error delineated California as an island . . . , and drew a Sea of California where there is none, for it comes up no higher than to thirty-two and a half degrees. 2. 'Dry land appeared even in the Red Sea' (*Terra aparuit arida et in Mari Rubro*). Many call the Sea of California the Red Sea; 'a way without hindrance' (*Via sine impedimento*) as chants our Holy Mother Church on the 8th of August and the day of the saints who have for their gospel (3), 'Go ye unto all the world and preach the Gospel unto every creature' (*Euntes in mundum universum. Predicate Evangelium omni creaturae*)." Kino, *Hist. Mem.*, II, 86–88.

Sons of Italy

CXXXVII

MINUTULI INSTALLED AT TUBUTAMA

F OR A YEAR OR MORE Kino had been confined to his home tasks. But with the churches completed he was soon again on the trail.
A new missionary came to Pima Land, and as usual it fell to Kino to install him. In December, 1703, when friends of the Pima missions least expected it, the wholly unlooked for worker arrived. He was Father Gerónimo Minutuli. He came "of his own accord, or to speak more truly, by disposition and control of the celestial favors of our Father." He had been missionary in California. But the mainland looked more promising, so he crossed the Gulf to Pimería Alta—with permission, of course.

Landing in Sinaloa, Minutuli came north to talk with Father Leal. He stopped to spend the Christmas holiday with Gilg at his Seri mission of Santa María del Pópulo, then continued north with his outfit. On the way he fell in with Kino's mayordomo, and by him sent word that from Valle de Sonora he intended to go to Dolores. There was an exchange of letters. Leal assigned Minutuli to the mission of Tubutama to take the place of Iturmendi, and Kino, in keeping with his rôle, went to meet the newcomer at Opodepe and escorted him to Dolores. On the way opponents of the missions had tried to scare Minutuli out or discourage him. "Throughout the journey from Cinaloa to Sonora, and even to . . . Dolores, his Reverence encountered great opposition and many obstacles. But since he was sent and came more by divine than by human disposition, he was always very constant, not fearing any of the thousand difficulties and obstacles which by so many routes and so repeatedly, and by plots so persistent, were placed in his way for almost an entire year." Kino thanked God for another man with stamina.

Minutuli arrived just in time for the dedication of the new churches, so he obtained at the start a most favorable impression of the Pimería. While engaged in the ceremonies Kino made plans for establishing him in his new charge. Minutuli went forward by way of San Ignacio; Father Eusebio returned from Cocóspora to Dolores and followed after him. Kino had made preparations for the new missionary. In preceding weeks he had ordered the house at Tubutama repaired, a good field of wheat sown, space for an orchard cleared, and planted with various small Castilian trees, grapevines, peaches, pomegranates, fig trees, pear trees, and all kinds of garden produce. Minutuli was given a warm welcome by the natives and was "greatly pleased at seeing the people so affable, domestic, and docile, with their officers, servants, vestments with which to say Mass, household furniture, sheep, and goats." The cattle and horses were still at San Ygnacio, whither they evidently had been moved when Father Iturmendi died. Kino aided Minutuli with new buildings. "We made plans for a good and spacious church and a house, and I promised to build the church at my own expense." Thrifty Father Eusebio!

Leaving Father Gerónimo happily at work, Kino returned by way of Búsanic and Síboda to Dolores. When he reported the expedition, Visitor Leal replied, "I thank you heartily, and God will recompense your Reverence for the work of going to El Tubutama with Father Gerónimo, as well as for the news that the father is pleased with the neophytes and they with him. For your Reverence has given him great comfort thereby, and likewise by the charity which you show him in the alms and in the cost of building the church, as you promised him. All this is sowing in good soil to reap a bountiful harvest. The paymaster is trustworthy and able." [1]

CXXXVIII

A CONFERENCE WITH PICOLO AT GUAYMAS

When Kino started for Tubutama to install Minutuli, his head was filled with the problem of aiding California. He was sending new

[1] Kino, *Favores Celestiales*, Parte III, Lib. ii, Cap. 17; Lib. iii, Cap. 3; *Hist. Mem.*, II, 84–85, 89–90; Kino to González, Jan. 24, 1704.

supplies to Guaymas and he planned to go there soon to confer with Father Picolo. And he still hoped to reach Loreto by going around the head of the Gulf. Salvatierra was urging it. Opponents had requested Leal to withhold permission. But Kino appealed to Thirso González, still Father General in Rome. "I beg of your Paternity," he wrote on January 24, 1704, "that you grant me permission to go by land to California and to return by way of the sea and Hyaqui from Loreto Conchó, where Father Salvatierra is, and afterward to go to Mexico to print a good new map of all these new lands and nations, with a relation of everything, for the good of so many souls." The relation, called *Favores Celestiales,* was already partly written.[1]

The journey to Guaymas was made as planned. This harbor had taken on a special significance. Three years earlier Salvatierra had founded there the mission of San José as a base for California shipping. Till the land route could be opened a Sonora supply base was vital, and in the California drama Guaymas came to occupy the rôle formerly taken by Hyaqui. For a time the giant Father Juan Ugarte worked there, and now Father Picolo was in charge—all members of the Peninsular staff. Guaymas, then, was a child of California, or California of Guaymas.

Kino and Picolo exchanged letters. Father Eusebio sent to Father Francisco fifteen packloads of flour as a gift for the California missions. And now he made the promised visit, to conduct more supplies and at the same time open a shorter road from Dolores. Previously the camino real had run through Guépaca, Ures, and Mátape and down the Yaqui River, thence back up the coast to Guaymas. It was roundabout, and a new road was desirable.

Preparations for the journey were made in the midst of the extra duties of Holy Week, during which many Spaniards had come from the new and near-by mining camp of La Soledad. Kino started on March 25, that very morning having performed thirteen baptisms, the while packing supplies, loading mules, and giving orders to be observed during his absence. His route lay down the San Miguel River through Cucurpe to the Sonora River. At the Seri mission of

[1] Kino to González, January 24, 1704, Fondo Gesuitico al Gesù di Roma. Epist. Selectae, II. n. 90.

Santa María del Pópulo he was welcomed and given fresh provisions by Father Gilg, and at San Francisco and Pitquín (now Hermosillo) by Father San Martín, the man who formerly had been at Guébavi. Thus far Kino was on a long-used camino real; from here he was a pathfinder. His route was essentially that now followed by the Southern Pacific Railroad from Hermosillo to Guaymas, where the traveler looks out from the car window on a dry, level, cactus and mesquite-covered stretch, broken by small ranges. The natives on the way spoke partly Pima and partly Seri. As Kino jogged along he stopped at villages to preach to the friendly people. At Cerro Grande he found three or four runaways from the missions.

Guaymas was reached at last, the mules brayed with joy at relief from their loads, and Kino was welcomed by some five hundred natives. At the moment Picolo was absent among the missions on Río Yaqui some fifty miles further south. Kino wrote to him and the other fathers there; in reply they invited him to come for a visit. The invitation to Tórin, where he had been nineteen years before, when with Atondo he abandoned California, especially tempted him. But he had to hurry back to Dolores. So Picolo returned to Guaymas, and here they had a conference. Both natives of Italy, they had much to talk about. Four days were thus spent together. At Picolo's request Kino baptized many catechumens, "for most of them spoke the Pima language, and they were Pimas like those of this extensive Pimería which Father Rector Adamo Gil used to call the Pimería Alta." So it was Gilg who suggested this now familiar name? As they visited, the two fathers discussed plans for supporting California with supplies raised on the mainland, and the ever present problem of obtaining more missionaries for "so many heathen souls of all this vast North America, of this mainland and of the neighboring Californias, Baja and Alta."

Kino saw "a hundred very good things" which Picolo was doing at Guaymas. He inspected the "very pretty and suitable posts. One had the corral for the cattle, and I noted that from it they could be embarked alive to be taken to the very near-by California," for San José was on the estuary that enters Guaymas Bay. In that vicinity he reported more than 4,000 natives. All in all he was greatly pleased "at seeing so great an opportunity to obtain much glory for our Lord, the salvation of so many souls, and the advantage of splendid fishing grounds, salt-beds, lands, gardens, cattle, sheep, goats, and a church and house which are being successfully built." That church, or its successor, still stands in the plaza of San José de Guaymas. The pueblo is now, or was recently, a military barracks.

The four days were up, and Kino had to return to Dolores. En-route many new heathen came out to the trail from their more remote retreats to see him. At his suggestion they agreed to assemble, when fathers should come, at the old mining camp of San Marcial. At Cerro Grande he endeavored to induce the runaway Indians to return to their missions, but in vain. At Pitquín and San Francisco he was again assisted by Father San Martín, and at Santa María del Pópulo by Father Gilg. Turning aside from the direct road home, he ascended the Sonora River to Guépaca to consult Leal.

Reporting to Thirso González his visit to Guaymas, Kino said that in October Picolo or his mayordomo would come with vaqueros to Dolores for more supplies, "for this district . . . is giving a hun-dred beeves to the new settlement of . . . Guaymas and two hundred others for California which are going to the ranch of Guaymas. And it may be that I shall go at the same time to take another peep at that heathendom." The new road would soon become a beaten trail, tramped out by the stock sent by Father Eusebio for the missions of the Peninsula.[1]

CXXXIX

WOLVES ATTACK THE FOLD

On his return from Guaymas Kino found letters from Rome and Mexico, among which there were two from Thirso González, the Father General, and one from Manuel Pineyro, the visitor general

[1] Kino to Thirso González, Dolores, June 30, 1704. Original Spanish manuscript, Fondo Gesuitico al Gesù di Roma. Epist. Selectae, II. n. 90. Printed in *Archivum Historicum Societatis Jesu.* III (Rome, 1934), 261–263. Kino to Alonso Quirós, Dolores, June 30, 1704. Original Spanish manuscript in the Maggs Collection (London), No. 27.

and now acting provincial. The two delighted him; the one was less pleasing. Some three years previously Father Eusebio had been appointed a second time rector of Pimería Alta. "For," says Kino, "although I made a nomination for the charge they did not listen to me." Now Pineyro requested him to name a successor. Kino complied, but his suggestion was not heeded. So Father Eusebio remained in office for the time being. "But," he protests, "I continued to be, and God willing, shall always be, more desirous and fond of living without such charges, and with religious freedom to attend to the welfare of these innumerable, poor, and needy souls of this vast North America, and of advancing their salvation by all possible methods and means, by word, by writing, or otherwise, than of acting in the capacity of superior, or reporting about other persons and their work, when there is so much to do, and in a matter of so great scruple and care, and of having each year to give an account of their persons to our Lord." [1] Kino was an individualist. By temperament he was unfitted to be a cog in a bureaucratic wheel—and he had something more important to do.

Father Eusebio was soon relieved of the office of rector, but new worries quickly rapped at his door. More correctly speaking, they were old worries which, like ill-natured curs, having slept for a time, now awoke to bark at his heels again. Kino had scarcely returned to Dolores when he was disturbed by "some new and calumnious hostility." The knockers were busy again. The trouble was that Satan, "by means of some persons unfavorable to these new conversions, who already on many other occasions had opposed them . . . to advance their own cause and that of the Common Enemy, hinted it about that the natives of this Pimería were so evil-natured that they were plotting to kill one of the missionary fathers." But Kino had loyal friends. Captain Becerra made investigations. Finding no evidence of hostility, he branded the story as "one of the usual idle and calumnious tales of those ill-disposed toward this Pima nation."

But the gossips soon found something else to talk about. In Sep-

---

[1] The rectorate was called Nuestra Señora de los Dolores, of which Mission Dolores was the capital. Kino, *Favores Celestiales,* Parte III, Lib. iv, Caps. 1–8; *Hist. Mem.,* II, 97, 98, 106, 107, 109.

tember (1704) it was reported that Chief Duck Tail (Cola de Pato), governor of Cocóspora, was plotting trouble. Duck Tail had said, so it was rumored, "that with the staff of office he was not a man, but that with weapons he was one." Rumor added that he had withdrawn to the mountains to assemble gandules and attack some place. Leal was disturbed and he asked Kino about it. "Over here it is said that the governor of Cocóspora has sent your Reverence the staff of office, saying that he intended to avenge the death of his kinsfolk, and that he has revolted with all Cocóspora. I beg your Reverence for information."

With his usual energy Kino proceeded to scotch the stories. He would expose the gossips. He would confront the tale bearers with the accused. He would take Duck Tail to Cucurpe for a hearing. "Knowing how foreign to all charity all these darnels were," he summoned the chief and his two sons, "both good cowboys." The call was promptly obeyed, and with Cola de Pato and his sons Kino rode to Cucurpe—a diverting picture they made—"that his calumniators might see him and be satisfied in the presence of many Spaniards." He convinced the investigators. This done he was on the point of continuing to Guépaca, to convince Leal and all the rest. Spaniards at Cucurpe, however, assured him that this was not necessary, "saying that they would there satisfy the father rector, the father visitor, and the alcalde mayor in regard to the innocence and loyalty of the governor of Cocóspora."

Duck Tail was vindicated, and Kino was cheered by many friendly letters. "I told you so," the chorus now rang. "I have always been confident that this about the governor of Cocóspora is false, and that they are powder flashes and whirlwinds of lies, whose source your Reverence knows. I have never given them credit," wrote Captain Salazar from Bacanuche. "I greatly rejoice that . . . the imagined or feigned revolt has gone up in smoke," Gilg wrote from Mátape. The friendliness of the Pimas was now demonstrated by another triumph over the Apaches. "The victory has been notable," wrote Gilg. "Blessed be God, who again has rescued the Pimas, proving that they are not such as they wish perforce to make them out."

When in trouble Kino was usually able to stem the tide of criticism by putting on a good show. And his Pimas were willing and loyal actors. The year ended with a Christmas celebration at Cocóspora which was both a new vindication of the Pimas and a love feast between them and the soldiery.

The Master of Dolores had triumphed again. But it was a constant fight. The wolves could be frightened off, but they always lurked about. The New Year brought a personal attack on Kino and an outrage on his missions. An "indiscreet lieutenant"—Father Eusebio does not tell his name—spread the report that Kino had sent out native officials to take Indians from other pueblos to Dolores, offering presents or other inducements. The "indiscreet lieutenant" did not stop here. He proceeded to restore the immigrants to their former villages. He went to Dolores "repeatedly, violently, and with great harshness, many stripes and serious threats of hanging, of death, etc., and took from us many Indians, more than ninety on one occasion alone." [1]

Kino was up in arms. This was the worst thing that had ever happened to him. He demanded an investigation. In the course of it the native justices of Dolores denied the charge of gifts and coaxing. The immigrants were then taken aside and questioned. All except three declared that no bribes or other inducements had been offered; they had moved to Dolores of their own free will, and they begged to be permitted to remain there. Nevertheless, a few days later, in Kino's absence, many of the immigrants were taken away, again "with much violence, with insults, harsh punishment, stripes, and threats of death." But most of them, Kino wrote with great satisfaction four years later, "after a little time returned to this pueblo of . . . Dolores, where they are found to this day."

Many persons were scandalized over these outrages. Polici wrote Kino, "On the one hand, I am greatly grieved by the persecution, so iniquitous, and on the other hand I envy your Reverence your patience and virtue." Father Minutuli went to Guépaca to protest, for his mission of Tubutama had been raided. Father Leal "having investigated everything . . . was amazed." Incensed, he appealed to the alcalde mayor for redress.

---

[1] Kino, *Favores Celestiales*, Parte III, Lib. iv, Caps. 4–9; *Hist. Mem.*, II, 102–113 *passim*.

Before this offense was punished another trouble for Kino was raised. Coro was now under fire. The same "indiscreet lieutenant" went to Santa María to barter for maize, boasting "that for this he had requested and obtained the lieutenancy of this Pimería." Such things have happened more recently and in other countries than Mexico. Chief Coro advised him not to treat the Pimas so harshly, lest they flee to the mountains, or even join the Jocomes and Apaches. Angry at what he regarded as impudence, the lieutenant spread a new tale. He reported that Coro and Duck Tail were in rebellion, and about to attack Sonora. Everybody was excited and urged the missionaries to flee for their lives.

The anxiety of the superiors is revealed by a communication written by Leal to Kino on March 25, 1705. "I desired a letter from there, because of the bad news which has arrived that Coro was coming to kill fathers and whomsoever he might encounter. I heard of this last night and I immediately reported to the alcalde mayor, who now will believe, and to General Retana. I am awaiting replies. . . . If there is danger, . . . set out at once and secure the things of the churches and whatever is possible. . . . If you should have any news regarding the matter, impart it immediately to the fathers, and secure their lives and whatever else is possible."

Meanwhile soldiers started for the scene of the supposed rebellion to save the lives of the fathers and punish the offenders. Miguel de Abajo, alcalde mayor of Sonora, set out for Cocóspora with twelve soldiers. At Bacanuche he learned from Kino that the rumor was a false alarm. Two days later he reached Cocóspora and found Cola de Pato and all his people quiet and friendly. Kino went to Cocóspora and summoned Coro thither. The chief came in friendship, bringing a following of his people. Terán, with soldiers and citizens from Opodepe, started for the scene of the supposed revolt. When they reached Cocóspora they found Kino calm, and Coro and Cola de Pato "perfectly quiet."

The affair ended in another love feast. All now went together to spend Holy Week and Easter at Dolores, where a great concourse of citizens, soldiers, and Indians were assembled. Kino had put on another impressive show for the benefit of his Pimas. To complete the triumph he sent Coro and Cola de Pato to Sonora to see General Retana. The General regaled them, "with much clothing, cloth, skirts, hats, knives, ribbons, etc., and they returned very well content consoled, and edified." When the alcalde mayor removed the "indiscreet lieutenant" Kino's victory was complete. By his generalship he had passed another crisis. The Indians were restored to their pueblos.

CXL

PICOLO BRINGS CHEER

Kino's victory over the "indiscreet lieutenant" synchronized with another favorable circumstance. Salvatierra had become provincial of all New Spain. He in turn appointed Father Picolo visitor of Sonora, and for a time now the fortunes of Pimería Alta were largely in the hands of four Italian friends: Salvatierra, head of all Jesuit Mexico; Picolo, visitor of Sonora; Kino, free lance of Dolores; and Minutuli, missionary at Tubutama, the key to the Altar Valley. They formed a notable quartet. All four were sons of Italy and they understood each other. All had labored in California, and their purposes harmonized. This augured well for Pima Land. From Mexico City Father Loyola wrote Kino: "Having a father provincial all Pima and all missionary, your Reverence will no doubt obtain whatever you may desire for the great good of those your beloved missions."[1] On the face of things it was a reasonable prophecy.

Picolo threw himself whole-heartedly into the promotion of the Pima missions, and Salvatierra lent what aid he could. Picolo on his way north wrote Kino from Mátape: "In spite of the Devil, who seeks confusion, those apostolic missions are going to be founded and advanced. Have fortitude, your Reverence, and patience, for I trust in the Lord that all will be adjusted and composed, and that the machinations of all Hell against the Pimería shall not prevail. Tomorrow, Wednesday, God willing, I shall go to Los Ures. I take that

---

[1] Kino, *Favores Celestiales*, Parte IV, Lib. ii, Cap. 7; *Hist. Mem.*, II, 150–151. Soon a fifth Italian, Father Crescoli, joined the group for a time.

route in order as soon as possible to be with your Reverence and with my Father Gerónimo Minutuli, whom I heartily salute." [1]

On the eve of Ascension Day Picolo reached Dolores, finding it in holiday attire. To welcome him and to participate in the festivities Kino had assembled "a concourse of natives, captains and governors, some of whom had come from far in the interior." To the edification of the Indians, the Padre Grande officiated in the ceremonies. "His Reverence chanted Solemn High Mass, accompanied by the good choir of singers" of which Kino was duly proud. In the chapel he preached a fervid sermon in the Pima tongue. One wonders how many native languages Picolo commanded. He had worked among the Tarahumares, the Cuchimíes of California, the Seris, and the Pimas. What linguists!

There were many things for the two veterans to talk about. The chief subjects the reader can easily guess. "We discussed the conversion of this extensive nation and of its neighbors, and the succor of California, his Reverence promising us many fathers." Could he guarantee them? That remained to be seen. "His Reverence was pleased to see this good and large church with good bells and ornaments, a good house, and a good garden" down by the riverside below the mission cliff. Kino might have listed also the fine irrigated fields and the pastures filled with well-fed stock.

Picolo spent three days at Dolores. Then, escorted by Kino, he set forth to inspect the other Pima missions. Together they crossed the mountains to San Ignacio. Halfway on the road they were met by Campos, glad to do honor to the distinguished visitor. "And in his second pueblo, that of Santa María Magdalena, where he was building the church and the house, they welcomed us with all kindness," says the chronicle. Kino now returned to Dolores, and Campos, the younger man, accompanied Picolo on the hard ride to Tubutama. Here they visited Minutuli, and with him went down the river to inspect his second and third pueblos, Atí and Oquitoa. Kino was still actively assisting these valley missions. In all places "building was going on," he says, "I have taken under my charge the erection of the church of . . . Tubutama, because, thanks be to the

[1] On Picolo's visits to Pima Land see, Kino, *Hist. Mem.*, II, 129–182, *passim*.

Lord, I had now finished the three pueblos under my own administration."

The visitor wrote Kino that he would be back at Dolores in time for the Feast of Corpus Christi. He needed advice. "I have received letters from the father provincial"—this was Salvatierra—"and we must have a talk." Bartíromo and Campos also would go to Dolores for the fiesta. "On Wednesday, God willing, we shall be at Santa Magdalena, on our return trip. Father Agustín and Father Gerónimo salute your Reverence heartily. . . . *Vale mey memor.*" Such letters as this, beaming with fraternal love, did much to mitigate the loneliness that so often came upon these exiles in the desert.

Picolo did not continue to Caborca, for there was no missionary there. Returning east, he and Campos visited Imuris. Here Kino met them and together the apostolic trio threaded the shady canyon to Remedios and Cocóspora, "where the fathers were rejoiced to see the two good and spacious new churches." Kino did not neglect to add, "both having transepts." Together they now turned south to finish the circuit at Dolores. Father Bartíromo came up from Tuape and the four Black Robes, all veterans, one in the prime of life and the others aging, told good stories, talked of "old times," and planned for the future.

Meanwhile a crowd of red, brown, and white men and women were assembling from all directions. "And with the concourse of many Spaniards . . . who came from the neighboring mining camps, and many nations from the interior, we held a solemn feast and procession of Corpus Christi, with a reliquary of gilded silver which in these past years Father Phelipe Esgrecho had presented as a gift to this mission." Writing four years after the event, Kino added with pardonable pride, "In the following year I bought at Mátape another very good reliquary or ceryl with wheat from this productive mission." The beauty of church ornaments was always a matter of greatest concern to the missionaries. By means of them they instilled in the natives added reverence for the Faith, for all beauty is a manifestation of the divine.

The solemnities over, Picolo went on his way, accompanied by Kino, Campos, and Bartíromo as far as Cucurpe, where Corpus Christi was celebrated on Sunday the octave. Kino and Campos returned to their missions, and Picolo went to Saracachi, the famous ranch near Cucurpe.

Kino, his garden, his missions, his wine, and his fruit, had made a deep impression on Picolo. Such hospitality was rare on that crude frontier. To Saracachi Father Eusebio sent the visitor "some trifles." Picolo replied: "I am in receipt of your Reverence's most welcome letter telling of your arrival at your most beautiful mission of . . . Dolores, which I bear graven upon my heart, together with all the other missions of the Pimería. . . . I am ready to serve your Reverence in any respect whatsoever, being very grateful to you, not so much for favors, caresses, and kindnesses which I have received in those holy houses of your Reverence, as for the love which I owe and have in my heart for you; and your Reverence's rare and most religious talents deserve it. I received the wine and the fruit from the fertile garden." These evidently were among the trifles. "Your Reverence's gifts still accompany me, and your garden, it seems, follows me with its choicest fruits. In truth, its apricots have come to me at Saracachi, perhaps as the farewell."

Picolo continued east and south, over mountain and valley, inspecting other Sonora missions. As he traveled the long circuit he wrote encouraging words to Kino, cheering the heart of the man who had met so many obstacles. From Oposura: "Although far from the Pimería I am there in heart; and oh! that my necessary occupations would permit me to labor and aid your Reverence in something!" From Mátape: "I salute your Reverence's governors and all the children. God grant me grace to return as soon as possible to see them all." From Batuco: "I should like to serve your Reverence as a muleteer on your apostolic journeys. . . . Those missions being the gateway to nations and people so extensive, it is necessary, my best beloved Father Eusebio, to put all our care upon them." [1]

Salvatierra added a word of encouragement. He had proved that he was indeed "all missionary" by returning for a moment to Cali-

[1] Kino, *Hist. Mem.,* II, 129–130, 146–147; Picolo to Kino, Tubutama, May 31, 1705 (Kino, *Hist. Mem.,* II, 136–137); Picolo to Kino, Saracachi, June 15, 1705 (*ibid.,* 138); Picolo to Kino, Batuco, January 19, 1706 (*ibid.,* 156–157); *Favores Celestiales,* Parte IV, Libs. i-iii.

fornia. Everybody marveled, for "no one ever heard of another provincial who had so apostolically come to such remote new missions." On his departure for Mexico again, he wrote to Kino expressing satisfaction with Picolo's report "of the good state of these missions of the Pimería, of the labors which have been and are being performed therein, and of the harmony and charity with which at present the fathers thereof deal with one another." It was an improvement. "For this I have given thanks, hoping now that each day we may make progress, because, all being united in God for one and the same end, we can better advance the service of God and the welfare of souls. . . . The fathers over here, who recognize your Reverence as their benefactor and apostolic model in your indefatigable labors, salute your Reverence."[1] No better testimony to Kino's qualities could be given.

CXLI

THE BUILDERS' PARADE

Salvatierra's encouragement did not end with words. He appointed Kino procurator, that is, purveyor, of the Pima missions. The title, it might be said, merely made official a function which the free lance of Dolores had been performing unofficially on all the frontier for nearly twenty years. But it was a recognition of his business ability, and it gave him more authority and more funds to work with. In the second place, Salvatierra sent Father Domingo Crescoli—another Italian, by the way—to reoccupy Caborca.

In the middle of January, 1706, Kino escorted Father Domingo to his new mission. At Tubutama they were joined by Minutuli. It was some time since Kino had been at Caborca, but the place had not been abandoned. After Iturmendi departed, Campos and Minutuli kept the sparks of Christianity alive. Messengers had gone before, and elaborate preparations for the visitors had been made by the natives. The three Jesuits were welcomed with all pleasure on the

---

[1] Salvatierra to Kino, Loreto, October 15, 1705 (Kino, *Favores Celestiales*, Parte IV, Lib. ii, Cap. 8; *Hist. Mem.*, II, 152–153).

part of more than a thousand Indians. They were waiting with arches and crosses placed along the roads, and had ready "a house in which to live, a church . . . , with a good and large hall, store-room, bakery, oven, kitchen, beginnings of a garden, with maize ready for harvest, a good field of wheat sown and sprouted, and also cattle, sheep and goats, saddle horses, droves of mares, etc." Kino adds, "We solemnized many baptisms of little ones and adults." After an excursion to the Gulf coast, Minutuli returned to Tubutama and Kino to Dolores, leaving Father Crescoli with his neophytes.[1]

The reoccupation of Caborca was the beginning of a missionary revival in the Pimería, carried through by these sons of Italy. As procurator, Kino now directed a vigorous program of building, both in the Altar Valley and to the north of Cocóspora. Of his work he left us a precious record. He started the new enterprise on Ash Wednesday. Having given ashes and confessed communicants at Dolores, he set out to do the same elsewhere. With him he took servants and *guasinques,* or native builders, for he had six churches to build or repair. And there were orchards and gardens to plant. While he was giving spiritual instruction at Remedios and Cocóspora, his servants planted at each place "a good garden of quinces, pome-granates, fig trees, peaches, grapevines for wine for the Masses, and many kinds of garden stuff, in all of which the garden of . . . Dolores greatly abounds."

From Cocóspora Kino went down to Magdalena and inspected the "squaring of the timbers for the building and the arches of the sanctu-ary of the very good church" which Father Campos had under way. Turning north he went up to Síboda, where he gave ashes to about thirty persons "in the little new church," said Mass, and preached a sermon on the significance of ashes. He heard confessions by resi-dents of Síboda and by various outsiders, some of whom had come from Búsanic and even from San Xavier.

While at Síboda Kino rounded up a drove of twenty mares, with their jack and burro, for the ranch at Caborca. Driving the mares to Aquimuri, thence he sent them direct to Caborca, while he pro-ceeded with his train to Búsanic, traveling till midnight, "in order

[1] Kino, *Hist. Mem.,* II, 159–161.

not to fail to say Mass the following day, the Third Sunday in Lent, for the children in their little church; for we had notified them before hand that I would give ashes and hear confessions of holy Lent." Kino did not hold his office lightly.

At Búsanic and in each of the other pueblos as he descended the river he rendered the same services—gave ashes, said Mass, preached, heard confessions, baptized, and solemnized marriages. While he gave spiritual ministry, he directed his builders. His expedition was a typical combination of the functions which every frontier Jesuit had to perform. "As they already had in San Ambrosio del Búsanic a good supply of adobes and some timbers, we raised the walls of a good, spacious church." From dawn to dark, hammer, saw, and trowel beat a cheerful tattoo, and as the hours lengthened the adobe walls rose higher. "We wrought and placed in the doors of the church, and of the sacristy and of the baptistry, the entablatures of very good timbers, and arranged that they should continue on the building of the church of San Ambrosio del Búsanic, and on the neighboring one of Santa Gertrudis del Sáric, since for both there were crops of maize, and cattle, sheep, and goats, and whatever else was necessary." Only missionaries were lacking.

Bizarre incidents sometimes varied the program of building and christening. At Búsanic Kino was given a scalp brought by a Quíquima chief from the Colorado River. It had graced the pate of a neighboring ponze or priest, and the only one there who had opposed Kino's teachings, hence the hair-raising. With the lock had come blue shells and an invitation to go to convert the Quíquimas. From this rare happening, said Kino, "may be inferred the great ripeness of the very extensive harvests of the very many souls that the celestial favors of our Lord are continually giving us with full hands."

At Tubutama Kino was again welcomed by Minutuli "with his accustomed great charity." For three days the guasinques worked on the church, "laying the foundations of a good sacristy and of the baptistry, and of a good, spacious hall, as well as raising the walls of the church, and especially of the sacristy, and cutting and working the timbers, brackets, beams, and arches or lintels, etc. Also we looked after the very good garden of Castilian fruit trees, vines for wine for masses, and all kinds of garden stuff." Rare data for the history of the spread of European culture.

Kino continued to Caborca, "where the very courteous children" gave him an affectionate welcome. From this I infer that Crescoli was not there. Was he too a bird of passage in the Pimería? Over these matters Father Eusebio usually spread the veil of charity. While he gave ashes and heard confessions, the guasinques worked on the Caborca church, "laying the foundations of its buildings and raising their walls and those of the sanctuary, and on the church of San Diego del Pitquí." Having received a letter from Father Picolo, saying that he would soon come again to the Pimería, Kino hurried back to Dolores.

The parade of the builders was not over. After the celebration of Holy Week at Dolores early in April, which was attended by four chiefs from San Xavier del Bac, Kino went northward on a pastoral and building tour similar to the one he had just made to the Altar Valley. He took with him the captain of Dolores, the governor of Remedios, a temastián or native catechist, three guasinques, and three other servants. His cowboys drove a herd of cattle for San Lázaro. Of course he had the necessary pack train with the outfit.

At Remedios, Cocóspora, San Lázaro, and Santa María, Kino heard confessions, instructed catechumens, preached, baptized, and solemnized marriages. Meanwhile the masons and carpenters were performing their more material tasks. At Santa María, Kino tells us, "we laid the foundations of a good, spacious hall and of two good lodges, and we began to raise their walls, for already some little storerooms had been made, and a little hall; and the foundations were also already made of a good and large church, with its transept, for which the guasinques cut twenty pine beams and forty oak brackets, and other wall timbers for the house. And an order was left that they should continue making adobes and building and finishing the spacious hall, that it might serve as a little church in which to say Mass with decency while the great church was being built." These are precious details regarding the interesting old pueblo of Santa María, now Santa Cruz, which still stands on the same site. San Lázaro was the scene of like activity. There, says Kino, "we began another

little hall with two lodges. It is a post very suitable for a good pueblo
and for a very good ranch,[1] and, indeed, some corrals had already
been made. We left at that post twenty-three beef cattle, with their
cowboys."

Still the parade was not over. In May Kino and his guasinques
went again to Tubutama and Caborca on a missionary and building
tour. At Caborca, he tells us, "on the 23d of May, as the walls of the
church, and particularly those of the sanctuary, were already high, we
adorned and roofed them with branches, straw and flowers, as best
we could, and held the feast and solemn procession of Corpus Christi,
taking from . . . Dolores the good choir of singers, and the ornaments, hangings, canopy, censer, clarion-players, wax, etc. There was
a great concourse of people, Christians, as well as catechumens." There
were many baptisms, "among them that of the governor of the very
great Ranchería del Humucan." This was Unuicut, near Pitquín,
home of the famous Chief Soba. Father Minutuli, who went with Kino
to Caborca, "catechized and instructed all those children very well,
before baptism and at the time of baptism." Returning to Dolores
Kino celebrated the Feast of Corpus Christi, with a great concourse
of visiting Spaniards and natives.[2]

Kino soon had another task on his hands. Picolo was moving
heaven and earth to obtain for the Pimería a goodly number of new
missionaries. Salvatierra gave all the aid he could without injuring his
California. In the summer of 1706 news arrived that more workers
were coming from Europe, and Picolo seized the opportunity. Pima
Land must get her share. For data on which to base a new request
he turned of course to Kino. To whom else could he turn? "Now
I beseech your Reverence," he wrote from Belén de Guaymas on
July 18—"Now I beesech your Reverence to please inform me by a
messenger how many are the missions founded in the Pimería, and
how many fathers are necessary. Let the report be made with all detail, because I earnestly desire to see the Pimería advanced in my
time; and it will not remain backward if my efforts, labors, and sweat

---

[1] Today San Lázaro is indeed a "very good ranch," and there I enjoyed delightful hospitality during my researches in the vicinity.
[2] Kino, *Favores Celestiales*, Parte IV, Lib. iii, Caps. 2–11; *Hist. Mem.*, II, 159–160, 165–
167, 169–170, 172–173, 175–176.

may avail." The letter was sent through Bartíromo, the rector. He forwarded it, asked *albricias* (a reward) for the good news, and seconded the request for information on proposed new missions. "Report them with the names of the places and posts as well as of the saints to whom they are dedicated. . . . It is important because workers are coming from Spain!"

More reports! Kino might well have groaned. Instead he complied with the enthusiasm of renewed hopes. There should be no slip on his account. The required document was drawn up promptly and dispatched by special messenger to Picolo at Guaymas. The manuscript included a long account of all the good sites in the Pimería, a map of the nine missions already under Kino, Campos, and Minutuli, and a request for at least five new missionaries for fifteen new pueblos.

The nine active missions, of course, were Dolores, Remedios, Cocóspora (Kino), San Ignacio, Magdalena, Imuris (Campos), Tubutama, Santa Teresa, and Oquitoa (Minutuli). For the five new fathers Kino proposed the following pueblos: 1. Caborca, Pitquín and San Valentín (a few leagues west of Caborca). 2. Santa María, San Lázaro, and San Luís Bacoancos. 3. Búsanic, Sáric, and Aquimuri. 4. San Xavier del Bac, San Agustín, and Santa Rosalía of the Sobaípuris. 5. Santa Ana del Quíburi, San Joachín (Huachuca), and Santa Cruz, "where lives the famous Captain Coro." The old chief had returned to the San Pedro, once more to challenge the Apaches.

For these missions the groundwork had already been laid. "For in all these posts or pueblos named above there are very good beginnings of Christianity; houses in which to live, churches in which to say Mass, fields and crops of wheat and maize, and the cattle, sheep, goats, and horses which for years the natives have been tending with all fidelity for the fathers whom they ask and hope to receive." This report is a good summary of the status of missionary work in the Pimería in the middle of 1706. Picolo was pleased with it and hurried it to Salvatierra, who sped it to Rome.[1]

As procurator Kino's business transactions increased. In the fall of this year he went to Fronteras and purchased a supply of clothing for his new missions from the store of General Fuensaldaña. The

[1] Kino, *Favores Celestiales*, Parte IV, Lib. iv, Cap. 1; *Hist. Mem.*, II, 170, 181, 182.

bill was $3,000. It was to be paid for in "provisions, flour, maize, horses, mules, etc., with which these conversions generally abound; all of which he gave me very willingly, not asking me for a single peso in silver, which they are accustomed to demand in the stores of other traders." Father Eusebio's credit was good.[1]

[1] Kino, *Favores Celestiales,* Parte IV, Lib. v, Cap. 1; *Hist. Mem.,* II, 194.

The California Problem Once More

CXLII

ON THE TEPOCA COAST

A FIRE WHICH HAS BEEN SMOTHERED before consuming all the fuel, on being opened to the air will burst forth into a new flame. So it was with Kino's zeal for exploration. It had been checked by opposition and official restraint. But it needed only a new breath to cause it to blaze forth again. Salvatierra, Picolo and Ugarte now furnished the oxygen of encouragement.

With renewed hopes, and with prospects for more missionaries, Kino was bitten again with the wanderlust. It had struck him when with Minutuli he went to install Crescoli at Caborca. This was just before he undertook his great building tours. Down the coast lived heathen Pimas and Tepocas, and by gathering them into the fold Caborca could be made a great pueblo. Some of them had already settled there. The rest should be brought in. Or perhaps new missions could be founded on the coast. So Kino again took the trail, to explore "the part and district and heathendom which appeared to be the newest and most needy, and whither as yet no white man, perhaps, had ever entered." That is to say, it was beyond the region explored in that direction by Manje twelve years before.

With pack train and servants, on January 19, 1706, Minutuli and Kino set out southwest, leaving Father Crescoli to begin his work. Traveling more than a hundred leagues over level plains peopled with heathen, part of whom were Pimas, they "arrived at the very Sea of California," in the vicinity of Tiburón Island. In the course of the journey, there and back, they saw more than fifteen hundred Indians, some of them Pimas, but mainly Tepocas and Seris. They were "very affable and gentle, for many of them in these preceding years had come to us at Caborca" and some even to Dolores. "Everywhere they received us with all friendliness, in many places with crosses and arches placed along the roads and little houses provided in which to live and say Mass with decency."

It was the old story repeated. Kino's wizardry carried all before him. "And we having in all parts preached the principal mysteries of our Holy Faith, they promised what we counseled and asked of them, namely, that inasmuch as these coasts were somewhat sterile, they should go to live in the very fertile and very convenient fields of . . . La Concepción [at Caborca], since now we had brought them a missionary father. They gave us many infants and some sick adults to baptize. And since, even without this, most of these natives, called by the justices . . . of Caborca, had come to the tasks of sowing, harvesting, and building at La Concepción, they agreed that little by little they would join themselves completely to that settlement." After a short stay on the coast the wayfarers returned home, Minutuli to Tubutama and Kino to Dolores. They had added a new paragraph to the history of North American exploration.

The Gulf littoral was not so barren as had been supposed, and Kino saw its beauties with a desert man's understanding eyes. "On this coast of the Sea of California the spring was now coming on, after its fashion," he says, "for many of those plains were beginning to grow green and blossom. There were many birds which live on the . . . fish with which this coast very greatly abounds. There was much medicinal jojoba, which is like the almond, and a very salutary and effective remedy for different kinds of sickness, and is in demand as far as Mexico, Puebla, Parral, New Mexico, etc. On this coast it usually bears all the year, and in fact we found it on this occasion, for on some shrubs it was now ripe, on others still somewhat immature."

In the course of his exploration on the coast Kino saw something of more interest to him than birds, fish, and desert flowers. In latitude 31°—as Kino estimated it—he discovered in the Gulf "a great island, which must be about three leagues in width from east to west, and about seven or eight leagues in length from north to south, and no more than about six or seven leagues from this our terra firma." In honor of the day of the discovery, January 21, it was called

Santa Inés. It was Tiburón Island, which, seeing it from the south twenty-one years previously, Kino and Guzmán had called a peninsula. It is not surprising that he did not recognize it now.

What was on the other side of the Gulf was quite as interesting to Kino as this island. "About three leagues to the northwest of this island of Santa Ynés, we very plainly discovered next day, . . . from a slight elevation, another large piece of land, apparently a part of California." Of this he was not quite sure. It was evidently the island called Angel de la Guarda. "We saw that it was no more than nine or ten leagues from us. What we knew to be very certain from all the surrounding natives, now, in this journey, as well as on many other occasions when we have inquired of these Pimas and maritime Zeris, with repeated and minute examinations of this Gulf of California, was and is that all this point and its environs are very thickly settled with people, for by night fires are continually seen from this side, and by day their smoke. As we discovered this point, so near by, on January 22, . . . we named it San Vizente, with apologies to the inhabitants, owners, and commanders of San Vizente in Europe."

The discovery of the Island of Santa Inés and San Vicente Point started the California bee a-buzzing in Kino's head once more. If missions were established at populous San Vicente Point they would serve as a halfway station between Loreto and the head of the Gulf, and thus promote the opening of the much desired land route to California. Moreover, San Vicente and Santa Inés taken together might offer a short route across the Gulf. If it were opened it would facilitate succor for Loreto by making unnecessary the long land journey by way of Guaymas with supplies from the Pima missions. They could be sent directly across the Gulf. A double triumph was in sight. So Father Eusebio returned with new zeal to his boat building in the desert.

Kino's discovery set others besides himself talking and writing. Minutuli helped spread the news. Kino tells us, "All those who look with favor upon the new conquests and new conversions of this Pimería as well as of California, have considered it very fortunate that this point of San Vizente should be so very close and this island of Santa

Ynés in this convenient halfway latitude of thirty-one degrees, to promote the communication, which, God willing, in His time can be opened in California between the fathers who actually live in the missions of . . . Loreto Conchó, . . . and the fathers who will be able to live in the land passage to California and in the very populous missions which can be had on the very populous and large-volumed Río Colorado." Kino was badly off in his latitudes. Tiburón Island (Santa Inés) is near 29° instead of 31°. But he was correct in thinking it about halfway between Loreto and the head of the Gulf.[1]

CXLIII

UGARTE GIVES GOOD ADVICE

Ugarte, the giant missionary now rector in California, was the person most interested in a short Gulf route, and he kept his eyes and ears open. Minutuli wrote him of the matter, suggesting a reconnaissance on the California side, and reported to Kino the reply. "Father . . . Ugarte has rejoiced at the discovery which your Reverence made of the new island of Santa Ynés and of the Cape of San Vicente. . . . His Reverence says that when he has enough provisions he will go on to explore it, but that the succor which is detained in Guaimas has not yet arrived. Therefore he greatly desires the commerce and nearer aid of the Pimería. . . . This in substance is what his Reverence says, and it has seemed to me well to impart it to your Reverence as soon as possible, in order that . . . this Pima-California gate may be opened soon."

Kino wrote Ugarte two letters "both very gratifying" to Father Juan. In reply Ugarte thanked him for his "laudable zeal . . . for the opening of communication through a port near to that province." Ugarte was a man of much experience with ships on the Gulf, some of it bitter, and he felt that Kino needed advice. Father Eusebio was

[1] Kino, *Hist. Mem.*, II, 159–161, 163, 164. There are indications that someone "doctored" these latitudes, as was done for that of the head of the Gulf, in both cases the latitudes being raised two degrees. In 1685 Kino and Guzmán correctly put the latitude of Kino Bay (opposite Tiburón Island) at 29°.

planning now to return to his boat-building project. "Taking for granted the determination of your Reverence," Ugarte wrote, "it is necessary for me, as one who at great cost has had experience with vessels, to advise your Reverence, so that your worthy desire and its fulfillment may not be delayed, but rather facilitated. Let me say, then, that although your Reverence may have timbers, and men, and even artisans to build; although you may have iron, sails, cables, towropes, bars, and on the beach a good place to launch the vessel, there would necessarily always be anxiety and expenditure of time." It would be better "to buy a launch already made, with anchors, cables, and sails." This would save more than half the expense, "and, what is the most . . . precious, time."

Ugarte gave examples out of his own sad experience with Gulf craft. They illuminate the story of planting the Faith on the rim of Christendom. "The cost to us of repairing a single launch in Acapulco was more than a thousand and four hundred pesos." Again, "It was cheaper for us to buy a Peruvian vessel at Acapulco than to repair the one which we had, and so it went to the bottom." It cost General Resaval "to build his little sloop, they say, fifteen thousand pesos, and more than four years of time, while the little launch which Captain Martín de Verástegui purchased cost only two thousand pesos." If Kino could raise that amount Ugarte would arrange for the purchase of a vessel. And Father Juan was not looking for a rakeoff; he wished to save time and get something done. Yes, *Por Dios,* get something done! For "with that we shall await only the good season for ascending to the latitude of the Seris and of the Pimería." Ugarte saw in the proposed Gulf route an advantage to Kino's missions as well as to his own. "Your Reverence will have, besides the fish, the salt in the Bay of La Concepción, without going down to the Island of El Carmen." Perhaps after all, he added, "with a vessel we shall see accomplished what has not been possible by land."

Kino did not adopt Ugarte's recommendation. He had a launch well under way, and he had long wished to try it out. It was a perhaps quixotic notion which he could not get out of his head. With all his great virtues, we should not begrudge him this hobby. "In regard to obtaining a small but adequate vessel for this very short crossing, of eight or nine or ten leagues of quiet and sheltered sea," he replied, "we shall not have great difficulty, for I have here on hand . . . the greater part of the timbers prepared for a little bark, already squared, which we shall be able, with some good pack mules, easily to carry to the shore of this gulf, together with the other planks which I have at . . . Cavorca, already near the sea." These were the timbers for the launch which had so scandalized Father Mora. They must have been well seasoned by now. In any case, he said, rich Pimería must assist poor California. "We eat nothing except to divide with her, for our sister is little and hath no breasts—*Soror enim nostra parvula, et ubera non habet.*" [1] If only he could get a substitute for himself at Dolores he would devote all his time to lending a hand to this little sister across the Gulf. [2] But as was the case nine years before, he could not be spared.

It ought to be added that all this discussion of a water route was somewhat beside the point, since it was based on the assumption that San Vicente was a part of the Peninsula, when as a matter of fact it was the island called Angel de la Guarda. But history has witnessed many earnest discussions based on equally erroneous assumptions. Eliminate all these and the covers of historical books would not be so far apart.

CXLIV

A LAST LOOK AT THE LAND PASSAGE

Kino's interest in the short Gulf route did not eclipse that in the land passage. In his mind the two were complementary. Moreover, the Quíquima Indians would not permit him to forget them and their neighbors. They poured in on him a constant stream of petitions. In April, 1706, Minutuli sent to Kino thirteen curious balls and some blue shells from the opposite coast. . . . "I am keeping three," he said. He was starting a little collection. Several Quíquimas had come from

[1] Canticles VIII. 8.
[2] Kino, *Favores Celestiales,* Parte IV, Lib. iii, Cap. 11; Lib. vi, Cap. 6; *Hist. Mem.,* II, 176–192.

California Alta to the vicinity of Sonóita. Here some got tired, others were afraid to cross Pima Land. So they sent these gifts and a message begging Kino to go to Sonóita to meet them. Meanwhile the poor souls lived on sea food for more than two months. Kino was too busy to visit the petitioners at the time, and they returned home disconsolate. "And," he wrote, "only the coming of the necessary fathers will be able to assuage such pitiful grief. The little ones asked for bread and there was none to break it unto them." In August another message from the Quíquimas gave a similar tug at his heart strings.

Just at this time Picolo was making strenuous efforts to obtain for the Pimería a new contingent of missionaries, and the prospect of success set objectors to voicing anew their doubts regarding Kino's view of the peninsularity of California. Manje, indeed, was one of the skeptics and he was now a man of influence. So Kino felt that he must plod once more to the northwest, to answer the call of the Quíquimas, and to bring fresh evidence regarding the land passage to California. They would not let him rest.

To take this step Kino was encouraged by General Fuensaldaña, now captain of the presidio of Fronteras. When Father Eusebio went to that post early in October to purchase a stock of clothing for his new missions they talked things over. Kino spoke with grief of the obstinate objectors, and of his intention to go once more to the Colorado. "Go ahead, I'll back you," Fuensaldaña said in effect. And "his Grace, considering as certain that which was very certain, that California was not an island, decided to furnish some soldiers to go with me, to be eyewitnesses and inform themselves of everything for the purpose of reporting juridically to Mexico." Fuensaldaña went even further. He offered to dispatch a courier at his own expense, "in order also to help bring the fathers so necessary for these new conversions." [1]

Then and there Kino prepared for his journey. Fuensaldaña detailed as escort Alférez Juan Matheo Ramírez and Antonio Durán. Fray Manuel de Oyuela, a Franciscan who was in Sonora soliciting alms, decided to accompany them. Kino's whole concern now was

[1] Kino, *Favores Celestiales*, Parte IV, Libs. iii–iv; *Hist. Mem.*, II, 174–175, 185, 194–195; Manje to Kino, September 15, 1706 (*ibid.*, 183–184).

to bring back authenticated testimony. So Ramírez was required by the General to keep a careful diary, signed by himself, Kino, Oyuela, and Durán, in order that it might be sent as evidence to Mexico "and even to His Royal Majesty." It is chiefly from this diary that we learn the story of the expedition.[1]

On October 13 the little party set forth southwestward, and three days later reached Dolores. There Ramírez saw exhibit No. 1, consisting of Indians who had come from the interior "with gifts of blue shells from the opposite coast, and with a holy cross which the people of the Quíquima nation sent." Kino showed him his museum of mementos of the northwest, "a great number of little crosses and blue shells, curious balls, and other gifts which on various occasions the Quíquimas of California Alta and the other natives of the land passage had sent" to him. The collection was a witness to the missionary's dearest dreams.

Five days were spent at Dolores making preparations for the long journey. Kino wrote letters, prepared supplies and pack animals, and sent couriers to report his coming. Ramírez went ahead with the pack train to Remedios to obtain more equipment. Next day Kino and Oyuela overtook him there; thence they continued together to Síboda.

This journey by Kino through the western pueblos is of special interest because it is the last one of his for which we have a detailed record. It was another typical tour of ministry, building, and exploration. As he went through the missions he performed his usual spiritual functions. In his train he took from Dolores a corps of workmen to build at different places on the way. Unfortunately we cannot stop to watch them at their labors.

Kino was as efficient as ever. At Síboda he obtained dried beef for the journey and forty horses and mules to supplement his twenty-five. From here also he took twenty-five head of wild cattle for Búsanic, to replace the gentle ones he had sent ahead from there to the ranch at Sonóita, for the new move toward the northwest involved a strengthening of that halfway station.

---

[1] Alférez Juan Ramírez, "Diary of the Journey to the Land Passage to California, from October 13 to November 16, 1706" (in Kino, *Favores Celestiales*, Parte IV, Lib. v, Caps. 3–6; *Hist. Mem.*, II, 197–209).

Minutuli had shown great energy in the Altar Valley, where he had come to occupy a place like that filled by Campos in the San Ignacio Valley. At Tubutama he welcomed the travelers and furnished them fresh supplies. He longed to join the expedition but was prevented by pressing duties. He had made with Kino that exhilarating journey down the Tepoca coast, and now the northbound trail beckoned like a siren. He dared not yield to the temptation, but, says Kino, "his Reverence with great love and generosity supplied us with wine for masses, with wax candles, chocolate, bread, and biscuit, pinole, mutton, beef, and even with his own saddle mule." No greater test of friendship can be put to a horseman.

So Kino continued to Caborca. Turning north, after a three days' ride over the familiar trail he reached Sonóita. At the very same moment the cattle arrived by a direct route from Búsanic. Kino was welcomed by a great concourse of Indians from the surrounding country, among them Yuma chiefs who had come all the way from the Colorado. The natives at Sonóita had proved faithful to their promise. They now had "a little church, with its very neat altar, whitewashed and painted," and they "tended for Father Kino his forty head of cattle, and wheat, maize, beans, etc., for the father whom these very affable and friendly natives are awaiting." Father Eusebio's men now helped them sow a goodly field of wheat for the Church.

Father Oyuela marveled at the hypnotic touch of the Master of Dolores. Kino preached to the assembled natives a fervent sermon. "So effective was it that two of the captains told him that since he had deprived them of so much good he ought to baptize them." The heathen gods having been put to rout by the eloquent preacher, he must give them a new one. Kino replied that they must first be instructed, and in consequence several natives accompanied him on his return all the way to Dolores to be taught and catechized. This was not the full measure of the fervor aroused by Kino's sermon. "We were there a day and a half," says Oyuela, "when I saw a thing very worthy of pondering in a people so ignorant." It was this: "After the father had preached to them, one of their captains continued admonishing them with such force and energy that it seems that the Lord must have given him words to enable him to speak so long, for he harangued them for a space of two hours, a difficult thing even for a great preacher. Afterward another took up the thread and continued in the other languages. In this manner day dawned upon them; and the following night it was the same." It was a veritable revival meeting.[1]

By now Kino had decided not to go to the Colorado River, but instead to ascend Santa Clara Mountain and from there convince Ramírez and Oyuela regarding the land passage. Having sent messengers to bring Quíquimas to meet him, he descended the river to El Carrizal. He had a tough climb ahead, and he drove his animals forward with all the vigor of his earlier days. The Old Man was still iron. On the 5th of November, setting out at dawn, he rode four leagues to a water hole, halted, said Mass, "breakfasted, drank chocolate, and mounted." Traveling ten more leagues to the skirts of Cerro de Santa Clara (Pinacate Mountain), he halted at a tank in the rocks and ate lunch. Here he left the extra horses with some boys and Durán, who was ill. Then, selecting the best mules, he and the rest climbed the four leagues up the steep and difficult trail. By now the mules were all in.

It was a terrific day's travel, even for a young man—forty-five miles, part way up a mountainside—and Kino was sixty-one. But he must reach the very summit before finishing the day. "On this peak three others are piled up," says Ramírez. "We ascended the one which slopes to the south, whence was seen the sea, which was exactly south of us." This is correct. "As far as the eye could reach there was no sea ascending toward the north or the northwest. This, too, is essentially correct.

Next morning, the Feast of San Bruno,[2] they ascended the highest peak. Says Oyuela: "I did so at the cost of a very great toil because it was so high, and was a sort of rubbish heap of tlesontle stone, like all this very great mountain, so that I seemed likely to end my life sooner than the undertaking." From this summit they saw again "with even more detail, what we had seen the afternoon before, and that with this continuity of both lands there is a passage by land to California. And

---

[1] Fray Manuel de Oyuela y Velarde, "Certification . . . of having seen the Land Passage to California," Dolores, November 29, 1706 (Kino, *Favores Celestiales*, Parte, IV, Lib. v. Cap. 7).
[2] Exactly twenty-three years since Kino and Atondo had begun their work at San Bruno in California.

we saw that the Sierra Madre of California runs from north to south to where the sea ends, and that a point shuts in a bay which Fray Manuel calls the estuary, because it is the mouth of the Río Colorado, at the head of the Sea of California."

They were convinced and ready to return, for it all was as plain as day. Saddling up, they descended the four leagues to the tank, where they rejoined Durán. "There the father said Mass in thanksgiving for the so plainly discovered certainty of the passage." Kino would have his authenticated testimony. It was for this that they had come. Taking breakfast here, they mounted and returned to El Carrizal. Two strenuous days had become history.

CXLV

DRAKE IN INFERNO

The back track slid quickly under the wiry mules. At Sonóita Kino found a Cocomaricopa chief from the Gila River, by whom he sent tender messages to his people. Continuing east they passed through Actúm and San Martín to Santa Biviana. Here the honest natives delivered two beeves left in their care by the vaqueros on the way to Sonóita. At Ootcam they found "a little church, or chapel, of adobe." Minutuli had been spreading the Faith into Pápago Land. Imuris and Remedios soon lay behind, and on November 16 the travelers dismounted at Dolores.

Ramírez here wrote out his record in fair hand and signed it, preparatory to sending it to Fronteras. Then Kino met a serious disappointment. "Just when the diary was to go to General Don Jacinto de Fuensaldaña, in order that Christianly authenticated by his hand it might go, for the good of so many souls, with papers of his own, to Mexico and even to Spain, we learned to our great sorrow that our Lord had just taken the General to Himself." This was hard luck for Kino. His project had lost an ardent supporter, and he a generous creditor.

Fuensaldaña's testimony might have carried more weight at Court than Oyuela's, but it could not have been more emphatic. In a separate declaration Fray Manuel left no room for skeptics. He correctly stated that in shape the head of the Gulf resembled the right foot of a man, the mouth of the Colorado corresponding to the big toe. His description of what he saw was essentially the same as that given by Ramírez, but his conclusion was stated in much stronger terms. "Therefore," he writes, "California is not an island but only a peninsula, as long since very well and correctly has been said and written by Father Eusevio Francisco Kino, who took us that we might be witnesses of this fact. From the foregoing I have seen that the heretic Drake is author of the lie whereby he will have it that this Sea of California ascends to the North Sea, wishing to discredit the ancient Spaniards who depicted California as terra firma with this land, as it really is." This of course was true.

Fray Manuel had a very personal grievance against the English Dragon. He was tired and saddle-galled from the long, grueling journey, made necessary by people who had swallowed and repeated Drake's lie, as Oyuela regarded it. "Because of this malevolent heretic we have toiled so much." But there was retribution. Drake was already smoking for it. "He is well punished in this life and also in the next, dying at the hand of a Spaniard here in Galicia, and paying forever for his evil deeds there in Inferno." Father Oyuela was manifestly not well informed regarding Drake's earthly career.[1] The friar was careful not to be misunderstood through lack of emphasis. "And always, as Father Kino says, California Alta will remain terra firma with the mainland. . . . And since this is the truth, I sign it at this pueblo of . . . Dolores, November 29, 1706." This made it water-tight.

Renewed congratulations for Kino from many sources. Father Rector Bartíromo wrote "more with tears than with ink . . . not of pain but of joy . . . 'The Lord be to thee a reward exceeding great.[2] —*Dominus sit tibi merces magna nimis.*' "[3]

---

[1] Oyuela, "Certification," Nov. 29, 1706 (Kino, *Favores Celestiales*, Parte IV, Lib. v, Cap. 7; *Hist. Mem.*, II, 209–214). Drake died of illness on board ship near the Isthmus of Panamá in 1596 and was buried in the Caribbean Sea.

[2] Kino, *Hist. Mem.*, II, 215.

[3] Perhaps suggested by Genesis XV. I: *Ego protector tuus sum, et merces tua magna nimis.* "I am thy protector and thy reward exceeding great."

With Spirit Undaunted

CXLVI

MANJE EXPLODES A BOMB

PIMA LAND WAS NOW GIVEN A SENSATION such as it had not experienced since Coro's victory over the Apaches. This one was quite different in kind. It came from a most unexpected source, and reflects the highly charged atmosphere in which Kino now labored.

As early as 1699 Manje was writing a book on the history of Sonora, including an account of his travels with Kino. With a gift for naming things, he called it "Light on the Unknown Lands of North America"—*Luz de Tierra Incógnita en la América Septentrional*.[1] In September, 1706, he was given a new impulse for his task. By now he was General Manje, and a man of influence. At this time the viceroy was considering the addition of thirty soldiers to the military force in Sonora, and he asked for Manje's journals as evidence bearing on the question. Manje wrote to Kino saying that he had already copied five of his diaries, but lacked the one for the journey with Leal. "Let me ask your Reverence to send it to me, and if you do not find it, please send me a short account from the day we set out until the day we returned."[2]

By the end of the year Manje had finished a draft of his book, which he dedicated to Viceroy Alburquerque. He closed the treatise with a chapter entitled "Conclusion of this work and a note on the present state, spiritual and temporal, of these missions of the province

---

[1] He tells us this in his Epitome of the expedition of February–March, 1699, dated at Dolores, May 16, 1699.

[2] Kino, *Favores Celestiales*, Parte IV, Lib. iv, Cap. 3; *Hist. Mem.*, II, 184. Manje included in his *Luz de Tierra Incógnita*, 273–281, a diary of this expedition written by himself. Whether or not it was one sent to him by Kino I cannot say.

557

of Sonora, and setting forth how important it would be to found a new presidio of forty or more soldiers to restrain and prevent the ravages and invasions of the hostile nations and the many murders of Christians which they commit along the roads." He suggested Bacanuche, his own residence, as a good place for the proposed garrison. Perhaps he hoped for the command.

In this concluding chapter the General described the Pima missions, voiced the need of more missionaries, spoke in most complimentary terms of the Jesuits in general, and of Kino, Campos, and Minutuli in particular. He described in glowing words the former wealth of the mines of Sonora, estimating that in its time the province had produced fifty million pesos of silver. In the two years only while he was alcalde mayor (1701–1703) more than half a million pesos left the province through his own office. And this did not include large shipments through Alamos.

Such were some of the glories of Sonora. But there were serious drawbacks. And here Manje stepped on dangerous ground. The missions, he said monopolized the best agricultural lands, leaving to the Spaniards only the poorest, "a reason why many of them are unable to . . . maintain themselves." He proposed a remedy. Since the Indian population in the older missions had greatly declined, some of them had "a superabundance of lands." In some missions where at first there had been ten thousand Indians, "today there will be a hundred, and the rest in proportion."

The moral was plain, said Manje. The government ought to survey the mission lands, leave the Indians generous fields, and assign the excess to the Spaniards, those pioneers who had defended the province at the cost of their estates, with shield, arquebus, horses, and other arms, offensive and defensive. Since the establishment of the Flying Company, some thirteen years previously, these citizens had left military campaigns chiefly to the soldiers, but for their past services they ought to be given lands for agriculture. Besides, he said, they should be granted the privilege enjoyed by the settlers of New Mexico. He referred to the repartimiento system by which Indians were practically enslaved.

The province suffered other afflictions. Sonora, a district five hundred leagues in periphery, had only three parish priests, whose respective capitals were the mining towns of San Juan, Nacozari, and Horcasitas. Of course three priests could not properly cover so large a circuit. As a result spiritual conditions in some places were deplorable. In remote regions a year often passed between visits of the curate, leaving Spaniards without Mass, confession, or communion, since their nakedness and the dangers of the road prevented them from making long journeys to the parish church for spiritual ministrations. Some Spaniards died without confession, and some were even buried by Indians without Church rites. Plainly more parish curates were needed. Anybody could see this.

Things would not be as bad if it were not for an impasse between the Jesuits and the bishop of Durango. Here in fact was the nub of the difficulty. The missionaries, said Manje, used to care generously for isolated Spaniards at their missions, and this without stipend. "But in the present state of things the Jesuit fathers have refused the administration of the sacraments to the Spanish citizens, and even to the Indian servants of the Spaniards. . . . In some missions they have denied Christian burial to persons who have died and been brought to them for interment. . . . They have even refused to baptize infants when carried to them a distance of ten leagues."

Such a situation was insupportable! How could it be defended? "These fathers exculpate themselves by saying that an impudent curate wrote" to the bishop of Durango "impugning their honor," and for this reason their prelate or visitor—this was Picolo—had ordered them not to minister to Spaniards.

And now Manje's old friend and mentor was brought into the story. "For better corroboration of this statement," he continued, "I will insert here incidentally a paragraph of a letter from Father Eusebio Francisco Kino, who writes the following: 'I am sorry not to be able to go to minister to those gentlemen of Bacanuchi' "—this was Manje's home town—" 'because a curate reported to the bishop against us, for which reason the superiors, through the father visitor, have again ordered us not to mix in the affairs of the curates.' " Evidently some citizens of Bacanuche had called on Kino for spiritual ministrations, and he had refused to go, for the reasons given. Whether the matter became a personal one between these two old companions on the trail does not appear. Let us hope not.

Manje here indulges in a sermon. "Oh, the unhappiness of these times, when for this idol of honor and credit one tramples on the honor of God and hinders the salvation of His souls redeemed with the excessive price of the Blood of the Lamb!" Of course the Jesuits were bound by the vow of obedience, he said, but only "in what is lawful, and not in what is unlawful."

Finally, to encourage mining, said Manje, "ancient Christian Indians" ought to be assigned "to labor for the Spanish miners." For, "in this province there are no slaves or other people to work the mines unless it be Indians." This suggestion had a timeliness which does not appear on the surface. Almost exactly two decades previously Kino had obtained royal protection for his Pima neophytes for a period of twenty years against forced labor in mines or on haciendas. The twenty years were about to expire.

Don Matheo must have realized that this document was loaded with dynamite, but it made a noise that was probably louder than he expected. It was signed at Bacanuche on December 3, 1706, shortly after Kino returned from Santa Clara Mountain.[1] Soon after this Manje sent a report, similar to, if not identical with, the "Conclusion," to the Audiencia of Guadalajara, and to the bishop of Durango. It was signed by several citizens of Bacanuche. This means that the document aired what was regarded as a public grievance.

Picolo got wind of Manje's report, and to say that he was incensed is to put it mildly. He expressed his feelings to Governor Córdova of Parral in a letter dated at Bacanuche on August 19, 1707. He had made inquiries on the ground. He and his fellow Jesuits "were disconsolate, hurt, and mortified" by what Manje had written and others had signed, for it was "a calumny against the priestly, religious, and apostolic office which they fill, . . . contrary to the honor of the Society, contrary to the good name of the missionaries, contrary to the welfare of the Indians, contrary to the well-being of everybody, and such as would not be heaped upon even the most dissolute men in all the

---

[1] Such is the story gleaned from a manuscript recently discovered by myself in an archive in Spain. The sequel comes from another manuscript subsequently discovered by Dr. Carl Sauer in an archive in Mexico. Truly, the materials of history are scattered to the ends of the earth.

world!" Moreover, unless there was a remedy for the insult he would "order all the father missionaries to leave that province."

Whether or not the Governor was surprised by the communication we cannot say. In any case, Picolo's threat was effective. On December 29, 1707, Córdova drew up a document in which he recited the contents of the visitor's complaint. In view of the evils which would follow "if such workers were lacking in the province," and to provide a remedy for the scandal, he forthwith ordered Manje arrested, an embargo placed upon all his goods, personal and real, and that the charges made by him be investigated. He issued orders also to inquire whether or not the signers of the document were influenced or suborned by Manje or anybody else.

Lively times now followed and Manje found himself in the limelight—and then in a dark hole. To effect the arrest, Córdova appointed Corporal Domínguez. The order required that Manje be sent a prisoner "with great caution and in handcuffs" to Parral. To sequestrate the goods and make the inquiry, Captain Zevallos was named.[1] On or before January 21, 1708, at the mines of Basochuca, near Bacanuche, the arrest was made. On that day Zevallos went to Manje's residence and ordered Simón Romo de Bibar, Manje's agent, to list all of the General's property. He did the job thoroughly, drawing up an inventory covering several pages—a most interesting record of what a prominent citizen of Sonora possessed.[2]

According to Manje, Domínguez executed his orders "with the greatest harshness, publicity, ignominy, and haste," and with contempt for his person, for the offices which he had held, and the privileges of his house. The General's dignity was offended, and this was not the worst of it. Manje was ordered to mount, "on a strange mule which happened to be at hand," not giving him time to obtain steeds of his own "gait" or to obtain suitable clothing or equipment for the long journey. Domínguez was abusive in every way, leaving Manje's house, wife and family "in the greatest affliction and confusion." Don Matheo obeyed, traveled a prisoner two hundred leagues on a hard-

---

[1] Córdova, order for Manje's arrest, Parral, December 29, 1707; order for sequestration of Manje's goods and for the investigation, same date (*Expediente* relative to the arrest and imprisonment of Manje, 1706–1707. Original manuscripts in the archives of Parral, Legajo 1707).

[2] Certificate of Zevallos, Basochuca, January 21, 1708. *Ibid.*

riding mule, and reached Parral on the last day of February. His arrival at the plaza was a spectacle.

Zevallos proceeded with his inquiry at Bacanuche. Being sworn, Romo made a deposition, as one of the signers of the offensive document. He testified that Manje wrote a report to the bishop of Durango, and that he as one of the citizens had signed it. So far as he remembered, it contained nothing derogatory to the Jesuits, either in general or in particular. "What he remembers is that they informed the bishop of the great lack of spiritual care in this province due to the shortage of priests which it suffers, and that the reverend fathers excused themselves from administering the holy sacraments to the citizens and residents near their districts. And likewise they made known the lack of Indians in repartimiento for the labor and cultivation of the lands of this deponent and other citizens of the valley of Bacanuche who occupy themselves in agriculture. And that for lack of such Indians, they lost many crops, as a result of which there was a great delinquency and shrinkage in the tithes of the Holy Cathedral Church of the city of Durango; and other things, which, because it was a good many days ago that he signed the report, he does not remember exactly. But he is certain that he did not in any manner speak ill of or to the discredit of the sacred religion of the Society of Jesus, nor of any one of their reverences in particular; and that he does not know and has not heard that General Juan Matheo Manje has written any other report whatsoever, except one for the Royal Audiencia of Guadalajara, which was of the same tenor as the one the deponent has described." Several other citizens made depositions identical with Romo's, except that two added that the Jesuits "did not wish to give burial in their churches to those who died outside of their pueblos."

It is thus clear that the contents of the report of which Picolo complained were essentially the same as those of the "Conclusion." It is clear, too, that Manje and the other citizens of Bacanuche were looking to the bishop for help in what they regarded as a common grievance against the Jesuits. They had started something.

Manje, in prison at Parral, was foaming with rage when release came through an unexpected influence. The Jesuits evidently feared that they had over-reached themselves. Córdova tells us that "some religious and superiors" of the order wrote him, requesting him to suspend the prosecution . . . without making any charge or complaint . . . because of the inconveniences which . . . might result from the publication of the sentence." One wonders if Kino did not intercede for his old friend. It is comforting to believe so. Complying again, Córdova ordered Manje dismissed and his goods restored. The General was informed of his release verbally by a messenger, and ordered "to return to his house without asking the reason for his imprisonment."

Red-blooded Manje would be damned if he would! This was arbitrary dealing. He knew perfectly well why he was arrested, but he wished written evidence of Córdova's high-handed procedure. So he drew up a protest, and demanded that he be told in writing the cause of his incarceration.

The General was still in Parral on April 27, but was no longer in jail. On that day in a conversation with the governor he recounted the story of his rough treatment. We may picture the scene as taking place on the plaza, in the angle between the church and the palacio. Close by a silver-laden mountain towered above the actors, symbolic of the height of the General's rage. He still writhed with anger, and he voiced an opinion of the Jesuits. They were too sure of themselves. "He had a letter from the province of Sonora in which he was informed that as soon as they had brought him here a prisoner, the religious of the Society of Jesus had assembled the Indians of their pueblos and preached to them that they could do anything" they wished, citing Manje's arrest as an example. This was a serious charge. The governor asked him if he could prove it. "Yes," replied Manje. "Produce the letter," said Córdova. Manje answered that he did not wish to do so. Córdova ordered him to show the letter or go back to jail. "To this Juan Matheo replied that the governor might do whatever he pleased, even to cutting off his head, but in that case all the province of Sonora would be in revolt and lost."

Córdova was not frightened by the threat. Suiting action to the word, his secretary tells us, he clapped Manje in jail again, declaring "that as a punishment for his disobedience he should remain a pris-

oner in that jail until his Lordship thought the punishment equiva-
lent to his guilt." The measure of Manje's guilt—that is to say the
length of his stay in jail—has not come to light.[1]

Just what happened after this point is not clear. But we get some
hints. In 1720 Manje completed a somewhat revised version of his
Luz de Tierra Incógnita. It is one of the classic books on North
American history. In the preface he tells of preparing the draft whch
in 1706 he had sent to the viceroy. "And at the conclusion I inserted
a manifest of the temporal and spiritual state of the missions, militia,
and mines of this province of Sonora, which true relation was the cause
of making against me surreptitious reports, encouraged by a facile,
vain, and vulgar credulity. But my assertions having been examined
by learned, wise, pious, prudent, and circumspect men, in the crucible
of the celebrated investigation, they approved and defended them and
declared for my innocence." So Manje was exonerated. Somewhere
in the archives there must be records of this "celebrated investigation."
When discovered they are likely to throw a flood of light on many
matters. And they may cause another sensation.

Manje next tells of revising his book. "Because a part of the re-
forms which I urgently requested were made as a necessary remedy,
I omit them, and proceed to set forth succinctly . . . what has not
been reformed." This statement is interesting in the light of the fact
that Manje's "Conclusion," written in 1706, was omitted from his
final draft, and in its place was put a description of Sonora by the
Jesuit Father Velarde.[2] Thus it is clear that Manje and the Jesuits
came to an understanding. Kino continued to speak well of Manje,
and Don Matheo in his 1720 manuscript speaks in highest terms of
the Jesuits. Speculation as to what happened in the interim is vain.
One would like to believe that there never was a breach between the
great missionary and the worthy General, or that if one occurred it
was thoroughly healed.

In reading this story of Manje, the Jesuits, and the bishop, one
should not judge anybody concerned too harshly. They were parties

---

[1] Depositions of Romo and others; Córdova, order for Manje's release, Parral, March 11,
1708; Manje's protest, on or after March 11, 1708; Certificate of Matheo Cuen, April 27;
Córdova, order for Manje's imprisonment, April 27, 1708. *Ibid.*

[2] Manje, *Luz de Tierra Incógnita*, Prólogo, p. 10.

to an inevitable conflict. The missionaries controlled the agricultural lands and the Indian labor. Spanish settlers demanded part of the soil and the customary right to use forced Indian labor. As a question of morals, they were in a position analogous to that of the slaveholders in the Anglo-American Old South. The bishop of Durango was interested in tithes, but he could not legally collect them from Indians still in the missions. Bishop and settlers often united to hasten secularization. The Jesuits, to protect their wards from exploitation, stubbornly resisted. We honor them. But Manje, too, had given ample proof of upright, Christian citizenship.

CXLVII

FAME IN EUROPE

In the midst of all this din of battle the Master of Dolores went serenely forward, refusing to be deflected from his life work either by the glamour of office or the distractions of strife. The story of Kino thus far set forth tells mainly of a man of action. And this he was. But he also found time to write and to make maps. Indeed, the products of his pen were nearly as outstanding as his deeds, and almost unknown to himself his work by now was winning high approval in Europe. One famous geographer flattered him by pirating one of his most important maps and publishing it under his own name. Of this, more below.

In the early days, as royal cartographer in California Kino drew several maps, some of which are still extant. Gradually they have come out of their hiding places, and some of them have been printed. One, showing the work of Atondo and himself at La Paz and San Bruno[1] to December, 1683, was first published in 1919—certainly not a speed record. The map is a credit to its author and a landmark in historical geography. A plan of the settlement of San Bruno made by

---

[1] Delineación de la Nueva Provincia de S. Andrés del Puerto de la Paz, y de las Islas circumvecinas de las Californias, ó Carolinas. San Bruno, Dec. 21, 1683. Original manuscript map A.G.I. 1–1–2/31, Patronato 31. Printed in Kino, *Hist. Mem.*, I, facing p. 48 (Berkeley, 1919).

Father Eusebio at the same time is still extant and in 1932 it helped me to identify and interpret the ruins there. It also was first published in 1919.

After his expedition across the Peninsula to the Pacific Ocean— where he first saw the blue shells—Kino made a map of wider sweep. It showed the Jesuit missions of all the West Coast mainland and brought the California story down to 1685. Now for the first time a map showed the River of Santo Tomás and other places discovered on that strenuous expedition. Kino had enlarged the known world. Eighteen years passed before this map appeared in print. In this case there was no piracy, for the precious manuscript fell into the hands of a cherished personal friend. In 1703 Father Heinrich Scherer, Kino's former teacher at Ingolstadt, published in Latin his great treatise called *Geographia Hierarchica,* an historical geography of the Catholic World, illustrated with many beautiful maps. He was proud to include in Volume II the work of one of his own disciples. In a chapter on "The Islands of California, or Carolina" he quotes a letter written him from the Peninsula by Kino in 1684. "A former pupil of mine," he affectionately calls him. He adds: "He sent me also a map drawn first by his own hand. I show it in somewhat more elegant form in Fol. D.C.D." Thus generously Scherer makes known the authorship of the *Delineatio Nova et Vera,*[1] as the rare map is called. As printed it is indeed beautiful, a joy to the cartographer's eye.

Quite different was the fate of another of Kino's maps. It will be remembered that Father Eusebio wrote a history of the martyrdom of Father Saeta, and illustrated it with a large map of all western New Spain—the *Teatro de los Trabajos.*[2] On the left margin he wrote a chronological summary of all the notable expeditions to California down to 1695. Four years later he sent a copy of this summary to his friend Thirso González, the Father General. This was on October 17, 1699.

---

[1] *Delineatio Nova et Vera Partis Australis Novi Mexici cum Australi Parte Insulae Californiae Saeculo Priori ab Hispanis Detectae.* Redrawn and printed in Scherer, *Geographia Hierarchica* (Monachii, 1703), II, fol. D.C.D. between pp. 98 and 99.

[2] Teatro de los Trabajos Apostólicos de la Compa. de Jesús en la América Septentrional, 1696. Original manuscript, in Kino's hand, in the central archives of the Jesuit Order.

By the time the report reached Spain an important event in European politics had occurred. A French prince had become King Philip V at Madrid. France now regarded Spain as something like a dependency. Since it was all in the family, Louis XIV felt privileged to make himself at home in his grandson's archives. Philip was complacent, but he would have deserved more praise had he thumbed his nose at the Grand Monarque. Louis was just now founding Louisiana and taking a new interest in all of Western America. So Kino's summary of California voyages was soon in the hands of Claude Delisle, the famous royal geographer of France. That he thought it important may be inferred from that fact that, busy man as he was, he made a copy of it with his own hand.[1]

Soon Kino's remarkable map also, the precious *Teatro de los Trabajos,* was in Paris. It was sent to Spain by the viceroy of Mexico, and reached France through the good offices of the Duque de Escalona, who sent it to M. Regis, as a gift to the French Academy of Sciences. Regis in turn sent it to Delisle and asked his opinion of it. The geographer was delighted. This man Kino had done something new. "A map of that kind is not common in this country, where people are profoundly ignorant of those things." Englishmen in London or in Boston could have said the same with equal truth. "In it I have noticed not only Indian peoples of which I did not know . . . but I have even imagined myself exploring the regions where the Spaniards are established among them."[2] Perhaps he also imagined French adventurers from Louisiana using the map as a guide to fabulous Spanish mines.

But Delisle's interest in the manuscript was largely geographical, for he, too, was making maps of North America. By it he was convinced of the falsity of Friar Marcos's story of Cíbola, and he was pleased to know the course of the western rivers, especially of the Río

---

[1] Kino, Varias Navegaciones y entradas . . . a las Californias ó Carolinas, 1695. Sent by Kino to Thirso González on October 17, 1699. Copy in the hand of Claude Delisle, royal geographer of France, c. 1700, in Bibliothèque Nationale, Paris, Service Hydrographique, Paris, 115, XI, No. 5A. Transmitted in 1752 to Father Patouillet. Bibliothèque Nationale, Paris, Service Hydrographique, Paris, 115, XI, No. 5C. Claude Delisle was the father of the more famous cartographer, Guillaume Delisle.

[2] Delisle to Regis, Comments on Kino's map, Teatro de los Trabajos, c. 1700. French manuscript in Bibliothèque Nationale, Paris, Archives du Service Hydrographique de la Marine, 115, X, No. 17C.

Grande del Coral. He criticized the map on seven counts, all but one of which concerned things beyond the range of Kino's own observations. It showed California as an island which, said the geographer, was uncertain. This is interesting, since at that very moment Kino was gathering data and making maps which proved California to be a peninsula. The *Teatro* placed the mouth of the Mississippi too far west. Delisle had hoped for more details concerning the Chihuahua country. Of course Kino had not made the map for the Frenchman's benefit. It put Gran Quivira west of New Mexico instead of east of it. Delisle thought Gran Teguayo was misplaced, but that will o' the wisp still troubles geographers and historians. Why did not Kino "fill out the void which appears between the Sobas and the Río del Coral with the names of some people who are in the province of Sonora, such as the Sumas, Heris [Seris], Pimas and others?" Kino might have replied, "because the Sumas and Heris do not inhabit the void." Moreover, he had not yet explored this region. Finally, the map, said Delisle, did not show the Río de Buena Guía, unless it were the one called by Kino the Río del Tizón—which, as it happened, was the case.

Whatever its faults, Kino's map was worth stealing, and stolen it was. Delisle himself was not the thief, although he may have been implicated. It was Nicolas de Fer who appropriated the precious manuscript. In 1705 he published in Paris *L'Atlas Curieux*.[1] One of its beautiful plates was none other than Kino's *Teatro de los Trabajos,* but it was not so labeled, nor did Kino's name appear. Fer had simply helped himself. The legend says: "This map of California and New Mexico is drawn from the one which was sent by a grandee of Spain to be presented to the gentlemen of the Royal Academy of Sciences. By N. de Fer, Geographer of Monseigneur the Dauphin. With the permission of the King, 1705." Scherer had just before this given Kino credit for the *Delineatio.* Fer was not equally generous.

But "murder will out." Recently a holograph of Kino's *Teatro de los Trabajos* was found in Europe. That it was the original of Fer's map was plain to me at a glance, although in places where the manu-

---

[1] *L'Atlas Curieux, ou le Monde Réprésenté dans des Cartes Générales et Particulières du Ciel et de la Térre.* Par. N. del Fer (Paris, 1705). Father Constantino Bayle, S.J., used the manuscript *Teatro de los Trabajos.* See his *Historia de los Descubrimientos y Colonización de los Padres de la Compañía de Jesús en la Baja California* (Madrid, 1933), p. 35.

script is crowded Fer has numbers and a name key instead of names, and the summary of California expeditions is left off. The discovery in Paris of Delisle's letter to Regis by Dr. Nasatir at almost the same time disclosed the name of the "grandee of Spain"—the Duque de Escalona—and the circumstances under which the map went to Paris. Whether or not Kino ever knew of the piracy I cannot say. Imitation is said to be the best flattery, but perhaps theft has a better claim.

Time passed, Kino died, Fer became bolder, and in 1720 he reprinted the map with its original title restored, and with the summary of California expeditions translated into French—but again with Kino's name omitted![1] So this precious map made by Father Eusebio has for over two and a third centuries been associated with the name of Nicolas de Fer.

A better fortune fell to Kino's *Paso por Tierra á la California,* the map drawn after his arduous journeys to the Colorado River. It was soon published under Kino's name and in its variant forms was many times reprinted.[2] This is Kino's most famous map, or better, perhaps, the one from which he won the most fame. It was made especially to show that California was "not an island but a peninsula," but it incorporated also the results of all of Kino's explorations between 1696 and 1702. The assertion sometimes made that it was printed in 1701 is apparently an error. The earliest known print is a French edition, called *Passage par Terre a la Californie,* published in Paris in May, 1705—the very same year when Fer first pirated the *Teatro de los Trabajos.* Thus within two years three rare Kino maps were published in Europe, two of them under his own name. In 1707, a Spanish version and in 1708 an English version of the *Paso por Tierra* was published, and thereafter it was reprinted many times in various languages. Not only did European scholars print and reprint Kino's maps, but they talked and wrote about his remarkable work. For example, on February 9, 1708/9, at a meeting of the Royal Society of London, "a paper was read of yᵉ discovery of California whereby it

---

[1] *La Californie ou Nouvelle Caroline. Teatro de los Trabajos Apostólicos de la Compa. de Jesús en la America Sept¹.* Printed in Paris by Nicolas de Fer, 1720. Wagner, the learned cartographer of the Pacific Coast, in 1932 attributed Fer's map to Sigüenza y Góngora on account of its data on New Mexico. "Note on the Fer Map," in Leonard, I. A., *The Mercurio Volante of Don Carlos Sigüenza y Góngora* (Los Angeles, 1932), p. 89.

[2] Kino made several manuscript drafts of this map, perhaps no two exactly alike.

appears not to be an Island." [1] Kino had become an international figure. His appointment as royal cosmographer was fully justified.

These maps are well known, but not so some others. At least two additional Kino maps have been preserved and are now published for the first time. One, evidently drawn in Mexico City before Kino went to California, shows the Jesuit missions of western New Spain. The inference is that he made it in 1681 while preparing for the California expedition—that time when he borrowed and forgot to return some of Sigüenza's charts. The other map is contemporaneous with the *Teatro* and was sent by Kino to Thirso González, the Father General, with a letter dated June 3, 1697. It shows northern Sonora and the Pimería with essentially the same data as the *Teatro* for the corresponding area, but is decorated with a drawing to illustrate the martyrdom of Father Saeta, the martyr kneeling to receive the arrows of two Pima bowmen. It is a gem. [2]

So Kino's mathematics had not gone for naught, after all. He had become a great explorer and cartographer, not of China, as he had hoped, but of even less known regions, more remote than the heart of Tibet. His name resounded in Europe. Of this Kino knew little. News traveled slowly across the wide Atlantic, and not till 1709 was he apprised—by Father Bayerca—of the publication of his *Paso por Tierra*. Presumably he had already been told of the publication of the *Delineatio*. [3]

CXLVIII

FAVORES CELESTIALES

Even more impressive than Kino's maps were his writings. He kept diaries of his travels, wrote letters to friends in Europe, America, and Asia, discussed geographical problems, defended his Pima friends

---

[1] Information furnished by Dr. Fulmer Mood.

[2] Kino, The Martyrdom of Father Saeta, Map of Pimería Alta and Northern Sonora, *circa* 1696. Original manuscript in the central archives of the Jesuit Order. Illustrating with drawings the martyrdom of Father Saeta. It was sent to the Father General, Thirso González, on June 3, 1697. It was manifestly drawn before the expedition of 1697 down the San Pedro River. The data are almost identical with those on the corresponding parts of the *Teatro de los Trabajos*, drawn in 1695–1696. González to Kino, Dec. 27, 1698, in *Hist. Mem.*, II, 157–158.

[3] *Hist. Mem.*, II, 115–116.

against slander and oppression, bombarded his superiors with accounts of the successes and the needs of his missions, pleaded constantly for more workers, and painted glowing pictures of lands and peoples yet outside the Christian fold. Besides these multitudinous and miscellaneous writings, three major items have come down to us intact. The first of these is the *Exposición Astronómica de el Cometa,* which so disturbed Sigüenza. The second is the history of the martyrdom of Father Saeta whose long title begins, *Inocente, Apostólica, y Gloriosa Muerte.* This rare manuscript has never yet been published. The third and by far the most important for the historian is the *Favores Celestiales.*[1] This great book amounts to an autobiography of Kino and a chronicle of the border from the time when he began his missionary work in Pimería Alta down to 1706. He was not only the apostle but also the historian of Pima Land.

The *Favores Celestiales* is not a unified production, nor was it written primarily as a history. Neither is it a monument to great literary skill. It was compiled in the heat of battle for practical purposes, a fact which gives it all the greater value as a human document. It was prepared in the form of separate reports written from time to time as a means of making known the needs of the missions and the opportunities for greater triumphs of the Faith.

In the writing of the *Favores* Kino was stimulated by Father Thirso González, his friend of Sevilla days, when Father Eusebio had exercised his mechanical skill by making a sundial for Father Thirso.

[1] The full title of the work (translated into English) is *Celestial Favors of Jesus, Most Holy Mary, and the Most Glorious Apostle of the Indies, San Francisco Xavier, Experienced in the New Conquests and New Conversions of the New Kingdom of Nueva Navarra of this Unknown North America; and the Land-Passage to California in thirty-five degrees of Latitude; with the new Cosmographic Map of these New and Extensive Lands which hitherto have been unknown. Dedicated to the Royal Majesty of Philip V, Very Catholic King and Grand Monarch of the Spains and the Indies.* It was published in English in 1919 under the title of *Kino's Historical Memoir of Pimería Alta.* Edited by Herbert Eugene Bolton (Cleveland). Kino mentions several compositions by himself which have not come down to us. Of one he wrote in February, 1702: "The Treatise on California Baxa, entitled *Novae Carolinae,* because with the so Catholic expenses of Don Carlos II, this conquest was begun, is already written. There only lacks to add to it the best, which is the present permanence and perseverance, thanks to the Lord, of the conquest and of its new conversions and missions" (Kino to Thirso González, Dolores, February 2, 1702.) In his dedication of the *Favores Celestiales* dated November 21, 1708, he says, "I have just written another small treatise called "Manifiesto Cosmográfico de que la California no es Ysla, sino Penisla, o Continente con esta Nueva España" (Cosmographic Proof that California is not an Island, but a Peninsula, and is Continuous with this New Spain) . . . and, with its map, I am sending it to Mexico to the father provincial, as his Reverence asks me to do." I have never seen this document, and I assume that it has never been printed (*Hist. Mem.,* I, 91). The substance of this work, it is inferred, is contained in the *Favores Celestiales,* Parte II, Lib. iv, Cap. 8.

When González became General this early friendship worked to the advantage of the Pima missions. Fired by Kino's glowing reports from the distant American frontier, González encouraged, indeed he requested, him to write an account of what had been accomplished. He even suggested a name for the work, which Kino adopted. Stimulation nearer home was contributed by Fathers Leal and Campos.

So Kino set about the task. When it reached its final form the manuscript consisted of five divisions. Part I was written late in 1699 and brought the story down to that date.[1] Thus Kino's *Favores Celestiales* and Manje's *Luz de Tierra Incógnita* were begun about the same time.[2] Three years passed. González in Rome acknowledged the receipt of Part I of the manuscript and urged Kino to carry the account forward. It was a fresh breath from the missionary frontier and gave a vivid glimpse of the Rim of Christendom. "I read it all, without omitting a word, and I affectionately charge your Reverence that as soon as possible you write the second part." Such praise from the head of the Order thrilled the humble missionary in the wilds of America. Just at this time Provincial Arteaga asked Kino for a report to use in an appeal for missionaries. Impetuous Campos urged him to write it and make it vigorous. "Say as much as you wish . . . petition, petition again; clamor, clamor again!" All these things, says Kino "impel me with great force to write this second part, as my continued and multitudinous occupations permit." So he took up his pen again and wrote two more sections. Part II reached to the end of 1702 and Part III to the end of 1704.[3]

Meanwhile, in May, 1704, Kino finished a short report on the Pima missions in the form of a dedication of the *Favores Celestiales* to King Philip V.[4] That is, it was regarded as a dedication of Parts I, II, and III. In it, with obvious flattery, Kino proposed a new name for Pima Land. Why not call it NEW PHILIPPINES? Surely the fifth Philip was as deserving as the third. In view of the royal cédula issued by Philip V in 1701 favoring the California and Sonora missions, he says, "one cannot refrain from giving them the renowned name of the

---

[1] Kino, *Favores Celestiales*, Parte I; *Hist. Mem.*, I, 103–224.
[2] Perhaps one was suggested by the other.
[3] Kino, *Favores Celestiales*, Partes II and III; *Hist. Mem.*, I, 225–379; II, 25–111.
[4] Dated May 1, 1704. It is nearly identical with the Dedicatory of Nov. 21, 1708, included in the *Favores Celestiales*. The original manuscript is in the Maggs Collection (London), No. 26.

New Philippines of the Western Indies of the very extensive North America, with the same and even more propriety than that with which, on account of the Catholic zeal of Philip III,[1] the conquered islands of the Eastern Indies in Asia were called the Philippines." The reigning monarch doubtless would agree.

There was another hiatus. Then, with new encouragement from various persons, Kino continued the narrative as Part IV, carrying the story to the end of 1706.[2] On November 21, 1708, he signed a new dedication of the work to Philip V.[3] It closely follows that of 1704, but there are innovations. For one thing, he proposes still another name for the new spiritual conquests. This for the Bourbon eye! Now, he says, the new conversions might appropriately be called the New Philippines,—"unless your Royal Majesty prefers, . . . that these new conquests . . . should be decorated with the name of the NEW KINGDOM OF NEW NAVARRE. . . . For this new kingdom of the American New Navarre might unite still other neighboring kingdoms which are being conquered with those already conquered, just as the kingdom of Navarre in Europe lies between and unites the crowns and realms of France and Spain." Was Father Eusebio suggesting that New France and New Spain might thus be joined? The conquerors of the "other neighboring kingdoms" to which Kino alluded were of course the Black Robes of New France.

Kino did not continue the chronological narrative of his work beyond the end of 1706, where he had left it in Part IV. This means that for the last five years of his career we lack a detailed account of his doings such as we have for the preceding twenty. But he did add to his chronicle a fifth part. It was not originally written as a division of the *Favores Celestiales,* but was incorporated as a suitable conclusion. It is a report to the king, dedicated in 1710, and consists of an extended plea for the promotion of conquests in the northwest and the establishment there of the kingdom to be called New Navarre.[4]

The Master of Dolores attributed all his successes, and indeed, all his tribulations, to the heavenly favors which had been so liberally

---

[1] It was Philip II for whom the Philippines were named.
[2] Kino, *Favores Celestiales,* Parte IV; *Hist. Mem.,* II, 113–220.
[3] Kino, *Favores Celestiales,* Dedication and Prologue; *Hist. Mem.,* II, 85–95.
[4] Kino, *Favores Celestiales,* Parte V; *Hist. Mem.,* II, 221–275.

bestowed upon him. So he called his book *Favores Celestiales,* as
González had suggested. These heavenly favors are extolled with
gratitude throughout the work, but are especially set forth in the Prologue. In this preface Kino's writing reached a plane which may well
be called inspired, for its beauty of thought and its exaltation of spirit.[1]

CXLIX

THE VISION

Just as Kino considered all blessings as celestial favors, he regarded
past achievements merely as preludes to future triumphs of the Faith.
This view of his work he maintained to the end of his days. In spite
of the weight of years, arduous toils, frontier privations, and ceaseless
opposition, he continued down to the very last with spirit unbroken,
able to dream and plan and work and promote, as he had dreamed
and planned and worked and promoted for a third of a century. In
the last chapters of the *Favores Celestiales* he paints a picture of the
glories, spiritual and temporal, yet to be achieved in Pima Land and,
particularly, in the vast regions *más allá.* This part V of his history,
written mainly in 1708 but signed only a year before his death, illustrates the dauntless optimism of the astounding man. It may be taken
as representing the vision of the near future which he nursed in his
last days and carried with him when he departed. It also reflects his
geographical outlook on North America and Asia.[2]

These new lands, with their numerous and gentle tribes, he said,

---

[1] Kino, *Favores Celestiales,* Prologue; *Hist. Mem.,* I, 97–102. Regarding the *Favores Celestiales* there was one unfortunate circumstance. Kino at some time in his later years seems to have
lost faith in his own findings as to the latitude of the head of the Gulf. He had explored diligently, made frequent astronomical observations, and correctly placed the head of the Gulf near
32 degrees. His maps of the *Paso por Tierra* were based on these findings and are surprisingly
accurate. Yet, after all this, for some unaccountable reason Kino concluded that the land passage
was near 35°. Moreover, at some time that has not been determined he went through the manuscript of the *Favores Celestiales* and in several places changed 32° to 35°. That the alterations
were made by Kino himself is beyond a doubt, for they are in his well-known hand. While these
changes mar the treatise they do not discredit it. Kino's latitudes as determined by his own observations were generally accurate and generally consistent. When the great work is again edited
the altered latitudes should be restored, thus giving the treatise the consistency which it had before
it was doctored.

[2] Kino, *Favores Celestiales,* Parte V, Libs. iii–iv; *Hist. Mem.,* II, 254–275.

offered so grand an opportunity to spread the Faith and the power of Spain that seven Christian kingdoms might be formed to replace the ancient heathen Seven Cities. These new kingdoms might be called Nueva Vizcaya, Nuevo Mexico, California Baja, Nueva Navarra, California Alta, Gran Quivira, "and Gran Teguayo or Nueva Borboña, which is to the north of us, beyond Moqui, and extends to the Sea of the North[1] which Hudson discovered." He means Hudson Bay. His vision was expansive. Nueva Borboña, or New Bourbon, was intended as a name for New France—or was it meant for a new jurisdiction in the heart of the continent, embracing the vast prairie regions of the Mississippi Valley and Canada?

And so, as a conclusion for his book, he sets forth "the very great advantages to both Majesties which can be obtained by the promotion of these new conquests and conversions." It is an enticing vision which he portrays—and is so intended. In part it is the same picture which he drew in 1702 after his return from the mouth of the Colorado River. He appears at his best as a writer of promotion literature.

Kino saw in the missions both temporal and spiritual benefits. At the same time that they spread the Faith they promoted Christian civilization. They would serve, as they had always done, to protect Sonora from the inroads of Apaches and their fellow bandits, who were now penetrating more and more deeply into the heart of the provinces. The Sobaípuris of the San Pedro Valley were still the surest reliance. Chief Coro was still the Spaniards' ablest ally. He should be encouraged. A mission at his village of Quíburi, with a fortification for its defense, would enable Coro to chastise the enemy, "as he is accustomed to do, winning very good victories as always, and even much greater, for the total relief of the province in general, and of Bazeraca in particular."

But it was *más allá* that opportunity lay. Beyond! There was glory for God and the king. Yes, for the old dreamer there was romance! New missions would be the means not only of preserving present provinces, but of adding new ones to the realm. "For there are prudent and weighty persons, zealous for the service of their Majesties, who are of the opinion that in these more than two hundred leagues

[1] Kino, *Favores Celestiales*, Dedication; *Hist. Mem.*, I, 90–91.

of rich new lands, inhabited by Indians industrious, recently conquered and reduced, a new kingdom with ease can be founded." And
it might be called New Navarre, "as others are called New Biscay,
New Galicia, New León."

Kino even dreamed of converting the indomitable Apaches, a hope
which required supreme optimism. But he had it. "By promoting the
new conversions of this extensive Pimería, with the favor of Heaven
we shall be able shortly to enter upon the reduction and conversion
of the neighboring Apachería, which lies northeast and north of us.
and extends northwest to the very large Colorado River, or Río del
Norte, . . . for, we having sent messages to those natives up the
Colorado River, already they have invited us to enter and see them,
and already they give us certain reports that soon, in imitation of
the rest, over here, they will be won to our friendship and to the desire
of receiving our holy Catholic Faith."

With Apache Land subdued and in the fold the gate would be
wide open. "By way of the same Apachería . . . we shall be able,
with the divine grace, to enter and trade with New Mexico, and with
its nearest provinces, Moqui and Zuñi . . . for we have also certain
reports that before the revolt of New Mexico the Spaniards of those
provinces used to come by way of the Apachería to these . . . Sobaí-
poris to barter maize for hatchets, cloth, sackcloth, blankets, chomites,
knives, etc." From New Mexico it would be just a step to the limit-
less beyond: "northward to Gran Teguayo; northwest to Gran Quibira;
and west to California Alta . . . and the South Sea, and to its great
Bay of the Eleven Thousand Virgins; [1] to the famous port of Monte
Rey; . . . and to the very renowned Cape Mendozino." With the aid
of Kino's zeal and imagination new kingdoms now were rising fast.

Still beyond. From New Mexico communication would follow
with New France—this again for the Bourbon eye—and with the Jesuits
there, "and with the new conquests, conversions, and missions which
at present they are making with their glorious and apostolic journeys
from east to west." A road to Canada would offer a short cut from
Sonora to Spain and France, "only half as long as the road which we
are accustomed to travel by way of the City of Mexico and . . . Vera

---

[1] San Quintín Bay.

Cruz; for if the one road is much more than two thousand leagues, the other will be little more than one thousand."

Kino's vision was not limited by the Pacific Ocean. Alluring prospects beckoned still further northwest—"a convenient land route to Asia, and to Great Tartary, and to Great China, since to the westward of Cape Mendosino and connected therewith follow the land of Jesso; . . . the Tierra de la Compañía . . . and the lands nearest Japan; and afterward the narrow Strait of Anian, which is no more than ten or twelve leagues across, and has the convenience of an island in the middle by which to pass to Great Tartary and from there to Great China: . . . And it is patent that there is no other Strait of Anian than this one which I mention here. For although Drake, in order to carry his point that California was an island, would feign another Strait of Anian, with another much talked of Sea of the North over here above California, . . . it is all a lie." Drake was done for.

Closer home there could be a port of call for the Manila Galleon and direct trade with it overland from Sonora by the land passage now discovered. "These new conversions and this new province of Sonora and all the Kingdom of Nueva Biscaia . . . by the land route to California, will be able to provide a port of call for the China Ship and trade with her, and succor with fresh food persons whom she is accustomed to bring ill with the very painful disease of scurvy, originating from their salt, dry, and stale food; all with very great advantages and gains for everybody," and obviating the very long and costly overland transportation from Acapulco. "And this port of call, with all due deference to the navigators of the China ships, . . . might be at the Bay of Todos Santos [now Ensenada], or at the famous neighboring port of San Diego."

Then, too, the age-old dream of one fold with one shepherd could now be realized, said Kino. "By the Catholic promotion of these new conquests and conversions . . . of this New Navarre, the Catholic empire of the Catholic royal crown and of our Holy Mother, the Roman Catholic Church, will be happily extended, so that all the world may be one fold with one shepherd—*ut fiat unum ovile et unus pastor* [1]

---

[1] John X. 16: *Et fiet unum ovile, et unus pastor.*—"And there shall be one fold and one shepherd."

—and this, by the divine grace, without great expenditure from the royal chests, and with only the accustomed alms for the missionary fathers."

Finally, with the advance of the mission frontier, the geographical data acquired would make it possible to correct the maps, as Kino already had done in so many particulars, and to dispel the myths which flitted about and cast a deceptive glow across the horizon. "If we continue with the promotion and advancement of these new conversions we shall be able to continue to make accurate maps of North America, the greater part of which has been unknown, or practically unknown. For some ancients blot the map with so many and such errors and with such fictitious grandeurs and feigned riches as a crowned king whom they carry in chairs of gold, with walled cities, and with lakes of quicksilver and gold or amber, and of corals. With reason Father Mariana rebukes them for deceiving us with these riches which do not exist.[1] But they do not say a word about the principal riches that exist there, namely the innumerable souls ransomed by the most precious blood of our Redeemer, Jesus Christ."

This was the vision. And there were means in sight for making it a reality. The celestial favors would be supplied, of course, by divine benevolence. The temporal means at hand Kino now proceeded to enumerate. The list of them constituted a description of the Pima missions and their resources. It was a summary of Kino's own achievement. He trusted in God, but assumed the immediate responsibility himself.

Among the assets at hand for realizing these spiritual and temporal glories, the old promoter listed even the humble cabbage and the lowly garlic. "There are already very rich and abundant fields, plantings and crops of wheat, maize, frijoles, chick peas, beans, lentils, bastard chick peas, etc. There are good gardens, . . . vineyards for wine for masses, and cane-fields of sweet cane for syrup and panocha, and with the favor of heaven, before long for sugar.[2] There are many Castilian fruit trees, such as fig trees, quinces, oranges, pomegranates, peaches, apricots, pears, apples, mulberries, pecans, tunas, etc.; all sorts of garden stuff, such as cabbages, melons, watermelons, white cabbage, lettuce, onions,

---

[1] Mariana, Juan de, *Historiae de rebus Hispaniae* (Toleti, 1592).
[2] Farther south on the Pacific Coast there were numerous sugar mills at this time.

leeks, garlic, anise, pepper, mustard, mint, Castilian roses, white lilies, etc., and very good timber for all kinds of building, such as pine, ash, cypress, walnut, China-trees, mesquite, alders, poplar, willow, and tamarind."

Quite apart from its relation to Kino's vision, the enumeration is eloquent testimony to the part which he and his associates had played in the transit of European culture to the deserts of Pima Land.

CL

STILL IN THE SADDLE

The calendar warned Kino that he was no longer young. But he went constructively forward. He by no means rusted out. His soaring dreams were only partially realized, and for lack of missionaries his vast plans for expansion did not take effect in his day. But he did not cease to labor vigorously at Dolores and in the promotion of new foundations. His ranches still prospered and he continued to aid California. Chiefs and their followers—Pimas, Cocomaricopas, Yumas, and Quíquimas—continued to come long distances to attend Church fiestas, bringing their infant sons for baptism by Padre Eusebio, and to appeal for missionaries. Kino forwarded their petitions to the superiors, and even as of yore escorted the supplicants to see them.

Two examples will suffice. In the fall of 1707 Picolo made another visit to the Pimería. Just after he left Dolores "more than thirty governors, captains, alcaldes, fiscales, etc., all on horseback," came to see the Padre Grande. They were too late, and Kino was touched by their disappointment. In spite of the weight of his sixty-two years he put foot in stirrup and with the disconsolate children of the desert he pursued the Father Visitor. "As his Reverence had just set out from this Pimería, they all went, and I with them, to overtake his Reverence, as far as Cucurpe, where he promised them that the necessary fathers, for whom they anxiously prayed, should come to them." Here was a hard forty-mile ride just to give pleasure to his Pima friends. A much longer jaunt now followed.

Late in the same year Kino rode once more over the mountain trail to escort a band of Cocomaricopa chiefs to Bazeraca to see Father Polici. From there he wrote to Father Tamburini, the new Father General in Rome—for his friend González was no more, and Kino had to educate another Father General in American ways. He wrote in Latin now.[1] "I have no doubt Father Orazio Police has written to your Reverence regarding the *regulos*—the governors or captains—of the Cocomaricopa nation. In order to visit the father and ask for the Faith and for missionaries, these chiefs traveled two hundred and fifty leagues, coming all the way from their own country to the residence of Father Oracio." He says nothing of his own grueling ride. "They are still with us, but will presently return to their homes, traveling another two hundred and fifty leagues. Their feeling is shared by the other tribes, such as the Yumas, Quíquimas, etc., who live along the large river called the Hila, and"—this in underscored Spanish, for emphasis—"*and on the very large-volumed Río Colorado, which is the true Río del Norte of the ancients.* If your Reverence so desires, within a little while and without difficulty this whole country will be ours." Only missionaries were lacking. Here was Tamburini's chance!

With the letter Kino and the Indians sent a little present,—a curiosity from the America wilderness. Perhaps it would pique the new Father General's interest. It is not blue shells now, but those medicinal treasures from the stomachs of ruminants which were then highly prized. "We—that is to say, these tribes and myself—are sending your Reverence with this letter three bezoar stones, as they are called, weighing about twenty ounces, or a pound and a half. We have rarely found or seen stones of such size and weight." Another Jesuit tells us that in Sonora these bezoar stones were used as cures "in poisonous epidemics, for melancholy, and for other purposes." They were found in the stomachs of "roebucks as well as does," and were especially plentiful in Pápago Land, whose heat and lack of water were thought by the natives to promote their formation.[2] Kino continues: "I pray your Reverence to pardon the triviality of this little gift which these poor

---

[1] Kino to Tamburini, Bazeraca, Dec. 14, 1707. Original Latin manuscript in Fondo Gesuitico al Gesù di Roma, Epist. Selectae, II. n. 90. Printed in *Archivum Historicum Societatis Jesu*, III (Rome, 1934), 263–264. Kino, *Favores Celestiales*, Parte III, Lib. v, Cap. 9; *Hist. Mem.*, II, 218.

[2] Pfefferkorn, Ignaz, *Beschreibung der Landschaft Sonora*, Part V, Caption, "Bezoar."

folks now send you. Perhaps at some future time, God willing, we shall be able to do better, and to deliver into your Reverence's holy hands a present of greater value. But all of us, by the sacred wounds of Jesus Christ, entreat you to send us laborers conspicuous for their zeal; and to send us many of them, for this vineyard is very large!" Again the refrain, more help! [1]

No help came, but Kino, with Campos and Minutuli, still kept the spark of Christianity alive in the outlying villages. Caborca and Búsanic in the Altar Valley, and Santa María in the Santa Cruz Valley, were centers of interest now. And they were going concerns. Bac, though it had no resident missionary, was an active visita.

Santa María now became the object of Kino's special attention on the border, and his efforts there were in keeping with his usual vigor and competence. His arm had not shortened. Dolores had not yielded her place as Mother of Missions. Her bounty was still nothing short of munificent. "This first mission of . . . Dolores is at present arranging for the delivery of a decent equipment for founding the new mission of Santa María de Bogata," he writes. "That is, new vestments with which to say Mass, three hundred head of cattle for their ranch, one hundred head of sheep and goats, a drove of mares, a drove of horses, a house in which to live, the beginnings of a church, with provisions and the necessary furnishings for a house, and the beginnings of sowing and crops of wheat, maize, etc." Perhaps Kino had Mora in mind when he added: "Almost as much was given, to the value of three thousand pesos, from the stock of . . . Dolores, a few years ago, for the founding and equipment of the mission of San Ygnacio." [2]

Encouraged by the great salesman, others now offered to help. Another boom was in prospect. Promotion of the conversions, Kino wrote "is greatly facilitated by the fact that different benefactors, missionary fathers of the old missions of the Society of Jesus, as well as secular gentlemen, promise very good aid." Gifts already offered amounted to the snug sum of more than twenty thousand pesos. Pima Land, as well as California, could have a Fondo Piadoso.

---

[1] We trust that the Father General received the bezoar stones and proudly showed them to his colleagues.
[2] Report dated Feb. 2, 1710, in *Favores Celestiales*, Parte V, Lib. iv, Cap. 13.

Quíburi, Coro's village on the Apache border, was the objective point next beyond Santa María. "One person alone,"—Kino does not tell us who—"offers five thousand pesos in suitable goods, with some silver, for the founding of the church, house, and fortification of the settlement or great mission of Santa Ana de Quíbori, where Captain Coro lives; because it is notorious that those his people will be able to continue to pursue the neighboring avowed enemies, the Hocomes, Janos, and Apaches, for the very great and total relief, or remedy, of all this province of Sonora." Thus was recognized the defensive character of missions.

The government was hard up. So Kino himself offered not only to equip new missions, but also to help pay the expenses of outfitting new missionaries in Mexico if only they could be sent. "What I especially come again to beg of your Reverence and of my Father Provincial," he wrote on September 16, 1709, to the procurator in Mexico, "is that we be aided with six or seven father missionaries for these new conversions and new incipient missions, and also that a few hundred pesos be spent on my account for providing the outfit for these fathers, for these rich missions will pay these expenses." [1] If necessary he would pay even the salaries of the new missionaries as well as outfit them. He would provide the *sínodos* which the government usually contributed. This offer may be taken as a measure of Kino's zeal, his thrift, or his self-confidence. In any case, he was competent, and he was game.

Father Eusebio's thrift continued up to the last. At the same time that he endowed the Holy Sepulcher, founded missions, and made gifts to the Province, he added to the permanent equipment of his mission. New bells and towers were acquired for Dolores. In the communication last cited he wrote the procurator: "By special messenger I am dispatching this letter to Fronteras, to go with one hundred marks of silver. Probably the same amount, which is owing me and is promised by reliable persons, will be assembled and collected and added on the way." It was to be forwarded by the captain of the presidio and placed to Kino's credit. From it the procurator was to

[1] Kino to Juan de Yturberoaga, procurator general, Dolores, September 16, 1709. With draft of reply, Feb. 1, 1710. Original Spanish manuscript in the Stevens Collection.

deduct the price of fifty pounds of chocolate owed on a former shipment of goods, and $300 as a gift to the Province. Out of the balance, "You may have sent to me the large and good bell of fourteen or sixteen arrobas [350 or 400 pounds] for this church, and a good turret,[1] and the other things which I requested in my memorandum. . . . And I hope that in a short time I shall be able to send more silver, because the year seems to promise to be fruitful." Dolores and her daughters had thrived.

Bulls and horses as well as silver, Kino continued to toss into the missionary hopper. Three months later he repeated to the procurator essentially what he had previously written. Through the captain of the presidio he had sent about two hundred marks or $1400 in silver. One thousand pesos were for the Province, the balance to be placed to his credit. Part of it he hoped would be used to outfit new missionaries. What he lacked in silver he could supply in stock from his prosperous ranches. "I added to the alms of one thousand pesos for the Province, one hundred bulls and young bulls and twenty-five horses, and these promptly, in order to aid it with all love and all my life."

California continued to be Kino's beneficiary. There was a conflict of affection, but Kino was able to solve it. "Father Rector Juan María de Salvatierra [now back at Loreto] gives me to understand that by disposition of our Father General my principal obligation is to succor California, and I am now sending thither also a goodly quantity of provisions and cattle, which is what they are asking of me." "P.S. . . . I very urgently recommend the sending of a bell of fourteen or fifteen or sixteen arrobas, and pardon me, your Reverence." It is plain that Father Eusebio was optimistic, active, and able to the very last.[2]

To Kino's letter of September 16, 1709, the procurator replied with shocking news. Father Eusebio might not need the requested missionaries or the new bells! The bishop of Durango was demanding that all the missions of the Society in New Spain be suppressed! What was worse, it was reported that the king had yielded to the demand.

---

[1] The ornamental turret-shaped counter-weight attached to the bell.
[2] Kino to Juan de Yturberoaga, Dolores, December 7, 1709. Original Spanish manuscript in the Stevens Collection.

Moreover, the Father General had obediently ordered the Provincial "that as soon as . . . he is informed of the suppression or that the king desires the alms, . . . at once all the missionary fathers of the Province shall retire and be placed in the colleges." How then, "can your Reverence expect to obtain what you request?" Indeed, how could he?

This ominous letter was written in Mexico on February 1, 1710.[1] Kino died at Magdalena thirteen months later. It is perhaps too much to hope that the mails were so slow that he did not receive it, and therefore never learned the distressing news.

CLI

THE LAST RIDE

One day near the middle of March, 1711, Kino rode over the familiar trail to Magdalena to dedicate a chapel in honor of his patron saint. It was the very season of the year when first he had threaded that mountain gap just twenty-four years previously. Spring flowers were in bloom and Nature was at her best. Magdalena, too, was in festive garb for the great occasion. But suddenly holiday colors were exchanged for the black of mourning. In the very midst of the dedication ceremony, in which he took a leading part, Kino became desperately ill and soon afterward died. It was fitting that his fellow-player in the final scene of the drama should be Father Campos, for eighteen years his co-laborer. Father Eusebio's last moments are described by Father Luís Velarde, his companion for eight years and his successor at Dolores.

"Father Kino died in the year 1711, having spent twenty-four years in glorious labors in this Pimería, which he entirely covered in forty expeditions made as best they could be made by two or three zealous workers. When he died he was almost seventy years old." As a matter of fact he was only sixty-six. "He died as he had lived, with extreme

---

[1] Yturberoaga to Kino, Mexico, Feb. 1, 1710. Draft of reply to Kino's letter of Sept. 16, 1709, written on the back. Original Spanish manuscript in the Stevens Collection. The threatened suppression did not take place at this time.

humility and poverty. In token of this, during his last illness he did not undress. His death bed, as his bed always, consisted of two calf-skins for a mattress, two blankets such as the Indians use for covers, and a pack saddle for a pillow. Nor did the entreaties of Father Agustín move him to anything else. He died in the house of the Father where he had gone to dedicate a finely made chapel in his pueblo of Santa Magdalena, consecrated to San Francisco Xavier. . . . When he was singing the Mass of the dedication he felt indisposed, and it seems that the Holy Apostle, to whom he was ever devoted, was calling him, in order that, being buried in his chapel, he might accompany him, as we believe, in glory." [1]

It fell to Father Campos to consign Father Kino to the grave. The original record of the event, written in Father Agustín's own hand and signed with his well-known rubric, lies before me at this moment. It contains an epitome of the great Black Robe's repute in the land where he had run his remarkable career.

"THE YEAR 1711

"Padre Eusebio Franco. Kino.—On the fifteenth of March, a little after midnight, Father Eusebio Francisco Kino died with great peace and edification in this house and pueblo of Santa Magdalena at the age of seventy years, having been for nearly twenty-four years missionary of Nuestra Señora de los Dolores, which he himself founded. He worked tirelessly in continuous peregrinations and in the reduction of all this Pimería. He discovered the Casa Grande, the rivers Jila and Colorado, the Cocomaricopa and Suma nations, and the Quicimaspa of the Island. And now, resting in the Lord, he is buried in a coffin in this chapel of San Francisco Xavier on the Gospel side where fall the second and third choir seats. He was German by nationality and of the province to which Bavaria belongs, before he entered the Pimería having been missionary and cosmographer in California, in the time of Admiral Don Ysidro de Otondo.

AGUSTIN DE CAMPOS [rubric]." [2]

---

[1] Velarde, in Manje, *Luz de Tierra Incógnita,* 382.
[2] Original manuscript in the Bancroft Library.

The irony of fate! Kino spent a decade in man-killing explorations and endless demonstrations that California was a peninsula. The biographer has produced unimpeachable evidence of Kino's baptism in the Italian village of Segno. He has explained with scholastic pride, tempered by due modesty, his discovery of the way in which the *A* was dropped out of Admiral Atondo's name. And now, at the end, in the very obituary of his hero, written by the hero's companion of eighteen years, California is referred to as "the Island"; and the biographer has to read that Kino was "German by nationality" and that he was in California with Otondo. It was not fair for Campos to treat either Kino or the biographer so. He should have been better informed. He had listened to Father Eusebio's critics. He had never made long weary journeys to and across the Colorado; he had never seen the sun rise over the Gulf; and he had never read this book.

A year after Kino's death Campos went to Tubutama and moved to Magdalena the remains of Manuel González. Father Eusebio and his first friend in Pima Land now rested side by side. With Kino's passing his fame at Magdalena grew. The statue of his patron saint installed in the chapel whose dedication was his last earthly act, became a shrine which until recently drew crowds of worshippers each year from Sonora, Arizona, and places even more remote. A few months ago the statue was removed and its veneration suppressed. But Kino's renown waxes greater. The folklore built around his name would fill another book.

CLII

WHAT HE HAD WROUGHT

If this story is too long, Kino himself is to blame, so many and so continued were his activities. Some men rise like a rocket, illuminate the scene for a moment, then disappear from view. Kino was not one of these. His light, beginning modestly as a candle flame, burned ever more brightly, lasted through decades, reached its maximum in his mature life, and was in full glow when suddenly he died. Kino was

Church at Magdalena. Successor to the one in which Kino was buried in 1711

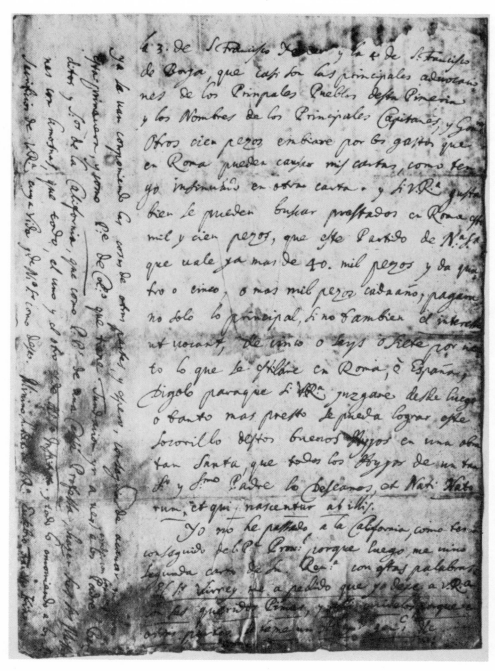

Last page of a letter by Kino to Thirso González, Father General of the Jesuit Order.
Undated, but written late in December, 1697

(From the original Spanish manuscript in the Fondo Jesuítico al Gesù di Roma)

a marked man during forty years, from his student days at Ingolstadt to his last Mass at Magdalena. In Germany he won recognition for his mathematics. His early letters to Rome revealed to the Father General a man of unusual religious fervor. In Spain his vigorous personality arrested the attention of a princely patroness of missions. On his first arrival in Mexico his knowledge of astronomy was requisitioned—and challenged. Each of these stages of his growth is clearly marked.

Before he came to California Kino's career was in preparation. There he became a personality. Without Kino to shed light upon them, Atondo, Goñi, and Copart would now be dim figures. They were good and useful men. But it was Kino's presence that lifted them and their deeds above the commonplace. On the Peninsula Father Eusebio revealed his gifts as an inimitable missionary, an exuberant explorer, a superb diarist, and a trained cartographer. On his return to the Mexican capital, where he dealt face to face with provincial and viceroy, he demonstrated his power to influence men—a power based on a magnetic personality, sound knowledge, and the courage of his convictions.

But not till he reached Pima Land did Kino's outstanding qualities blossom forth into full flower. There his peculiar genius found its opportunity. He was an individualist, restive of restraint, fitted best to flourish outside the range of stereotyped society. He was most himself on the frontier. The Jesuit precept of obedience he always acknowledged, but with him obedience was never divorced from responsibility. In Pima Land he was beyond the realm of fixed routine, in surroundings where initiative was at a premium. Here his boundless zeal, his vaulting imagination, and his astounding energy found room, though often hampered by misinformed superiors, by the honest fears or the petty jealousies of smaller calibered associates, and by the secret or open hostility of secular neighbors whose desire to exploit the Indians made him their natural enemy.

Kino's achievements on the Rim of Christendom were manifold. He was great as missionary, church builder, explorer, ranchman, Indian diplomat, cartographer, and historian. He personally baptized more than four thousand Indians, a number which writers persistently exaggerate to forty thousand, merely because an early chronicler mistook a cauldron for a cipher.[1] By Kino directly or under his supervision, missions were founded on both sides of the Sonora-Arizona boundary, on the San Ignacio, Altar, Sonóita, and Santa Cruz rivers. The occupation of California by the Jesuits was the direct result of Kino's former residence there and of his persistent efforts in its behalf, for it was from Kino that Salvatierra, founder of the permanent California missions, got his inspiration. Father Juan took up the work where Father Eusebio left off.

To Kino is due the credit for first traversing in detail and accurately mapping important sections of California and the whole of Pimería Alta. Considered quantitatively alone, his work of exploration was astounding. During his twenty-four years of residence at the mission of Dolores he made more than fifty journeys inland, an average of more than two per year. These tours varied from a hundred to nearly a thousand miles in length. They were all made on horseback. In the course of them he crossed and recrossed repeatedly and at varying angles all of the two hundred miles of country between the San Ignacio and the Gila and the two hundred and fifty miles between the San Pedro and the Colorado. When he first opened them most of his trails were either absolutely untrod by civilized man or had been altogether forgotten. His explorations were made through countries inhabited by unknown tribes who might but fortunately did not offer him personal violence, though they sometimes proved too threatening for the nerve of his companions. One of his routes was over a forbidding, waterless waste which later became the graveyard of scores of travelers who died of thirst because they lacked Father Kino's pioneering skill. I refer to the Camino del Diablo, or Devil's Highway, from Sonóita to the Gila. In the prosecution of these journeys Kino's energy and hardihood were almost beyond belief.

In estimating these feats of exploration we must remember the limited means with which he performed them. He was not supported and encouraged by hundreds of horsemen and a great retinue of

[1] In 1708 Kino wrote: "In these twenty-one years . . . I have baptized here in these new conquests and new conversions about four thousand five hundred souls, and I could have baptized twelve or fifteen thousand if we had not suspended further baptisms until our Lord should bring us necessary fathers to aid us in instructing and ministering to so many new subjects of your Majesty and parishioners of our Holy Mother Church." (*Favores Celestiales*, Dedication.)

friendly Indians as were De Soto and Coronado. In all but two cases he went almost unaccompanied by military aid, and more than once he traveled without a single white man. In one expedition, made in 1697 to the Gila, he was accompanied by Lieutenant Manje, Captain Bernal, and twenty-two soldiers. In 1701 he was escorted by Manje and ten soldiers. At other times he had no other military escort than Lieutenant Manje or Captain Carrasco, without soldiers. Once Father Gilg and Manje accompanied him; once two Black Robes and two citizens. His last great exploration to the Colorado was made with only one other white man in his party, while three times he reached the Gila with no living soul save his Indian servants. But he was usually well equipped with horses and mules from his own ranches, for he took at different times as many as fifty, sixty, eighty, ninety, one hundred and five, and even one hundred and thirty head. A Kino cavalcade was a familiar sight in Pima Land.

The work which Father Kino did as ranchman would alone stamp him as an unusual business man and make him worthy of remembrance. He was easily the cattle king of his day and region. From the small outfit supplied him from the older missions to the east and south, within fifteen years he established the beginnings of ranching in the valleys of the San Ignacio, the Altar, the Santa Cruz, the San Pedro, and the Sonóita. The stock-raising industry of nearly twenty places on the modern map owes its beginnings on a considerable scale to this indefatigable man. Ranches were established by him or directly under his supervision at Dolores, Caborca, Tubutama, San Ignacio, Imuris, Magdalena, Quíburi, Tumacácori, Cocóspora, San Xavier del Bac, Bacoancos, Guébavi, Síboda, Búsanic, Sonóita, San Lázaro, Sáric, Santa Bárbara, and Santa Eulalia.

It must not be supposed that Kino did this work for private gain, for he did not own a single animal. It was to furnish a food supply for the neophytes of the missions established, give them economic independence, and train the Indians in the rudiments of civilized life. And it must not be forgotten that Kino conducted this cattle industry with Indian labor, almost without the aid of a single white man. An illustration of his method and of his difficulties is found in the fact that the important ranch at Tumacácori was founded with cattle and sheep driven, at Kino's orders, a hundred miles or more across the country from Caborca, by the very Indians who had recently murdered Father Saeta. There was always the danger that the mission Indians would revolt and run off the stock, as they did in 1695; and the danger, more imminent, that the hostile Apaches would do this damage, and add to it the destruction of life, as experience often proved.

Kino's endurance in the saddle would make a seasoned cowboy green with envy. This is evident from the bare facts with respect to the long journeys which he made. Here figures become eloquent. When he went to the City of Mexico in the fall of 1695, being then at the age of fifty-one, Kino made the journey in fifty-three days. The distance, via Guadalajara, is no less than fifteen hundred miles, making his average, not counting the stops which he made at Guadalajara and other important places, nearly thirty miles per day. In November, 1697, when he went to the Gila, he rode seven or eight hundred miles in thirty days, not counting out the stops. On his journey next year to the Gila he made an average of twenty-five or more miles a day for twenty-six days, over an unknown country. In 1699 he made the trip to and from the lower Gila, about eight or nine hundred miles, in thirty-five days, an average of ten leagues a day, or twenty-five to thirty miles. In October and November of the same year, he rode two hundred and forty leagues in thirty-nine days. In September and October, 1700, he rode three hundred and eighty-four leagues, or perhaps a thousand miles, in twenty-six days. This was an average of nearly forty miles a day. Next year he made over four hundred leagues, or some eleven hundred miles, in thirty-five days.

Thus it was customary for Kino when on these missionary tours to make an average of thirty or more miles a day for weeks in a stretch, and out of this time are to be counted the long stops which he made to preach, baptize the Indians, say Mass, and give instructions for building and planting.

A special instance of his hard riding is found in the journey which he made in November, 1699, with Leal, Gonzalvo, and Manje. After twelve days of continuous travel, supervising, baptizing, and preaching up and down the Santa Cruz Valley, going the while at the average rate of twenty-three miles (nine leagues) a day, Kino left Father Leal at Batki to go home by a more direct route, while he and Manje sped *á la ligera* to the west and northwest, to see if there were any sick Indians to baptize. Going thirteen leagues (thirty-three miles) on the eighth, he baptized two infants and two adults at the village of San Rafael. On the ninth he rode nine leagues to another village, made a census of four hundred Indians, preached to them, and continued sixteen more leagues to another village, making nearly sixty miles for the day. On the tenth he made a census of the assembled throng of three hundred persons, preached, baptized three sick persons, distributed presents, and then rode thirty-three leagues (some seventy-five miles) over a pass in the mountains to Sonóita, arriving there in the night, having stopped to make a census of, preach to, and baptize in, two villages on the way. Next day he baptized and preached, and then rode, that day and night, the fifty leagues (a hundred and twenty-five miles) that lie between Sonóita and Búsanic, where he overtook Father Leal. During the last three days he had ridden no less than one hundred and eight leagues, or over two hundred and fifty miles, counting, preaching to, and baptizing in five villages on the way. And yet after four hours' sleep he was up next morning, preaching, baptizing, and supervising the butchering of cattle for supplies. Truly this was strenuous work for a man of fifty-five.

Kino's physical courage is attested by his whole career in America, spent in exploring unknown wilds and laboring among untamed heathen. One illustration, chosen out of many, will suffice. In March and April, 1695, it will be remembered, the Pimas of the Altar Valley rose in revolt. At Caborca Father Saeta was killed and became the protomartyr of Pimería Alta. At Caborca and Tubutama seven servants of the mission were slain, and at Caborca, Tubutama, Imuris, San Ignacio and Magdalena—the whole length of the Altar and San Ignacio valleys—mission churches and other buildings were burned and the stock killed or stampeded. The missionary of Tubutama fled over the mountains to Cucurpe. San Ignacio being attacked by three hundred warriors, Father Campos fled to the same refuge.

At Dolores Father Kino, Lieutenant Manje, and three citizens of Bacanuche awaited the onslaught. An Indian who had been stationed on the mountains, seeing the smoke at San Ignacio, fled to Dolores with the news that Father Campos and all the soldiers had been killed. Manje sped to Opodepe to get aid; the three citizens hurried home to Bacanuche, and Kino was left alone. When Manje returned next day, together they hid the treasures of the church in a cave, but in spite of the soldier's entreaties that they should flee, Kino insisted on returning to the mission to await death, which they did. It is indicative of the modesty of this great soul that in his autobiography this incident in his life is passed over in complete silence. But Manje, who was weak or wise enough to wish to flee, was also generous and brave enough to record the padre's heroism and his own fears.

Kino was a significant cartographer. His maps of Lower California illumined many dark spots in a *tierra incógnita*. His *Teatro de los Trabajos,* or map of the Jesuit missions of New Spain, was so important that it was plagiarized and copied for generations. His *Paso por Tierra* was the first map of northern Pimería based on actual exploration, and for nearly a century and a half was the principal one of the region in existence. More especially, it turned the tide from the insular to the peninsular theory of California geography. Kino did not kill the notion outright, but he dealt it a body blow.

As historian Kino's contribution was even greater. Scholars have long known a few precious items from his pen. More recently a large body of his correspondence and his history of the Pima uprising in 1695 have come to light. Most important of all is the *Favores Celestiales,* a complete history, written by Kino himself at his mission of Dolores, covering a large part of his career in America. It was used by the early Jesuit historians, but lay forgotten for over a century and a half. Since its rediscovery it is found to be the source of practically all that hitherto had been known of the work of Kino and his companions, and to contain much that never was known before. Kino, therefore, was not only the first great missionary, ranchman, explorer, and geographer of the Pimería Alta, but his book was the first and will be for all time the principal history of Pima Land during his quarter century.

Kino was in the fullest sense a pioneer of civilization. But to him all this was incidental. His one burning ambition was to save souls and push outward the Rim of Christendom.

Epilogue

CLIII

THOSE WHO CAME AFTER

K INO HAD GONE. Velarde remained in charge at Dolores. A year ahead of Kino Leal had been called to his last reward. The old veteran Polici survived Kino two years, dying at Bazeraca in 1713 after some four decades of service there. Campos held the fort at San Ignacio more than a score of years after Father Eusebio departed. Manje was still active in 1726 and the date of his death is not known. Mora outlived Kino nine years, dying at Arizpe in 1720, at the age of fifty-eight. He too had become a veteran. For twenty-six years he had cared for Arizpe and its two *visitas* of Bacoache and Chinapa. His obituary calls him "godly, learned, and charitable." To the last he was punctilious in matters of religious observance. In his final moments, at his urgent insistence, he was permitted to crawl from his bed to the church to say Mass. No priest being at hand to confess him, he had sworn witnesses testify that he had begged for the rite. This being down in ink, he died in the arms of Captain Juan Bautista de Anza, famous father of a more famous son. Almost at the same time that Kino was called beyond, his staunch old friend Chief Coro died with his boots on, slain in a hand-to-hand fight. Four years later Chief Cola de Pato was instantly killed at Cocóspora in an accident.

Salvatierra, in California, outlasted Kino by six years. By the time of his death (1717) he and his associates had founded seven flourishing missions among almost savage Indians on a rocky tongue of land scarcely capable of sustaining civilized life. Ugarte now carried the Cross to the hostile people in the lower end of the Peninsula, where the names of Carranco and Tamaral were added to the already long list of Jesuit martyrs. In the mid-century new foundations were made in the north, until nearly a score of successful missions were in operation, and many thousand Indians were baptized and given a touch of civilized life. During their stay of seven decades in California more than fifty Black Robes, all told, labored in exile in this barren cactus patch.

The last three and the northernmost of the Jesuit missions in California were made possible by a Borgian heiress. The tale is told that when she made the gift she was asked in what country she wished the missions established. "In the most outlandish place in the world," she replied. The Jesuits consulted their atlases and returned the answer: "The most outlandish place in all the world is California." So in California the three missions were founded. Of course this is just a story.

The early eighteenth century witnessed a great shortage of missionaries. Then came a revival. In the far south the Black Robes took over the difficult Coras of Nayarit. In the north a new missionary host, mainly north Europeans,—the kind of men for whom Kino had begged—entered the field on both sides of the Gulf. In Sonora and Pimería Alta the Jesuit annals record the eighteenth century labors of Black Robes with the very un-Spanish names of Bentz, Fraedenberg, Gerstner, Grashofer, Hoffenrichter, Hawe, Keller, Klever, Kolub, Kürtzel, Middendorff, Miner, Nentuig, Och, Paver, Rhuen, Sedelmayr, Segesser, Slesac, Steb, Steiger, Wazet, and Weis. In California in these days labored Baegert, Bischoff, Consag, Ducrue, Gasteiger, Gordon, Helen, Link, Neumayer, Retz, Tempis, Tuersch, and Wagner, all of north European extraction.[1]

By these men Kino's old missions were restored and new ones founded. Keller and Sedelmayr retraced some of Father Eusebio's journeys to the Gila and Colorado Rivers. They, Consag, and Link, revived Kino's plan to extend missions to the Colorado, and to supply California by a land route around the head of the Gulf. Consag explored the Gulf coast on the California side all the way to the mouth of the Colorado River, and thus clinched Kino's conclusion that "California no es isla, sino penisla." Father Eusebio had scotched the island

---

[1] For the history of the Jesuits on the Pacific Coast after Kino's day see the works of Alegre, Baegert, Clavigero, Decorme, Ducrue, Ortega, Venegas, and Engelhardt. For the coming of the Franciscans and the founding of Alta California see the writings of Bancroft, Bolton, Chapman, Coues, Crespi, Engelhardt, and Palóu.

myth, Consag delivered its death blow. In the midst of these labors the Pimas rose once more in rebellion, and killed Tello at Caborca and Rhuen at Sonóita. The West Coast martyrs now numbered more than a score.

A large missionary province, the result of many years of development, was like a palm tree. The fresh growth was near the top. So it was with the Jesuit Province of New Spain. The roots of the plant were the central organization in Europe and Mexico. The colleges and other permanent foundations at the principal centers on the way north represented the trunk. This stem, though not devoid of life, gradually became bare of missionary verdure. Between Durango and California there were now missions in all stages of evolution, some already secularized, others old and stable, but without new blood from heathendom; still others, on the periphery, were filled with the vigor of youth.

The Jesuits had always labored under a degree of insecurity due to causes other than Indian revolts. Frequently there was pressure for secularizing the missions, a step which was contemplated in the system. This urge came from bishops for various reasons, from the government which wished to collect tribute, or from secular neighbors who were greedy for Indian lands or the right to exploit Indian labor. In the middle eighteenth century the missions among Tepehuanes and in Tarahumara Baja were thus turned over to the parish clergy.

Then came the final blow—the Expulsion. For reasons best known to himself, Carlos III decided to drive the Jesuits from the whole of the Spanish Empire. The edict fell in 1767. All Black Robes in New Spain were arrested, dispossessed, hurried to Vera Cruz, carried to Spain, imprisoned there, or distributed in other lands. Many of the expatriates died of disease or hardship on the way. A work of two centuries was at an end.

But the service of the Black Robes to the land of their toil did not cease even now. Many of them spent their prison hours writing of the country and the people they so dearly loved. Clavigero composed his history of California, Baegert his *Nachrichten,* Pfefferkorn his book on Sonora, Ducrue his story of the Expulsion. These and other works were published. Still others remain in manuscript and await the historian, for whom they will constitute a fresh fountain of knowledge and a well-spring of inspiration.

Some of the Jesuit missions thus left vacant were secularized—that is to say, they were put into the hands of the parish clergy. Others were entrusted to the Franciscans. Junípero Serra and his matchless band went to the Peninsula, whence with Portolá they soon advanced to San Diego and to Monterey. In Pima Land Francisco Garcés became the unique figure of the new era. A contemporary of Daniel Boone, he was like him a wanderer. Sallying forth from San Xavier del Bac, the mission to which he was assigned, he warmed old trails long cold and blazed new ones in the *Más Allá* of which Kino had talked and written. As guide and companion of Anza, he joined the expeditions which opened a land route from Sonora to California, founded San Francisco, and thus brought to a realization one of Kino's fondest dreams—that the Pimería might lend a hand to California, her little sister beyond the Colorado.

Garcés, with three companions, soon won the crown of martyrdom among the Yumas. In Sonora, Arizona, and elsewhere his successors carried on. The fine old churches still standing at San Xavier del Bac, Tumacácori, San Ignacio and other places in Pima Land are in part or mainly Franciscan structures erected on foundations laid by the Padre on Horseback. They are monuments both to the Black Robes and to the Grey Robes who came after them.

Bibliography

PRINCIPAL ARCHIVES CITED

A.G.I.—Archivo General de Indias, Sevilla, Spain.
A.G.P.M.—Archivo General y Público, Mexico.
B.H.M.—Bayerische Hauptstaatsarchiv, München, Germany.
B.L.—Bancroft Library, Berkeley, California.
B.N.E.—Biblioteca Nacional de España, Madrid.
B.N.F.—Bibliothèque Nationale de France, Paris.
B.N.M.—Biblioteca Nacional de México.
B.N.P.—Biblioteca Nacional del Perú, Lima.
B.S.M.—Bayerische Staatsbibliothek, München, Germany.
C.A.J.O.—Central Archives of the Jesuit Order, Rome.
C.L.—Clark Library, University of California at Los Angeles.
F.G.G.R.—Fondo Gesuitico al Gesù di Roma, Rome.
H.L.—Huntington Library, San Marino, California.
L.C.—Library of Congress, Washington, D.C.
M.A.P.—Municipal Archives of Parral, Chihuahua.
P.S.B.—Preussische Staatsbibliothek, Berlin, Germany.
R.A.H.—Real Academia de Historia, Madrid.
S.C.—Stevens Collection, Mexico.
V.H.C.—Van Houten Collection, Berkeley, California.
W.C.—Wagner Collection, San Marino, California.

I. *Kino Writings and Correspondence* [1]

MANUSCRIPTS [2]

Record of Kino's baptism. Segno, August 10, 1645. Original Latin manuscript in the baptismal register of the parish archive at Torra, Italy.

Kino's will. Ingolstadt, December 10, 1667. Original Latin manuscript in the possession of Father Simone Weber. Trento, Italy.

Division of the Kino family property, Enneberg, August 27, 1668. Original

---

[1] With the addition of Kino's birth and death certificates. This list does not include as separate items numerous letters and diaries included in the manuscript of the *Favores Celestiales*.

[2] The original manuscript or a facsimile of the original of every document in this list has been used. In case a manuscript has been published the printed text also is cited here. All the documents in this list are in preparation for publication.

manuscript (Latin, Italian and German) in the possession of Maestro Benedetto Chini, Rovereto, Italy.

Kino to Oliva, the Father General. Ingolstadt, June 1, 1670. Original Latin manuscript in Fondo Gesuitico al Gesù di Roma. Codex Germaniae Superiori Indipetae, 1661–1730, folio 69. Printed in *Studi Trentini,* Annata XI (Trento, 1930), 9–10.

Kino to Oliva, Ala, Innsbruck, January 31, 1672. Original Latin manuscript in Fondo Gesuitico al Gesù di Roma. Cod. Germ. Sup. Indipetae, 1661–1730, folio 99. Printed in *Studi Trentini,* Annata XI (Trento, 1930), 11–12.

Kino to Oliva, Ala, Innsbruck, June 18, 1673. Original Latin manuscript in Fondo Gesuitico al Gesù di Roma. Cod. Germ. Sup. Indipetae, 1661–1730, folio 121. Printed in *Studi Trentini,* Annata XI (Trento, 1930), 12–13.

Kino to Oliva, Ingolstadt, February 25, 1675. Original Latin manuscript in Fondo Gesuitico al Gesù di Roma. Cod. Germ. Sup. Indipetae, 1661–1730, folio 139. Printed in *Studi Trentini,* Annata XI (Trento, 1930), 13–14.

Kino to Oliva, Ingolstadt, April 7, 1676. Original Latin manuscript in Fondo Gesuitico al Gesù di Roma. Cod. Germ. Sup. Indipetae, 1661–1730, folio 141. Printed in *Archivum Historicum Societatis Jesu,* III (Rome, 1934), 250–251.

Kino to Oliva, Oettingen, March 17, 1678. Original Latin manuscript in Fondo Gesuitico al Gesù di Roma. Cod. Germ. Sup. Indipetae, 1661–1730, folio 190. Printed in *Studi Trentini,* Annata XI (Trento, 1930), 15–16.

Kino to Schnurnburg, Ala, Innsbruck, April 12, 1678. Original Latin manuscript in Bayerische Staatsbibliothek, München. Codex Latinus Monacensis No. 26472, folio 259.

Kino to Oliva, Genoa, May 6, 1678. Original Latin manuscript in Fondo Gesuitico al Gesù di Roma. Cod. Germ. Sup. Indipetae, 1661–1730, folio 179. Printed in *Studi Trentini,* Annata XI (Trento, 1930), 16–17.

Kino to Lucca, Genoa, May 10, 1678. Original Italian manuscript in the possession of Maestro Benedetto Chini, Rovereto, Italy.

Kino, Diary of his voyage from Genoa to Sevilla, Genoa, June 12, 1678–Sevilla, July 27, 1678. Original Latin manuscript in Bayerische Hauptstaatsarchiv, München, Jesuitica, Nos. 293–294.

Kino to Leinberer, Sevilla, October 17, 1679. Original Latin manuscript in Bayerische Hauptstaatsarchiv, München. Jesuitica Nos. 293–294.

Kino to the Duchess of Aveiro y Arcos, Cádiz, August 18, 1680. Original Italian manuscript in the Huntington Library, San Marino, California.

Kino to the Duchess of Aveiro y Arcos, Cádiz, September 15, 1680. Original Spanish manuscript in the Huntington Library.

Kino to the Duchess of Aveiro y Arcos Cádiz, November 16, 1680. Original Latin manuscript in the Huntington Library.

Kino to the Duchess of Aveiro y Arcos, Cádiz, December 6, 1680. Original Latin manuscript in the Huntington Library.

Kino to the Duchess of Aveiro y Arcos, Cádiz, December 14, 1680. Original Latin manuscript in the Huntington Library.

Kino to the Duchess of Aveiro y Arcos, Cádiz, December 28, 1680. Original Latin manuscript in the Huntington Library.

Kino to Espinosa, Cádiz, January 8, 1681. Original Spanish manuscript in the Huntington Library.

Kino to the Duchess of Aveiro y Arcos, Cádiz, January 11, 1681. Original Latin manuscript in the Huntington Library.

Kino to the Duchess of Aveiro y Arcos, Cádiz, January 26, 1681. Original Latin manuscript in the Huntington Library.

Kino to the Duchess of Aveiro y Arcos, near the Canary Islands, February 24, 1681. Original Latin manuscript in the Huntington Library.

Kino to the Duchess of Aveiro y Arcos, Mexico, July 4, 1681. Original Latin manuscript in the Huntington Library.

Kino's license as curate and vicar, Guadalajara, November 15, 1681. Testimonio de Título de Cura y Vicario. Spanish manuscript in A.G.I. 67–4–2. Sobre Pertenencia del Govierno Espiritual de Californias. (See March 18, 1724, *post.,* p. 618.) Cited as Sobre Pertenencia.

Kino's license from the Bishop of Nueva Vizcaya, Durango, May 24, 1682. Spanish manuscript in A.G.I. 67–4–2. Sobre Pertenencia.

Kino to the Duchess of Aveiro y Arcos, Nuestra Señora del Rosario, June 3, 1682. Original Spanish manuscript in the Huntington Library, San Marino, California.

Kino to the Duchess of Aveiro y Arcos. Chacala, November 3, 1682. Original Spanish manuscript in the Huntington Library, San Marino, California.

The Bishop of Guadalajara to Suárez, Kino and Goñi, Guadalajara, November 26, 1682. Spanish manuscript in A.G.I. 67–4–2. Sobre Pertenencia.

The Bishop of Guadalajara to Suárez, Kino and Goñi, Guadalajara, December 5, 1682. Spanish manuscript in A.G.I. 67–4–2. Sobre Pertenencia.

Roberto y Sierra to Suárez, Guadalajara, December 7, 1682. Spanish manuscript in A.G.I. 67–4–2. Sobre Pertenencia.

The Bishop of Guadalajara to Kino, Guadalajara, December 10, 1682. Spanish manuscript in A.G.I. 67–4–2. Sobre Pertenencia.

Kino to Pardo, Mazatlán, February 7, 1683. Original Spanish manuscript in the central archives of the Jesuit Order.

Kino to Pardo, Sinaloa, March 16, 1683. Original Spanish manuscript in the central archives of the Jesuit Order.

Kino and Goñi. Act of taking spiritual possession. Toma de Poseción, La Paz, April 5, 1683. Spanish manuscript in A.G.I. 67–4–2.

Kino to Martínez, La Paz, April 20, 1683. Original Spanish manuscript in the Huntington Library, San Marino, California. Official copy in the central archives of the Jesuit Order.

Kino to Martínez, Copia de un Capítulo de una carta del Padre Kino. La Paz, April 20, 1683. Spanish manuscript in the Huntington Library. Copy of part of the above letter signed by Kino.

[Kino and Atondo], Relación Puntual de la Entrada que han hecho los Españoles . . . en la Grande Ysla de la California. Spanish manuscript in the Biblioteca Nacional, Mexico. Californias, Legajo 53. Based on letters of Atondo (April 20, 1683) and Kino (April 22, 1683). This manuscript was printed in Mexico in 1686 under the same title. A fragment of the rare print is in the collection of Henry R. Wagner. The manuscript is the basis of Verbiest's *Nouvelle Descente des Espagnols* printed in 1685, and of Lockman's *A Descent Made by the Spaniards* printed in 1743 (q.v.).

Kino to Martínez, La Paz, April 23, 1683. Original Spanish manuscript in the Huntington Library.

Kino to Martínez, San Lucas, Sinaloa, July 27, 1683. Original Spanish manuscript in the Huntington Library. Not all in Kino's hand.

Kino to Pardo, San Lucas, Sinaloa, August 10, 1683. Spanish manuscript in A.G.I. 58–4–23, Mexico 56.

Kino to the Duchess of Aveiro y Arcos, San Lucas, Sinaloa, August 12, 1683. Original Spanish manuscript in the Huntington Library.

Kino to Zingnis, San Lucas, Sinaloa, August 30, 1683. Original Latin manuscript in the Bayerische Hauptstaatsarchiv, München. Jesuitica, Nos. 293–294. Printed in *Archivum Historicum Societatis Iesu*, III (Rome, 1934), 116–121.

Kino to Zingnis (?), Diary of the second voyage to California, San Lucas, September 29–San Bruno, December 15, 1683. Original Latin manuscript in Bayerische Hauptstaatsarchiv, München, Jesuitica, Nos. 293–294.

Kino, Relación de la segunda Navegazión a las Californias del Año de 1683 y de las entradas de 20 leguas la tierra adentro. San Lucas, September 29–San Bruno, December 15, 1683. Beautiful contemporary copy in the central archives of the Jesuit Order.

Kino, Segunda Entrada en la California a 1° de Dize de 1683. Original Spanish manuscript in the central archives of the Jesuit Order. This is a continuation of the item next above.

Kino to the Duchess of Aveiro y Arcos. San Bruno, December 15, 1683. Original Spanish manuscript in the Huntington Library. An extract is in the central archives of the Jesuit Order. Another original of the account of the same date, not addressed to anyone, but signed by Kino is in Bayerische Hauptstaatsarchiv, München, Jesuitica, Nos. 293–294.

Kino, the San Bruno Diary, December 21, 1683–May 8, 1684. Known as the Tercera Entrada en 21 de Diciembre de 1683 because it opens with this heading, which in fact covers only a small part of the Diary. Manuscript, not in Kino's handwriting, in the Archivo General y Público, Mexico. Sección de Historia, Tomo 17. Printed in *Documentos para la Historia de México*. Cuarta série Tomo I, 405–468. (Mexico, 1857.)

Kino to Scherer, on board ship, San Bruno, September 25, 1684. Original Latin manuscript in Bayerische Hauptstaatsarchiv, München, Jesuitica Nos. 293–294. Printed in *Archivum Historicum Societatis Iesu*, III (Rome, 1934), 121–126.

Kino to Zingnis, San Bruno, October 6, 1684. Original Latin manuscript. In No. 14 Literae P. Francisi Eusebii Kinus ad P. Paulum Zignis ex Insulis Californiis Seu Carolinis 6 Octob. Ao. 1684. Bayerische Hauptstaatsarchiv, München, Jesuitica No. 282.

Kino to Zingnis, San Bruno, October 6, 1684. Original Latin manuscript in Bayerische Hauptstaatsarchiv, München, Jesuitica Nos. 293–294. Practically identical with the above except for the opening and closing paragraphs.

Kino to the Duchess of Aveiro y Arcos, San Bruno, October 25, 1684. Original Spanish manuscript in the Huntington Library. Signed by Kino. Text in another hand.

Kino to the Viceroy, December 6, 1684. Spanish manuscript in A.G.I. 1-1-2/31, Patronato 31, Autos sobre los Parajes.

Kino to the Duchess of Aveiro y Arcos, San Bruno, December 8, 1684. Original Spanish manuscript in the Huntington Library. There are two letters of the same date, or one written at two sittings. The first is in a copyist's hand. The other, continuing on the same sheet, is in Kino's hand and signed by him.

Kino to Bishop Garabito, San Bruno, December 8, 1684. Spanish manuscript A.G.I. 1-1-2/31, Patronato 31, Autos sobre los Parajes.

Kino, Relación de la Segunda Entrada de las Californias, ó Carolinas, deste año de 1685, hazia al Sur. February 16–March 8, 1685. Spanish manuscript in the Huntington Library. Unsigned. Apparently not in Kino's hand, but clearly written by him.

Kino, Parecer, *circa* April 6, 1685. Original Spanish manuscript in A.G.I. 1-1-2/31, Patronato 31. Autos de la Ultima Entrada (I).

Kino to Wolfgang Leinberer, San Bruno, April 9, 1685. Latin manuscript, not in Kino's hand, in Bayerische Hauptstaatsarchiv, München, Jesuitica No. 282. Printed in *Archivum Historicum Societatis Iesu,* III (Rome, 1934), 126–128.

Kino to the Bishop of Guadalajara, Tórin, May 30, 1685. Spanish manuscript in A.G.I. 67-3-28, Guadalajara 134. El Obispo da quenta.

Kino to the Bishop of Guadalajara, October 10, 1685. Spanish manuscript in A.G.I. 67-3-28, Guadalajara 134. El Obispo da quenta.

Kino to the Bishop of Guadalajara, Compostela, November 5, 1685. Spanish manuscript in A.G.I. 67-3-28, Guadalajara 134. El Obispo da quenta.

Kino to the Bishop of Guadalajara, Matanchel, November 15, 1685. Spanish manuscript in A.G.I. 67-3-28, Guadalajara 134. El Obispo da quenta.

Kino to the Bishop of Guadalajara, On board the Almiranta, December 2, 1685. Spanish manuscript in A.G.I. 67-3-28, Guadalajara 134. El Obispo da quenta.

Kino, Parecer, Mexico, January 21, 1686. Official copy in A.G.I. 58-4-23, Mexico 56, Autos de la Ultima Entrada (II).

Kino to the Bishop of Guadalajara, Casa Profesa, Mexico, February 15, 1686. Spanish manuscript in A.G.I. 67-3-28, Guadalajara 134, El Obispo da quenta.

Kino to the Duchess of Aveiro y Arcos, Casa Profesa, Mexico, July 19, 1686. Original Spanish manuscript in the Huntington Library.

Kino to the Duchess of Aveiro y Arcos, Mexico, November 16, 1686. Original Spanish manuscript in the Huntington Library. The body of the letter is in a copyist's hand, but the P.S. and the signature are in Kino's.

Kino, Petition to exempt mission Indians from forced labor. Guadalajara, December 16, 1686. Spanish manuscript in A.G.I. 67-1-36, Guadalajara, 69.

Opinion of the Fiscal concerning Kino's petition. Guadalajara, December 16, 1686. Original Spanish manuscript, A.G.I. 67-1-36, Guadalajara, 69.

Auto granting Kino's petition. Guadalajara, December 16, 1686. Original Spanish manuscript, A.G.I. 67-1-36, Guadalajara, 69.

Kino to the Duchess of Aveiro y Arcos. Conicari, February 15, 1687. Original Spanish manuscript in the Huntington Library. Most of the letter is in a copyist's hand, the remainder and the signature in Kino's.

Kino to Juan Marín, Conicari, February 15, 1687. Original Spanish manuscript in the central archives of the Jesuit Order. Body of letter in a copyist's hand, signature and postscript in Kino's.

Kino to Mansilla, Dolores, June 30, 1687. Original Spanish manuscript in the Huntington Library. Salutation, closing paragraph, and signature in Kino's hand.

Kino to Mansilla, Dolores, August 6, 1687. Original Spanish manuscript in the Huntington Library. In Kino's hand. This letter begins on the same sheet where the one of June 30 ends.

Kino to the Viceroy, Conde de Monclova, Dolores, August 30, 1687. Original Spanish manuscript in the Biblioteca Nacional, Lima, Perú. The body of the letter is in a copyist's hand, the signature in Kino's. Printed in *Revista Histórica del Perú*, IX (Lima, 1928), pp. 97-99. Edited by Bertram T. Lee.

Kino to ———. Dolores, March 15, 1688. Original Latin manuscript in Litterae Astronomicae Jesuitarum ab anno 1619 usque 1753. Preussische Staatsbibliothek, Berlin. Handschr. Abtl.

Kino to De Soto, Provincial of Mexico, Dolores, June 15, 1689. Original Spanish manuscript in the central archives of the Jesuit Order.

Kino, Certificate of services of Captain Francisco Ramírez, Dolores, March 27, 1692. Original Spanish manuscript, A.G.I. 67-4-11, Audiencia de Guadalajara. Autos de Guerra Tocantes al Capitán franco. Ramírez de Salazar.

Kino, Inocente, Apostólica y Gloriosa Muerte del V. Pe. Francisco Xavier Saeta, de la Compa. de Jesus, Missionero en la Nueva Conversión de la Concepción de Na. Sa. del Cabotca de la Pimería en la Provincia de Sonora. Dictamenes Apostólicos del mismo V. Pe. en orden a Hazer Nuevas Conquistas y Conversiones de Almas. Como tambien del Estado presente destas las Nuevas Naciones, con el Mappa Universal de todas las Missiones, intitulado Theatro de los Trabajos Apostólicos de la Compa. de Jesus en la América Septentrional, 1695. Por el Pe. Eusebio Francisco Kino de la Compa. de Jesus. Original manuscript in Kino's own hand, p. 110. In the Biblioteca Nacional, Mexico.

Kino, Varias navegaciones y entradas que se han hecho a las Californias ó Carolinas, 1695. Sent by Kino to Thirso González on October 17, 1699. Copy in the hand of Claude Delisle, royal geographer of France, c. 1700. In Bibliothèque Nationale, Paris, Service Hydrographique, 115, XI, No. 5A. This document contains essentially the data given in the summary of voyages written on Kino's map called Teatro de los Trabajos, made in 1695, from which it was doubtless copied. A summary of the document, written in Latin, was sent in 1752 from Rome to Father Patouillet. It is this document which gives us the date October 17, 1699. (Bibliothèque Nationale, Paris, Service Hydrographique, 115, XI, No. 5C.)

Kino to Thirso González, Dolores, after December 3, 1697. Original Spanish manuscript, in Kino's hand. Fondo Gesuitico al Gesù di Roma. Epist. Selectae, II,

n. 90. Printed in *Archivum Historicum Societatis Jesu,* III (Rome, 1934), 252–254.

[Kino], Bernal, et al. Relación del estado de la Pimería que remite el Pe. Visitador Horacio Polici: y es copia de Carta que le escribe el Capitan Dn. Christóval Martín, Bernal. Dec. 3 and 4, 1697. Original MS. in A.G.P.M. Printed in *Documentos para la Historia de México,* Tercera Série (Mexico, 1856), pp. 797–799. Signed by Bernal, Kino and others. Listed also on p. 610.

Expediente concerning the expedition of Kino and Carrasco to the Pápagos, 1698. Original Spanish manuscript A.G.I. 67–3–28, Guadalajara, 134.

Mora Contra Kino. A report by Mora to Palacios, Arizpe, May 28, 1698. Original Spanish manuscript in the Biblioteca Nacional, Mexico. Californias, Legajo 53. This document contains extracts of so much Kino correspondence that I include it in this list, although it was not addressed to him.

Bernal, Christóbal, to Kino, Tubutama, August 10, 1698. Quoted by Kino in Relasión Diaria de la Entrada al Nortueste, Entry for October 16, 1698. Original Spanish manuscript in the Archivo General y Público, Mexico, Historia, Tomo 393.

Kino, Colocación de Nuestra Sa. de los Remedios en su nueva Capilla de su nuevo pueblo de las nuevas conversiones de la Pimería en 15 de Setiembre de [16]98 años. Dolores, September 16, 1698. Original Spanish manuscript, Archivo General y Público, Mexico, Misiones, Tomo 26. Printed in *Doc. Hist. Mex.,* Tercera Série (Mexico, 1856), pp. 814–816.

Kino, Relasión Diaria de la Entrada al Nortueste, que fue de Ida y Buelta mas de 300 leguas, desde 21 de setiembre hasta 18 de otobre de 1698; descubrimento del desemboque del río grande a la Mar de la California, y del Puerto de Sa. Clara. Original Spanish manuscript, Archivo General y Público, Mexico, Historia, Tomo 393. Printed in *Publicaciones del Archivo General de la Nación,* Vol. VIII (Mexico, 1922).

Kino, Del Estado, grasias al Señor, Pasifico y quieto, de esta dilatada Pimería y de la Provia. de Sonora. Dolores, October 18, 1698. Original Spanish manuscript in Archivo General y Público, Mexico, Historia, Tomo 393. This is a continuation of Kino's Relasión Diaria of the same date. Printed in *Publicaciónes del Archivo General de la Nación,* Vol. VIII (Mexico, 1922).

Kino, Breve Relación de la insigne victoria que los pimas sobayporis en 30 de Marzo de 1698 an conseguido contra los enemigos de esta provincia de Sonora. Dolores, May 3, 1698. With a postscript dated October 25. Original Spanish manuscript. Postscript and signature in Kino's hand; the rest in another hand. Fondo Gesuitico al Gesù di Roma, Epist. Selectae, II, n. 90. Printed in *Archivum Historicum Societatis Jesu,* III (Rome, 1934), 254–257. Another MS., in the archives of Mexico, is printed in *Doc. Hist. Mex.,* Tercera Série (Mexico, 1856), pp. 810–813.

Kino to Polici, Dolores, October 18, 1698. Carta del Padre Eusevio Kino al Padre Visitador Horacio Polici acerca de una entrada al Noroeste y mar de California en compañía del Capitán Diego Carrasco, actual Teniente desta dilatada Pimería que fue de hida y buelta de mas de trecientas leguas a 22 de Septiembre de 1698 años. Spanish manuscript in the Archivo General y Público,

Mexico, Historia, Tomo 16. Printed in *Doc. Hist. Mex.,* Tercera Série (Mexico, 1856), pp. 817–819.

Kino to Jironza, Dedicatoria al Sor. Gral. Dn. Domingo Gironza Petris de Cruzat, Governador de las Armas de esta Prova. de Sonora, Theniente de Capitán General y Alcalde Mayor de ella por su Magd. Dolores, December 8, 1698. Spanish manuscript in the Bibliothèque Nationale, Paris. Mexicain, 174, 16 pp. Followed by an incomplete copy of Kino's diary of the expedition with Carrasco.

Kino to the Father General, October 17, 1699. A report on North America with a chronological list of the expeditions to California between 1533 and 1699. The report has not been seen, but a summary of it, sent from Rome by the P. to Father Patouillet in 1752, is in the Bibliothèque Nationale, Paris, Archives du Service Hydrographique de la Marine, Vol. 115, XI, No. 5C.

Kino, Favores Celestiales de Iesus y de María SS^{ma} y del Gloriosissimo Apostol de las Indias S. Francisco Xavier Experimentados en las Nuevas Conquistas y Nuevas Conversiones del Nuevo Reino de la Nueva Navarra desta América Septentrional Yncognita, y Passo por tierra á la California en 35 grados de altura. Con su Nuevo Mapa Cosmográfico de estas Nuevas y Dilatadas Tierras que hasta aora havian sido Yncognitas. Dedicados a la Rl. Magd. de Felipo V, Mui Católico Rey y Gran Monarca de las Españas y de las Yndias. [1699–1710.] Original Spanish manuscript in the Archivo General y Público, Mexico, Misiones, Tomo 27. 183 folios. This manuscript has been twice printed entire and once in part. I discovered it in 1907. In 1916 I published in English Part V as "Report and Relation of the New Conversions" in *Spanish Exploration in the Southwest* (New York, 1916). Three years later I published in English the entire manuscript under the title of *Kino's Historical Memoir of Pimería Alta* (Cleveland, 1919) 2 vols. Subsequently the manuscript was published in Spanish by Francisco Fernández del Castillo and Emilio Batres as *Las Misiones de Sonora y Arizona* (Mexico, 1922).

Kino to Thirso González, Dolores, October 18, 1701. Original Spanish manuscript in the central archives of the Jesuit Order.

Kino to Leal. Tanto de la Carta que escriví al Pe. Visitador Anto. Leal De Buelta del Passo por Tierra Firme a las Californias. Dolores, Dec. 8, 1701. Original Spanish manuscript in the central archives of the Jesuit Order. Heading and signature in Kino's hand, the rest in a copyist's. Printed in Bolton, *Kino's Historical Memoir of Pimería Alta,* I, 232–234.

Kino to Thirso González, February 2, 1702. Original Spanish manuscript in the central archives of the Jesuit Order.

Kino to Thirso González, Dolores, February 3, 1702. Original Spanish manuscript in Fondo Gesuitico al Gesù di Roma, Epist. Selectae, II, n. 90. Printed in *Archivum Historicum Societatis Jesu,* III (Rome, 1934), 258.

Kino to Thirso González, January 24, 1704. Original Spanish manuscript in Fondo Gesuitico al Gesù di Roma, Epist. Selectae, II, n. 90. Printed in *Archivum Historicum Societatis Jesu,* III (Rome, 1934), 259–261.

Kino, Introduction to the *Favores Celestiales,* Dolores, May 10, 1704. Original Spanish manuscript in the Maggs Collection (London) No. 26. Signed by Kino; the text in another hand. Another original draft is in the central archives of the Jesuit Order. Signed by Kino; the text in a different hand. This introduction is a dedication, and is incorporated with some changes in the complete manuscript of the *Favores Celestiales,* as printed in Bolton, Herbert Eugene, *Kino's Historical Memoir of Pimería Alta.*

Kino to Alonso Quirós, Procurator of the Province of Mexico. Dolores, June 30, 1704. Original Spanish manuscript in the Maggs Collection (London), No. 27. Copy in the Huntington Library (HM 4095).

Kino to Thirso González, Dolores, June 30, 1704. Original Spanish manuscript in Fondo Gesuitico al Gesù di Roma, Epist. Selectae, II, n. 90. Printed in *Archivum Historicum Societatis Jesu,* III (Rome, 1934), 261–263.

Kino to Tamburini, Bazeraca, December 14, 1707. Original Latin manuscript in Fondo Gesuitico al Gesù di Roma, Epist. Selectae, II, n. 90. Printed in *Archivum Historicum Societatis Jesu,* III (Rome, 1934), 263–264.

Kino to Juan de Yturberoaga, Procurator General. Dolores, September 16, 1709. With draft of reply, February 1, 1710. Original Spanish manuscript in the W. B. Stevens Collection.

Kino to Juan de Yturberoaga. Dolores, December 7, 1709. Original Spanish manuscript in the Stevens Collection.

Juan de Yturberoaga to Kino. Mexico, February 1, 1710. Draft of reply to Kino's letter of September 16, 1709. Original Spanish manuscript in the Stevens Collection.

Record of the Burial of Father Kino. Magdalena, March 15, 1711. Church Register of San Ignacio and Magdalena, Sonora. Original in the Bancroft Library. He was buried by Father Agustín de Campos, who wrote the record and signed it with his own hand.

PRINTED [1]

Kino, Eusebio Francisco. Exposición Astronómica de el Cometa que el Año de 1680, por los meses de Noviembre y Diziembre, y este Año de 1681, por los meses de Enero y Febrero, se ha visto en todo el mundo, y le ha observado en la Ciudad de Cádiz El P. Eusebio Francisco Kino de la Compañía de Jesús. Con Licencia en México por Francisco Rodríguez Lupercio, 1681, 4° ffnc. 28, 1 carte.

[Kino and Atondo]. Nouvelle Descente des Espagnols, in Verbiest, Ferdinand. *Voyages de L'Empereur de la Chine dans la Tartarie Auquels on a Joint une nouvelle decouverte au Mexique* (Paris, 1685). Based on the Relación Puntual.

[Kino and Atondo]. A Descent made by the Spaniards, in the Island of California in 1683. Based on the Relación Puntual of Kino and Atondo. In Lockman, John, *Travels of the Jesuits into various Parts of the World: Compiled from their letters* (London, 1743), Vol. I.

Kino, Eusebio Francisco. Letter to Father Henricus Scherer, San Bruno,

---

[1] This is a list of printed Kino writings the original manuscripts of which are not known to me. It does not include as separate items numerous letters and diaries printed in Kino's *Historical Memoir of Pimería Alta.*

October 6, 1684. Printed in Latin in Scherer, *Geographia Hierarchica* (Monachii, 1703), Pars. II, pp. 99–103. As a matter of fact, the extract is not a single letter, "but a gathering of several letters of Kino."

Kino, Eusebio Francisco. Letter to the procurator of the Province of Mexico. Cucurpe, May 13, 1687. Quoted by Father Gilg in a letter dated at Mexico, October 8, 1687. Printed in German in Stöcklein, *Neue Welt-Bott,* I, No. 33, pp. 107–110 (Augsburg and Gratz, 1726).

A WORK ERRONEOUSLY ATTRIBUTED TO KINO

Arte de la Lengua Névome, que se dice Pima, Propia de Sonora. Con la Doctrina Christiana y Confesionario Añadidos. San Augustín de la Florida, 1862.

The added title-page reads: Grammar of the Pima or Névome, a language of Sonora, from a Manuscript of the XVIII Century. Edited by Buckingham Smith. New York, Cramoisy Press, 1862.

The Library of Congress catalogues reads: "Kino, Eusebio Francisco, 1644–1711, supposed author," quoting from Platzmann, who writes: "Der Verfasser dieser 'Arte' ist ohne zweifel der in der geschichte der californischen missionen so berühmte Jesuitenpater Kino." This would seem to be a very bad guess on the part of Herr Platzmann. In the first place, Kino had the reputation of not knowing the Pima tongue very well. In the second place, the Névomes are Lower Pima people, amongst whom Kino never lived.

II. *Kino Maps*

Kino made numerous maps and sketches of the regions in which he labored, several of which have come down to us. The rest are still in hiding or have disappeared forever. His maps were long a primary source of data for contemporary and later cartographers. Several of them have been printed in Kino's name, one of them many times. One of his most important productions was printed in Europe with his name left off. For obvious reasons I have included in this list the Guzmán map of the voyage to Kino Bay. The maps are here listed in groups determined by the dates of the basic manuscripts rather than those of publication. Each group represents a different map.

A

Kino, Map of northwestern New Spain, showing Nueva Vizcaya, Sinaloa, Sonora, and part of New Mexico. *Circa* 1681. Original manuscript in the central archives of the Jesuit Order. This map is in Kino's well-known hand but is unsigned and undated. It evidently antedates his expedition to California (1683), for it shows the shoreline of the southern end of the Peninsula with no details. On the mainland it reaches north only to Cotzari, and clearly antedates the founding of Mission Dolores there in 1687. It bears numbers from 1 to 54, which apparently stand for Jesuit missions. The inference is that there was a key to these numbers which is not now with the map.

B

Kino, Delineacion de la Nueva Provincia de S. Andres, del Puerto de la Paz, y de las Islas circumvecinas de las Californias, o Carolinas, que Al Excellmo Señor D. Thomas Antonio Lorenzo Manuel Manrique de la Zerda Enríquez Afan de Ribera, Porto Carrero y Cárdenas, Conde de Paredes, Marqués de la Laguna, Comendador de la Moraleja en la Orden y Cavalleria de Alcántara, del Consejo de su Magestad, Camara, y Junta de Guerra de Indias, su Virrey, Lugar Teniente, Governador, y Capitán General de la Nueba España, y Presidente de la R! Audiencia y Chanzelleria della, Dedica y Consagra la Mission de la Compª de Jesus de dichas Californias o Carolinas, en 21 de Dice, dia del Glorioso Apóstol de las Indias S. Thomas, de 1683 años. Original manuscript in A.G.I. 1–1–2/31, Patronato 31. Transmitted to the king by the viceroy March 26, 1685. Torres Lanzas, No. 76. Printed in Bolton, *Kino's Historical Memoir of Pimería Alta,* I, facing p. 48. (Cleveland, 1919).

C

Kino, Description de la Fortificacion y Rl. de S. Bruno de Californias, 1683. Transmitted to the King of Spain by the Viceroy of Mexico, March 26, 1685. Original manuscript drawing, A.G.I. 1–1–2/31. Torres Lanzas No. 77. Printed in Bolton, *Kino's Historical Memoir of Pimería Alta,* I, facing p. 40.

D

Kino, Delineatio Nova et Vera Partis Australis Novi Mexici, cum Australi Parte Insulae Californiae Saeculo Priori ab Hispanis Detectae: Drawn by Kino in 1685. Redrawn and printed in the *Geographia Hierarchica* of Father Henricus Scherer, S.J., Monachii, 1703. Pars. II, Fol. D.C.D., between pp. 98 and 99. This map shows the lower part of the Peninsula of California with the data acquired by the Atondo-Kino expeditions, including the one across the Peninsula, December 1684–January, 1685.

E

Guzmán, Blas, [and Kino], Descripción de la nueva situacion del Golfo de California que hizo el Capⁿ Dⁿ. Blas de Gusman en su descubrimiento. 1685. Manuscript in the Biblioteca Nacional, Lima, Perú. This is a map of the Guzmán-Kino voyage to Kino Bay in the summer of 1685, Guzmán being the commander of the vessel. The map and the diary of the expedition give complete historical justification for the name of Kino Bay on the Sonora Coast.

F

Kino, Teatro de los Trabajos Apostólicos de la Compª de Jesús en la America Septentrional, 1696. Original manuscript, in Kino's hand, in the central archives of the Jesuit Order. Prepared to illustrate Kino's book on the martyrdom of Father

Saeta. Drawn partly or entirely in 1695, but the decorative title is dated 1696.

This map was sent by the viceroy of Mexico to the Duque de Escalona; by him to M. Regis as a gift to the Royal Academy of Paris; by him to Claude Delisle for comment; by him was discussed in a letter to Regis (c. 1700). The map was pirated by Nicolas de Fer and at least twice published under his name. Delisle to Regis, c. 1700. Bibliothèque Nationale, Paris. Service Hydrographique, 115–XI–No. 170. See below, 1705, 1720. Claude Delisle was royal geographer of France and father of the more famous cartographer, Guillaume Delisle.

Fer, N., Carte de Californie et du Nouveau Mexique. A pirated version of Kino's Teatro de los Trabajos Apostólicos. Redrawn and printed by Nicolas de Fer, in *L'Atlas Curieux, ou Le Monde Réprésenté dans des Cartes Générales et Particuliéres du Ciel et de la Térre. . . .* Par N. de Fer. Géografe de Monseigneur le Dauphin. Paris, 1705.

The legend on the map says "Cette Carte de Californie et du Nouveau Mexique est tirée de celle qui a été envoyée par un grand d'Espagne pour être communiquée a Mrs de l'Academie Royale des Sciences. Par N. de Fer, Geographe de Monseigneur le Dauphin. Avec privilege du Roy, 1705." By good fortune, we have been able to identify the "grand d'Espagne" who sent Kino's map to the French Academy. In 1700 a Bourbon ascended the Spanish throne and the relations of the two courts were now close. France was just founding Louisiana, and taking a new interest in Western North America, and in Spanish maps of the region. On October 17, 1699, Kino sent the Father General, Thirso González, a summary of Spanish voyages to California. It was nearly identical with the summary written on Kino's *Teatro*, 1695–96. Soon afterward it was copied in the hand of Claude Delisle, the French geographer. Bibliothèque Nationale, Paris. Service Hydrographique, 115–ix–No. 5A.

Fer, N., La Californie ou Nouvelle Caroline. Teatro de los Trabajos Apostólicos de la Compa. e [*sic*] Jesus en la America Septe Dressée sur celle que le Viceroy de la Nouvelle Espagne envoya il y a peu d'Années a Mrs de l'Academie des Sciences. Par N. de Fer Geographe de sa Majesté Catolique. Paris, 1720. The lettering looks like hand work rather than printing from type. This is another pirated version of Kino's Teatro de los Trabajos Apostólicos by Nicolas de Fer. Kino was now dead and his title of the map was restored, but his name does not appear. The summary of voyages on Kino's *Teatro de los Trabajos* was omitted by De Fer from his 1705 map but was restored, in French translation, in this 1720 editon.

G

Kino, The Martyrdom of Father Saeta. Map of Pimería Alta and Northern Sonora, 1697. Illustrating with drawings the martyrdom of Father Saeta and intended to accompany Kino's book on that subject. Original manuscript in the central archives of the Jesuit Order. The data are almost identical with those on the corresponding parts of Kino's *Teatro de los Trabajos,* drawn in 1695–96. It was sent by Kino to Thirso González, the Father General of the Order, with a letter dated Dolores, June 3, 1697.

H

Kino, Paso por Tierra á la California, 1700–1702.

In its various printed forms this is Kino's most famous map. It was drawn especially to show that California was a peninsula, but it incorporated the results of all of Kino's explorations between 1696 and 1702. It therefore represents the next step in Kino cartography after the *Teatro de los Trabajos Apostólicos* of 1695–96.

Under essentially the above title Kino drew several maps, as is plain from his correspondence, one at least showing the results of each of his three expeditions to Cerro de Santa Clara and the Colorado River in 1701–1702. One version, drawn after his return from Santa Clara to Dolores in 1701, is the prototype of the printed Land Passage maps bearing the dates "1698 to 1701"; one drawn after the last journey is presumably the prototype of those bearing the added date "1702." Except for this variation in title these maps do not differ greatly. The assertion that the *Paso por Tierra* was published in 1701 is an error. The earliest known print was published in 1705. A few of the early and one recent print of the map are listed here:

Kino, Passage par Terre a la Californie Decouvert par le Rev. Pere Eusebe-François Kino Jesuite depuis 1698 jusqu'a 1701 ou l'on voit encore les Nouvelles Missions des PP. de la Compagє de Jesus. Printed in *Mémoires pour l'Histoire des Sciences et des Beaux Arts.* Op. p. 746. Paris, May, 1705. Another print of the same map, evidently from the same plate, appeared in Paris the same year in *Le Gobien, Lettres Edifiantes et Curieuses,* V Recueil (Paris, 1705). Thereafter this map was frequently reprinted.

Kino, Passo por Tierra á la California y sus Confinantes Nuevas Naciones y Nuevas Missiones de la Compª de Jesus en la America Septentrional. 1701. Printed at Leipzig and Hamburg, 1707.

This map, the basic manuscript of the Paso por Tierra, was made by Kino after his journey with Salvatierra to Cerro de Santa Clara in March, 1701, and was sent by him to Father Kappus. The map was folded and on the back of it was the following inscription: "Eusebius Franciscus Kinus, S.J., commends himself earnestly to the reverend Father Marcus Antonius Kappus, S.J., rector of the College of Mátape, patron and benefactor of these new regions and missions." Kappus forwarded the manuscript to a Jesuit in Austria with a letter dated at Mátape, Sonora, June 8, 1701. The map was printed in 1707 in the *Nova Litteraria Germaniae Aliorumque Europae Regnorum Anni MDCCVII. Collecta Hamburgi. Lipsiae et Francofurte apud Christianum Liebezeit.* ("Literary News of Germany and of other European Kingdoms in the year 1707. Collection of Hamburg. At Leipzig and Frankfort, in the house of Christian Liebezeit.")

Kino, A passage by Land to California Discovered by the Rev. Father Eusebius Francis Kino, Jesuite, between ye years 1698 and 1701. *Philosophical Transactions* (Number 318) *for the Months of November and December, 1708.* London. The place names on the map are a mixture of Spanish, French, Indian, and English.

Kino, Tabula Californiae Anno 1702. Ex autopticâ observatione delineata á R.P. Chino è S.I. *or* Via Terrestris in Californiam comperta et detecta Per R. Patrem Eusebium Fran Chino è S.I. Germanum. Adnotatis novis Missionibus ejusdem Soctis ab Anno 1698 ad Annum 1701. Printed in Stöcklein, *Neue Welt-Bott,* I, between documents 52 and 53 (Augsburg and Gratz, 1726). This is evidently the map sent by Kino to Thirso González, February 2, 1702.

Kino, Paso por Tierra a la California y sus confinantes Nuevas naciones y Misiones nuevas de la Compañía de JHS en la America Septentrional. Descubierto, andado y demarcado por el Padre Eusebio Francisco Kino, Jesuita, desde el año de 1698 hasta el de 1701. Original manuscript A.G.I. 67–3–39. Listed in Torres Lanzas, No. 95; Lowery, p. 215. Certain data on this map make it appear to be a middle eighteenth century reproduction of the original Kino map. Printed in Bolton, *Kino's Historical Memoir of Pimería Alta,* I, facing p. 330 (Berkeley, 1919).

III. *Manje, Bernal, and Carrasco Manuscripts*

With one exception the following diaries and letters of Juan Matheo Manje, Christóbal Bernal, and Diego Carrasco, companions of Kino on the trail, have been used in this book, and they are in preparation for publication in the immediate future. Since they constitute so distinctive a body of material, and are so intimately related to Kino's career, they deserve to be listed here as a special group, apart from the general list of supplementary documents. Most of them have been hitherto unknown to scholars.

Manje, Juan Matheo. Diary of the expedition down the San Pedro and the Gila, Nov. 2–Dec. 2, 1697. Original Spanish manuscript in possession of Carlos Linga.

Bernal, Christóbal, Diary of the expedition down the San Pedro and the Gila, November 5–December 4, 1697. Original Spanish manuscript in the Archivo General y Público, Mexico, Sección de Misiones, Tomo 26. Signed by Bernal, Kino, Acuña, Escalante, Barselona, and Barios. Printed in *Doc. Hist. Mex.,* Tercera Série (Mexico, 1856), pp. 799–809.

Bernal, Christóbal, to Horacio Polici. Relación del Estado de la Pimería que remitte el Pe. Visitador, y es copia de carta que le escribe el Capitán Dn. Christóval Martín Bernal, Dolores, December 3–4, 1697. Original Spanish manuscript in the Archivo General y Público, Mexico, Misiones, Tomo 26. Printed in *Doc. Hist. Mex.,* Tercera Série (Mexico, 1856), pp. 797–799.

Jironza to the Viceroy of Mexico, Sonora, May 16, 1698. A.G.I. 67–3–28, Guadalajara 134.

Jironza to Carrasco, appointing him to go with Kino on the Pápago expedition, Sept. 15, 1698. A.G.I. 67–3–28, Guadalajara 134.

Carrasco, Diego. Diario fho. por el Capitn. Diego Carrazco Thente. de alcalde mr. y Cappn. a guerra de todos los pueblos y rancherías de la nación Pima y sus distritos y juron. por su Magd. que in Virtud de orden que va . . . del Gral. Don Domingo Jironza Petris de Cruzat . . . me puse a hacer desde el dia 22 de Septiembre hasta el dia diez y ocho de Octubre de el año de mill ssos. y noventa y ocho para el descubrimto. del desemboque del río grande a la mar de la California y puertto de Santta Clara. A.G.I. 67–3–28, Guadalajara 134.

Carrasco to Jironza, Dolores, October 18, 1698. Carta del Señor Theniente de la Pimería, Diego Carrasco, al Señor General Domingo Gironza Petríz de Cruzat, de la entrada al Norueste. Original Spanish manuscript A.G.I. 67–3–28, Guadalajara 134.

Jironza to the Viceroy of New Spain [San Juan Bautista de], Sonora, March 8, 1699. A.G.I. 67–3–28, Guadalajara 134. Expediente concerning the Kino-Carrasco expedition.

Manje, Juan Matheo, Relación Ytineraria del Nuevo Descubrimiento qe hizimos los Ros. Ps. Eusevio franco. Kino y Adamo gil y el Capn. Ju. Matheo Manje, llevando el Cargo de the. de alcalde Mar. y Capn. a guerra, a descubrir las Nuevas Naciones Cocopas, Yumas y Pimas, desde 1 de febrero hasta 14 de Marzo deste presente año de 1699, Caminando de ida y buelta 360 legs., Como consta en la Diaria Relación. Original Spanish manuscript in the Biblioteca Nacional, Madrid.

Manje, Juan Matheo, Epitome en qe. se compendian las Materias y Médula de la Relación del descubrimiento a la parte del Norueste y Naciones Pimas, Yumas y Cocopas qe. hizieron los Pas. Jesuitas en compa. del Capitán Ju. Matheo Manje desde 1 de febo. a 14 de Marzo de 1699 ans. que queda atras Referida. This is a continuation or summary of the foregoing Relación Ytineraria. Original Spanish manuscript in the Biblioteca Nacional, Madrid.

The fiscal to the viceroy of New Spain, Mexico, October 16, 1699. A.G.I. 67–3–28, Guadalajara 134. Expediente concerning the Kino-Carrasco expedition.

Manje, Juan Matheo. Ytinerario de la Entra. qe. hizimos al descubrimto. de las Naciones Pimas y Sobaypuris del Norte, Norueste, y Poniente deste Prova. de Sonora, los PPs. Visitador Antto. Leal, Eusevio franco. Kino, franco. Gonzalvo, Jesuitas, y Yo el Capn. Jn. Matheo Manje, Autor desta Relación y el Capn. Antto. Cortés, con otros soldados, desde 24 de Octubre hasta 18 de Novre, de 1699 años, Caminando de ida y buelta 280 leguas, en que. se hizieron 25 bauptismos de Gentiles Adultos y Parvulos de ambos sexos. Original manuscript in the Biblioteca Nacional, Madrid.

Manje, Juan Matheo. Relación Ytineraria del descubrimiento que hizieron el Pe. Rev. Ju. María Salvatierra y el Pe. Eusevio franco. Kino, Jesuitas, en Compañía del Capn. Ju. Matheo Manje y el ayudante Nicolás Bohórques, con otros 10 Compañeros y soldados, estos a costa del Genl. Dn. Domingo Jironza Petris de Cruzatt, pa. el septentrion de esta América, consiguiendos (segun el digtamen y parecer de los Pas.) Paso por tierra a Californias contra la opinion de ms. cosmographos qe. en sus mapas la han delineado por hisla; el qual hizimos por los meses de Febrero, Marzo, y Abril deste presente Año de 1701. Original manuscript in the Biblioteca Nacional, Madrid.

Manje, Juan Matheo. Epitome ó Resunta del descubrimento que ysieron el Pe. Vtor. y Consultor Manl. Gonzalez y el Pe. Eusebio Franco. Kino, Jesuitas, a indagar la tierra continente deste America septentrional con las Californias que prebiamte. saca el Capn. Ju. Matheo Manje, quien por la ócupacion de Alce. Mor. en servicio de su Magd. no pudo acompañar a las PPs. que hisieron [*sic*] de 200 leguas desde cinco de Febrero asta los quinse de Abril de este año de 1702. Original Spanish manuscript in the Biblioteca Nacional, Madrid. Unsigned. Seems to be incomplete.

Manje, Juan Matheo. Conclusion de esta óbra y nota del estado presste. espiritual y temporal que tienen estas misiones de la Prova. de Sonora, y lo mucho que combendra el fundar un nuebo Presidio de quarenta ó mas soldados para reprimir y obiar las ostilidades, ymbasiones de las nasiones enemigos de los muchos robos y muertes de Crisptianos que assen por los caminos. Signed by Manje at Real de Minas del Santo Nombre de Jesus de Bacanuchi, Sonora, Dec. 3, 1706. Original Spanish manuscript in the Biblioteca Nacional, Madrid.

Expediente relative to the arrest and imprisonment of Manje, 1706–1707. Original manuscripts in the archives of Parral, Legajo 1707.

Manje, Juan Matheo (?), Conquista de la Sonora. Descripcion de las Provincias y Costas del Mar del Sur de esta Governacion. Luz de la Tierra Incógnita por el Norte, y Noruoeste de la Proa. de Sonora. Manuscript in the Franciscan archives in Rome. K. Leg. 14, No. 52. Incomplete, unsigned, 41 pp. Includes nine chapters of Tratado I. The subtitle, the subject, and the chapter headings lead me to surmise that this is a draft of part of Manje's *Luz de Tierra Incógnita*. It evidently came from the archives of the College of the Holy Cross of Querétaro.

Mange (Manje), Juan Matheo, Libro Segundo. Luz de Tierra Yncógnita en la América Septentrional de todos los Viajes de Tierra, Ríos, y Naciones que Descubrieron Varios Padres de la Comp ª de Jesús con el Cap ª Juan Matheo Manje, Autor de la Presente Obra; y Anuales Muertes, Rovos, e Yncendios q. los primeros años q. Gov ᵑᶜ el Genl. D. Domingo Jironza la Comp ª Volante q. dotó su Magd. pa. su defensa desde fines del año de 1693 hasta el de 1721. Original Spanish manuscript in the Archivo General y Público, Mexico. Historia, Tomo 393. Printed in Mexico in 1926.

Manje, Juan Matheo. Declaration containing an account of the Apache attack on Quíburi in 1698. Parral, February 9, 1723. Original Spanish manuscript in the archives of Parral, Legajo 1723.

IV. *Other Manuscripts*

The supplementary manuscript materials used in the preparation of this work are much more voluminous than the writings of Kino. Of these additional materials the most extensive single group are those contained in the Archivo General de Indias. They deal with many phases of the history of New Spain directly or indirectly connected with Kino's career, especially with the Atondo expedition, in which Kino took part. Besides many *expedientes,* or unified groups of documents dealing with specific episodes, I used in the Archivo General de Indias hundreds of individual manuscripts scattered through the vast collection, many of which are cited in the footnotes of this work. It would be impractical to include here a calendar of all the individual items consulted in that archive. I therefore indicate the principal *legajos* or bundles in which they are found, as follows: 1–1–2/31, Patronato 31; 54–4–18, México 51; 58–4–20, México 33; 58–4–21, México 54; 58–4–23, México 56; 67–1–30, Guadalajara 63;

67–1–35, 67–4–7, Guadalajara 147; 87–5–10, México 1031; 87–5–10, México 1073.

Next in importance to the Archivo General de Indias for my purposes were the Central Archives of the Jesuit Order; the Archivo General y Público, Mexico; the Biblioteca Nacional, Madrid; the State Archives of Munich; the Bancroft Library, at the University of California; the Huntington Library, at San Marino.

Here follows a selected list of individual manuscript items used. Unless otherwise indicated, all archive items cited in this list are original Spanish manuscripts or official copies of the originals.

The viceroy of Mexico to the king of Spain, August 3, 1678. Reports Pinadero's proposal for colonizing California. Is looking for a suitable leader. A.G.I. 58–4–18, Mexico 51.

Atondo to the viceroy, Mexico, November 8, 1678. Proposal to colonize California. A.G.I. 58–4–18, Mexico 51.

Atondo to the viceroy, Mexico, November 23, 1678. Second proposal. A.G.I. 58–4–18, Mexico 51.

Escritura de asiento de la California, 1678–1679. Official proceedings relative to Atondo's proposal. A.G.I. 1–1–2/31, Patronato 31.

The viceroy to the king, February 12, 1679. Reporting the contract with Atondo for colonizing California. A.G.I. 1–1–2/31, Patronato 31.

The king to the viceroy, Madrid, October 8, 1679. Approving Atondo's contract. A.G.I. 58–4–18, Mexico 51.

Kerschpamer to a Father in Bavaria, Sevilla, Jan. 24, 1680. Original Latin manuscript in Bayerische Hauptstaatsarchiv, München, Codex Monacensis, Jesuitica No. 293–294.

The viceroy to the king, Mexico, February 28, 1681. El Virrey de la Na. España da quenta a V. Mgd. de las asistencias que ha dado para la conquista, poblazon, Combersion y entrada del Reyno de la California, y estado de ella, en conformidad del asiento hecho con Dn. Ysidro Otondo y Antillón, confirmado por Vra. Mgd. February 28, 1681. A.G.I. 1–1–2/31, Patronato 31.

The viceroy to the Juezes Oficiales regarding supplies for Atondo, Mexico, May 21, 1681. Two despatches of the same date. Original Spanish manuscripts in the Clark Library, University of California at Los Angeles.

Officials of Vera Cruz to the viceroy, April 23, 1681. Two letters. Original Spanish manuscripts in the Clark Library, University of California at Los Angeles.

The viceroy to the king, Mexico, July 12, 1681. El Virrey de la na. España da qta. a V M de lo que se a executado despues de la que dió en carta de 28 de febrero para la conqta., a cargo de Dn. Ysidro de Atondo, July 12, 1681. A.G.I. 1–1–2/31, Patronato 31.

The bishop of Durango to the bishop of Guadalajara, Durango, July 14, 1681. Regarding spiritual jurisdiction over California. A.G.I. 67–1–30, Guadalajara 63.

Joseph Gregorio to the Duchess of Aveiro y Arcos, Mexico, October 9, 1681. Original Spanish manuscript in the Huntington Library (HM 22488). Described in Parish, *California Books and Manuscripts in the Huntington Library,* pp. 21–22, San Marino, 1935.

The king of Spain to the viceroy of Mexico, Madrid, December 31, 1681. A.G.I. 87-5-10, Mexico 1073.

Klein to the Father Superior at Ingolstadt, Mexico, February 16, 1682. Original Latin manuscript in the Huntington Library.

License to Suárez, Guadalajara, August 13, 1682. A.G.I. 67-4-2. Sobre Pertenencia.

The viceroy to the king. Mexico, October 13, 1682. A.G.I. 58-4-20, Mexico 33.

Atondo and others. Correspondence concerning the appointment of missionaries for California, 1682-1683. A.G.I. 67-1-35, Guadalajara 68.

Ximénez to the Duchess of Aveiro y Arcos, Mexico, December 11, 1682. Original Spanish manuscript in the Huntington Library.

Proclamation regarding pearl fishing, La Paz, April 1, 1683. A.G.I. 1-1-2/31, Patronato 31.

The king to the viceroy, Madrid, June 16, 1683. A.G.I. 87-5-10, Mexico 1031.

The viceroy to the king, Mexico, July 17, 1683. A.G.I. 58-4-21, Mexico 54.

Testimonio de Auttos sobre los Socorros hechos a la Armadilla que Passa a las Californias, y de haverse hecho a la Vela este presente año. Vino con carta del Sor. Virrey, Conde de Paredes, de 17 de Julio de 1683 No 5o. A.G.I. 58-4-21, Mexico 54, pp. 77.

Mansilla to the Duchess of Aveiro y Arcos, Mexico, August 13, 1683. Original Spanish manuscript in the Huntington Library.

Atondo to the viceroy, San Lucas, September 25, 1683. A.G.I. 58-4-23, Mexico 56. Autos sobre la Entrada Primera.

Atondo, Diary of the expedition to the Plains of San Xavier, December 1-8, 1683. A.G.I. 58-4-23. Mexico 56. Entrada Primera, pp. 254-260.

The Consejo de Indias to the king, Madrid, February 28, 1684. A.G.I. 58-4-23, Mexico 56. Autos sobre la Entrada Primera.

Autos sobre la Entrada Primera q. hizo el Almirante Dn. Ysidro de Atondo y Antillón en unos paraxes de la California, y de haverse retirado al Puerto de San Lucas, 50 leguas de Sinaloa, de donde ymbió a pedir Gentte, Armas, Munisiones, Bastimentos, y otros generos, y peltrechos, para bolver a dha. ysla California. Y de la segunda entrada que hizo, y el Paraxe donde oy existe, y a comenzado a Poblar y fortificar, y los socorros que se le an hecho. Vino con carta del Sr. Virrey Conde de Paredes de 11 de Agto de 1684. No. 12. A.G.I. 58-4-23, Mexico 56, pp. 462.

The viceroy to the king, August 11, 1684. El Virrey participa las Noticias que le ha dado el Almirante Dn. Ysidro de Atondo, de las entradas que a hecho a diferentes paraxes de las Islas Californias. A.G.I. 58-4-23, Mexico 56. Autos sobre la Entrada Primera. Summarizes both Atondo expeditions.

Atondo to the viceroy, Río Grande, California, October 12, 1684. A.G.I. 58-4-23, Mexico 56. Autos sobre la Entrada Primera.

Atondo to the viceroy, Río Grande, October 15, 1684. A.G.I. 58-4-23, Mexico 56. Autos sobre la Entrada Primera.

Atondo. Proclamation concerning pearl fishing, San Bruno, October 23, 1684. A.G.I. 1-1-2/31.

Florencia to the Duchess of Aveiro y Maqueda, Mexico, November 1, 1684. Original Spanish manuscript in the Huntington Library.

Atondo, account of Indian Ceremonies at San Isidro, Nov. 12, 1684. A.G.I. 1–1–2/31, Patronato 31. Autos sobre los Parajes.

Atondo, Diary of the expedition to the Contra Costa of California. December 14, 1684–January 14, 1685. A.G.I. 1–1–1/23, Patronato 31. Autos de la Ultima Entrada (I).

Atondo, Diary of the expedition to the South, February 16–March 8, 1685. A.G.I. 1–1–2/31, Patronato 31. Autos de la Ultima Entrada (I).

Autos sobre los Parajes q ha descubierto en las Yslas Californias el Almirante D. Ysidro de Atondo y la Ultima entrada q esta pa. executar en ellos. Y los socorros qe. pa. ello se le han hecho de Rl. hazda, conforme ordenes de S. Magd. Vino con carta del Sr. Virrey Conde de Paredes de 26 de Mzo. de 1685. No. 2º. A.G.I. 1–1–2/31, Patronato 31.

El Virrey de la Na. España da qta, a V.M. Con Testimonio de Autos y Mapas que remite de los Parajes que ha descubierto en las Islas Californias el Almte. Don Isidro de Atondo y en las que se ha fortificado, y los socorros y medios de Rl. hazienda con que se le ha asistido pa. este efecto y pa. la Ultima Entrada que esta para executar en dhas. Islas. March 26, 1685. A.G.I. 1–1–2/31, Patronato 31.

El Obispo de Guadalaxara da qta del estado en que esta la conquista y conversión de las islas Californias despues de haver buelto las Naos que fueron a hazerla. A.G.I. 67–3–28, Guadalajara 134. Cited as El Obispo da quenta.

The viceroy to the king, Mexico, July 30, 1685. A.G.I. 1–1–2/31, Patronato 31.

El Virrey da quenta a V. Magd. de la Ultima Entrada que hizo en las Islas Californias el Almte, Dn. Ysidro de Atondo. September 3, 1685. A.G.I. 67–3–28, Guadalajara 134. Cited as El Virrey da quenta.

Goñi to the bishop of Guadalajara, San Ignacio, Sinaloa, September 22, 1685. A.G.I. 67–3–28, Guadalajara 134. El Obispo da quenta.

Guzmán, Diary of the voyage up the Gulf, San Bruno, May 8–Matanchel, September 17, 1685. A.G.I. 1–1–2/31, Patronato 31. Autos de la Ultima Entrada (I).

Atondo, Diary of his pearl fishing voyage on the Gulf, 1685. May–September, 1685. A.G.I. 1–1–2/31, Patronato 31. Autos de la Ultima Entrada (I).

Testimonio de Autos de la Ultima Entrada que hizo en las yslas de la California el Almirante Don Ysidro de Atondo y Antillón lo que de ella Resulttó, y la Resolución de Junta Gral, en que consta la providencia y medios que se an elexido, (I). Vino con carta del Sor. Virrey Conde de Paredes de 3 de Otbe, de 1685. No. 2. A.G.I. 1–1–2/31, Patronato 31, pp. 537.

The Viceroy of Mexico to the king of Spain, October 3, 1685. El Virrey . . . da quenta a V Magd de la Ultima entrada que hizo en las islas Californias el Almirante Dn. Ysidro de Atondo. A.G.I. 1–1–2/31, Patronato 31. Cited as El Virrey da quenta de la Ultima entrada.

The King of Spain to the Viceroy of Mexico, Royal Cédula, Madrid, December 22, 1685, suspending the California project because of Indian troubles in Tarahumara. A.G.I. 67–3–28, Guadalajara 134. Another copy is in A.G.I. 67–4–7, Guadalajara 147.

La Audiencia de Guadalaxara da quenta de las dilixencias fechas en virtud de la Real Zedula de catorse de Maio de el año proximo pasado de ochenta y seis sobre el fomento de las misiones y combersiones nuebas de los Indios, 1686–1687. A.G.I. 67–1–36, Guadalajara 69.

Atondo to the bishop of Guadalajara, Mexico, February 10, 1686. A.G.I. 67–3–28, Guadalajara 134, El Obispo da quenta.

Atondo to the bishop of Guadalajara, Mexico, February 16, 1686. A.G.I. 67–3–28, Guadalajara 134, El Obispo da quenta.

El Obispo de Guadalaxara. Da qta a V. Magd. (por lo q. le toca) del estado en que esta la conquista y combersion de las Californias. Guadalajara, February 18, 1686. With accompanying documents. A.G.I. 67–3–28, Guadalajara 134.

The bishop of Guadalajara to Kino, Guadalajara, March 10, 1686. A.G.I. 67–3–28, Guadalajara 134. This is a postscript to the letter of February 18.

Mansilla to the Duchess of Aveiro y Arcos, Mexico, March 13, 1686. Original Spanish manuscript in the Huntington Library.

The viceroy to the king. El Señor Virrey de la Na. Espa. da quenta a V.M. de la Ultima ressolución con acuerdo de Junta General sobre continuarse la combersion de los Gentiles de las Yslas Californias, modificando su gasto para este efecto del que hastta aqui tenia, y reduziendolo solo al de ttreynta mill ps. cada año pr. aora y en el interim q. V.M. con vista del testimonio de auttos q. remite mda. lo que fuere de su mayor agrado. March 15, 1686. A.G.I. 58–4–23, Mexico 56. Cited as El Señor Virrey da quenta de la ultima resolución.

Testimo. de Autos de la Ultima Entrada qe. hizo en las Yslas Californias el Almirante D. Ysidro de Atondo. Y de la Ultima Resoluzión de Junta Gl. sobre la Continuaon. de dha. Converzión (II). Vino con carta del Sr. Virrey Conde de Paredes, de 15 de Marzo de 1686, No. 7. A.G.I. 58–4–23, Mexico 56, pp. 228.

Autos sobre los Parajes q ha descubierto en las Yslas Californias el Almirante D. Ysidro de Atondo y la ultima entrada q esta pa. executar en ellas; y los socorros q pa. ello se le han hecho de Rl. hazda. Vino con carta del Sor. Virrey Conde de Paredes de 26 de Mzo. de 1685. No. 2. A.G.I. 1–1–2/31, Patronato 31, pp. 188.

Mansilla to the Duchess of Aveiro y Arcos, Mexico, April 4, 1686. Original Spanish manuscript in the Huntington Library.

Royal order concerning conversions, Buen Retiro, Madrid, May 14, 1686. A.G.I. 67–1–36, Guadalajara 69.

Neumann to Stowasser, Sisokitschick (Sisoguichic), Tarahumara, July 29, 1686. Latin manuscript in the city archives of Prague. Printed in German in Stöcklein, *Neue Welt-Bott*, I, No. 32, pp. 102–106.

Auto y Obedecimiento, Guadalajara, September 27, 1686. A.G.I. 67–1–36, Guadalajara 69.

Azcarrazo to King of Spain, Guadalajara, October 9, 1686. A.G.I. 67–1–36, Guadalajara 69.

Mansilla to the Duchess of Aveiro, Maqueda, y Arcos, Mexico, November 29, 1686. Original Spanish manuscript in the Huntington Library.

Roxas to Bernabé de Soto, Provincial of Mexico. Ures, March 31, 1688. Copia de una carta del Pe. Antonio de Roxas al Pe. Bernabe de Soto, Provl. de la Prova. de Na. Espa. escrita desde las Missiones de Sonora. Spanish manuscript in the central archives of the Jesuit Order.

Año de 1689. Cartas y informes sobre el estado en que se halla la Provincia de Sonora, escritas á el Sr. Don. Jno. Ysidro de Pardiñas Villar de Francos, Cavo. del horden de Santiago, Govor. y Capn. Genl. de la Nueva Viscaya. Expediente No. 5. Original manuscript in Archivo General y Público, Mexico, Provincias Internas, Tomo 30.

Año de 1689. Autos sobre el estado en que se hallan los Yndios de Sinaloa y Río Yaqui. Por el Sr. Don Juan de Pardiñas Villar de Francos, Cavo. del horden de Santiago, Govor, y Capn. Genl. de la Na. Viscaya. Expediente No. 7. Original manuscript in Archivo General y Público, Mexico, Provincias Internas, Tomo 30.

Testtimonio de Auttos de Guerra fechos por los Capitanes Juan Fernandes de la Fuentte, Don Domingo Therán de los Rios, y Don Domingo Gironza Petris de Cruzati, Sobre las Guerras de las Nassiones Janos, Jocomes, Sumas, Chinarras, Mansos, y Apaches, y la pasificazn. de los Pimas. Año de 1695. Archives of Parral, Chihuahua, 202 folios. This is the diary of the expedition from Janos to the Altar Valley to pacify the Pimas after the murder of Father Saeta.

Testimonio de Autos de Guerra Tocantes al Capitan Francisco Ramírez de Salazar con los motivos y Resolucion de Junta para la formacion de la Compañía Volante de Sonora con el numero de Cinquenta Soldados que oy sirve Dn. Domingo Jironza Petris de Cruzate. Vino con carta del Virrey de 6 de Enero de 1696. A.G.I. 67–4–11, Audiencia de Guadalajara.

El Virrey de la Nva. Espa. Da qta. a V.M. de la entrada que ha hecho a las Islas Californias El. P. Jn. María de Salbatierra de la Compa. de Jhs., los buenos efectos que han resultado, y los demas qe. propone sre. la continuazon. de esta conquista. Mexico, May 5, 1698. Accompanied by action of the Council, Madrid, June 14, 1699. A.G.I. 67–3–28, Guadalajara 134.

El Virrey de la Nueva España pone en la Real noticia de Vuestra Magestad haverse continuado subcesivos los favorables avisos de los progresos y buenos efectos de la redución de gentiles en las Yslas Californias en el servicio de Dios y agrado de Vuestra Magestad, y que sera propio de su Real piedad se asista á los religiosos con alguna ayuda de costa de la Real Hazienda en la forma que propone. Mexico, October 20, 1699. A.G.I. 67–3–28, Guadalajara 134.

Ugarte, Salvatierra, and Picolo Correspondence, 1699–1702. A.G.I. 67–3–28, Guadalajara 134.

De l'Isle, Claude. A Mr Regis sur la carte que M. le Duc d'Escalone lui a envoiée. (c. 1700). Manuscript in the Bibliothèque Nationale, Paris. Archives du Service Hydrographique de la Marine, Vol. 15, x. No. 17. C. Comments on Kino's map of 1695–96 called *Teatro de los Trabajos.*

Expediente concerning the legacy from Alonzo Fernández de la Torre (1701–1706). A.G.I. 67–3–28, Guadalajara 134.

The Consejo de Indias to the King. Recommending aid for the California missions, since litigation over the Fernández de la Torre legacy has been settled and troubles in Sinaloa, Sonora and Nueva Vizcaya have subsided. July 4, 1701. A.G.I. 67–3–28, Audiencia de Guadalajara 134.

Consejo de Indias a 9 de Jullio de 1701. Representa á V. Mgd. lo que ha passado en la conquista, poblazón, y reduzión de las Californias desde su principio; El Estado que oy tiene, y las providenzias que combendrá se den para acalorar á los Religiosos de la Compañía que se han encargado de esta empresa y la tienen adelantada. July 9, 1701. A.G.I. 67–1–37. Gives a summary of California history.

Bernardo Rolandegui, procurator general of the Province of New Spain. Urging support for the California missions. Referred to the relator, May 29, 1701. Approved July 4, 1701. A.G.I. 67–3–28, Guadalajara 134. This communication evidently resulted in the royal cédula of July 17, 1701.

Royal Cédula, to the bishop of Guadalajara, reporting the decision to contribute 6000 pesos a year for the support of the California missions. With related documents. Madrid, July 17, 1701. A.G.I. 67–3–28. Guadalajara 134.

Record of the Burial of Father Gonzalvo. San Ignacio, August 10, 1702. Libro de Entierros, Mission San Ignacio. Original manuscript in the Bancroft Library.

Luis Velarde, Cathólogo de esta Missión de Na. Sra. de los Dolores en la Pimería Alta desde el año de 1716. By Luis Velarde, Kino's successor, September 10, 1720. Original manuscript in the central archives of the Jesuit Order. Velarde describes the condition of Dolores, Remedios, and Cocóspora in 1720.

Sobre Pertenencia del Govierno Espiritual de California. Vino con Carta del Cavildo Eclesiástico de Guadalaxara de 18 de Marzo de 1724. A.G.I. 67–4–2. Cited as Sobre Pertenencia. This expediente covers a long period of time, and incidentally contains copies of Kino's licenses for his work in California.

Consag to Escobar, San Ignacio, October 31, 1746. Official copy A.G.I. 67–3–28, Guadalajara 134.

Balthasar, Juan Antonio. Carta circular del Pe. Provl. de Mexico. a los PP. Provinciales de la Asistencia de España en Europa. Mexico, May 15, 1752. Original manuscript in the Biblioteca Nacional, Madrid. It gives a glowing eulogy of Kino, four decades after his death.

Venegas, Miguel. Empressas Apostólicas de los PP. Missioneros de la Compañía de Jesús de la Provincia de Nueva España Obradas en la Conquista de Californias, debida y Consagradas al Patrocinio de María Santissima, Conquistadora de Nuevas Gentes en su Sagrada Imagen de Loreto. Historiadas por el Padre Miguel Venegas de la Misma Compañía de Jesús. 682 pp. "Se acabó esta Historia en Sabbado 7 de Noviembre de 1739." A beautiful contemporary manuscript copy is in the Maggs Collection, London. Another copy is in the library of the Real Academia de la Historia, Madrid. Sommervogel, VIII (1898), 561, mentions still another copy in the library of the college of San Gregorio, in Mexico.

Baegert, Father Jacob, S.J. Brief eines Elsassers aus Californien in Nord Amerika, an seinem Bruder in Schlettstadt 1752 von Pater Jacob Bägert, d.G.J. Aus dem Patriotischen Elsasser, Strassburg und Colmar, 1777. Californien, in der

Mission des H. Aloysii den 11ten September 1752. Transcript in the Bancroft Library with an English translation by Mary J. Price.

Decorme, G.S.J. La Obra de los Jesuitas en Mexico en la Epoca Colonial. 1572–1767. Compendio Histórico, c. 1931. Bancroft Library.

V. *Other Printed Works*

BOOKS

Agricola, Georgius. De Re Metallica (Chemnitz, Saxony, 1556). Translated into English by Herbert Clark Hoover and Lou Henry Hoover (London, 1912).

Alegre, Francisco Javier. Historia de la Compañía de Jesús en Nueva-España. Edited by Carlos Bustamante (Mexico, 1841–1842), 3 vols.

Astrain, P. Antonio. Historia de la Compañía de Jesús en la Asistencia de España. Tomo II (Madrid, 1905); Tomo VI (Madrid, 1920).

Ayer, Mrs. E. E. Memorial of Fray Alonso de Benavides, 1630. Translated by Mrs. Edward E. Ayer. Annotated by Frederick Webb Hodge and Charles Fletcher Lummis (Chicago, 1916).

Baegert, J. J. Nachrichten von der Amerikanischen Halbinsel Californien (Mannheim, 1772).

Bancroft, Hubert Howe. History of Arizona and New Mexico (San Francisco, 1889).

Bancroft, Hubert Howe. History of the North Mexican States and Texas (San Francisco, 1884), 2 vols.

Bayle, Constantino, S. I. Historia de los Descubrimientos y Colonización de los Padres de la Compañía de Jesús en la Baja California (Madrid, 1933). Contains an excellent list of unpublished documents.

Beals, Ralph. The Acaxee. A Mountain Tribe of Durango and Sinaloa (Berkeley, 1933).

Beristáin y Souza, José Mariano. Biblioteca Hispano-Americana Septentrional, por el Doctor D. José Mariano Beristáin y Souza. Segunda edición. Publícala el Presbítero Br. Fortino Hipolito Vera (Amecameca, 1883), 4 vols.

Beristáin y Souza, José Mariano. Biblioteca Hispano-Americana Septentrional. Adiciones y Correcciones (Mexico, 1898).

Bolton, Herbert Eugene. Anza's California Expeditions (Berkeley, 1930), 5 vols.

Bolton, Herbert Eugene. Guide to Materials for the History of the United States in the Principal Archives of Mexico (Washington, 1913).

Bolton, Herbert Eugene. Kino's Historical Memoir of Pimería Alta, 1683–1711 (Cleveland, 1919), 2 vols.

Bolton, Herbert Eugene. Outpost of Empire (New York, 1931).

Bolton, Herbert Eugene. Spanish Exploration in the Southwest, 1542–1706 (New York, 1916).

Bolton, Herbert Eugene. The Padre on Horseback. A Sketch of Eusebio Francisco Kino, S.J., Apostle to the Pimas (San Francisco, 1932).

Bolton, Herbert Eugene. The Spanish Borderlands (New Haven, Toronto, London, Oxford, 1921).

Braun, Bartholomé. Carta del P. Bartholomé Braun, Visitador de la Provincia Tarahumara, a los PP. Superiores de esta Provincia de Nueva España, sobre la Apostólica Vida, Virtudes, y Santa Muerte del P. Francisco Hermano Glandorff. Con las licencias necessarias: Impressa en el Real y mas antiguo Colegio de San Ildefonso de México, Año de 1764.

Buelna, Eustaquio. Compendio Histórico de Sinaloa (Mexico, 1877).

Campbell, Thomas J., S.J. Pioneer Priests of North America (New York, 1914), 3 vols.

Campbell, Thomas J., S.J. The Jesuits, 1534–1921; A History of the Society of Jesus (New York, 1921), 2 vols.

Catrou, et al. (editors). Mémoires pour l'Histoire des Sciences et des Beaux-Arts (Trévoux, 1701–1714), 16 vols.

Caughey, John Walton. History of the Pacific Coast (Los Angeles. Privately published by the author, 1933).

Chapman, Charles Edward. Catalogue of Materials in the Archivo General de Indias for the history of the Pacific coast and the American Southwest (Berkeley, 1919).

Chapman, Charles Edward. The Founding of Spanish California (New York, 1916).

Clavigero, Francisco J. Historia de la Antigua ó Baja California (Mexico, 1852).

Clavijero, Francesco S. Storia della California (Venezia, 1789), 2 vols.

Cuevas, Mariano, S. J. Historia de la Iglesia en México (México, 1928), 4 vols.

Ducrue, P. Bennone Francisco. Relatio Expulsionis Societatis Iesu ex Provincia Mexicana, et Maxime e California a. 1767, Cum Aliis Scitu Dignis Notitiis. Scripta a P. Bennone Francisco Ducrue Eiusdem Provinciae, per viginti annos Missionario. In Jour. für Kunst u. Litterat. XII, Theil. t XII. pp. 217–267 du Journal de Christoph von Murr. A French translation is in pp. 353–396, of Documents Inédits of P. Carayon. Document P. Poctiers, Oudin, 1857.

Duhr, Bernhard, S.J. Geschichte der Jesuiten in den Ländern Deutscher Zunge (Freiburg im Breisgau und St. Louis, 1907–1913), 2 vols.

Dunn, William Edward. Spanish and French Rivalry in the Gulf Region of the United States, 1678–1702 (Austin, 1917).

Engelhardt, Fr. Zephyrin. Missions and Missionaries of California (San Francisco, 1908), Vol. 1.

Fer, Nicolás de. L'Atlas Curieux, ou le Monde Réspenté dans des cartes Générales et Particulières du Ciel et de la Terre. Par N. de Fer (Paris, 1705).

Florencia, Francisco de. Historia de la Provincia de la Compañía de Jesús de Nueva España. Tomo Primero (Mexico, 1694).

Fluviá, Francisco J. See Ortega, Apostólicos Afanes. Bayle, in his *Historia de los Descubrimientos y Colonización de los Padres de la Compañía de Jesús en la Baja California* (Madrid, 1933), pp. 82–85, critically discusses the authorship of the work attributed to Ortega, and Fluviá's part in it.

Furlong, Guillermo, S.J. Los Jesuitas y la Cultura Ríoplatense. Montevideo, 1933.

Gerstl to his father. Extracts from letters, Spain, June 30, 1678–Puebla de los Angeles, Mexico, July 14, 1681. Printed in German in Stöcklein, *Der Neue Welt-Bott,* I, No. 31, pp. 90–102 (Augsburg and Gratz, 1726).

Gilg, Adamo, letter to the procurator, Mexico, October 8, 1687. Printed in German in Stöcklein, *Neue Welt-Bott,* I, No. 33, pp. 107–110 (Augsburg and Gratz, 1726).

Gobien, Charles Le, *et al.* Cartas Edificantes, y Curiosas, Escritas de las Missiones Estranjeras, por Algunos Missioneros de la Compañía de Jesus: Traducidas del Idioma Francés por el Padre Diego Davin (Madrid, 1753–1757), 16 vols.

Gobien, Charles Le, *et al.* Lettres Edifiantes et Curieuses, Écrites des Missions Estrangères. Nouvelle edition, ornée de cinquante belles gravures. Mémoires d'Amérique (Lyon, 1819), 14 vols.

Hackett, Charles Wilson. Historical documents relating to New Mexico, Nueva Vizcaya, and approaches thereto . . . (Washington, D. C., 1923–1926), Vols. I and II. Others to follow.

Hackett, Charles Wilson. Pichardo's treatise on the limits of Louisiana and Texas. . . . Published for the first time from a transcript of the original manuscript in the Mexican archives; translated into English by Charles Wilson Hackett, Ph.D., Charmion Clair Shelby, M.A., and Mary Ruth Splawn, M.A., and edited and annotated by Charles Wilson Hackett (Austin, 1931–1934), Vols. I and II. Two more to follow.

Hammond, George P. Don Juan de Oñate and the Founding of New Mexico (Santa Fé, 1927).

Hervas, Lorenzo. Catálogo de las Lenguas (Mexico, 1860).

Hodge, Frederick Webb. Handbook of American Indians North of Mexico (Washington, 1907–1910).

Hughes, Anne. The Beginnings of Spanish Settlement in the El Paso District (Berkeley, 1914).

Hughes, Thomas, S.J. History of the Society of Jesus in North America (London, 1910–1917), 4 vols.

Huonder, Anton, S.J. Deutsche Jesuitenmissionäre des 17. und 18. Jahrhunderts (Freiburg, 1899).

Kenny, Rev. Michael. The Romance of the Floridas (New York, Milwaukee, Chicago, 1934).

Kroeber, Alfred L. Handbook of the Indians of California (Washington, 1925).

Kroeber, Alfred L. Native Culture of the Southwest (Berkeley, 1928).

Kroeber, Alfred L. The Seri (Los Angeles, 1931).

Kroeber, Alfred L. Uto-Aztecan Languages of Mexico (Berkeley, 1934).

Leonard, Irving A. Don Carlos de Sigüenza y Gónogora, a Mexican Savant of the Seventeenth Century (Berkeley, 1929).

Lockwood, Frank C. Arizona Characters (Los Angeles, 1928).

Lockwood, Frank C. Pioneer Days in Arizona from the Spanish occupation to statehood (New York, 1932).

Lockwood, Frank C. Story of the Spanish Missions of the Middle Southwest (Santa Ana, 1934).

Lockwood, Frank C., and Page, D. W. Tucson, the Old Pueblo (Phoenix, 1930).

Lockwood, Frank C. With Padre Kino on the Trail (Tucson, 1934).

Lumholtz, Carl. New Trails in Mexico: an account of one year's exploration in Northwestern Sonora, Mexico, and Southwestern Arizona, 1909–1910 (New York, 1912).

Mancker—letter to Schiel, Mexico, February 25, 1681. Printed in German in Stöcklein, *Neue Welt-Bott,* I, No. 30, pp. 85–90 (Augsburg and Gratz, 1726).

Manje (Mange). Luz de Tierra Incógnita en la América Septentrional y Díario de las Exploraciones en Sonora, por el Capitán Juan Matheo Mange (Mexico, 1926).

Manje, Juan Matheo. Historia de la Pimería Alta. In *Documentos para la Historia de México,* Cuarta Série, Tomo I, 226–402. The same as Manje's Luz de Tierra Incógnita, Libro II.

McGee, W.J. The Seri Indians (Washington, 1898).

Medina, José Toribio. Noticias Bio-Bibliográficas de los Jesuitas Expulsos de América en 1767 (Santiago de Chile, 1914).

Mémoires de Trévoux (see Catrou).

Mota Padilla, D. Matías. Historia de la Conquista de la Nueva-Galicia. Escrita por el Lic. D. Matías de la Mota Padilla en 1742. Publicada por la Sociedad Mexicana de Geografía y Estadística (Mexico, 1870).

Murr, Christopher von. Nachrichten von verscheidenen Ländern des Spanischen Amerika (Halle, 1809). See "Ducrue."

Nentuig, Juan (?). Rudo Ensayo. Tentativo de una prebencional Descripción Geographica de la Provincia de Sonora, sus terminos y confines; ó mejor, colección de materiales para hacerla quien lo supiere mejor. Compilada así de noticias adquiridas por el Colector en sus Viages por casi toda ella, como Subministradas por los Padres Missioneros y Practicos de la Tierra. Dirigida al Remedio de ella, por un Amigo del Bien Común (San Augustín de la Florida, Año de 1863). Edited by Buckingham Smith. Internal evidence makes it appear that the author was Father Juan Nentuig, missionary of Guasavas, Sonora. *Cf.* an original MS. in A.G.P.M., Historia, 393.

Neumann, Joseph. Historia Seditionum quas Adversùs Societatis Jesu Missionarios, Eorúmqu; Auxiliares Moverunt Nationes Indicae, ac Potissimùm Tarahumara in America Septemtrionali, Regnóque Novae Cantabriae, Jam toto ad fidem Catholicam propemodùm redacto, Authore P. Josepho Neymanno Ejusdem Societatis Jesu in Partibus Tarahumarorum Missionario. Pragae, Typis Univers. Carolo-Ferd. Soc. Jesu. ad S. Clem. No date on title page. Preface dated April 15, 1724.

Orozco y Berra, Manuel. Geografía de las Lenguas (Mexico, 1864).

Ortega, José de. Apostólicos Afanes de la Compañía de Jesús escritos por un padre de la misma sagrada religion de su provincia de México (Barcelona, 1754). See "Fluviá, Francisco J.," above.

Ortega, José de. Historia del Nayarit, Sonora, Sinaloa, y ambas Californias. Que con el Título de "Apostólicos Afanes de la compañía de Jesús, en la América Septentrional" se Publicó Anónima en Barcelona el año de 1754, siendo su autor el padre José Ortega. Edited by Manuel de Olaguibel (Mexico, 1887).

Paz, Julián. Manuscritos sobre México en la Biblioteca Nacional de Madrid.

Sacada del Catálogo de Manuscritos de América de Don Julián Paz. Cuadernos Mexicanos de la Embajada de México en España (1933).

Pérez de Ribas, Andrés. Historia de los trivmphos de nuestra santa fee entre gentes las mas barbaras y fieras del nueuo orbe; conseguidos por los soldados de la milicia de la Compañía de Iesvs en las missiones de la prouincia de Nueua-España. Refierense assimismo las costvmbres, ritos, y supersticiones que vsauan estas gentes; sus puestos, y templo; las victorias que de algunas dellas alcançaron con las armas los católicos españoles, quando les obligaron á tomarles: y las muertes de veinte religiosos de la Compañía, que en varios puestos, y a manos de varias naciones, dieron sus vidas por la predicación del santo euangelio. . . . Escrita por el padre Andrés Pérez de Ribas (Madrid, A. de Paredes, 1645).

Pérez de Ribas, Andrés. Crónica y Historia Religiosa de la Provincia de la Compañía de Jesús de México en Nueva España . . . (Mexico, 1896), 2 vols.

Pfefferkorn, Ignaz. Beschreibung der Landschaft Sonora samt andern merkwürdigen Nachrichten von den innern Theilen Neu-Spaniens, und Reise aus Amerika bis in Deutschland, nebst einer Landcharte von Sonora. Von Ignaz Pfefferkorn eilfjahrigen Missionar daselbst . . . Köln am Rhein, auf Kosten des Verfassers gedrukt in der Langenschen Buchhandlung, 1794–95. 2 vols., fold map. i8cm.

Picolo, Francisco María. Informe del Estado de la Nueva Christiandad de California, que pidió por auto, la Real Audiencia de Guadalaxara, Obedeciendo á la Real Cédula de N. Rey y Señor, D. Phelipe V. Fecha en Madrid, á 17. de Julio de 1701. En Qve Ordena SV Magestad, Se le Informe individualmente, àcerca de la Nueva Christiandad, del Progresso, Augmento y Población de aquel Nuevo Reyno. Dado, Y Respondido, á dicha Real Audiencia de Guadalaxara Por el P. Francisco María Picolo de la Compañía Vno de los primeros fundadores de dichas Missiones de California, en las quales ha vivido en compañía del Padre Rector Juan María de Salvatierra estos cinco años que entraron en aquellas tierras (Mexico, 1702).

Pimentel, Francisco. Cuadro descriptivo y comparativo de las lenguas indígenas de México (Mexico, 1862–1865), 2 vols.

Platzweg, Carl. Lebensbilder deutscher Jesuiten in auswärtigen Missionen (Paderborn, 1882).

Priestley, Herbert Ingram. José de Gálvez, Visitor-General of New Spain, 1765–1771 (Berkeley, 1916).

Ratkay to Avancinus, Mexico, November 16, 1680. Printed in German in Stöcklein, *Neue Welt-Bott*, I, No. 28, pp. 77–81. (Augsburg and Gratz, 1726.)

Ratkay to Avancinus, Frontiers of New Mexico (the Tarahumara), February 25, 1681. Printed in German in Stöcklein, *Neue Welt-Bott*, I, No. 29, pp. 81–84 (Augsburg and Gratz, 1726).

Report of the Boundary Commission upon the Survey and Re-marking of the Boundary between the United States and Mexico West of the Río Grande, 1891 to 1896. Parts I and II (Washington, 1898).

Ricci, Eugenia. Il Padre Eusebio Chini, Esploratore Missionario della California e dell' Arizona. Con 16 Ilustrazioni e una Carta (Milano, 1930). Contains facsimile of record of Kino's baptism.

Rossaro, D. A. Brevi Cenni sul Gesuita P. Eusebio Francesco Chini di Segno in Val di Non (Rovereto, 1929). On p. 12 is a facsimile of a letter by Kino to D. Pietro Lucca of Caldero, May 10, 1678.

Russell, Frank. The Pima Indians. In United States Bureau of American Ethnology, Annual Report, 1904–1905 (Washington, 1908).

Salvatierra, Juan María. Letter to the Duquesa de Sesar, Nov. 26, 1697. In *Documentos para la Historia de México,* Segunda Série, Tomo I, 107–109.

Salvatierra, Juan María. Letter to Juan de Ugarte, Nov. 27, 1697; *ibid.,* 109–154.

Salvatierra, Juan María. Letter to Juan Cavallero y Osio, Nov. 27, 1697; *ibid.,* 154–157.

Salvatierra, Juan María. Letter to the viceroy, Conde de Montezuma, Nov. 28, 1697; *ibid.,* 103–107.

Salvatierra, Juan María. Letter to Francisco de Arteaga (May, 1702?); *ibid.,* Cuarta Série, Tomo IV, 105–156.

Sauer, Carl. Aboriginal Population of Northwestern Mexico (Berkeley, 1935).

Sauer, Carl. The Distribution of Aboriginal Tribes and Languages in Northwestern Mexico (Berkeley, 1934).

Sauer, Carl. The Road to Cíbola (Berkeley, 1932).

Sauer, Carl, and Brand, Donald. Aztatlán (Berkeley, 1932).

Sauer, Carl, and Brand, Donald. Prehistoric Settlements of Sonora, with Special Reference to Cerros de Trincheras (Berkeley, 1931).

Scherer, P. Henricus. Geographia Hierarchica sive Status Ecclesiastici Romano-Catholici per Orbem Universum Distributi Succincta Descriptio Historico-Geographica. Authore P. Henrico Scherer, Societatis Jesu. Pars II Sumptibus Joannis Caspari Bencard, Bibliopolae Academiae Dilinganae (Monachii, 1703).

Shiels, William Eugene, S.J. Gonzalo de Tapia (1561–1594), founder of the first permanent Jesuit mission in North America (New York, 1934).

Sigüenza y Góngora, Carlos de. Libra astronómica y Philosóphica en que D. Carlos de Sigüenza y Góngora, Cosmógrapho, y mathemático regio en la Acadmia Mexicana, examina no solo lo que à su manifiesto philosophico contra los cometas opuso el R. P. Eusebio Francisco Kino de la Compañía de Jesus, sino lo que el mismo R. P. opino, y pretendio haver demonstrado en su exposición astronómica del cometa del año de 1681 (México. Sacala à luz D. Sebastián de Guzmán y Córdova . . . c. 1690).

Simpson, Lesley Byrd, The Encomienda in New Spain (Berkeley, 1929).

Simpson, Lesley Byrd. Studies in the Administration of the Indians in New Spain (Berkeley, 1929, 1934—).

Sommervogel, C. Bibliothèque de la Compagnie de Jésus. Première partie: Bibliographie par . . . Augustin et Aloys de Backer. Seconde partie: Histoire par . . . Auguste Carayon. Nouv. éd. par. C. Sommervogel, publ. par la Province de Belgique . . . (Bruxelles, O. Schepens; Paris, A. Picard, 1890–1932), 11 vols., fol. In double columns, numbered.

Sonora, Materiales para la Historia. In *Documentos para la Historia de México,* Tercera Série; Cuarta Série, Tomo I.

Stitz, Peter. Deutsche Jesuiten als Geographen in Niederkalifornien und Nord-mexiko im 17 und 18. Jahrhundert (1680–1767/68). (Hausen Verlogs—gesellschaft m.b. H. Saarlouis, 1932).

Stöcklein, Joseph. Der Neue Welt-Bott mit Allerhand Nachrichten dern Mis-sionariorum Soc. Jesu. (The full title page of Bund I reads): Allerhand so lehr als geistreiche Brief Schriften und Reis-Beschreibungen welche von denen Mis-sionarii der Gesellschafft Jesu aus Beyden Indien und andern über Meer gele-genen Ländern Seit An. 1642 bisz auf das jahr 1726 in Europa angelangt seynd. jetzt zum Erstenmal theils aus Handschrifftlichen Urkunden, theils aus denen Französischen Lettres Edifiantes verteutscht und zusammen getragen von Joseph Stöcklein gedachter Societät Jesu Priester. Erster Bund oder die 8 erste Theil. Cum Privilegio Caesareo et Superiorum Facultate ac Indice locupletissimo (Augsburg und Grätz, 1726).

Thoelen, Heinrich, S.J. Menologium, oder Lebensbilder aus der Geschichte der deutschen Ordensprovinz der Gesellschaft Jesu (Roermond, 1901).

Thomas, C. and Swanton, J. R. The Indian Languages of Mexico (Washington, 1911).

Torres Lanzas, Pedro. Relación Descriptiva de los Mapas y Planos de México y Floridas Existentes en el Archivo General de Indias (Sevilla, 1900), 2 vols.

Velarde, Luís, Descripción del sitio, longitud, y latitud de las naciónes de la Pimería y sus adjacentes Septentrionales, y seno Californio, y otras noticias y observaciones, por el R. Padre Luís Velarde de la Compañía de Jesús, Rector y Ministro de dicha Pimería. In Manje, *Luz de Tierra Incógnita,* Segunda Parte, capitulos, IX–XII (Mexico, 1926).

Velasco, José F. Noticias Estadísticas de Sonora (Mexico, 1850).

Venegas, Miguel (Burriel). Noticia de la California, y de su conquista tem-poral, y espiritual, hasta el tiempo presente. Sacada de la Historia Manu-crita formada in México, año de 1739, por el Padre Miguèl Venegas, de la Compañía de Jesús; y de Otras Noticias, y Relaciones antiguas, y modernas. Añadida de Algunos Mapas particulares, y uno general de la América Sep-tentrional. Asia Oriental, y Mar del Súr intermedio, formados sobre las Memorias mas recientes, y exactas, que se publican juntamente. Dedicada Al Rey Ntro. Señor por la Provincia de Nueva-España, de la Compañía de Jesús (Madrid, 1757), 3 vols.

Venegas, Miguel (Burriel). Natural and Civil History of California. English translation of the above (London, 1759), 2 vols.

Venegas (Miguel) and Juan Antonio de Oviedo. El Apóstol Mariano, repre-sentado en la vida del V.P. Juan María de Salvatierra, de la Compañía de Jesús, fervoroso Missionero en la provincia de Nueva España, y Conquistador apostólico de las Californias (Mexico, 1754), 3 vols. See translation by Wilbur.

Verbiest, Ferdinand. Voyages de L'Empereur de la Chine dans la Tartarie Auquels on a Joint une nouvelle decouverte au Mexique (Paris, 1685). Con-tains "Nouvelle Descente des Espagnols," 79–110.

Walsh, James J. American Jesuits (New York, 1934).

Weber, Simone. Nazionalità e Cognome di P. Eusebio Chini (Trento, 1930).

Wilbur, Marguerite Eyer. Juan María de Salvatierra of the Company of Jesus; Missionary in the Province of New Spain, and Apostolic Conqueror of the Californias. By Miguel Venegas. Translated into English, edited and annotated by Marguerite Eyer Wilbur (Cleveland, 1929).

Wright, Harold Bell. Long Ago Told (Huh-kew ah-kah). Legends of the Pápago Indians (London and New York, 1929).

Wyllys, Rufus Kay. Pioneer Padre. Life and Times of Eusebio Francisco Kino (Dallas, 1935).

Zárate Salmerón, Gerónimo. Relaciones de todas las cosas que en el Nuevo-Mexico se han visto y sabido, asi por mar como por tierra, desde el año de 1538 hasta el de 1626. In *Documentos para la historia de México*. Tercera Série (Mexico, 1856), pp. 1–225.

ARTICLES IN MAGAZINES AND ENCYCLOPEDIAS

Bollettino della R. Società Geografica Italiano (Trento, Luglio—Agusto, 1928). Article on Kino.

Bolton, Herbert Eugene. Father Escobar's Relation of the Oñate Expedition. *Catholic Historical Review*, Vol. V, 19–41 (Washington, D. C., April, 1919).

Bolton, Herbert Eugene. Father Kino's lost History, its Discovery and its Value. *Papers of the Bibliographical Society of America*, vol. vi, 1911.

Bolton, Herbert Eugene, The Black Robes of New Spain. *Catholic Historical Review*, Vol. XXI, 257–282 (Washington, October, 1935).

Bolton, Herbert Eugene. The Mission as a Frontier Institution in the Spanish American Colonies. *American Historical Review*, XXIII, No. 2, pp. 42–61 (Washington, October, 1917).

Campbell, Thomas J. Eusebio Kino, 1644–1711. *Catholic Historical Review* V, 353–376 (Washington, 1920).

Catholic Encyclopedia (New York, 1907–1914), 16 vols. Article on Kino in Vol. VIII, p. 660.

Chapman, Charles E. The Jesuits in Baja California (1697–1768). *Catholic Historical Review*, VI, No. 1 (April, 1920) pp. 46–58.

Dunne, Peter, S.J. The Literature of the Jesuits of New Spain. *Catholic Historical Review*, Vol. XX, pp. 248–259 (Washington, D. C., 1934).

Galindo y Villa. Ing. Jesús, El Padre Eusebio Kino. *Memorias y Revista de la Academia Nacional de Ciencias Antonio Alzate*. Tomo 53, pp. 1–14 (Mexico, 1934). Contains photograph of the Kino monument erected in Trent, Italy, Sept. 12, 1930. Facing p. 8.

Hackett, Charles Wilson. The Revolt of the Pueblo Indians of New Mexico in 1680. Texas State Historical Association *Quarterly*, Vol. XV, 93–147 (Austin, 1912).

Hackett, Charles Wilson. The Retreat of the Spaniards from New Mexico in 1680 and the Beginnings of El Paso. *Southwestern Historical Quarterly*, Vol. XVI, 137–168 (Austin, 1913).

Hammond, George P. Pimería Alta after Kino's Time. *New Mexico Historical Review*, IV, No. 3, pp. 220–238 (July, 1929).

Holweck, F. J. Communication relative to Kino's nationality. *Catholic Historical Review*, Vol. VI, pp. 378–379 (Washington, October, 1920).

Il Monumento Alla Memoria di Padre Eusebio Chini (Relates to the plan for a Kino Monument in Tucson). *L'Italia. The Italian Daily News. Organo Degl' Interessi delle Colonie Italiane della Costa del Pacifico.* (San Francisco, California, March 13, 1932.)

Lockwood, Frank C. When Kino led the Way to California. *Touring Topics.* Vol. XXV, No. 8 (Los Angeles, July, 1932).

Mosna, Ezio, P. Eusebio Francesco Chini, Grande Esploratore Trentino: Quaderno della Rivista *Trentino*, N. 2, pp. 3–7 (Trento, 1930). Contains facsimiles copied from Ricci. This is a reprint of the article by Trozzi cited below.

Ricci, Eugenia. P. F. E. Chini. *Studi Trentini di Scienze Naturali*, Anno XI (Trento, 1930). Contains facsimile of record of Kino's baptism.

Rizzatti, Ferraccio. L'Italiano Padre Eusebio Chini, Pionere, Esploratore, Civilizzatore. *L'Illustrazione Italiana* VIII, pp. 911–913 (Milano, May 25, 1930).

Rowland, Donald. The Sonora Frontier, 1735–1745. In *New Spain and the Anglo-American West* (2 vols. Los Angeles, 1932). Vol. I, pp. 147–164.

Stitz, Dr. Peter. Kalifornische Briefe des P. Eusebio Francisco Kino (Chini) Nach der oberdeutschen Provinz, 1683–1685, von Dr. Peter Stitz. *Archivum Historicum Societatis Jesu* III (Romae, Burgo Santo Spirito, 5, 1934), pp. 108–128. Contains facsimiles of Kino's map in Scherer and of Passage par Terre.

Tacchi- Venturi, Pietro, S.I. Nuove Lettere Inédite del P. Eusebio Francesco Chino d.C.d.G. *Archivum Historicum Societatis Jesu*, III, pp. 248–264 (Rome, 1934).

Tacchi-Venturi, Pietro, S.I. Sei Lettere inédite del P. Eusebio Chino al P. Gian Paolo Oliva. Gen. d.C.d.G. *Studi Trentini di Scienze Storiche*, Annata XI, pp. 3–17 (Trento, 1930).

Trozzi, Ugo. P. Eusebio Francesco Chini, Grande Esploratore Trentino. In *Trentino: Rivista della Legione Trentina.* Anno VI, N.S., pp. 73–77 (Trento, 1930). Contains baptismal record and other facsimiles copied from Ricci.

Was Father Francis Eusebius Kinus an Italian? *Catholic Historical Review*, New Series, II, pp. 275–277 (Washington, July, 1922).

Weber, Simone. Eusebio Francesco Chini. Apostolo degli Indiani del Messico. *Strenna Trentine*, 1928, pp. 27–30 (Trento, 1928).

Weber, Simone. P. Eusebio F. Chini, Apostolo ed Esploratore del Nord America. *Bolletino del Clero dell' Arcidiocesi di Trento* (Trento, Luglio–Agosto, 1930).

Weber, Simone. Letter of June 21, 1920, concerning Kino's nationality. *Catholic Historical Review*, Vol. VI, 379–380 (Washington, October, 1920).

Wyllys, Rufus Kay. Kino of Pimería Alta. A series of articles in the *Arizona Historical Review*, Vol. V (Tucson, April, 1932–January, 1933).

Wyllys, Rufus Kay. Translation of Padre Luís Velarde's Relación of Pimería Alta. *New Mexico Historical Review*, Vol. VI, pp. 111–157 (Santa Fé, April, 1931).

Index